Artificial Intelligence
Foundations of Computational Agents

Artificial Intelligence: Foundations of Computational Agents is about the science of artificial intelligence (AI). It presents AI as the study of the design of intelligent computational agents. The book is structured as a textbook, but it is accessible to a wide audience of professionals and researchers.

The past decades have witnessed the emergence of AI as a serious science and engineering discipline. This book provides the first accessible synthesis of the field aimed at undergraduate and graduate students. It provides a coherent vision of the foundations of the field as it is today, in terms of a multidimensional design space that has been partially explored. As with any science worth its salt, AI has a coherent, formal theory and a rambunctious experimental wing. The book balances theory and experiment, showing how to link them intimately together. It develops the science of AI together with its engineering applications.

David L. Poole is Professor of Computer Science at the University of British Columbia. He is a coauthor of *Computational Intelligence: A Logical Approach* (1998), cochair of the Twenty-Fourth AAAI Conference on Artificial Intelligence (AAAI-10), and coeditor of the *Proceedings of the Tenth Conference in Uncertainty in Artificial Intelligence* (1994). Poole is a former associate editor of the *Journal of Artificial Intelligence Research*. He is an associate editor of *Artificial Intelligence* and on the editorial boards of *AI Magazine* and AAAI Press. He is the secretary of the Association for Uncertainty in Artificial Intelligence and is a Fellow of the Association for the Advancement of Artificial Intelligence.

Alan K. Mackworth is Professor of Computer Science and Canada Research Chair in Artificial Intelligence at the University of British Columbia. He has authored more than 100 papers and coauthored the text *Computational Intelligence: A Logical Approach*. He was President and Trustee of International Joint Conferences on AI (IJCAI) Inc. Mackworth was vice president and president of the Canadian Society for Computational Studies of Intelligence (CSCSI). He has served as president of the AAAI. He also served as the founding director of the UBC Laboratory for Computational Intelligence. He is a Fellow of the Canadian Institute for Advanced Research, AAAI, and the Royal Society of Canada.

Artificial Intelligence

Foundations of Computational Agents

David L. Poole

University of British Columbia

Alan K. Mackworth

University of British Columbia

CAMBRIDGE
UNIVERSITY PRESS

CAMBRIDGE UNIVERSITY PRESS
Cambridge, New York, Melbourne, Madrid, Cape Town,
Singapore, São Paulo, Delhi, Tokyo, Mexico City

Cambridge University Press
32 Avenue of the Americas, New York, NY 10013-2473, USA

www.cambridge.org
Information on this title: www.cambridge.org/9780521519007

First published 2010
Reprinted 2011

A catalog record for this publication is available from the British Library.

Library of Congress Cataloging in Publication Data

Poole, David L. (David Lynton), 1958–
Artificial intelligence : foundations of computational agents / David L. Poole, Alan K. Mackworth.
   p. cm.
Includes bibliographical references and index.
ISBN 978-0-521-51900-7 (hardback)
1. Computational intelligence – Textbooks. 2. Artificial intelligence – Textbooks. I. Mackworth, Alan K.
II. Title.
Q342.P66   2010
006.3 – dc22   2009039895

ISBN 978-0-521-51900-7 Hardback

To our families for their love, support, and patience

Jennifer, Alexandra, and Shannon

Marian and Bryn

Contents

Preface   **xiii**

I Agents in the World: What Are Agents and How Can They Be Built? **1**

1 Artificial Intelligence and Agents   **3**

   1.1   What Is Artificial Intelligence? 3
   1.2   A Brief History of AI 6
   1.3   Agents Situated in Environments 10
   1.4   Knowledge Representation 11
   1.5   Dimensions of Complexity 19
   1.6   Prototypical Applications 29
   1.7   Overview of the Book 39
   1.8   Review 40
   1.9   References and Further Reading 40
   1.10   Exercises 42

2 Agent Architectures and Hierarchical Control   **43**

   2.1   Agents 43
   2.2   Agent Systems 44
   2.3   Hierarchical Control 50
   2.4   Embedded and Simulated Agents 59
   2.5   Acting with Reasoning 60
   2.6   Review 65

2.7   References and Further Reading   66
2.8   Exercises   66

II Representing and Reasoning   **69**

3 States and Searching   **71**
3.1   Problem Solving as Search   71
3.2   State Spaces   72
3.3   Graph Searching   74
3.4   A Generic Searching Algorithm   77
3.5   Uninformed Search Strategies   79
3.6   Heuristic Search   87
3.7   More Sophisticated Search   92
3.8   Review 106
3.9   References and Further Reading 106
3.10 Exercises 107

4 Features and Constraints   **111**
4.1   Features and States 111
4.2   Possible Worlds, Variables, and Constraints 113
4.3   Generate-and-Test Algorithms 118
4.4   Solving CSPs Using Search 119
4.5   Consistency Algorithms 120
4.6   Domain Splitting 125
4.7   Variable Elimination 127
4.8   Local Search 130
4.9   Population-Based Methods 141
4.10 Optimization 144
4.11 Review 151
4.12 References and Further Reading 151
4.13 Exercises 152

5 Propositions and Inference   **157**
5.1   Propositions 157
5.2   Propositional Definite Clauses 163
5.3   Knowledge Representation Issues 174
5.4   Proving by Contradictions 185
5.5   Complete Knowledge Assumption 193
5.6   Abduction 199
5.7   Causal Models 204
5.8   Review 206
5.9   References and Further Reading 207
5.10 Exercises 208

6   Reasoning Under Uncertainty   **219**
   6.1   Probability   219
   6.2   Independence   232
   6.3   Belief Networks   235
   6.4   Probabilistic Inference   248
   6.5   Probability and Time   266
   6.6   Review   274
   6.7   References and Further Reading   274
   6.8   Exercises   275

III Learning and Planning   **281**

7   Learning: Overview and Supervised Learning   **283**
   7.1   Learning Issues   284
   7.2   Supervised Learning   288
   7.3   Basic Models for Supervised Learning   298
   7.4   Composite Models   313
   7.5   Avoiding Overfitting   320
   7.6   Case-Based Reasoning   324
   7.7   Learning as Refining the Hypothesis Space   327
   7.8   Bayesian Learning   334
   7.9   Review   340
   7.10 References and Further Reading   341
   7.11 Exercises   342

8   Planning with Certainty   **349**
   8.1   Representing States, Actions, and Goals   350
   8.2   Forward Planning   356
   8.3   Regression Planning   357
   8.4   Planning as a CSP   360
   8.5   Partial-Order Planning   363
   8.6   Review   366
   8.7   References and Further Reading   367
   8.8   Exercises   367

9   Planning Under Uncertainty   **371**
   9.1   Preferences and Utility   373
   9.2   One-Off Decisions   381
   9.3   Sequential Decisions   386
   9.4   The Value of Information and Control   396
   9.5   Decision Processes   399
   9.6   Review   412
   9.7   References and Further Reading   413
   9.8   Exercises   413

10 Multiagent Systems   **423**
   10.1   Multiagent Framework 423
   10.2   Representations of Games 425
   10.3   Computing Strategies with Perfect Information 430
   10.4   Partially Observable Multiagent Reasoning 433
   10.5   Group Decision Making 445
   10.6   Mechanism Design 446
   10.7   Review 449
   10.8   References and Further Reading 449
   10.9   Exercises 450

11 Beyond Supervised Learning   **451**
   11.1   Clustering 451
   11.2   Learning Belief Networks 458
   11.3   Reinforcement Learning 463
   11.4   Review 485
   11.5   References and Further Reading 486
   11.6   Exercises 486

IV Reasoning About Individuals and Relations   **489**

12 Individuals and Relations   **491**
   12.1   Exploiting Structure Beyond Features 492
   12.2   Symbols and Semantics 493
   12.3   Datalog: A Relational Rule Language 494
   12.4   Proofs and Substitutions 506
   12.5   Function Symbols 512
   12.6   Applications in Natural Language Processing 520
   12.7   Equality 532
   12.8   Complete Knowledge Assumption 537
   12.9   Review 541
   12.10 References and Further Reading 542
   12.11 Exercises 542

13 Ontologies and Knowledge-Based Systems   **549**
   13.1   Knowledge Sharing 549
   13.2   Flexible Representations 550
   13.3   Ontologies and Knowledge Sharing 563
   13.4   Querying Users and Other Knowledge Sources 576
   13.5   Implementing Knowledge-Based Systems 579
   13.6   Review 591
   13.7   References and Further Reading 591
   13.8   Exercises 592

14 Relational Planning, Learning, and Probabilistic Reasoning   597
   14.1   Planning with Individuals and Relations 598
   14.2   Learning with Individuals and Relations 606
   14.3   Probabilistic Relational Models 611
   14.4   Review 618
   14.5   References and Further Reading 618
   14.6   Exercises 620

V   The Big Picture   623

15 Retrospect and Prospect   625
   15.1   Dimensions of Complexity Revisited 625
   15.2   Social and Ethical Consequences 629
   15.3   References and Further Reading 632

A   Mathematical Preliminaries and Notation   633
   A.1   Discrete Mathematics 633
   A.2   Functions, Factors, and Arrays 634
   A.3   Relations and the Relational Algebra 635

Bibliography   637

Index   653

Preface

Artificial Intelligence: Foundations of Computational Agents is a book about the science of artificial intelligence (AI). The view we take is that AI is the study of the design of intelligent computational agents. The book is structured as a textbook, but it is designed to be accessible to a wide audience.

We wrote this book because we are excited about the emergence of AI as an integrated science. As with any science worth its salt, AI has a coherent, formal theory and a rambunctious experimental wing. Here we balance theory and experiment and show how to link them intimately together. We develop the science of AI together with its engineering applications. We believe the adage "There is nothing so practical as a good theory." The spirit of our approach is captured by the dictum "Everything should be made as simple as possible, but not simpler." We must build the science on solid foundations; we present the foundations, but only sketch, and give some examples of, the complexity required to build useful intelligent systems. Although the resulting systems will be complex, the foundations and the building blocks should be simple.

The book works as an introductory text on AI for advanced undergraduate or graduate students in computer science or related disciplines such as computer engineering, philosophy, cognitive science, or psychology. It will appeal more to the technically minded; parts are technically challenging, focusing on learning by doing: designing, building, and implementing systems. Any curious scientifically oriented reader will benefit from studying the book. Previous experience with computational systems is desirable, but prior study of the foundations on which we build, including logic, probability, calculus, and control theory, is not necessary, because we develop the concepts as required.

The serious student will gain valuable skills at several levels ranging from expertise in the specification and design of intelligent agents to skills for implementing, testing, and improving real software systems for several challenging application domains. The thrill of participating in the emergence of a new science of intelligent agents is one of the attractions of this approach. The practical skills of dealing with a world of ubiquitous, intelligent, embedded agents are now in great demand in the marketplace.

The focus is on an intelligent agent acting in an environment. We start with simple agents acting in simple, static environments and gradually increase the power of the agents to cope with more challenging worlds. We explore nine dimensions of complexity that allow us to introduce, gradually and with modularity, what makes building intelligent agents challenging. We have tried to structure the book so that the reader can understand each of the dimensions separately, and we make this concrete by repeatedly illustrating the ideas with four different agent tasks: a delivery robot, a diagnostic assistant, a tutoring system, and a trading agent.

The agent we want the student to envision is a hierarchically designed agent that acts intelligently in a stochastic environment that it can only partially observe – one that reasons about individuals and the relationships among them, has complex preferences, learns while acting, takes into account other agents, and acts appropriately given its own computational limitations. Of course, we can't start with such an agent; it is still a research question to build such agents. So we introduce the simplest agents and then show how to add each of these complexities in a modular way.

We have made a number of design choices that distinguish this book from competing books, including the earlier book by the same authors:

- We have tried to give a coherent framework in which to understand AI. We have chosen not to present disconnected topics that do not fit together. For example, we do not present disconnected logical and probabilistic views of AI, but we have presented a multidimensional design space in which the students can understand the big picture, in which probabilistic and logical reasoning coexist.

- We decided that it is better to clearly explain the foundations on which more sophisticated techniques can be built, rather than present these more sophisticated techniques. This means that a larger gap exists between what is covered in this book and the frontier of science. It also means that the student will have a better foundation to understand current and future research.

- One of the more difficult decisions we made was how to linearize the design space. Our previous book (Poole, Mackworth, and Goebel, 1998) presented a relational language early and built the foundations in terms of this language. This approach made it difficult for the students to appreciate work that was not relational, for example, in reinforcement learning that is developed in terms of states. In this book, we have chosen a relations-late approach. This approach probably reflects better the research over the past few decades in which there has been much progress in feature-based representations. It also allows the student to understand that probabilistic and logical reasoning are complementary. The book, however, is structured so that an instructor can present relations earlier.

This book uses examples from AIspace.org (http://www.aispace.org), a collection of pedagogical applets that we have been involved in designing. To gain further experience in building intelligent systems, a student should also experiment with a high-level symbol-manipulation language, such as LISP or Prolog. We also provide implementations in AILog, a clean logic programming language related to Prolog, designed to demonstrate many of the issues in this book. This connection is not essential to an understanding or use of the ideas in this book.

Our approach, through the development of the power of the agent's capabilities and representation language, is both simpler and more powerful than the traditional approach of surveying and cataloging various applications of AI. However, as a consequence, some applications, such as the details of computational vision or computational linguistics, are not covered in this book.

We have chosen not to present an encyclopedic view of AI. Not every major idea that has been investigated is presented here. We have chosen some basic ideas on which other, more sophisticated, techniques are based and have tried to explain the basic ideas in detail, sketching how these can be expanded.

Figure 1 (page xvi) shows the topics covered in the book. The solid lines give prerequisites. Often the prerequisite structure does not include all subtopics. Given the medium of a book, we have had to linearize the topics. However, the book is designed so that the topics can be taught in any order satisfying the prerequisite structure.

The references given at the end of each chapter are not meant to be comprehensive: we have referenced works that we have directly used and works that we think provide good overviews of the literature, by referencing both classic works and more recent surveys. We hope that no researchers feel slighted by their omission, and we are happy to have feedback where someone feels that an idea has been misattributed. Remember that this book is *not* a survey of AI research.

We invite you to join us in an intellectual adventure: building a science of intelligent agents.

David Poole
Alan Mackworth

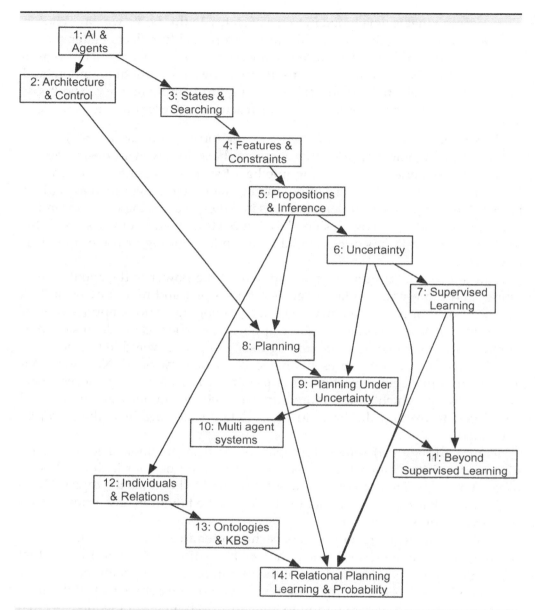

Figure 1: Overview of chapters and dependencies

Acknowledgments

Thanks to Randy Goebel for valuable input on this book. We also grate-fully acknowledge the helpful comments on earlier drafts of this book re-ceived from Giuseppe Carenini, Cristina Conati, Mark Crowley, Pooyan Fazli, Holger Hoos, Manfred Jaeger, Mohammad Reza Khojasteh, Jacek Kisyński, Bob Kowalski, Kevin Leyton-Brown, Marian Mackworth, Gabriel Murray, Alessandro Provetti, Marco Valtorta, and the anonymous reviewers. Thanks to the students who pointed out many errors in earlier drafts.

Thanks to Jen Fernquist for the web site design, and to Tom Sgouros for hyperlatex fixes. We are grateful to James Falen for permission to quote his poem on constraints. Thanks to our editor Lauren Cowles and the staff at Cam-bridge University Press for all their support, encouragement, and help. All the mistakes remaining are ours.

Part I

Agents in the World: What Are Agents and How Can They Be Built?

Chapter 1

Artificial Intelligence and Agents

The history of AI is a history of fantasies, possibilities, demonstrations, and promise. Ever since Homer wrote of mechanical "tripods" waiting on the gods at dinner, imagined mechanical assistants have been a part of our culture. However, only in the last half century have we, the AI community, been able to build experimental machines that test hypotheses about the mechanisms of thought and intelligent behavior and thereby demonstrate mechanisms that formerly existed only as theoretical possibilities.

– Bruce Buchanan [2005]

This book is about artificial intelligence, a field built on centuries of thought, which has been a recognized discipline for over 50 years. As Buchanan points out in the quote above, we now have the tools to test hypotheses about the nature of thought itself, as well as solve practical problems. Deep scientific and engineering problems have already been solved and many more are waiting to be solved. Many practical applications are currently deployed and the potential exists for an almost unlimited number of future applications. In this book, we present the principles that underlie intelligent computational agents. Those principles can help you understand current and future work in AI and equip you to contribute to the discipline yourself.

1.1   What Is Artificial Intelligence?

Artificial intelligence, or **AI**, is the field that studies *the synthesis and analysis of computational agents that act intelligently*. Let us examine each part of this definition.

An **agent** is something that acts in an environment – it does something. Agents include worms, dogs, thermostats, airplanes, robots, humans, companies, and countries.

We are interested in what an agent does; that is, how it **acts**. We judge an agent by its actions.

An agent acts **intelligently** when

- what it does is appropriate for its circumstances and its goals,
- it is flexible to changing environments and changing goals,
- it learns from experience, and
- it makes appropriate choices given its perceptual and computational limitations. An agent typically cannot observe the state of the world directly; it has only a finite memory and it does not have unlimited time to act.

A **computational** agent is an agent whose decisions about its actions can be explained in terms of computation. That is, the decision can be broken down into primitive operation that can be implemented in a physical device. This computation can take many forms. In humans this computation is carried out in "wetware"; in computers it is carried out in "hardware." Although there are some agents that are arguably not computational, such as the wind and rain eroding a landscape, it is an open question whether all intelligent agents are computational.

The central **scientific goal** of AI is to understand the principles that make intelligent behavior possible in natural or artificial systems. This is done by

- the **analysis** of natural and artificial agents;
- formulating and testing hypotheses about what it takes to construct intelligent agents; and
- designing, building, and experimenting with computational systems that perform tasks commonly viewed as requiring intelligence.

As part of science, researchers build empirical systems to test hypotheses or to explore the space of possibilities. These are quite distinct from applications that are built to be useful for an application domain.

Note that the definition is not for intelligent *thought*. We are only interested in **thinking** intelligently insofar as it leads to better performance. The role of thought is to affect action.

The central **engineering goal** of AI is the **design** and **synthesis** of useful, intelligent artifacts. We actually want to build agents that act intelligently. Such agents are useful in many applications.

1.1.1 Artificial and Natural Intelligence

Artificial intelligence (AI) is the established name for the field, but the term "artificial intelligence" is a source of much confusion because artificial intelligence may be interpreted as the opposite of real intelligence.

Interrogator: In the first line of your sonnet which reads "Shall I compare thee to a summer's day," would not "a spring day" do as well or better?

Witness: It wouldn't scan.

Interrogator: How about "a winter's day," That would scan all right.

Witness: Yes, but nobody wants to be compared to a winter's day.

Interrogator: Would you say Mr. Pickwick reminded you of Christmas?

Witness: In a way.

Interrogator: Yet Christmas is a winter's day, and I do not think Mr. Pickwick would mind the comparison.

Witness: I don't think you're serious. By a winter's day one means a typical winter's day, rather than a special one like Christmas.

Figure 1.1: A possible dialog for the Turing test (from Turing [1950])

For any phenomenon, you can distinguish real versus fake, where the fake is non-real. You can also distinguish natural versus artificial. Natural means occurring in nature and artificial means made by people.

Example 1.1 A tsunami is a large wave in an ocean caused by an earthquake or a landslide. Natural tsunamis occur from time to time. You could imagine an artificial tsunami that was made by people, for example, by exploding a bomb in the ocean, yet which is still a real tsunami. One could also imagine fake tsunamis: either artificial, using computer graphics, or natural, for example, a mirage that looks like a tsunami but is not one.

It is arguable that intelligence is different: you cannot have *fake* intelligence. If an agent behaves intelligently, it is intelligent. It is only the external behavior that defines intelligence; acting intelligently is being intelligent. Thus, artificial intelligence, if and when it is achieved, will be real intelligence created artificially.

This idea of intelligence being defined by external behavior was the motivation for a test for intelligence designed by Turing [1950], which has become known as the **Turing test**. The Turing test consists of an imitation game where an interrogator can ask a witness, via a text interface, any question. If the interrogator cannot distinguish the witness from a human, the witness must be intelligent. Figure 1.1 shows a possible dialog that Turing suggested. An agent that is not really intelligent could not fake intelligence for arbitrary topics.

There has been much debate about the Turing test. Unfortunately, although it may provide a test for how to recognize intelligence, it does not provide a way to get there; trying each year to fake it does not seem like a useful avenue of research.

The obvious naturally intelligent agent is the human being. Some people might say that worms, insects, or bacteria are intelligent, but more people would say that dogs, whales, or monkeys are intelligent (see Exercise 1 (page 42)). One class of intelligent agents that may be more intelligent than humans is the class of *organizations*. Ant colonies are a prototypical example of organizations. Each individual ant may not be very intelligent, but an ant colony can act more intelligently than any individual ant. The colony can discover food and exploit it very effectively as well as adapt to changing circumstances. Similarly, companies can develop, manufacture, and distribute products where the sum of the skills required is much more than any individual could master. Modern computers, from low-level hardware to high-level software, are more complicated than any human can understand, yet they are manufactured daily by organizations of humans. Human *society* viewed as an agent is arguably the most intelligent agent known.

It is instructive to consider where human intelligence comes from. There are three main sources:

biology: Humans have evolved into adaptable animals that can survive in various habitats.

culture: Culture provides not only language, but also useful tools, useful concepts, and the wisdom that is passed from parents and teachers to children.

life-long learning: Humans learn throughout their life and accumulate knowledge and skills.

These sources interact in complex ways. Biological evolution has provided stages of growth that allow for different learning at different stages of life. We humans and our culture have evolved together so that humans are helpless at birth, presumably because of our culture of looking after infants. Culture interacts strongly with learning. A major part of lifelong learning is what people are taught by parents and teachers. Language, which is part of culture, provides distinctions in the world that should be noticed for learning.

1.2 A Brief History of AI

Throughout human history, people have used technology to model themselves. There is evidence of this from ancient China, Egypt, and Greece that bears witness to the universality of this activity. Each new technology has, in its turn, been exploited to build intelligent agents or models of mind. Clockwork, hydraulics, telephone switching systems, holograms, analog computers, and digital computers have all been proposed both as technological metaphors for intelligence and as mechanisms for modeling mind.

About 400 years ago people started to write about the nature of thought and reason. Hobbes (1588–1679), who has been described by Haugeland [1985,

p. 85] as the "Grandfather of AI," espoused the position that thinking was symbolic reasoning like talking out loud or working out an answer with pen and paper. The idea of symbolic reasoning was further developed by Descartes (1596–1650), Pascal (1623–1662), Spinoza (1632–1677), Leibniz (1646–1716), and others who were pioneers in the philosophy of mind.

The idea of symbolic operations became more concrete with the development of computers. The first general-purpose computer designed (but not built until 1991, at the Science Museum of London) was the **Analytical Engine** by Babbage (1792–1871). In the early part of the 20th century, there was much work done on understanding computation. Several models of computation were proposed, including the Turing machine by Alan Turing (1912–1954), a theoretical machine that writes symbols on an infinitely long tape, and the lambda calculus of Church (1903–1995), which is a mathematical formalism for rewriting formulas. It can be shown that these very different formalisms are equivalent in that any function computable by one is computable by the others. This leads to the **Church–Turing thesis**:

> Any effectively computable function can be carried out on a Turing machine (and so also in the lambda calculus or any of the other equivalent formalisms).

Here **effectively computable** means following well-defined operations; "computers" in Turing's day were people who followed well-defined steps and computers as we know them today did not exist. This thesis says that all computation can be carried out on a Turing machine or one of the other equivalent computational machines. The Church–Turing thesis cannot be proved but it is a hypothesis that has stood the test of time. No one has built a machine that has carried out computation that cannot be computed by a Turing machine. There is no evidence that people can compute functions that are not Turing computable. An agent's actions are a function of its abilities, its history, and its goals or preferences. This provides an argument that computation is more than just a metaphor for intelligence; reasoning *is* computation and computation can be carried out by a computer.

Once real computers were built, some of the first applications of computers were AI programs. For example, Samuel [1959] built a checkers program in 1952 and implemented a program that learns to play checkers in the late 1950s. Newell and Simon [1956] built a program, Logic Theorist, that discovers proofs in propositional logic.

In addition to that for high-level symbolic reasoning, there was also much work on low-level learning inspired by how neurons work. McCulloch and Pitts [1943] showed how a simple thresholding "formal neuron" could be the basis for a Turing-complete machine. The first learning for these neural networks was described by Minsky [1952]. One of the early significant works was the Perceptron of Rosenblatt [1958]. The work on neural networks went into decline for a number of years after the 1968 book by Minsky and Papert [1988],

Does Afghanistan border China?

What is the capital of Upper_Volta?

Which country's capital is London?

Which is the largest african country?

How large is the smallest american country?

What is the ocean that borders African countries and that borders Asian countries?

What are the capitals of the countries bordering the Baltic?

How many countries does the Danube flow through?

What is the total area of countries south of the Equator and not in Australasia?

What is the average area of the countries in each continent?

Is there more than one country in each continent?

What are the countries from which a river flows into the Black_Sea?

What are the continents no country in which contains more than two cities whose population exceeds 1 million?

Which country bordering the Mediterranean borders a country that is bordered by a country whose population exceeds the population of India?

Which countries with a population exceeding 10 million border the Atlantic?

Figure 1.2: Some questions CHAT-80 could answer

which argued that the representations learned were inadequate for intelligent action.

These early programs concentrated on learning and search as the foundations of the field. It became apparent early that one of the main problems was how to represent the knowledge needed to solve a problem. Before learning, an agent must have an appropriate target language for the learned knowledge. There have been many proposals for representations from simple feature-based representations to complex logical representations of McCarthy and Hayes [1969] and many in between such as the frames of Minsky [1975].

During the 1960s and 1970s, success was had in building natural language understanding systems in limited domains. For example, the STUDENT program of Daniel Bobrow [1967] could solve high school algebra problems expressed in natural language. Winograd's [1972] SHRDLU system could, using restricted natural language, discuss and carry out tasks in a simulated blocks world. CHAT-80 [Warren and Pereira, 1982] could answer geographical questions placed to it in natural language. Figure 1.2 shows some questions that CHAT-80 answered based on a database of facts about countries, rivers, and so on. All of these systems could only reason in very limited domains using restricted vocabulary and sentence structure.

During the 1970s and 1980s, there was a large body of work on **expert systems**, where the aim was to capture the knowledge of an expert in some domain so that a computer could carry out expert tasks. For example, **DENDRAL** [Buchanan and Feigenbaum, 1978], developed from 1965 to 1983 in the field of organic chemistry, proposed plausible structures for new organic compounds. **MYCIN** [Buchanan and Shortliffe, 1984], developed from 1972 to 1980, diagnosed infectious diseases of the blood, prescribed antimicrobial therapy, and explained its reasoning. The 1970s and 1980s were also a period when AI reasoning became widespread in languages such as **Prolog** [Colmerauer and Roussel, 1996; Kowalski, 1988].

During the 1990s and the 2000s there was great growth in the subdisciplines of AI such as perception, probabilistic and decision-theoretic reasoning, planning, embodied systems, machine learning, and many other fields. There has also been much progress on the foundations of the field; these form the foundations of this book.

1.2.1 Relationship to Other Disciplines

AI is a very young discipline. Other disciplines as diverse as philosophy, neurobiology, evolutionary biology, psychology, economics, political science, sociology, anthropology, control engineering, and many more have been studying intelligence much longer.

The science of AI could be described as "synthetic psychology," "experimental philosophy," or "computational epistemology"– **epistemology** is the study of knowledge. AI can be seen as a way to study the old problem of the nature of knowledge and intelligence, but with a more powerful experimental tool than was previously available. Instead of being able to observe only the external behavior of intelligent systems, as philosophy, psychology, economics, and sociology have traditionally been able to do, AI researchers experiment with executable models of intelligent behavior. Most important, such models are open to inspection, redesign, and experiment in a complete and rigorous way. Modern computers provide a way to construct the models about which philosophers have only been able to theorize. AI researchers can experiment with these models as opposed to just discussing their abstract properties. AI theories can be empirically grounded in implementation. Moreover, we are often surprised when simple agents exhibit complex behavior. We would not have known this without implementing the agents.

It is instructive to consider an analogy between the development of flying machines over the past few centuries and the development of thinking machines over the past few decades. There are several ways to understand flying. One is to dissect known flying animals and hypothesize their common structural features as necessary fundamental characteristics of any flying agent. With this method, an examination of birds, bats, and insects would suggest that flying involves the flapping of wings made of some structure covered with feathers or a membrane. Furthermore, the hypothesis could be tested by strapping feathers to one's arms, flapping, and jumping into the air, as Icarus did. An alternate methodology is to try to understand the principles of flying without restricting oneself to the natural occurrences of flying. This typically involves the construction of artifacts that embody the hypothesized principles, even if they do not behave like flying animals in any way except flying. This second method has provided both useful tools – airplanes – and a better understanding of the principles underlying flying, namely *aerodynamics*.

AI takes an approach analogous to that of aerodynamics. AI researchers are interested in testing general hypotheses about the nature of intelligence by building machines that are intelligent and that do not necessarily mimic humans or organizations. This also offers an approach to the question, "Can computers really think?" by considering the analogous question, "Can airplanes really fly?"

AI is intimately linked with the discipline of computer science. Although there are many non-computer scientists who are doing AI research, much, if not most, AI research is done within computer science departments. This is appropriate because the study of computation is central to AI. It is essential to understand algorithms, data structures, and combinatorial complexity to build intelligent machines. It is also surprising how much of computer science started as a spinoff from AI, from timesharing to computer algebra systems.

Finally, AI can be seen as coming under the umbrella of *cognitive science*. Cognitive science links various disciplines that study cognition and reasoning, from psychology to linguistics to anthropology to neuroscience. AI distinguishes itself within cognitive science by providing tools to build intelligence rather than just studying the external behavior of intelligent agents or dissecting the inner workings of intelligent systems.

1.3 Agents Situated in Environments

AI is about practical reasoning: reasoning in order to do something. A coupling of perception, reasoning, and acting comprises an **agent**. An agent acts in an **environment**. An agent's environment may well include other agents. An agent together with its environment is called a **world**.

An agent could be, for example, a coupling of a computational engine with physical sensors and actuators, called a **robot**, where the environment is a physical setting. It could be the coupling of an advice-giving computer – an **expert system** – with a human who provides perceptual information and carries out the task. An agent could be a program that acts in a purely computational environment – a **software agent**.

Figure 1.3 shows the inputs and outputs of an agent. At any time, what an agent does depends on its

- **prior knowledge** about the agent and the environment;
- **history** of interaction with the environment, which is composed of

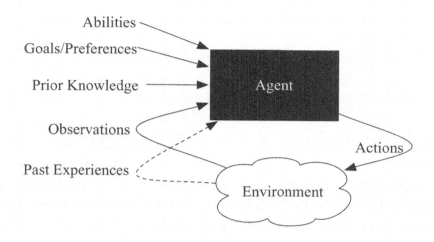

Figure 1.3: An agent interacting with an environment

- **observations** of the current environment and
- **past experiences** of previous actions and observations, or other data, from which it can learn;
- **goals** that it must try to achieve or preferences over states of the world; and
- **abilities**, which are the primitive actions it is capable of carrying out.

Two deterministic agents with the same prior knowledge, history, abilities, and goals should do the same thing. Changing any one of these can result in different actions.

Each agent has some internal state that can encode beliefs about its environment and itself. It may have goals to achieve, ways to act in the environment to achieve those goals, and various means to modify its beliefs by reasoning, perception, and learning. This is an all-encompassing view of intelligent agents varying in complexity from a simple thermostat, to a team of mobile robots, to a diagnostic advising system whose perceptions and actions are mediated by human beings, to society itself.

1.4 Knowledge Representation

Typically, a problem to solve or a task to carry out, as well as what constitutes a solution, is only given informally, such as "deliver parcels promptly when they arrive" or "fix whatever is wrong with the electrical system of the house."

The general framework for solving problems by computer is given in Figure 1.4 (on the next page). To solve a problem, the designer of a system must

- flesh out the task and determine what constitutes a solution;
- represent the problem in a language with which a computer can reason;

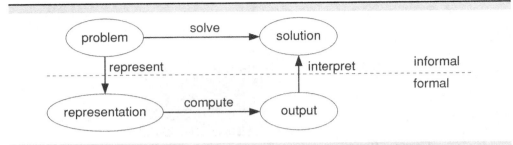

Figure 1.4: The role of representations in solving problems

- use the computer to compute an output, which is an answer presented to a user or a sequence of actions to be carried out in the environment; and

- interpret the output as a solution to the problem.

Knowledge is the information about a domain that can be used to solve problems in that domain. To solve many problems requires much knowledge, and this knowledge must be represented in the computer. As part of designing a program to solve problems, we must define how the knowledge will be represented. A **representation scheme** is the form of the knowledge that is used in an agent. A **representation** of some piece of knowledge is the internal representation of the knowledge. A representation scheme specifies the form of the knowledge. A **knowledge base** is the representation of all of the knowledge that is stored by an agent.

A good representation scheme is a compromise among many competing objectives. A representation should be

- rich enough to express the knowledge needed to solve the problem.

- as close to the problem as possible; it should be compact, natural, and maintainable. It should be easy to see the relationship between the representation and the domain being represented, so that it is easy to determine whether the knowledge represented is correct. A small change in the problem should result in a small change in the representation of the problem.

- amenable to efficient computation, which usually means that it is able to express features of the problem that can be exploited for computational gain and able to trade off accuracy and computation time.

- able to be acquired from people, data and past experiences.

Many different representation schemes have been designed. Many of these start with some of these objectives and are then expanded to include the other objectives. For example, some are designed for learning and then expanded to allow richer problem solving and inference abilities. Some representation schemes are designed with expressiveness in mind, and then inference and learning are added on. Some schemes start from tractable inference and then are made more natural, and more able to be acquired.

Some of the questions that must be considered when given a problem or a task are the following:

- What is a solution to the problem? How good must a solution be?
- How can the problem be represented? What distinctions in the world are needed to solve the problem? What specific knowledge about the world is required? How can an agent acquire the knowledge from experts or from experience? How can the knowledge be debugged, maintained, and improved?
- How can the agent compute an output that can be interpreted as a solution to the problem? Is worst-case performance or average-case performance the critical time to minimize? Is it important for a human to understand how the answer was derived?

These issues are discussed in the next sections and arise in many of the representation schemes presented later in the book.

1.4.1 Defining a Solution

Given an informal description of a problem, before even considering a computer, a knowledge base designer should determine what would constitute a solution. This question arises not only in AI but in any software design. Much of **software engineering** involves refining the specification of the problem.

Typically, problems are not well specified. Not only is there usually much left unspecified, but also the unspecified parts cannot be filled in arbitrarily. For example, if you ask a trading agent to find out all the information about resorts that may have health issues, you do not want the agent to return the information about all resorts, even though all of the information you requested is in the result. However, if the trading agent does not have complete knowledge about the resorts, returning all of the information may be the only way for it to guarantee that all of the requested information is there. Similarly, you do not want a delivery robot, when asked to take all of the trash to the garbage can, to take everything to the garbage can, even though this may be the only way to guarantee that all of the trash has been taken. Much work in AI is motivated by **commonsense reasoning**; we want the computer to be able to make commonsense conclusions about the unstated assumptions.

Given a well-defined problem, the next issue is whether it matters if the answer returned is incorrect or incomplete. For example, if the specification asks for all instances, does it matter if some are missing? Does it matter if there are some extra instances? Often a person does not want just any solution but the best solution according to some criteria. There are four common classes of solutions:

Optimal solution An **optimal solution** to a problem is one that is the best solution according to some measure of solution quality. This measure is typically specified as an **ordinal**, where only the order matters. However, in some situations, such as when combining multiple criteria or when reasoning under uncertainty, you need a **cardinal** measure, where the relative magnitudes also matter. An example of an ordinal measure is for the robot to take out as much trash as possible; the more trash it can take out, the better. As an example of a cardinal measure, you may want the delivery robot to take as much of the trash as possible to the garbage can, minimizing the distance traveled, and explicitly specify a trade-off between the effort required and the proportion of the trash taken out. It may be better to miss some trash than to waste too much time. One general cardinal measure of desirability, known as **utility**, is used in decision theory (page 373).

Satisficing solution   Often an agent does not need the best solution to a problem but just needs some solution. A **satisficing solution** is one that is good enough according to some description of which solutions are adequate. For example, a person may tell a robot that it must take all of trash out, or tell it to take out three items of trash.

Approximately optimal solution   One of the advantages of a cardinal measure of success is that it allows for approximations. An **approximately optimal solution** is one whose measure of quality is close to the best that could theoretically be obtained. Typically agents do not need optimal solutions to problems; they only must get close enough. For example, the robot may not need to travel the optimal distance to take out the trash but may only need to be within, say, 10% of the optimal distance.

For some problems, it is much easier computationally to get an approximately optimal solution than to get an optimal solution. However, for other problems, it is (asymptotically) just as difficult to guarantee finding an approximately optimal solution as it is to guarantee finding an optimal solution. Some approximation algorithms guarantee that a solution is within some range of optimal, but for some algorithms no guarantees are available.

Probable solution   A **probable solution** is one that, even though it may not actually be a solution to the problem, is likely to be a solution. This is one way to approximate, in a precise manner, a satisficing solution. For example, in the case where the delivery robot could drop the trash or fail to pick it up when it attempts to, you may need the robot to be 80% sure that it has picked up three items of trash. Often you want to distinguish the **false-positive error** rate (the proportion of the answers given by the computer that are not correct) from the **false-negative error** rate (which is the proportion of those answers not given by the computer that are indeed correct). Some applications are much more tolerant of one of these errors than of the other.

These categories are not exclusive. A form of learning known as probably approximately correct (PAC) learning considers probably learning an approximately correct concept (page 332).

1.4.2 Representations

Once you have some requirements on the nature of a solution, you must represent the problem so a computer can solve it.

Computers and human minds are examples of **physical symbol systems**. A **symbol** is a meaningful pattern that can be manipulated. Examples of symbols are written words, sentences, gestures, marks on paper, or sequences of bits. A **symbol system** creates, copies, modifies, and destroys symbols. Essentially, a symbol is one of the patterns manipulated as a unit by a symbol system.

The term physical is used, because symbols in a physical symbol system are physical objects that are part of the real world, even though they may be internal to computers and brains. They may also need to physically affect action or motor control.

Much of AI rests on the **physical symbol system hypothesis** of Newell and Simon [1976]:

> A physical symbol system has the necessary and sufficient means
> for general intelligent action.

This is a strong hypothesis. It means that any intelligent agent is necessarily a physical symbol system. It also means that a physical symbol system is all that is needed for intelligent action; there is no magic or an as-yet-to-be-discovered quantum phenomenon required. It does not imply that a physical symbol system does not need a body to sense and act in the world. The physical symbol system hypothesis is an empirical hypothesis that, like other scientific hypotheses, is to be judged by how well it fits the evidence, and what alternative hypotheses exist. Indeed, it could be false.

An intelligent agent can be seen as manipulating symbols to produce action. Many of these symbols are used to refer to things in the world. Other symbols may be useful concepts that may or may not have external meaning. Yet other symbols may refer to internal states of the agent.

An agent can use physical symbol systems to model the world. A **model** of a world is a representation of the specifics of what is true in the world or of the dynamic of the world. The world does not have to be modeled at the most detailed level to be useful. All models are **abstractions**; they represent only part of the world and leave out many of the details. An agent can have a very simplistic model of the world, or it can have a very detailed model of the world. The **level of abstraction** provides a partial ordering of abstraction. A lower-level abstraction includes more details than a higher-level abstraction. An agent can have multiple, even contradictory, models of the world. The models are judged not by whether they are correct, but by whether they are useful.

Example 1.2 A delivery robot can model the environment at a high level of abstraction in terms of rooms, corridors, doors, and obstacles, ignoring distances, its size, the steering angles needed, the slippage of the wheels, the weight of parcels, the details of obstacles, the political situation in Canada, and virtually everything else. The robot could model the environment at lower levels of abstraction by taking some of these details into account. Some of these details may be irrelevant for the successful implementation of the robot, but some may be crucial for the robot to succeed. For example, in some situations the size of the robot and the steering angles may be crucial for not getting stuck around a particular corner. In other situations, if the robot stays close to the center of the corridor, it may not need to model its width or the steering angles.

Choosing an appropriate level of abstraction is difficult because

- a high-level description is easier for a human to specify and understand.
- a low-level description can be more accurate and more predictive. Often high-level descriptions abstract away details that may be important for actually solving the problem.
- the lower the level, the more difficult it is to reason with. This is because a solution at a lower level of detail involves more steps and many more possible courses of action exist from which to choose.
- you may not know the information needed for a low-level description. For example, the delivery robot may not know what obstacles it will encounter or how slippery the floor will be at the time that it must decide what to do.

It is often a good idea to model an environment at multiple levels of abstraction. This issue is further discussed in Section 2.3 (page 50).

Biological systems, and computers, can be described at multiple levels of abstraction. At successively lower levels are the neural level, the biochemical level (what chemicals and what electrical potentials are being transmitted), the chemical level (what chemical reactions are being carried out), and the level of physics (in terms of forces on atoms and quantum phenomena). What levels above the neuron level are needed to account for intelligence is still an open question. Note that these levels of description are echoed in the hierarchical structure of science itself, where scientists are divided into physicists, chemists, biologists, psychologists, anthropologists, and so on. Although no level of description is more important than any other, we conjecture that you do not have to emulate every level of a human to build an AI agent but rather you can emulate the higher levels and build them on the foundation of modern computers. This conjecture is part of what AI studies.

The following are two levels that seem to be common to both biological and computational entities:

- The **knowledge level** is a level of abstraction that considers what an agent knows and believes and what its goals are. The knowledge level considers what an agent knows, but not how it reasons. For example, the delivery agent's behavior can be described in terms of whether it knows that a parcel has arrived or not and whether it knows where a particular person is or not. Both human and robotic agents can be described at the knowledge level. At this level, you do not specify how the solution will be computed or even which of the many possible strategies available to the agent will be used.

- The **symbol level** is a level of description of an agent in terms of the reasoning it does. To implement the knowledge level, an agent manipulates symbols to produce answers. Many cognitive science experiments are designed to determine what symbol manipulation occurs during reasoning. Note that whereas the knowledge level is about what the agent believes about the external world and what its goals are in terms of the outside world, the symbol level is about what goes on inside an agent to reason about the external world.

1.4.3 Reasoning and Acting

The manipulation of symbols to produce action is called **reasoning**.

One way that AI representations differ from computer programs in traditional languages is that an AI representation typically specifies **what** needs to be computed, not **how** it is to be computed. We might specify that the agent should find the most likely disease a patient has, or specify that a robot should get coffee, but not give detailed instructions on how to do these things. Much AI reasoning involves searching through the space of possibilities to determine how to complete a task.

In deciding what an agent will do, there are three aspects of computation that must be distinguished: (1) the computation that goes into the design of the agent, (2) the computation that the agent can do before it observes the world and needs to act, and (3) the computation that is done by the agent as it is acting.

- **Design time reasoning** is the reasoning that is carried out to design the agent. It is carried out by the designer of the agent, not the agent itself.

- **Offline computation** is the computation done by the agent before it has to act. It can include compilation and learning. Offline, the agent takes background knowledge and data and compiles them into a usable form called a **knowledge base**. **Background knowledge** can be given either at design time or offline.

- **Online computation** is the computation done by the agent between observing the environment and acting in the environment. A piece of information obtained online is called an **observation**. An agent typically must use both its knowledge base and its observations to determine what to do.

It is important to distinguish between the knowledge in the mind of the designer and the knowledge in the mind of the agent. Consider the extreme cases:

- At one extreme is a highly specialized agent that works well in the environment for which it was designed, but it is helpless outside of this niche. The designer may have done considerable work in building the agent, but the agent may not need to do very much to operate well. An example is a thermostat. It may be difficult to design a thermostat so that it turns on and off at exactly the right temperatures, but the thermostat itself does not have to do much computation. Another example is a painting robot that always paints the same parts in an automobile factory. There may be much design time or offline computation to get it to work perfectly, but the painting robot can paint parts with little online computation; it senses that there is a part in position, but then it carries out its predefined actions. These very specialized agents do not adapt well to different environments or to changing goals. The painting robot would not notice if a different sort of part were present and, even if it did, it would not know what to do with it. It would have to be redesigned or reprogrammed to paint different parts or to change into a sanding machine or a dog washing machine.

- At the other extreme is a very flexible agent that can survive in arbitrary environments and accept new tasks at run time. Simple biological agents such as insects can adapt to complex changing environments, but they cannot carry out arbitrary tasks. Designing an agent that can adapt to complex environments and changing goals is a major challenge. The agent will know much more about the particulars of a situation than the designer. Even biology has not produced many such agents. Humans may be the only extant example, but even humans need time to adapt to new environments.

Even if the flexible agent is our ultimate dream, researchers have to reach this goal via more mundane goals. Rather than building a universal agent, which can adapt to any environment and solve any task, they have built particular agents for particular environmental niches. The designer can exploit the structure of the particular niche and the agent does not have to reason about other possibilities.

Two broad strategies have been pursued in building agents:

- The first is to simplify environments and build complex reasoning systems for these simple environments. For example, factory robots can do sophisticated tasks in the engineered environment of a factory, but they may be hopeless in a natural environment. Much of the complexity of the problem can be reduced by simplifying the environment. This is also important for building practical systems because many environments can be engineered to make them simpler for agents.

- The second strategy is to build simple agents in natural environments. This is inspired by seeing how **insects** can survive in complex environments even though they have very limited reasoning abilities. Researchers then make the agents have more reasoning abilities as their tasks become more complicated.

One of the advantages of simplifying environments is that it may enable us to prove properties of agents or to optimize agents for particular situations. Proving properties or optimization typically requires a model of the agent and its environment. The agent may do a little or a lot of reasoning, but an observer or designer of the agent may be able to reason about the agent and the environment. For example, the designer may be able to prove whether the agent can achieve a goal, whether it can avoid getting into situations that may be bad for the agent (**safety goals**), whether it will get stuck somewhere (**liveness**), or whether it will eventually get around to each of the things it should do (**fairness**). Of course, the proof is only as good as the model.

The advantage of building agents for complex environments is that these are the types of environments in which humans live and want our agents to live.

Fortunately, research along both lines is being carried out. In the first case, researchers start with simple environments and make the environments more complex. In the second case, researchers increase the complexity of the behaviors that the agents can carry out.

1.5 Dimensions of Complexity

Agents acting in environments range in complexity from thermostats to companies with multiple goals acting in competitive environments. A number of dimensions of complexity exist in the design of intelligent agents. These dimensions may be be considered separately but must be combined to build an intelligent agent. These dimensions define a **design space** of AI; different points in this space can be obtained by varying the values of the dimensions.

Here we present nine dimensions: modularity, representation scheme, planning horizon, sensing uncertainty, effect uncertainty, preference, number of agents, learning, and computational limits. These dimensions give a coarse division of the design space of intelligent agents. There are many other design choices that must be made to build an intelligent agent.

1.5.1 Modularity

The first dimension is the level of modularity.

Modularity is the extent to which a system can be decomposed into interacting modules that can be understood separately.

Modularity is important for reducing complexity. It is apparent in the structure of the brain, serves as a foundation of computer science, and is an important part of any large organization.

Modularity is typically expressed in terms of a hierarchical decomposition. For example, a human's visual cortex and eye constitute a module that takes in light and perhaps higher-level goals and outputs some simplified description of a scene. Modularity is hierarchical if the modules are organized into smaller modules, which, in turn, can be organized into even smaller modules, all the way down to primitive operations. This hierarchical organization is part of what biologists investigate. Large organizations have a hierarchical organization so that the top-level decision makers are not overwhelmed by details and do not have to micromanage all details of the organization. Procedural abstraction and object-oriented programming in computer science are designed to enable simplification of a system by exploiting modularity and abstraction.

In the **modularity dimension**, an agent's structure is one of the following:

- **flat**: there is no organizational structure;
- **modular**: the system is decomposed into interacting modules that can be understood on their own; or
- **hierarchical**: the system is modular, and the modules themselves are decomposed into interacting modules, each of which are hierarchical systems, and this recursion grounds out into simple components.

In a flat or modular structure the agent typically reasons at a single level of abstraction. In a hierarchical structure the agent reasons at multiple levels of abstraction. The lower levels of the hierarchy involve reasoning at a lower level of abstraction.

Example 1.3 In taking a trip from home to a holiday location overseas, an agent, such as yourself, must get from home to an airport, fly to an airport near the destination, then get from the airport to the destination. It also must make a sequence of specific leg or wheel movements to actually move. In a flat representation, the agent chooses one level of abstraction and reasons at that level. A modular representation would divide the task into a number of subtasks that can be solved separately (e.g., booking tickets, getting to the departure airport, getting to the destination airport, and getting to the holiday location). In a hierarchical representation, the agent will solve these subtasks in a hierarchical way, until the problem is reduced to simple problems such a sending an http request or taking a particular step.

A hierarchical decomposition is important for reducing the complexity of building an intelligent agent that acts in a complex environment. However, to explore the other dimensions, we initially ignore the hierarchical structure and assume a flat representation. Ignoring hierarchical decomposition is often fine for small or moderately sized problems, as it is for simple animals, small organizations, or small to moderately sized computer programs. When problems or systems become complex, some hierarchical organization is required.

How to build hierarchically organized agents is discussed in Section 2.3 (page 50).

1.5.2 Representation Scheme

The **representation scheme dimension** concerns how the world is described.

The different ways the world could be to affect what an agent should do are called **states**. We can factor the state of the world into the agent's internal state (its belief state) and the environment state.

At the simplest level, an agent can reason explicitly in terms of individually identified states.

> **Example 1.4** A thermostat for a heater may have two belief states: *off* and *heating*. The environment may have three states: *cold, comfortable*, and *hot*. There are thus six states corresponding to the different combinations of belief and environment states. These states may not fully describe the world, but they are adequate to describe what a thermostat should do. The thermostat should move to, or stay in, *heating* if the environment is *cold* and move to, or stay in, *off* if the environment is *hot*. If the environment is *comfortable*, the thermostat should stay in its current state. The agent heats in the *heating* state and does not heat in the *off* state.

Instead of enumerating states, it is often easier to reason in terms of the state's features or propositions that are true or false of the state. A state may be described in terms of **features**, where a feature has a value in each state [see Section 4.1 (page 112)].

> **Example 1.5** An agent that has to look after a house may have to reason about whether light bulbs are broken. It may have features for the position of each switch, the status of each switch (whether it is working okay, whether it is shorted, or whether it is broken), and whether each light works. The feature *pos_s2* may be a feature that has value *up* when switch *s2* is up and has value *down* when the switch is down. The state of the house's lighting may be described in terms of values for each of these features.

A **proposition** is a Boolean feature, which means that its value is either *true* or *false*. Thirty propositions can encode $2^{30} = 1,073,741,824$ states. It may be easier to specify and reason with the thirty propositions than with more than a billion states. Moreover, having a compact representation of the states indicates understanding, because it means that an agent has captured some regularities in the domain.

> **Example 1.6** Consider an agent that has to recognize letters of the alphabet. Suppose the agent observes a binary image, a 30×30 grid of pixels, where each of the 900 grid points is either on or off (i.e., it is not using any color or gray scale information). The action is to determine which of the letters $\{a, \ldots, z\}$ is drawn in the image. There are 2^{900} different states of the image, and so $26^{2^{900}}$ different functions from the image state into the characters $\{a, \ldots, z\}$. We cannot even represent such functions in terms of the state space. Instead, we define features of the image, such as line segments, and define the function from images to characters in terms of these features.

When describing a complex world, the features can depend on relations and individuals. A relation on a single individual is a property. There is a feature for each possible relationship among the individuals.

> **Example 1.7** The agent that looks after a house in Example 1.5 could have the lights and switches as individuals, and relations *position* and *connected_to*. Instead of the feature *position_s1* = *up*, it could use the relation *position*(s_1, up).

This relation enables the agent to reason about all switches or for an agent to have knowledge about switches that can be used when the agent encounters a switch.

Example 1.8 If an agent is enrolling students in courses, there could be a feature that gives the grade of a student in a course, for every student–course pair where the student took the course. There would be a *passed* feature for every student–course pair, which depends on the *grade* feature for that pair. It may be easier to reason in terms of individual students, courses and grades, and the relations *grade* and *passed*. By defining how *passed* depends on *grade* once, the agent can apply the definition for each student and course. Moreover, this can be done before the agent knows of any of the individuals and so before it knows any of the features.

Thus, instead of dealing with features or propositions, it is often more convenient to have **relational descriptions** in terms of **individuals** and **relations** among them. For example, one binary relation and 100 individuals can represent $100^2 = 10,000$ propositions and 2^{10000} states. By reasoning in terms of relations and individuals, an agent can specify reason about whole classes of individuals without ever enumerating the features or propositions, let alone the states. An agent may have to reason about infinite sets of individuals, such as the set of all numbers or the set of all sentences. To reason about an unbounded or infinite number of individuals, an agent cannot reason in terms of states or features; it must reason at the relational level.

In the **representation scheme dimension**, the agent reasons in terms of

- states,
- features, or
- relational descriptions, in terms of individuals and relations.

Some of the frameworks will be developed in terms of states, some in terms of features and some relationally.

Reasoning in terms of states is introduced in Chapter 3. Reasoning in terms of features is introduced in Chapter 4. We consider relational reasoning starting in Chapter 12.

1.5.3 Planning Horizon

The next dimension is how far ahead in time the agent plans. For example, when a dog is called to come, it should turn around to start running in order to get a reward in the future. It does not act only to get an immediate reward. Plausibly, a dog does not act for goals arbitrarily far in the future (e.g., in a few months), whereas people do (e.g., working hard now to get a holiday next year).

How far the agent "looks into the future" when deciding what to do is called the **planning horizon**. That is, the planning horizon is how far ahead the agent considers the consequences of its actions. For completeness, we include the non-planning case where the agent is not reasoning in time. The time points considered by an agent when planning are called **stages**.

In the **planning horizon dimension**, an agent is one of the following:

- A **non-planning** agent is an agent that does not consider the future when it decides what to do or when time is not involved.

- A **finite horizon** planner is an agent that looks for a fixed finite number of time steps ahead. For example, a doctor may have to treat a patient but may have time for some testing and so there may be two stages: a testing stage and a treatment stage to plan for. In the degenerate case where an agent only looks one time step ahead, it is said to be **greedy** or **myopic**.

- An **indefinite horizon** planner is an agent that looks ahead some finite, but not predetermined, number of steps ahead. For example, an agent that must get to some location may not know *a priori* how many steps it will take to get there.

- An **infinite horizon** planner is an agent that plans on going on forever. This is often called a **process**. For example, the stabilization module of a legged robot should go on forever; it cannot stop when it has achieved stability, because the robot has to keep from falling over.

1.5.4 Uncertainty

An agent could assume there is no uncertainty, or it could take uncertainty in the domain into consideration. Uncertainty is divided into two dimensions: one for uncertainty from sensing and one for uncertainty about the effect of actions.

Sensing Uncertainty

In some cases, an agent can observe the state of the world directly. For example, in some board games or on a factory floor, an agent may know exactly the state of the world. In many other cases, it may only have some noisy perception of the state and the best it can do is to have a probability distribution over the set of possible states based on what it perceives. For example, given a patient's symptoms, a medical doctor may not actually know which disease a patient may have and may have only a probability distribution over the diseases the patient may have.

The **sensing uncertainty dimension** concerns whether the agent can determine the state from the observations:

- **Fully observable** is when the agent knows the state of the world from the observations.

- **Partially observable** is when the agent does not directly observe the state of the world. This occurs when many possible states can result in the same observations or when observations are noisy.

Assuming the world is fully observable is often done as a simplifying assumption to keep reasoning tractable.

Effect Uncertainty

In some cases an agent knows the effect of an action. That is, given a state and an action, it can accurately predict the state resulting from carrying out that action in that state. For example, an agent interacting with a file system may be able to predict the effect of deleting a file given the state of the file system. In many cases, it is difficult to predict the effect of an action, and the best an agent can do is to have a probability distribution over the effects. For example, a person may not know the effect of calling his dog, even if he knew the state of the dog, but, based on experience, he has some idea of what it will do. The dog owner may even have some idea of what another dog, that he has never seen before, will do if he calls it.

The **effect uncertainty dimension** is that the dynamics can be

- **deterministic** – when the state resulting from an action is determined by an action and the prior state or

- **stochastic** – when there is only a probability distribution over the resulting states.

This dimension only makes sense when the world is fully observable. If the world is partially observable, a stochastic system can be modeled as a deterministic system where the effect of an action depends on some unobserved feature. It is a separate dimension because many of the frameworks developed are for the fully observable, stochastic action case.

Planning with deterministic actions is considered in Chapter 8. Planning with stochastic actions and with partially observable domains is considered in Chapter 9.

1.5.5   Preference

Agents act to have better outcomes for themselves. The only reason to choose one action over another is because the preferred action will lead to more desirable outcomes.

An agent may have a simple goal, which is a state to be reached or a proposition to be true such as getting its owner a cup of coffee (i.e., end up in a state where she has coffee). Other agents may have more complex preferences. For example, a medical doctor may be expected to take into account suffering, life expectancy, quality of life, monetary costs (for the patient, the doctor, and society), the ability to justify decisions in case of a lawsuit, and many other desiderata. The doctor must trade these considerations off when they conflict, as they invariably do.

The **preference dimension** is whether the agent has

- **goals**, either **achievement goals** to be achieved in some final state or **maintenance goals** that must be maintained in all visited states. For example, the goals for a robot may be to get two cups of coffee and a banana, and not to make a mess or hurt anyone.

- **complex preferences** involve trade-offs among the desirability of various outcomes, perhaps at different times. An **ordinal preference** is where only the ordering of the preferences is important. A **cardinal preference** is where the magnitude of the values matters. For example, an ordinal preference may be that Sam prefers cappuccino over black coffee and prefers black coffee over tea. A cardinal preference may give a trade-off between the wait time and the type of beverage, and a mess–taste trade-off, where Sam is prepared to put up with more mess in the preparation of the coffee if the taste of the coffee is exceptionally good.

Goals are considered in Chapter 8. Complex preferences are considered in Chapter 9.

1.5.6 Number of Agents

An agent reasoning about what it should do in an environment where it is the only agent is difficult enough. However, reasoning about what to do when there are other agents who are also reasoning is much more difficult. An agent in a multiagent setting should reason strategically about other agents; the other agents may act to trick or manipulate the agent or may be available to cooperate with the agent. With multiple agents, is often optimal to act randomly because other agents can exploit deterministic strategies. Even when the agents are cooperating and have a common goal, the problem of coordination and communication makes multiagent reasoning more challenging. However, many domains contain multiple agents and ignoring other agents' strategic reasoning is not always the best way for an agent to reason.

Taking the point of view of a single agent, the **number of agents dimension** considers whether the agent does

- **single agent** reasoning, where the agent assumes that any other agents are just part of the environment. This is a reasonable assumption if there are no other agents or if the other agents are not going to change what they do based on the agent's action.

- **multiple agent** reasoning, where the agent takes the reasoning of other agents into account. This happens when there are other intelligent agents whose goals or preferences depend, in part, on what the agent does or if the agent must communicate with other agents.

Reasoning in the presence of other agents is much more difficult if the agents can act simultaneously or if the environment is only partially observable. Multiagent systems are considered in Chapter 10.

1.5.7   Learning

In some cases, a designer of an agent may have a good model of the agent and its environment. Often a designer does not have a good model, and an agent should use data from its past experiences and other sources to help it decide what to do.

The **learning dimension** determines whether

- **knowledge is given** or
- **knowledge is learned** (from data or past experience).

Learning typically means finding the best model that fits the data. Sometimes this is as simple as tuning a fixed set of parameters, but it can also mean choosing the best representation out of a class of representations. Learning is a huge field in itself but does not stand in isolation from the rest of AI. There are many issues beyond fitting data, including how to incorporate background knowledge, what data to collect, how to represent the data and the resulting representations, what learning biases are appropriate, and how the learned knowledge can be used to affect how the agent acts.

Learning is considered in Chapters 7, 11, and 14.

1.5.8   Computational Limits

Sometimes an agent can decide on its best action quickly enough for it to act. Often there are computational resource limits that prevent an agent from carrying out the best action. That is, the agent may not be able to find the best action quickly enough within its memory limitations to act while that action is still the best thing to do. For example, it may not be much use to take 10 minutes to derive what was the best thing to do 10 minutes ago, when the agent has to act *now*. Often, instead, an agent must trade off how long it takes to get a solution with how good the solution is; it may be better to find a reasonable solution quickly than to find a better solution later because the world will have changed during the computation.

The **computational limits dimension** determines whether an agent has

- **perfect rationality**, where an agent reasons about the best action without taking into account its limited computational resources; or
- **bounded rationality**, where an agent decides on the best action that it can find given its computational limitations.

Computational resource limits include computation time, memory, and numerical accuracy caused by computers not representing real numbers exactly.

An **anytime algorithm** is an algorithm whose solution quality improves with time. In particular, it is one that can produce its current best solution at any time, but given more time it could produce even better solutions. We can ensure that the quality doesn't decrease by allowing the agent to store the best solution found so far and return that when asked for a solution. However, waiting to act

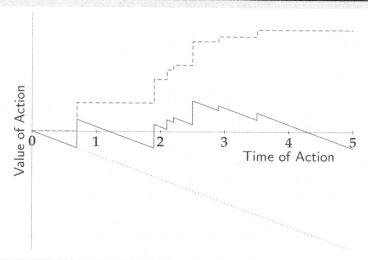

Figure 1.5: Solution quality as a function of time for an anytime algorithm. The agent has to choose an action. As time progresses, the agent can determine better actions. The value to the agent of the best action found so far, if it had been carried out initially, is given by the dashed line. The reduction in value to the agent by waiting to act is given by the dotted line. The net value to the agent, as a function of the time it acts, is given by the solid line.

has a cost; it may be better for an agent to act before it has found what would have been the best solution.

Example 1.9 Figure 1.5 shows how the computation time of an anytime algorithm can affect the solution quality. The agent has to carry out an action but can do some computation to decide what to do. The absolute solution quality, had the action been carried out at time zero, shown as the dashed line at the top, is improving as the agent takes time to reason. However, there is a penalty associated with taking time to act. In this figure, the penalty, shown as the dotted line at the bottom, is proportional to the time taken before the agent acts. These two values can be added to get the discounted quality, the time-dependent value of computation; this is the solid line in the middle of the graph. For the example of Figure 1.5 , an agent should compute for about 2.5 time units, and then act, at which point the discounted quality achieves its maximum value. If the computation lasts for longer than 4.3 time units, the resulting discounted solution quality is worse than if the algorithm just outputs the initial guess it can produce with virtually no computation. It is typical that the solution quality improves in jumps; when the current best solution changes, there is a jump in the quality. However, the penalty associated with waiting is often not as simple as a straight line.

To take into account bounded rationality, an agent must decide whether it should act or think more. This is challenging because an agent typically does not know how much better off it would be if it only spent a little bit more time

Dimension	Values
Modularity	flat, modular, hierarchical
Representation scheme	states, features, relations
Planning horizon	non-planning, finite stage, indefinite stage, infinite stage
Sensing uncertainty	fully observable, partially observable
Effect uncertainty	deterministic, stochastic
Preference	goals, complex preferences
Learning	knowledge is given, knowledge is learned
Number of agents	single agent, multiple agents
Computational limits	perfect rationality, bounded rationality

Figure 1.6: Dimensions of complexity

reasoning. Moreover, the time spent thinking about whether it should reason may detract from actually reasoning about the domain. However, bounded rationality can be the basis for approximate reasoning.

1.5.9   Interaction of the Dimensions

Figure 1.6 summarizes the dimensions of complexity. Unfortunately, we cannot study these dimensions independently because they interact in complex ways. Here we give some examples of the interactions.

The representation dimension interacts with the modularity dimension in that some modules in a hierarchy may be simple enough to reason in terms of a finite set of states, whereas other levels of abstraction may require reasoning about individuals and relations. For example, in a delivery robot, a module that maintains balance may only have a few states. A module that must prioritize the delivery of multiple parcels to multiple people may have to reason about multiple individuals (e.g., people, packages, and rooms) and the relations between them. At a higher level, a module that reasons about the activity over the day may only require a few states to cover the different phases of the day (e.g., there might be three states: busy time, available for requests, and recharge time).

The planning horizon interacts with the modularity dimension. For example, at a high level, a dog may be getting an immediate reward when it comes and gets a treat. At the level of deciding where to place its paws, there may be a long time until it gets the reward, and so at this level it may have to plan for an indefinite stage.

Sensing uncertainty probably has the greatest impact on the complexity of reasoning. It is much easier for an agent to reason when it knows the state of the world than when it doesn't. Although sensing uncertainty with states is well understood, sensing uncertainty with individuals and relations is an active area of current research.

The effect uncertainty dimension interacts with the modularity dimension: at one level in a hierarchy, an action may be deterministic, whereas at another level, it may be stochastic. As an example, consider the result of flying to Paris with a companion you are trying to impress. At one level you may know where you are (in Paris); at a lower level, you may be quite lost and not know where you are on a map of the airport. At an even lower level responsible for maintaining balance, you may know where you are: you are standing on the ground. At the highest level, you may be very unsure whether you have impressed your companion.

Preference models interact with uncertainty because an agent must have a trade-off between satisfying a major goal with some probability or a less desirable goal with a higher probability. This issue is explored in Section 9.1 (page 373).

Multiple agents can also be used for modularity; one way to design a single agent is to build multiple interacting agents that share a common goal of making the higher-level agent act intelligently. Some researchers, such as Minsky [1986], argue that intelligence is an emergent feature from a "society" of unintelligent agents.

Learning is often cast in terms of learning with features – determining which feature values best predict the value of another feature. However, learning can also be carried out with individuals and relations. Much work has been done on learning hierarchies, learning in partially observable domains, and learning with multiple agents, although each of these is challenging in its own right without considering interactions with multiple dimensions.

Two of these dimensions, modularity and bounded rationality, promise to make reasoning more efficient. Although they make the formalism more complicated, breaking the system into smaller components, and making the approximations needed to act in a timely fashion and within memory limitations, should help build more complex systems.

1.6 Prototypical Applications

AI applications are widespread and diverse and include medical diagnosis, scheduling factory processes, robots for hazardous environments, game playing, autonomous vehicles in space, natural language translation systems, and tutoring systems. Rather than treating each application separately, we abstract the essential features of such applications to allow us to study the principles behind intelligent reasoning and action.

This section outlines four application domains that will be developed in examples throughout the book. Although the particular examples presented are simple – otherwise they would not fit into the book – the application domains are representative of the range of domains in which AI techniques can be, and are being, used.

The four application domains are as follows:

- An **autonomous delivery robot** roams around a building delivering packages and coffee to people in the building. This delivery agent should be able to find paths, allocate resources, receive requests from people, make decisions about priorities, and deliver packages without injuring people or itself.

- A **diagnostic assistant** helps a human troubleshoot problems and suggests repairs or treatments to rectify the problems. One example is an electrician's assistant that suggests what may be wrong in a house, such as a fuse blown, a light switch broken, or a light burned out, given some symptoms of electrical problems. Another example is a medical diagnostician that finds potential diseases, useful tests, and appropriate treatments based on knowledge of a particular medical domain and a patient's symptoms and history. This assistant should be able to explain its reasoning to the person who is carrying out the tests and repairs and who is ultimately responsible for their actions.

- A **tutoring system** interacts with a student, presenting information about some domain and giving tests of the student's knowledge or performance. This entails more than presenting information to students. Doing what a good teacher does, namely tailoring the information presented to each student based on his or her knowledge, learning preferences, and misunderstandings, is more challenging. The system must understand both the subject matter and how students learn.

- A **trading agent** knows what a person wants and can buy goods and services on her behalf. It should know her requirements and preferences and how to trade off competing objectives. For example, for a family holiday a travel agent must book hotels, airline flights, rental cars, and entertainment, all of which must fit together. It should determine a customer's trade-offs. If the most suitable hotel cannot accommodate the family for all of the days, it should determine whether they would prefer to stay in the better hotel for part of the stay or if they prefer not to move hotels. It may even be able to shop around for specials or to wait until good deals come up.

These four domains will be used for the motivation for the examples in the book. In the next sections, we discuss each application domain in detail.

1.6.1 An Autonomous Delivery Robot

Imagine a robot that has wheels and can pick up objects and put them down. It has sensing capabilities so that it can recognize the objects that it must manipulate and can avoid obstacles. It can be given orders in natural language and obey them, making reasonable choices about what to do when its goals conflict. Such a robot could be used in an office environment to deliver packages, mail, and/or coffee, or it could be embedded in a wheelchair to help disabled people. It should be useful as well as safe.

In terms of the black box characterization of an agent in Figure 1.3 (page 11), the autonomous delivery robot has the following as inputs:

- prior knowledge, provided by the agent designer, about its own capabilities, what objects it may encounter and have to differentiate, what requests mean, and perhaps about its environment, such as a map;

- past experience obtained while acting, for instance, about the effect of its actions, what objects are common in the world, and what requests to expect at different times of the day;

- goals in terms of what it should deliver and when, as well as preferences that specify trade-offs, such as when it must forgo one goal to pursue another, or the trade-off between acting quickly and acting safely; and

- observations about its environment from such input devices as cameras, sonar, touch, sound, laser range finders, or keyboards.

The robot's outputs are motor controls that specify how its wheels should turn, where its limbs should move, and what it should do with its grippers. Other outputs may include speech and a video display.

In terms of the dimensions of complexity, the simplest case for the robot is a flat system, represented in terms of states, with no uncertainty, with achievement goals, with no other agents, with given knowledge, and with perfect rationality. In this case, with an indefinite stage planning horizon, the problem of deciding what to do is reduced to the problem of finding a path in a graph of states. This is explored in Chapter 3.

Each dimension can add conceptual complexity to the task of reasoning:

- A hierarchical decomposition can allow the complexity of the overall system to be increased while allowing each module to be simple and able to be understood by itself. This is explored in Chapter 2.

- Modeling in terms of features allows for a much more comprehensible system than modeling explicit states. For example, there may be features for the robot's location, the amount of fuel it has, what it is carrying, and so forth. Reasoning in terms of the states, where a state is an assignment of a value to each feature, loses the structure that is provided by the features. Reasoning in terms of the feature representation can be exploited for computational gain. Planning in terms of features is discussed in Chapter 8. When dealing with multiple individuals (e.g., multiple people or objects to deliver), it may be easier to reason in terms of individuals and relations. Planning in terms of individuals and relations is explored in Section 14.1 (page 598).

- The planning horizon can be finite if the agent only looks ahead a few steps. The planning horizon can be indefinite if there is a fixed set of goals to achieve. It can be infinite if the agent has to survive for the long term, with ongoing requests and actions, such as delivering mail whenever it arrives and recharging its battery when its battery is low.

- There could be goals, such as "deliver coffee to Chris and make sure you always have power." A more complex goal may be to "clean up the lab, and put everything where it belongs." There can be complex preferences, such as

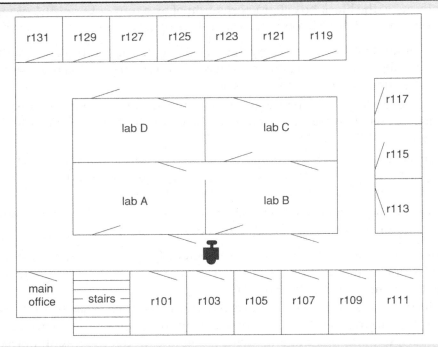

Figure 1.7: An environment for the delivery robot, which shows a typical laboratory environment. This also shows the locations of the doors and which way they open.

"deliver mail when it arrives and service coffee requests as soon as possible, but it is more important to deliver messages marked as important, and Chris really needs her coffee quickly when she asks for it."

- There can be sensing uncertainty because the robot does not know what is in the world based on its limited sensors.

- There can be uncertainty about the effects of an action, both at the low level, such as due to slippage of the wheels, or at the high level in that the agent might not know if putting the coffee on Chris's desk succeeded in delivering coffee to her.

- There can be multiple robots, which can coordinate to deliver coffee and parcels and compete for power outlets. There may also be children out to trick the robot.

- A robot has lots to learn, such as how slippery floors are as a function of their shininess, where Chris hangs out at different parts of the day and when she will ask for coffee, and which actions result in the highest rewards.

Figure 1.7 depicts a typical laboratory environment for a delivery robot. This environment consists of four laboratories and many offices. The robot can only push doors, and the directions of the doors in the diagram reflect the directions in which the robot can travel. Rooms require keys, and those keys can be obtained from various sources. The robot must deliver parcels, beverages, and dishes from room to room. The environment also contains a stairway that is potentially hazardous to the robot.

1.6.2 A Diagnostic Assistant

A **diagnostic assistant** is intended to advise a human about some particular system such as a medical patient, the electrical system in a house, or an automobile. The diagnostic assistant should advise about potential underlying faults or diseases, what tests to carry out, and what treatment to prescribe. To give such advice, the assistant requires a model of the system, including knowledge of potential causes, available tests, and available treatments, and observations of the system (which are often called symptoms).

To be useful, the diagnostic assistant must provide added value, be easy for a human to use, and not be more trouble than it is worth. A diagnostic assistant connected to the Internet can draw on expertise from throughout the world, and its actions can be based on the most up-to-date research. However, it must be able to justify why the suggested diagnoses or actions are appropriate. Humans are, and should be, suspicious of computer systems that are opaque and impenetrable. When humans are responsible for what they do, even if it is based on a computer system's advice, they should have reasonable justifications for the suggested actions.

In terms of the black box definition of an agent in Figure 1.3 (page 11), the diagnostic assistant has the following as inputs:

- prior knowledge, such as how switches and lights normally work, how diseases or malfunctions manifest themselves, what information tests provide, and the effects of repairs or treatments.

- past experience, in terms of data of previous cases that include the effects of repairs or treatments, the prevalence of faults or diseases, the prevalence of symptoms for these faults or diseases, and the accuracy of tests. These data are usually about similar artifacts or patients, rather than the actual one being diagnosed.

- goals of fixing the device and trade-offs, such as between fixing or replacing different components, or whether patients prefer to live longer if it means they will be in pain or be less coherent.

- observations of symptoms of a device or patient.

The output of the diagnostic assistant is in terms of recommendations of treatments and tests, along with a rationale for its recommendations.

Example 1.10 Figure 1.8 (on the next page) shows a depiction of an electrical distribution system in a house. In this house, power comes into the house through circuit breakers and then it goes to power outlets or to lights through light switches. For example, light l_1 is on if there is power coming into the house, if circuit breaker cb_1 is *on*, and if switches s_1 and s_2 are either both up or both down. This is the sort of model that normal householders may have of the electrical power in the house, and which they could use to determine what is

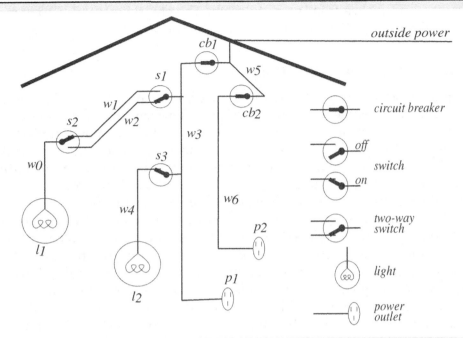

Figure 1.8: An electrical environment for the diagnostic assistant

wrong given evidence about the position of the switches and which lights are on and which are off. The diagnostic assistant is there to help a householder or an electrician troubleshoot electrical problems.

Each dimension is relevant to the diagnostic assistant:

- Hierarchical decomposition allows for very-high-level goals to be maintained while treating the lower-level causes and allows for detailed monitoring of the system. For example, in a medical domain, one module could take the output of a heart monitor and give higher-level observations such as notifying when there has been a change in the heart rate. Another module could take in this observation and other high-level observations and notice what other symptoms happen at the same time as a change in heart rate. In the electrical domain, Figure 1.8 is at one level of abstraction; a lower level could specify the voltages, how wires are spliced together, and the internals of switches.

- Most systems are too complicated to reason about in terms of the states, and so they are usually described in terms of the features or individual components and relations among them. For example, a human body may be described in terms of the values for features of its various components. Designers may want to model the dynamics without knowing the actual individuals. For example, designers of the electrical diagnosis system would model how lights and switches work before knowing which lights and switches exist in an actual house and, thus, before they know the features.

This can be achieved by modeling in terms of relations and their interaction and by adding the individual components when they become known.

- It is possible to reason about a static system, such as reasoning about what could be wrong when a light is off given the position of switches. It is also possible to reason about a sequence of tests and treatments, where the agents keep testing and treating until the problem is fixed, or where the agent carries out ongoing monitoring of a system, continuously fixing whatever gets broken.

- Sensing uncertainty is the fundamental problem that faces diagnosis. Diagnosis is required if an agent cannot directly observe the internals of the system.

- Effect uncertainty also exists in that an agent may not know the outcome of a treatment and, often, treatments have unanticipated outcomes.

- The goal may be as simple as "fix what is wrong," but often there are complex trade-offs involving costs, pain, life expectancy, the probability that the diagnosis is correct, and the uncertainty as to efficacy and side effects of the treatment.

- Although it is often a single-agent problem, diagnosis becomes more complicated when multiple experts are involved who perhaps have competing experience and models. There may be other patients with whom an agent must compete for resources (e.g., doctor's time, surgery rooms).

- Learning is fundamental to diagnosis. It is through learning that we understand the progression of diseases and how well treatments work or do not work. Diagnosis is a challenging domain for learning, because all patients are different, and each individual doctor's experience is only with a few patients with any particular set of symptoms. Doctors also see a biased sample of the population; those who come to see them usually have unusual or painful symptoms.

- Diagnosis often requires a quick response, which may not allow for the time to carry out exhaustive reasoning or perfect rationality.

1.6.3   An Intelligent Tutoring System

An **intelligent tutoring system** is a computer system that tutors students in some domain of study.

For example, in a tutoring system to teach elementary physics, such as mechanics, the system may present the theory and worked-out examples. The system can ask the student questions and it must be able to understand the student's answers, as well as determine the student's knowledge based on what answers were given. This should then affect what is presented and what other questions are asked of the student. The student can ask questions of the system, and so the system should be able to solve problems in the physics domain.

In terms of the black box definition of an agent in Figure 1.3 (page 11), an intelligent tutoring system has the following as inputs:

- prior knowledge, provided by the agent designer, about the subject matter being taught, teaching strategies, possible errors, and misconceptions of the students.

- past experience, which the tutoring system has acquired by interacting with students, about what errors students make, how many examples it takes to learn something, and what students forget. This can be information about students in general or about a particular student.

- preferences about the importance of each topic, the level of achievement of the student that is desired, and costs associated with usability. There are often complex trade-offs among these.

- observations of a student's test results and observations of the student's interaction (or non-interaction) with the system. Students can also ask questions or provide new examples with which they want help.

The output of the tutoring system is the information presented to the student, tests the students should take, answers to questions, and reports to parents and teachers.

Each dimension is relevant to the tutoring system:

- There should be both a hierarchical decomposition of the agent and a decomposition of the task of teaching. Students should be taught the basic skills before they can be taught higher-level concepts. The tutoring system has high-level teaching strategies, but, at a much lower level, it must design the details of concrete examples and specific questions for a test.

- A tutoring system may be able to reason in terms of the state of the student. However, it is more realistic to have multiple features for the student and the subject domain. A physics tutor may be able to reason in terms of features that are known at design time if the examples are fixed and it is only reasoning about one student. For more complicated cases, the tutoring system should refer to individuals and relations. If the tutoring system or the student can create examples with multiple individuals, the system may not know the features at design time and will have to reason in terms of individuals and relations.

- In terms of planning horizon, for the duration of a test, it may be reasonable to assume that the domain is static and that the student does not learn while taking a test. For some subtasks, a finite horizon may be appropriate. For example, there may be a teach, test, reteach sequence. For other cases, there may be an indefinite horizon where the system may not know at design time how many steps it will take until the student has mastered some concept. It may also be possible to model teaching as an ongoing process of learning and testing with appropriate breaks, with no expectation of the system finishing.

- Uncertainty will have to play a large role. The system cannot directly observe the knowledge of the student. All it has is some sensing input, based on questions the student asks or does not ask, and test results. The system will not know for certain the effect of a particular teaching episode.

- Although it may be possible to have a simple goal such as to teach some particular concept, it is more likely that complex preferences must be taken into account. One reason is that, with uncertainty, there may be no way to guarantee that the student knows the concept being taught; any method that tries to maximize the probability that the student knows a concept will be very annoying, because it will continue to repeatedly teach and test if there is a slight chance that the student's errors are due to misunderstanding as opposed to fatigue or boredom. More complex preferences would enable a trade-off among fully teaching a concept, boring the student, the time taken, and the amount of retesting. The user may also have a preference for a teaching style that should be taken into account.

- It may be appropriate to treat this as a single-agent problem. However, the teacher, the student, and the parent may all have different preferences that must be taken into account. Each of these agents may act strategically by not telling the truth.

- We would expect the system to be able to learn about what teaching strategies work, how well some questions work at testing concepts, and what common mistakes students make. It could learn general knowledge, or knowledge particular to a topic (e.g., learning about what strategies work for teaching mechanics) or knowledge about a particular student, such as learning what works for Sam.

- One could imagine that choosing the most appropriate material to present would take a lot of computation time. However, the student must be responded to in a timely fashion. Bounded rationality would play a part in ensuring that the system does not compute for a long time while the student is waiting.

1.6.4 A Trading Agent

A **trading agent** is like a robot, but instead of interacting with a physical environment, it interacts with an information environment. Its task is to procure goods and services for a user. It must be able to be told the needs of a user, and it must interact with sellers (e.g., on the Web). The simplest trading agent involves proxy bidding for a user on an auction site, where the system will keep bidding until the user's price limit is reached. A more complicated trading agent will buy multiple complementary items, like booking a flight, a hotel, and a rental car that fit together, in addition to trading off competing preferences. Another example of a trading agent is one that monitors how much food and groceries are in a household, monitors the prices, and orders goods before they are needed, keeping costs to a minimum.

In terms of the black box definition of an agent in Figure 1.3 (page 11), the trading agent has the following as inputs:

- prior knowledge about types of goods and services, selling practices, and how auctions work;

- past experience about where is the best place to look for specials, how prices vary in time in an auction, and when specials tend to turn up;
- preferences in terms of what the user wants and how to trade off competing goals; and
- observations about what items are available, their price, and, perhaps, how long they are available.

The output of the trading agent is either a proposal to the user that they can accept or reject or an actual purchase.

The trading agent should take all of the dimensions into account:

- Hierarchical decomposition is essential because of the complexity of domains. Consider the problem of making all of the arrangements and purchases for a custom holiday for a traveler. It is simpler to have a module that can purchase a ticket and optimize connections and timing, rather than to do this at the same time as determining what doors to go through to get to the taxi stand.

- The state space of the trading agent is too large to reason in terms of individual states. There are also too many individuals to reason in terms of features. The trading agent will have to reason in terms of individuals such as customers, days, hotels, flights, and so on.

- A trading agent typically does not make just one purchase, but must make a sequence of purchases, often a large number of sequential decisions (e.g., purchasing one hotel room may require booking ground transportation, which may in turn require baggage storage), and often plans for ongoing purchasing, such as for an agent that makes sure a household has enough food on hand at all times.

- There is often sensing uncertainty in that a trading agent does not know all of the available options and their availability, but must find out information that can become old quickly (e.g., if some hotel becomes booked up). A travel agent does not know if a flight will be canceled or delayed or whether the passenger's luggage will be lost. This uncertainty means that the agent must plan for the unanticipated.

- There is also effect uncertainty in that the agent does not know if an attempted purchase will succeed.

- Complex preferences are at the core of the trading agent. The main problem is in allowing users to specify what they want. The preferences of users are typically in terms of functionality, not components. For example, typical computer buyers have no idea of what hardware to buy, but they know what functionality they want and they also want the flexibility to be able to use new features that might not yet exist. Similarly, in a travel domain, what activities a user may want may depend on the location. Users also may want the ability to participate in a local custom at their destination, even though they may not know what these customs are.

- A trading agent has to reason about other agents. In commerce, prices are governed by supply and demand; this means that it is important to reason about the other competing agents. This happens particularly in a world where many items are sold by auction. Such reasoning becomes particularly difficult when there are items that must complement each other, such as flights and hotel booking, and items that can substitute for each other, such as bus transport or taxis.

- A trading agent should learn about what items sell quickly, which of the suppliers are reliable, where to find good deals, and what unanticipated events may occur.

- A trading agent faces severe communication limitations. In the time between finding that some item is available and coordinating the item with other items, the item may have sold out. This can sometimes be alleviated by sellers agreeing to hold some items (not to sell them to someone else in the meantime), but sellers will not be prepared to hold an item indefinitely if others want to buy it.

Because of the personalized nature of the trading agent, it should be able to do better than a generic purchaser that, for example, only offers packaged tours.

1.7 Overview of the Book

The rest of the book explores the design space defined by the dimensions of complexity. It considers each dimension separately, where this can be done sensibly.

Chapter 2 analyzes what is inside the black box of Figure 1.3 (page 11) and discusses the modular and hierarchical decomposition of intelligent agents.

Chapter 3 considers the simplest case of determining what to do in the case of a single agent that reasons with explicit states, no uncertainty, and has goals to be achieved, but with an indefinite horizon. In this case, the problem of solving the goal can be abstracted to searching for a path in a graph. It is shown how extra knowledge of the domain can help the search.

Chapters 4 and 5 show how to exploit features. In particular, Chapter 4 considers how to find possible states given constraints on the assignments of values to features represented as variables. Chapter 5 shows how to determine whether some proposition must be true in all states that satisfy a given set of constraints.

Chapter 6 shows how to reason with uncertainty.

Chapter 7 shows how an agent can learn from past experiences and data. It covers the most common case of learning, namely supervised learning with features, where a set of observed target features are being learned.

Chapter 8 considers the problem of planning, in particular representing and reasoning with feature-based representations of states and actions. Chapter 9 considers the problem of planning with uncertainty, and Chapter 10 expands the case to multiple agents.

Chapter 11 introduces learning under uncertainty and reinforcement learning.

Chapter 12 shows how to reason in terms of individuals and relations. Chapter 13 discusses ontologies and how to build knowledge-based systems. Chapter 14 shows how reasoning about individuals and relations can be combined with planning, learning, and probabilistic reasoning.

Chapter 15 reviews the design space of AI and shows how the material presented can fit into that design space. It also presents ethical considerations involved in building intelligent agents.

1.8 Review

The following are the main points you should have learned from this chapter:

- Artificial intelligence is the study of computational agents that act intelligently.
- An agent acts in an environment and only has access to its prior knowledge, its history of observations, and its goals and preferences.
- An intelligent agent is a physical symbol system that manipulates symbols to determine what to do.
- A designer of an intelligent agent should be concerned about modularity, how to describe the world, how far ahead to plan, uncertainty in both perception and the effects of actions, the structure of goals or preferences, other agents, how to learn from experience, and the fact that all real agents have limited computational resources.
- To solve a problem by computer, the computer must have an effective representation with which to reason.
- To know when you have solved a problem, an agent must have a definition of what constitutes an adequate solution, such as whether it has to be optimal, approximately optimal, or almost always optimal, or whether a satisficing solution is adequate.
- In choosing a representation, you should find a representation that is as close as possible to the problem, so that it is easy to determine what it is representing and so it can be checked for correctness and be able to be maintained. Often, users want an explanation of why they should believe the answer.

1.9 References and Further Reading

The ideas in this chapter have been derived from many sources. Here, we will try to acknowledge those that are explicitly attributable to particular authors. Most of the other ideas are part of AI folklore; trying to attribute them to anyone would be impossible.

Haugeland [1997] contains a good collection of articles on the philosophy behind artificial intelligence, including that classic paper of Turing [1950] that proposes the Turing test. Cohen [2005] gives a recent discussion of the Turing test.

Nilsson [2009] gives a detailed description of the history of AI. Chrisley and Begeer [2000] present many classic papers on AI.

The physical symbol system hypothesis was posited by Newell and Simon [1976]. See also Simon [1996], who discusses the role of symbol systems in a multidisciplinary context. The distinctions between real, synthetic, and artificial intelligence are discussed by Haugeland [1985], who also provides useful introductory material on interpreted, automatic formal symbol systems and the Church–Turing thesis. For a critique of the symbol-system hypothesis see Brooks [1990] and Winograd [1990]. Nilsson [2007] evaluates the hypothesis in terms of recent criticisms.

The use of anytime algorithms is due to Horvitz [1989] and Boddy and Dean [1994]. See Dean and Wellman [1991, Chapter 8], Zilberstein [1996], and Russell [1997] for introductions to bounded rationality.

For discussions on the foundations of AI and the breadth of research in AI see Kirsh [1991a], Bobrow [1993], and the papers in the corresponding volumes, as well as Schank [1990] and Simon [1995]. The importance of knowledge in AI is discussed in Lenat and Feigenbaum [1991] and Smith [1991].

For overviews of cognitive science and the role that AI and other disciplines play in that field, see Gardner [1985], Posner [1989], and Stillings, Feinstein, Garfield, Rissland, Rosenbaum, Weisler, and Baker-Ward [1987].

Purchasing agents can become very complex. Sandholm [2007] describes how AI can be used for procurement of multiple goods with complex preferences.

A number of AI texts are valuable as reference books complementary to this book, providing a different perspective on AI. In particular, Russell and Norvig [2010] give a more encyclopedic overview of AI and provide a complementary source for many of the topics covered in this book. They provide an outstanding review of the scientific literature, which we do not try to duplicate.

The *Encyclopedia of Artificial Intelligence* [Shapiro, 1992] is an encyclopedic reference on AI written by leaders in the field and still provides background on some of the classic topics. There are also a number of collections of classic research papers. The general collections of most interest to readers of this book include Webber and Nilsson [1981] and Brachman and Levesque [1985]. More specific collections are given in the appropriate chapters.

The Association for the Advancement of Artificial Intelligence (AAAI) provides introductory material and news at their *AI Topics* web site (http://www.aaai.org/AITopics/html/welcome.html). *AI Magazine*, published by AAAI, often has excellent overview articles and descriptions of particular applications. *IEEE Intelligent Systems* also provides accessible articles on AI research.

There are many journals that provide in-depth research contributions and conferences where the most up-to-date research is found. These include the journals *Artificial Intelligence*, the *Journal of Artificial Intelligence Research*, *IEEE Transactions on Pattern Analysis and Machine Intelligence*, and *Computational Intelligence*, as well as more specialized journals such as *Neural Computation*, *Computational Linguistics*, *Machine Learning*, the *Journal of Automated Reasoning*, the

Journal of Approximate Reasoning, *IEEE Transactions on Robotics and Automation*, and the *Theory and Practice of Logic Programming*. Most of the cutting-edge research is published first in conferences. Those of most interest to a general audience are the biennial International Joint Conference on Artificial Intelligence (IJCAI), the AAAI Annual Conference, the European Conference on AI (ECAI), the Pacific Rim International Conference on AI (PRICAI), various national conferences, and many specialized conferences and workshops.

1.10 Exercises

Exercise 1.1 For each of the following, give five reasons why:

(a) A dog is more intelligent than a worm.

(b) A human is more intelligent than a dog.

(c) An organization is more intelligent than an individual human.

Based on these, give a definition of what "more intelligent" may mean.

Exercise 1.2 Give as many disciplines as you can whose aim is to study intelligent behavior of some sort. For each discipline, find out what aspect of behavior is investigated and what tools are used to study it. Be as liberal as you can regarding what defines intelligent behavior.

Exercise 1.3 Find out about two applications of AI (not classes of applications, but specific programs). For each application, write, at most, one typed page describing it. You should try to cover the following questions:

(a) What does the application actually do (e.g., control a spacecraft, diagnose a photocopier, provide intelligent help for computer users)?

(b) What AI technologies does it use (e.g., model-based diagnosis, belief networks, semantic networks, heuristic search, constraint satisfaction)?

(c) How well does it perform? (According to the authors or to an independent review? How does it compare to humans? How do the authors know how well it works?)

(d) Is it an experimental system or a fielded system? (How many users does it have? What expertise do these users require?)

(e) Why is it intelligent? What aspects of it makes it an intelligent system?

(f) [optional] What programming language and environment was it written in? What sort of user interface does it have?

(g) References: Where did you get the information about the application? To what books, articles, or web pages should others who want to know about the application refer?

Exercise 1.4 Choose four pairs of dimensions that were not covered in the book. For each pair, give one commonsense example of where the dimensions interact.

Chapter 2

Agent Architectures and Hierarchical Control

By a hierarchic system, or hierarchy, I mean a system that is composed of interrelated subsystems, each of the latter being in turn hierarchic in structure until we reach some lowest level of elementary subsystem. In most systems of nature it is somewhat arbitrary as to where we leave off the partitioning and what subsystems we take as elementary. Physics makes much use of the concept of "elementary particle," although the particles have a disconcerting tendency not to remain elementary very long . . .

Empirically a large proportion of the complex systems we observe in nature exhibit hierarchic structure. On theoretical grounds we would expect complex systems to be hierarchies in a world in which complexity had to evolve from simplicity.

– Herbert A. Simon [1996]

This chapter discusses how an intelligent agent can perceive, reason, and act over time in an environment. In particular, it considers the internal structure of an agent. As Simon points out in the quote above, hierarchical decomposition is an important part of the design of complex systems such as intelligent agents. This chapter presents ways to design agents in terms of hierarchical decompositions and ways that agents can be built, taking into account the knowledge that an agent needs to act intelligently.

2.1 Agents

An **agent** is something that acts in an environment. An agent can, for example, be a person, a robot, a dog, a worm, the wind, gravity, a lamp, or a computer program that buys and sells.

Purposive agents have preferences. They prefer some states of the world to other states, and they act to try to achieve the states they prefer most. The non-purposive agents are grouped together and called **nature**. Whether or not an agent is purposive is a modeling assumption that may, or may not, be appropriate. For example, for some applications it may be appropriate to model a dog as purposive, and for others it may suffice to model a dog as non-purposive.

If an agent does not have preferences, by definition it does not care what world state it ends up in, and so it does not matter what it does. The only reason to design an agent is to instill it with preferences – to make it prefer some world states and try to achieve them. An agent does not have to know its preferences. For example, a thermostat is an agent that senses the world and turns a heater either on or off. There are preferences embedded in the thermostat, such as to keep the occupants of a room at a pleasant temperature, even though the thermostat arguably does not know these are its preferences. The preferences of an agent are often the preferences of the designer of the agent, but sometimes an agent can be given goals and preferences at run time.

Agents interact with the environment with a **body**. An **embodied** agent has a physical body. A **robot** is an artificial purposive embodied agent. Sometimes agents that act only in an information space are called robots, but we just refer to those as agents.

This chapter considers how to build purposive agents. We use robots as a main motivating example, because much of the work has been carried out in the context of robotics and much of the terminology is from robotics. However, the discussion is intended to cover all agents.

Agents receive information through their **sensors**. An agent's actions depend on the information it receives from its sensors. These sensors may, or may not, reflect what is true in the world. Sensors can be noisy, unreliable, or broken, and even when sensors are reliable there is still ambiguity about the world based on sensor readings. An agent must act on the information it has available. Often this information is very weak, for example, "sensor s appears to be producing value v."

Agents act in the world through their **actuators** (also called **effectors**). Actuators can also be noisy, unreliable, slow, or broken. What an agent controls is the message (command) it sends to its actuators. Agents often carry out actions to find more information about the world, such as opening a cupboard door to find out what is in the cupboard or giving students a test to determine their knowledge.

2.2 Agent Systems

Figure 2.1 depicts the general interaction between an agent and its environment. Together the whole system is known as an agent system.

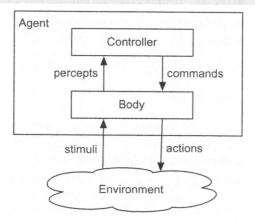

Figure 2.1: An agent system and its components

An **agent system** is made up of an agent and its environment. The agent receives **stimuli** from the environment and carries out **actions** in the environment.

An **agent** is made up of a **body** and a **controller**. The controller receives **percepts** from the body and sends **commands** to the body.

A body includes **sensors** that convert stimuli into percepts and **actuators** that convert commands into actions.

Stimuli include light, sound, words typed on a keyboard, mouse movements, and physical bumps. The stimuli can also include information obtained from a web page or from a database.

Common sensors include touch sensors, cameras, infrared sensors, sonar, microphones, keyboards, mice, and XML readers used to extract information from web pages. As a prototypical sensor, a camera senses light coming into its lens and converts it into a two-dimensional array of intensity values called **pixels**. Sometimes multiple pixel arrays exist for different colors or for multiple cameras. Such pixel arrays could be the percepts for our controller. More often, percepts consist of higher-level features such as lines, edges, and depth information. Often the percepts are more specialized – for example, the positions of bright orange dots, the part of the display a student is looking at, or the hand signals given by a human.

Actions include steering, accelerating wheels, moving links of arms, speaking, displaying information, or sending a post command to a web site. Commands include low-level commands such as to set the voltage of a motor to some particular value, and high-level specifications of the desired motion of a robot, such as "stop" or "travel at 1 meter per second due east" or "go to room 103." Actuators, like sensors, are typically noisy. For example, stopping takes time; a robot is governed by the laws of physics and has momentum, and messages take time to travel. The robot may end up going only approximately

1 meter per second, approximately east, and both speed and direction may fluctuate. Even traveling to a particular room may fail for a number of reasons.

The controller is the brain of the agent. The rest of this chapter is about how to build controllers.

2.2.1   The Agent Function

Agents are situated in time: they receive sensory data in time and do actions in time. The action that an agent does at a particular time is a function of its inputs (page 10). We first consider the notion of time.

Let T be the set of **time** points. Assume that T is totally ordered and has some metric that can be used to measure the temporal distance between any two time points. Basically, we assume that T can be mapped to some subset of the real line.

T is **discrete** if there exist only a finite number of time points between any two time points; for example, there is a time point every hundredth of a second, or every day, or there may be time points whenever interesting events occur. T is **dense** if there is always another time point between any two time points; this implies there must be infinitely many time points between any two points. Discrete time has the property that, for all times, except perhaps a last time, there is always a next time. Dense time does not have a "next time." Initially, we assume that time is discrete and goes on forever. Thus, for each time there is a next time. We write $t + 1$ to be the next time after time t; it does not mean that the time points are equally spaced.

Assume that T has a starting point, which we arbitrarily call 0.

Suppose P is the set of all possible percepts. A **percept trace**, or **percept stream**, is a function from T into P. It specifies what is observed at each time.

Suppose C is the set of all commands. A **command trace** is a function from T into C. It specifies the command for each time point.

Example 2.1 Consider a household trading agent that monitors the price of some commodity (e.g., it checks online for special deals and for price increases for toilet paper) and how much the household has in stock. It must decide whether to buy more and how much to buy. The percepts are the price and the amount in stock. The command is the number of units the agent decides to buy (which is zero if the agent does not buy any). A percept trace specifies for each time point (e.g., each day) the price at that time and the amount in stock at that time. Percept traces are given in Figure 2.2. A command trace specifies how much the agent decides to buy at each time point. An example command trace is given in Figure 2.3.

The action of actually buying depends on the command but may be different. For example, the agent could issue a command to buy 12 rolls of toilet paper at a particular price. This does not mean that the agent actually buys 12 rolls because there could be communication problems, the store could have run out of toilet paper, or the price could change between deciding to buy and actually buying.

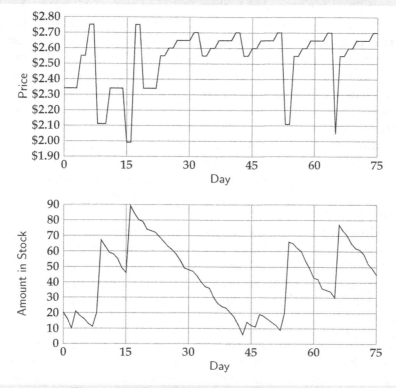

Figure 2.2: Percept traces for Example 2.1

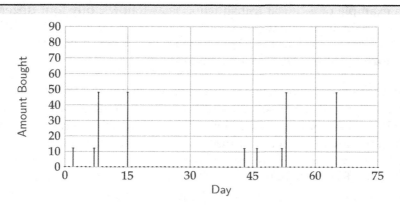

Figure 2.3: Command trace for Example 2.1

A percept trace for an agent is thus the sequence of all past, present, and future percepts received by the controller. A command trace is the sequence of all past, present, and future commands issued by the controller. The commands can be a function of the history of percepts. This gives rise to the concept of a **transduction**, a function that maps percept traces into command traces.

Because all agents are situated in time, an agent cannot actually observe full percept traces; at any time it has only experienced the part of the trace up to *now*. It can only observe the value of the trace at time $t \in T$ when it gets to time t. Its command can only depend on what it has experienced.

A transduction is **causal** if, for all times t, the command at time t depends only on percepts up to and including time t. The causality restriction is needed because agents are situated in time; their command at time t cannot depend on percepts after time t.

A **controller** is an implementation of a causal transduction.

The **history** of an agent at time t is the percept trace of the agent for all times before or at time t and the command trace of the agent before time t.

Thus, a **causal transduction** specifies a function from the agent's history at time t into the command at time t. It can be seen as the most general specification of an agent.

Example 2.2　Continuing Example 2.1 (page 46), a causal transduction specifies, for each time, how much of the commodity the agent should buy depending on the price history, the history of how much of the commodity is in stock (including the current price and amount in stock) and the past history of buying.

An example of a causal transduction is as follows: buy four dozen rolls if there are fewer than five dozen in stock and the price is less than 90% of the average price over the last 20 days; buy a dozen more rolls if there are fewer than a dozen in stock; otherwise, do not buy any.

Although a causal transduction is a function of an agent's history, it cannot be directly implemented because an agent does not have direct access to its entire history. It has access only to its current percepts and what it has remembered.

The **belief state** of an agent at time t is all of the information the agent has remembered from the previous times. An agent has access only to its history that it has encoded in its belief state. Thus, the belief state encapsulates all of the information about its history that the agent can use for current and future commands. At any time, an agent has access to its belief state and its percepts.

The belief state can contain any information, subject to the agent's memory and processing limitations. This is a very general notion of belief; sometimes we use a more specific notion of belief, such as the agent's belief about what is true in the world, the agent's beliefs about the dynamics of the environment, or the agent's belief about what it will do in the future.

Some instances of belief state include the following:

- The belief state for an agent that is following a fixed sequence of instructions may be a program counter that records its current position in the sequence.

- The belief state can contain specific facts that are useful – for example, where the delivery robot left the parcel in order to go and get the key, or where it has already checked for the key. It may be useful for the agent to remember anything that is reasonably stable and that cannot be immediately observed.

- The belief state could encode a model or a partial model of the state of the world. An agent could maintain its best guess about the current state of the world or could have a probability distribution over possible world states; see Section 5.6 (page 199) and Chapter 6.

- The belief state could be a representation of the dynamics of the world and the meaning of its percepts, and the agent could use its perception to determine what is true in the world.

- The belief state could encode what the agent **desires**, the **goals** it still has to achieve, its **beliefs** about the state of the world, and its **intentions**, or the steps it intends to take to achieve its goals. These can be maintained as the agent acts and observes the world, for example, removing achieved goals and replacing intentions when more appropriate steps are found.

A controller must maintain the agent's belief state and determine what command to issue at each time. The information it has available when it must do this includes its belief state and its current percepts.

A **belief state transition function** for discrete time is a function

$$remember : S \times P \rightarrow S$$

where S is the set of belief states and P is the set of possible percepts; $s_{t+1} = remember(s_t, p_t)$ means that s_{t+1} is the belief state following belief state s_t when p_t is observed.

A **command function** is a function

$$do : S \times P \rightarrow C$$

where S is the set of belief states, P is the set of possible percepts, and C is the set of possible commands; $c_t = do(s_t, p_t)$ means that the controller issues command c_t when the belief state is s_t and when p_t is observed.

The belief-state transition function and the command function together specify a causal transduction for the agent. Note that a causal transduction is a function of the agent's history, which the agent doesn't necessarily have access to, but a command function is a function of the agent's belief state and percepts, which it does have access to.

Example 2.3 To implement the causal transduction of Example 2.2, a controller must keep track of the rolling history of the prices for the previous 20 days. By keeping track of the average (*ave*), it can update the average using

$$ave := ave + \frac{new - old}{20}$$

where *new* is the new price and *old* is the oldest price remembered. It can then discard *old*. It must do something special for the first 20 days.

A simpler controller could, instead of remembering a rolling history in order to maintain the average, remember just the average and use the average as a surrogate for the oldest item. The belief state can then contain one real number (*ave*). The state transition function to update the average could be

$$ave := ave + \frac{new - ave}{20}$$

This controller is much easier to implement and is not sensitive to what happened 20 time units ago. This way of maintaining estimates of averages is the basis for temporal differences in reinforcement learning (page 467).

If there exists a finite number of possible belief states, the controller is called a **finite state controller** or a **finite state machine**. A **factored representation** is one in which the belief states, percepts, or commands are defined by features (page 21). If there exists a finite number of features, and each feature can only have a finite number of possible values, the controller is a **factored finite state machine**. Richer controllers can be built using an unbounded number of values or an unbounded number of features. A controller that has countably many states can compute anything that is computable by a Turing machine.

2.3   Hierarchical Control

One way that you could imagine building an agent depicted in Figure 2.1 (page 45) is to split the body into the sensors and a complex perception system that feeds a description of the world into a reasoning engine implementing a controller that, in turn, outputs commands to actuators. This turns out to be a bad architecture for intelligent systems. It is too slow, and it is difficult to reconcile the slow reasoning about complex, high-level goals with the fast reaction that an agent needs, for example, to avoid obstacles. It also is not clear that there is a description of a world that is independent of what you do with it (see Exercise 1 (page 66)).

An alternative architecture is a hierarchy of controllers as depicted in Figure 2.4. Each layer sees the layers below it as a **virtual body** from which it gets percepts and to which it sends commands. The lower-level layers are able to run much faster, react to those aspects of the world that need to be reacted to quickly, and deliver a simpler view of the world to the higher layers, hiding inessential information.

In general, there can be multiple features passed from layer to layer and between states at different times.

There are three types of inputs to each layer at each time:

- the features that come from the belief state, which are referred to as the remembered or previous values of these features;
- the features representing the percepts from the layer below in the hierarchy; and
- the features representing the commands from the layer above in the hierarchy.

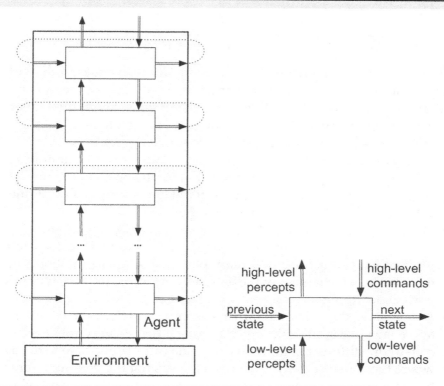

Figure 2.4: An idealized hierarchical agent system architecture. The unlabeled rect-angles represent layers, and the double lines represent information flow. The dotted lines show how the output at one time is the input for the next time.

There are three types of outputs from each layer at each time:

- the higher-level percepts for the layer above,
- the lower-level commands for the layer below, and
- the next values for the belief-state features.

An implementation of a layer specifies how the outputs of a layer are a func-tion of its inputs. Computing this function can involve arbitrary computation, but the goal is to keep each layer as simple as possible.

To implement a controller, each input to a layer must get its value from somewhere. Each percept or command input should be connected to an out-put of some other layer. Other inputs come from the remembered beliefs. The outputs of a layer do not have to be connected to anything, or they could be connected to multiple inputs.

High-level reasoning, as carried out in the higher layers, is often discrete and qualitative, whereas low-level reasoning, as carried out in the lower lay-ers, is often continuous and quantitative (see box on page 52). A controller that reasons in terms of both discrete and continuous values is called a **hybrid system**.

| Qualitative Versus Quantitative Representations |

Much of science and engineering considers **quantitative reasoning** with numerical quantities, using differential and integral calculus as the main tools. **Qualitative reasoning** is reasoning, often using logic, about qualitative distinctions rather than numerical values for given parameters.

Qualitative reasoning is important for a number of reasons:

- An agent may not know what the exact values are. For example, for the delivery robot to pour coffee, it may not be able to compute the optimal angle that the coffee pot needs to be tilted, but a simple control rule may suffice to fill the cup to a suitable level.
- The reasoning may be applicable regardless of the quantitative values. For example, you may want a strategy for a robot that works regardless of what loads are placed on the robot, how slippery the floors are, or what the actual charge is of the batteries, as long as they are within some normal operating ranges.
- An agent needs to do qualitative reasoning to determine which quantitative laws are applicable. For example, if the delivery robot is filling a coffee cup, different quantitative formulas are appropriate to determine where the coffee goes when the coffee pot is not tilted enough for coffee to come out, when coffee comes out into a non-full cup, and when the coffee cup is full and the coffee is soaking into the carpet.

Qualitative reasoning uses discrete values, which can take a number of forms:

- **Landmarks** are values that make qualitative distinctions in the individual being modeled. In the coffee example, some important qualitative distinctions include whether the coffee cup is empty, partially full, or full. These landmark values are all that is needed to predict what happens if the cup is tipped upside down or if coffee is poured into the cup.
- **Orders-of-magnitude reasoning** involves approximate reasoning that ignores minor distinctions. For example, a partially full coffee cup may be full enough to deliver, half empty, or nearly empty. These **fuzzy terms** have ill-defined borders. Some relationship exists between the actual amount of coffee in the cup and the qualitative description, but there may not be strict numerical divisors.
- **Qualitative derivatives** indicate whether some value is increasing, decreasing, or staying the same.

A flexible agent needs to do qualitative reasoning before it does quantitative reasoning. Sometimes qualitative reasoning is all that is needed. Thus, an agent does not always need to do quantitative reasoning, but sometimes it needs to do both qualitative and quantitative reasoning.

Example 2.4 Consider a delivery robot (page 32) able to carry out high-level navigation tasks while avoiding obstacles. Suppose the delivery robot is required to visit a sequence of named locations in the environment of Figure 1.7 (page 32), avoiding obstacles it may encounter.

Assume the delivery robot has wheels like a car, and at each time can either go straight, turn right, or turn left. It cannot stop. The velocity is constant and the only command is to set the steering angle. Turning the wheels is instantaneous, but adjusting to a certain direction takes time. Thus, the robot can only travel straight ahead or go around in circular arcs with a fixed radius.

The robot has a position sensor that gives its current coordinates and orientation. It has a single whisker sensor that sticks out in front and slightly to the right and detects when it has hit an obstacle. In the example below, the whisker points 30° to the right of the direction the robot is facing. The robot does not have a map, and the environment can change (e.g., obstacles can move).

A layered controller for such a delivery robot is depicted in Figure 2.5 (on the next page). The robot is given a high-level plan to execute. The plan is a sequence of named locations to visit in order. The robot needs to sense the world and to move in the world in order to carry out the plan. The details of the lower layer are not shown in this figure.

The top layer, called *follow plan*, is described in Example 2.6 (page 56). That layer takes in a plan to execute. The plan is a list of named locations to visit in order. The locations are selected in order. Each selected location becomes the current target. This layer determines the x-y coordinates of the target. These coordinates are the target position for the lower level. The upper level knows about the names of locations, but the lower levels only know about coordinates.

The top layer maintains a belief state consisting of a list of names of locations that the robot still needs to visit and the coordinates of the current target. It issues commands to the middle layer in terms of the coordinates of the current target.

The middle layer, which could be called *go to target and avoid obstacles*, tries to keep traveling toward the current target position, avoiding obstacles. The middle layer is described in Example 2.5 (page 55). The target position, *target_pos*, is obtained from the top layer. When the middle layer has arrived at the target position, it signals to the top layer that it has achieved the target by setting *arrived* to be true. This signal can be implemented either as the middle layer issuing an interrupt to the top layer, which was waiting, or as the top layer continually monitoring the middle layer to determine when *arrived* becomes true. When *arrived* becomes true, the top layer then changes the target position to the coordinates of the next location on the plan. Because the top layer changes the current target position, the middle layer must use the *previous* target position to determine whether it has arrived. Thus, the middle layer must get both the current and the previous target positions from the top layer: the previous target position to determine whether it has arrived, and the current target position to travel to.

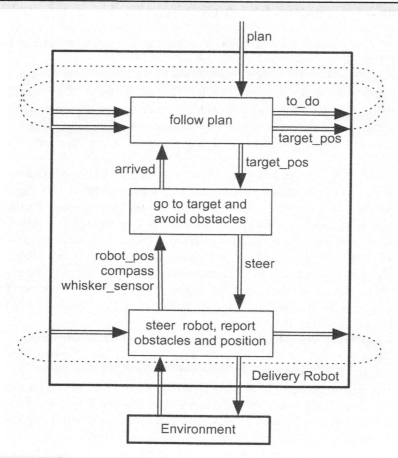

Figure 2.5: A hierarchical decomposition of the delivery robot

The middle layer can access the robot's current position and direction and can determine whether its single whisker sensor is on or off. It can use a simple strategy of trying to head toward the target unless it is blocked, in which case it turns left.

The middle layer is built on a lower layer that provides a simple view of the robot. This lower layer could be called *steer robot and report obstacles and position*. It takes in steering commands and reports the robot's position, orientation, and whether the sensor is on or off.

Inside a layer are features that can be functions of other features and of the inputs to the layers. There is an arc into a feature from the features or inputs on which it is dependent. The graph of how features depend on each other must be acyclic. The acyclicity of the graph allows the controller to be implemented by running a program that assigns the values in order. The features that make up the belief state can be written to and read from memory.

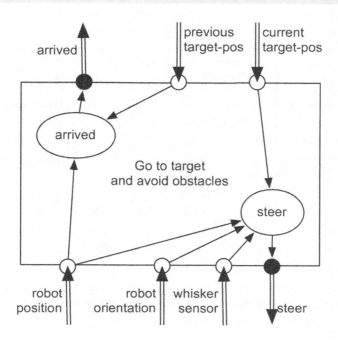

Figure 2.6: The middle layer of the delivery robot

Example 2.5 The middle *go to location and avoid obstacles* layer steers the robot to avoid obstacles. The inputs and outputs of this layer are given in Figure 2.6.

The robot has a single whisker sensor that detects obstacles touching the whisker. The one bit value that specifies whether the whisker sensor has hit an obstacle is provided by the lower layer. The lower layer also provides the robot position and orientation. All the robot can do is steer left by a fixed angle, steer right, or go straight. The aim of this layer is to make the robot head toward its current target position, avoiding obstacles in the process, and to report when it has arrived.

This layer of the controller maintains no internal belief state, so the belief state transition function is vacuous. The command function specifies the robot's steering direction as a function of its inputs and whether the robot has arrived.

The robot has arrived if its current position is close to the previous target position. Thus, *arrived* is assigned a value that is a function of the robot position and previous target position, and a threshold constant:

$$arrived := distance(previous\_target\_pos, robot\_pos) < threshold$$

where := means assignment, *distance* is the Euclidean distance, and *threshold* is a distance in the appropriate units.

The robot steers left if the whisker sensor is on; otherwise it heads toward the target position. This can be achieved by assigning the appropriate value to

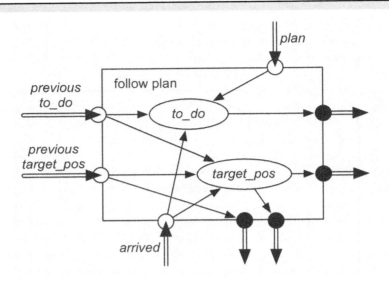

Figure 2.7: The top layer of the delivery robot controller

the *steer* variable:

    if *whisker_sensor* = *on*

        then *steer* := *left*

    else if *straight_ahead*(*robot_pos*, *robot_dir*, *current_target_pos*)

        then *steer* := *straight*

    else if *left_of*(*robot_position*, *robot_dir*, *current_target_pos*)

        then *steer* := *left*

    else *steer* := *right*

    end if

where *straight_ahead*(*robot_pos*, *robot_dir*, *current_target_pos*) is true when the robot is at *robot_pos*, facing the direction *robot_dir*, and when the current target position, *current_target_pos*, is straight ahead of the robot with some threshold (for later examples, this threshold is 11° of straight ahead). The function *left_of* tests if the target is to the left of the robot.

This layer is purely quantitative. It reasons in terms of numerical quantities rather than discrete values.

Example 2.6 The top layer, *follow plan*, is given a plan – a list of named locations to visit in order. These are the kinds of targets that could be produced by a planner, such as those developed in Chapter 8. The top layer is also told when the robot has arrived at the previous target. It must output target coordinates to the middle layer, and remember what it needs to carry out the plan. The layer is shown in Figure 2.7.

This layer maintains an internal belief state. It remembers the current target position and what locations it still has to visit. The *to_do* feature has as its value a list of all pending locations to visit. The *target_pos* feature maintains the position for the current target.

Once the robot has arrived at its previous target, the next target position is the coordinate of the next location to visit. The top-level plan given to the robot is in terms of named locations, so these must be translated into coordinates for the middle layer to use. The following code shows how the target position and the *to_do* list are changed when the robot has arrived at its previous target position:

> if *arrived* and not *empty*(*to_do*)
>
> > then
> >
> > > *target_pos'* := *coordinates*(*head*(*to_do*))
> > > *to_do'* := *tail*(*to_do*)
> >
> > end if

where *to_do'* is the next value for the *to_do* feature, and *target_pos'* is the next target position. Here *head*(*to_do*) is the first element of the *to_do* list, *tail*(*to_do*) is the rest of the *to_do* list, and *empty*(*to_do*) is true when the *to_do* list is empty.

In this layer, if the *to_do* list becomes empty, the robot does not change its target position. It keeps going around in circles. See Exercise 2.3 (page 67).

This layer determines the coordinates of the named locations. This could be done by simply having a database that specifies the coordinates of the locations. Using such a database is sensible if the locations do not move and are known a priori. However, if the locations can move, the lower layer must be able to tell the upper layer the current position of a location. The top layer would have to ask the lower layer the coordinates of a given location. See Exercise 2.8 (page 68).

To complete the controller, the belief state variables must be initialized, and the top-level plan must be input. This can be done by initializing the *to_do* list with the tail of the plan and the *target_pos* with the location of the first location.

A simulation of the plan [*goto*(*o109*), *goto*(*storage*), *goto*(*o109*), *goto*(*o103*)] with one obstacle is given in Figure 2.8 (on the next page). The robot starts at position $(0, 5)$ facing $90°$ (north), and there is a rectangular obstacle between the positions $(20, 20)$ and $(35, -5)$.

2.3.1 Agents Modeling the World

The definition of a belief state is very general and does not constrain what should be remembered by the agent. Often it is useful for the agent to maintain some model of the world, even if its model is incomplete and inaccurate. A **model** of a world is a representation of the state of the world at a particular time and/or the dynamics of the world.

One method is for the agent to maintain its belief about the world and to update these beliefs based on its commands. This approach requires a model of both the state of the world and the dynamics of the world. Given the state at one time, and the dynamics, the state at the next time can be predicted. This

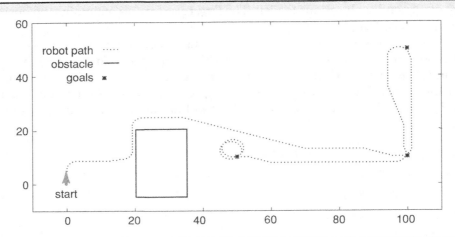

Figure 2.8: A simulation of the robot carrying out the plan of Example 2.6

process is known as **dead reckoning**. For example, a robot could maintain its estimate of its position and update it based on its actions. When the world is dynamic or when there are noisy actuators (e.g., a wheel slips, it is not of exactly the right diameter, or acceleration is not instantaneous), the noise accumulates, so that the estimates of position soon become so inaccurate that they are useless. However, if the model is accurate at some level of abstraction, this may be an appropriate model of that level of abstraction.

An alternative is to use **perception** to build a model of the relevant part of the world. Perception is the use of sensing information to understand the world. This could, for example, involve using vision to detect features of the world and use these features to determine the position of a robot and obstacles or packages to be picked up. Perception tends to be ambiguous and noisy. It is difficult to build a model of a three-dimensional world based on a single image of the world.

A more promising approach is to combine the agent's prediction of the world state with sensing information. This can take a number of forms:

- If both the noise of forward prediction and sensor noise are modeled, the next belief state can be estimated using Bayes' rule (page 227). This is known as **filtering** (page 267).

- With more complicated sensors such as vision, a model can be used to predict where visual features can be found, and then vision can be used to look for these features close to the predicted location. This makes the vision task much simpler and vision can greatly reduce the errors in position arising from forward prediction alone.

A control problem is **separable** if the best action can be obtained by first finding the best model of the world and then using that model to determine the best action. Unfortunately, most control problems are not separable. This means that the agent should consider multiple models to determine what to do, and what information it gets from the world depends on what it will do with that information. Usually, there is no best model of the world that is independent of what the agent will do with the model.

2.4 Embedded and Simulated Agents

There are a number of ways an agent's controller can be used:

- An **embedded agent** is one that is run in the real world, where the actions are carried out in a real domain and where the sensing comes from a domain.

- A **simulated agent** is one that is run with a simulated body and environment; that is, where a program takes in the commands and returns appropriate percepts. This is often used to debug a controller before it is deployed.

- A **agent system model** is where there are models of the controller (which may or may not be the actual code), the body, and the environment that can answer questions about how the agent will behave. Such a model can be used to prove properties of agents before they are built, or it can be used to answer hypothetical questions about an agent that may be difficult or dangerous to answer with the real agent.

Each of these is appropriate for different purposes.

- Embedded mode is how the agent must run to be useful.

- A simulated agent is useful to test and debug the controller when many design options must be explored and building the body is expensive or when the environment is dangerous or inaccessible. It also allows us to test the agent under unusual combinations of conditions that may be difficult to arrange in the actual world.

    How good the simulation is depends on how good the model of the environment is. Models always have to abstract some aspect of the world. Appropriate abstraction is important for simulations to be able to tell us whether the agent will work in a real environment.

- A model of the agent, a model of the set of possible environments, and a specification of correct behavior allow us to prove theorems about how the agent will work in such environments. For example, we may want to prove that a robot running a particular controller will always get within a certain distance of the target, that it will never get stuck in mazes, or that it will never crash. Of course, whether what is proved turns out to be true depends on how accurate the models are.

- Given a model of the agent and the environment, some aspects of the agent can be left unspecified and can be adjusted to produce the desired or optimal behavior. This is the general idea behind optimization and planning.

- In reinforcement learning (page 463), the agent improves its performance while interacting with the real world.

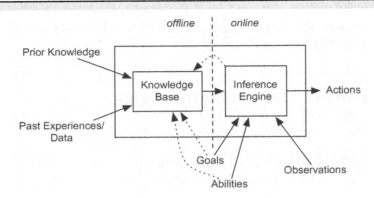

Figure 2.9: Offline and online decomposition of an agent

2.5   Acting with Reasoning

The previous sections assumed that an agent has some belief state that it maintains through time. For an intelligent agent, the belief state can be very complex, even for a single layer.

Experience in studying and building intelligent agents has shown that an intelligent agent requires some internal representation of its belief state. **Knowledge** is the information about a domain that is used for solving problems in that domain. Knowledge can include general knowledge that can be applied to particular situations. Thus, it is more general than the beliefs about a specific state. A **knowledge-based system** is a system that uses knowledge about a domain to act or to solve problems.

Philosophers have defined knowledge as true, justified belief. AI researchers tend to use the terms knowledge and belief more interchangeably. Knowledge tends to mean general information that is taken to be true. Belief tends to mean information that can be revised based on new information. Often beliefs come with measures of how much they should be believed and models of how the beliefs interact. In an AI system, knowledge is typically not necessarily true and is justified only as being useful. This distinction often becomes blurry when one module of an agent may treat some information as true but another module may be able to revise that information.

Figure 2.9 shows a refinement of Figure 1.3 (page 11) for a knowledge-based agent. A **knowledge base** is built offline and is used online to produce actions. This decomposition of an agent is orthogonal to the layered view of an agent; an intelligent agent requires both hierarchical organization and knowledge bases.

Online (page 17), when the agent is acting, the agent uses its knowledge base, its observations of the world, and its goals and abilities to choose what to do and to update its knowledge base. The **knowledge base** is its **long-term**

memory, where it keeps the knowledge that is needed to act in the future. This knowledge comes from prior knowledge and is combined with what is learned from data and past experiences. The **belief state** (page 48) is the **short-term memory** of the agent, which maintains the model of current environment needed between time steps. A clear distinction does not always exist between general knowledge and specific knowledge; for example, an outside delivery robot could learn general knowledge about a particular city. There is feedback from the inference engine to the knowledge base, because observing and acting in the world provide more data from which to learn.

Offline, before the agent has to act, it can build the knowledge base that is useful for it to act online. The role of the offline computation is to make the online computation more efficient or effective. The knowledge base is built from prior knowledge and from data of past experiences (either its own past experiences or data it has been given). Researchers have traditionally considered the case involving lots of data and little prior knowledge in the field of **machine learning**. The case of lots of prior knowledge and little or no data from which to learn has been studied under the umbrella of **expert systems**. However, for most non-trivial domains, the agent must use whatever information is available, and so it requires both rich prior knowledge and lots of data.

The goals and abilities are given offline, online, or both, depending on the agent. For example, a delivery robot could have general goals of keeping the lab clean and not damaging itself or other objects, but it could get other delivery goals at runtime. The online computation can be made more efficient if the knowledge base is tuned for the particular goals and abilities. However, this is often not possible when the goals and abilities are only available at runtime.

Figure 2.10 (on the next page) shows more detail of the interface between the agents and the world.

2.5.1 Design Time and Offline Computation

The knowledge base required for online computation can be built initially at design time and then augmented offline by the agent.

An **ontology** is a specification of the meaning of the symbols used in an information system. It specifies what is being modeled and the vocabulary used in the system. In the simplest case, if the agent is using explicit state-based representation with full observability, the ontology specifies the mapping between the world and the state. Without this mapping, the agent may know it is in, say, state 57, but, without the ontology, this information is just a meaningless number to another agent or person. In other cases, the ontology defines the features or the individuals and relationships. It is what is needed to convert raw sense data into something meaningful for the agent or to get meaningful input from a person or another knowledge source.

Ontologies are built by communities, often independently of a particular knowledge base or specific application. It is this shared vocabulary that

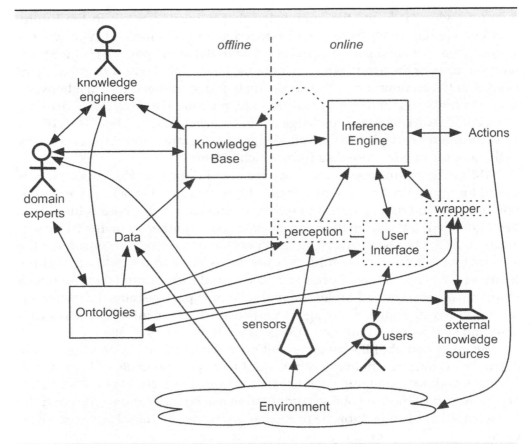

Figure 2.10: Internals of an agent, showing roles

allows for effective communication and interoperation of the data from multiple sources (sensors, humans, and databases). Ontologies for the case of individuals and relationships are discussed in Section 13.3 (page 563).

The ontology logically comes before the data and the prior knowledge: we require an ontology to have data or to have knowledge. Without an ontology, data are just sequences of bits. Without an ontology, a human does not know what to input; it is the ontology that gives the data meaning. Often the ontology evolves as the system is being developed.

The ontology specifies a level or levels of abstraction. If the ontology changes, the data must change. For example, a robot may have an ontology of obstacles (e.g., every physical object is an obstacle to be avoided). If the ontology is expanded to differentiate people, chairs, tables, coffee mugs, and the like, different data about the world are required.

The knowledge base is typically built offline from a combination of expert knowledge and data. It is usually built before the agent knows the particulars of the environment in which it must act. Maintaining and tuning the knowledge base is often part of the online computation.

Offline, there are three major **role**s involved with a knowledge-based system:

- **Software engineers** build the inference engine and user interface. They typically know nothing about the contents of the knowledge base. They need not be experts in the use of the system they implement; however, they must be experts in the use of a programming language like Java, Lisp, or Prolog rather than in the knowledge representation language of the system they are designing.

- **Domain experts** are the people who have the appropriate prior knowledge about the domain. They know about the domain, but typically they know nothing about the particular case that may be under consideration. For example, a medical domain expert would know about diseases, symptoms, and how they interact but would not know the symptoms or the diseases of the particular patient. A delivery robot domain expert may know the sort of individuals that must be recognized, what the battery meter measures, and the costs associated with various actions. Domain experts typically do not know the particulars of the environment the agent would encounter – for example, the details of the patient for the diagnostic assistant or the details of the room a robot is in.

   Domain experts typically do not know about the internal workings of the AI system. Often they have only a semantic view of the knowledge (page 161) and have no notion of the algorithms used by the inference engine. The system should interact with them in terms of the domain, not in terms of the steps of the computation. For example, it is unreasonable to expect that domain experts could debug a knowledge base if they were presented with traces of how an answer was produced. Thus, it is not appropriate to have debugging tools for domain experts that merely trace the execution of a program.

- **Knowledge engineers** design, build, and debug the knowledge base in consultation with domain experts. They know about the details of the system and about the domain through the domain expert. They know nothing about any particular case. They should know about useful inference techniques and how the complete system works.

The same people may fill multiple roles: A domain expert who knows about AI may act as a knowledge engineer; a knowledge engineer may be the same person who writes the system. A large system may have many different software engineers, knowledge engineers, and experts, each of whom may specialize in part of the system. These people may not even know they are part of the system; they may publish information for anyone to use.

Offline, the agent can combine the expert knowledge and the data. At this stage, the system can be tested and debugged. The agent is able to do computation that is not particular to the specific instance. For example, it can compile parts of the knowledge base to allow more efficient inference.

2.5.2 Online Computation

Online, the information about the particular case becomes available, and the agent has to act. The information includes the observations of the domain and often information about the available actions and the preferences or goals. The agent can get observations from sensors, users, and other information sources (such as web sites), but we assume it does not have access to the domain experts or knowledge engineer.

An agent typically has much more time for offline computation than for online computation. However, during online computation it can take advantage of particular goals and particular observations.

For example, a medical diagnosis system only has the details of a particular patient online. Offline, it can acquire knowledge about how diseases and symptoms interact and do some debugging and compilation. It can only do the computation about a particular patient online.

Online the following roles are involved:

- A **user** is a person who has a need for expertise or has information about individual cases. Users typically are not experts in the domain of the knowledge base. They often do not know what information is needed by the system. Thus, it is unreasonable to expect them to volunteer the information about a particular case. A simple and natural interface must be provided because users do not typically understand the internal structure of the system. They often, however, must make an informed decision based on the recommendation of the system; thus, they require an explanation of why the recommendation is appropriate.

- **Sensors** provide information about the environment. For example, a thermometer is a sensor that can provide the current temperature at the location of the thermometer. Sensors may be more sophisticated, such as a vision sensor. At the lowest level, a vision sensor may simply provide an array of 720×480 pixels at 30 frames per second. At a higher level, a vision system may be able to answer specific questions about the location of particular features, whether some type of individual is in the environment, or whether some particular individual is in the scene. An array of microphones can be used at a low level of abstraction to provide detailed vibration information. It can also be used as a component of a higher-level sensor to detect an explosion and to provide the type and the location of the explosion.

  Sensors come in two main varieties. A **passive sensor** continuously feeds information to the agent. Passive sensors include thermometers, cameras, and microphones. The designer can typically choose where the sensors are or where they are pointing, but they just feed the agent information. In contrast, an **active sensor** is controlled or asked for information. Examples of an active sensor include a medical probe able to answer specific questions about a patient or a test given to a student in an intelligent tutoring system. Often sensors that are passive sensors at lower levels of abstraction can be seen as active sensors at higher levels of abstraction. For example, a camera could be asked whether a particular person is in the room. To do this it may need to zoom in on the faces in the room, looking for distinguishing features of the person.

- An **external knowledge source**, such as a web site or a database, can typically be asked questions and can provide the answer for a limited domain. An agent can ask a weather web site for the temperature at a particular location or an airline web site for the arrival time of a particular flight. The knowledge sources have various protocols and efficiency trade-offs. The interface between an agent and an external knowledge source is called a **wrapper**. A wrapper translates between the representation the agent uses and the queries the external knowledge source is prepared to handle. Often wrappers are designed so that the agent can ask the same query of multiple knowledge sources. For example, an agent may want to know about airplane arrivals, but different airlines or airports may require very different protocols to access that information. When web sites and databases adhere to a common ontology, they can be used together because the same symbols have the same meaning. Having the same symbols mean the same thing is called **semantic interoperability**. When they use different ontologies, there must be mappings between the ontologies to allow them to interoperate.

Again, these roles are separate, even though the people in these roles may overlap. The domain expert, for example, may act as a user to test or debug the system. Each of the roles has different requirements for the tools they need. The tools that explain to a user how the system reached a result can be the same tools that the domain experts use to debug the knowledge.

2.6 Review

The main points you should have learned from this chapter are as follows:

- An agent system is composed of an agent and an environment.
- Agents have sensors and actuators to interact with the environment.
- An agent is composed of a body and interacting controllers.
- Agents are situated in time and must make decisions of what to do based on their history of interaction with the environment.
- An agent has direct access not to its history, but to what it has remembered (its belief state) and what it has just observed. At each point in time, an agent decides what to do and what to remember based on its belief state and its current observations.
- Complex agents are built modularly in terms of interacting hierarchical layers.
- An intelligent agent requires knowledge that is acquired at design time, offline or online.

2.7 References and Further Reading

The model of agent systems is based on the constraint nets of Zhang and Mackworth [1995], also on Rosenschein and Kaelbling [1995]. The hierarchcical control is based on Albus [1981] and the subsumption architecture of Brooks [1986]. *Turtle Geometry*, by Abelson and DiSessa [1981], investigates mathematics from the viewpoint of modeling simple reactive agents. Luenberger [1979] is a readable introduction to the classical theory of agents interacting with environments. Simon [1996] argues for the importance of hierarchical control.

For more detail on agent control see Dean and Wellman [1991], Latombe [1991], and Agre [1995].

The methodology for building intelligent agents is discussed by Haugeland [1985], Brooks [1991], Kirsh [1991b], and Mackworth [1993].

Qualitative reasoning is described by Forbus [1996] and Kuipers [2001]. Weld and de Kleer [1990] contains many seminal papers on qualitative reasoning. See also Weld [1992] and related discussion in the same issue. For a recent review see Price, Travé-Massuyàs, Milne, Ironi, Forbus, Bredeweg, Lee, Struss, Snooke, Lucas, Cavazza, and Coghill [2006].

2.8 Exercises

Exercise 2.1 Section 2.3 (page 50) argued that it was impossible to build a representation of a world that is independent of what the agent will do with it. This exercise lets you evaluate this argument.

Choose a particular world, for example, what is on some part of your desk at the current time.

  i) Get someone to list all of the things that exist in this world (or try it yourself as a thought experiment).

  ii) Try to think of twenty things that they missed. Make these as different from each other as possible. For example, the ball at the tip of the rightmost ballpoint pen on the desk, or the spring in the stapler, or the third word on page 66 of a particular book on the desk.

  iii) Try to find a thing that cannot be described using natural language.

  iv) Choose a particular task, such as making the desk tidy, and try to write down all of the things in the world at a level of description that is relevant to this task.

Based on this exercise, discuss the following statements:

  (a) What exists in a world is a property of the observer.

  (b) We need ways to refer to individuals other than expecting each individual to have a separate name.

  (c) What individuals exist is a property of the task as well as of the world.

  (d) To describe the individuals in a domain, you need what is essentially a dictionary of a huge number of words and ways to combine them to describe

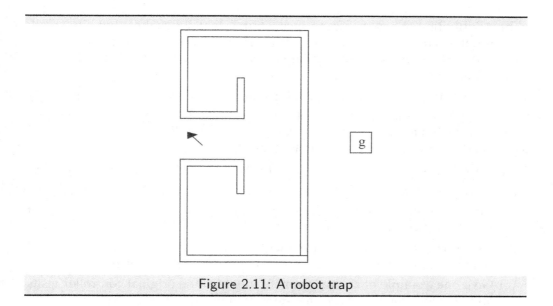

Figure 2.11: A robot trap

individuals, and this should be able to be done independently of any particular domain.

Exercise 2.2   Explain why the middle layer in Example 2.5 (page 55) must have both the previous target position and the current target position as inputs. Suppose it had only one of these as input; which one would it have to be, and what would the problem with this be?

Exercise 2.3   The definition of the target position in Example 2.6 (page 56) means that, when the plan ends, the robot will just keep the last target position as its target position and keep circling forever. Change the definition so that the robot goes back to its home and circles there.

Exercise 2.4   The obstacle avoidance implemented in Example 2.5 (page 55) can easily get stuck.

(a) Show an obstacle and a target for which the robot using the controller of Example 2.5 (page 55) would not be able to get around (and it will crash or loop).

(b) Even without obstacles, the robot may never reach its destination. For example, if it is next to its target position, it may keep circling forever without reaching its target. Design a controller that can detect this situation and find its way to the target.

Exercise 2.5   Consider the "robot trap" in Figure 2.11.

(a) Explain why it is so tricky for a robot to get to location g. You must explain what the current robot does as well as why it is difficult to make a more sophisticated robot (e.g., one that follows the wall using the "right-hand rule": the robot turns left when it hits an obstacle and keeps following a wall, with the wall always on its right) to work.

(b) An intuition of how to escape such a trap is that, when the robot hits a wall, it follows the wall until the number of right turns equals the number of left turns. Show how this can be implemented, explaining the belief state, the belief-state transition function, and the command function.

Exercise 2.6 When the user selects and moves the current target location, the robot described in this chapter travels to the original position of that target and does not try to go to the new position. Change the controller so that the robot will try to head toward the current location of the target at each step.

Exercise 2.7 The current controller visits the locations in the *todo* list sequentially.

(a) Change the controller so that it is opportunistic; when it selects the next location to visit, it selects the location that is closest to its current position. It should still visit all of the locations.

(b) Give one example of an environment in which the new controller visits all of the locations in fewer time steps than the original controller.

(c) Give one example of an environment in which the original controller visits all of the locations in fewer time steps than the modified controller.

(d) Change the controller so that, at every step, the agent heads toward whichever target location is closest to its current position.

(e) Can the controller from part (d) get stuck in a loop and never reach a target in an example where the original controller will work? Either give an example in which it gets stuck in a loop and explain why it cannot find a solution, or explain why it does not get into a loop.

Exercise 2.8 Change the controller so that the robot senses the environment to determine the coordinates of a location. Assume that the body can provide the coordinates of a named location.

Exercise 2.9 Suppose you have a new job and must build a controller for an intelligent robot. You tell your bosses that you just have to implement a command function and a state transition function. They are very skeptical. Why these functions? Why only these? Explain why a controller requires a command function and a state transition function, but not other functions. Use proper English. Be concise.

Part II

Representing and Reasoning

Chapter 3

States and Searching

Have you ever watched a crab on the shore crawling backward in search of the Atlantic Ocean, and missing? That's the way the mind of man operates.

– H. L. Mencken (1880–1956)

The previous chapter discussed how an agent perceives and acts, but not how its goals affect its actions. An agent could be programmed to act in the world to achieve a fixed set of goals, but then it may not adapt to changing goals and so would not be intelligent. Alternatively, an agent could reason about its abilities and its goals to determine what to do. This chapter shows how the problem of an agent deciding what to do can be cast as the problem of searching to find a path in a graph, and it presents a number of ways that such problems can be solved on a computer. As Mencken suggests in the quote above, the mind uses search to solve problems, although not always successfully.

3.1 Problem Solving as Search

In the simplest case of an agent reasoning about what it should do, the agent has a state-based model of the world, with no uncertainty and with goals to achieve. This is either a flat (non-hierarchical) representation or a single level of a hierarchy. The agent can determine how to achieve its goals by searching in its representation of the world state space for a way to get from its current state to a goal state. It can find a sequence of actions that will achieve its goal before it has to act in the world.

This problem can be abstracted to the mathematical problem of finding a path from a start node to a goal node in a directed graph. Many other problems can also be mapped to this abstraction, so it is worthwhile to consider this level of abstraction. Most of this chapter explores various algorithms for finding such paths.

This notion of search is computation inside the agent. It is different from searching in the world, when it may have to act in the world, for example, an agent searching for its keys, lifting up cushions, and so on. It is also different from searching the web, which involves searching for information. Searching in this chapter means searching in an internal representation for a path to a goal.

The idea of search is straightforward: the agent constructs a set of potential partial solutions to a problem that can be checked to see if they truly are solutions or if they could lead to solutions. Search proceeds by repeatedly selecting a partial solution, stopping if it is a path to a goal, and otherwise extending it by one more arc in all possible ways.

Search underlies much of artificial intelligence. When an agent is given a problem, it is usually given only a description that lets it recognize a solution, not an algorithm to solve it. It has to search for a solution. The existence of NP-complete problems (page 170), with efficient means to recognize answers but no efficient methods for finding them, indicates that searching is, in many cases, a necessary part of solving problems.

It is often believed that humans are able to use intuition to jump to solutions to difficult problems. However, humans do not tend to solve general problems; instead they solve specific instances about which they may know much more than the underlying search space. Problems in which little structure exists or in which the structure cannot be related to the physical world are very difficult for humans to solve. The existence of public key encryption codes, where the search space is clear and the test for a solution is given – for which humans nevertheless have no hope of solving and computers cannot solve in a realistic time frame – demonstrates the difficulty of search.

The difficulty of search and the fact that humans are able to solve some search problems efficiently suggests that computer agents should exploit knowledge about special cases to guide them to a solution. This extra knowledge beyond the search space is **heuristic knowledge**. This chapter considers one kind of heuristic knowledge in the form of an estimate of the cost from a node to a goal.

3.2 State Spaces

One general formulation of intelligent action is in terms of **state space**. A **state** contains all of the information necessary to predict the effects of an action and to determine if it is a goal state. State-space searching assumes that

- the agent has perfect knowledge of the state space and can observe what state it is in (i.e., there is full observability);

- the agent has a set of actions that have known deterministic effects;

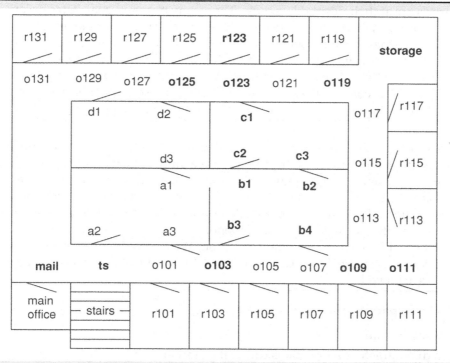

Figure 3.1: The delivery robot domain with interesting locations labeled

- some states are goal states, the agent wants to reach one of these goal states, and the agent can recognize a goal state; and

- a **solution** is a sequence of actions that will get the agent from its current state to a goal state.

Example 3.1 Consider the robot delivery domain and the task of finding a path from one location to another in Figure 3.1. This can be modeled as a state-space search problem, where the states are locations. Assume that the agent can use a lower-level controller to carry out the high-level action of getting from one location to a neighboring location. Thus, at this level of abstraction, the actions can involve deterministic traveling between neighboring locations.

An example problem is where the robot is outside room $r103$, at position $o103$, and the goal is to get to room $r123$. A solution is a sequence of actions that will get the robot to room $r123$.

Example 3.2 In a more complicated example, the delivery robot may have a number of parcels to deliver to various locations. In this case, the state may consist of the location of the robot, the parcels the robot is carrying, and the locations of the other parcels. The possible actions may be for the robot to move, to pick up parcels that are at the same location as the robot, or to put down whatever parcels it is carrying. A goal state may be one in which some specified parcels are at their desired locations. There may be many goal states because we may not care where the robot is or where some of the other parcels are.

Notice that this representation has ignored many details, for example, how the robot is carrying the parcels (which may affect whether it can carry other parcels), the battery level of the robot, whether the parcels are fragile or damaged, and the color of the floor. By not having these as part of the state space, we assume that these details are not relevant to the problem at hand.

Example 3.3 In a tutoring system, a state may consist of the set of topics that the student knows. The action may be teaching a particular lesson, and the result of a teaching action may be that the student knows the topic of the lesson as long as the student knows the topics that are prerequisites for the lesson being taught. The aim is for the student to know some particular set of topics.

If the effect of teaching also depends on the aptitude of the student, this detail must be part of the state space, too. We do not have to model what the student is carrying if that does not affect the result of actions or whether the goal is achieved.

A **state-space problem** consists of

- a set of states;
- a distinguished set of states called the **start states**;
- a set of actions available to the agent in each state;
- an **action function** that, given a state and an action, returns a new state;
- a set of goal states, often specified as a Boolean function, $goal(s)$, that is true when s is a goal state; and
- a criterion that specifies the quality of an acceptable solution. For example, any sequence of actions that gets the agent to the goal state may be acceptable, or there may be costs associated with actions and the agent may be required to find a sequence that has minimal total cost. This is called an **optimal** solution. Alternatively, it may be satisfied with any solution that is within 10% of optimal.

This framework is extended in subsequent chapters to include cases where an agent can exploit the internal features of the states, where the state is not fully observable (e.g., the robot does not know where the parcels are, or the teacher does not know the aptitude of the student), where the actions are stochastic (e.g., the robot may overshoot, or the student perhaps does not learn a topic that is taught), and where complex preferences exist in terms of rewards and punishments, not just goal states.

3.3   Graph Searching

In this chapter, we abstract the general mechanism of searching and present it in terms of searching for paths in directed graphs. To solve a problem, first define the underlying search space and then apply a search algorithm to that search space. Many problem-solving tasks can be transformed into the problem of finding a path in a graph. Searching in graphs provides an appropriate level of abstraction within which to study simple problem solving independent of a particular domain.

A (directed) graph consists of a set of nodes and a set of directed arcs between nodes. The idea is to find a path along these arcs from a start node to a goal node.

The abstraction is necessary because there may be more than one way to represent a problem as a graph. Whereas the examples in this chapter are in terms of state-space searching, where nodes represent states and arcs represent actions, future chapters consider different ways to represent problems as graphs to search.

3.3.1 Formalizing Graph Searching

A directed **graph** consists of

- a set N of **nodes** and
- a set A of ordered pairs of nodes called **arcs**.

In this definition, a node can be anything. All this definition does is constrain arcs to be ordered pairs of nodes. There can be infinitely many nodes and arcs. We do not assume that the graph is represented explicitly; we require only a procedure that can generate nodes and arcs as needed.

The arc $\langle n_1, n_2 \rangle$ is an **outgoing arc** from n_1 and an **incoming arc** to n_2.

A node n_2 is a **neighbor** of n_1 if there is an arc from n_1 to n_2; that is, if $\langle n_1, n_2 \rangle \in A$. Note that being a neighbor does not imply symmetry; just because n_2 is a neighbor of n_1 does not mean that n_1 is necessarily a neighbor of n_2. Arcs may be **labeled**, for example, with the action that will take the agent from one state to another.

A **path** from node s to node g is a sequence of nodes $\langle n_0, n_1, \ldots, n_k \rangle$ such that $s = n_0$, $g = n_k$, and $\langle n_{i-1}, n_i \rangle \in A$; that is, there is an arc from n_{i-1} to n_i for each i. Sometimes it is useful to view a path as the sequence of arcs, $\langle n_0, n_1 \rangle$, $\langle n_1, n_2 \rangle, \ldots, \langle n_{k-1}, n_k \rangle$, or a sequence of labels of these arcs.

A **cycle** is a nonempty path such that the end node is the same as the start node – that is, a cycle is a path $\langle n_0, n_1, \ldots, n_k \rangle$ such that $n_0 = n_k$ and $k \neq 0$. A directed graph without any cycles is called a **directed acyclic graph (DAG)**. This should probably be an **acyclic directed graph**, because it is a directed graph that happens to be acyclic, not an acyclic graph that happens to be directed, but DAG sounds better than ADG!

A **tree** is a DAG where there is one node with no incoming arcs and every other node has exactly one incoming arc. The node with no incoming arcs is called the **root** of the tree and nodes with no outgoing arcs are called **leaves**.

To encode problems as graphs, one set of nodes is referred to as the **start nodes** and another set is called the **goal nodes**. A **solution** is a path from a start node to a goal node.

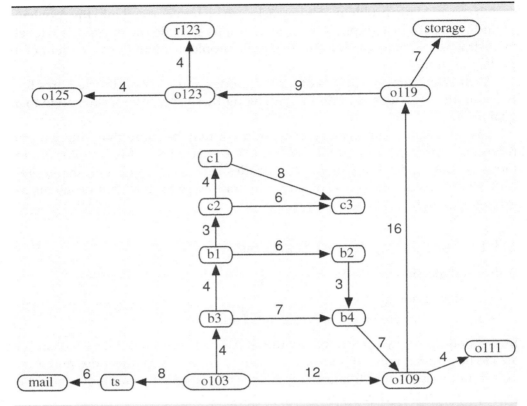

Figure 3.2: A graph with arc costs for the delivery robot domain

Sometimes there is a **cost** – a positive number – associated with arcs. We write the cost of arc $\langle n_i, n_j \rangle$ as $cost(\langle n_i, n_j \rangle)$. The costs of arcs induces a cost of paths.

Given a path $p = \langle n_0, n_1, \ldots, n_k \rangle$, the cost of path p is the sum of the costs of the arcs in the path:

$$cost(p) = cost(\langle n_0, n_1 \rangle) + \cdots + cost(\langle n_{k-1}, n_k \rangle)$$

An **optimal solution** is one of the least-cost solutions; that is, it is a path p from a start node to a goal node such that there is no path p' from a start node to a goal node where $cost(p') < cost(p)$.

Example 3.4 Consider the problem of the delivery robot finding a path from location $o103$ to location $r123$ in the domain depicted in Figure 3.1 (page 73). In this figure, the interesting locations are named. For simplicity, we consider only the locations written in bold and we initially limit the directions that the robot can travel. Figure 3.2 shows the resulting graph where the nodes represent locations and the arcs represent possible single steps between locations. In this figure, each arc is shown with the associated cost of getting from one location to the next.

In this graph, the nodes are $N = \{mail, ts, o103, b3, o109, \ldots\}$ and the arcs are $A = \{\langle ts, mail \rangle, \langle o103, ts \rangle, \langle o103, b3 \rangle, \langle o103, o109 \rangle, \ldots\}$. Node $o125$ has no neighbors. Node ts has one neighbor, namely $mail$. Node $o103$ has three neighbors, namely ts, $b3$, and $o109$.

There are three paths from $o103$ to $r123$:

$$\langle o103, o109, o119, o123, r123 \rangle$$
$$\langle o103, b3, b4, o109, o119, o123, r123 \rangle$$
$$\langle o103, b3, b1, b2, b4, o109, o119, o123, r123 \rangle$$

If $o103$ were a start node and $r123$ were a goal node, each of these three paths would be a solution to the graph-searching problem.

In many problems the search graph is not given explicitly; it is dynamically constructed as needed. All that is required for the search algorithms that follow is a way to generate the neighbors of a node and to determine if a node is a goal node.

The **forward branching factor** of a node is the number of arcs leaving the node. The **backward branching factor** of a node is the number of arcs entering the node. These factors provide measures of the complexity of graphs. When we discuss the time and space complexity of the search algorithms, we assume that the branching factors are bounded from above by a constant.

Example 3.5 In the graph of Figure 3.2, the forward branching factor of node $o103$ is three; there are three arcs coming out of node $o103$. The backward branching factor of node $o103$ is zero; there are no arcs coming into node $o103$. The forward branching factor of $mail$ is zero and the backward branching factor of $mail$ is one. The forward branching factor of node $b3$ is two and the backward branching factor of $b3$ is one.

The branching factor is important because it is a key component in the size of the graph. If the forward branching factor for each node is b, and the graph is a tree, there are b^n nodes that are n arcs away from any node.

3.4   A Generic Searching Algorithm

This section describes a generic algorithm to search for a solution path in a graph. The algorithm is independent of any particular search strategy and any particular graph.

The intuitive idea behind the generic search algorithm, given a graph, a set of start nodes, and a set of goal nodes, is to incrementally explore paths from the start nodes. This is done by maintaining a **frontier** (or **fringe**) of paths from the start node that have been explored. The frontier contains all of the paths that could form initial segments of paths from a start node to a goal node. (See Figure 3.3 (on the next page), where the frontier is the set of paths to the gray shaded nodes.) Initially, the frontier contains trivial paths containing no

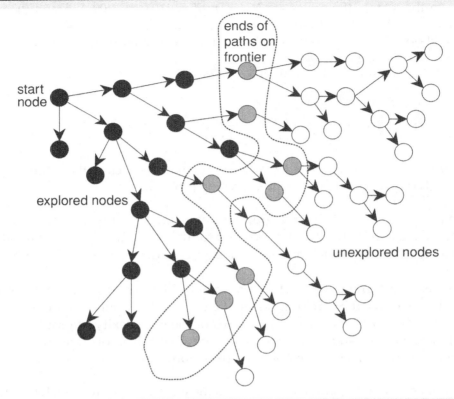

Figure 3.3: Problem solving by graph searching

arcs from the start nodes. As the search proceeds, the frontier expands into the unexplored nodes until a goal node is encountered. To expand the frontier, the searcher selects and removes a path from the frontier, extends the path with each arc leaving the last node, and adds these new paths to the frontier. A search strategy defines which element of the frontier is selected at each step.

The generic search algorithm is shown in Figure 3.4. Initially, the frontier is the set of empty paths from start nodes. At each step, the algorithm advances the frontier by removing a path $\langle s_0, \ldots, s_k \rangle$ from the frontier. If $goal(s_k)$ is true (i.e., s_k is a goal node), it has found a solution and returns the path that was found, namely $\langle s_0, \ldots, s_k \rangle$. Otherwise, the path is extended by one more arc by finding the neighbors of s_k. For every neighbor s of s_k, the path $\langle s_0, \ldots, s_k, s \rangle$ is added to the frontier. This step is known as **expanding** the node s_k.

This algorithm has a few features that should be noted:

- The selection of a path at line 13 is non-deterministic. The choice of path that is selected can affect the efficiency; see the box on page 170 for more details on our use of "select". A particular search strategy will determine which path is selected.

- It is useful to think of the *return* at line 15 as a temporary return; another path to a goal can be searched for by continuing to line 16.

1: **procedure** *Search*(*G*, *S*, *goal*)
2:     **Inputs**
3:         *G*: graph with nodes *N* and arcs *A*
4:         *S*: set of start nodes
5:         *goal*: Boolean function of states
6:     **Output**
7:         path from a member of *S* to a node for which *goal* is true
8:         or ⊥ if there are no solution paths
9:     **Local**
10:         *Frontier*: set of paths
11:     *Frontier* ← {⟨*s*⟩ : *s* ∈ *S*}
12:     **while** *Frontier* ≠ {} **do**
13:         **select** and **remove** ⟨s_0, . . . , s_k⟩ from *Frontier*
14:         **if** *goal*(s_k) **then**
15:             **return** ⟨s_0, . . . , s_k⟩
16:         *Frontier* ← *Frontier* ∪ {⟨s_0, . . . , s_k, *s*⟩ : ⟨s_k, *s*⟩ ∈ *A*}
17:     **return** ⊥

Figure 3.4: Generic graph searching algorithm

- If the procedure returns ⊥, no solutions exist (or there are no remaining solutions if the proof has been retried).

- The algorithm only tests if a path ends in a goal node *after* the path has been selected from the frontier, not when it is added to the frontier. There are two main reasons for this. Sometimes a very costly arc exists from a node on the frontier to a goal node. The search should not always return the path with this arc, because a lower-cost solution may exist. This is crucial when the least-cost path is required. The second reason is that it may be expensive to determine whether a node is a goal node.

If the path chosen does not end at a goal node and the node at the end has no neighbors, extending the path means removing the path. This outcome is reasonable because this path could not be part of a path from a start node to a goal node.

3.5   Uninformed Search Strategies

A problem determines the graph and the goal but not which path to select from the frontier. This is the job of a search strategy. A search strategy specifies which paths are selected from the frontier. Different strategies are obtained by modifying how the selection of paths in the frontier is implemented.

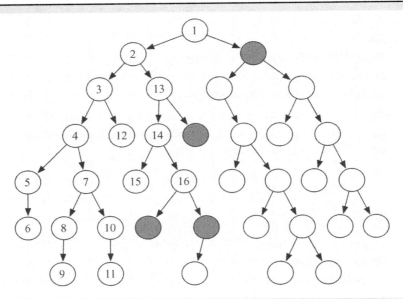

Figure 3.5: The order nodes are expanded in depth-first search

This section presents three **uninformed search strategies** that do not take into account the location of the goal. Intuitively, these algorithms ignore where they are going until they find a goal and report success.

3.5.1   Depth-First Search

The first strategy is **depth-first search**. In depth-first search, the frontier acts like a last-in first-out **stack**. The elements are added to the stack one at a time. The one selected and taken off the frontier at any time is the last element that was added.

Example 3.6 Consider the tree-shaped graph in Figure 3.5. Suppose the start node is the root of the tree (the node at the top) and the nodes are ordered from left to right so that the leftmost neighbor is added to the stack last. In depth-first search, the order in which the nodes are expanded does not depend on the location of the goals. The first sixteen nodes expanded are numbered in order of expansion in Figure 3.5. The shaded nodes are the nodes at the ends of the paths on the frontier after the first sixteen steps.

Notice how the first six nodes expanded are all in a single path. The sixth node has no neighbors. Thus, the next node that is expanded is a child of the lowest ancestor of this node that has unexpanded children.

Implementing the frontier as a stack results in paths being pursued in a depth-first manner – searching one path to its completion before trying an alternative path. This method is said to involve **backtracking**: The algorithm selects a first alternative at each node, and it *backtracks* to the next alternative when it has pursued all of the paths from the first selection. Some paths may be infinite when the graph has cycles or infinitely many nodes, in which case a depth-first search may never stop.

This algorithm does not specify the order in which the neighbors are added to the stack that represents the frontier. The efficiency of the algorithm is sensitive to this ordering.

Example 3.7 Consider depth-first search from $o103$ in the graph given in Figure 3.2. The only goal node is $r123$. In this example, the frontier is shown as a list of paths with the top of the stack at the beginning of the list.

Initially, the frontier contains the trivial path $\langle o103 \rangle$.

At the next stage, the frontier contains the following paths:

$$[\langle o103, ts \rangle, \langle o103, b3 \rangle, \langle o103, o109 \rangle].$$

Next, the path $\langle o103, ts \rangle$ is selected because it is at the top of the stack. It is removed from the frontier and replaced by extending it by one arc, resulting in the frontier

$$[\langle o103, ts, mail \rangle, \langle o103, b3 \rangle, \langle o103, o109 \rangle].$$

Next, the first path $\langle o103, ts, mail \rangle$ is removed from the frontier and is replaced by the set of paths that extend it by one arc, which is the empty set because $mail$ has no neighbors. Thus, the resulting frontier is

$$[\langle o103, b3 \rangle, \langle o103, o109 \rangle].$$

At this stage, the path $\langle o103, b3 \rangle$ is the top of the stack. Notice what has happened: depth-first search has pursued all paths from ts and, when all of these paths were exhausted (there was only one), it backtracked to the next element of the stack. Next, $\langle o103, b3 \rangle$ is selected and is replaced in the frontier by the paths that extend it by one arc, resulting in the frontier

$$[\langle o103, b3, b1 \rangle, \langle o103, b3, b4 \rangle, \langle o103, o109 \rangle].$$

Then $\langle o103, b3, b1 \rangle$ is selected from the frontier and is replaced by all one-arc extensions, resulting in the frontier

$$[\langle o103, b3, b1, c2 \rangle, \langle o103, b3, b1, b2 \rangle, \langle o103, b3, b4 \rangle,$$
$$\langle o103, o109 \rangle].$$

Now the first path is selected from the frontier and is extended by one arc, resulting in the frontier

$$[\langle o103, b3, b1, c2, c3 \rangle, \langle o103, b3, b1, c2, c1 \rangle,$$
$$\langle o103, b3, b1, b2 \rangle, \langle o103, b3, b4 \rangle, \langle o103, o109 \rangle].$$

Node $c3$ has no neighbors, and thus the search "backtracks" to the last alternative that has not been pursued, namely to the path to $c1$.

Suppose $\langle n_0, \dots, n_k \rangle$ is the selected path in the frontier. Then every other element of the frontier is of the form $\langle n_0, \dots, n_i, m \rangle$, for some index $i < n$ and some node m that is a neighbor of n_i; that is, it follows the selected path for a number of arcs and then has exactly one extra node.

To understand the complexity (see the box on page 83) of depth-first search, consider an analogy using family trees, where the neighbors of a node correspond to its children in the tree. At the root of the tree is a start node. A branch down this tree corresponds to a path from a start node. Consider the node at the end of path at the top of the frontier. The other elements of the frontier correspond to children of ancestors of that node – the "uncles," "great uncles," and so on. If the branching factor is b and the first element of the list has length n, there can be at most $n \times (b-1)$ other elements of the frontier. These elements correspond to the $b-1$ alternative paths from each node. Thus, for depth-first search, the space used is linear in the depth of the path length from the start to a node.

If there is a solution on the first branch searched, then the time complexity is linear in the length of the path; it considers only those elements on the path, along with their siblings. The worst-case complexity is infinite. Depth-first search can get trapped on infinite branches and never find a solution, even if one exists, for infinite graphs or for graphs with loops. If the graph is a finite tree, with the forward branching factor bounded by b and depth n, the worst-case complexity is $O(b^n)$.

Example 3.8 Consider a modification of the delivery graph, in which the agent has much more freedom in moving between locations. The new graph is presented in Figure 3.6 (page 84). An infinite path leads from ts to $mail$, back to ts, back to $mail$, and so forth. As presented, depth-first search follows this path forever, never considering alternative paths from $b3$ or $o109$. The frontiers for the first five iterations of the path-finding search algorithm using depth-first search are

$$[\langle o103 \rangle]$$
$$[\langle o103, ts \rangle, \langle o103, b3 \rangle, \langle o103, o109 \rangle]$$
$$[\langle o103, ts, mail \rangle, \langle o103, ts, o103 \rangle, \langle o103, b3 \rangle, \langle o103, o109 \rangle]$$
$$[\langle o103, ts, mail, ts \rangle, \langle o103, ts, o103 \rangle, \langle o103, b3 \rangle, \langle o103, o109 \rangle]$$
$$[\langle o103, ts, mail, ts, mail \rangle, \langle o103, ts, mail, ts, o103 \rangle, \langle o103, ts, o103 \rangle,$$
$$\langle o103, b3 \rangle, \langle o103, o109 \rangle]$$

Depth-first search can be improved by not considering paths with cycles (page 93).

Because depth-first search is sensitive to the order in which the neighbors are added to the frontier, care must be taken to do it sensibly. This ordering can be done statically (so that the order of the neighbors is fixed) or dynamically (where the ordering of the neighbors depends on the goal).

Depth-first search is appropriate when either

- space is restricted;
- many solutions exist, perhaps with long path lengths, particularly for the case where nearly all paths lead to a solution; or
- the order of the neighbors of a node are added to the stack can be tuned so that solutions are found on the first try.

Comparing Algorithms

Algorithms (including search algorithms) can be compared on
- the time taken,
- the space used, and
- the quality or accuracy of the results.

The time taken, space used, and accuracy of an algorithm are a function of the inputs to the algorithm. Computer scientists talk about the **asymptotic complexity** of algorithms, which specifies how the time or space grows with the input size of the algorithm. An algorithm has time (or space) complexity $O(f(n))$ – read "big-oh of $f(n)$" – for input size n, where $f(n)$ is some function of n, if there exist constants n_0 and k such that the time, or space, of the algorithm is less than $k \times f(n)$ for all $n > n_0$. The most common types of functions are exponential functions such as 2^n, 3^n, or 1.015^n; polynomial functions such as n^5, n^2, n, or $n^{1/2}$; and logarithmic functions, $\log n$. In general, exponential algorithms get worse more quickly than polynomial algorithms which, in turn, are worse than logarithmic algorithms.

An algorithm has time or space complexity $\Omega(f(n))$ for input size n if there exist constants n_0 and k such that the time or space of the algorithm is greater than $k \times f(n)$ for all $n > n_0$. An algorithm has time or space complexity $\Theta(n)$ if it has complexity $O(n)$ and $\Omega(n)$. Typically, you cannot give an $\Theta(f(n))$ complexity on an algorithm, because most algorithms take different times for different inputs. Thus, when comparing algorithms, one has to specify the class of problems that will be considered.

Algorithm A is better than B, using a measure of either time, space, or accuracy, could mean:
- the worst case of A is better than the worst case of B; or
- A works better in practice, or the average case of A is better than the average case of B, where you average over typical problems; or
- you characterize the class of problems for which A is better than B, so that which algorithm is better depends on the problem; or
- for every problem, A is better than B.

The worst-case asymptotic complexity is often the easiest to show, but it is usually the least useful. Characterizing the class of problems for which one algorithm is better than another is usually the most useful, if it is easy to determine which class a given problem is in. Unfortunately, this characterization is usually very difficult.

Characterizing when one algorithm is better than the other can be done either theoretically using mathematics or empirically by building implementations. Theorems are only as valid as the assumptions on which they are based. Similarly, empirical investigations are only as good as the suite of test cases and the actual implementations of the algorithms. It is easy to disprove a conjecture that one algorithm is better than another for some class of problems by showing a counterexample, but it is much more difficult to prove such a conjecture.

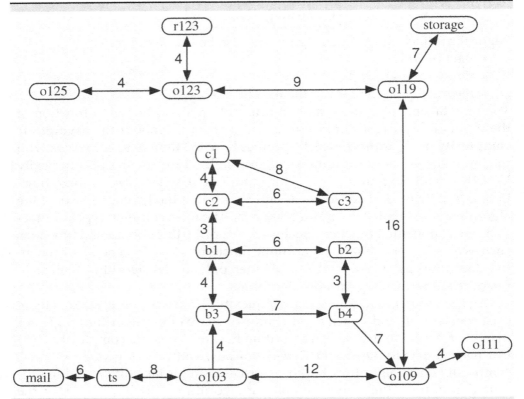

Figure 3.6: A graph, with cycles, for the delivery robot domain. Edges of the form $X \longleftrightarrow Y$ means there is an arc from X to Y and an arc from Y to X. That is, $\langle X, Y \rangle \in A$ and $\langle Y, X \rangle \in A$.

It is a poor method when

- it is possible to get caught in infinite paths; this occurs when the graph is infinite or when there are cycles in the graph; or
- solutions exist at shallow depth, because in this case the search may look at many long paths before finding the short solutions.

Depth-first search is the basis for a number of other algorithms, such as iterative deepening (page 95).

3.5.2   Breadth-First Search

In **breadth-first search** the frontier is implemented as a FIFO (first-in, first-out) queue. Thus, the path that is selected from the frontier is the one that was added earliest.

This approach implies that the paths from the start node are generated in order of the number of arcs in the path. One of the paths with the fewest arcs is selected at each stage.

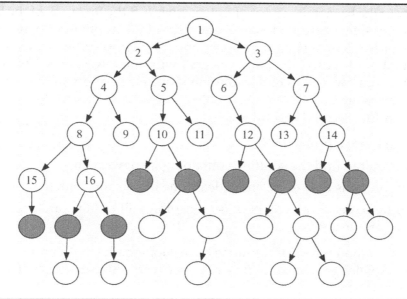

Figure 3.7: The order in which nodes are expanded in breadth-first search

Example 3.9 Consider the tree-shaped graph in Figure 3.7. Suppose the start node is the node at the top. In breadth-first search, as in depth-first search, the order in which the nodes are expanded does not depend on the location of the goal. The first sixteen nodes expanded are numbered in order of expansion in the figure. The shaded nodes are the nodes at the ends of the paths of the frontier after the first sixteen steps.

Example 3.10 Consider breadth-first search from $o103$ in the graph given in Figure 3.2 (page 76). The only goal node is $r123$. Initially, the frontier is $[\langle o103 \rangle]$. This is extended by $o103$'s neighbors, making the frontier $[\langle o103, ts \rangle, \langle o103, b3 \rangle, \langle o103, o109 \rangle]$. These are the nodes one arc away from $o013$. The next three paths chosen are $\langle o103, ts \rangle$, $\langle o103, b3 \rangle$, and $\langle o103, o109 \rangle$, at which stage the frontier contains

$$[\langle o103, ts, mail \rangle, \langle o103, b3, b1 \rangle, \langle o103, b3, b4 \rangle,$$
$$\langle o103, o109, o111 \rangle, \langle o103, o109, o119 \rangle].$$

These are the paths containing two arcs and starting at $o103$. These five paths are the next elements of the frontier chosen, at which stage the frontier contains the paths of three arcs away from $o103$, namely,

$$[\langle o103, b3, b1, c2 \rangle, \langle o103, b3, b1, b2 \rangle, \langle o103, b3, b4, o109 \rangle,$$
$$\langle o103, o109, o119, storage \rangle, \langle o103, o109, o119, o123 \rangle].$$

Note how each of the paths on the frontier has approximately the same number of arcs. For breadth-first search, the number of arcs in the paths on the frontier always differs by, at most, one.

Suppose the branching factor of the search is b. If the first path of the frontier contains n arcs, there are at least b^{n-1} elements of the frontier. All of these paths contain n or $n+1$ arcs. Thus, both space and time complexities are exponential in the number of arcs of the path to a goal with the fewest arcs. This method is guaranteed, however, to find a solution if one exists and will find a solution with the fewest arcs.

Breadth-first search is useful when

- space is not a problem;
- you want to find the solution containing the fewest arcs;
- few solutions may exist, and at least one has a short path length; and
- infinite paths may exist, because it explores all of the search space, even with infinite paths.

It is a poor method when all solutions have a long path length or there is some heuristic knowledge available. It is not used very often because of its space complexity.

3.5.3   Lowest-Cost-First Search

When a non-unit cost is associated with arcs, we often want to find the solution that minimizes the total cost of the path. For example, for a delivery robot, costs may be distances and we may want a solution that gives the minimum total distance. Costs for a delivery robot may be resources required by the robot to carry out the action represented by the arc. The cost for a tutoring system may be the time and effort required by the students. In each of these cases, the searcher should try to minimize the total cost of the path found to reach the goal.

The search algorithms considered thus far are not guaranteed to find the minimum-cost paths; they have not used the arc cost information at all. Breadth-first search finds a solution with the fewest arcs first, but the distribution of arc costs may be such that a path of fewest arcs is not one of minimal cost.

The simplest search method that is guaranteed to find a minimum cost path is similar to breadth-first search; however, instead of expanding a path with the fewest number of arcs, it selects a path with the minimum cost. This is implemented by treating the frontier as a priority queue ordered by the *cost* function (page 76).

Example 3.11 Consider a lowest-cost-first search from $o103$ in the graph given in Figure 3.2 (page 76). The only goal node is $r123$. In this example, paths are denoted by the end node of the path. A subscript shows the cost of the path.

Initially, the frontier is $[o103_0]$. At the next stage it is $[b3_4, ts_8, o109_{12}]$. The path to $b3$ is selected, with the resulting frontier

$$[b1_8, ts_8, b4_{11}, o109_{12}].$$

The path to $b1$ is then selected, resulting in frontier

$$[ts_8, c2_{11}, b4_{11}, o109_{12}, b2_{14}].$$

Then the path to ts is selected, and the resulting frontier is

$$[c2_{11}, b4_{11}, o109_{12}, mail_{14}, b2_{14}].$$

Then $c2$ is selected, and so forth. Note how the lowest-cost-first search grows many paths incrementally, always expanding the path with lowest cost.

If the costs of the arcs are bounded below by a positive constant and the branching factor is finite, the lowest-cost-first search is guaranteed to find an optimal solution – a solution with lowest path cost – if a solution exists. Moreover, the first path to a goal that is found is a path with least cost. Such a solution is optimal, because the algorithm generates paths from the start in order of path cost. If a better path existed than the first solution found, it would have been selected from the frontier earlier.

The bounded arc cost is used to guarantee the lowest-cost search will find an optimal solution. Without such a bound there can be infinite paths with a finite cost. For example, there could be nodes $n_0, n_1, n_2, \ldots$ with an arc $\langle n_{i-1}, n_i \rangle$ for each $i > 0$ with cost $1/2^i$. Infinitely many paths of the form $\langle n_0, n_1, n_2, \ldots, n_k \rangle$ exist, all of which have a cost of less than 1. If there is an arc from n_0 to a goal node with a cost greater than or equal to 1, it will never be selected. This is the basis of Zeno's paradoxes that Aristotle wrote about more than 2,300 years ago.

Like breadth-first search, lowest-cost-first search is typically exponential in both space and time. It generates *all* paths from the start that have a cost less than the cost of the solution.

3.6 Heuristic Search

All of the search methods in the preceding section are uninformed in that they did not take into account the goal. They do not use any information about where they are trying to get to unless they happen to stumble on a goal. One form of heuristic information about which nodes seem the most promising is a heuristic function $h(n)$, which takes a node n and returns a non-negative real number that is an estimate of the path cost from node n to a goal node. The function $h(n)$ is an *underestimate* if $h(n)$ is less than or equal to the actual cost of a lowest-cost path from node n to a goal.

The heuristic function is a way to inform the search about the direction to a goal. It provides an informed way to guess which neighbor of a node will lead to a goal.

There is nothing magical about a heuristic function. It must use only information that can be readily obtained about a node. Typically a trade-off exists between the amount of work it takes to derive a heuristic value for a node and how accurately the heuristic value of a node measures the actual path cost from the node to a goal.

A standard way to derive a heuristic function is to solve a simpler problem and to use the actual cost in the simplified problem as the heuristic function of the original problem.

Example 3.12 For the graph of Figure 3.2 (page 76), the straight-line distance in the world between the node and the goal position can be used as the heuristic function.

The examples that follow assume the following heuristic function:

$$
\begin{array}{rclcrclcrcl}
h(mail) & = & 26 & \quad h(ts) & = & 23 & h(o103) & = & 21 \\
h(o109) & = & 24 & \quad h(o111) & = & 27 & h(o119) & = & 11 \\
h(o123) & = & 4 & \quad h(o125) & = & 6 & h(r123) & = & 0 \\
h(b1) & = & 13 & \quad h(b2) & = & 15 & h(b3) & = & 17 \\
h(b4) & = & 18 & \quad h(c1) & = & 6 & h(c2) & = & 10 \\
h(c3) & = & 12 & \quad h(storage) & = & 12 & & &
\end{array}
$$

This h function is an underestimate because the h value is less than or equal to the exact cost of a lowest-cost path from the node to a goal. It is the exact cost for node $o123$. It is very much an underestimate for node $b1$, which seems to be close, but there is only a long route to the goal. It is very misleading for $c1$, which also seems close to the goal, but no path exists from that node to the goal.

Example 3.13 Consider the delivery robot of Example 3.2 (page 73), where the state space includes the parcels to be delivered. Suppose the cost function is the total distance traveled by the robot to deliver all of the parcels. One possible heuristic function is the largest distance of a parcel from its destination. If the robot could only carry one parcel, a possible heuristic function is the sum of the distances that the parcels must be carried. If the robot could carry multiple parcels at once, this may not be an underestimate of the actual cost.

The h function can be extended to be applicable to (non-empty) paths. The heuristic value of a path is the heuristic value of the node at the end of the path. That is:

$$ h(\langle n_o, \ldots, n_k \rangle) = h(n_k) $$

A simple use of a heuristic function is to order the neighbors that are added to the stack representing the frontier in depth-first search. The neighbors can be added to the frontier so that the best neighbor is selected first. This is known as **heuristic depth-first search**. This search chooses the locally best path, but it explores all paths from the selected path before it selects another path. Although it is often used, it suffers from the problems of depth-fist search.

Another way to use a heuristic function is to always select a path on the frontier with the lowest heuristic value. This is called **best-first search**. It

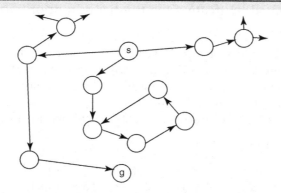

Figure 3.8: A graph that is bad for best-first search

usually does not work very well; it can follow paths that look promising because they are close to the goal, but the costs of the paths may keep increasing.

Example 3.14 Consider the graph shown in Figure 3.8, where the cost of an arc is its length. The aim is to find the shortest path from s to g. Suppose the Euclidean distance to the goal g is used as the heuristic function. A heuristic depth-first search will select the node below s and will never terminate. Similarly, because all of the nodes below s look good, a best-first search will cycle between them, never trying an alternate route from s.

3.6.1 A^* Search

A^* **search** is a combination of lowest-cost-first and best-first searches that considers both path cost and heuristic information in its selection of which path to expand. For each path on the frontier, A^* uses an estimate of the total path cost from a start node to a goal node constrained to start along that path. It uses $cost(p)$, the cost of the path found, as well as the heuristic function $h(p)$, the estimated path cost from the end of p to the goal.

For any path p on the frontier, define $f(p) = cost(p) + h(p)$. This is an estimate of the total path cost to follow path p then go to a goal node.

If n is the node at the end of path p, this can be depicted as follows:

$$\underbrace{\underbrace{start \xrightarrow{\text{actual}} n}_{cost(p)} \underbrace{\xrightarrow{\text{estimate}} goal}_{h(p)}}_{f(p)}$$

If $h(n)$ is an underestimate of the path costs from node n to a goal node, then $f(p)$ is an underestimate of a path cost of going from a start node to a goal node via p.

A^* is implemented by treating the frontier as a priority queue ordered by $f(p)$.

Example 3.15 Consider using A^* search in Example 3.4 (page 76) using the heuristic function of Figure 3.12 (page 88). In this example, the paths on the frontier are shown using the final node of the path, subscripted with the f-value of the path. The frontier is initially $[o103_{21}]$, because $h(o103) = 21$ and the cost of the path is zero. It is replaced by its neighbors, forming the frontier

$$[b3_{21}, ts_{31}, o109_{36}].$$

The first element represents the path $\langle o103, b3 \rangle$; its f-value is $f(\langle o103, b3 \rangle) = cost(\langle o103, b3 \rangle) + h(b3) = 4 + 17 = 21$. Next $b3$ is selected and replaced by its neighbors, forming the frontier

$$[b1_{21}, b4_{29}, ts_{31}, o109_{36}].$$

Then the path to $b1$ is selected and replaced by its neighbors, forming the frontier

$$[c2_{21}, b4_{29}, b2_{29}, ts_{31}, o109_{36}].$$

Then the path to $c2$ is selected and replaced by its neighbors, forming

$$[c1_{21}, b4_{29}, b2_{29}, c3_{29}, ts_{31}, o109_{36}].$$

Up to this stage, the search has been continually exploring what seems to be the direct path to the goal. Next the path to $c1$ is selected and is replaced by its neighbors, forming the frontier

$$[b4_{29}, b2_{29}, c3_{29}, ts_{31}, c3_{35}, o109_{36}].$$

At this stage, there are two different paths to the node $c3$ on the queue. The path to $c3$ that does not go through $c1$ has a lower f-value than the one that does. Later (page 93), we consider the situation when one of these paths can be pruned.

There are two paths with the same f-value. The algorithm does not specify which is selected. Suppose the path to $b4$ is selected next and is replaced by its neighbors, forming

$$[b2_{29}, c3_{29}, ts_{31}, c3_{35}, o109_{36}, o109_{42}].$$

Then the path to $b2$ is selected and replaced by its neighbors, which is the empty set, forming

$$[c3_{29}, ts_{31}, c3_{35}, b4_{35}, o109_{36}, o109_{42}].$$

Then the path to $c3$ is removed and has no neighbors; thus, the new frontier is

$$[ts_{31}, c3_{35}, b4_{35}, o109_{36}, o109_{42}].$$

Note how A^* pursues many different paths from the start.

A lowest-cost path is eventually found. The algorithm is forced to try many different paths, because several of them temporarily seemed to have the lowest cost. It still does better than either lowest-cost-first search or best-first search.

Example 3.16 Consider Figure 3.8 (page 89), which was a problematic graph for the other heuristic methods. Although it initially searches down from s because of the heuristic function, eventually the cost of the path becomes so large that it picks the node on an actual optimal path.

The property that A^* always finds an optimal path, if one exists, and that the first path found to a goal is optimal is called the **admissibility** of A^*. Admissibility means that, even when the search space is infinite, if solutions exist, a solution will be found and the first path found will be an optimal solution – a lowest-cost path from a start node to a goal node.

Proposition 3.1. *(A^* admissibility): If there is a solution, A^* always finds a solution, and the first solution found is an optimal solution, if*

- *the branching factor is finite (each node has only a finite number of neighbors),*
- *arc costs are greater than some $\epsilon > 0$, and*
- *$h(n)$ is a lower bound on the actual minimum cost of the lowest-cost path from n to a goal node.*

Proof. **Part A:** A solution will be found. If the arc costs are all greater than some $\epsilon > 0$, eventually, for all paths p in the frontier, $cost(p)$ will exceed any finite number and, thus, will exceed a solution cost if one exists (at depth in the search tree no greater than m/ϵ, where m is the solution cost). Because the branching factor is finite, only a finite number of nodes must be expanded before the search tree could get to this size, but the A^* search would have found a solution by then.

Part B: The first path to a goal selected is an optimal path. The f-value for any node on an optimal solution path is less than or equal to the f-value of an optimal solution. This is because h is an underestimate of the actual cost from a node to a goal. Thus, the f-value of a node on an optimal solution path is less than the f-value for any non-optimal solution. Thus, a non-optimal solution can never be chosen while a node exists on the frontier that leads to an optimal solution (because an element with minimum f-value is chosen at each step). So, before it can select a non-optimal solution, it will have to pick all of the nodes on an optimal path, including each of the optimal solutions. □

It should be noted that the admissibility of A^* does not ensure that every intermediate node selected from the frontier is on an optimal path from the start node to a goal node. Admissibility relieves the algorithm from worrying about cycles and ensures that the first solution found will be optimal. It does not ensure that the algorithm will not change its mind about which partial path is the best while it is searching.

To see how the heuristic function improves the efficiency of A^*, suppose c is the cost of a shortest path from a start node to a goal node. A^*, with an admissible heuristic, expands every path from a start node in the set

$$\{p : cost(p) + h(p) < c\}$$

Strategy	Selection from Frontier	Halts?	Space
Depth-first	Last node added	No	Linear
Breadth-first	First node added	Yes	Exponential
Best-first	Globally minimal $h(p)$	No	Exponential
Lowest-cost-first	Minimal $cost(p)$	Yes	Exponential
A^*	Minimal $cost(p) + h(p)$	Yes	Exponential

"Halts?" means "Is the method guaranteed to halt if there is a path to a goal on a (possibly infinite) graph with a finite number of neighbors for each node and where the arc costs have a positive lower bound?" Those search strategies where the answer is "Yes" have worst-case time complexity which increases exponentially with the size of the path length. Those algorithms that are not guaranteed to halt have infinite worst-case time complexity.

Space refers to the space complexity, which is either "Linear" in the path length or "Exponential" in the path length.

Figure 3.9: Summary of search strategies

and some of the paths in the set

$$\{p : cost(p) + h(p) = c\}.$$

Improving h affects the efficiency of A^* if it reduces the size of the first of these sets.

3.6.2 Summary of Search Strategies

The table in Figure 3.9 gives a summary of the searching strategies presented so far.

The depth-first methods are linear in space with respect to the path lengths explored but are not guaranteed to find a solution if one exists. Breadth-first, lowest-cost-first, and A^* may be exponential in both space and time, but they are guaranteed to find a solution if one exists, even if the graph is infinite (as long as there are finite branching factors and positive non-trivial arc costs).

Lowest-cost-first and A^* searches are guaranteed to find the least-cost solution as the first solution found.

3.7   More Sophisticated Search

A number of refinements can be made to the preceding strategies. First, we present two methods that are applicable when there are cycles in the graph; one checks explicitly for cycles, whereas the other method checks for multiple paths to a node. Next, we present iterative deepening and depth-first branch-and-bound searches, which are general methods that are guaranteed to find a solution (even an optimal solution), like breadth-first search or A^* search, but using the space advantages of depth-first search. We present problem-reduction methods to break down a search problem into a number of smaller search problems, each of which may be much easier to solve. Finally, we show how dynamic programming can be used for path finding and for constructing heuristic functions.

3.7.1   Cycle Checking

It is possible for a graph representing a search space to include cycles. For example, in the robot delivery domain of Figure 3.6 (page 84), the robot can go back and forth between nodes $o103$ and $o109$. Some of the aforementioned search methods can get trapped in cycles, continuously repeating the cycle and never finding an answer even in finite graphs. The other methods can loop though cycles, but eventually they still find a solution.

The simplest method of pruning the search tree, while guaranteeing that a solution will be found in a finite graph, is to ensure that the algorithm does not consider neighbors that are already on the path from the start. A **cycle check** or **loop check** checks for paths where the last node already appears on the path from the start node to that node. With a cycle check, only the paths $\langle s_0, \ldots, s_k, s \rangle$, where $s \notin \{s_0, \ldots, s_k\}$, are added to the frontier at line 16 of Figure 3.4 (page 79). Alternatively, the check can be made after a node is selected; paths with a cycle can be thrown away.

The computational complexity of a cycle check depends on the search method being used. For depth-first methods, where the graph is explicitly stored, the overhead can be as low as a constant factor; a bit can be added to each node in the graph that is assigned a value of 1 when the node is expanded, and assigned a value of 0 on backtracking. A search algorithm can avoid cycles by never expanding a node with its bit set to 1. This approach works because depth-first search maintains a single current path. The elements on the frontier are alternative branches from this path. Even if the graph is generated dynamically, as long as an efficient indexing structure is used for the nodes on the current path, a cycle check can be done efficiently.

For the search strategies that maintain multiple paths – namely, all of those with exponential space in Figure 3.9 – a cycle check takes time linear in the length of the path being searched. These algorithms cannot do better than searching up the partial path being considered, checking to ensure they do not add a node that already appears in the path.

3.7.2   Multiple-Path Pruning

There is often more than one path to a node. If only one path is required, a search algorithm can prune from the frontier any path that leads to a node to which it has already found a path.

Multiple-path pruning can be implemented by keeping a **closed list** of nodes that have been expanded. When a path is selected at line 13 of Figure 3.4 (page 79), if its last node is in the closed list, the path can be discarded. Otherwise', its last node is added to the closed list, and the algorithm proceeds as before.

This approach does not necessarily guarantee that the shortest path is not discarded. Something more sophisticated may have to be done to guarantee that an optimal solution is found. To ensure that the search algorithm can still find a lowest-cost path to a goal, one of the following can be done:

- Make sure that the first path found to any node is a lowest-cost path to that node, then prune all subsequent paths found to that node, as discussed earlier.

- If the search algorithm finds a lower-cost path to a node than one already found, it can remove all paths that used the higher-cost path to the node (because these cannot be on an optimal solution). That is, if there is a path p on the frontier $\langle s, \ldots, n, \ldots, m \rangle$, and a path p' to n is found that is shorter than the portion of the path from s to n in p, then p can be removed from the frontier.

- Whenever the search finds a lower-cost path to a node than a path to that already found, it can incorporate a new initial section on the paths that have extended the initial path. Thus, if there is a path $p = \langle s, \ldots, n, \ldots, m \rangle$ on the frontier, and a path p' to n is found that is shorter than the portion of p from s to n, then p' can replace the initial part of p to n.

The first of these alternatives allows the use of the closed list without losing the ability to find an optimal path. The others require more sophisticated algorithms.

In lowest-cost-first search, the first path found to a node (i.e., when the node is selected from the frontier) is the least-cost path to the node. Pruning subsequent paths to that node cannot remove a lower-cost path to that node, and thus pruning subsequent paths to each node still enables an optimal solution to be found.

As described earlier, A^* (page 89) does not guarantee that when a path to a node is selected for the first time it is the lowest cost path to that node. Note that the admissibility theorem (page 91) guarantees this for every path to a *goal* node but not for every path. To see when pruning subsequent paths to a node can remove the optimal solution, suppose the algorithm has selected a path p to node n for expansion, but there exists a lower-cost path to node n, which it has not found yet. Then there must be a path p' on the frontier that is the initial part of the lower-cost path. Suppose path p' ends at node n'. It must be that $f(p) \leq f(p')$, because p was selected before p'. This means that

$$cost(p) + h(n) \leq cost(p') + h(n').$$

If the path to n via p' has a lower cost than the path p,

$$cost(p') + d(n', n) < cost(p),$$

where $d(n', n)$ is the actual cost of the shortest path from node n' to n. From these two equations, we can derive

$$d(n', n) < cost(p) - cost(p') \leq h(p') - h(p) = h(n') - h(n).$$

Thus, we can ensure that the first path found to any node is the lowest-cost path if $|h(n') - h(n)| \leq d(n', n)$ for any two nodes n and n'. The **monotone restriction** on h is that $|h(n') - h(n)| \leq d(n', n)$ for any two nodes n and n'. That is, the difference in the heuristic values for two nodes must be less than or equal to the actual cost of the lowest-cost path between the nodes. It is applicable to, for example, the heuristic function of Euclidean distance (the straight-line distance in an n-dimensional Euclidean space) between two points when the cost function is distance. It is also typically applicable when the heuristic function is a solution to a simplified problem that has shorter solutions.

With the monotone restriction, the f-values on the frontier are monotonically non-decreasing. That is, when the frontier is expanded, the f-values do not get smaller. Thus, with the monotone restriction, subsequent paths to any node can be pruned in A^* search.

Multiple-path pruning subsumes a cycle check, because a cycle is another path to a node and is therefore pruned. Multiple-path pruning can be done in constant time, if the graph is explicitly stored, by setting a bit on each node to which a path has been found. It can be done in logarithmic time (in the number of nodes expanded, as long as it is indexed appropriately), if the graph is dynamically generated, by storing the closed list of all of the nodes that have been expanded. Multiple-path pruning is preferred over cycle checking for breadth-first methods where virtually all of the nodes considered have to be stored anyway. For depth-first search strategies, however, the algorithm does not otherwise have to store all of the nodes already considered. Storing them makes the method exponential in space. Therefore, cycle checking is preferred over multiple-path checking for depth-first methods.

3.7.3 Iterative Deepening

So far, none of the methods discussed have been ideal; the only ones that guarantee that a path will be found require exponential space (see Figure 3.9 (page 92)). One way to combine the space efficiency of depth-first search with the optimality of breadth-first methods is to use **iterative deepening**. The idea is to recompute the elements of the frontier rather than storing them. Each recomputation can be a depth-first search, which thus uses less space.

Consider making a breadth-first search into an iterative deepening search. This is carried out by having a depth-first searcher, which searches only to a limited depth. It can first do a depth-first search to depth 1 by building paths of length 1 in a depth-first manner. Then it can build paths to depth 2, then depth 3, and so on. It can throw away all of the previous computation each time and start again. Eventually it will find a solution if one exists, and, as it is enumerating paths in order, the path with the fewest arcs will always be found first.

When implementing an iterative deepening search, you have to distinguish between

- failure because the depth bound was reached and

- failure that does not involve reaching the depth bound.

In the first case, the search must be retried with a larger depth bound. In the second case, it is a waste of time to try again with a larger depth bound, because no path exists no matter what the depth. We say that failure due to reaching the depth bound is **failing unnaturally**, and failure without reaching the depth bound is **failing naturally**.

An implementation of iterative-deepening search, *IdSearch*, is presented in Figure 3.10. The local procedure *dbsearch* implements a depth-bounded depth-first search (using recursion to keep the stack) that places a limit on the length of the paths for which it is searching. It uses a depth-first search to find all paths of length $k + b$, where k is the path length of the given path from the start and b is a non-negative integer. The iterative-deepening searcher calls this for increasing depth bounds. This program finds the paths to goal nodes in the same order as does the breadth-first search. As in the generic graph searching algorithm, to find more solutions after the *return* on line 22, the search can continue from line 23.

The iterative-deepening search fails whenever the breadth-first search would fail. When asked for multiple answers, it only returns each successful path once, even though it may be rediscovered in subsequent iterations. Halting is achieved by keeping track of when increasing the bound could help find an answer:

- The depth bound is increased if the depth bound search was truncated by reaching the depth bound. In this case, the search failed *unnaturally*. The search failed *naturally* if the search did not prune any paths due to the depth bound. In this case, the program can stop and report no (more) paths.

- The search only reports a solution path if that path would not have been reported in the previous iteration. Thus, it only reports paths whose length is the depth bound.

The obvious problem with iterative deepening is the wasted computation that occurs at each step. This, however, may not be as bad as one might think, particularly if the branching factor is high. Consider the running time of the algorithm. Assume a constant branching factor of $b > 1$. Consider the search where the bound is k. At depth k, there are b^k nodes; each of these has been generated once. The nodes at depth $k - 1$ have been generated twice, those at depth $k - 2$ have been generated three times, and so on, and the nodes at depth 1 have been generated k times. Thus, the total number of nodes

1: **procedure** *IdSearch*(*G*, *s*, *goal*)
2:   **Inputs**
3:     *G*: graph with nodes *N* and arcs *A*
4:     *s*: set of start nodes
5:     *goal*: Boolean function on states
6:   **Output**
7:     path from *s* to a node for which *goal* is true
8:     or ⊥ if there is no such path
9:   **Local**
10:    *natural_failure*: Boolean
11:    *bound*: integer
12:    **procedure** *dbsearch*($\langle n_0, \ldots, n_k \rangle$, *b*)
13:      **Inputs**
14:        $\langle n_0, \ldots, n_k \rangle$: path
15:        *b*: integer, $b \geq 0$
16:      **Output**
17:        path to goal of length $k + b$
18:      **if** $b > 0$ **then**
19:        **for each** arc $\langle n_k, n \rangle \in A$ **do**
20:          *dbsearch*($\langle n_0, \ldots, n_k, n \rangle$, $b - 1$)
21:      **else if** *goal*(n_k) **then**
22:        **return** $\langle n_0, \ldots, n_k \rangle$
23:      **else if** n_k has any neighbors **then**
24:        *natural_failure* := *false*
25:    *bound* := 0
26:    **repeat**
27:      *natural_failure* := *true*
28:      *dbsearch*($\{\langle s \rangle : s \in S\}$, *bound*)
29:      *bound* := *bound* + 1
30:    **until** natural_failure
31:    **return** ⊥

Figure 3.10: Iterative deepening search

generated is

$$b^k + 2b^{k-1} + 3b^{k-2} + \cdots + kb$$
$$= b^k(1 + 2b^{-1} + 3b^{-2} + \cdots + kb^{1-k})$$
$$\leq b^k \left(\sum_{i=1}^{\infty} ib^{(1-i)} \right)$$
$$= b^k \left(\frac{b}{b-1} \right)^2.$$

There is a constant overhead $(b/(b-1))^2$ times the cost of generating the nodes at depth n. When $b = 2$ there is an overhead factor of 4, and when $b = 3$ there is an overhead of 2.25 over generating the frontier. This algorithm is $O(b^k)$ and there cannot be an asymptotically better uninformed search strategy. Note that, if the branching factor is close to 1, this analysis does not work (because then the denominator would be close to zero); see Exercise 3.9 (page 109).

Iterative deepening can also be applied to an A^* search. **Iterative deepening A^*** (IDA*) performs repeated depth-bounded depth-first searches. Instead of the bound being on the number of arcs in the path, it is a bound on the value of $f(n)$. The threshold starts at the value of $f(s)$, where s is the starting node with minimal h-value. IDA* then carries out a depth-first depth-bounded search but never expands a node with a higher f-value than the current bound. If the depth-bounded search fails *unnaturally*, the next bound is the minimum of the f-values that exceeded the previous bound. IDA* thus checks the same nodes as A^* but recomputes them with a depth-first search instead of storing them.

3.7.4   Branch and Bound

Depth-first **branch-and-bound** search is a way to combine the space saving of depth-first search with heuristic information. It is particularly applicable when many paths to a goal exist and we want an optimal path. As in A^* search, we assume that $h(n)$ is less than or equal to the cost of a lowest-cost path from n to a goal node.

The idea of a branch-and-bound search is to maintain the lowest-cost path to a goal found so far, and its cost. Suppose this cost is *bound*. If the search encounters a path p such that $cost(p) + h(p) \geq bound$, path p can be pruned. If a non-pruned path to a goal is found, it must be better than the previous best path. This new solution is remembered and *bound* is set to the cost of this new solution. It then keeps searching for a better solution.

Branch-and-bound search generates a sequence of ever-improving solutions. Once it has found a solution, it can keep improving it.

Branch-and-bound search is typically used with depth-first search, where the space saving of the depth-first search can be achieved. It can be implemented similarly to depth-bounded search, but where the bound is in terms of path cost and reduces as shorter paths are found. The algorithm remembers the lowest-cost path found and returns this path when the search finishes.

The algorithm is shown in Figure 3.11. The internal procedure *cbsearch*, for cost-bounded search, uses the global variables to provide information to the main procedure.

Initially, *bound* can be set to infinity, but it is often useful to set it to an overestimate, *bound$_0$*, of the path cost of an optimal solution. This algorithm

---

1: **procedure** $DFBranchAndBound(G, s, goal, h, bound_0)$
2:     **Inputs**
3:         G: graph with nodes N and arcs A
4:         s: start node
5:         $goal$: Boolean function on nodes
6:         h: heuristic function on nodes
7:         $bound_0$: initial depth bound (can be ∞ if not specified)
8:     **Output**
9:         a least-cost path from s to a goal node if there is a solution with cost less than $bound_0$
10:         or $\perp$ if there is no solution with cost less than $bound_0$
11:     **Local**
12:         $best\_path$: path or $\perp$
13:         $bound$: non-negative real
14:         **procedure** $cbsearch(\langle n_0, \ldots, n_k \rangle)$
15:             **if** $cost(\langle n_0, \ldots, n_k \rangle) + h(n_k) < bound$ **then**
16:                 **if** $goal(n_k)$ **then**
17:                     $best\_path := \langle n_0, \ldots, n_k \rangle$
18:                     $bound := cost(\langle n_0, \ldots, n_k \rangle)$
19:                 **else**
20:                     **for each** arc $\langle n_k, n \rangle \in A$ **do**
21:                         $cbsearch(\langle n_0, \ldots, n_k, n \rangle)$
22:     $best\_path := \perp$
23:     $bound := bound_0$
24:     $cbsearch(\langle s \rangle)$
25:     **return** $best\_path$

Figure 3.11: Depth-first branch-and-bound search

will return an optimal solution – a least-cost path from the start node to a goal node – if there is a solution with cost less than the initial bound $bound_0$.

If the initial bound is slightly above the cost of a lowest-cost path, this algorithm can find an optimal path expanding no more arcs than A^* search. This happens when the initial bound is such that the algorithm prunes any path that has a higher cost than a lowest-cost path; once it has found a path to the goal, it only explores paths whose the f-value is lower than the path found. These are exactly the paths that A^* explores when it finds one solution.

If it returns $\perp$ when $bound_0 = \infty$, there are no solutions. If it returns $\perp$ when $bound_0$ is some finite value, it means no solution exists with cost less than $bound_0$. This algorithm can be combined with iterative deepening to increase the bound until either a solution is found or it can be shown there is no solution. See Exercise 3.13 (page 109).

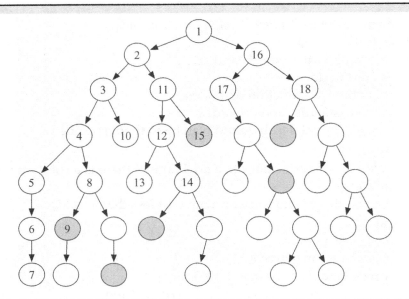

Figure 3.12: The nodes expanded in depth-first branch-and-bound search

Example 3.17 Consider the tree-shaped graph in Figure 3.12. The goal nodes are shaded. Suppose that each arc has length 1, and there is no heuristic information (i.e., $h(n) = 0$ for each node n). In the algorithm, suppose $depth_0 = \infty$ and the depth-first search always chooses the leftmost child first. This figure shows the order in which the nodes are checked to determine if they are a goal node. The nodes that are not numbered are not checked for being a goal node.

The subtree under the node numbered "5" does not have a goal and is explored fully (or up to depth $depth_0$ if it had a finite value). The ninth node checked is a goal node. It has a path cost of 5, and so the bound is set to 5. From then on, only paths with a length of less than 5 are checked for being a solution. The fifteenth node checked is also a goal. It has a path cost of 3, and so the bound is reduced to 3. There are no other goal nodes found, and so the path to the node labeled 15 is returned. It is an optimal path. There is another optimal path that is pruned; the algorithm never checks the children of the node labeled with 18.

If there was heuristic information, it could be used to prune parts of the search space, as in A^* search.

3.7.5 Direction of Search

The size of the search space of the generic search algorithm on finite uniform graphs is b^k, where b is the branching factor and k is the path length. Anything that can be done to reduce k or b can potentially give great savings.

The abstract definition of the graph-searching method of problem solving is symmetric in the sense that the algorithm can either begin with a start node and search forward for a goal node or begin with a goal node and search backward for a start node in the inverse graph. Note that in many applications the goal is determined implicitly by a Boolean function that returns *true* when a goal is found, and not explicitly as a set of nodes, so backward search may not be possible.

For those cases where the goal nodes are explicit, it may be more efficient to search in one direction than in the other. The size of the search space is exponential in the branching factor. It is typically the case that forward and backward searches have different branching factors. A general principle is to search forward or backward, depending on which has the smaller branching factor.

The following sections consider some ways in which search efficiency can be improved beyond this for many search spaces.

Bidirectional Search

The idea of a bidirectional search is to reduce the search time by searching forward from the start and backward from the goal simultaneously. When the two search frontiers intersect, the algorithm can reconstruct a single path that extends from the start state through the frontier intersection to the goal.

A new problem arises during a bidirectional search, namely ensuring that the two search frontiers actually meet. For example, a depth-first search in both directions is not likely to work well because its small search frontiers are likely to pass each other by. Breadth-first search in both directions would be guaranteed to meet.

A combination of depth-first search in one direction and breadth-first search in the other would guarantee the required intersection of the search frontiers, but the choice of which to apply in which direction may be difficult. The decision depends on the cost of saving the breadth-first frontier and searching it to check when the depth-first method will intersect one of its elements.

There are situations where a bidirectional search can result in substantial savings. For example, if the forward and backward branching factors of the search space are both b, and the goal is at depth k, then breadth-first search will take time proportional to b^k, whereas a symmetric bidirectional search will take time proportional to $2b^{k/2}$. This is an exponential savings in time, even though the time complexity is still exponential. Note that this complexity analysis assumes that finding the intersection of frontiers is free, which may not be a valid assumption for many applications (see Exercise 3.10 (page 109)).

Island-Driven Search

One of the ways that search may be made more efficient is to identify a limited number of places where the forward search and backward search can meet. For example, in searching for a path from two rooms on different floors, it may be appropriate to constrain the search to first go to the elevator on one level, then to the elevator on the goal level. Intuitively, these designated positions are **islands** in the search graph, which are constrained to be on a solution path from the start node to a goal node.

When islands are specified, an agent can decompose the search problem into several search problems, for example, one from the initial room to the elevator, one from the elevator on one level to the elevator on the other level, and one from the elevator to the destination room. This reduces the search space by having three simpler problems to solve. Having smaller problems helps to reduce the combinatorial explosion of large searches and is an example of how extra knowledge about a problem can be used to improve efficiency of search.

To find a path between s and g using islands:

1. Identify a set of islands $i_0, ..., i_k$;

2. Find paths from s to i_0, from i_{j-1} to i_j for each j from 1 to k, and from i_k to g.

Each of these searching problems should be correspondingly simpler than the general problem and therefore easier to solve.

The identification of islands is extra knowledge which may be beyond that which is in the graph. The use of inappropriate islands may make the problem more difficult (or even impossible to solve). It may also be possible to identify an alternate decomposition of the problem by choosing a different set of islands and search through the space of possible islands. Whether this works in practice depends on the details of the problem.

Searching in a Hierarchy of Abstractions

The notion of islands can be used to define problem-solving strategies that work at multiple levels of detail or multiple levels of abstraction.

The idea of searching in a hierarchy of abstractions first involves abstracting the problem, leaving out as many details as possible. A partial solution to a problem may be found – one that requires further details to be worked out. For example, the problem of getting from one room to another requires the use of many instances of turning, but an agent would like to reason about the problem at a level of abstraction where the details of the actual steering are omitted. It is expected that an appropriate abstraction solves the problem in broad strokes, leaving only minor problems to be solved. The route planning problem for the delivery robot is too difficult to solve by searching without leaving out details until it must consider them.

One way this can be implemented is to generalize island-driven search to search over possible islands. Once a solution is found at the island level, subproblems can be solved recursively in the same manner. Information that is found at the lower level can inform higher levels that some potential solution does not work as well as expected. The higher level can then use that information to replan. This process typically does not result in a guaranteed optimal solution because it only considers some of the high-level decompositions.

Searching in a hierarchy of abstractions depends very heavily on *how* one decomposes and *abstracts* the problem to be solved. Once the problems are abstracted and decomposed, any of the search methods can be used to solve them. It is not easy, however, to recognize useful abstractions and problem decompositions.

3.7.6 Dynamic Programming

Dynamic programming is a general method for optimization that involves storing partial solutions to problems, so that a solution that has already been found can be retrieved rather than being recomputed. Dynamic programming algorithms are used throughout AI.

Dynamic programming can be used for finding paths in graphs. Intuitively, **dynamic programming** for graph searching can be seen as constructing the *perfect* heuristic function so that A^*, even if it keeps only one element of the frontier, is guaranteed to find a solution. This cost-to-goal function represents the exact cost of a minimal-cost path from each node to the goal.

A **policy** is a specification of which arc to take from each node. The cost-to-goal function can be computed offline and can be used to build an optimal policy. Online, an agent can use this policy to determine what to do at each point.

Let *cost_to_goal*(n) be the actual cost of a lowest-cost path from node n to a goal; *cost_to_goal*(n) can be defined as

$$cost\_to\_goal(n) = \begin{cases} 0 & \text{if } is\_goal(n), \\ \min_{\langle n,m \rangle \in A}(cost(\langle n, m \rangle) + cost\_to\_goal(m)) & \text{otherwise.} \end{cases}$$

The general idea is to start at the goal and build a table of the *cost_to_goal*(n) value for each node. This can be done by carrying out a lowest-cost-first search, with multiple-path pruning, from the goal nodes in the *inverse graph*, which is the graph with all arcs reversed. Rather than having a goal to search for, the dynamic programming algorithm records the *cost_to_goal* values for each node found. It uses the inverse graph to compute the costs from each node to the goal and not the costs from the goal to each node. In essence, dynamic programming works backward from the goal by trying to build the lowest-cost paths to the goal from each node in the graph.

For a particular goal, once the *cost_to_goal* value for each node has been recorded, an agent can use the *cost_to_goal* value to determine the next arc on an optimal path. From node n it should go to a neighbor m that minimizes $cost(\langle n, m \rangle) + cost\_to\_goal(m)$. Following this policy will take the agent from any node to a goal along a lowest-cost path. Given *cost_to_goal*, determining which arc is optimal takes constant time with respect to the size of the graph, assuming a bounded number of neighbors for each node. Dynamic programming takes time and space linear in the size of the graph to build the *cost_to_goal* table.

Dynamic programming is useful when

- the goal nodes are explicit (the previous methods only assumed a function that recognizes goal nodes);
- a lowest-cost path is needed;
- the graph is finite and small enough to be able to store the *cost_to_goal* value for each node;
- the goal does not change very often; and
- the policy is used a number of times for each goal, so that the cost of generating the *cost_to_goal* values can be amortized over many instances of the problem.

The main problems with dynamic programming are that

- it only works when the graph is finite and the table can be made small enough to fit into memory,
- an agent must recompute a policy for each different goal, and
- the time and space required is linear in the size of the graph, where the graph size for finite graphs is typically exponential in the path length.

Example 3.18 For the graph given in Figure 3.2 (page 76), the cost from $r123$ to the goal is 0; thus,

$$cost\_to\_goal(r123) = 0.$$

Continuing with a lowest-cost-first search from $r123$:

$$cost\_to\_goal(o123) = 4$$
$$cost\_to\_goal(o119) = 13$$
$$cost\_to\_goal(o109) = 29$$
$$cost\_to\_goal(b4) = 36$$
$$cost\_to\_goal(b2) = 39$$
$$cost\_to\_goal(o103) = 41$$
$$cost\_to\_goal(b3) = 43$$
$$cost\_to\_goal(b1) = 45$$

At this stage the backward search halts. Two things can be noticed here. First, if a node does not have a *cost_to_goal* value, then no path to the goal exists from that node. Second, an agent can quickly determine the next arc on a lowest-cost path to the goal for any node. For example, if the agent is at $o103$, to determine a lowest-cost path to $r123$ it compares $4 + 43$ (the cost of going via $b3$) with $12 + 29$ (the cost of going straight to $o109$) and can quickly determine to go to $o109$.

When building the *cost_to_goal* function, the searcher has implicitly determined which neighbor leads to the goal. Instead of determining at run time which neighbor is on an optimal path, it can store this information.

Optimality of the A^* algorithm

A search algorithm is **optimal** if no other search algorithm uses less time or space or expands fewer nodes, both with a guarantee of solution quality. The optimal search algorithm would be one that picks the correct node at each choice. However, this specification is not effective because we cannot directly implement it. Whether such an algorithm is possible is an open question (as to whether $P = NP$). There does, however, seem to be a statement that can be proved.

Optimality of A^*: Among search algorithms that only use arc costs and a heuristic estimate of the cost from a node to a goal, no algorithm expands fewer nodes than A^* and guarantees to find a lowest-cost path.

Proof sketch: Given only the information about the arc costs and the heuristic information, unless the algorithm has expanded each path p, where $f(p)$ is less than the cost of an optimal path, it does not know whether p leads to a lower-cost path. More formally, suppose an algorithm A' found a path for a problem P where some path p was not expanded such that $f(p)$ was less than the solution found. Suppose there was another problem P', which was the same as P, except that there really was a path via p with cost $f(p)$. The algorithm A' cannot tell P' from P, because it did not expand the path p, so it would report the same solution for P' as for P, but the solution found for P would not be optimal for P' because the solution found has a higher cost than the path via p. Therefore, an algorithm is not guaranteed to find a lowest-cost path unless it explores all paths with f-values less than the value of an optimal path; that is, it must explore all the paths that A^* explores.

Counterexample: Although this proof seems reasonable, there are algorithms that explore fewer nodes. Consider an algorithm that does a forward A^*-like search and a backward dynamic programming search, where the steps are interleaved in some way (e.g., by alternating between the forward steps and the backward steps). The backward search builds a table of $cost\_to\_goal(n)$ values of the actual discovered cost from n to a goal, and it maintains a bound b, where it has explored all paths of cost less than b to a goal. The forward search uses a priority queue on $cost(p) + c(n)$, where n is the node at the end of the path p, and $c(n)$ is $cost\_to\_goal(n)$ if it has been computed; otherwise, $c(n)$ is $max(h(n), b)$. The intuition is that, if a path exists from the end of path p to a goal node, either it uses a path that has been discovered by the backward search or it uses a path that costs at least b. This algorithm is guaranteed to find a lowest-cost path and often expands fewer nodes than A^* (see Exercise 3.11 (page 109)).

Conclusion: Having a counterexample would seem to mean that the optimality of A^* is false. However, the proof does seem to have some appeal and perhaps it should not be dismissed outright. A^* is not optimal out of the class of all algorithms, but the proof seems right for the class of algorithms that only do forward search. See Exercise 3.12 (page 109).

Dynamic programming can be used to construct heuristics for A^* and branch-and-bound searches. One way to build a heuristic function is to simplify the problem (e.g., by leaving out some details) until the simplified problem has a small enough state space. Dynamic programming can be used to find the optimal path length to a goal in the simplified problem. This information can then be used as a heuristic for the original problem.

3.8   Review

The following are the main points you should have learned from this chapter:

- Many problems can be abstracted as the problem of finding paths in graphs.
- Breadth-first and depth-first searches can find paths in graphs without any extra knowledge beyond the graph.
- A^* search can use a heuristic function that estimates the cost from a node to a goal. If this estimate underestimates the actual cost, A^* is guaranteed to find a least-cost path first.
- Iterative deepening and depth-first branch-and-bound searches can be used to find least-cost paths with less memory than methods such as A^*, which store multiple paths.
- When graphs are small, dynamic programming can be used to record the actual cost of a least-cost path from each node to the goal, which can be used to find the next arc in an optimal path.

3.9   References and Further Reading

There is a lot of information on search techniques in the literature of operations research, computer science, and AI. Search was seen early on as one of the foundations of AI. The AI literature emphasizes heuristic search.

Basic search algorithms are discussed in Nilsson [1971]. For a detailed analysis of heuristic search see Pearl [1984]. The A^* algorithm was developed by Hart, Nilsson, and Raphael [1968].

Depth-first iterative deepening is described in Korf [1985].

Branch-and-bound search was developed in the operations research community and is described in Lawler and Wood [1966].

Dynamic programming is a general algorithm that will be used as a dual to search algorithms in other parts of the book. The specific algorithm presented here was invented by Dijkstra [1959]. See Cormen, Leiserson, Rivest, and Stein [2001] for more details on the general class of dynamic programming algorithms.

The idea of using dynamic programming as a source of heuristics for A^* search was proposed by Culberson and Schaeffer [1998] and further developed by Felner, Korf, and Hanan [2004].

Minsky [1961] discussed islands and problem reduction.

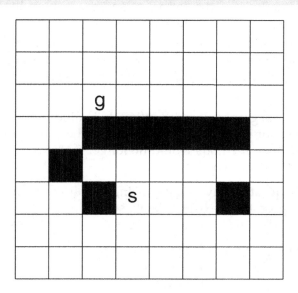

Figure 3.13: A grid-searching problem

3.10 Exercises

Exercise 3.1 Comment on the following quote: "One of the main goals of AI should be to build general heuristics that can be used for any graph-searching problem."

Exercise 3.2 Which of the path-finding search procedures are fair in the sense that any element on the frontier will eventually be chosen? Consider this for question finite graphs without loops, finite graphs with loops, and infinite graphs (with finite branching factors).

Exercise 3.3 Consider the problem of finding a path in the grid shown in Figure 3.13 from the position s to the position g. A piece can move on the grid horizontally and vertically, one square at a time. No step may be made into a forbidden shaded area.

(a) On the grid shown in Figure 3.13, number the nodes expanded (in order) for a depth-first search from s to g, given that the order of the operators is up, left, right, then down. Assume there is a cycle check.

(b) For the same grid, number the nodes expanded, in order, for a best-first search from s to g. Manhattan distance should be used as the evaluation function. The Manhattan distance between two points is the distance in the x-direction plus the distance in the y-direction. It corresponds to the distance traveled along city streets arranged in a grid. Assume multiple-path pruning. What is the first path found?

(c) On the same grid, number the nodes expanded, in order, for a heuristic depth-first search from s to g, given Manhattan distance as the evaluation function. Assume a cycle check. What is the path found?

(d) Number the nodes in order for an A^* search, with multiple-path pruning, for the same graph. What is the path found?

(e) Show how to solve the same problem using dynamic programming. Give the *dist* value for each node, and show which path is found.

(f) Based on this experience, discuss which algorithms are best suited for this problem.

(g) Suppose that the graph extended infinitely in all directions. That is, there is no boundary, but *s*, *g*, and the blocks are in the same positions relative to each other. Which methods would no longer find a path? Which would be the best method, and why?

Exercise 3.4 This question investigates using graph searching to design video presentations. Suppose there exists a database of video segments, together with their length in seconds and the topics covered, set up as follows:

Segment	Length	Topics covered
seg0	10	[welcome]
seg1	30	[skiing, views]
seg2	50	[welcome, artificial_intelligence, robots]
seg3	40	[graphics, dragons]
seg4	50	[skiing, robots]

Suppose we represent a node as a pair:

$$\langle To\_Cover, Segs \rangle,$$

where *Segs* is a list of segments that must be in the presentation, and *To_Cover* is a list of topics that also must be covered. Assume that none of the segments in *Segs* cover any of the topics in *To_Cover*.

The neighbors of a node are obtained by first selecting a topic from *To_Cover*. There is a neighbor for each segment that covers the selected topic. [Part of this exercise is to think about the exact structure of these neighbors.]

For example, given the aforementioned database of segments, the neighbors of the node $\langle [welcome, robots], [] \rangle$, assuming that *welcome* was selected, are $\langle [], [seg2] \rangle$ and $\langle [robots], [seg0] \rangle$.

Thus, each arc adds exactly one segment but can cover one or more topics. Suppose that the cost of the arc is equal to the time of the segment added.

The goal is to design a presentation that covers all of the topics in *MustCover*. The starting node is $\langle MustCover, [] \rangle$, and the goal nodes are of the form $\langle [], Presentation \rangle$. The cost of the path from a start node to a goal node is the time of the presentation. Thus, an optimal presentation is a shortest presentation that covers all of the topics in *MustCover*.

(a) Suppose that the goal is to cover the topics [*welcome, skiing, robots*]. Suppose the algorithm always select the leftmost topic to find the neighbors for each node. Draw the search space expanded for a lowest-cost-first search until the first solution is found. This should show all nodes expanded, which node is a goal node, and the frontier when the goal was found.

(b) Give a non-trivial heuristic function h that is an underestimate of the real cost. [Note that $h(n) = 0$ for all n is the trivial heuristic function.] Does it satisfy the monotone restriction for a heuristic function?

Exercise 3.5 Draw two different graphs, indicating start and goal nodes, for which forward search is better in one and backward search is better in the other.

Exercise 3.6 Implement iterative-deepening A^*. This should be based on the iterative deepening searcher of Figure 3.10 (page 97).

Exercise 3.7 Suppose that, rather than finding an optimal path from the start to a goal, we wanted a path with a cost not more than, say, 10% greater than the least-cost path. Suggest an alternative to an iterative-deepening A^* search that would guarantee this outcome. Why might this be advantageous to iterative-deepening A^* search?

Exercise 3.8 How can depth-first branch-and-bound be modified to find a path with a cost that is not more than, say, 10% greater than the least-cost path. How does this algorithm compare to the variant of A^* from the previous question?

Exercise 3.9 The overhead for iterative deepening with $b - 1$ on the denominator (page 97) is not a good approximation when $b \approx 1$. Give a better estimate of the complexity of iterative deepening when $b = 1$. What is the complexity of the other methods given in this chapter? Suggest a way that iterative deepening can have a lower overhead when the branching factor is close to 1.

Exercise 3.10 Bidirectional search must be able to determine when the frontiers intersect. For each of the following pairs of searches specify how to determine when the frontiers intersect:

(a) Breadth-first search and depth-bounded depth-first search.

(b) Iterative deepening search and depth-bounded depth-first search.

(c) A^* and depth-bounded depth-bounded search.

(d) A^* and A^*.

Exercise 3.11 Consider the algorithm sketched in the counterexample of the box on page 105:

(a) When can the algorithm stop? (Hint: it does not have to wait until the forward search finds a path to a goal).

(b) What data structures should be kept?

(c) Specify the algorithm in full.

(d) Show that it finds the optimal path.

(e) Give an example where it expands (many) fewer nodes than A^*.

Exercise 3.12 Give a statement of the optimality of A^* that specifies the class of algorithms for which A^* is optimal. Give the formal proof.

Exercise 3.13 The depth-first branch and bound of Figure 3.11 (page 99) is like a depth-bounded search in that it only finds a solution if there is a solution with cost less than *bound*. Show how this can be combined with an iterative deepening search to increase the depth bound if there is no solution for a particular depth bound. This algorithm must return ⊥ in a finite graph if there is no solution. The algorithm should allow the bound to be incremented by an arbitrary amount and still return an optimal (least-cost) solution when there is a solution.

Chapter 4

Features and Constraints

Every task involves constraint,
Solve the thing without complaint;
There are magic links and chains
Forged to loose our rigid brains.
Structures, strictures, though they bind,
Strangely liberate the mind.

– James Falen

Instead of reasoning explicitly in terms of states, it is often better to describe states in terms of features and then to reason in terms of these features. Often these features are not independent and there are **hard constraints** that specify legal combinations of assignments of values to variables. As Falen's elegant poem emphasizes, the mind discovers and exploits constraints to solve tasks. Common examples occur in planning and scheduling, where an agent must assign a time for each action that must be carried out; typically, there are constraints on when actions can be carried out and constraints specifying that the actions must actually achieve a goal. There are also often preferences over values that can be specified in terms of **soft constraints**. This chapter shows how to generate assignments that satisfy a set of hard constraints and how to optimize a collection of soft constraints.

4.1 Features and States

For any practical problem, an agent cannot reason in terms of states; there are simply too many of them. Moreover, most problems do not come with an explicit list of states; the states are typically described implicitly in terms of

features. When describing a real state space, it is usually more natural to describe the features that make up the state rather than explicitly enumerating the states.

The definitions of states and features are intertwined; we can describe either in terms of the other.

- States can be defined in terms of features: features can be primitive and a state corresponds to an assignment of a value to each feature.

- Features can be defined in terms of states: the states can be primitive and a feature is a function of the states. Given a state, the function returns the value of the feature on that state.

Each feature has a **domain** that is the set of values that it can take on. The domain of the feature is the range of the function on the states.

Example 4.1 In the electrical environment of Figure 1.8 (page 34), there may be a feature for the position of each switch that specifies whether the switch is up or down. There may be a feature for each light that specifies whether the light is lit or not. There may be a feature for each component specifying whether it is working properly or if it is broken. A state consists of the position of every switch, the status of every device, and so on.

If the features are primitive, a state is an assignment of a value to each feature. For example, a state may be described as switch 1 is up, switch 2 is down, fuse 1 is okay, wire 3 is broken, and so on.

If the states are primitive, the functions may be, for example, the position of switch 1. The position is a function of the state, and it may be *up* in some states and *down* in other states.

One main advantage of reasoning in terms of features is the computational savings. For a **binary feature** the domain has two values. Many states can be described by a few features:

- 10 binary features can describe $2^{10} = 1,024$ states.

- 20 binary features can describe $2^{20} = 1,048,576$ states.

- 30 binary features can describe $2^{30} = 1,073,741,824$ states.

- 100 binary features can describe $2^{100} = 1,267,650,600,228,229,401,496,$ $703,205,376$ states.

Reasoning in terms of thirty features may be easier than reasoning in terms of more than a billion states. One hundred features is not that many, but reasoning in terms of more than 2^{100} states explicitly is not possible. Many problems have thousands if not millions of features.

Typically the features are not independent, in that there may be constraints on the values of different features. One problem is to determine what states are possible given the features and the constraints.

4.2 Possible Worlds, Variables, and Constraints

To keep the formalism simple and general, we develop the notion of features without considering time explicitly. Constraint satisfaction problems will be described in terms of possible worlds.

When we are not modeling change, there is a direct one-to-one correspondence between features and variables, and between states and possible worlds.

A **possible world** is a possible way the world (the real world or some imaginary world) could be. For example, when representing a crossword puzzle, the possible worlds correspond to the ways the crossword could be filled out. In the electrical environment, a possible world specifies the position of every switch and the status of every component.

Possible worlds are described by algebraic variables. An **algebraic variable** is a symbol used to denote features of possible worlds. Algebraic variables will be written starting with an upper-case letter. Each algebraic variable V has an associated **domain**, $dom(V)$, which is the set of values the variable can take on.

For this chapter, we refer to an algebraic variable simply as a **variable**. These algebraic variables are different from the variables used in logic, which are discussed in Chapter 12. Algebraic variables are the same as the random variables used in probability theory, which are discussed in Chapter 6.

A **discrete variable** is one whose domain is finite or countably infinite. One particular case of a discrete variable is a **Boolean variable**, which is a variable with domain {*true, false*}. If X is a Boolean variable, we write $X = true$ as its lower-case equivalent, x, and write $X = false$ as $\bar{x}$. We can also have variables that are not discrete; for example, a variable whose domain corresponds to a subset of the real line is a **continuous variable**.

Example 4.2 The variable *Class_time* may denote the starting time for a particular class. The domain of *Class_time* may be the following set of possible times:

$$dom(Class\_time) = \{8, 9, 10, 11, 12, 1, 2, 3, 4, 5\}.$$

The variable *Height_joe* may refer to the height of a particular person at a particular time and have as its domain the set of real numbers, in some range, that represent the height in centimeters. *Raining* may be a Boolean random variable with value *true* if it is raining at a particular time.

Example 4.3 Consider the electrical domain depicted in Figure 1.8 (page 34).

- S_1_pos may be a discrete binary variable denoting the position of switch s_1 with domain {*up, down*}, where $S_1\_pos = up$ means switch s_1 is up, and $S_1\_pos = down$ means switch s_1 is down.
- S_1_st may be a variable denoting the status of switch s_1 with domain {*ok, upside_down, short, intermittent, broken*}, where $S_1\_st = ok$ means switch s_1 is working normally, $S_1\_st = upside\_down$ means switch s_1 is installed upside down, $S_1\_st = short$ means switch s_1 is shorted and acting as a wire, $S_1\_st = intermittent$ means switch S_1 is working intermittently, and $S_1\_st = broken$ means switch s_1 is broken and does not allow electricity to flow.

- *Number_of_broken_switches* may be an integer-valued variable denoting the number of switches that are broken.

- *Current_w_1* may be a real-valued variable denoting the current, in amps, flowing through wire w_1. *Current_w_1* $= 1.3$ means there are 1.3 amps flowing through wire w_1. We also allow inequalities between variables and constants as Boolean features; for example, *Current_w_1* ≥ 1.3 is true when there are at least 1.3 amps flowing through wire w_1.

Symbols and Semantics

Algebraic variables are symbols.

Internal to a computer, a **symbol** is just a sequence of bits that can be distinguished from other symbols. Some symbols have a fixed interpretation, for example, symbols that represent numbers and symbols that represent characters. Symbols that do not have fixed meaning appear in many programming languages. In Java, starting from Java 1.5, they are called *enumeration types*. Lisp refers to them as *atoms*. Usually, they are implemented as indexes into a symbol table that gives the name to print out. The only operation performed on these symbols is equality to determine if two symbols are the same or not.

To a **user** of a computer, symbols have meanings. A person who inputs constraints or interprets the output associates meanings with the symbols that make up the constraints or the outputs. He or she associates a symbol with some concept or object in the world. For example, the variable *HarrysHeight*, to the computer, is just a sequence of bits. It has no relationship to *HarrysWeight* or *SuesHeight*. To a person, this variable may mean the height, in particular units, of a particular person at a particular time.

The meaning associated with a variable–value pair must satisfy the **clarity principle**: an **omniscient agent** – a fictitious agent who knows the truth and the meanings associated with all of the symbols – should be able to determine the value of each variable. For example, the *height of Harry* only satisfies the clarity principle if the particular person being referred to and the particular time are specified as well as the units. For example, we may want to reason about the height, in centimeters, of Harry Potter at the start of the second movie of J. K. Rowling's book. This is different from the height, in inches, of Harry Potter at the end of the same movie (although they are, of course, related). If you want to refer to Harry's height at two different times, you must have two different variables.

You should have a consistent meaning. When stating constraints, you must have the same meaning for the same variable and the same values, and you can use this meaning to interpret the output.

The bottom line is that symbols can have meanings because we give them meanings. For this chapter, assume that the computer does not know what the symbols mean. A computer can only know what a symbol means if it can perceive and manipulate the environment.

Example 4.4 A classic example of a constraint satisfaction problem is a crossword puzzle. There are two different representations of crossword puzzles in terms of variables:

1. In one representation, the variables are the numbered squares with the direction of the word (down or across), and the domains are the set of possible words that can be put in. A possible world corresponds to an assignment of a word for each of the variables.

2. In another representation of a crossword, the variables are the individual squares and the domain of each variable is the set of letters in the alphabet. A possible world corresponds to an assignment of a letter to each square.

Possible worlds can be defined in terms of variables or variables can be defined in terms of possible worlds:

- Variables can be primitive and a **possible world** corresponds to a **total assignment** of a value to each variable.
- Worlds can be primitive and a variable is a function from possible worlds into the domain of the variable; given a possible world, the function returns the value of that variable in that possible world.

Example 4.5 If there are two variables, A with domain $\{0, 1, 2\}$ and B with domain $\{true, false\}$, there are six possible worlds, which you can name $w_0, \ldots, w_5$. One possible arrangement of variables and possible worlds is
- $w_0 : A = 0$ and $B = true$
- $w_1 : A = 0$ and $B = false$
- $w_2 : A = 1$ and $B = true$
- $w_3 : A = 1$ and $B = false$
- $w_4 : A = 2$ and $B = true$
- $w_5 : A = 2$ and $B = false$

Example 4.6 The trading agent, in planning a trip for a group of tourists, may be required to schedule a given set of activities. There can be two variables for each activity: one for the date, for which the domain is the set of possible days for the activity, and one for the location, for which the domain is the set of possible towns where it may occur. A possible world corresponds to an assignment of a date and a town for each activity.

4.2.1 Constraints

In many domains, not all possible assignments of values to variables are permissible. A **hard constraint**, or simply constraint, specifies legal combinations of assignments of values to the variables.

A **scope** or **scheme** is a set of variables. A **tuple** on scope S is an assignment of a value to each variable in S. A **constraint** c on a scope S is a set of tuples on S. A constraint is said to **involve** each of the variables in its scope.

If S' is a set of variables such that $S \subseteq S'$, and t is a tuple on S', constraint c is said to **satisfy** t if t, restricted to S, is in c.

Constraints can be defined using the terminology of relational databases (page 635). The main difference between constraints and database relations is that a constraint specifies legal values, whereas a database relation specifies what happens to be true in some situation. Constraints are also often defined **intensionally**, in terms of predicates (Boolean functions), to recognize legal assignments rather than **extensionally** by representing each assignment explicitly in a table. Extensional definitions can be implemented either by representing the legal assignments or by representing the illegal assignments.

Example 4.7 Consider a constraint on the possible dates for three activities. Let A, B, and C be variables that represent the date of each activity. Suppose the domain of each variable is $\{1, 2, 3, 4\}$.

The constraint could be written as a table that gives the legal combinations:

A	B	C
2	2	4
1	1	4
1	2	3
1	2	4

which has scope $\{A, B, C\}$. Each row is a tuple that specifies a legal assignment of a value to each variable in the scope of the constraint. The first tuple is

$$\{A = 2, B = 2, C = 4\}.$$

This tuple, which assigns A the value of 2, B the value of 2, and C the value of 4, specifies one of the four legal assignments of the variables.

This constraint satisfies the tuple $\{A = 1, B = 2, C = 3, D = 3, E = 1\}$, because that tuple assigns legal values to the variables in the scope.

This constraint could also be described intensionally by using a predicate – a logical formula – to specify the legal assignments. The preceding constraint could be specified by

$$(A \leq B) \wedge (B < 3) \wedge (B < C) \wedge \neg(A = B \wedge C = 3),$$

where $\wedge$ means *and*, and $\neg$ means *not*. This formula says that A is on the same date or before B, and B is before 3, and B is before C, and it cannot be that A and B are on the same date and C is on day 3.

A **unary constraint** is a constraint on a single variable (e.g., $X \neq 4$). A **binary constraint** is a constraint over a pair of variables (e.g., $X \neq Y$). In general, a k-ary constraint has a scope of size k.

A possible world w **satisfies** a set of constraints if, for every constraint, the values assigned in w to the variables in the scope of the constraint satisfy the constraint. In this case, we say that the possible world is a **model** of the constraints. That is, a **model** is a possible world that satisfies all of the constraints.

Example 4.8 Suppose the delivery robot must carry out a number of delivery activities, a, b, c, d, and e. Suppose that each activity happens at any of times 1, 2, 3, or 4. Let A be the variable representing the time that activity a will occur, and similarly for the other activities. The variable domains, which represent possible times for each of the deliveries, are

$$dom(A) = \{1,2,3,4\}, dom(B) = \{1,2,3,4\}, dom(C) = \{1,2,3,4\},$$
$$dom(D) = \{1,2,3,4\}, dom(E) = \{1,2,3,4\}.$$

Suppose the following constraints must be satisfied:

$$\{(B \neq 3), (C \neq 2), (A \neq B), (B \neq C), (C < D), (A = D),$$

$$(E < A), (E < B), (E < C), (E < D), (B \neq D)\}$$

The aim is to find a model, an assignment of a value to each variable, such that all the constraints are satisfied.

Example 4.9 Consider the constraints for the two representations of crossword puzzles of Example 4.4.

1. For the case in which the domains are words, the constraint is that the letters where a pair of words intersect must be the same.
2. For the representation in which the domains are the letters, the constraint is that contiguous sequences of letters must form legal words.

Example 4.10 In Example 4.6 (page 115), consider some typical constraints. It may be that certain activities have to be on different days or that other activities have to be in the same town on the same day. There may also be constraints that some activities must occur before other activities, or that there must be a certain number of days between two activities, or that there cannot be three activities on three consecutive days.

4.2.2 Constraint Satisfaction Problems

A **constraint satisfaction problem** (CSP) consists of

- a set of variables,
- a domain for each variable, and
- a set of constraints.

The aim is to choose a value for each variable so that the resulting possible world satisfies the constraints; we want a model of the constraints.

A finite CSP has a finite set of variables and a finite domain for each variable. Many of the methods considered in this chapter only work for finite CSPs, although some are designed for infinite, even continuous, domains.

The multidimensional aspect of these problems, where each variable can be seen as a separate dimension, makes them difficult to solve but also provides structure that can be exploited.

Given a CSP, there are a number of tasks that can be performed:

- Determine whether or not there is a model.
- Find a model.
- Find all of the models or enumerate the models.
- Count the number of models.
- Find the best model, given a measure of how good models are; see Section 4.10 (page 144).
- Determine whether some statement holds in all models.

This chapter mostly considers the problem of finding a model. Some of the methods can also determine if there is no solution. What may be more surprising is that some of the methods can find a model if one exists, but they cannot tell us that there is no model if none exists.

CSPs are very common, so it is worth trying to find relatively efficient ways to solve them. Determining whether there is a model for a CSP with finite domains is NP-hard (see box on page 170) and no known algorithms exist to solve such problems that do not use exponential time in the worst case. However, just because a problem is NP-hard does not mean that all instances are difficult to solve. Many instances have structure that can be exploited.

4.3   Generate-and-Test Algorithms

Any finite CSP can be solved by an exhaustive generate-and-test algorithm. The **assignment space**, D, is the set of assignments of values to all of the variables; it corresponds to the set of all possible worlds. Each element of D is a total assignment of a value to each variable. The algorithm returns those assignments that satisfy all of the constraints.

Thus, the **generate-and-test** algorithm is as follows: check each total assignment in turn; if an assignment is found that satisfies all of the constraints, return that assignment.

Example 4.11   In Example 4.8 the assignment space is

$$D = \{ \quad \{A = 1, B = 1, C = 1, D = 1, E = 1\},$$
$$\{A = 1, B = 1, C = 1, D = 1, E = 2\}, \ldots,$$
$$\{A = 4, B = 4, C = 4, D = 4, E = 4\}\}.$$

In this case there are $|D| = 4^5 = 1,024$ different assignments to be tested. In the crossword example of Exercise 1 (page 152) there are $40^6 = 4,096,000,000$ possible assignments.

If each of the n variable domains has size d, then D has d^n elements. If there are e constraints, the total number of constraints tested is $O(ed^n)$. As n becomes large, this very quickly becomes intractable, and so we must find alternative solution methods.

4.4 Solving CSPs Using Search

Generate-and-test algorithms assign values to all variables before checking the constraints. Because individual constraints only involve a subset of the variables, some constraints can be tested before all of the variables have been assigned values. If a partial assignment is inconsistent with a constraint, any complete assignment that extends the partial assignment will also be inconsistent.

Example 4.12 In the delivery scheduling problem of Example 4.8 (page 117), the assignments $A = 1$ and $B = 1$ are inconsistent with the constraint $A \neq B$ regardless of the values of the other variables. If the variables A and B are assigned values first, this inconsistency can be discovered before any values are assigned to C, D, or E, thus saving a large amount of work.

An alternative to generate-and-test algorithms is to construct a search space from which the search strategies of the previous chapter can be used. The search problem can be defined as follows:

- The nodes are assignments of values to some subset of the variables.
- The neighbors of a node N are obtained by selecting a variable V that is not assigned in node N and by having a neighbor for each assignment of a value to V that does not violate any constraint.

  Suppose that node N represents the assignment $X_1 = v_1, \ldots, X_k = v_k$. To find the neighbors of N, select a variable Y that is not in the set $\{X_1, \ldots, X_k\}$. For each value $y_i \in dom(Y)$, such that $X_1 = v_1, \ldots, X_k = v_k, Y = y_i$ is consistent with the constraints, $X_1 = v_1, \ldots, X_k = v_k, Y = y_i$ is a neighbor of N.

- The start node is the empty assignment that does not assign a value to any variables.
- A goal node is a node that assigns a value to every variable. Note that this only exists if the assignment is consistent with the constraints.

In this case, it is not the path that is of interest, but the goal nodes.

Example 4.13 Suppose you have a CSP with the variables A, B, and C, each with domain $\{1, 2, 3, 4\}$. Suppose the constraints are $A < B$ and $B < C$. A possible search tree is shown in Figure 4.1 (on the next page). In this figure, a node corresponds to all of the assignments from the root to that node. The potential nodes that are pruned because they violate constraints are labeled with ✗.

The leftmost ✗ corresponds to the assignment $A = 1$, $B = 1$. This violates the $A < B$ constraint, and so it is pruned.

This CSP has four solutions. The leftmost one is $A = 1$, $B = 2$, $C = 3$. The size of the search tree, and thus the efficiency of the algorithm, depends on which variable is selected at each time. A static ordering, such as always splitting on A then B then C, is less efficient than the dynamic ordering used here. The set of answers is the same regardless of the variable ordering.

In the preceding example, there would be $4^3 = 64$ assignments tested in a generate-and-test algorithm. For the search method, there are 22 assignments generated.

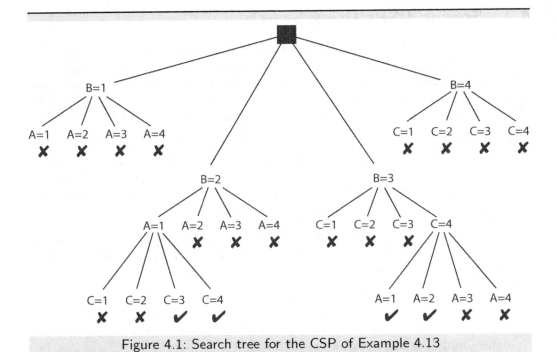

Figure 4.1: Search tree for the CSP of Example 4.13

Searching with a depth-first search, typically called **backtracking**, can be much more efficient than generate and test. Generate and test is equivalent to not checking constraints until reaching the leaves. Checking constraints higher in the tree can prune large subtrees that do not have to be searched.

4.5   Consistency Algorithms

Although depth-first search over the search space of assignments is usually a substantial improvement over generate and test, it still has various inefficiencies that can be overcome.

Example 4.14   In Example 4.13, the variables A and B are related by the constraint $A < B$. The assignment $A = 4$ is inconsistent with each of the possible assignments to B because $dom(B) = \{1, 2, 3, 4\}$. In the course of the backtrack search (see Figure 4.1), this fact is rediscovered for different assignments to B and C. This inefficiency can be avoided by the simple expedient of deleting 4 from $dom(A)$, once and for all. This idea is the basis for the consistency algorithms.

The consistency algorithms are best thought of as operating over the network of constraints formed by the CSP:

- There is a node for each variable. These nodes are drawn as ovals.
- There is a node for each constraint. These nodes are drawn as rectangles.
- Associated with each variable, X, is a set D_X of possible values. This set of values is initially the domain of the variable.

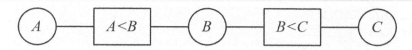

Figure 4.2: Constraint network for the CSP of Example 4.15

- For every constraint c, and for every variable X in the scope of c, there is an arc $\langle X, c \rangle$.

Such a network is called a **constraint network**.

Example 4.15 Consider Example 4.13 (page 119). There are three variables A, B, and C, each with domain $\{1, 2, 3, 4\}$. The constraints are $A < B$ and $B < C$. In the constraint network, shown in Figure 4.2, there are four arcs:

$\langle A, A < B \rangle$
$\langle B, A < B \rangle$
$\langle B, B < C \rangle$
$\langle C, B < C \rangle$

Example 4.16 The constraint $X \neq 4$ has one arc:

$\langle X, X \neq 4 \rangle$

The constraint $X + Y = Z$ has three arcs:

$\langle X, X + Y = Z \rangle$
$\langle Y, X + Y = Z \rangle$
$\langle Z, X + Y = Z \rangle$

The simplest case is when the constraint has just one variable in its scope. In this case, the arc is **domain consistent** if every value of the variable satisfies the constraint.

Example 4.17 The constraint $B \neq 3$ has scope $\{B\}$. With this constraint, and with $D_B = \{1, 2, 3, 4\}$, the arc $\langle B, B \neq 3 \rangle$ is not domain consistent because $B = 3$ violates the constraint. If the value 3 were removed from the domain of B, then it would be domain consistent.

Suppose constraint c has scope $\{X, Y_1, \ldots, Y_k\}$. Arc $\langle X, c \rangle$ is **arc consistent** if, for each value $x \in D_X$, there are values $y_1, \ldots, y_k$ where $y_i \in D_{Y_i}$, such that $c(X = x, Y_1 = y_1, \ldots, Y_k = y_k)$ is satisfied. A network is arc consistent if all its arcs are arc consistent.

Example 4.18 Consider the network of Example 4.15. None of the arcs are arc consistent. The first arc is not arc consistent because for $A = 4$ there is no corresponding value for B for which $A < B$. If 4 were removed from the domain of A, then it would be arc consistent. The second arc is not arc consistent because there is no corresponding value for A when $B = 1$.

```
1:  procedure GAC(V, dom, C)
2:      Inputs
3:          V: a set of variables
4:          dom: a function such that dom(X) is the domain of variable X
5:          C: set of constraints to be satisfied
6:      Output
7:          arc-consistent domains for each variable
8:      Local
9:          D_X is a set of values for each variable X
10:         TDA is a set of arcs
11:     for each variable X do
12:         D_X ← dom(X)
13:         TDA ← {⟨X, c⟩ | c ∈ C and X ∈ scope(c)}
14:     while TDA ≠ {} do
15:         select ⟨X, c⟩ ∈ TDA;
16:         TDA ← TDA \ {⟨X, c⟩};
17:         ND_X ← {x | x ∈ D_X and some {X = x, Y_1 = y_1, …, Y_k = y_k} ∈ c
        where y_i ∈ D_{Y_i} for all i}
18:         if ND_X ≠ D_X then
19:             TDA ← TDA ∪ {⟨Z, c′⟩ | X ∈ scope(c′), c′ is not c, Z ∈ scope(c′) \
        {X}}
20:             D_X ← ND_X
21:     return {D_X | X is a variable}
```

Figure 4.3: Generalized arc consistency algorithm

If an arc $\langle X, c \rangle$ is *not* arc consistent, there are some values of X for which there are no values for $Y_1, \ldots, Y_k$ for which the constraint holds. In this case, all values of X in D_X for which there are no corresponding values for the other variables can be deleted from D_X to make the arc $\langle X, c \rangle$ consistent.

The **generalized arc consistency algorithm** is given in Figure 4.3. It makes the entire network arc consistent by considering a set of potentially inconsistent arcs, the *to-do* arcs, in the set TDA. TDA initially consists of all the arcs in the graph. While the set is not empty, an arc $\langle X, c \rangle$ is removed from the set and considered. If the arc is not consistent, it is made consistent by pruning the domain of variable X. All of the previously consistent arcs that could, as a result of pruning X, have become inconsistent are placed back into the set TDA. These are the arcs $\langle Z, c' \rangle$, where c' is a constraint different from c that involves X, and Z is a variable involved in c' other than X.

Example 4.19 Consider the algorithm GAC operating on the network from Example 4.15. Initially, all of the arcs are in the TDA set. Here is one possible sequence of selections of arcs:

- Suppose the algorithm first selects the arc $\langle A, A < B \rangle$. For $A = 4$, there is no value of B that satisfies the constraint. Thus, 4 is pruned from the domain of A. Nothing is added to TDA because there is no other arc currently outside TDA.

- Suppose that $\langle B, A < B \rangle$ is selected next. The value 1 can be pruned from the domain of B. Again no element is added to TDA.

- Suppose that $\langle B, B < C \rangle$ is selected next. The value 4 can be removed from the domain of B. Because the domain of B has been reduced, the arc $\langle A, A < B \rangle$ must be added back into the TDA set because the domain of A could potentially be reduced further now that the domain of B is smaller.

- If the arc $\langle A, A < B \rangle$ is selected next, the value $A = 3$ can be pruned from the domain of A.

- The remaining arc on TDA is $\langle C, B < C \rangle$. The values 1 and 2 can be removed from the domain of C. No arcs are added to TDA and TDA becomes empty.

The algorithm then terminates with $D_A = \{1,2\}$, $D_B = \{2,3\}$, $D_C = \{3,4\}$. Although this has not fully solved the problem, it has greatly simplified it.

Example 4.20 Consider applying GAC to the scheduling problem of Example 4.8 (page 117). The network shown in Figure 4.4 (on the next page) has already been made domain consistent (the value 3 has been removed from the domain of B and 2 has been removed from the domain of C). Suppose arc $\langle D, C < D \rangle$ is considered first. The arc is not arc consistent because $D = 1$ is not consistent with any value in D_C, so 1 is deleted from D_D. D_D becomes $\{2,3,4\}$ and arcs $\langle A, A = D \rangle$, $\langle B, B \neq D \rangle$, and $\langle E, E < D \rangle$ could be added to TDA but they are on it already.

Suppose arc $\langle C, E < C \rangle$ is considered next; then D_C is reduced to $\{3,4\}$ and arc $\langle D, C < D \rangle$ goes back into the TDA set to be reconsidered.

Suppose arc $\langle D, C < D \rangle$ is next; then D_D is further reduced to the singleton $\{4\}$. Processing arc $\langle C, C < D \rangle$ prunes D_C to $\{3\}$. Making arc $\langle A, A = D \rangle$ consistent reduces D_A to $\{4\}$. Processing $\langle B, B \neq D \rangle$ reduces D_B to $\{1,2\}$. Then arc $\langle B, E < B \rangle$ reduces D_B to $\{2\}$. Finally, arc $\langle E, E < B \rangle$ reduces D_E to $\{1\}$. All arcs remaining in the queue are consistent, and so the algorithm terminates with the TDA set empty. The set of reduced variable domains is returned. In this case, the domains all have size 1 and there is a unique solution: $A = 4$, $B = 2$, $C = 3$, $D = 4$, $E = 1$.

Regardless of the order in which the arcs are considered, the algorithm will terminate with the same result, namely, an arc-consistent network and the same set of reduced domains. Three cases are possible, depending on the state of the network upon termination:

- In the first case, one domain is empty, indicating there is no solution to the CSP. Note that, as soon as any one domain becomes empty, all the domains of connected nodes will become empty before the algorithm terminates.

- In the second case, each domain has a singleton value, indicating that there is a unique solution to the CSP, as in Example 4.20.

- In the third case, every domain is non-empty and at least one has multiple values left in it. In this case, we do not know whether there is a solution or

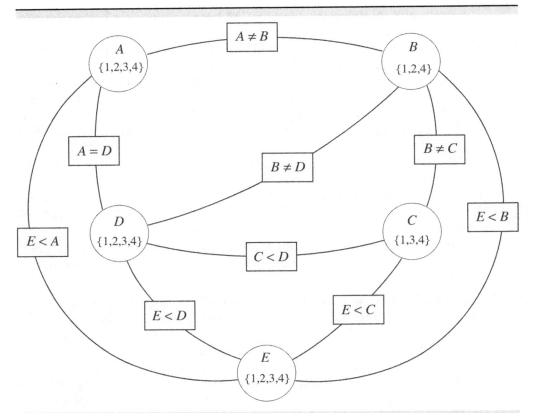

Figure 4.4: Domain-consistent constraint network. The variables are depicted as circles or ovals with their corresponding domain. The constraints are represented as rectangles. There is an arc between each variable and each constraint that involves that variable.

what the solutions look like. We require some other methods to solve the problem; some such methods are explored in the following sections.

The following example shows that it is possible for a network to be arc consistent even though there is no solution.

Example 4.21 Suppose there are three variables, A, B and C, each with the domain $\{1, 2, 3\}$. Consider the constraints $A = B$, $B = C$, and $A \neq C$. This is arc consistent: no domain can be pruned using any single constraint. However, there are no solutions. There is no assignment to the three variables that satisfies the constraints.

If each variable domain is of size d and there are e constraints to be tested, then the algorithm *GAC* does $O(ed^3)$ consistency checks. For some CSPs, for example, if the constraint graph is a tree, *GAC* alone solves the CSP and does it in time linear in the number of variables.

Various extensions to the arc-consistency technique are also possible. The domains need not be finite; they may be specified using descriptions, not just lists of their values. It is also possible to prune the constraints if the constraints are represented extensionally: if a value has been pruned for a variable X, this value can be pruned from all constraints that involve X. Higher-order consistency techniques, such as **path consistency**, consider k-tuples of variables at a time, not just pairs of variables that are connected by a constraint. For example, by considering all three variables, you can recognize that there is no solution in Example 4.21. These higher-order methods are often less efficient for solving a problem than using arc consistency augmented with the methods described below.

4.6 Domain Splitting

Another method for simplifying the network is **domain splitting** or **case analysis**. The idea is to split a problem into a number of disjoint cases and solve each case separately. The set of all solutions to the initial problem is the union of the solutions to each case.

In the simplest case, suppose there is a binary variable X with domain $\{t, f\}$. All of the solutions either have $X = t$ or $X = f$. One way to find them is to set $X = t$, find all of the solutions with this assignment, and then assign $X = f$ and find all solutions with this assignment. Assigning a value to a variable gives a smaller *reduced* problem to solve.

If the domain of a variable has more than two elements, for example if the domain of A is $\{1, 2, 3, 4\}$, there are a number of ways to split it:

- Split the domain into a case for each value. For example, split A into the four cases $A = 1$, $A = 2$, $A = 3$, and $A = 4$.
- Always split the domain into two disjoint subsets. For example, split A into the two cases $A \in \{1, 2\}$ and the case $A \in \{3, 4\}$.

The first approach makes more progress with one split, but the second may allow for more pruning with fewer steps. For example, if the same values for B can be pruned whether A is 1 or 2, the second case allows this fact to be discovered once and not have to be rediscovered for each element of A. This saving depends on how the domains are split.

Recursively solving the cases using domain splitting, recognizing when there is no solution based on the assignments, is equivalent to the search algorithm of Section 4.4 (page 119). We can be more efficient by interleaving arc consistency with the search.

One effective way to solve a CSP is to use arc consistency to simplify the network before each step of domain splitting. That is, to solve a problem,

- simplify the problem using arc consistency; and,
- if the problem is not solved, select a variable whose domain has more than one element, split it, and recursively solve each case.

One thing to notice about this algorithm is that it does not require a restart of the arc consistency from scratch after domain splitting. If the variable X has its domain split, *TDA* can start with just the arcs that are possibly no longer arc consistent as a result of the split; these are only the arcs of the form $\langle Y, r \rangle$, where X appears in r and Y is a variable, other than X, that appears in constraint r.

Example 4.22 In Example 4.19 (page 122), arc consistency simplified the network, but did not solve the problem. After arc consistency had completed, there were multiple elements in the domains. Suppose B is split. There are two cases:

- $B = 2$. In this case $A = 2$ is pruned. Splitting on C produces two of the answers.
- $B = 3$. In this case $C = 3$ is pruned. Splitting on A produces the other two answers.

This search tree should be contrasted with the search tree of Figure 4.1 (page 120). The search space with arc consistency is much smaller, and it was not as sensitive to the selection of variable orderings. [Figure 4.1 (page 120) would be much bigger with different variable orderings.]

One other enhancement can make domain splitting much more efficient. If assigning values to the variables disconnects the graph, each disconnected component can be solved separately. The solution to the complete problem is the cross product of the solutions to each component. This can save much computation when one is counting the number of solutions or finding all solutions. For example, if one component has 100 solutions and the other component has 20 solutions, there are 2,000 solutions. This is a more efficient way to count than finding each of the 2,000 solutions separately.

4.6.1   Exploiting Propositional Structure

A fundamental idea in AI is to exploit structure in a domain. One form of structure for CSPs arises from the exploitation of aspects of restricted classes of variables and constraints. One such class is the class of **propositional satisfiability** problems. These problems are characterized by

- Boolean variables: a Boolean variable (page 113) is a variable with domain $\{true, false\}$. Given a Boolean variable *Happy*, the proposition *happy* means *Happy* = *true*, and $\overline{happy}$ means *Happy* = *false*.
- clausal constraints: a **clause** is an expression of the form $l_1 \vee l_2 \vee \cdots \vee l_k$, where each l_i is a literal. A **literal** is an assignment of a value to a Boolean variable. A clause is satisfied, or true, in a possible world if and only if at least one of the literals that makes up the clause is true in that possible world.

For example, the clause *happy* $\vee$ *sad* $\vee$ $\overline{living}$ is a constraint among the variables *Happy*, *Sad*, and *Living*, which is true if *Happy* has value *true*, *Sad* has value *true*, or *Living* has value *false*.

A clause is a constraint on a set of Boolean variables that removes one of the assignments from consideration – the assignment that makes all literals false. Thus, the clause *happy* $\vee$ *sad* $\vee$ $\overline{living}$ specifies that the assignment $\overline{happy}$, $\overline{sad}$, *living* is not allowed.

When there are only two values, pruning a value from the domain is equivalent to assigning the opposite value. Thus, if X has domain $\{true, false\}$, pruning *true* from the domain of X is the same as assigning X to have value *false*.

Arc consistency can be used to prune the set of values and the set of constraints. Assigning a value to a Boolean variable can simplify the set of constraints:

- If X is assigned *true*, all of the clauses with $X = true$ become redundant; they are automatically satisfied. These clauses can be removed. Similarly, assigning the X the value of *false* can remove the clauses containing $X = false$.

- If X is assigned the value of *true*, any clause with $X = false$ can be simplified by removing $X = false$ from the clause. Similarly, if X is assigned the value of *false*, then $X = true$ can be removed from any clause it appears in. This step is called **unit resolution**.

Following some steps of pruning the clauses, clauses may exist that contain just one assignment, $Y = v$. In this case, the other value can be removed from the domain of Y. The aforementioned procedure can be repeated for the assignment of $Y = v$. If all of the assignments are removed from a clause, the constraints are unsatisfiable.

Example 4.23 Consider the clause $\bar{x} \vee y \vee \bar{z}$. When X is assigned to *true*, the clause can be simplified to $y \vee \bar{z}$. If Y is then assigned to *false*, the clause can be simplified to $\bar{z}$. Thus, *true* can be pruned from the domain of Z.

If, instead, X is assigned to *false*, the preceding clause can be removed.

If a variable has the same value in all remaining clauses, and the algorithm must only find one model, it can assign that value to that variable. For example, if variable Y only appears as $Y = true$ (i.e., $\bar{y}$ is not in any clause), then Y can be assigned the value *true*. That assignment does not remove all of the models; it only simplifies the problem because the set of clauses remaining after setting $Y = true$ is a subset of the clauses that would remain if Y were assigned the value *false*. A variable that only has one value in all of the clauses is called a **pure symbol**.

It turns out that pruning the domains and constraints, domain splitting, assigning pure symbols, and efficiently managing the constraints (i.e., determining when all but one of the disjuncts are false) turns out to be a very efficient algorithm. It is called the **DPLL** algorithm, after its authors.

4.7 Variable Elimination

Arc consistency simplifies the network by removing values of variables. A complementary method is **variable elimination** (**VE**), which simplifies the network by removing variables.

The idea of VE is to remove the variables one by one. When removing a variable X, VE constructs a new constraint on some of the remaining variables reflecting the effects of X on all of the other variables. This new constraint replaces all of the constraints that involve X, forming a reduced network that does not involve X. The new constraint is constructed so that any solution to the reduced CSP can be extended to a solution of the larger CSP that contains X. In addition to creating the new constraint, VE provides a way to construct a solution to the CSP that contains X from a solution to the reduced CSP.

The following algorithm is described using the relational algebra calculations of join and project (page 635).

When eliminating X, the influence of X on the remaining variables is through the constraint relations that involve X. First, the algorithm collects all of the constraints that involve X. Let the join of all of these relations be the relation $r_X(X, \overline{Y})$, where $\overline{Y}$ is the set of other variables in the scope of r_X. It then projects r_X onto $\overline{Y}$; this relation can replace all of the relations that involve X. It now has a reduced CSP that involves one less variable, which it can solve recursively. Once it has a solution for the reduced CSP, it can extend that solution to a solution for the original CSP by joining the solution with r_X.

When only one variable is left, it returns those domain elements that are consistent with the constraints on this variable.

Example 4.24   Consider a CSP that contains the variables A, B, and C, each with domain $\{1, 2, 3, 4\}$. Suppose the constraints that involve B are $A < B$ and $B < C$. There may be many other variables, but if B does not have any constraints in common with these variables, eliminating B will not impose any new constraints on these other variables. To remove B, first join on the relations that involve B:

A	B
1	2
1	3
1	4
2	3
2	4
3	4

$\bowtie$

B	C
1	2
1	3
1	4
2	3
2	4
3	4

$=$

A	B	C
1	2	3
1	2	4
1	3	4
2	3	4

To get the relation on A and C induced by B, project this join onto A and C, which gives

A	C
1	3
1	4
2	4

This relation on A and C contains all of the information about the constraints on B that affect the solutions of the rest of the network.

The original constraints on B are replaced with the new constraint on A and C. It then solves the rest of the network, which is now simpler because it does not involve the variable B. It must remember the joined relation to construct a solution that involves B from a solution to the reduced network.

```
 1: procedure VE_CSP(V, C)
 2:     Inputs
 3:         V: a set of variables
 4:         C: a set of constraints on V
 5:     Output
 6:         a relation containing all of the consistent variable assignments
 7:     if V contains just one element then
 8:         return the join of all the relations in C
 9:     else
10:         select variable X to eliminate
11:         V' := V \ {X}
12:         C_X := {T in C : T involves X}
13:         let R be the join of all of the constraints in C_X
14:         let R' be R projected onto the variables other than X
15:         S := VE_CSP(V', (C \ C_X) ∪ {R'})
16:         return R ⋈ S
```

Figure 4.5: Variable elimination for CSPs

Figure 4.5 gives a recursive algorithm for variable elimination, VE_CSP, to find all solutions for a CSP.

The base case of the recursion occurs when only one variable is left. In this case (line 8), a solution exists if and only if there are rows in the join of the final relations. Note that these relations are all relations on a single variable, and so they are the sets of legal values for this variable. The join of these relations is the intersection of these sets.

In the non-base case, a variable X is selected for elimination (line 10). Which variable is selected does not affect the correctness of the algorithm, but it may affect the efficiency. To eliminate variable X, the algorithm propagates the effect of X onto those variables that X is directly related to. This is achieved by joining all of the relations in which X is involved (line 13) and then projecting X out of the resulting relation (line 14). Thus, a simplified problem (with one less variable) has been created that can be solved recursively. To get the possible values for X, the algorithm joins the solution of the simplified problem with the relation R that defines the effect of X.

If you only wanted to find one solution, instead of returning $R \bowtie S$, the algorithm can return one element of the join. No matter which element it returns, that element is guaranteed to be part of a solution. If any value of R in this algorithm contains no tuples, there are no solutions.

The efficiency of the VE algorithm depends on the order in which variables are selected. The intermediate structure – which variables the intermediate relations are over – depends not on the actual content of relations but only on the graph structure of the constraint network. The efficiency of this algorithm can be determined by considering the graphical structure. In general, VE is efficient when the constraint network is sparse. The number of variables in the largest relation returned for a particular variable ordering is called the **treewidth** of the graph for that variable ordering. The treewidth of a graph is the minimum treewidth for any ordering. The complexity of VE is exponential in treewidth and linear in the number of variables. This can be compared to searching [see Section 4.4 (page 119)], which is exponential in the number of variables.

Finding an elimination ordering that results in the smallest treewidth is NP-hard. However, some good heuristics exist. The two most common are

- **min-factor**: at each stage, select the variable that results in the smallest relation.

- **minimum deficiency** or **minimum fill**: at each stage, select the variable that adds the smallest number of arcs to the remaining constraint network. The deficiency of a variable X is the number of pairs of variables that are in a relationship with X that are not in a relationship with each other. The intuition is that it is okay to remove a variable that results in a large relation as long as it does not make the network more complicated.

The minimum deficiency has usually been found empirically to give a smaller treewidth than min-factor, but it is more difficult to compute.

VE can also be combined with arc consistency; whenever VE removes a variable, arc consistency can be used to further simplify the problem. This approach can result in smaller intermediate tables.

4.8   Local Search

The previous sections have considered algorithms that systematically search the space. If the space is finite, they will either find a solution or report that no solution exists. Unfortunately, many search spaces are too big for systematic search and are possibly even infinite. In any reasonable time, systematic search will have failed to consider enough of the search space to give any meaningful results. This section and the next consider methods intended to work in these very large spaces. The methods do not systematically search the whole search space but they are designed to find solutions quickly on average. They do not guarantee that a solution will be found even if one exists, and so they are not able to prove that no solution exists. They are often the method of choice for applications where solutions are known to exist or are very likely to exist.

Local search methods start with a complete assignment of a value to each variable and try to iteratively improve this assignment by improving steps, by taking random steps, or by restarting with another complete assignment. A wide variety of local search techniques has been proposed. Understanding when these techniques work for different problems forms the focus of a number of research communities, including those from both operations research and AI.

The generic local search algorithm for CSPs is given in Figure 4.6. A specifies an assignment of a value to each variable. The first *for each* loop assigns a

1: **procedure** *Local-Search*(V, *dom*, C)
2:     **Inputs**
3:         V: a set of variables
4:         *dom*: a function such that $dom(X)$ is the domain of variable X
5:         C: set of constraints to be satisfied
6:     **Output**
7:         complete assignment that satisfies the constraints
8:     **Local**
9:         $A[V]$ an array of values indexed by V
10:     **repeat**
11:         **for each** variable X **do**
12:             $A[X] \leftarrow$ a random value in $dom(X)$;
13:         **while** stopping criterion not met & A is not a satisfying assignment
    do
14:             Select a variable Y and a value $V \in dom(Y)$
15:             Set $A[Y] \leftarrow V$
16:         **if** A is a satisfying assignment **then**
17:             **return** A
18:     **until** termination

Figure 4.6: Local search for finding a solution to a CSP

random value to each variable. The first time it is executed is called a **random initialization**. Each iteration of the outer loop is called a **try**. A common way to implement a new try is to do a **random restart**. An alternative to random initialization is to use a construction heuristic that guesses a solution, which is then iteratively improved.

The while loop does a **local search**, or a **walk**, through the assignment space. It maintains a current assignment S, considers a set of **neighbors** of the current assignment, and selects one to be the next current assignment. In Figure 4.6, the neighbors of a total assignment are those assignments that differ in the assignment of a single variable. Alternate sets of neighbors can also be used and will result in different search algorithms.

This walk through assignments continues until either a satisfying assignment is found and returned or some stopping criterion is satisfied. The stopping criterion is used to decide when to stop the current local search and do a random restart, starting again with a new assignment. A stopping criterion could be as simple as stopping after a certain number of steps.

This algorithm is not guaranteed to halt. In particular, it goes on forever if there is no solution, and it is possible to get trapped in some region of the search space. An algorithm is **complete** if it finds an answer whenever there is one. This algorithm is incomplete.

One instance of this algorithm is **random sampling**. In this algorithm, the stopping criterion is always true so that the while loop is never executed. Random sampling keeps picking random assignments until it finds one that satisfies the constraints, and otherwise it does not halt. Random sampling is complete in the sense that, given enough time, it guarantees that a solution will be found if one exists, but there is no upper bound on the time it may take. It is very slow. The efficiency depends only on the product of the domain sizes and how many solutions exist.

Another instance is a **random walk**. In this algorithm the while loop is only exited when it has found a satisfying assignment (i.e., the stopping criterion is always false and there are no random restarts). In the while loop it selects a variable and a value at random. Random walk is also complete in the same sense as random sampling. Each step takes less time than resampling all variables, but it can take more steps than random sampling, depending on how the solutions are distributed. Variants of this algorithm are applicable when the domain sizes of the variables differ; a random walk algorithm can either select a variable at random and then a value at random, or select a variable–value pair at random. The latter is more likely to select a variable when it has a larger domain.

4.8.1 Iterative Best Improvement

In **iterative best improvement**, the neighbor of the current selected node is one that optimizes some **evaluation function**. In **greedy descent**, a neighbor is chosen to minimize an evaluation function. This is also called **hill climbing** or **greedy ascent** when the aim is to maximize. We only consider minimization; if you want to maximize a quantity, you can minimize its negation.

Iterative best improvement requires a way to evaluate each total assignment. For constraint satisfaction problems, a common evaluation function is the number of constraints that are violated by the total assignment that is to be minimized. A violated constraint is called a **conflict**. With the evaluation function being the number of conflicts, a solution is a total assignment with an evaluation of zero. Sometimes this evaluation function is refined by weighting some constraints more than others.

A **local optimum** is an assignment such that no neighbor improves the evaluation function. This is also called a local minimum in greedy descent, or a local maximum in greedy ascent.

Example 4.25 Consider the delivery scheduling in Example 4.8 (page 117). Suppose gradient descent starts with the assignment $A = 2, B = 2, C = 3, D = 2, E = 1$. This assignment has an evaluation of 3, because it does not satisfy $A \neq B$, $B \neq D$, and $C < D$. Its neighbor with the minimal evaluation has $B = 4$ with an evaluation of 1 because only $C < D$ is unsatisfied. This is now a local minimum. A random walk can then change D to 4, which has an evaluation of 2. It can change A to 4, with an evaluation of 2, and then change B to 2 with an evaluation of zero, and a solution is found.

The following gives a trace of the assignments through the walk:

A	B	C	D	E	evaluation
2	2	3	2	1	3
2	4	3	2	1	1
2	4	3	4	1	2
4	4	3	4	1	2
4	2	3	4	1	0

Different initializations, or different choices when multiple assignments have the same evaluation, give different results.

If the variables have small finite domains, a local search algorithm can consider all other values of the variable when considering a neighbor. If the domains are large, the cost of considering all other values may be too high. An alternative is to consider only a few other values, often the close values, for one of the variables. Sometimes quite sophisticated methods are used to select an alternative value.

Local search typically considers the best neighboring assignment even if it is equal to or even worse than the current assignment. It is often better to make a quick choice than to spend a lot of time making the best choice. There are many possible variants of which neighbor to choose:

- Select the value and variable together. Out of all of the different assignments to any of the variables, select one of them that minimizes the evaluation function. If more than one has the minimum value; pick one of them at random.

- Select a variable, then select its value. To select a variable, there are a number of possibilities:

  - Maintain how many violated constraints each variable is involved in, and pick one of the variables involved in the most violated constraints.
  - Select randomly a variable involved in any violated constraint.
  - Select a variable at random.

  Once the variable has been selected, it can either select one of the values that has the best evaluation or just select a value at random.

- Select a variable and/or value at random and accept the change if it improves the evaluation.

Optimizing over all variable–value pairs makes bigger improvements than the other methods but it is more computationally expensive. Although some theoretical results exist, deciding which method works better in practice is an empirical question.

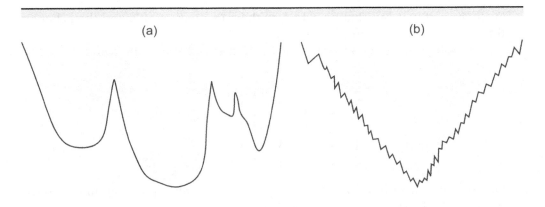

Figure 4.7: Two search spaces; find the minimum

4.8.2 Randomized Algorithms

Iterative best improvement randomly picks one of the best neighbors of the current assignment. Randomness can also be used to escape local minima that are not global minima in two main ways:

- random restart, in which values for all variables are chosen at random. This lets the search start from a completely different part of the search space.
- random walk, in which some random steps are taken interleaved with the optimizing steps. With greedy descent, this process allows for upward steps that may enable random walk to escape a local minimum that is not a global minimum.

A random walk is a local random move, whereas a random restart is a global random move. For problems involving a large number of variables, a random restart can be quite expensive.

A mix of greedy descent with random moves is an instance of a class of algorithms known as **stochastic local search**.

Unfortunately, it is very difficult to visualize the search space to understand what algorithms you expect to work because there are often thousands of dimensions, each with a discrete set of values. Some of the intuitions can be gleaned from lower-dimensional problems. Consider the two one-dimensional search spaces in Figure 4.7, where we try to find the minimum value. Suppose that a neighbor is obtained by a small step, either left or right of the current position. To find the global minimum in the search space (a), we would expect the greedy descent with random restart to find the optimal value quickly. Once a random choice has found a point in the deepest valley, greedy descent quickly leads to the global minimum. One would not expect a random walk to work well in this example, because many random steps are required to exit one of the local, but not global, minima. However, for search space (b), a random restart quickly gets stuck on one of the jagged peaks and does not work very well. However, a random walk combined with greedy descent enables it to escape these local minima. One or two random steps may be enough to escape a local minimum. Thus, you would expect that a random walk would work better in this search space.

As presented, the local search has no memory. It does not remember anything about the search as it proceeds. A simple way to use memory to improve a local search is a **tabu list**, which is a list of the most recently changed variable–value assignments. The idea is, when selecting a new assignment, not to select a variable–value pair that is on the tabu list. This prevents cycling among a few assignments. A tabu list is typically of a small fixed size; the size of the tabu list is one of the parameters that can be optimized. A tabu list of size 1 is equivalent to not allowing the same assignment to be immediately revisited.

Algorithms can differ in how much work they require to guarantee the best improvement step. At one extreme, an algorithm can guarantee to select a new assignment that gives the best improvement out of all of the neighbors. At the other extreme, an algorithm can select a new assignment at random and reject the assignment if it makes the situation worse. The rest of this section gives some typical algorithms that differ in how much computational effort they put in to ensure that they make the best improvement. Which of these methods works best is, typically, an empirical question.

Most Improving Step

The first method is to always select the variable–value pair that makes the best improvement. The naive way of doing this is to linearly scan the variables; for each value of each variable, determine how many fewer constraints would be violated with this assignment compared to the current assignment to all variables, then select one of the variable–value pairs that results in the best improvement, even if that improvement is negative. The complexity of one step is $O(ndr)$, where n is the number of variables, d is the average domain size, and r is the number of neighbors of an assignment.

A more sophisticated alternative is to have a priority queue of variable–value pairs. For any variable X, and value v in the domain of X such that X is not assigned to v in the current assignment, the pair $\langle X, v \rangle$ would be in the priority queue; the weight of the pair is the evaluation of the current total assignment minus the evaluation of the total assignment if X, instead, had value v. That is, it maintains the change in the evaluation for each alternate value. At each stage, the algorithm selects a value with minimum weight, which is the neighbor that gives the biggest improvement.

Once a variable X has been given a new value, the weights of all variables that participate in a constraint that has been made satisfied or unsatisfied by the new assignment to X must have their weights changed and must be reinserted into the priority queue.

The complexity of one step of this algorithm is $O(\log nd + rd \log nd)$, where n is the number of variables, d is the average domain size, and r is the number of neighbors of an assignment.

This algorithm spends much time maintaining the data structures to ensure that the most improving step is taken at each time.

Two-Stage Choice

An alternative is to split the choice of a variable–value pair into first choosing a variable to change and then choosing a value.

This algorithm maintains a priority queue of variables, where the weight of a variable is the number of conflicts in which it participates. At each time, the algorithm selects a variable with maximum weight. Once a variable has been chosen, it can be assigned a value that minimizes the number of conflicts. For each conflict that has its value changed as a result of this new assignment, the other variables participating in the conflict must have their weight changed.

The complexity of one step of this algorithm is $O(\log n + r \log n)$. Compared to selecting the best variable–value pair, this does less work for each step and so more steps are achievable for any fixed time period. However, the steps tend to give less improvement, and so a trade-off exists between the number of steps and the complexity per step that must be evaluated empirically.

Any Conflict

An even simpler alternative, instead of choosing the best step, is to select any variable participating in a conflict and change its value. At each step, one of the variables involved in a violated constraint is selected at random. The algorithm assigns to that variable one of the values that minimizes the number of violated constraints.

To implement this alternative, we require a data structure to represent the set C of variables involved in a conflict. This data structure should be designed for quick selection of a random member of C. When a variable X has its value changed, each constraint in which X is involved is checked. For each such constraint that has become violated, all of the variables involved in the constraint are added to C. For each such constraint that is no longer violated, those variables involved in that constraint, but not involved in another violated constraint, are removed from C. One way to check whether a variable is involved in another conflict is to maintain a count of the number of conflicts for each variable, which is incremented when a constraint becomes violated and decremented when a constraint is no longer violated.

Each of the preceding algorithms can be combined with random steps, random restarts, and a tabu mechanism.

Simulated Annealing

The last method maintains no data structure of conflicts; instead it picks a neighbor at random and either rejects or accepts the new assignment.

Annealing is a process in metallurgy where metals are slowly cooled to make them reach a state of low energy where they are very strong. Simulated

Temperature	Probability of acceptance		
	1-worse	2-worse	3-worse
10	0.9	0.82	0.74
1	0.37	0.14	0.05
0.25	0.018	0.0003	0.000006
0.1	0.00005	2×10^{-9}	9×10^{-14}

Figure 4.8: Probability of simulated annealing accepting worsening steps

annealing is an analogous method for optimization. It is typically described in terms of thermodynamics. The random movement corresponds to high temperature; at low temperature, there is little randomness. Simulated annealing is a process where the temperature is reduced slowly, starting from a random search at high temperature eventually becoming pure greedy descent as it approaches zero temperature. The randomness should tend to jump out of local minima and find regions that have a low heuristic value; greedy descent will lead to local minima. At high temperatures, worsening steps are more likely than at lower temperatures.

Simulated annealing maintains a current assignment of values to variables. At each step, it picks a variable at random, then picks a value at random. If assigning that value to the variable is an improvement or does not increase the number of conflicts, the algorithm accepts the assignment and there is a new current assignment. Otherwise, it accepts the assignment with some probability, depending on the temperature and how much worse it is than the current assignment. If the change is not accepted, the current assignment is unchanged.

To control how many worsening steps are accepted, there is a positive real-valued temperature T. Suppose A is the current assignment of a value to each variable. Suppose that $h(A)$ is the evaluation of assignment A to be minimized. For solving constraints, h is typically the number of conflicts. Simulated annealing selects a neighbor at random, which gives a new assignment A'. If $h(A') \leq h(A)$, it accepts the assignment and A' becomes the new assignment. Otherwise, the assignment is only accepted randomly with probability

$$e^{(h(A)-h(A'))/T}.$$

Thus, if $h(A')$ is close to $h(A)$, the assignment is more likely to be accepted. If the temperature is high, the exponent will be close to zero, and so the probability will be close to 1. As the temperature approaches zero, the exponent approaches $-\infty$, and the probability approaches zero.

Figure 4.8 shows the probability of accepting worsening steps at different temperatures. In this figure, k-worse means that $h(A') - h(A) = k$. For example, if the temperature is 10 (i.e., $T = 10$), a change that is one worse (i.e., if $h(a) - h(a') = -1$) will be accepted with probability $e^{-0.1} \approx 0.9$; a change that is two worse will be accepted with probability $e^{-0.2} \approx 0.82$. If the temperature T is 1, accepting a change that is one worse will happen with probability

$e^{-1} \approx 0.37$. If the temperature is 0.1, a change that is one worse will be accepted with probability $e^{-10} \approx 0.00005$. At this temperature, it is essentially only performing steps that improve the value or leave it unchanged.

If the temperature is high, as in the $T = 10$ case, the algorithm tends to accept steps that only worsen a small amount; it does not tend to accept very large worsening steps. There is a slight preference for improving steps. As the temperature is reduced (e.g., when $T = 1$), worsening steps, although still possible, become much less likely. When the temperature is low (e.g., 0.1), it is very rare that it chooses a worsening step.

Simulated annealing requires an **annealing schedule**, which specifies how the temperature is reduced as the search progresses. Geometric cooling is one of the most widely used schedules. An example of a geometric cooling schedule is to start with a temperature of 10 and multiply by 0.97 after each step; this will have a temperature of 0.48 after 100 steps. Finding a good annealing schedule is an art.

4.8.3   Evaluating Randomized Algorithms

It is difficult to compare randomized algorithms when they give a different result and a different run time each time they are run, even for the same problem. It is especially difficult when the algorithms sometimes do not find an answer; they either run forever or must be stopped at an arbitrary point.

Unfortunately, summary statistics, such as the mean or median run time, are not very useful. For example, if you were to compare algorithms on the mean run time, you must consider how to average in unsuccessful runs (where no solution was found). If you were to ignore these unsuccessful runs in computing the average, then an algorithm that picks a random assignment and then stops would be the best algorithm; it does not succeed very often, but when it does, it is very fast. If you were to treat the non-terminating runs as having infinite time, then all algorithms that do not find a solution will have infinite averages. If you use the stopping time as the time for the non-terminating runs, the average is more of a function of the stopping time than of the algorithm itself, although this does allow for a crude trade-off between finding some solutions fast versus finding more solutions.

If you were to compare algorithms using the median run time, you would prefer an algorithm that solves the problem 51% of the time but very slowly over one that solves the problem 49% of the time but very quickly, even though the latter is more useful. The problem is that the median (the 50th percentile) is just an arbitrary value; you could just as well consider the 47th percentile or the 87th percentile.

One way to visualize the run time of an algorithm for a particular problem is to use a **run-time distribution**, which shows the variability of the run time of a randomized algorithm on a single problem instance. On the x-axis is either the number of steps or the run time. The y-axis shows, for each value of x, the number of runs or proportion of the runs solved within that run time or number of steps. Thus, it provides a cumulative distribution of how often the problem was solved within some number of steps or run time. For example, you can find the run time of the 30th percentile of the runs by finding the x-value that maps to 30% on the y-scale. The run-time distribution can be plotted (or approximated) by running the algorithm for a large number of times (say, 100 times for a rough approximation or 1,000 times for a reasonably accurate plot) and then by sorting the runs by run time.

Example 4.26 Four empirically generated run-time distributions for a single problem are shown in Figure 4.9 (on the next page). On the x-axis is the number of steps, using a logarithmic scale. On the y-axis is the number of instances that were successfully solved out of 1,000 runs. This shows four run-time distributions on the same problem instance. Algorithms 1 and 2 solved the problem 40% of the time in 10 or fewer steps. Algorithm 3 solved the problem in about 50% of the runs in 10 or fewer steps. Algorithm 4 found a solution in 10 or fewer steps in about 12% of the runs. Algorithms 1 and 2 found a solution in about 58% of the runs. Algorithm 3 could find a solution about 80% of the time. Algorithm 4 always found a solution. This only compares the number of steps; the time taken would be a better evaluation but is more difficult to measure for small problems and depends on the details of the implementation.

One algorithm strictly dominates another for this problem if its run-time distribution is to the left (and above) the run-time distribution of the second algorithm. Often two algorithms are incomparable under this measure. Which algorithm is better depends on how much time you have or how important it is to actually find a solution.

A run-time distribution allows us to predict how the algorithm will work with random restart after a certain number of steps. Intuitively, a random restart will repeat the lower left corner of the run-time distribution, suitably scaled down, at the stage where the restart occurs. A random restart after a certain number of greedy descent steps will make any algorithm that sometimes finds a solution into an algorithm that always finds a solution, given that one exists, if it is run for long enough.

Example 4.27 In the run-time distributions of Figure 4.9 (on the next page), Algorithm 3 dominates algorithms 1 and 2. Algorithms 1 and 2 are actually different sets of runs of the same algorithm with the same settings. This shows the errors that are typical of multiple runs of the same stochastic algorithm on the same problem instance. Algorithm 3 is better than Algorithm 4 up to 60 steps, after which Algorithm 4 is better.

By looking at the graph, you can see that Algorithm 3 can often solve the problem in its first four or five steps, after which it is not as effective. This may lead you to try to suggest using Algorithm 3 with a random restart after five steps and this does, indeed, dominate all of the algorithms for this problem instance, at least in the number of steps (counting a restart as a single step). However, because the random restart is an expensive operation, this algorithm may not be the most efficient. This also does not necessarily predict how well the algorithm will work in other problem instances.

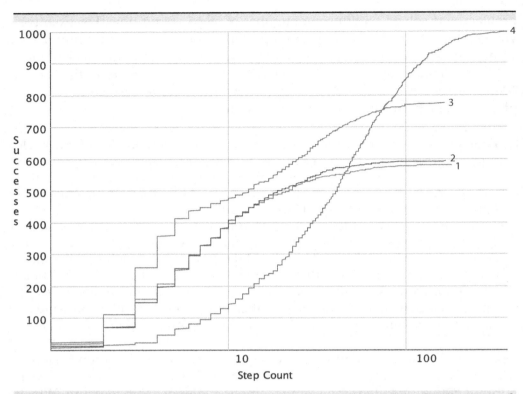

Figure 4.9: Run-time distributions. These are empirical run-time distributions of 1,000 runs, with each run having a limit of 1,000 steps. On the x-axis is the number of steps (using a logarithmic scale), and on the y-axis is the number of successes out of 1,000 runs. This is for the sample CSP, "Scheduling Problem 1," of Alspace. org. Distributions 1 and 2 are two separate runs for the two-stage greedy descent. Distribution 3 is for the one-stage greedy descent. Distribution 4 is a greedy descent with random walk, where first a random node that participates in a conflict (a red node in Alspace.org) is chosen, then the best value for this variable is chosen with a 50% chance and a random value is chosen otherwise.

4.8.4 Exploiting Propositional Structure in Local Search

Stochastic local search is simpler for CSPs that are in the form of propositional satisfiability problems (page 126), with Boolean variables and constraints that are clauses. Each local search step can be made more efficient for three main reasons:

- Because only one alternative value exists for each assignment to a variable, the algorithm does not have to search through the alternative values.

- Changing any value in an unsatisfied clause makes the clause satisfied. As a result, it is easy to satisfy a clause, but this may make other clauses unsatisfied.

- If a variable is changed to be true, only those clauses where it appears negatively can be made unsatisfied and similarly for variables becoming false. This enables fast indexing of clauses.

It is possible to convert any finite CSP into a propositional satisfiable problem. A variable Y with domain $\{v_1, \ldots, v_k\}$ can be converted into k Boolean variables $\{Y_1, \ldots, Y_k\}$, where Y_i is true when Y has value v_i and is false otherwise. Each Y_i is called an **indicator variable**. There is a clause for each false tuple in each constraint, which specifies which assignments to the Y_i are not allowed by the constraint. There are also constraints that specify that Y_i and Y_j cannot both be true when $i \neq j$. There is also a constraint that one of the variables Y_i must have value *true*. Converting a CSP into a propositional satisfiability problem has three potential advantages:

- Each local step can be simpler and therefore implemented more efficiently.
- The search space is expanded. In particular, before a solution has been found, more than one Y_i could be true (which corresponds to Y having multiple values) or all of the Y_i variables could be false (which corresponds to Y having no values). This can mean that some assignments that were local minima in the original problem may not be local minima in the new representation.
- Satisfiability has been studied much more extensively than most other types of CSPs and more efficient solvers are currently known because more of the space of potential algorithms has been explored by researchers.

Whether the conversion makes search performance better for a particular example is, again, an empirical question.

4.9 Population-Based Methods

The preceding local search algorithms maintain a single current assignment. This section considers algorithms that maintain multiple assignments. The first method, beam search, maintains the best k assignments. The next algorithm, stochastic beam search, selects which assignments to propagate stochastically. In genetic algorithms, which are inspired by biological evolution, the k assignments forming a population interact in various ways to produce the new population. In these algorithms, a total assignment of a value to each variable is called an **individual** and the set of current individuals is a **population**.

Beam search is a method similar to iterative best improvement, but it maintains up to k assignments instead of just one. It reports success when it finds a satisfying assignment. At each stage of the algorithm, it selects the k best neighbors of the current individuals (or all of them if there are less than k) and picks randomly in the case of ties. It repeats with this new set of k total assignments.

Beam search considers multiple assignments at the same time. Beam search is useful for memory-bounded cases, where k can be selected depending on the memory available.

Stochastic beam search is an alternative to beam search, which, instead of choosing the best k individuals, selects k of the individuals at random; the individuals with a better evaluation are more likely to be chosen. This is done by making the probability of being chosen a function of the evaluation function. A standard way to do this is to use a **Gibbs distribution** or **Boltzmann distribution** and to select an assignment A with probability proportional to

$$e^{-h(A)/T},$$

where $h(A)$ is the evaluation function and T is a temperature.

Stochastic beam search tends to allow more diversity in the k individuals than does plain beam search. In terms of evolution in biology, the evaluation function reflects the fitness of the individual; the fitter the individual, the more likely it is to pass that part of its variable assignment that is good onto the next generation. Stochastic beam search is like asexual reproduction; each individual gives slightly mutated children and then stochastic beam search proceeds with survival of the fittest. Note that under stochastic beam search it is possible for an individual to be selected multiple times at random.

Genetic algorithms further pursue the evolution analogy. Genetic algorithms are like stochastic beam searches, but each new element of the population is a combination of a pair of individuals – its parents. In particular, genetic algorithms select pairs of individuals and then create new offspring by taking some of the values for the offspring's variables from one of the parents and the rest from the other parent, loosely analogous to how DNA is spliced in sexual reproduction.

The new operation that occurs in genetic algorithms is called **crossover**. Uniform crossover selects two individuals (the parents) and creates two new individuals, called the **children**. The value for each variable in a child comes from one of the parents. A common method is **one-point crossover**, which assumes a total ordering of the variables. An index i is selected at random. One of the children is constructed by selecting the values for the variables before i from one of the parents, and the values for variables after i from the other parent. The other child gets the other values. The effectiveness of the crossover depends on the total ordering of the variables. The ordering of the variables is part of the design of the genetic algorithm.

Assume that you have a population of k individuals (where k is even). A basic genetic algorithm proceeds by maintaining k individuals as a generation and then using these individuals to generate a new generation via the following steps:

- Randomly select pairs of individuals where the fitter individuals are more likely to be chosen. How much more likely a fit individual is to be chosen than a less fit individual depends on the difference in fitness levels and a temperature parameter.

1: **procedure** $GeneticAlgorithm(V, dom, C, S, k)$
2:     **Inputs**
3:         V: a set of variables
4:         dom: a function; $dom(X)$ is the domain of variable X
5:         C: set of constraints to be satisfied
6:         S: a cooling schedule for the temperature
7:         k: population size – an even integer
8:     **Output**
9:         complete assignment that satisfies the constraints
10:     **Local**
11:         Pop: a set of assignments
12:         T: real
13:     $Pop \leftarrow k$ complete random assignments
14:     T is assigned a value according to S
15:     **repeat**
16:         **if** some $A \in Pop$ satisfies all constraints in C **then**
17:             **return** A
18:         $Npop \leftarrow \{\}$
19:         **repeat** $k/2$ **times**
20:             $A_1 \leftarrow RandomSelection(Pop, T)$
21:             $A_1 \leftarrow RandomSelection(Pop, T)$
22:             $N_1, N_2 \leftarrow combine(A_1, A_2)$
23:             $Npop \leftarrow Npop \cup \{mutate(N_1), mutate(N_2)\}$
24:         $Pop \leftarrow Npop$
25:         T is updated according to S
26:     **until** termination
27: **procedure** $RandomSelection(Pop, T)$
28:     select A from Pop with probability proportional to $e^{-h(A)/T}$
29:     **return** A
30: **procedure** $Combine(A_1, A_2)$
31:     select integer i, $1 \leq i < |V|$ at random
32:     Let $N_1 \leftarrow \{(X_j = v_j) \in A_1 \text{ for } j \leq i\} \cup \{(X_j = v_j) \in A_2 \text{ for } j > i\}$
33:     Let $N_2 \leftarrow \{(X_j = v_j) \in A_2 \text{ for } j \leq i\} \cup \{(X_j = v_j) \in A_1 \text{ for } j > i\}$
34:     **return** N_1, N_2

Figure 4.10: Genetic algorithm for finding a solution to a CSP

- For each pair, perform a crossover.

- Randomly mutate some (very few) values by choosing other values for some randomly chosen variables. This is a random walk step.

It proceeds in this way until it has created k individuals, and then the operation proceeds to the next generation. The algorithm is shown in Figure 4.10.

Example 4.28 Consider Example 4.8 (page 117). Suppose we use the same evaluation function as in Example 4.25 (page 132), namely the number of unsatisfied constraints. The individual $A = 2, B = 2, C = 3, D = 1, E = 1$ has an evaluation of 4. It has a low value mainly because $E = 1$. Its offspring that preserve this property will tend to have a lower evaluation than those that do not and, thus, will be more likely to survive. Other individuals may have low values for different reasons; for example, the individual $A = 4, B = 2, C = 3, D = 4, E = 4$ also has an evaluation of 4. It is low mainly because of the assignment of values to the first four variables. Again, offspring that preserve this property will be fitter and more likely to survive than those that do not. If these two were to mate, some of the offspring would inherit the bad properties of both and would die off. Some, by chance, would inherit the good properties of both. These would then have a better chance of survival.

As in other stochastic local search algorithms, it is difficult to design features and the evaluation function so that the algorithm does not get trapped in local minima. Efficiency is very sensitive to the variables used to describe the problem and the ordering of the variables. Getting this to work is an art. As with many other heuristic algorithms, evolutionary algorithms have many degrees of freedom and, therefore, are difficult to configure or tune for good performance. Also, analogies to natural evolution can be very misleading, because what is at work in nature is not always the best strategy for solving combinatorial decision or optimization problems.

A large community of researchers are working on genetic algorithms to make them practical for real problems and there have been some impressive results. What we have described here is only one of the possible genetic algorithms.

4.10   Optimization

Instead of just having possible worlds satisfy constraints or not, we often have a **preference** relation over possible worlds, and we want a best possible world according to the preference. The preference is often to minimize some error.

An **optimization problem** is given

- a set of variables, each with an associated domain;
- an **objective function** that maps total assignments to real numbers; and
- an **optimality criterion**, which is typically to find a total assignment that minimizes or maximizes the objective function.

The aim is to find a total assignment that is optimal according to the optimality criterion. For concreteness, we assume that the optimality criterion is to minimize the objective function.

A **constrained optimization problem** is an optimization problem that also has hard constraints specifying which variable assignments are possible. The aim is to find a best assignment that satisfies the hard constraints.

A huge literature exists on optimization. There are many techniques for particular forms of constrained optimization problems. For example, linear programming is the class of constrained optimization where the variables are real valued, the objective function is a linear function of the variables, and the hard constraints are linear inequalities. We do not cover these specific techniques. Although they have many applications, they have limited applicability in the space of all optimization problems. We do cover some general techniques that allow more general objective functions. However, if the problem you are interested in solving falls into one of the classes for which there are more specific algorithms, or can be transformed into one, it is generally better to use those techniques than the general algorithms presented here.

In a **constraint optimization problem**, the objective function is factored into a set of functions of subsets of the variables called soft constraints. A **soft constraint** assigns a cost for each assignment of values to some subset of the variables. The value of the objective function on a total assignment is the sum of the costs given by the soft constraints on that total assignment. A typical optimality criterion is to minimize the objective function.

Like a hard constraint (page 115), a soft constraint has a **scope** that is a set of variables. A soft constraint is a function from the domains of the variables in its scope into a real number, called its **evaluation**. Thus, given an assignment of a value to each variable in its scope, this function returns a real number.

Example 4.29 Suppose a number of delivery activities must be scheduled, similar to Example 4.8 (page 117), but, instead of hard constraints, there are preferences on times for the activities. The soft constraints are costs associated with combinations of times. The aim is to find a schedule with the minimum total sum of the costs.

Suppose variables A, C, D, and E have domain $\{1,2\}$, and variable B has domain $\{1,2,3\}$. The soft constraints are

c_1:	A	B	Cost		c_2:	B	C	Cost		c_3:	B	D	Cost
	1	1	5			1	1	5			1	1	3
	1	2	2			1	2	2			1	2	0
	1	3	2			2	1	0			2	1	2
	2	1	0			2	2	4			2	2	2
	2	2	4			3	1	2			3	1	2
	2	3	3			3	2	0			3	2	4

Thus, the scope of c_1 is $\{A,B\}$, the scope of c_2 is $\{B,C\}$, and the scope of c_3 is $\{B,D\}$. Suppose there are also constraints $c_4(C,E)$ and $c_5(D,E)$.

An assignment to some of the variables in a soft constraint results in a soft constraint that is a function of the other variables. In the preceding example, $c_1(A=1)$ is a function of B, which when applied to $B=2$ evaluates to 2.

Given a total assignment, the evaluation of the total assignment is the sum of the evaluations of the soft constraints applied to the total assignment.

One way to formalize this is to define operations on the soft constraints. Soft constraints can be added pointwise. The sum of two soft constraints is a soft constraint with scope that is the union of their scopes. The value of any assignment to the scope is the sum of the two functions on that assignment.

Example 4.30 Consider functions c_1 and c_2 in the previous example. $c_1 + c_2$ is a function with scope $\{A, B, C\}$, given by

$c_1 + c_2$:	A	B	C	Cost
	1	1	1	10
	1	1	2	7
	1	2	1	2
	...	...	...	...

The second value is computed as follows:

$$(c_1 + c_2)(A{=}1, B{=}1, C{=}2)$$
$$= c_1(A{=}1, B{=}1) + c_2(B{=}1, C{=}2)$$
$$= 5 + 2$$
$$= 7$$

One way to find the optimal assignment, corresponding to **generate and test** (page 118), is to compute the sum of the soft constraints and to choose an assignment with minimum value. Later we consider other, more efficient, algorithms for optimization.

Hard constraints can be modeled as having a cost of infinity for violating a constraint. As long as the cost of an assignment is finite, it does not violate a hard constraint. An alternative is to use a large number – larger than the sum of the soft constraints could be – as the cost of violating a hard constraint. Then optimization can be used to find a solution with the fewest number of violated hard constraints and, among those, one with the lowest cost.

Optimization problems have one difficulty that goes beyond constraint satisfaction problems. It is difficult to know whether an assignment is optimal. Whereas, for a CSP, an algorithm can check whether an assignment is a solution by just considering the assignment and the constraints, in optimization problems an algorithm can only determine if an assignment is optimal by comparing it to other assignments.

Many of the methods for solving hard constraints can be extended to optimization problems, as outlined in the following sections.

4.10.1 Systematic Methods for Optimization

Arc consistency (page 121) can be generalized to optimization problems by allowing pruning of dominated assignments. Suppose $c_1, \ldots, c_k$ are the soft constraints that involve X. Let soft constraint $c = c_1 + \cdots + c_k$. Suppose Y are the variables, other than X, that are involved in c. A value v for variable X is

strictly dominated if, for all values y of Y, some value v' of X exists such that $c(X = v', Y = y) < c(X = v, Y = y)$. Pruning strictly dominated values does not remove an optimal solution. The pruning of domains can be done repeatedly, as in the GAC algorithm (page 122).

Weakly dominated has the same definition as strictly dominated, but with "less than" replaced by "less than or equal to." If only one solution is required, weakly dominated values can be pruned sequentially. Which weakly dominated values are removed may affect which optimal solution is found, but removing a weakly dominated value does not remove all optimal solutions. As with arc consistency for hard constraints, pruning (strictly or weakly) dominated values can greatly simplify the problem but does not, by itself, always solve the problem.

Domain splitting (page 125) can be used to build a search tree. Domain splitting picks some variable X and considers each value of X. Assigning a value to X allows the constraints that involve X to be simplified and values for other variables to be pruned. In particular, pruning weakly dominated values means that, when there is only one variable left, a best value for that variable can be computed. Repeated domain splitting can build a search tree, as in Figure 4.1 (page 120), but with values at the leaves. By assigning costs when they can be determined, search algorithms such as A^* or branch-and-bound can be used to find an optimal solution.

Domain splitting can be improved via two techniques. First, if, under a split on X, an assignment to another variable does not depend on the value of X, the computation for that variable can be shared among the subtrees for the values of X; the value can be computed once and cached. Second, if removing a set of variables would disconnect the constraint graph, then when those variables have been assigned values, the disconnected components can be solved independently.

Variable elimination is the dynamic programming variant of domain splitting. The variables are eliminated one at a time. A variable X is eliminated as follows. Let R be the set of constraints that involve X. T is a new constraint whose scope is the union of the scopes of the constraints in R and whose value is the sum of the values of R. Let $V = scope(T) \setminus \{X\}$. For each value of the variables in V, select a value of X that minimizes T, resulting in a new soft constraint, N, with scope V. The constraint N replaces the constraints in R. This results in a new problem, with fewer variables and a new set of constraints, which can be solved recursively. A solution, S, to the reduced problem is an assignment to the variables in V. Thus, $T(S)$, the constraint T under the assignment S, is a function of X. An optimal value for X is obtained by choosing a value that results in the minimum value of $T(S)$.

Figure 4.11 (on the next page) gives pseudocode for the VE algorithm. The elimination ordering can be given a priori or can be computed on the fly, for example, using the elimination ordering heuristics discussed for CSP VE (page 130). It is possible to implement this without storing T and only by constructing an extensional representation of N.

```
 1:  procedure VE_SC(Vs, Fs)
 2:      Inputs
 3:          Vs: set of variables
 4:          Fs: set of constraints
 5:      Output
 6:          an optimal assignment to Vs.
 7:      if Vs contains a single element or Fs contains a single constraint then
 8:          let F be the sum of the constraints in Fs
 9:          return assignment with minimum value in F
10:      else
11:          select X ∈ Vs according to some elimination ordering
12:          R = {F ∈ Fs : F involves X}
13:          let T be the sum of the constraints in R
14:          N := min_X T
15:          S := VE_SC(Vs \ {X}, Fs \ R ∪ {N})
16:          X_opt := arg min_X T(S)
17:          return S ∪ {X = X_opt}
```

Figure 4.11: Variable elimination for optimizing with soft constraints

Example 4.31   Consider Example 4.29 (page 145). First consider eliminating A. It appears in only one constraint, $c_1(A, B)$. Eliminating A gives

$c_6(B) = \arg\min_A c_1(A, B)$:

B	Cost
1	0
2	2
3	2

The constraint $c_1(A, B)$ is replaced by $c_6(B)$.

Suppose B is eliminated next. B appears in three constraints: $c_2(B, C)$, $c_3(B, D)$, and $c_6(B)$. These three constraints are added, giving

$c_2(B, C) + c_3(B, D) + c_6(B)$:

B	C	D	Cost
1	1	1	8
1	1	2	5
		...	
2	1	1	4
2	1	2	4
		...	
3	1	1	6
3	1	2	8

The constraints c_2, c_3, and c_6 are replaced by

$c_7(C, D) = \min_B (c_2(B, C) + c_3(B, D) + c_6(B))$:

C	D	Cost
1	1	4
1	2	4
	...	

There are now three remaining constraints: $c_4(C, E)$, $C_5(D, E)$, and $c_7(C, D)$. These can be optimized recursively.

Suppose the recursive call returns the solution $C = 1$, $D = 2$, $E = 2$. An optimal value for B is the value that gives the minimum in $c_2(B, C = 1) + c_3(B, D = 2) + c_6(B)$, which is $B = 2$.

From $c_1(A, B)$, the value of A that minimizes $c_1(A, B = 2)$ is $A = 1$. Thus, an optimal solution is $A = 1$, $B = 2$, $C = 1$, $D = 2$, $E = 2$.

The complexity of VE depends on the structure of the constraint graph, as it does with hard constraints (page 129). Sparse graphs may result in small intermediate constraints in VE algorithms, including VE_SC. Densely connected graphs result in large intermediate constraints.

4.10.2 Local Search for Optimization

Local search is directly applicable to optimization problems, using the objective function of the optimization problem as the evaluation function of the local search. The algorithm runs for a certain amount of time (perhaps including random restarts to explore other parts of the search space), always keeping the best assignment found thus far, and returning this as its answer.

Local search for optimization has one extra complication that does not arise with only hard constraints: it is difficult to determine whether a total assignment is the best possible solution. A **local minimum** is a total assignment that is at least as good, according to the optimality criterion, as any of its neighbors. A **global minimum** is a total assignment that is at least as good as all of the other total assignments. Without systematically searching the other assignments, the algorithm may not know whether the best assignment found so far is a global optimum or whether a better solution exists in a different part of the search space.

When solving constrained optimization problems, with both hard and soft constraints, there could be a trade-off between violating hard constraints and making the evaluation function worse. We typically do not treat a violated constraint as having a cost of infinity, because then the algorithms would not distinguish violating one hard constraint from violating many. It is sometimes good to allow hard constraints to be temporarily violated in the search.

Continuous Domains

For optimization where the domains are continuous, a local search becomes more complicated because it is not obvious what the neighbors of a total assignment are. This problem does not arise with hard constraint satisfaction problems because the constraints implicitly discretize the space.

For optimization, **gradient descent** can be used to find a minimum value, and **gradient ascent** can be used to find a maximum value. Gradient descent is like walking downhill and always taking a step in the direction that goes down the most. The general idea is that the neighbor of a total assignment is to step downhill in proportion to the slope of the evaluation function h. Thus, gradient

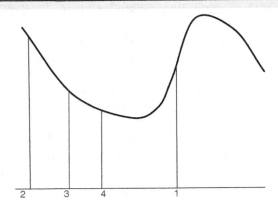

Figure 4.12: Gradient descent

descent takes steps in each direction proportional to the negative of the partial derivative in that direction.

In one dimension, if X is a real-valued variable with the current value of v, the next value should be

$$v - \eta \times \left(\frac{dh}{dX} \right) (v),$$

where

- η, the **step size**, is the constant of proportionality that determines how fast gradient descent approaches the minimum. If η is too large, the algorithm can overshoot the minimum; if η is too small, progress becomes very slow.

- $\frac{dh}{dX}$, the derivative of h with respect to X, is a function of X and is evaluated for $X = v$.

Example 4.32 Figure 4.12 shows a typical one-dimensional example for finding a local minimum of a one-dimensional function. It starts at a position marked as 1. The derivative is a big positive value, so it takes a step to the left to position 2. Here the derivative is negative, and closer to zero, so it takes a smaller step to the right to position 3. At position 3, the derivative is negative and closer to zero, so it takes a smaller step to the right. As it approaches the local minimum value, the slope becomes closer to zero and it takes smaller steps.

For multidimensional optimization, when there are many variables, gradient descent takes a step in each dimension proportional to the partial derivative of that dimension. If $\langle X_1, \ldots, X_n \rangle$ are the variables that have to be assigned values, a total assignment corresponds to a tuple of values $\langle v_1, \ldots, v_n \rangle$. Assume that the evaluation function, h, is differentiable. The next neighbor of the total assignment $\langle v_1, \ldots, v_n \rangle$ is obtained by moving in each direction in proportion to the slope of h in that direction. The new value for X_i is

$$v_i - \eta \times \left(\frac{\partial h}{\partial X_i} \right) (v_1, \ldots, v_n),$$

where η is the **step size**. The partial derivative, $\frac{\partial h}{\partial X_i}$, is a function of $X_1, \ldots, X_n$. Applying it to the point $(v_1, \ldots, v_n)$ gives

$$\left(\frac{\partial h}{\partial X_i}\right)(v_1, \ldots, v_n) = \lim_{\epsilon \to \infty} \frac{h(v_1, \ldots, v_i + \epsilon, \ldots, v_n) - h(v_1, \ldots, v_i, \ldots, v_n)}{\epsilon}.$$

If the partial derivative of h can be computed analytically, it is usually good to do so. If not, it can be estimated using a small value of ϵ.

Gradient descent is used for parameter learning (page 304), in which there may be thousands of real-valued parameters to be optimized. There are many variants of this algorithm that we do not discuss. For example, instead of using a constant step size, the algorithm could do a binary search to determine a locally optimal step size.

4.11   Review

The following are the main points you should have learned from this chapter:

- Instead of reasoning explicitly in terms of states, it is almost always much more efficient for an agent solving realistic problems to reason in terms of a set of features that characterize a state.
- Many problems can be represented as a set of variables, corresponding to the set of features, domains of possible values for the variables, and a set of hard and/or soft constraints. A solution is an assignment of a value to each variable that satisfies a set of hard constraints or optimizes some function.
- Arc consistency and search can often be combined to find assignments that satisfy some constraints or to show that there is no assignment.
- Stochastic local search can be used to find satisfying assignments, but not to show there are no satisfying assignments. The efficiency depends on the trade-off between the time taken for each improvement and how much the value is improved at each step. Some method must be used to allow the search to escape local minima that are not solutions.
- Optimization can use systematic methods when the constraint graph is sparse. Local search can also be used, but the added problem exists of not knowing when the search is at a global optimum.

4.12   References and Further Reading

Constraint satisfaction techniques are described in Dechter [2003] and Freuder and Mackworth [2006]. The *GAC* algorithm was invented by Mackworth [1977].

The DPLL algorithm (page 127) was invented by Davis, Logemann, and Loveland [1962].

VE for propositional satisfiability was proposed by Davis and Putnam [1960]. VE for optimization has been called **non-serial dynamic programming** and was invented by Bertelè and Brioschi [1972].

A1,D1	D2	D3
A2		
A3		

Word list:
add, ado, age, ago, aid,
ail, aim, air, and, any,
ape, apt, arc, are, ark,
arm, art, ash, ask, auk,
awe, awl, aye, bad, bag,
ban, bat, bee, boa, ear,
eel, eft, far, fat, fit,
lee, oaf, rat, tar, tie.

Figure 4.13: A crossword puzzle to be solved with six words

Stochastic local search is described by Spall [2003] and Hoos and Stützle [2004]. The any-conflict heuristic is based on the min-conflict heuristic of Minton, Johnston, Philips, and Laird [1992]. Simulated annealing was invented by Kirkpatrick, Gelatt, and Vecchi [1983].

Genetic algorithms were pioneered by Holland [1975]. A huge literature exists on genetic algorithms; for overviews see Goldberg [1989], Koza [1992], Mitchell [1996], Bäck [1996], Whitley [2001], and Goldberg [2002].

4.13   Exercises

Exercise 4.1 Consider the crossword puzzle shown in Figure 4.13. You must find six three-letter words: three words read across (A1, A2, and A3) and three words read down (D1, D2, and D3). Each word must be chosen from the list of forty possible words shown. Try to solve it yourself, first by intuition, then by hand using first domain consistency and then arc consistency.

There are at least two ways to represent the crossword puzzle shown in Figure 4.13 as a constraint satisfaction problem.

The first is to represent the word positions (A1, A2, A3, D1, D2, and D3) as variables, with the set of words as possible values. The constraints are that the letter is the same where the words intersect.

The second is to represent the nine squares as variables. The domain of each variable is the set of letters of the alphabet, $\{a, b, \ldots, z\}$. The constraints are that there is a word in the word list that contains the corresponding letters. For example, the top-left square and the center-top square cannot both have the value a, because there is no word starting with aa.

(a) Give an example of pruning due to domain consistency using the first representation (if one exists).

(b) Give an example of pruning due to arc consistency using the first representation (if one exists).

(c) Are domain consistency plus arc consistency adequate to solve this problem using the first representation? Explain.

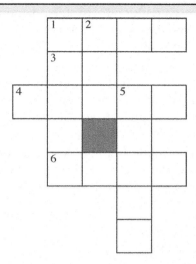

Figure 4.14: A crossword puzzle to be solved with seven words

(d) Give an example of pruning due to domain consistency using the second representation (if one exists).

(e) Give an example of pruning due to arc consistency using the second representation (if one exists).

(f) Are domain consistency plus arc consistency adequate to solve this problem using the second representation?

(g) Which representation leads to a more efficient solution using consistency-based techniques? Give the evidence on which you are basing your answer.

Exercise 4.2 Suppose you have a relation $v(N, W)$ that is true if there is a vowel (one of: a, e, i, o, u) as the N-th letter of word W. For example, $v(2, cat)$ is true because there is a vowel ("a") as the second letter of the word "cat"; $v(3, cat)$ is false, because the third letter of "cat" is "t", which is not a vowel; and $v(5, cat)$ is also false because there is no fifth letter in "cat".

Suppose the domain of N is $\{1, 3, 5\}$ and the domain of W is $\{added, blue, fever, green, stare\}$.

(a) Is the arc $\langle N, v \rangle$ arc consistent? If so, explain why. If not, show what element(s) can be removed from a domain to make it arc consistent.

(b) Is the arc $\langle W, v \rangle$ arc consistent? If so, explain why. If not, show what element(s) can be removed from a domain to make it arc consistent.

Exercise 4.3 Consider the crossword puzzle shown in Figure 4.14 . The available words that can be used are

at, eta, be, hat, he, her, it, him, on, one, desk, dance, usage, easy, dove, first, else, loses, fuels, help, haste, given, kind, sense, soon, sound, this, think.

(a) Given the representation with nodes for the positions (1-across, 2-down, etc.) and words for the domains, specify the network after domain consistency and arc consistency have halted.

(b) Consider the dual representation, in which the squares on the intersection of words are the variables and their domains are the letters that could go in these positions. Give the domains after this network has been made arc consistent. Does the result after arc consistency in this representation correspond to the result in part (a)?

(c) Show how variable elimination can be used to solve the crossword problem. Start from the arc-consistent network from part (a).

(d) Does a different elimination ordering affect the efficiency? Explain.

Exercise 4.4 Consider how stochastic local search can solve Exercise 4.3. You should use the "stochastic local search" Alspace.org applet to answer this question. Start with the arc-consistent network.

(a) How well does random walking work?

(b) How well does hill climbing work?

(c) How well does the combination work?

(d) Give a set of parameter settings that works best.

Exercise 4.5 Consider a scheduling problem, where there are five activities to be scheduled in four time slots. Suppose we represent the activities by the variables A, B, C, D, and E, where the domain of each variable is $\{1, 2, 3, 4\}$ and the constraints are $A > D$, $D > E$, $C \neq A$, $C > E$, $C \neq D$, $B \geq A$, $B \neq C$, and $C \neq D + 1$.

[Before you start this, try to find the legal schedule(s) using your own intutions.]

(a) Show how backtracking can be used to solve this problem. To do this, you should draw the search tree generated to find all answers. Indicate clearly the valid schedule(s). Make sure you choose a reasonable variable ordering.

To indicate the search tree, write it in text form with each branch on one line. For example, suppose we had variables X, Y, and Z with domains t, f and constraints $X \neq Y$ and $Y \neq Z$. The corresponding search tree can be written as:

```
X=t Y=t failure
    Y=f Z=t solution
        Z=f failure
X=f Y=t Z=t failure
        Z=f solution
    Y=f failure
```

[Hint: It may be easier to write a program to generate such a tree for a particular problem than to do it by hand.]

(b) Show how arc consistency can be used to solve this problem. To do this you must

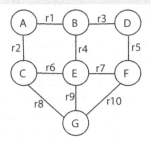

Figure 4.15: Abstract constraint network

- draw the constraint graph;
- show which elements of a domain are deleted at each step, and which arc is responsible for removing the element;
- show explicitly the constraint graph after arc consistency has stopped; and
- show how splitting a domain can be used to sove this problem.

Exercise 4.6 Which of the following methods can

(a) determine that there is no model, if there is not one?

(b) find a model if one exists?

(c) guarantee to find all models?

The methods to consider are

i) arc consistency with domain splitting.

ii) variable elimination.

iii) stochastic local search.

iv) genetic algorithms.

Exercise 4.7 Explain how arc consistency with domain splitting can be used to return all of the models and not just one. Give the algorithm.

Exercise 4.8 Explain how VE can be used to return one of the models rather than all of them. Give the algorithm. How is finding one easier than finding all?

Exercise 4.9 Explain how arc consistency with domain splitting can be used to count the number of models.

Exercise 4.10 Explain how VE can be used to count the number of models, without enumerating them all. [Hint: You do not need the backward pass, but instead you can pass forward the number of solutions there would be.]

Exercise 4.11 Consider the constraint graph of Figure 4.15 with named binary constraints [e.g., r_1 is a relation on A and B, which we can write as $r_1(A, B)$]. Consider solving this network using VE.

(a) Suppose you were to eliminate variable A. Which constraints are removed? A constraint is created on which variables? (You can call this r_{11}).

(b) Suppose you were to subsequently eliminate B (i.e., after eliminating A). Which relations are removed? A constraint is created on which variables?

Exercise 4.12 Pose and solve the crypt-arithmetic problem $SEND + MORE = MONEY$ as a CSP. In a crypt-arithmetic problem, each letter represents a different digit, the leftmost digit cannot be zero (because then it would not be there), and the sum must be correct considering each sequence of letters as a base ten numeral. In this example, you know that $Y = (D + E)$ mod 10 and that $E = (N + R + ((D + E) \div 10))$ mod 10, and so on.

Chapter 5

Propositions and Inference

For when I am presented with a false theorem, I do not need to examine or even to know the demonstration, since I shall discover its falsity a posteriori by means of an easy experiment, that is, by a calculation, costing no more than paper and ink, which will show the error no matter how small it is ...

And if someone would doubt my results, I should say to him: "Let us calculate, Sir," and thus by taking to pen and ink, we should soon settle the question.

– Gottfried Wilhelm Leibniz [1677]

This chapter considers a simple form of a knowledge base that is told facts about what is true in the world. An agent can use such a knowledge base, together with its observations, to determine what else must be true in the world. When an agent is queried about what is true given a knowledge base, it can answer the query without enumerating the possible worlds, or even generating any possible worlds. This chapter presents a number of reasoning formalisms that use propositions. They differ in what is being proved, what background knowledge must be provided, and how the observations that the agent receives online are handled.

5.1 Propositions

Writing constraints extensionally as tables of legal values for variables is not very intuitive. It is difficult to see what the tables are saying. It is also difficult to debug the knowledge, and small changes in the problem can mean big changes to the tables. One way to write constraints intensionally is in terms of propositions.

There are a number of reasons for using propositions for specifying constraints and queries:

- It is often more concise and readable to give a logical statement about the relationship between some variables than to use an extensional representation.

- The kind of queries an agent may have to answer may be richer than single assignments of values to variables.

- This language is extended to reason about individuals and relations in Chapter 12.

We first give the syntax and the semantics of a language called **propositional calculus**.

5.1.1 Syntax of Propositional Calculus

A **proposition** is a sentence, written in a language, that has a truth value (i.e., it is true or false) in a world. A proposition is built from atomic propositions using logical connectives.

An **atomic proposition**, or just an **atom**, is a symbol (page 114) that starts with a lower-case letter. Intuitively, an atom is something that is true or false.

For example, ai_is_fun, lit_l_1, $live\_outside$, and $sunny$ can all be atoms.

In terms of the algebraic variables of the preceding chapter, an atom can be seen as a statement that a variable has a particular value or that the value is in a set of values. For example, the proposition $classtimeAfter3$ may mean $ClassTime > 3$, which is true when the variable $ClassTime$ has value greater than 3 and is false otherwise. It is traditional in propositional calculus not to make the variable explicit and we follow that tradition. A direct connection exists to **Boolean variables** (page 113), which are variables with domain $\{true, false\}$. An assignment $X = true$ is written as the proposition x, using the variable name, but in lower case. So the proposition $happy$ can mean there exists a Boolean variable $Happy$, where $happy$ means $Happy = true$.

Propositions can be built from simpler propositions using logical connectives. A **proposition** is either

- an atomic proposition or
- a **compound proposition** of the form

    $\neg p$ (read "not p")—the **negation** of p
    $p \wedge q$ (read "p and q")—the **conjunction** of p and q
    $p \vee q$ (read "p or q")—the **disjunction** of p and q
    $p \rightarrow q$ (read "p implies q")—the **implication** of q from p
    $p \leftarrow q$ (read "p if q")—the **implication** of p from q
    $p \leftrightarrow q$ (read "p if and only if q" or "p is equivalent to q")

  where p and q are propositions.

The precedence of the operators is in the order they are given above. That is, a compound proposition can be disambiguated by adding parentheses to

p	q	$\neg p$	$p \wedge q$	$p \vee q$	$p \leftarrow q$	$p \rightarrow q$	$p \leftrightarrow q$
true	true	false	true	true	true	true	true
true	false	false	false	true	true	false	false
false	true	true	false	true	false	true	false
false	false	true	false	false	true	true	true

Figure 5.1: Truth table defining $\neg$, $\wedge$, $\vee$, $\leftarrow$, $\rightarrow$, and $\leftrightarrow$

the subexpressions in the order the operations are defined above. Thus, for example,

$$\neg a \vee b \wedge c \rightarrow d \wedge \neg e \vee f$$

is an abbreviation for

$$((\neg a) \vee (b \wedge c)) \rightarrow ((d \wedge (\neg e)) \vee f).$$

5.1.2   Semantics of the Propositional Calculus

Semantics specifies how to put symbols of the language into correspondence with the world. Semantics can be used to understand sentences of the language. The semantics of propositional calculus is defined below.

An **interpretation** consists of a function π that maps atoms to $\{true, false\}$. If $\pi(a) = true$, we say atom a is **true** in the interpretation, or that the interpretation assigns $true$ to a. If $\pi(a) = false$, we say a is **false** in the interpretation. Sometimes it is useful to think of π as the set of atoms that map to $true$, and that the rest of the atoms map to $false$.

The interpretation maps each proposition to a **truth value**. Each proposition is either **true** in the interpretation or **false** in the interpretation. An atomic proposition a is true in the interpretation if $\pi(a) = true$; otherwise, it is false in the interpretation. The truth value of a compound proposition is built using the truth table of Figure 5.1.

Note that we only talk about the truth value in an interpretation. Propositions may have different truth values in different interpretations.

Example 5.1   Suppose there are three atoms: ai_is_fun, $happy$, and $light\_on$.

Suppose interpretation I_1 assigns $true$ to ai_is_fun, $false$ to $happy$, and $true$ to $light\_on$. That is, I_1 is defined by the function π_1 defined by $\pi_1(ai\_is\_fun) = true$, $\pi_1(happy) = false$, and $\pi_1(light\_on) = true$. Then

- ai_is_fun is true in I_1.
- $\neg ai\_is\_fun$ is false in I_1.
- $happy$ is false in I_1.
- $\neg happy$ is true in I_1.
- $ai\_is\_fun \vee happy$ is true in I_1.
- $ai\_is\_fun \leftarrow happy$ is true in I_1.

- *happy ← ai_is_fun* is false in I_1.
- *ai_is_fun ← happy ∧ light_on* is true in I_1.

Suppose interpretation I_2 assigns *false* to *ai_is_fun*, *true* to *happy*, and *false* to *light_on*:

- *ai_is_fun* is false in I_2.
- *¬ai_is_fun* is true in I_2.
- *happy* is true in I_2.
- *¬happy* is false in I_2.
- *ai_is_fun ∨ happy* is true in I_2.
- *ai_is_fun ← happy* is false in I_2.
- *ai_is_fun ← light_on* is true in I_2.
- *ai_is_fun ← happy ∧ light_on* is true in I_2.

A **knowledge base** is a set of propositions that the agent is given as being true. An element of the knowledge base is an **axiom**.

A **model** of a set of propositions is an interpretation in which all the propositions are true.

If *KB* is a knowledge base and *g* is a proposition, *g* is a **logical consequence** of *KB*, written as

$$KB \models g$$

if *g* is true in every model of *KB*.

That is, no interpretation exists in which *KB* is true and *g* is false. The definition of logical consequence places no constraints on the truth value of *g* in an interpretation where *KB* is false.

If $KB \models g$ we also say *g* **logically follows** from *KB*, or *KB* **entails** *g*.

Example 5.2 Suppose *KB* is the following knowledge base:

> *sam_is_happy.*
> *ai_is_fun.*
> *worms_live_underground.*
> *night_time.*
> *bird_eats_apple.*
> *apple_is_eaten ← bird_eats_apple.*
> *switch_1_is_up ← sam_is_in_room ∧ night_time.*

Given this knowledge base,

> $KB \models bird\_eats\_apple.$
> $KB \models apple\_is\_eaten.$

KB does not entail *switch_1_is_up* as there is a model of the knowledge base where *switch_1_is_up* is false. Note that *sam_is_in_room* must be false in that interpretation.

Humans' View of Semantics

The description of semantics does not tell us why semantics is interesting or how it can be used as a basis to build intelligent systems. The basic idea behind the use of logic is that, when a knowledge base designer has a particular world to characterize, the designer can choose that world as an **intended interpretation**, choose meaning for the symbols with respect to that world, and write propositions about what is true in that world. When the system computes a logical consequence of a knowledge base, the designer can interpret this answer with respect to the intended interpretation. A designer should communicate this meaning to other designers and users so that they can also interpret the answer with respect to the meaning of the symbols.

The logical entailment "$KB \models g$" is a semantic relation between a set of propositions (KB) and a proposition it entails, g. Both KB and g are symbolic, and so they can be represented in the computer. The meaning may be with reference to the world, which need not be syntactic. The $\models$ relation is not about computation or proofs; it simply provides the specification of what follows from some statements about what is true.

The methodology used by a knowledge base designer to represent a world can be expressed as follows:

Step 1 A knowledge base designer chooses a task domain or world to represent, which is the intended interpretation. This could be some aspect of the real world (for example, the structure of courses and students at a university, or a laboratory environment at a particular point in time), some imaginary world (such as the world of Alice in Wonderland, or the state of the electrical environment if a switch breaks), or an abstract world (for example, the world of numbers and sets). The designer also must choose which propositions are of interest.

Step 2 The knowledge base designer selects atoms to represent some aspects of the world. Each atom has a precise meaning with respect to the intended interpretation.

Step 3 The knowledge base designer **tells** the system propositions that are true in the intended interpretation. This is often called **axiomatizing** the domain, where the given propositions are the **axioms** of the domain.

Step 4 The KB designer can now **ask** questions about the intended interpretation. The system can answer these questions. The designer is able to interpret the answers using the meaning assigned to the symbols.

Within this methodology, the designer does not actually tell the computer anything until step 3. The first two steps are carried out in the head of the designer.

Designers should document the meanings of the symbols so that they can make their representations understandable to other people, so that they remember what each symbol means, and so that they can check the truth of the given propositions. A specification of meaning of the symbols is called an **ontology**. Ontologies can be informally specified in comments, but they are increasingly specified in formal languages to enable semantic interoperability – the ability to use symbols from different knowledge bases together so the same symbol means the same thing. Ontologies are discussed in detail in Chapter 13.

Step 4 can be carried out by other people as long as they understand the ontology. Other people who know the meaning of the symbols in the question and the answer, and who trust the knowledge base designer to have told the truth, can interpret answers to their questions as being true in the world under consideration.

The Computer's View of Semantics

The knowledge base designer who provides information to the system has an intended interpretation and interprets symbols according to that intended interpretation. The designer states knowledge, in terms of propositions, about what is true in the intended interpretation. The computer does not have access to the intended interpretation – only to the propositions in the knowledge base. As will be shown, the computer is able to tell if some statement is a logical consequence of a knowledge base. The intended interpretation is a model of the axioms if the knowledge base designer has been truthful according to the meaning assigned to the symbols. Assuming the intended interpretation is a model of the knowledge base, if a proposition is a logical consequence of the knowledge base, it is true in the intended interpretation because it is true in all models of the knowledge base.

The concept of logical consequence seems like exactly the right tool to derive implicit information from an axiomatization of a world. Suppose KB represents the knowledge about the intended interpretation; that is, the intended interpretation is a model of the knowledge base, and that is all the system knows about the intended interpretation. If $KB \models g$, then g must be true in the intended interpretation, because it is true in all models of the knowledge base. If $KB \not\models g$ – that is, if g is not a logical consequence of KB – a model of KB exists in which g is false. As far as the computer is concerned, the intended interpretation may be the model of KB in which g is false, and so it does not know whether g is true in the intended interpretation.

Given a knowledge base, the models of the knowledge base correspond to all of the ways that the world could be, given that the knowledge base is true.

Example 5.3 Consider the knowledge base of Example 5.2 (page 160). The user could interpret these symbols as having some meaning. The computer does not know the meaning of the symbols, but it can still make conclusions based on what it has been told. It can conclude that *apple_is_eaten* is true in the intended interpretation. It cannot conclude *switch_1_is_up* because it does not know if *sam_is_in_room* is true or false in the intended interpretation.

If the knowledge base designer tells lies – some axioms are false in the intended interpretation – the computer's answers are not guaranteed to be true in the intended interpretation.

It is very important to understand that, until we consider computers with perception and the ability to act in the world, the computer does not know the meaning of the symbols. It is the human that gives the symbols meaning. All the computer knows about the world is what it is told about the world. However, because the computer can provide logical consequences of the knowledge base, it can make conclusions that are true in the intended interpretation.

5.2 Propositional Definite Clauses

The language of **propositional definite clauses** is a sublanguage of propositional calculus that does not allow uncertainty or ambiguity. In this language, propositions have the same meaning as in propositional calculus, but not all compound propositions are allowed in a knowledge base.

The **syntax** of **propositional definite clauses** is defined as follows:

- An **atomic proposition** or **atom** is the same as in propositional calculus.
- A **body** is an atom or a conjunction of atoms. Defined recursively, a body is either an atom or of the form $a \wedge b$, where a is an atom and b is a body.
- A **definite clause** is either an atom a, called an **atomic clause**, or of the form $a \leftarrow b$, called a **rule**, where a, the **head**, is an atom and b is a body.
- A **knowledge base** is a set of definite clauses.

Example 5.4   The elements of the knowledge base in Example 5.2 (page 160) are all definite clauses.

The following are *not* definite clauses:

$apple\_is\_eaten \wedge bird\_eats\_apple.$

$sam\_is\_in\_room \wedge night\_time \leftarrow switch\_1\_is\_up.$

$Apple\_is\_eaten \leftarrow Bird\_eats\_apple.$

$happy \vee sad \vee \neg alive.$

The third proposition is not a definite clause because an atom must start with a lower-case letter.

Note that a definite clause is a restricted form of a clause (page 126). For example, the definite clause

$a \leftarrow b \wedge c \wedge d.$

is equivalent to the clause

$a \vee \neg b \vee \neg c \vee \neg d.$

In general, a definite clause is equivalent to a clause with exactly one positive literal (non-negated atom). Propositional definite clauses cannot represent disjunctions of atoms (e.g., $a \vee b$) or disjunctions of negated atoms (e.g., $\neg c \vee \neg d$).

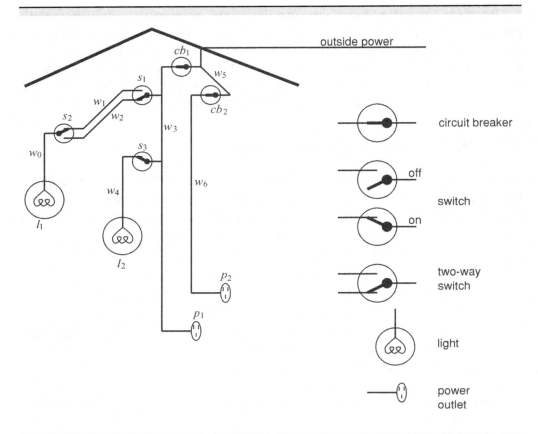

Figure 5.2: An electrical environment with components named

Example 5.5 Consider how to axiomatize the electrical environment of Figure 5.2 following the methodology for the user's view of semantics (page 161). This axiomatization will allow us to simulate the electrical system. It will be expanded in later sections to let us diagnose faults based on observed symptoms.

Assume the representation will be used to determine whether lights are on or off, based on switch positions and the status of circuit breakers, and, eventually, to be able to diagnose what is wrong with wires, switches, and circuit breakers if something unexpected is observed. Assume you are not concerned here with the color of the wires, the design of the switches, the length or weight of the wire, the date of manufacture of the lights and the wires, or any of the other myriad of detail one could imagine about the domain.

We must choose a level of abstraction. The aim is to represent the domain at the most general level that will enable the diagnostic assistant to solve the problems it must solve. We also want to represent the domain at a level that the agent will have information about. For example, we could represent the actual voltages and currents, but exactly the same reasoning would be done if this were a 12-volt DC system or a 120-volt AC system; the voltages and frequencies are irrelevant for questions about how switches affect whether lights are on.

Instead, we represent this domain at a commonsense level that non-electricians may use to describe the domain, in terms of wires being live and currents flowing from the outside through wires to the lights, and that circuit breakers and light switches connect wires if they are turned on and working.

We have to choose what to represent. Suppose we want to represent propositions about whether lights are lit, whether wires are live, whether switches are up or down, and whether components are broken.

We then choose atoms with a specific meaning in the world. We can use descriptive names for these, such as up_s_2 to represent whether switch s_2 is up and $live\_l_1$ to represent whether light l_1 is live (i.e., has power coming into it). The computer does not know the meaning of these names and does not have access to the components of the atom's name.

At this stage, we have not told the computer anything. It does not know what the atoms are, let alone what they mean.

Once we have decided which symbols to use and what they mean, we tell the system, using definite clauses, background knowledge about what is true in the world. The simplest forms of definite clauses are those without bodies – the atomic clauses – such as

$light\_l_1$.
$light\_l_2$.
ok_l_1.
ok_l_2.
ok_cb_1.
ok_cb_2.
$live\_outside$.

The designer may look at part of the domain and know that light l_1 is live if wire w_0 is live, because they are connected together, but may not know if w_0 is live. Such knowledge is expressible in terms of rules:

$live\_l_1 \leftarrow live\_w_0$.
$live\_w_0 \leftarrow live\_w_1 \wedge up\_s_2$.
$live\_w_0 \leftarrow live\_w_2 \wedge down\_s_2$.
$live\_w_1 \leftarrow live\_w_3 \wedge up\_s_1$.
$live\_w_2 \leftarrow live\_w_3 \wedge down\_s_1$.
$live\_l_2 \leftarrow live\_w_4$.
$live\_w_4 \leftarrow live\_w_3 \wedge up\_s_3$.
$live\_p_1 \leftarrow live\_w_3$.
$live\_w_3 \leftarrow live\_w_5 \wedge ok\_cb_1$.
$live\_p_2 \leftarrow live\_w_6$.
$live\_w_6 \leftarrow live\_w_5 \wedge ok\_cb_2$.
$live\_w_5 \leftarrow live\_outside$.
$lit\_l_1 \leftarrow light\_l_1 \wedge live\_l_1 \wedge ok\_l_1$.
$lit\_l_2 \leftarrow light\_l_2 \wedge live\_l_2 \wedge ok\_l_2$.

At run time, the user is able to input the observations of the current switch positions, such as

> $down\_s_1$.
>
> up_s_2.
>
> up_s_3.

The knowledge base consists of all of the definite clauses, whether specified as background knowledge or as observations.

5.2.1   Questions and Answers

One reason to build a description of a world is to be able to determine what else must be true in that world. After the computer is given a knowledge base about a particular domain, a user might like to ask the computer questions about that domain. The computer can answer whether or not a proposition is a logical consequence of the knowledge base. If the user knows the meaning of the atoms, the user can interpret the answer in terms of the domain.

A **query** is a way of asking whether a proposition is a logical consequence of a knowledge base. Once the system has been provided with a knowledge base, a query is used to ask whether a formula is a logical consequence of the knowledge base. Queries have the form

> ask b.

where b is a body (page 163).

A query is a question that has the **answer** *"yes"* if the body is a logical consequence of the knowledge base, or the answer *"no"* if the body is not a consequence of the knowledge base. The latter does not mean that *body* is false in the intended interpretation but rather that it is impossible to determine whether it is true or false based on the knowledge provided.

Example 5.6   Once the computer has been told the knowledge base of Example 5.5 (page 164), it can answer queries such as

> ask $light\_l_1$.

for which the answer is *yes*. The query

> ask $light\_l_6$.

has answer *no*. The computer does not have enough information to know whether or not l_6 is a light. The query

> ask lit_l_2.

has answer *yes*. This atom is true in all models.

The user can interpret this answer with respect to the intended interpretation.

5.2.2   Proofs

So far, we have specified what an answer is, but not how it can be computed. The definition of $\models$ specifies what propositions should be logical consequences of a knowledge base but not how to compute them. The problem of **deduction** is to determine if some proposition is a logical consequence of a knowledge base. Deduction is a specific form of **inference**.

A **proof** is a mechanically derivable demonstration that a proposition logically follows from a knowledge base. A **theorem** is a provable proposition. A **proof procedure** is a – possibly non-deterministic – algorithm for deriving consequences of a knowledge base. See the box on page 170 for a description of non-deterministic choice.

Given a proof procedure, $KB \vdash g$ means g can be **proved** or **derived** from knowledge base KB.

A proof procedure's quality can be judged by whether it computes what it is meant to compute.

A proof procedure is **sound** with respect to a semantics if everything that can be derived from a knowledge base is a logical consequence of the knowledge base. That is, if $KB \vdash g$, then $KB \models g$.

A proof procedure is **complete** with respect to a semantics if there is a proof of each logical consequence of the knowledge base. That is, if $KB \models g$, then $KB \vdash g$.

We present two ways to construct proofs for propositional definite clauses: a bottom-up procedure and a top-down procedure.

Bottom-Up Proof Procedure

The first proof procedure is a **bottom-up proof procedure** to derive logical consequences. It is called bottom-up as an analogy to building a house, where we build on top of the structure we already have. The bottom-up proof procedure builds on atoms that have already been established. It should be contrasted with a top-down approach (page 169), which starts from a query and tries to find definite clauses that support the query. Sometimes we say that a bottom-up procedure is **forward chaining** on the definite clauses, in the sense of going forward from what is known rather than going backward from the query.

The general idea is based on one **rule of derivation**, a generalized form of the rule of inference called *modus ponens*:

If "$h \leftarrow b_1 \wedge \ldots \wedge b_m$" is a definite clause in the knowledge base, and each b_i has been derived, then h can be derived.

This rule also covers the case when $m = 0$; the bottom-up proof procedure can always immediately derive the atom at the head of a definite clause with no body.

Figure 5.3 (on the next page) gives a procedure for computing the **consequence set** C of a set KB of definite clauses. Under this proof procedure, if g is

---

```
1: procedure DCDeductionBU(KB)
2:     Inputs
3:         KB: a set of definite clauses
4:     Output
5:         Set of all atoms that are logical consequences of KB
6:     Local
7:         C is a set of atoms
8:     C := {}
9:     repeat
10:        select "h ← b₁ ∧ ... ∧ bₘ" in KB where bᵢ ∈ C for all i, and h ∉ C
11:        C := C ∪ {h}
12:    until no more definite clauses can be selected
13:    return C
```

Figure 5.3: Bottom-up proof procedure for computing consequences of KB

an atom, $KB \vdash g$ if $g \in C$ at the end of the $DCDeductionBU$ procedure. For a conjunction, $KB \vdash g_1 \wedge \cdots \wedge g_k$, if $g_i \in C$ for each i such that $0 < i \leq k$.

Example 5.7 Suppose the system is given the knowledge base KB:

$$a \leftarrow b \wedge c.$$
$$b \leftarrow d \wedge e.$$
$$b \leftarrow g \wedge e.$$
$$c \leftarrow e.$$
$$d.$$
$$e.$$
$$f \leftarrow a \wedge g.$$

One trace of the value assigned to C in the bottom-up procedure is

$$\{\}$$
$$\{d\}$$
$$\{e, d\}$$
$$\{c, e, d\}$$
$$\{b, c, e, d\}$$
$$\{a, b, c, e, d\}.$$

The algorithm terminates with $C = \{a, b, c, e, d\}$. Thus, $KB \vdash a$, $KB \vdash b$, and so on.

The last rule in KB is never used. The bottom-up proof procedure cannot derive f or g. This is as it should be because a model of the knowledge base exists in which f and g are both false.

There are a number of properties that can be established for the proof procedure of Figure 5.3:

Soundness Every atom in C is a logical consequence of KB. That is, if $KB \vdash g$ then $KB \models g$. To show this, assume that an atom exists in C that is not a logical consequence of KB. If such an element exists, there must be a first element added to C that is not true in every model of KB. Suppose this is h, and suppose it is not true in model I of KB; h must be the first element generated that is false in I. Because h has been generated, there must be some definite clause in KB of the form $h \leftarrow b_1 \wedge \ldots \wedge b_m$ such that $b_1 \ldots b_m$ are all in C (which includes the case where h is an atomic clause and so $m = 0$). The b_i are generated before h and so are all true in I. This clause's head is false in I, and its body is true in I; therefore, by the definition of truth of clauses, this clause is false in I. This is a contradiction to the fact that I is a model of KB. Thus, every element of C is a logical consequence of KB.

Complexity The algorithm of Figure 5.3 halts, and the number of times the loop is repeated is bounded by the number of definite clauses in KB. This can be seen easily because each definite clause can only be used once. Thus, the time complexity of the preceding algorithm is linear in the size of the knowledge base if it can index the definite clauses so that the inner loop can be carried out in constant time.

Fixed Point The final C generated in the algorithm of Figure 5.3 is called a **fixed point** because any further application of the rule of derivation does not change C. C is the **minimum fixed point** because there is no smaller fixed point.

Let I be the interpretation in which every atom in the minimum fixed point is true and every atom not in the minimum fixed point is false. To show that I must be a model of KB, suppose "$h \leftarrow b_1 \wedge \ldots \wedge b_m$" $\in KB$ is false in I. The only way this could occur is if $b_1, \ldots, b_m$ are in the fixed point, and h is not in the fixed point. By construction, the rule of derivation can be used to add h to the fixed point, a contradiction to it being the fixed point. Thus, there can be no definite clause in KB that is false in an interpretation defined by a fixed point. Thus, I is a model of KB.

Completeness Suppose $KB \models g$. Then g is true in every model of KB, so it is true in the model I defined by the minimum fixed point, and so it is in C, and so $KB \vdash g$.

The model I defined above by the minimum fixed point is a **minimum model** in the sense that it has the fewest true propositions. Every other model must also assign the atoms in I to be true.

Top-Down Proof Procedure

An alternative proof method is to search *backward* or *top-down* from a query to determine if it is a logical consequence of the given definite clauses. This procedure is called **propositional definite clause resolution** or **SLD resolution**, where SL stands for Selecting an atom using a Linear strategy, and D stands for Definite clauses. It is an instance of the more general **resolution** method.

Non-deterministic Choice

In many AI programs, we want to separate the definition of a solution from how it is computed. Usually, the algorithms are **non-deterministic**, which means that there are choices in the program that are left unspecified. There are two sorts of non-determinism:

- **Don't-care non-determinism** is exemplified by the "select" in Figure 5.3 (page 168). In this form of non-determinism, if one selection does not lead to a solution there is no point in trying any other alternatives. Don't-care non-determinism is used in resource allocation, where a number of requests occur for a limited number of resources, and a scheduling algorithm has to select who gets which resource at each time. The correctness is not affected by the selection, but efficiency and termination may be. When there is an infinite sequence of selections, a selection mechanism is **fair** if a request that is repeatedly available to be selected will eventually be selected. The problem of an element being repeatedly not selected is called **starvation**. We want to make sure that any selection is fair.

- **Don't-know non-determinism** is exemplified by the "choose" in Figure 5.4 (page 172). Just because one choice did not lead to a solution does not mean that other choices will not work. Often we speak of an **oracle** that can specify, at each point, which choice will lead to a solution. Because our agent does not have such an oracle, it has to search through the space of alternate choices. Chapter 3 presents algorithms to search the space.

  Don't-know non-determinism plays a large role in computational complexity theory. The class of P problems contains the problems solvable with time complexity polynomial in the size of the problem. The class of NP problems contains the problems that could be solved in polynomial time with an **oracle** that chooses the correct value at each time or, equivalently, if a solution is verifiable in polynomial time. It is widely conjectured that $P \neq NP$, which would mean that no such oracle can exist. One great result of complexity theory is that the hardest problems in the NP class of problems are all equally complex; if one can be solved in polynomial time, they all can. These problems are **NP-complete**. A problem is **NP-hard** if it is at least as hard as an NP-complete problem.

In this book, we consistently use the term **select** for don't-care non-determinism and **choose** for don't-know non-determinism. In a **non-deterministic procedure**, we assume that an oracle makes an appropriate choice at each time. Thus, a *choose* statement will result in a choice that will led to success, or will **fail** if there are no such choices. A non-deterministic procedure may have multiple answers, where there are multiple choices that succeed, and will fail if there are no applicable choices. We can also explicitly **fail** a choice that should not succeed. The oracle is implemented by search.

The top-down proof procedure can be understood in terms of answer clauses. An **answer clause** is of the form

$$yes \leftarrow a_1 \wedge a_2 \wedge \ldots \wedge a_m.$$

where *yes* is a special atom. Intuitively, *yes* is going to be true exactly when the answer to the query is "yes."

If the query is

$$\mathsf{ask}\ q_1 \wedge \ldots \wedge q_m.$$

the initial answer clause is

$$yes \leftarrow q_1 \wedge \ldots \wedge q_m.$$

Given an answer clause, the top-down algorithm selects an atom in the body of the answer clause. Suppose it selects a_i. The atom selected is called a **goal**. The algorithm proceeds by doing steps of **resolution**. In one step of resolution, it chooses a definite clause in *KB* with a_i as the head. If there is no such clause, it fails. The **resolvent** of the above answer clause on the selection a_i with the definite clause

$$a_i \leftarrow b_1 \wedge \ldots \wedge b_p.$$

is the answer clause

$$yes \leftarrow a_1 \wedge \ldots \wedge a_{i-1} \wedge b_1 \wedge \ldots \wedge b_p \wedge a_{i+1} \wedge \ldots \wedge a_m.$$

That is, the goal in the answer clause is replaced by the body of the chosen definite clause.

An **answer** is an answer clause with an empty body ($m = 0$). That is, it is the answer clause $yes \leftarrow$.

An **SLD derivation** of a query "ask $q_1 \wedge \ldots \wedge q_k$" from knowledge base *KB* is a sequence of answer clauses $\gamma_0, \gamma_1, \ldots, \gamma_n$ such that

- γ_0 is the answer clause corresponding to the original query, namely the answer clause $yes \leftarrow q_1 \wedge \ldots \wedge q_k$;
- γ_i is the resolvent of γ_{i-1} with a definite clause in *KB*; and
- γ_n is an answer.

Another way to think about the algorithm is that the top-down algorithm maintains a collection *G* of atoms to prove. Each atom that must be proved is a **goal**. Initially, *G* is the set of atoms in the query. A clause $a \leftarrow b_1 \wedge \ldots \wedge b_p$ means goal *a* can be replaced by goals $b_1, \ldots, b_p$. Each b_i is a **subgoal** of *a*. The *G* to be proved corresponds to the answer clause $yes \leftarrow G$.

The procedure in Figure 5.4 (on the next page) specifies a procedure for solving a query. It follows the definition of a derivation. In this procedure, *G* is the set of atoms in the body of the answer clause. The procedure is non-deterministic in that a point exists in the algorithm where it has to *choose* a

```
1: non-deterministic procedure DCDeductionTD(KB,Query)
2:     Inputs
3:         KB: a set definite clauses
4:         Query: a set of atoms to prove
5:     Output
6:         yes if KB ⊨ Query and the procedure fails otherwise
7:     Local
8:         G is a set of atoms
9:     G := Query
10:    repeat
11:        select an atom a in G
12:        choose definite clause "a ← B" in KB with a as head
13:        replace a with B in G
14:    until G = {}
15:    return yes
```

Figure 5.4: Top-down definite clause proof procedure

definite clause to resolve against. If there are choices that result in G being the empty set, it returns *yes*; otherwise it fails.

This algorithm treats the body of a clause as a set of atoms; G is also a set of atoms. It can be implemented by treating G as a set, where duplicates are removed. It can also be implemented with G as an ordered list of atoms, perhaps with an atom appearing a number of times.

Note that the algorithm requires a selection strategy of which atom to select at each time. It does not have to search over the different selections, but the selections affect the efficiency. One common selection strategy is to select the leftmost atom in some ordering of the atoms. This is not a fair strategy; it is possible for it to get into an infinite loop, when a different strategy would fail. The best selection strategy is to select the atom that is most likely to fail.

Example 5.8 Suppose the system is given the knowledge base

$a \leftarrow b \wedge c.$

$b \leftarrow d \wedge e.$

$b \leftarrow g \wedge e.$

$c \leftarrow e.$

$d.$

$e.$

$f \leftarrow a \wedge g.$

It is asked the following query:

ask $a.$

The following shows a derivation that corresponds to the sequence of assignments to G in the repeat loop of Figure 5.4. We assume that G is represented as an ordered list, and it always selects the leftmost atom in G:

$$yes \leftarrow a.$$
$$yes \leftarrow b \wedge c.$$
$$yes \leftarrow d \wedge e \wedge c.$$
$$yes \leftarrow e \wedge c.$$
$$yes \leftarrow c.$$
$$yes \leftarrow e.$$
$$yes \leftarrow .$$

The following shows a sequence of choices, where the second definite clause for b was chosen, which fails to provide a proof:

$$yes \leftarrow a.$$
$$yes \leftarrow b \wedge c.$$
$$yes \leftarrow g \wedge e \wedge c.$$

If g is selected, there are no rules that can be chosen. This proof attempt is said to *fail*.

When the top-down procedure has derived the answer, the rules used in the derivation can be used in a bottom-up proof procedure to infer the query. Similarly, a bottom-up proof of an atom can be used to construct a corresponding top-down derivation. This equivalence can be used to show the soundness and completeness of the top-down proof procedure. As defined, the top-down proof procedure may spend extra time re-proving the same atom multiple times, whereas the bottom-up procedure proves each atom only once. However, the bottom-up procedure proves every atom, but the top-down procedure proves only atoms that are relevant to the query.

The non-deterministic top-down algorithm of Figure 5.4 together with a selection strategy induces a search graph, which is a tree. Each node in the search graph represents an answer clause. The neighbors of a node $yes \leftarrow a_1 \wedge \ldots \wedge a_m$, where a_i is the selected atom, represent all of the possible answer clauses obtained by resolving on a_i. There is a neighbor for each definite clause whose head is a_i. The goal nodes of the search are of the form $yes \leftarrow .$

Example 5.9 Given the knowledge base

$a \leftarrow b \wedge c.$	$a \leftarrow g.$	$a \leftarrow h.$
$b \leftarrow j.$	$b \leftarrow k.$	$d \leftarrow m.$
$d \leftarrow p.$	$f \leftarrow m.$	$f \leftarrow p.$
$g \leftarrow m.$	$g \leftarrow f.$	$k \leftarrow m.$
$h \leftarrow m.$	$p.$	

and the query

    ask $a \wedge d.$

The search graph for an SLD derivation, assuming the leftmost atom is selected in each answer clause, is shown in Figure 5.5 (on the next page).

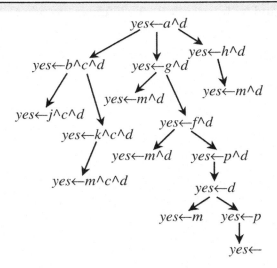

Figure 5.5: A search graph for a top-down derivation

For most problems, the search graph is not given statically, because this would entail anticipating every possible query. More realistically, the search graph is dynamically constructed as needed. All that is required is a way to generate the neighbors of a node. Selecting an atom in the answer clause defines a set of neighbors. A neighbor exists for each rule with the selected atom as its head.

Any of the search methods of Chapter 3 can be used to search the search space. Because we are only interested in whether the query is a logical consequence, we just require a path to a goal node; an optimal path is not necessary. There is a different search space for each query. A different selection of which atom to resolve at each step will result in a different search space.

5.3   Knowledge Representation Issues

5.3.1   Background Knowledge and Observations

An **observation** (page 17) is a piece of information received online from users, sensors, or other knowledge sources. For this chapter, we assume an observation is an atomic proposition. Observations are implicitly conjoined, so a set of observations is a conjunction of atoms. Neither users nor sensors provide rules directly from observing the world. The background knowledge allows the agent to do something useful with these observations.

In many reasoning frameworks, the observations are added to the background knowledge. But in other reasoning frameworks (e.g, in abduction, probabilistic reasoning, and learning), observations are treated separately from background knowledge.

Users (page 64) cannot be expected to tell us everything that is true. First, they do not know what is relevant, and second, they do not know what vocabulary to use. An **ontology** (page 61) that specifies the meaning of the symbols, and a graphical user interface to allow the user to click on what is true, may help to solve the vocabulary problem. However, many problems are too big; what is relevant depends on other things that are true, and there are too many possibly relevant truths to expect the user to specify everything that is true, even with a sophisticated graphical user interface.

Similarly, passive sensors (page 64) are able to provide direct observations of conjunctions of atomic propositions, but active sensors may have to be queried by the agent for the information that is necessary for a task.

5.3.2 Querying the User

At design time or offline, there is typically no information about particular cases. This information arrives online (page 64) from users, sensors, and external knowledge sources. For example, a medical-diagnosis program may have knowledge represented as definite clauses about the possible diseases and symptoms but it would not have knowledge about the actual symptoms manifested by a particular patient. You would not expect that the user would want to, or even be able to, volunteer all of the information about a particular case because often the user does not know what information is relevant or know the syntax of the representation language. The user would prefer to answer explicit questions put to them in a more natural language. The idea of **querying the user** is that the system can treat the user as a source of information and ask the user specific questions about a particular case. The proof procedure can determine what information is relevant and will help to prove a query.

The simplest way to get information from a user is to incorporate an **ask-the-user** mechanism into the top-down proof procedure (page 169). In such a mechanism, an atom is **askable** if the user would know the truth value at run time. The top-down proof procedure, when it has selected an atom to prove, either can use a clause in the knowledge base to prove it, or, if the atom is askable, can ask the user whether or not the atom is true. The user is thus only asked about atoms that are relevant for the query. There are three classes of atoms that can be selected:

- atoms for which the user is not expected to know the answer, so the system never asks.
- askable atoms for which the user has not already provided an answer. In this case, the user should be asked for the answer, and the answer should be recorded.
- askable atoms for which the user has already provided an answer. In this case, that answer should be used, and the user should not be asked again about this atom.

A bottom-up proof procedure can also be adapted to ask a user, but it should avoid asking about all askable atoms; see Exercise 5.5 (page 210).

It is important to note that a symmetry exists between roles of the user and roles of the system. They can both ask questions and give answers. At the top level, the user asks the system a question, and at each step the system asks a question, which is answered either by finding the relevant definite clauses or by asking the user. The whole system can be characterized by a protocol of questions and answers.

Example 5.10   In the electrical domain of Example 5.5 (page 164), one would not expect the designer of the house to know the switch positions or expect the user to know which switches are connected to which wires. It is reasonable that all of the definite clauses of Example 5.5 (page 164), except for the switch positions, should be given by the designer. The switch positions can then be made askable.

Here is a possible dialog, where the user asks a query and answers yes or no. The user interface here is minimal to show the basic idea; a real system would use a more sophisticated user-friendly interface.

ailog: ask lit_l_1.
Is up_s_1 true? [yes,no,unknown,why,help]: no.
Is $down\_s_1$ true? [yes,no,unknown,why,help]: yes.
Is $down\_s_2$ true? [yes,no,unknown,why,help]: yes.
Answer: lit_l_1.

The system only asks the user questions that the user is able to answer and that are relevant to the task at hand.

Instead of answering questions, it is sometimes preferable for a user to be able to specify if there is something strange or unusual going on. For example, a patient may not be able to specify everything that is true about them but can specify what is unusual. For example, a patient may come in and say that their left knee hurts; it is unreasonable to expect them to volunteer that their left elbow doesn't hurt and, similarly, for every other part that does not hurt. It may be possible for a sensor to specify that something has changed in a scene, even though it may not be able to recognize what is in a scene.

Given that a user specified everything that is exceptional, an agent can often infer something from the lack of knowledge. The normality will be a **default** that can be overridden with exceptional information. This idea of allowing for defaults and exceptions to the defaults is explored in Section 5.5 (page 193).

5.3.3   Knowledge-Level Explanation

The explicit use of semantics allows explanation and debugging at the **knowledge level** (page 16). To make a system usable by people, the system cannot just give an answer and expect the user to believe it. Consider the case of a system advising doctors who are legally responsible for the treatment that they carry out based on the diagnosis. The doctors must be convinced that the diagnosis is appropriate. The system must be able to justify that its answer is correct. The same features are used to explain how the system found a result and to debug the knowledge base.

Three complementary means of interrogation are used to explain the relevant knowledge: (1) a **how question** is used to explain how an answer was derived, (2) a **why question** is used to ask the system why it is asking the user a question, and (3) a **whynot question** is used to ask why an atom was not able to be proved.

To explain how an answer was derived, a "how" question can be asked by a user when the system has returned the answer. The system provides the definite clause used to deduce the answer. For any atom in the body of the definite clause, the user can ask how the system derived that atom.

The user can ask "why" in response to being asked a question. The system replies by giving the rule that produced the question. The user can then ask why the head of that rule was being proved. Together these rules allow the user to traverse a proof or a partial proof of the top-level query.

A "whynot" question can be used to ask why a particular atom was not able to be proved.

How Did the System Prove a Goal?

The first explanation procedure allows the user to ask "how" a goal was derived. If there is a proof for g, either g must be an atomic clause or there must be a rule

$$g \leftarrow a_1 \wedge \ldots \wedge a_k.$$

such that a proof exists for each a_i.

If the system has derived g, and the user asks how in response, the system can display the clause that was used to prove g. If this clause was a rule, the user can then ask

> how i.

which will give the rule that was used to prove a_i. The user can continue using the how command to explore how g was derived.

Example 5.11 In the axiomatization of Example 5.5 (page 164), the user can ask the query ask lit_l2. In response to the system proving this query, the user can ask how. The system would reply:

> $lit\_l2 \leftarrow$
>> $light\_l2 \wedge$
>> $live\_l2 \wedge$
>> $ok\_l2.$

This is the top-level rule used to prove lit_l2. To find out how $live\_l2$ was proved, the user can ask

> how 2.

The system can return the rule used to prove $live\_l_2$, namely,

> $live\_l_2 \leftarrow$
>> $live\_w_4.$

To find how $live\_w_4$ was proved, the user can ask

> how 1.

The system presents the rule

> $live\_w_4 \leftarrow$
>> $live\_w_3 \wedge$
>>
>> $up\_s_3.$

To find how first atom in the body was proved, the user can ask

> how 1.

The first atom, $live\_w_3$, was proved using the following rule:

> $live\_w_3 \leftarrow$
>> $live\_w_5 \wedge$
>>
>> $ok\_cb_1.$

To find how the second atom in the body was proved, the user can ask

> how 2.

The system will report that ok_cb_1 is explicitly given.

Notice that the explanation here was only in terms of the knowledge level, and it only gave the relevant definite clauses it has been told. The user does not have to know anything about the proof procedure or the actual computation.

Why Did the System Ask a Question?

Another useful explanation is for why a question was asked. This is useful because

- We want the system to appear intelligent. Knowing why a question was asked will increase a user's confidence that the system is working sensibly.
- One of the main measures of complexity of an interactive system is the number of questions asked of a user; you want to keep this to a minimum. Knowing why a question was asked will help the knowledge designer reduce this complexity.
- An irrelevant question is usually a symptom of a deeper problem.
- The user may learn something from the system by knowing why the system is doing something. This learning is much like an apprentice asking a master why the master is doing something.

When the system asks the user a question (q), there must be a rule used by the system that contains q in the body. The user can ask

> why.

This is read as "Why did you ask me that question?" The answer can be simply the rule that contains q in the body. If the user asks why again, the system should explain why the goal at the head of the rule was asked, and so forth. Repeatedly asking why will eventually give the path of goals to the top-level query. If all of these rules are reasonable, this justifies why the system's question to the user is reasonable.

Example 5.12 Consider the dialog of Example 5.10 (page 176). The following shows how repeated use of why can repeatedly find higher-level goals. The following dialog is for the query ask lit_l_1, with user asking the initial query, and responding with "why":

> ailog: ask lit_l_1.
> Is up_s_1 true? why.
> up_s_1 is used in the rule $live\_w_1 \leftarrow live\_w_3 \wedge up\_s_1$: why.
> $live\_w_1$ is used in the rule $live\_w_0 \leftarrow live\_w_1 \wedge up\_s_2$: why.
> $live\_w_0$ is used in the rule $live\_l_1 \leftarrow live\_w_0$: why.
> $live\_l_1$ is used in the rule $lit\_l_1 \leftarrow light\_l_1 \wedge live\_l_1 \wedge ok\_l_1$: why.
> Because that is what you asked me!

Typically, how and why are used together; how moves from higher-level to lower-level goals, and why moves from lower-level to higher-level goals. Together they let the user traverse a **proof tree**, where nodes are atoms, and a node together with its children corresponds to a clause in the knowledge base.

Example 5.13 As an example of the need to combine how and why, consider the previous example where the user asked why up_s_1. The system gave the following rule:

$$live\_w_1 \leftarrow live\_w_3 \wedge up\_s_1.$$

This means that up_s_1 was asked because the system wants to know $live\_w_1$ and is using this rule to try to prove up_s_1. The user may think it is reasonable that the system wants to know $live\_w_1$ but may think it is inappropriate that up_s_1 be asked because the user may doubt that $live\_w_3$ should have succeeded. In this case it is useful for the user to ask how $live\_w_3$ was derived.

5.3.4 Knowledge-Level Debugging

Just as in other software, there can be errors and omissions in knowledge bases. Domain experts and knowledge engineers must be able to debug a knowledge base and add knowledge. In knowledge-based systems, debugging is difficult because the domain experts and users who have the domain knowledge required to detect a bug do not necessarily know anything about the internal working of the system, nor do they want to. Standard debugging tools, such as providing traces of the execution, are useless because they require a knowledge of the mechanism by which the answer was produced. In this section, we show how the idea of semantics (page 159) can be exploited to provide powerful debugging facilities for knowledge-based systems. Whoever is debugging the system is required only to know the meaning of the symbols and whether specific atoms are true or not. This is the kind of knowledge that a domain expert and a user may have.

Knowledge-level debugging is the act of finding errors in knowledge bases with reference only to what the symbols mean. One of the goals of building knowledge-based systems that are usable by a range of domain experts is that a discussion about the correctness of a knowledge base should be a discussion about the knowledge domain. For example, debugging a medical knowledge base should be a question of medicine that medical experts, who are not experts in AI, can answer. Similarly, debugging a knowledge base about house wiring should be with reference to the particular house, not about the internals of the system reasoning with the knowledge base.

Four types of non-syntactic errors can arise in rule-based systems:

- An incorrect answer is produced; that is, some atom that is false in the intended interpretation was derived.

- Some answer was not produced; that is, the proof failed when it should have succeeded (some particular true atom was not derived).

- The program gets into an infinite loop.

- The system asks irrelevant questions.

Ways to debug the first three types of error are examined below. Irrelevant questions can be investigated using the why questions as described earlier.

Incorrect Answers

An **incorrect answer** is an answer that has been proved yet is false in the intended interpretation. It is also called a **false-positive error**. An incorrect answer can only be produced by a sound proof procedure if an incorrect definite clause was used in the proof.

Assume that whoever is debugging the knowledge base, such as a domain expert or a user, knows the intended interpretation of the symbols of the language and can determine whether a particular proposition is true or false in the intended interpretation. The person does not have to know how the answer was derived. To debug an incorrect answer, a domain expert needs only to answer yes-or-no questions.

Suppose there is an atom g that was proved yet is false in the intended interpretation. Then there must be a rule $g \leftarrow a_1 \wedge \ldots \wedge a_k$ in the knowledge base that was used to prove g. Either

- one of the a_i is false in the intended interpretation, in which case it can be debugged in the same way, or

- all of the a_i are true in the intended interpretation. In this case, the definite clause $g \leftarrow a_1 \wedge \ldots \wedge a_k$ must be incorrect.

```
1:  procedure Debug(g, KB)
2:      Inputs
3:          KB a knowledge base
4:          g an atom: KB ⊢ g and g is false in intended interpretation
5:      Output
6:          clause in KB that is false
7:      Find definite clause g ← a₁ ∧ ... ∧ aₖ ∈ KB used to prove g
8:      for each aᵢ do
9:          ask user whether aᵢ is true
10:         if user specifies aᵢ is false then
11:             return Debug(aᵢ, KB)
12:     return g ← a₁ ∧ ... ∧ aₖ
```

Figure 5.6: An algorithm to debug incorrect answers

This leads to an algorithm, presented in Figure 5.6, to debug a knowledge base when an atom that is false in the intended interpretation is derived. This only requires the person debugging the knowledge base to be able to answer yes-or-no questions.

This procedure can also be carried out by the use of the *how* command (page 177). Given a proof for g that is false in the intended interpretation, a user can ask how that atom was proved. This will return the definite clause that was used in the proof. If the clause was a rule, the user could use *how* to ask about an atom in the body that was false in the intended interpretation. This will return the rule that was used to prove that atom. The user can repeat this until a definite clause is found where all of the elements of the body are true (or there are no elements in the body). This is the incorrect definite clause. The method of debugging assumes that the user can determine whether an atom is true or false in the intended interpretation. The user does not have to know the proof procedure used.

Example 5.14 Consider Example 5.5 (page 164), involving the electrical domain, but assume there is a bug in the program. Suppose that the domain expert or user had inadvertently said that whether w_1 is connected to w_3 depends on the status of s_3 instead of s_1 (see Figure 1.8 (page 34)). Thus, the knowledge includes the following incorrect rule:

$$live\_w_1 \leftarrow live\_w_3 \land up\_s_3.$$

All of the other axioms are the same as in Example 5.5. Given this axiom set, the atom lit_l_1 can be derived, which is false in the intended interpretation. Consider how a user would go about finding this incorrect definite clause when they detected this incorrect answer.

Given that lit_l_1 is false in the intended interpretation, they ask how it was derived, which will give the following rule:

$$lit\_l_1 \leftarrow light\_l_1 \land live\_l_1 \land ok\_l_1.$$

They check the atoms in the body of this rule. $light\_l_1$ and ok_l_1 are true in the intended interpretation, but $live\_l_1$ is false in the intended interpretation. So they ask

> how 2.

The system presents the rule

> $live\_l_1 \leftarrow live\_w_0.$

$live\_w_0$ is false in the intended interpretation, so they ask

> how 1.

The system presents the rule

> $live\_w_0 \leftarrow live\_w_1 \wedge up\_s_2.$

$live\_w_1$ is false in the intended interpretation, so they ask

> how 1.

The system presents the rule

> $live\_w_1 \leftarrow live\_w_3 \wedge up\_s_3.$

Both elements of the body are true in the intended interpretation, so this is the buggy rule.

The user or domain expert can find the buggy definite clause without having to know the internal workings of the system or how the proof was found. They only require knowledge about the intended interpretation and the disciplined use of how.

Missing Answers

The second type of error occurs when an expected answer is not produced. This manifests itself by a failure when an answer is expected. A goal g that is true in the domain, but is not a consequence of the knowledge base, is called a **false-negative error**.

The preceding algorithm does not work in this case. There is no proof. We must look for why there is no proof for g.

An appropriate answer is not produced only if a definite clause or clauses are missing from the knowledge base. By knowing the intended interpretation of the symbols and by knowing what queries should succeed (i.e, what is true in the intended interpretation), a domain expert can debug a missing answer. Given an atom that failed when it should have succeeded, Figure 5.7 shows how to find an atom for which there is a missing definite clause.

Suppose g is an atom that should have a proof, but which fails. Because the proof for g fails, the bodies of all of the definite clauses with g in the head fail.

- Suppose one of these definite clauses for g should have resulted in a proof; this means all of the atoms in the body must be true in the intended interpretation. Because the body failed, there must be an atom in

```
 1: procedure DebugMissing(g, KB)
 2:    Inputs
 3:        KB a knowledge base
 4:        g an atom: KB ⊬ g and g is true in the intended interpretation
 5:    Output
 6:        atom for which there is a clause missing
 7:    if there is a definite clause g ← a₁ ∧ . . . ∧ aₖ ∈ KB such that all aᵢ are
    true in the intended interpretation then
 8:        select aᵢ that cannot be proved
 9:        DebugMissing(aᵢ, KB)
10:    else
11:        return g
```

Figure 5.7: An algorithm for debugging missing answers

the body that fails. This atom is then true in the intended interpretation, but fails. So we can recursively debug it.

- Otherwise, there is no definite clause applicable to proving g, so the user must add a definite clause for g.

Example 5.15 Suppose that, for the axiomatization of the electrical domain in Example 5.5 (page 164), the world of Figure 1.8 (page 34) actually had s_2 down. Thus, it is missing the definite clause specifying that s_2 is down. The axiomatization of Example 5.5 fails to prove lit_l_1 when it should succeed. Let's find the bug.

lit_l_1 failed, so we find all of the rules with lit_l_1 in the head. There is one such rule:

$$lit\_l_1 \leftarrow light\_l_1 \land live\_l_1 \land ok\_l_1.$$

The user can then verify that all of the elements of the body are true. $light\_l_1$ and ok_l_1 can both be derived, but $live\_l_1$ fails, so we debug this atom. There is one rule with $live\_l_1$ in the head:

$$live\_l_1 \leftarrow live\_w_0.$$

The atom $live\_w_0$ cannot be proved, but the user verifies that it is true in the intended interpretation. So we find the rules for $live\_w_0$:

$$live\_w_0 \leftarrow live\_w_1 \land up\_s_2.$$
$$live\_w_0 \leftarrow live\_w_2 \land down\_s_2.$$

The user can say that the body of the second rule is true. A proof exists for $live\_w_2$, but there are no definite clauses for $down\_s_2$, so this atom is returned. The correction is to add the appropriate atomic clause or rule for it.

Infinite Loops

There is an infinite loop in the top-down derivation if there is an atom a that is being proved as a subgoal of a. (Here we assume that being a subgoal is transitive; a subgoal of a subgoal is a subgoal). Thus, there can be an infinite loop only if the knowledge base is cyclic. A knowledge base is **cyclic** if there is an atom a such that there is a sequence of definite clauses of the form

$$a \leftarrow \ldots a_1 \ldots$$
$$a_1 \leftarrow \ldots a_2 \ldots$$
$$\ldots$$
$$a_n \leftarrow \ldots a \ldots$$

(where if $n = 0$ there is a single definite clause with a in the head and body).

A knowledge base is **acyclic** if there is an assignment of natural numbers (non-negative integers) to the atoms so that the atoms in the body of a definite clause are assigned a lower number than the atom in the head. All of the knowledge bases given previously in this chapter are acyclic. There cannot be an infinite loop in an acyclic knowledge base.

To detect a cyclic knowledge base, the top-down proof procedure can be modified to maintain the set of all **ancestors** for each atom in the proof. In the procedure in Figure 5.4 (page 172), the set A can contain pairs of an atom and its set of ancestors.

Initially the set of ancestors of each atom is empty. When the rule

$$a \leftarrow a_1 \wedge \ldots \wedge a_k$$

is used to prove a, the ancestors of a_i will be the ancestors of a together with a. That is,

$$ancestors(a_i) = ancestors(a) \cup \{a\}.$$

The proof can fail if an atom is in its set of ancestors. This failure only occurs if the knowledge base is cyclic. Note that this is a more refined version of cycle checking (page 93), where each atom has its own set of ancestors.

A cyclic knowledge base is often a sign of a bug. When writing a knowledge base, it is often useful to ensure an acyclic knowledge base by identifying a value that is being reduced at each iteration. For example, in the electrical domain, the number of steps away from the outside of the house is meant to be reduced by one each time through the loop. Disciplined and explicit use of a well-founded ordering can be used to prevent infinite loops in the same way that programs in traditional languages must be carefully programmed to prevent infinite looping.

Note that the bottom-up proof procedure does not get into an infinite loop, because it selects a rule only when the head has not been derived.

5.4 Proving by Contradictions

Definite clauses can be used in a proof by contradiction by allowing rules that give contradictions. For example, in the electrical wiring domain (page 164), it is useful to be able to specify that some prediction, such as light l_2 is on, is not true. This will enable diagnostic reasoning to deduce that some switches, lights, or circuit breakers are broken.

5.4.1 Horn Clauses

The definite clause language does not allow a contradiction to be stated. However, a simple expansion of the language can allow proof by contradiction.

An **integrity constraint** is a clause of the form

$$false \leftarrow a_1 \wedge \ldots \wedge a_k.$$

where the a_i are atoms and *false* is a special atom that is false in all interpretations.

A **Horn clause** is either a definite clause (page 163) or an integrity constraint. That is, a Horn clause has either *false* or a normal atom as its head.

Integrity constraints allow the system to prove that some conjunction of atoms is false in all models of a knowledge base – that is, to prove disjunctions of negations of atoms. Recall (page 158) that $\neg p$ is the **negation** of p, which is true in an interpretation when p is false in that interpretation, and $p \vee q$ is the **disjunction** of p and q, which is true in an interpretation if p is true or q is true or both are true in the interpretation. The integrity constraint $false \leftarrow a_1 \wedge \ldots \wedge a_k$ is logically equivalent to $\neg a_1 \vee \ldots \vee \neg a_k$.

A Horn clause knowledge base can imply negations of atoms, as shown in Example 5.16.

> **Example 5.16** Consider the knowledge base KB_1:
>
> $false \leftarrow a \wedge b.$
> $a \leftarrow c.$
> $b \leftarrow c.$
>
> The atom c is false in all models of KB_1. If c were true in model I of KB_1, then a and b would both be true in I (otherwise I would not be a model of KB_1). Because *false* is false in I and a and b are true in I, the first clause is false in I, a contradiction to I being a model of KB_1. Thus, c is false in all models of KB_1. This is expressed as
>
> $KB_1 \models \neg c$
>
> which means that $\neg c$ is true in all models of KB_1, and so c is false in all models of KB_1.

Although the language of Horn clauses does not allow disjunctions and negations to be input, disjunctions of negations of atoms can be derived, as Example 5.17 (on the next page) shows.

Example 5.17 Consider the knowledge base KB_2:

$false \leftarrow a \wedge b.$

$a \leftarrow c.$

$b \leftarrow d.$

$b \leftarrow e.$

Either c is false or d is false in every model of KB_2. If they were both true in some model I of KB_2, both a and b would be true in I, so the first clause would be false in I, a contradiction to I being a model of KB_2. Similarly, either c is false or e is false in every model of KB_2. Thus,

$KB_2 \models \neg c \vee \neg d.$

$KB_2 \models \neg c \vee \neg e.$

A set of clauses is **unsatisfiable** if it has no models. A set of clauses is provably **inconsistent** with respect to a proof procedure if $false$ can be derived from the clauses using that proof procedure. If a proof procedure is sound and complete, a set of clauses is provably inconsistent if and only if it is unsatisfiable.

It is always possible to find a model for a set of definite clauses. The interpretation with all atoms true is a model of any set of definite clauses. Thus, a definite-clause knowledge base is always satisfiable. However, a set of Horn clauses can be unsatisfiable.

Example 5.18 The set of clauses $\{a, false \leftarrow a\}$ is unsatisfiable. There is no interpretation that satisfies both clauses. Both a and $false \leftarrow a$ cannot be true in any interpretation.

Both the top-down and the bottom-up proof procedures can be used to prove inconsistency, by using $false$ as the query. That is, a Horn clause knowledge base is inconsistent if and only if $false$ can be derived.

5.4.2 Assumables and Conflicts

Reasoning from contradictions is a very useful tool. For many activities it is useful to know that some combination of assumptions is incompatible. For example, it is useful in planning to know that some combination of actions an agent is trying to do is impossible. It is useful in design to know that some combination of components cannot work together.

In a diagnostic application it is useful to be able to prove that some components working normally is inconsistent with the observations of the system. Consider a system that has a description of how it is supposed to work and some observations. If the system does not work according to its specification, a diagnostic agent must identify which components could be faulty.

To carry out these tasks it is useful to be able to make assumptions that can be proved to be false.

An **assumable** is an atom that can be assumed in a proof by contradiction. A proof by contradiction derives a disjunction of the negation of the assumables.

With a Horn clause knowledge base and explicit assumabes, if the system can prove a contradiction from some assumptions, it can extract combinations of assumptions that cannot all be true.

In a definite-clause knowledge base, a query (page 166) is used to ask if a proposition is a consequence of the knowledge base. Given a query, the system tries to construct a proof for the query. With a proof by contradiction, the system tries to prove *false*. The user must specify what is allowable as part of an answer.

If *KB* is a set of Horn clauses, a **conflict** of *KB* is a set of assumables that, given *KB*, implies *false*. That is, $C = \{c_1, \ldots, c_r\}$ is a conflict of *KB* if

$$KB \cup \{c_1, \ldots, c_r\} \models false.$$

In this case, an **answer** is

$$KB \models \neg c_1 \vee \ldots \vee \neg c_r.$$

A **minimal conflict** is a conflict such that no strict subset is also a conflict.

Example 5.19 In Example 5.17, if $\{c, d, e, f, g, h\}$ is the set of assumables, then $\{c, d\}$ and $\{c, e\}$ are minimal conflicts of KB_2; $\{c, d, e, h\}$ is also a conflict, but not a minimal conflict.

In the examples that follow, the assumables are specified using the assumable keyword followed by one or more assumable atoms separated by commas.

5.4.3 Consistency-Based Diagnosis

Making assumptions about what is working normally, and deriving what components could be abnormal, is the basis of **consistency-based diagnosis**. Suppose a **fault** is something that is wrong with a system. The aim of consistency-based diagnosis is to determine the possible faults based on a model of the system and observations of the system. By making the absence of faults assumable, conflicts can be used to prove what is wrong with the system.

Example 5.20 Consider the house wiring example depicted in Figure 5.2 (page 164) and represented in Example 5.5 (page 164). A background knowledge base suitable for consistency-based diagnosis is given in Figure 5.8 (on the next page). Normality assumptions are added to the clauses to make explicit the assumption that the components work. We have added conditions that switches, circuit breakers, and lights must be okay to work as expected. There are no clauses for the *ok* atoms, but they are made assumable.

The user is able to observe the switch positions and whether a light is lit or dark.

$light\_l_1$.

$light\_l_2$.

$live\_outside$.

$live\_l_1 \leftarrow live\_w_0$.

$live\_w_0 \leftarrow live\_w_1 \wedge up\_s_2 \wedge ok\_s_2$.

$live\_w_0 \leftarrow live\_w_2 \wedge down\_s_2 \wedge ok\_s_2$.

$live\_w_1 \leftarrow live\_w_3 \wedge up\_s_1 \wedge ok\_s_1$.

$live\_w_2 \leftarrow live\_w_3 \wedge down\_s_1 \wedge ok\_s_1$.

$live\_l_2 \leftarrow live\_w_4$.

$live\_w_4 \leftarrow live\_w_3 \wedge up\_s_3 \wedge ok\_s_3$.

$live\_p_1 \leftarrow live\_w_3$.

$live\_w_3 \leftarrow live\_w_5 \wedge ok\_cb_1$.

$live\_p_2 \leftarrow live\_w_6$.

$live\_w_6 \leftarrow live\_w_5 \wedge ok\_cb_2$.

$live\_w_5 \leftarrow live\_outside$.

$lit\_l_1 \leftarrow light\_l_1 \wedge live\_l_1 \wedge ok\_l_1$.

$lit\_l_2 \leftarrow light\_l_2 \wedge live\_l_2 \wedge ok\_l_2$.

$false \leftarrow dark\_l_1 \wedge lit\_l_1$.

$false \leftarrow dark\_l_2 \wedge lit\_l_2$.

assumable $ok\_cb_1, ok\_cb_2, ok\_s_1, ok\_s_2, ok\_s_3, ok\_l_1, ok\_l_2$.

Figure 5.8: Knowledge for Example 5.20

A light cannot be both lit and dark. This knowledge is stated in the following integrity constraints:

$false \leftarrow dark\_l_1 \wedge lit\_l_1$.

$false \leftarrow dark\_l_2 \wedge lit\_l_2$.

Suppose the user observes that all three switches are up, and that l_1 and l_2 are both dark. This is represented by the atomic clauses

up_s_1.

up_s_2.

up_s_3.

$dark\_l_1$.

$dark\_l_2$.

Given the knowledge of Figure 5.8 together with the observations, two minimal conflicts exist, namely

$$\{ok\_cb_1, ok\_s_1, ok\_s_2, ok\_l_1\} \text{ and}$$
$$\{ok\_cb_1, ok\_s_3, ok\_l_2\}.$$

Thus, it follows that

$$KB \models \neg ok\_cb_1 \vee \neg ok\_s_1 \vee \neg ok\_s_2 \vee \neg ok\_l_1$$
$$KB \models \neg ok\_cb_1 \vee \neg ok\_s_3 \vee \neg ok\_l_2,$$

which means that at least one of the components cb_1, s_1, s_2, or l_1 must not be okay, and least one of the components cb_1, s_3, or l_2 must not be okay.

Given the set of all conflicts, a user can determine what may be wrong with the system being diagnosed. However, given a set of conflicts, it is often difficult to determine if all of the conflicts could be explained by a few faults. Some of the questions that a user may want to know are whether all of the conflicts could be accounted for a by a single fault or a pair of faults.

Given a set of conflicts, a **consistency-based diagnosis** is a set of assumables that has at least one element in each conflict. A **minimal diagnosis** is a diagnosis such that no subset is also a diagnosis. For one of the diagnoses, all of its elements must be false in the world being modeled.

Example 5.21 Let's continue Example 5.20 (page 187). Because the disjunction of the negation of the two conflicts is a logical consequence of the clauses, the conjunction

$$(\neg ok\_cb_1 \vee \neg ok\_s_1 \vee \neg ok\_s_2 \vee \neg ok\_l_1)$$
$$\wedge (\neg ok\_cb_1 \vee \neg ok\_s_3 \vee \neg ok\_l_2)$$

follows from the knowledge base. This conjunction of disjunctions can be distributed into **disjunctive normal form (DNF)**, a disjunction of conjunctions of negated atoms:

$$\neg ok\_cb_1 \vee$$
$$(\neg ok\_s_1 \wedge \neg ok\_s_3) \vee (\neg ok\_s_1 \wedge \neg ok\_l_2) \vee$$
$$(\neg ok\_s_2 \wedge \neg ok\_s_3) \vee (\neg ok\_s_2 \wedge \neg ok\_l_2) \vee$$
$$(\neg ok\_l_1 \wedge \neg ok\_s_3) \vee (\neg ok\_l_1 \wedge \neg ok\_l_2).$$

Thus, either cb_1 is broken or there is at least one of six double faults.

The propositions that are disjoined together correspond to the seven minimal diagnoses: $\{ok\_cb_1\}$, $\{ok\_s_1, ok\_s_3\}$, $\{ok\_s_1, ok\_l_2\}$, $\{ok\_s_2, ok\_s_3\}$, $\{ok\_s_2, ok\_l_2\}$, $\{ok\_l_1, ok\_s_3\}$, $\{ok\_l_1, ok\_l_2\}$. The system has proved that one of these combinations must be faulty.

```
1: procedure ConflictBU(KB, Assumables)
2:    Inputs
3:        KB: a set Horn clauses
4:        Assumables: a set of atoms that can be assumed
5:    Output
6:        set of conflicts
7:    Local
8:        C is a set of pairs of an atom and a set of assumables
9:    C := {⟨a, {a}⟩ : a is assumable}
10:   repeat
11:       select clause "h ← b₁ ∧ ... ∧ bₘ" in KB such that
12:           ⟨bᵢ, Aᵢ⟩ ∈ C for all i and
13:           ⟨h, A⟩ ∉ C where A = A₁ ∪ ... ∪ Aₘ
14:       C := C ∪ {⟨h, A⟩}
15:   until no more selections are possible
16:   return {A : ⟨false, A⟩ ∈ C}
```

Figure 5.9: Bottom-up proof procedure for computing conflicts

5.4.4 Reasoning with Assumptions and Horn Clauses

This section presents a bottom-up implementation and a top-down implementation for finding conflicts in Horn clause knowledge bases.

Bottom-Up Implementation

The bottom-up implementation is an augmented version of the bottom-up algorithm for definite clauses presented in Section 5.2.2 (page 167).

The modification to that algorithm is that the conclusions are pairs $\langle a, A \rangle$, where a is an atom and A is a set of assumables that imply a in the context of Horn clause knowledge base KB.

Initially, the conclusion set C is $\{\langle a, \{a\} \rangle : a$ is assumable$\}$. Clauses can be used to derive new conclusions. If there is a clause $h \leftarrow b_1 \wedge \ldots \wedge b_m$ such that for each b_i there is some A_i such that $\langle b_i, A_i \rangle \in C$, then $\langle h, A_1 \cup \ldots \cup A_m \rangle$ can be added to C. Note that this covers the case of atomic clauses, with $m = 0$, where $\langle h, \{\} \rangle$ is added to C. Figure 5.9 gives code for the algorithm.

When the pair $\langle false, A \rangle$ is generated, the assumptions A form a conflict.

One refinement of this program is to prune supersets of assumptions. If $\langle a, A_1 \rangle$ and $\langle a, A_2 \rangle$ are in C, where $A_1 \subset A_2$, then $\langle a, A_2 \rangle$ can be removed from C or not added to C. There is no reason to use the extra assumptions to imply a. Similarly, if $\langle false, A_1 \rangle$ and $\langle a, A_2 \rangle$ are in C, where $A_1 \subseteq A_2$, then $\langle a, A_2 \rangle$ can be removed from C because A_1 and any superset – including A_2 – are inconsistent with the clauses given, and so nothing more can be learned from considering such sets of assumables.

Example 5.22 Consider the axiomatization of Figure 5.8 (page 188), discussed in Example 5.20 (page 187).

Initially, in the algorithm of Figure 5.9, C has the value

$$\{\langle ok\_l_1, \{ok\_l_1\}\rangle, \langle ok\_l_2, \{ok\_l_2\}\rangle, \langle ok\_s_1, \{ok\_s_1\}\rangle, \langle ok\_s_2, \{ok\_s_2\}\rangle,$$
$$\langle ok\_s_3, \{ok\_s_3\}\rangle, \langle ok\_cb_1, \{ok\_cb_1\}\rangle, \langle ok\_cb_2, \{ok\_cb_2\}\rangle\}.$$

The following shows a sequence of values added to C under one sequence of selections:

$\langle live\_outside, \{\}\rangle$
$\langle live\_w5, \{\}\rangle$
$\langle live\_w3, \{ok\_cb_1\}\rangle$
$\langle up\_s3, \{\}\rangle$
$\langle live\_w4, \{ok\_cb_1, ok\_s3\}\rangle$
$\langle live\_l_2, \{ok\_cb_1, ok\_s3\}\rangle$
$\langle light\_l_2, \{\}\rangle$
$\langle lit\_l_2, \{ok\_cb_1, ok\_s3, ok\_l_2\}\rangle$
$\langle dark\_l_2, \{\}\rangle$
$\langle false, \{ok\_cb_1, ok\_s3, ok\_l_2\}\rangle$.

Thus, the knowledge base entails

$$\neg ok\_cb_1 \vee \neg ok\_s3 \vee \neg ok\_l_2.$$

The other conflict can be found by continuing the algorithm.

Top-Down Implementation

The top-down implementation is similar to the top-down definite clause interpreter described in Figure 5.4 (page 172), except the top-level goal is to prove *false*, and the assumables encountered in a proof are not proved but collected.

1: **non-deterministic procedure** *ConflictTD*(KB,Assumables)
2:    **Inputs**
3:       *KB*: a set Horn clauses
4:       *Assumables*: a set of atoms that can be assumed
5:    **Output**
6:       A conflict
7:    **Local**
8:       *G* is a set of atoms (that implies false)
9:    $G := \{false\}$
10:    **repeat**
11:       **select** an atom a_i from G such that $a_i \notin Assumables$
12:       **choose** clause C in *KB* with a_i as head
13:       replace a_i in G by the atoms in the body of C
14:    **until** $G \subseteq Assumables$
15:    **return** G

Figure 5.10: Top-down Horn clause interpreter to find conflicts

The algorithm is shown in Figure 5.10. Different choices can lead to different conflicts being found. If no choices are available, the algorithm fails.

Example 5.23 Consider the representation of the circuit in Example 5.20 (page 187). The following is a sequence of the values of G for one sequence of selections and choices that leads to a conflict:

$\{false\}$
$\{dark\_l_1, lit\_l_1\}$
$\{lit\_l_1\}$
$\{light\_l_1, live\_l_1, ok\_l_1\}$
$\{live\_l_1, ok\_l_1\}$
$\{live\_w_0, ok\_l_1\}$
$\{live\_w_1, up\_s_2, ok\_s_2, ok\_l_1\}$
$\{live\_w_3, up\_s_1, ok\_s_1, up\_s_2, ok\_s_2, ok\_l_1\}$
$\{live\_w_5, ok\_cb_1, up\_s_1, ok\_s_1, up\_s_2, ok\_s_2, ok\_l_1\}$
$\{live\_outside, ok\_cb_1, up\_s_1, ok\_s_1, up\_s_2, ok\_s_2, ok\_l_1\}$
$\{ok\_cb_1, up\_s_1, ok\_s_1, up\_s_2, ok\_s_2, ok\_l_1\}$
$\{ok\_cb_1, ok\_s_1, up\_s_2, ok\_s_2, ok\_l_1\}$
$\{ok\_cb_1, ok\_s_1, ok\_s_2, ok\_l_1\}.$

The set $\{ok\_cb_1, ok\_s_1, ok\_s_2, ok\_l_1\}$ is returned as a conflict. Different choices of the clause to use can lead to another answer.

5.5 Complete Knowledge Assumption

A database is often complete in the sense that anything not stated is false.

> **Example 5.24** You may want the user to specify which switches are up and which circuit breakers are broken so that the system can conclude that any switch not mentioned as up is down and any circuit breaker not specified as broken is okay. Thus, down is the default value of switches, and okay is the default value for circuit breakers. It is easier for users to communicate using defaults than it is to specify the seemingly redundant information about which switches are down and which circuit breakers are okay. To reason with such defaults, an agent must assume it has complete knowledge; a switch's position is not mentioned because it is down, not because the agent does not know whether it is up or down.

The given definite-clause logic does not allow the derivation of a conclusion from a lack of knowledge or a failure to prove. It does not assume that the knowledge is complete. In particular, the negation of an atom can never be a logical consequence of a definite-clause knowledge base.

The **complete knowledge assumption** assumes that, for every atom, the clauses with the atom as the head cover all the cases when the atom is true. Under this assumption, an agent can conclude that an atom is false if it cannot derive that the atom is true. This is also called the **closed-world assumption**. It can be contrasted with the **open-world assumption**, which is that the agent does not know everything and so cannot make any conclusions from a lack of knowledge. The closed-world assumption requires that everything relevant about the world be known to the agent.

When there are rules for an atom, the assumption is that the rules for each atom cover all of the cases where the atom is true. In particular, suppose the rules for atom a are

$$a \leftarrow b_1.$$
$$\vdots$$
$$a \leftarrow b_n.$$

where an atomic clause a is the rule $a \leftarrow true$. The complete knowledge assumption says that if a is true in some interpretation then one of the b_i must be true in that interpretation; that is,

$$a \rightarrow b_1 \vee \ldots \vee b_n.$$

Because the clauses defining a are equivalent to

$$a \leftarrow b_1 \vee \ldots \vee b_n,$$

the meaning of the clauses can be seen as the conjunction of these two propositions, namely, the equivalence:

$$a \leftrightarrow b_1 \vee \ldots \vee b_n,$$

where $\leftrightarrow$ is read as "if and only if" (see Figure 5.1 (page 159)). This equivalence is called **Clark's completion** of the clauses for a. Clark's completion of a knowledge base is the completion for each atom in the knowledge base.

Clark's completion means that if there are no rules for an atom a, the completion of this atom is $a \leftrightarrow false$, which means that a is false.

Example 5.25 Consider the following clauses from Example 5.5 (page 164):

$down\_s_1.$

$up\_s_2.$

$live\_l_1 \leftarrow live\_w_0.$

$live\_w_0 \leftarrow live\_w_1 \wedge up\_s_2.$

$live\_w_0 \leftarrow live\_w_2 \wedge down\_s_2.$

$live\_w_1 \leftarrow live\_w_3 \wedge up\_s_1.$

Suppose that these are the only clauses for the atoms in the heads of these clauses, and there are no clauses for up_s_1 or $down\_s_2$. The completion of these atoms is

$down\_s_1 \leftrightarrow true.$

$up\_s_1 \leftrightarrow false.$

$up\_s_2 \leftrightarrow true.$

$down\_s_2 \leftrightarrow false.$

$live\_l_1 \leftrightarrow live\_w_0.$

$live\_w_0 \leftrightarrow (live\_w_1 \wedge up\_s_2) \vee (live\_w_2 \wedge down\_s_2).$

$live\_w_1 \leftrightarrow live\_w_3 \wedge up\_s_1.$

This implies that up_s_1 is false, and $live\_w_1$ is false.

With the completion, the system can derive negations, and so it is useful to extend the language to allow negations in the body of clauses. A **literal** is either an atom or the negation of an atom. The definition of a definite clause (page 163) can be extended to allow literals in the body rather than just atoms. We write the negation of atom a under the complete knowledge assumption as $\sim a$ to distinguish it from classical negation that does not assume the completion. This negation is often called **negation as failure**.

Under negation as failure, body g is a consequence of the knowledge base KB if $KB' \models g$, where KB' is Clark's completion of KB. A negation $\sim a$ in the body of a clause or the query becomes $\neg a$ in the completion. That is, a query following from a knowledge base under the complete knowledge assumption means that the query is a logical consequence of the completion of the knowledge base.

Example 5.26 Consider the axiomatization of Example 5.5 (page 164). Representing a domain can be made simpler by expecting the user to tell the system only what switches are up and by the system concluding that a switch is down if it has not been told the switch is up. This can be done by adding the following rules:

$down\_s_1 \leftarrow \sim up\_s_1.$

$down\_s_2 \leftarrow \sim up\_s_2.$

$down\_s_3 \leftarrow \sim up\_s_3.$

Similarly, the system may conclude that the circuit breakers are okay unless it has been told they are broken:

$ok\_cb_1 \leftarrow \sim broken\_cb_1.$

$ok\_cb_2 \leftarrow \sim broken\_cb_2.$

Although this may look more complicated than the previous representation, it means that is it easier for the user to specify what is occurring in a particular situation. The user has to specify only what is up and what is broken. This may save time if being down is normal for switches and being okay is normal for circuit breakers.

To represent the state of Figure 5.2 (page 164), the user specifies

$up\_s_2.$

$up\_s_3.$

The system can infer that s_1 must be down and both circuit breakers are okay. The completion of the knowledge base is

$down\_s_1 \leftrightarrow \neg up\_s_1.$

$down\_s_2 \leftrightarrow \neg up\_s_2.$

$down\_s_3 \leftrightarrow \neg up\_s_3.$

$ok\_cb_1 \leftrightarrow \neg broken\_cb_1.$

$ok\_cb_2 \leftrightarrow \neg broken\_cb_2.$

$up\_s_1 \leftrightarrow false.$

$up\_s_2 \leftrightarrow true.$

$up\_s_3 \leftrightarrow true.$

$broken\_cb_1 \leftrightarrow false.$

$broken\_cb_2 \leftrightarrow false.$

Notice that atoms in bodies of clauses but not in the head of any clauses are false in the completion.

Recall that a knowledge base is **acyclic** (page 184) if there is an assignment of natural numbers (non-negative integers) to the atoms so that the atoms in the body of a clause are assigned a lower number than the atom in the head. With negation as failure, non-acyclic knowledge bases become semantically problematic.

The following knowledge base is not acyclic:

$a \leftarrow \sim b.$

$b \leftarrow \sim a.$

Clark's completion of this knowledge base is equivalent to $a \leftrightarrow \neg b$, which just specifies that a and b have different truth values but not which one is true.

The following knowledge base is not acyclic:

$$a \leftarrow {\sim}a.$$

Clark's completion of this knowledge base is $a \leftrightarrow \neg a$, which is logically inconsistent.

Clark's completion of an acyclic knowledge base is always consistent and always gives a truth value to each atom. For the rest of this chapter, we assume that the knowledge bases are acyclic.

5.5.1 Non-monotonic Reasoning

The definite clause logic is **monotonic** in the sense that anything that could be concluded before a clause is added can still be concluded after it is added; adding knowledge does not reduce the set of propositions that can be derived.

A logic is **non-monotonic** if some conclusions can be invalidated by adding more knowledge. The logic of definite clauses with negation as failure is non-monotonic. Non-monotonic reasoning is useful for representing defaults. A **default** is a rule that can be used unless it overridden by an exception.

For example, to say that b is normally true if c is true, a knowledge base designer can write a rule of the form

$$b \leftarrow c \wedge {\sim}ab_a.$$

where ab_a is an atom that means abnormal with respect to some aspect a. Given c, the agent can infer b unless it is told ab_a. Adding ab_a to the knowledge base can prevent the conclusion of b. Rules that imply ab_a can be used to prevent the default under the conditions of the body of the rule.

Example 5.27 Suppose the purchasing agent is investigating purchasing holidays. A resort may be adjacent to a beach or away from a beach. This is not symmetric; if the resort was adjacent to a beach, the knowledge provider would specify this. Thus, it is reasonable to have the clause

$$away\_from\_beach \leftarrow {\sim}on\_beach.$$

This clause enables an agent to infer that a resort is away from the beach if the agent is not told it is adjacent to a beach.

A **cooperative system** tries to not mislead. If we are told the resort is on the beach, we would expect that resort users would have access to the beach. If they have access to a beach, we would expect them to be able to swim at the beach. Thus, we would expect the following defaults:

$$beach\_access \leftarrow on\_beach \wedge {\sim}ab_{beach\_access}.$$
$$swim\_at\_beach \leftarrow beach\_access \wedge {\sim}ab_{swim\_at\_beach}.$$

A cooperative system would tell us if a resort on the beach has no beach access or if there is no swimming. We could also specify that, if there is an enclosed bay and a big city, then there is no swimming, by default:

$$ab_{swim\_at\_beach} \leftarrow enclosed\_bay \wedge big\_city \wedge \sim ab_{no\_swimming\_near\_city}.$$

We could say that British Columbia is abnormal with respect to swimming near cities:

$$ab_{no\_swimming\_near\_city} \leftarrow in\_BC \wedge \sim ab_{BC\_beaches}.$$

Given only the preceding rules, an agent infers *away_from_beach*. If it is then told *on_beach*, it can no longer infer *away_from_beach*, but it can now infer *beach_access* and *swim_at_beach*. If it is also told *enclosed_bay* and *big_city*, it can no longer infer *swim_at_beach*. However, if it is then told *in_BC*, it can then infer *swim_at_beach*.

By having defaults of what is normal, a user can interact with the system by telling it what is abnormal, which allows for economy in communication. The user does not have to state the obvious.

One way to think about non-monotonic reasoning is in terms of **arguments**. The rules can be used as components of arguments, in which the negated abnormality gives a way to undermine arguments. Note that, in the language presented, only positive arguments exist that can be undermined. In more general theories, there can be positive and negative arguments that attack each other.

5.5.2 Proof Procedures for Complete Knowledge

Bottom-Up Procedure

The bottom-up procedure for negation as failure is a modification of the bottom-up procedure for definite clauses (page 167). The difference is that it can add literals of the form $\sim p$ to the set C of consequences that have been derived; $\sim p$ is added to C when it can determine that p must fail.

Failure can be defined recursively: p **fails** when every body of a clause with p as the head fails. A body fails if one of the literals in the body fails. An atom b_i in a body fails if $\sim b_i$ has been derived. A negation $\sim b_i$ in a body fails if b_i has been derived.

Figure 5.11 (on the next page) gives a bottom-up negation-as-failure interpreter for computing consequents of a ground KB. Note that this includes the case of a clause with an empty body (in which case $m = 0$, and the atom at the head is added to C) and the case of an atom that does not appear in the head of any clause (in which case its negation is added to C).

1: **procedure** *NAFBU(KB)*
2:     **Inputs**
3:         *KB*: a set of clauses that can include negation as failure
4:     **Output**
5:         set of literals that follow from the completion of *KB*
6:     **Local**
7:         *C* is a set of literals
8:     $C := \{\}$
9:     **repeat**
10:        **either**
11:            **select** $r \in KB$ such that
12:                *r* is "$h \leftarrow b_1 \wedge \ldots \wedge b_m$"
13:                $b_i \in C$ for all *i*, and
14:                $h \notin C$;
15:            $C := C \cup \{h\}$
16:        **or**
17:            **select** *h* such that $\sim h \notin C$ and
18:                where for every clause "$h \leftarrow b_1 \wedge \ldots \wedge b_m$" $\in KB$
19:                    either for some $b_i, \sim b_i \in C$
20:                    or some $b_i = \sim g$ and $g \in C$
21:            $C := C \cup \{\sim h\}$
22:    **until** no more selections are possible

Figure 5.11: Bottom-up negation as failure proof procedure

Example 5.28 Consider the following clauses:

$p \leftarrow q \wedge \sim r.$
$p \leftarrow s.$
$q \leftarrow \sim s.$
$r \leftarrow \sim t.$
$t.$
$s \leftarrow w.$

The following is a possible sequence of literals added to *C*:

$t,$
$\sim r,$
$\sim w,$
$\sim s,$
$q,$
$p,$

where t is derived trivially because it is given as an atomic clause; $\sim r$ is derived because $t \in C$; $\sim w$ is derived as there are no clauses for w, and so the "for every clause" condition of line 18 of Figure 5.11 trivially holds. Literal $\sim s$ is derived as $\sim w \in C$; and q and p are derived as the bodies are all proved.

Top-Down Negation-as-Failure Procedure

The top-down procedure for the complete knowledge assumption proceeds by **negation as failure**. It is similar to the top-down definite-clause proof procedure of Figure 5.4 (page 172). This is a non-deterministic procedure (see the box on page 170) that can be implemented by searching over choices that succeed. When a negated atom $\sim a$ is selected, a new proof for atom a is started. If the proof for a fails, $\sim a$ succeeds. If the proof for a succeeds, the algorithm fails and must make other choices. The algorithm is shown in Figure 5.12.

> **Example 5.29** Consider the clauses from Example 5.28. Suppose the query is ask p.
>
> Initially $G = \{p\}$.
>
> Using the first rule for p, G becomes $\{q, \sim r\}$.
>
> Selecting q, and replacing it with the body of the third rule, G becomes $\{\sim s, \sim r\}$.
>
> It then selects $\sim s$ and starts a proof for s. This proof for s fails, and thus G becomes $\{\sim r\}$.
>
> It then selects $\sim r$ and tries to prove r. In the proof for r, there is the subgoal $\sim t$, and thus it tries to prove t. This proof for t succeeds. Thus, the proof for $\sim t$ fails and, because there are no more rules for r, the proof for r fails. Thus, the proof for $\sim r$ succeeds.
>
> G is empty and so it returns *yes* as the answer to the top-level query.

Note that this implements **finite failure**, because it makes no conclusion if the proof procedure does not halt. For example, suppose there is just the rule $p \leftarrow p$. The algorithm does not halt for the query ask p. The completion, $p \leftrightarrow p$, gives no information. Even though there may be a way to conclude that there will never be a proof for p, a sound proof procedure should not conclude $\sim p$, as it does not follow from the completion.

5.6 Abduction

Abduction is a form of reasoning where assumptions are made to explain observations. For example, if an agent were to observe that some light was not working, it can hypothesize what is happening in the world to explain why the light was not working. An intelligent tutoring system could try to explain why a student gives some answer in terms of what the student understands and does not understand.

```
1: non-deterministic procedure NAFTD(KB,Query)
2:     Inputs
3:         KB: a set of clauses that can include negation as failure
4:         Query: a set of literals to prove
5:     Output
6:         yes if completion of KB entails Query and no otherwise
7:     Local
8:         G is a set of literals
9:     G := Query
10:    repeat
11:        select literal l ∈ G
12:        if l is of the form ∼a then
13:            if NAFTD(KB,a) fails then
14:                G := G \ {l}
15:            else
16:                fail
17:        else
18:            choose clause l ← B from KB
19:            replace l with B in G
20:    until G = {}
21:    return yes
```

Figure 5.12: Top-down negation-as-failure interpreter

The term **abduction** was coined by Peirce (1839–1914) to differentiate this type of reasoning from **deduction**, which involves determining what logically follows from a set of axioms, and **induction**, which involves inferring general relationships from examples.

In abduction, an agent hypothesizes what may be true about an observed case. An agent determines what implies its observations – what could be true to make the observations true. Observations are trivially implied by contradictions (as a contradiction logically implies everything), so we want to exclude contradictions from our explanation of the observations.

To formalize abduction, we use the language of Horn clauses and assumables (the same input that was used for proving from contradictions (page 185)). The system is given

- a knowledge base, *KB*, which is a set of of Horn clauses, and

- a set *A* of atoms, called the **assumables**; the assumables are the building blocks of hypotheses.

Instead of adding observations to the knowledge base, observations must be explained.

A **scenario** of $\langle KB, A \rangle$ is a subset H of A such that $KB \cup H$ is satisfiable. $KB \cup H$ is **satisfiable** if a model exists in which every element of KB and every element H is true. This happens if no subset of H is a conflict of KB.

An **explanation** of proposition g from $\langle KB, A \rangle$ is a scenario that, together with KB, implies g.

That is, an explanation of proposition g is a set H, $H \subseteq A$ such that

$$KB \cup H \models g \text{ and}$$
$$KB \cup H \not\models false.$$

A **minimal explanation** of g from $\langle KB, A \rangle$ is an explanation H of g from $\langle KB, A \rangle$ such that no strict subset of H is also an explanation of g from $\langle KB, A \rangle$.

Example 5.30 Consider the following simplistic knowledge base and assumables for a diagnostic assistant:

> $bronchitis \leftarrow influenza.$
> $bronchitis \leftarrow smokes.$
> $coughing \leftarrow bronchitis.$
> $wheezing \leftarrow bronchitis.$
> $fever \leftarrow influenza.$
> $soreThroat \leftarrow influenza.$
> $false \leftarrow smokes \wedge nonsmoker.$
> assumable $smokes, nonsmoker, influenza.$

If the agent observes *wheezing*, there are two minimal explanations:

> $\{influenza\}$ and $\{smokes\}$

These explanations imply *bronchitis* and *coughing*.

If *wheezing* $\wedge$ *fever* is observed, there is one minimal explanation:

> $\{influenza\}.$

The other explanation is no longer needed in a minimal explanation.

Notice how, when *wheezing* is observed, the agent reasons that it must be *bronchitis*, and so *influenza* and *smokes* are the hypothesized culprits. However, if *fever* were also observed, the patient must have influenza, so there is no need for the hypothesis of *smokes*; it has been **explained away**.

If *wheezing* $\wedge$ *nonsmoker* was observed instead, there is one minimal explanation:

> $\{influenza, nonsmoker\}$

The other explanation of *wheezing* is inconsistent with being a non-smoker.

Determining what is going on inside a system based on observations about the behavior is the problem of **diagnosis** or **recognition**. In **abductive diagnosis**, the agent hypothesizes diseases and malfunctions, as well as that some parts are working normally, to explain the observed symptoms. This differs from consistency-based diagnosis (page 187) in that the designer models faulty behavior in addition to normal behavior, and the observations are explained rather than added to the knowledge base. Abductive diagnosis requires more detailed modeling and gives more detailed diagnoses, because the knowledge base has to be able to actually prove the observations. It also allows an agent to diagnose systems in which there is no normal behavior. For example, in an intelligent tutoring system, by observing what a student does, the tutoring system can hypothesize what the student understands and does not understand, which can guide the action of the tutoring system.

Abduction can also be used for **design**, in which what is to be explained is a design goal and the assumables are the building blocks of the designs. The explanation is the design. Consistency means that the design is possible. The implication of the design goal means that the design provably achieved the design goal.

Example 5.31 Consider the electrical domain of Figure 5.2 (page 164). Similar to the representation of the example for consistency-based diagnosis in Example 5.20 (page 187), we axiomatize what follows from the assumptions of what may be happening in the system. In abductive diagnosis, we must axiomatize what follows both from faults and from normality assumptions. For each atom that could be observed, we axiomatize how it could be produced. In the following example, the assumable atoms are declared in-line using the "assumable" keyword.

A user could observe that l_1 is lit or is dark. We must write rules that axiomatize how the system must be to make these true. Light l_1 is lit if it is okay and there is power coming in. The light is dark if it is broken or there is no power. The system can assume l_1 is ok or broken, but not both:

$lit\_l_1 \leftarrow live\_w_0 \wedge ok\_l_1.$

$dark\_l_1 \leftarrow broken\_l_1.$

$dark\_l_1 \leftarrow dead\_w_0.$

assumable $ok\_l_1.$

assumable $broken\_l_1.$

$false \leftarrow ok\_l_1 \wedge broken\_l_1.$

Wire w_0 is live or dead depending on the switch positions and whether the wires coming in are alive or dead:

$live\_w_0 \leftarrow live\_w_1 \wedge up\_s_2 \wedge ok\_s_2.$

$live\_w_0 \leftarrow live\_w_2 \wedge down\_s_2 \wedge ok\_s_2.$

$dead\_w_0 \leftarrow broken\_s_2.$

$dead\_w_0 \leftarrow up\_s_2 \wedge dead\_w_1.$

$dead\_w_0 \leftarrow down\_s_2 \wedge dead\_w_2.$

assumable $ok\_s_2.$

assumable $broken\_s_2.$

$false \leftarrow ok\_s_2 \wedge broken\_s_2.$

The other wires are axiomatized similarly. Some of the wires depend on whether the circuit breakers are okay or broken:

$live\_w_3 \leftarrow live\_w_5 \wedge ok\_cb_1.$

$dead\_w_3 \leftarrow broken\_cb_1.$

$dead\_w_3 \leftarrow dead\_w_5.$

assumable $ok\_cb_1.$

assumable $broken\_cb_1.$

$false \leftarrow ok\_cb_1 \wedge broken\_cb_1.$

For the rest of this question, we assume that the other light and wires are represented analogously.

The outside power can be live or the power can be down:

$live\_w_5 \leftarrow live\_outside.$

$dead\_w_5 \leftarrow outside\_power\_down.$

assumable $live\_outside.$

assumable $outside\_power\_down.$

$false \leftarrow live\_outside \wedge outside\_power\_down.$

The switches can be assumed to be up or down:

assumable $up\_s_1.$

assumable $down\_s_1.$

$false \leftarrow up\_s_1 \wedge down\_s_1.$

There are two minimal explanations of lit_l_1:

$\{live\_outside, ok\_cb_1, ok\_l_1, ok\_s_1, ok\_s_2, up\_s_1, up\_s_2\}.$

$\{down\_s_1, down\_s_2, live\_outside, ok\_cb_1, ok\_l_1, ok\_s_1, ok\_s_2\}.$

This could be seen in design terms as a way to make sure the light is on: put both switches up or both switches down, and ensure the switches all work. It could also be seen as a way to determine what is going on if the agent observed that l_1 is lit; one of these two scenarios must hold.

There are ten minimal explanations of $dark\_l_1$:

$\{broken\_l_1\}$

$\{broken\_s_2\}$

$\{down\_s_1, up\_s_2\}$

$\{broken\_s_1, up\_s_2\}$

$\{broken\_cb_1, up\_s_1, up\_s_2\}$

$\{outside\_power\_down, up\_s_1, up\_s_2\}$

$\{down\_s_2, up\_s_1\}$

$\{broken\_s_1, down\_s_2\}$

$\{broken\_cb_1, down\_s_1, down\_s_2\}$

$\{down\_s_1, down\_s_2, outside\_power\_down\}$

There are six minimal explanations of $dark\_l_1 \wedge lit\_l_2$:

$\{broken\_l_1, live\_outside, ok\_cb_1, ok\_l_2, ok\_s_3, up\_s_3\}$

$\{broken\_s_2, live\_outside, ok\_cb_1, ok\_l_2, ok\_s_3, up\_s_3\}$

$\{down\_s_1, live\_outside, ok\_cb_1, ok\_l_2, ok\_s_3, up\_s_2, up\_s_3\}$

$\{broken\_s_1, live\_outside, ok\_cb_1, ok\_l_2, ok\_s_3, up\_s_2, up\_s_3\}$

$\{down\_s_2, live\_outside, ok\_cb_1, ok\_l_2, ok\_s_3, up\_s_1, up\_s_3\}$

$\{broken\_s_1, down\_s_2, live\_outside, ok\_cb_1, ok\_l_2, ok\_s_3, up\_s_3\}$

Notice how the explanations cannot include $outside\_power\_down$ or $broken\_cb_1$ because they are inconsistent with the explanation of l_2 being lit.

The bottom-up and top-down implementations for assumption-based reasoning with Horn clauses (page 190) can both be used for abduction. The bottom-up implementation of Figure 5.9 (page 190) computes, in C, the minimal explanations for each atom. The pruning discussed in the text can also be used. The top-down implementation can be used to find the explanations of any g by generating the conflicts and, using the same code and knowledge base, proving g instead of $false$. The minimal explanations of g are the minimal sets of assumables collected to prove g that are not subsets of conflicts.

5.7 Causal Models

A **primitive** atom is an atom that is stated as an atomic clause when it is true. A **derived** atom is one that uses rules to define when it is true. Typically the designer writes axioms for the derived atoms and then expects a user to specify which primitive atoms are true. Thus, the derived atoms will be inferred as necessary from the primitive atoms and other atoms that can be derived.

The designer of an agent must make many decisions when designing a knowledge base for a domain. For example, consider two propositions, a and b, both of which are true. There are many choices of how to write this. A designer could specify both a and b as atomic clauses, treating both as primitive. A designer could have a as primitive and b as derived, stating a as an atomic clause and giving the rule $b \leftarrow a$. Alternatively, the designer could specify the atomic clause b and the rule $a \leftarrow b$, treating b as primitive and a as derived. These representations are logically equivalent; they cannot be distinguished logically. However, they have different effects when the knowledge base is changed. Suppose a was no longer true for some reason. In the first and third representations, b would still be true, and in the second representation b would no longer true.

A **causal model**, or a model of **causality**, is a representation of a domain that predicts the results of interventions. An **intervention** is an action that forces a variable to have a particular value; that is, it changes the value in some way other than manipulating other variables in the model.

To predict the effect of interventions, a causal model represents how the cause implies its effect. When the cause is changed, its effect should be changed. An **evidential model** represents a domain in the other direction – from effect to cause. Note that we do not assume that there is "the cause" of an effect; rather there are many propositions, which together make the effect true.

Example 5.32 Consider the electrical domain depicted in Figure 1.8 (page 34). In this domain, switch $s3$ is up and light $l2$ is lit. There are many different ways to axiomatize this domain. Example 5.5 (page 164) contains causal rules such as

$$lit\_l_2 \leftarrow up\_s_3 \land live\_w_3.$$

Alternatively, we could specify in the evidential direction:

$$up\_s_3 \leftarrow lit\_l_2.$$
$$live\_w_3 \leftarrow lit\_l_2.$$

These are all statements that are true of the domain.

Suppose that wire w_3 was live and someone put switch s_3 up; we would expect that l_2 would become lit. However, if someone was to make s_3 lit by some mechanism outside of the model (and not by flipping the switch), we would not expect the switch to go up as a side effect.

Example 5.33 Consider the electrical domain depicted in Figure 1.8 (page 34). The following proposition describes an invariant on the relationship between switches s_1 and s_2 and light l_1, assuming all components are working properly:

$$up\_s_1 \leftrightarrow (lit\_l_1 \leftrightarrow up\_s_2). \tag{5.1}$$

This formula is symmetric between the three propositions; it is true if and only if an odd number of the propositions are true. However, in the world, the relationship between these propositions is not symmetric. Suppose all three atoms were true in some state. Putting s_1 down does not make s_2 go down to preserve lit_l_1. Instead, putting s_1 down makes lit_l_1 false, and up_s_2 remains true to preserve this invariant. Thus, to predict the result of interventions, we require more than proposition (5.1) above.

A causal model is

$$lit\_l_1 \leftarrow up\_s_1 \land up\_s_2.$$
$$lit\_l_1 \leftarrow \sim up\_s_1 \land \sim up\_s_2.$$

The completion of this is equivalent to proposition (5.1); however, it makes reasonable predictions when one of the values is changed.

An evidential model is

$$up\_s_1 \leftarrow lit\_l_1 \land up\_s_2.$$
$$up\_s_1 \leftarrow \sim lit\_l_1 \land \sim up\_s_2.$$

This can be used to answer questions about whether s_1 is up based on the position of s_2 and whether l_1 is lit. Its completion is also equivalent to formula (5.1). However, it does not accurately predict the effect of interventions.

A **causal model** consists of

- a set of **background variables**, sometimes called **exogenous variables**, which are determined by factors outside of the model;

- a set of **endogenous variables**, which are determined as part of the model; and

- a set of functions, one for each endogenous variable, that specifies how the endogenous variable can be determined from other endogenous variables and background variables. The function for a variable X is called the **causal mechanism** for X. The entire set of functions must have a unique solution for each assignment of values to the background variables.

When the variables are propositions, the function for a proposition can be specified as a set of clauses with the proposition as their head (under the complete knowledge assumption). One way to ensure a unique solution is for the knowledge base to be acyclic.

Example 5.34 In Example 5.33, Equation (5.1) can be the causal mechanism for lit_l_1. This can be expressed as the rules with lit_l_1 in the head specified in this model. There would be other causal mechanisms for up_s_1 and up_s_2, or perhaps these could be background variables that are not controlled in the model.

An **intervention** is an action to force a variable X to have a particular value v by some mechanism other than changing one of the other variables in the model. The effect of an intervention can be obtained by replacing the clausal mechanism for X by $X = v$. To intervene to force a proposition p to be true involves replacing the clauses for p with the atomic clause p. To intervene to force a proposition p to be false involves removing the clauses for p.

If the values of the background variables are not known, the background variables can be represented by assumables. An observation can be implemented by two stages:

1. abduction to explain the observation in terms of the background variables and

2. prediction to see what follows from the explanations.

Intuitively, abduction tells us what the world is like, given the observations. The prediction tells us the consequence of the action, given how the world is.

5.8   Review

The following are the main points you should have learned from this chapter:

- A definite clause knowledge base can be used to specify atomic clauses and rules about a domain when there is no uncertainty or ambiguity.

- Given a set of facts about a domain, the logical consequences characterize what else must be true.

- A sound and complete proof procedure can be used to determine the logical consequences of a knowledge base.

- Proof by contradiction can be used to make inference from a Horn clause knowledge base.

- Negation as failure can be used when the knowledge is complete (i.e., under the complete knowledge assumption).

- Abduction can be used to explain observations.

- A causal model predicts the effect of an intervention.

5.9 References and Further Reading

The semantics for propositional logic presented here was invented by Tarski [1956]. For introductions to logic see Copi [1982] for an informal overview, Enderton [1972] and Mendelson [1987] for more formal approaches, and Bell and Machover [1977] for advanced topics. For in-depth discussion of the use of logic in AI see the multivolume *Handbook of Logic in Artificial Intelligence and Logic Programming* [Gabbay, Hogger, and Robinson, 1993].

The tell-ask notion of a knowledge base is described by Levesque [1984].

Consistency-based diagnosis was formalized by de Kleer, Mackworth, and Reiter [1992].

Much of the foundation of definite and Horn clause reasoning was developed in the context of a richer logic that is presented in Chapter 12 and is studied under the umbrella of **logic programming**. Resolution was developed by Robinson [1965]. SLD resolution was pioneered by Kowalski [1974] and Colmerauer, Kanoui, Roussel, and Pasero [1973], building on previous work by Green [1969], Hayes [1973], and Hewitt [1969]. The fixed point semantics was developed by van Emden and Kowalski [1976]. For more detail on the semantics and properties of logic programs see Lloyd [1987].

The work on negation as failure (page 193) is based on the work of Clark [1978]. Apt and Bol [1994] provide a survey of different techniques and semantics for handling negation as failure. The bottom-up negation-as-failure proof procedure is based on the **truth maintenance system** of Doyle [1979], who also considered incremental addition and removal of clauses; see Exercise 5.15 (page 216). The use of abnormality for default reasoning was advocated by McCarthy [1986].

The abduction framework presented here is based on the assumption-based truth maintenance system (ATMS) of de Kleer [1986] and on Theorist [Poole, Goebel, and Aleliunas, 1987]. Abduction has been used for diagnosis [Peng and Reggia, 1990], natural language understanding [Hobbs, Stickel, Appelt, and Martin, 1993], and temporal reasoning [Shanahan, 1989]. Kakas, Kowalski, and Toni [1993] and Kakas and Denecker [2002] review abductive reasoning. For an overview of the work of Peirce, see Burch [2008].

Dung [1995] presents an abstract framework for arguments that provides a foundation for much of the work in this area. Dung, Mancarella, and Toni

[2007] present a recent argumentation framework. Chesnevar, Maguitman, and Loui [2000] and Besnard and Hunter [2008] survey work on arguments.

The bottom-up Horn implementation for finding explanations is based on the ATMS [de Kleer, 1986]. The ATMS is more sophisticated in that it considers the problem of incremental addition of clauses and assumables, which we ignored (see Exercise 5.16 (page 216)).

Causal models are discussed by Pearl [2000] and Spirtes, Glymour, and Scheines [2000].

5.10   Exercises

These exercises use AILog, a simple logical reasoning system that implements all of the reasoning discussed in this chapter. It is available from the book web site.

Exercise 5.1 Suppose we want to be able to reason about an electric kettle plugged into a power outlet for the electrical domain. Suppose a kettle must be plugged into a working power outlet, it must be turned on, and it must be filled with water, in order to heat.

Using AILog syntax, write axioms that let the system determine whether kettles are heating. AILog code for the electrical environment is available from the web.

You must

- Give the intended interpretation of all symbols used.

- Write the clauses so they can be loaded into AILog.

- Show that the resulting knowledge base runs in AILog.

Exercise 5.2 Consider the domain of house plumbing represented in the diagram of Figure 5.13.

In this example, $p1$, $p2$, and $p3$ denote cold water pipes; $t1$, $t2$, and $t3$ denote taps; $d1$, $d2$, and $d3$ denote drainage pipes; *shower* denotes a shower; *bath* denotes a bath; *sink* denotes a sink; and *floor* denotes the floor. Figure 5.13 is intended to give the denotation for the symbols.

Suppose we have the following atoms:

- *pressurized_p_i* is true if pipe p_i has mains pressure in it.
- *on_t_i* is true if tap t_i is on.
- *off_t_i* is true if tap t_i is off.
- *wet_b* is true if b is wet (b is either the sink, bath or floor).
- *flow_p_i* is true if water is flowing through p_i.
- *plugged_sink* is true if the sink has the plug in.
- *plugged_bath* is true if the bath has the plug in.
- *unplugged_sink* is true if the sink does not have the plug in.
- *unplugged_bath* is true if the bath does not have the plug in.

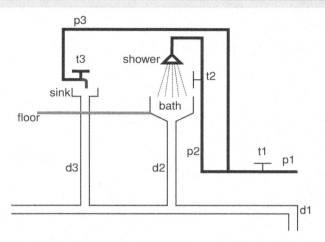

Figure 5.13: The plumbing domain

A definite-clause axiomatization for how water can flow down drain $d1$ if taps $t1$ and $t2$ are on and the bath is unplugged is

$pressurized\_p1$.

$pressurized\_p2 \leftarrow on\_t1 \land pressurized\_p1$.

$flow\_shower \leftarrow on\_t2 \land pressurized\_p2$.

$wet\_bath \leftarrow flow\_shower$.

$flow\_d2 \leftarrow wet\_bath \land unplugged\_bath$.

$flow\_d1 \leftarrow flow\_d2$.

on_t1.

on_t2.

$unplugged\_bath$.

(a) Finish the axiomatization for the sink in the same manner as the axiomatization for the bath. Test it in AILog.

(b) What information would you expect the user to be able to provide that the plumber, who is not at the house, cannot? Change the axiomatization so that questions about this information are asked of the user.

(c) Axiomatize how the floor is wet if the sink overflows or the bath overflows. They overflow if the plug is in and water is flowing in. You may invent new atomic propositions as long as you give their intended interpretation. (Assume that the taps and plugs have been in the same positions for one hour; you do not have to axiomatize the dynamics of turning on the taps and inserting and removing plugs.) Test it in AILog.

(d) Suppose a hot water system is installed to the left of tap $t1$. This has another tap in the pipe leading into it and supplies hot water to the shower and the sink (there are separate hot and cold water taps for each). Add this to your axiomatization. Give the denotation for all propositions you invent. Test it in AILog.

Exercise 5.3 You are given the following knowledge base:

$a \leftarrow b \wedge c.$
$a \leftarrow e \wedge f.$
$b \leftarrow d.$
$b \leftarrow f \wedge h.$
$c \leftarrow e.$
$d \leftarrow h.$
$e.$
$f \leftarrow g.$
$g \leftarrow c.$

(a) Give a model of the knowledge base.
(b) Give an interpretation that is not a model of the knowledge base.
(c) Give two atoms that are logical consequences of the knowledge base.
(d) Give two atoms that are not logical consequences of the knowledge base.

Exercise 5.4 You are given the knowledge base *KB* containing the following clauses:

$a \leftarrow b \wedge c.$
$b \leftarrow d.$
$b \leftarrow e.$
$c.$
$d \leftarrow h.$
$e.$
$f \leftarrow g \wedge b.$
$g \leftarrow c \wedge k.$
$j \leftarrow a \wedge b.$

(a) Show how the bottom-up proof procedure works for this example. Give all logical consequences of *KB*.
(b) *f* is not a logical consequence of *KB*. Give a model of *KB* in which *f* is false.
(c) *a* is a logical consequence of *KB*. Give a top-down derivation for the query ask *a*.

Exercise 5.5 A bottom-up proof procedure can incorporate an ask-the-user mechanism by asking the user about every askable atom. How can a bottom-up proof procedure still guarantee proof of all (non-askable) atoms that are a logical consequence of a definite-clause knowledge base without asking the user about every askable atom?

Exercise 5.6 This question explores how having an explicit semantics can be used to debug programs. The file `elect_bug2.ail` in the AILog distribution on the book web site is an axiomatization of the electrical wiring domain of Figure 5.2 (page 164), but it contains a buggy clause (one that is false in the intended interpretation shown in the figure). The aim of this exercise is to use AILog to find the buggy clause, given the denotation of the symbols given in Example 5.5 (page 164). To find the buggy rule, you won't even need to look at the knowledge base! (You can look at the knowledge base to find the buggy clause if you like, but that won't help you in this exercise.) All you must know is the meaning of the symbols in the program and what is true in the intended interpretation.

The query *lit_l1* can be proved, but it is false in the intended interpretation. Use the *how* questions of AILog to find a clause whose head is false in the intended interpretation and whose body is true. This is a buggy rule.

Exercise 5.7 Consider the following knowledge base and assumables aimed to explain why people are acting suspiciously:

> *goto_forest* ← *walking*.
> *get_gun* ← *hunting*.
> *goto_forest* ← *hunting*.
> *get_gun* ← *robbing*.
> *goto_bank* ← *robbing*.
> *goto_bank* ← *banking*.
> *fill_withdrawal_form* ← *banking*.
> *false* ← *banking* ∧ *robbing*.
> *false* ← *wearing_good_shoes* ∧ *goto_forest*.
> assumable *walking, hunting, robbing, banking*.

(a) Suppose *get_gun* is observed. What are all of the minimal explanations for this observation?

(b) Suppose *get_gun* ∧ *goto_bank* is observed. What are all of the minimal explanations for this observation?

(c) Is there something that could be observed to remove one of these as a minimal explanation? What must be added to be able to explain this?

(d) What are the minimal explanations of *goto_bank*?

(e) What are the minimal explanations of *goto_bank* ∧ *get_gun* ∧ *fill_withdrawal_form*?

Exercise 5.8 Suppose there are four possible diseases a particular patient may have: p, q, r, and s. p causes spots. q causes spots. Fever could be caused by one (or more) of q, r, or s. The patient has spots and fever. Suppose you have decided to use abduction to diagnose this patient based on the symptoms.

(a) Show how to represent this knowledge using Horn clauses and assumables.

(b) Show how to diagnose this patient using abduction. Show clearly the query and the resulting answer(s).

(c) Suppose also that p and s cannot occur together. Show how that changes your knowledge base from part (a). Show how to diagnose the patient using abduction with the new knowledge base. Show clearly the query and the resulting answer(s).

Exercise 5.9 Consider the following clauses and integrity constraints:

$false \leftarrow a \wedge b.$
$false \leftarrow c.$
$a \leftarrow d.$
$a \leftarrow e.$
$b \leftarrow d.$
$b \leftarrow g.$
$b \leftarrow h.$
$c \leftarrow h.$

Suppose the assumables are $\{d, e, f, g, h, i\}$. What are the minimal conflicts?

Exercise 5.10 Deep Space One (http://nmp.jpl.nasa.gov/ds1/), a spacecraft launched by NASA in October 1998, used AI technology for its diagnosis and control. For more details, see Muscettola, Nayak, Pell, and Williams [1998] or http://ic.arc.nasa.gov/projects/remote-agent/ (although these references are not necessary to complete this question).

Figure 5.14 depicts a part of the actual DS1 engine design. To achieve thrust in an engine, fuel and oxidizer must be injected. The whole design is highly redundant to ensure its operation even in the presence of multiple failures (mainly stuck or inoperative valves). Note that whether the valves are black or white, and whether or not they have a bar are irrelevant for this assignment.

Each valve can be okay (or not) and can be open (or not). The aim of this assignment is to axiomatize the domain so that we can do two tasks:

(a) Given an observation of the lack of thrust in an engine and given which valves are open, using consistency-based diagnosis, determine what could be wrong.

(b) Given the goal of having thrust and given the knowledge that some valves are okay, determine which valves should be opened.

For each of these tasks, you must think about what the clauses are in the knowledge base and what is assumable.

The atoms should be of the following forms:

- *open_V* is true if valve V is open. This the atoms should be *open_v1*, *open_v2*, and so on.

- *ok_V* is true if valve V is working properly.

- *pressurized_V* is true if the output of valve V is pressurized with gas. You should assume that *pressurized_t1* and *pressurized_t2* are true.

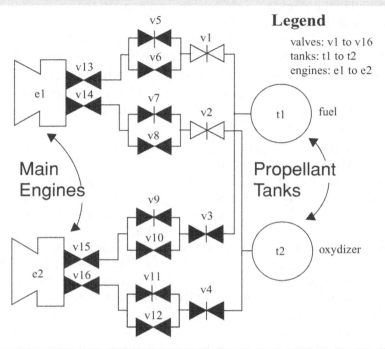

Figure 5.14: Deep Space One engine design

- *thrust_E* is true if engine *E* has thrust.

- *thrust* is true if no thrust exists in either engine.

- *nothrust* is true if there is no thrust.

To make this manageable, only write rules for the input into engine *e*1. Test your code using AILog on a number of examples.

Exercise 5.11 Consider using abductive diagnosis on the problem in the previous question.

Suppose the following:

- Valves can be *open* or *closed*. For some of them, we know if they are open or closed, and for some valves we do not know.

- A valve can be *ok*, in which case the gas will flow if the valve is open and not if it is closed; *broken*, in which case gas never flows; *stuck*, in which case gas flows independently of whether the valve is open or closed; or *leaking*, in which case gas flowing into the valve leaks out instead of flowing through.

- There are three gas sensors that can detect gas leaking (but not which gas); the first gas sensor detects gas from the rightmost valves ($v1, \ldots, v4$), the second gas sensor detects gas from the center valves ($v5, \ldots, v12$), and the third gas sensor detects gas from the leftmost valves ($v13, \ldots, v16$).

(a) Axiomatize the domain so the system can explain thrust or no thrust in engine $e1$ and the presence of gas in one of the sensors. For example, it should be able to explain why $e1$ is thrusting. It should be able to explain why $e1$ is not thrusting and there is a gas detected by the third sensor.

(b) Test your axiomatization on some non-trivial examples.

(c) For some of the queries, many explanations exist. Suggest how the number of explanations could be reduced or managed so that the abductive diagnoses are more useful.

Exercise 5.12 AILog has *askables*, which are atoms that are asked of the user, and *assumables*, which are collected in an answer.

Imagine you are axiomatizing the wiring in your home and you have an axiomatization similar to that of Example 5.3 (page 162). You are axiomatizing the domain for a new tenant who is going to sublet your home and may want to determine what may be going wrong with the wiring.

There are some atoms that you will know the rules for, some that the tenant will know, and some that neither will know. Divide the atomic propositions into these three categories, and suggest which should be made askable and which should be assumable. Show what the resulting interaction will look like under your division.

Exercise 5.13 In this question, consider using integrity constraints and consistency-based diagnosis in a purchasing agent that interacts with various information sources on the web. To answer a question, the purchasing agent will ask a number of the information sources for facts. However, information sources are sometimes wrong. It is useful to be able to automatically determine which information sources may be wrong when a user gets conflicting information.

In this question we consider how integrity constraints and assumables can be used to determine what errors are present in different information sources.

In this question, we use meaningless symbols such as $a, b, c, \ldots$, but in a real domain there will be meaning associated with the symbols, such as a meaning "there is skiing in Hawaii" and z meaning "there is no skiing in Hawaii", or a meaning "butterflies do not eat anything" and z meaning "butterflies eat nectar". We will use meaningless symbols in this question because the computer does not have access to the meanings and must simply treat them as meaningless symbols.

Suppose the following information sources and associated information are provided:

Source s_1: Source s_1 claims the following clauses are true:

$$a \leftarrow h.$$
$$d \leftarrow c.$$

Source s_2: Source s_2 claims the following clauses are true:

$$e \leftarrow d.$$
$$f \leftarrow k.$$
$$z \leftarrow g.$$
$$j.$$

Source s_3**:** Source s_3 claims the following clause is true:

$$h \leftarrow d.$$

Source s_4**:** Source s_4 claims the following clauses are true:

$$a \leftarrow b \wedge e.$$
$$b \leftarrow c.$$

Source s_5**:** Source s_5 claims the following clause is true:

$$g \leftarrow f \wedge j.$$

Yourself: Suppose that you know that the following clauses are true:

$$false \leftarrow a \wedge z.$$
$$c.$$
$$k.$$

Not every source can be believed, because together they produce a contradiction.

(a) Code the knowledge provided by the users into AILog using assumables. To use a clause provided by one of the sources, you must assume that the source is reliable.

(b) Use the program to find the conflicts about what sources are reliable. (To find conflicts you can just ask *false*.)

(c) Suppose you would like to assume that as few sources as possible are unreliable. Which single source, if it was unreliable, could account for a contradiction (assuming all other sources were reliable)?

(d) Which pairs of sources could account for a contradiction (assuming all other sources are reliable) such that no single one of them could account for the contradiction?

Exercise 5.14 Suppose you have a job at a company that is building online teaching tools. Because you have taken an AI course, your boss wants to know your opinion on various options under consideration.

They are planning on building an intelligent tutoring system for teaching elementary physics (e.g., mechanics and electromagnetism). One of the things that the system must do is to diagnose errors that a student may be making.

For each of the following, answer the explicit questions and use proper English. Answering parts not asked or giving more than one answer when only one is asked for will annoy the boss. The boss also does not like jargon, so please use straightforward English.

The boss has heard of consistency-based diagnosis and abductive diagnosis but wants to know what they involve *in the context of building an intelligent tutoring system for teaching elementary physics.*

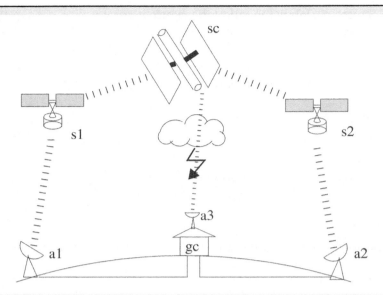

Figure 5.15: A space communication network

(a) Explain what knowledge (about physics and about students) is requried for consistency-based diagnosis.

(b) Explain what knowledge (about physics and about students) is requried for abductive diagnosis.

(c) What is the main advantage of using abductive diagnosis over consistency-based diagnosis in this domain?

(d) What is the main advantage of consistency-based diagnosis over abductive diagnosis in this domain?

Exercise 5.15 Consider the bottom-up negation-as-failure proof procedure of Figure 5.11 (page 198). Suppose we want to allow for incremental addition and deletion of clauses. How does C change as a clause is added? How does C change if a clause is removed?

Exercise 5.16 Suppose you are implementing a bottom-up Horn clause explanation reasoner and you want to incrementally add clauses or assumables. When a clause is added, how are the minimal explanations affected? When an assumable is added, how are the minimal explanations affected?

Exercise 5.17 Figure 5.15 shows a simplified redundant communication network between an unmanned spacecraft (sc) and a ground control center (gc). There are two indirect high-bandwidth (high-gain) links that are relayed through satellites ($s1$, $s2$) to different ground antennae ($a1$, $a2$). Furthermore, there is a direct, low-bandwidth (low-gain) link between the ground control center's antenna ($a3$) and the spacecraft. The low-gain link is affected by atmospheric disturbances – it works if there are no disturbances (no_dist) – and the spacecraft's low-gain transmitter (sc_lg) and antenna 3 are okay. The high-gain links always work if the spacecraft's high-gain transmitter (sc_hg), the satellites' antennae ($s1\_ant$, $s2\_ant$), the satellites' transmitters (*s1_trans*, *s2_trans*), and the ground antennae (*a1*, *a2*) are okay.

To keep matters simple, we consider only messages from the spacecraft going through these channels to the ground control center.

The following knowledge base formalizes the part of the communication network we are interested in:

$$send\_signal\_lg\_sc \leftarrow ok\_sc\_lg \wedge alive\_sc.$$
$$send\_signal\_hg\_sc \leftarrow ok\_sc\_hg \wedge alive\_sc.$$
$$get\_signal\_s1 \leftarrow send\_signal\_hg\_sc \wedge ok\_s1\_ant.$$
$$get\_signal\_s2 \leftarrow send\_signal\_hg\_sc \wedge ok\_s2\_ant.$$
$$send\_signal\_s1 \leftarrow get\_signal\_s1 \wedge ok\_s1\_trans.$$
$$send\_signal\_s2 \leftarrow get\_signal\_s2 \wedge ok\_s2\_trans.$$
$$get\_signal\_gc \leftarrow send\_signal\_s1 \wedge ok\_a1.$$
$$get\_signal\_gc \leftarrow send\_signal\_s2 \wedge ok\_a2.$$
$$get\_signal\_gc \leftarrow send\_signal\_lg\_sc \wedge ok\_a3 \wedge no\_dist.$$

Ground control is worried, because it has not received a signal from the spacecraft (*no_signal_gc*). It knows for sure that all ground antennae are okay (i.e., *ok_a1*, *ok_a2*, and *ok_a3*) and satellite *s1*'s transmitter is ok (*ok_s1_trans*). It is not sure about the state of the spacecraft, its transmitters, the satellites' antennae, *s2*'s transmitter, and atmospheric disturbances.

(a) Specify a set of assumables and an integrity constraint that model the situation.

(b) Using the assumables and the integrity constraints from part (a), what is the set of minimal conflicts?

(c) What is the consistency-based diagnosis for the given situation? In other words, what are the possible combinations of violated assumptions that could account for why the control center cannot receive a signal from the spacecraft?

Exercise 5.18

(a) Explain why NASA may want to use abduction rather than consistency-based diagnosis for the domain of Exercise 5.17.

(b) Suppose that an atmospheric disturbance *dist* could produce static or no signal in the low-bandwidth signal. To receive the static, antenna *a3* and the spacecraft's low-bandwidth transmitter *sc_lg* must be working. If *a3* or *sc_lg* are not working or *sc* is dead, there is no signal. What rules and assumables must be added to the knowledge base of Exercise 5.17 so that we can explain the possible observations *no_signal_gc*, *get_signal_gc*, or *static_gc*? You may ignore the high-bandwidth links. You can invent any symbols you need.

Chapter 6

Reasoning Under Uncertainty

It is remarkable that a science which began with the consideration of games of chance should become the most important object of human knowledge ... The most important questions of life are, for the most part, really only problems of probability ...

The theory of probabilities is at bottom nothing but common sense reduced to calculus.

– Pierre Simon de Laplace [1812]

All of the time, agents are forced to make decisions based on incomplete information. Even when an agent senses the world to find out more information, it rarely finds out the exact state of the world. A robot does not know exactly where an object is. A doctor does not know exactly what is wrong with a patient. A teacher does not know exactly what a student understands. When intelligent agents must make decisions, they have to use whatever information they have. This chapter considers reasoning under uncertainty: determining what is true in the world based on observations of the world. This is used in Chapter 9 as a basis for acting under uncertainty, where the agent must make decisions about what action to take even though it cannot precisely predict the outcomes of its actions. This chapter starts with probability, shows how to represent the world by making appropriate independence assumptions, and shows how to reason with such representations.

6.1 Probability

To make a good decision, an agent cannot simply assume what the world is like and act according to those assumptions. It must consider multiple possible contingencies and their likelihood. Consider the following example.

Example 6.1 Many people consider it sensible to wear a seat belt when traveling in a car because, in an accident, wearing a seat belt reduces the risk of serious injury. However, consider an agent that commits to assumptions and bases its decision on these assumptions. If the agent assumes it will not have an accident, it will not bother with the inconvenience of wearing a seat belt. If it assumes it will have an accident, it will not go out. In neither case would it wear a seat belt! A more intelligent agent may wear a seat belt because the inconvenience of wearing a seat belt is far outweighed by the increased risk of injury or death if it has an accident. It does not stay at home too worried about an accident to go out; the benefits of being mobile, even with the risk of an accident, outweigh the benefits of the extremely cautious approach of never going out. The decisions of whether to go out and whether to wear a seat belt depend on the likelihood of having an accident, how much a seat belt helps in an accident, the inconvenience of wearing a seat belt, and how important it is to go out. The various trade-offs may be different for different agents. Some people do not wear seat belts, and some people do not go out because of the risk of accident.

Reasoning under uncertainty has been studied in the fields of probability theory and decision theory. Probability is the calculus of **gambling**. When an agent makes decisions and uncertainties are involved about the outcomes of its action, it is gambling on the outcome. However, unlike a gambler at the casino, the agent cannot opt out and decide not to gamble; whatever it does – including doing nothing – involves uncertainty and risk. If it does not take the probabilities into account, it will eventually lose at gambling to an agent that does. This does not mean, however, that making the best decision guarantees a win.

Many of us learn probability as the theory of tossing coins and rolling dice. Although this may be a good way to present probability theory, probability is applicable to a much richer set of applications than coins and dice. In general, we want a calculus for belief that can be used for making decisions.

The view of probability as a measure of belief, as opposed to being a frequency, is known as **Bayesian probability** or **subjective probability**. The term *subjective* does not mean *arbitrary*, but rather it means "belonging to the subject." For example, suppose there are three agents, Alice, Bob, and Chris, and one die that has been tossed. Suppose Alice observes that the outcome is a "6" and tells Bob that the outcome is even, but Chris knows nothing about the outcome. In this case, Alice has a probability of 1 that the outcome is a "6," Bob has a probability of $\frac{1}{3}$ that it is a "6" (assuming Bob believes Alice and treats all of the even outcomes with equal probability), and Chris may have probability of $\frac{1}{6}$ that the outcome is a "6." They all have different probabilities because they all have different knowledge. The probability is about the outcome of this particular toss of the die, not of some generic event of tossing dice. These agents may have the same or different probabilities for the outcome of other coin tosses.

The alternative is the **frequentist** view, where the probabilities are long-run frequencies of repeatable events. The Bayesian view of probability is appropriate for intelligent agents because a measure of belief in particular situations is what is needed to make decisions. Agents do not encounter generic events but have to make a decision based on uncertainty about the particular circumstances they face.

Probability theory can be defined as the study of *how knowledge affects belief*. Belief in some proposition, α, can be measured in terms of a number between 0 and 1. The probability α is 0 means that α is believed to be definitely false (no new evidence will shift that belief), and a probability of 1 means that α is believed to be definitely true. Using 0 and 1 is purely a convention.

Adopting the belief view of probabilities does not mean that statistics are ignored. Statistics of what has happened in the past is knowledge that can be conditioned on and used to update belief. (See Chapter 7 for how to learn probabilities.)

We are assuming that the uncertainty is **epistemological** – pertaining to an agent's knowledge of the world – rather than **ontological** – how the world is. We are assuming that an agent's knowledge of the truth of propositions is uncertain, not that there are degrees of truth. For example, if you are told that someone is very tall, you know they have some height; you only have vague knowledge about the actual value of their height.

If an agent's probability of some α is greater than zero and less than one, this does not mean that α is true to some degree but rather that the agent is ignorant of whether α is true or false. The probability reflects the agent's ignorance.

For the rest of this chapter, we ignore the agent whose beliefs we are modeling and only talk about the probability.

6.1.1 Semantics of Probability

Probability theory is built on the same foundation of worlds and variables as constraint satisfaction [see Section 4.2 (page 113)]. Instead of having constraints that eliminate some worlds and treat every other world as possible, probabilities put a measure over the possible worlds. The variables in probability theory are referred to as **random variables**. The term *random variable* is somewhat of a misnomer because it is neither random nor variable. As discussed in Section 4.2 (page 113), worlds can be described in terms of variables; a world corresponds to an assignment of a value to each variable. Alternatively, variables can be described in terms of worlds; a variable is a function that returns a value on each world.

First we define probability as a measure on sets of worlds, then define probabilities on propositions, then on variables.

A **probability measure** over the worlds is a function μ from sets of worlds into the non-negative real numbers such that

- if Ω_1 and Ω_2 are disjoint sets of worlds (i.e., if $\Omega_1 \cap \Omega_2 = \{\}$), then $\mu(\Omega_1 \cup \Omega_2) = \mu(\Omega_1) + \mu(\Omega_2)$;
- if Ω is the set of all worlds, $\mu(\Omega) = 1$.

Note that the use of 1 as the probability of the set of all of the worlds is just by convention. You could just as well use 100.

It is possible to have infinitely many worlds when some variables have infinite domains or when infinitely many variables exist. When there are infinitely many worlds, we do not require a measure for all subsets of Ω – just for those sets that can be described using some language that we assume allows us to describe the intersection, union, and complement of sets. The set of subsets describable by these operations has the structure of what mathematicians call an **algebra**.

The measure μ can be extended to worlds by defining $\mu(\omega) = \mu(\{\omega\})$ for world ω. When finitely many worlds exist, the measure over individual worlds is adequate to define μ. When infinitely many worlds exist, it is possible that the measure of individual worlds is not enough information to define μ, or that it may not make sense to have a measure over individual worlds.

Example 6.2 Suppose the worlds correspond to the possible real-valued heights, in centimeters, of a particular person. In this example, there are infinitely many possible worlds. The measure of the set of heights in the range $[175, 180)$ could be 0.2 and the measure of the range $[180, 190)$ could be 0.3. Then the measure of the range $[175, 190)$ is 0.5. However, the measure of any particular height could be zero.

As described in Section 5.1 (page 157), a primitive proposition is an assignment of a value to a variable. Propositions are built from primitive propositions using logical connectives. We then use this property to define probability distributions over variables.

The **probability** of proposition α, written $P(\alpha)$, is the measure of the set of possible worlds in which α is true. That is,

$$P(\alpha) = \mu(\{\omega : \omega \models \alpha\}),$$

where $\omega \models \alpha$ means α is true in world ω. Thus, $P(\alpha)$ is the measure of the set of worlds in which α is true.

This use of the symbol $\models$ differs from its use in the previous chapter [see Section 5.1.2 (page 160)]. There, the left-hand side was a knowledge base; here, the left-hand side is a world. Which meaning is intended should be clear from the context.

A **probability distribution**, $P(X)$, over a random variable X is a function from the domain of X into the real numbers such that, given a value $x \in dom(X)$, $P(x)$ is the probability of the proposition $X = x$. We can also define a probability distribution over a set of variables analogously. For example, $P(X, Y)$ is a probability distribution over X and Y such that $P(X = x, Y = y)$, where $x \in dom(X)$ and $y \in dom(Y)$, has the value $P(X = x \wedge Y = y)$, where $X = x \wedge Y = y$ is a proposition and P is the function on propositions. We will use probability distributions when we want to treat a set of probabilities as a unit.

6.1.2 Axioms for Probability

The preceding section gave a semantic definition of probability. We can also give an axiomatic definition of probability that specifies axioms of what properties we may want in a calculus of belief.

| Probability Density Functions |

The definition of probability is sometimes specified in terms of probability density functions when the domain is continuous (e.g., a subset of the real numbers). A probability density function provides a way to give a measure over sets of possible worlds. The measure is defined in terms of an integral of a probability density function. The formal definition of an integral is the limit of the discretizations as the discretizations become finer.

The only non-discrete probability distribution we will use in this book is where the domain is the real line. In this case, there is a possible world for each real number. A **probability density function**, which we write as p, is a function from reals into non-negative reals that integrates to 1. The probability that a real-valued random variable X has value between a and b is given by

$$P(a \leq X \leq b) = \int_a^b p(X) \, dX.$$

A **parametric distribution** is one where the density function can be described by a formula. Although not all distributions can be described by formulas, all of the ones that we can represent are. Sometimes statisticians use the term parametric to mean the distribution can be described using a fixed, finite number of parameters. A **non-parametric distribution** is one where the number of parameters is not fixed. (Oddly, non-parametric typically means "many parameters").

A common parametric distribution is the **normal or Gaussian distribution** with mean μ and variance σ^2 defined by

$$p(X) = \frac{1}{\sqrt{2\pi}\sigma} e^{-\frac{1}{2}((X-\mu)/\sigma)^2},$$

where σ is the standard deviation. The normal distribution is used for measurement errors, where there is an average value, given by μ, and a variation in values specified by σ. The **central limit theorem**, proved by Laplace [1812], specifies that a sum of independent errors will approach the Gaussian distribution. This and its nice mathematical properties account for the widespread use of the normal distribution.

Other distributions, including the beta and Dirichlet distributions, are discussed in the Learning Under Uncertainty section (page 334).

Suppose P is a function from propositions into real numbers that satisfies the following three **axioms of probability**:

Axiom 1 $0 \leq P(\alpha)$ for any proposition α. That is, the belief in any proposition cannot be negative.

Axiom 2 $P(\tau) = 1$ if τ is a tautology. That is, if τ is true in all possible worlds, its probability is 1.

Axiom 3 $P(\alpha \vee \beta) = P(\alpha) + P(\beta)$ if α and β are contradictory propositions; that is, if $\neg(\alpha \wedge \beta)$ is a tautology. In other words, if two propositions cannot both be true (they are mutually exclusive), the probability of their disjunction is the sum of their probabilities.

These axioms are meant to be intuitive properties that we would like to have of any reasonable measure of belief. If a measure of belief follows these intuitive axioms, it is covered by probability theory, whether or not the measure is derived from actual frequency counts. These axioms form a sound and complete axiomatization of the meaning of probability. Soundness means that probability, as defined by the possible-worlds semantics, follows these axioms. Completeness means that any system of beliefs that obeys these axioms has a probabilistic semantics.

Proposition 6.1. *If there are a finite number of finite discrete random variables, Axioms 1, 2, and 3 are sound and complete with respect to the semantics.*

It is easy to check that these axioms are true of the semantics. In the other way around, you can use the axioms to compute any probability from the probability of worlds, because the descriptions of two worlds are mutually exclusive. The full proof is left as an exercise.

Proposition 6.2. *The following hold for all propositions α and β:*

(a) *Negation of a proposition:*

$$P(\neg\alpha) = 1 - P(\alpha).$$

(b) *If $\alpha \leftrightarrow \beta$, then $P(\alpha) = P(\beta)$. That is, logically equivalent propositions have the same probability.*

(c) *Reasoning by cases:*

$$P(\alpha) = P(\alpha \wedge \beta) + P(\alpha \wedge \neg\beta).$$

(d) *If V is a random variable with domain D, then, for all propositions α,*

$$P(\alpha) = \sum_{d \in D} P(\alpha \wedge V = d).$$

(e) *Disjunction for non-exclusive propositions:*

$$P(\alpha \vee \beta) = P(\alpha) + P(\beta) - P(\alpha \wedge \beta).$$

Proof.

(a) The propositions $\alpha \vee \neg\alpha$ and $\neg(\alpha \wedge \neg\alpha)$ are tautologies. Therefore, $1 = P(\alpha \vee \neg\alpha) = P(\alpha) + P(\neg\alpha)$. Rearranging gives the desired result.

(b) If $\alpha \leftrightarrow \beta$, then $\alpha \vee \neg\beta$ is a tautology, so $P(\alpha \vee \neg\beta) = 1$. α and $\neg\beta$ are contradictory statements, so we can use Axiom 3 to give $P(\alpha \vee \neg\beta) = P(\alpha) + P(\neg\beta)$. Using part (a), $P(\neg\beta) = 1 - P(\beta)$. Thus, $P(\alpha) + 1 - P(\beta) = 1$, and so $P(\alpha) = P(\beta)$.

(c) The proposition $\alpha \leftrightarrow ((\alpha \wedge \beta) \vee (\alpha \wedge \neg\beta))$ and $\neg((\alpha \wedge \beta) \wedge (\alpha \wedge \neg\beta))$ are tautologies. Thus, $P(\alpha) = P((\alpha \wedge \beta) \vee (\alpha \wedge \neg\beta)) = P(\alpha \wedge \beta) + P(\alpha \wedge \neg\beta)$.

(d) The proof is analogous to the proof of part (c).

(e) $(\alpha \vee \beta) \leftrightarrow ((\alpha \wedge \neg\beta) \vee \beta)$ is a tautology. Thus,

$$
\begin{aligned}
P(\alpha \vee \beta) &= P((\alpha \wedge \neg\beta) \vee \beta) \\
&= P(\alpha \wedge \neg\beta) + P(\beta).
\end{aligned}
$$

Part (c) shows $P(\alpha \wedge \neg\beta) = P(\alpha) - P(\alpha \wedge \beta)$. Thus,

$$
P(\alpha \vee \beta) = P(\alpha) - P(\alpha \wedge \beta) + P(\beta).
$$

$\square$

6.1.3 Conditional Probability

Typically, we do not only want to know the prior probability of some proposition, but we want to know how this belief is updated when an agent observes new evidence.

The measure of belief in proposition h based on proposition e is called the **conditional probability** of h **given** e, written $P(h|e)$.

A formula e representing the conjunction of *all* of the agent's **observations** of the world is called **evidence**. Given evidence e, the conditional probability $P(h|e)$ is the agent's **posterior probability** of h. The probability $P(h)$ is the **prior probability** of h and is the same as $P(h|true)$ because it is the probability before the agent has observed anything.

The posterior probability involves conditioning on *everything* the agent knows about a particular situation. All evidence must be conditioned on to obtain the correct posterior probability.

Example 6.3 For the diagnostic assistant, the patient's symptoms will be the evidence. The prior probability distribution over possible diseases is used before the diagnostic agent finds out about the particular patient. The posterior probability is the probability the agent will use after it has gained some evidence. When the agent acquires new evidence through discussions with the patient, observing symptoms, or the results of lab tests, it must update its posterior probability to reflect the new evidence. The new evidence is the conjunction of the old evidence and the new observations.

Example 6.4 The information that the delivery robot receives from its sensors is its evidence. When sensors are noisy, the evidence is what is known, such as the particular pattern received by the sensor, not that there is a person in front of the robot. The robot could be mistaken about what is in the world but it knows what information it received.

Semantics of Conditional Probability

Evidence e will rule out all possible worlds that are incompatible with e. Like the definition of logical consequence, the given formula e selects the possible worlds in which e is true. Evidence e induces a new measure, μ_e, over possible worlds where all worlds in which e is false have measure 0, and the remaining worlds are normalized so that the sum of the measures of the worlds is 1.

Here we go back to basic principles to define conditional probability. This basic definition is often useful when faced with unusual cases.

The definition of the measure follows from two intuitive properties:

- If S is a set of possible worlds, all of which have e true, define $\mu_e(S) = c \times \mu(S)$ for some constant c (which we derive below).

- If S is a set of worlds, all of which have e false, define $\mu_e(S) = 0$.

Other Possible Measures of Belief

Justifying other measures of belief is problematic. Consider, for example, the proposal that the belief in $\alpha \wedge \beta$ is some function of the belief in α and the belief in β. Such a measure of belief is called **compositional**. To see why this is not sensible, consider the single toss of a fair coin. Compare the case where α_1 is "the coin will land heads" and β_1 is "the coin will land tails" with the case where α_2 is "the coin will land heads" and β_2 is "the coin will land heads." For these two cases, the belief in α_1 would seem to be the same as the belief in α_2, and the belief in β_1 would be the same as the belief in β_2. But the belief in $\alpha_1 \wedge \beta_1$, which is impossible, is very different from the belief in $\alpha_2 \wedge \beta_2$, which is the same as α_2.

The conditional probability $P(f|e)$ is very different from the probability of the implication $P(e \rightarrow f)$. The latter is the same as $P(\neg e \vee f)$, which is the measure of the interpretations for which f is true or e is false. For example, suppose you have a domain where birds are relatively rare, and non-flying birds are a small proportion of the birds. Here $P(\neg flies|bird)$ would be the proportion of birds that do not fly, which would be low. $P(bird \rightarrow \neg flies)$ is the same as $P(\neg bird \vee \neg flies)$, which would be dominated by non-birds and so would be high. Similarly, $P(bird \rightarrow flies)$ would also be high, the probability also being dominated by the non-birds. It is difficult to imagine a situation where the probability of an implication is the kind of knowledge that is appropriate or useful.

We want μ_e to be a probability measure, so if Ω is the set of all possible worlds, $\mu_e(\Omega) = 1$. Thus, $1 = \mu_e(\Omega) = \mu_e(\{\omega : \omega \models e\}) + \mu_e(\{\omega : \omega \not\models e\}) = c \times \mu(\{\omega : \omega \models e\}) + 0 = c \times P(e)$. Therefore, $c = 1/P(e)$.

The conditional probability of formula h given evidence e is the measure, using μ_e, of the possible worlds in which h is true. That is,

$$
\begin{aligned}
P(h|e) &= \mu_e(\{\omega : \omega \models h\}) \\
&= \mu_e(\{\omega : \omega \models h \wedge e\}) + \mu_e(\{\omega : \omega \models h \wedge \neg e\}) \\
&= \frac{\mu(\{\omega : \omega \models h \wedge e\})}{P(e)} + 0 \\
&= \frac{P(h \wedge e)}{P(e)}.
\end{aligned}
$$

The last form above is usually given as the definition of conditional probability.

For the rest of this chapter, assume that, if e is the evidence, $P(e) > 0$. We do not consider the problem of conditioning on propositions with zero probability (i.e., on sets of worlds with measure zero).

A **conditional probability distribution**, written $P(X|Y)$ where X and Y are variables or sets of variables, is a function of the variables: given a value $x \in dom(X)$ for X and a value $y \in dom(Y)$ for Y, it gives the value $P(X = x|Y = y)$, where the latter is the conditional probability of the propositions.

The definition of conditional probability lets us decompose a conjunction into a product of conditional probabilities:

Proposition 6.3. *(Chain rule) Conditional probabilities can be used to decompose conjunctions. For any propositions $\alpha_1, \ldots, \alpha_n$:*

$$
\begin{aligned}
P(\alpha_1 \wedge \alpha_2 \wedge \ldots \wedge \alpha_n) &= P(\alpha_1) \times \\
& \quad P(\alpha_2|\alpha_1) \times \\
& \quad P(\alpha_3|\alpha_1 \wedge \alpha_2) \times \\
& \quad \vdots \\
& \quad P(\alpha_n|\alpha_1 \wedge \cdots \wedge \alpha_{n-1}) \\
&= \prod_{i=1}^{n} P(\alpha_i|\alpha_1 \wedge \cdots \wedge \alpha_{i-1}),
\end{aligned}
$$

where the right-hand side is assumed to be zero if any of the products are zero (even if some of them are undefined).

Note that any theorem about unconditional probabilities is a theorem about conditional probabilities if you add the same evidence to each probability. This is because the conditional probability measure is another probability measure.

Bayes' Rule

An agent must update its belief when it observes new evidence. A new piece of evidence is conjoined to the old evidence to form the complete set of evidence.

| Background Knowledge and Observation |

The difference between background knowledge and observation was described in Section 5.3.1 (page 174). When we use reasoning under uncertainty, the background model is described in terms of a probabilistic model, and the observations form evidence that must be conditioned on.

Within probability, there are two ways to state that a is true:

- The first is to state that the probability of a is 1 by writing $P(a) = 1$.
- The second is to condition on a, which involves using a on the right-hand side of the conditional bar, as in $P(\cdot|a)$.

The first method states that a is true in all possible worlds. The second says that the agent is only interested in worlds where a happens to be true.

Suppose an agent was told about a particular animal:

$$
\begin{aligned}
P(\textit{flies}|\textit{bird}) &= 0.8, \\
P(\textit{bird}|\textit{emu}) &= 1.0, \\
P(\textit{flies}|\textit{emu}) &= 0.001.
\end{aligned}
$$

If it determines the animal is an emu, it cannot add the statement $P(\textit{emu}) = 1$. No probability distribution satisfies these four assertions. If emu were true in all possible worlds, it would not be the case that in 0.8 of the possible worlds, the individual flies. The agent, instead, must condition on the fact that the individual is an emu.

To build a probability model, a knowledge base designer must take some knowledge into consideration and build a probability model based on this knowledge. All subsequent knowledge acquired must be treated as observations that are conditioned on.

Suppose the agent's observations at some time are given by the proposition k. The agent's subsequent belief states can be modeled by either of the following:

- construct a probability theory, based on a measure μ, for the agent's belief before it had observed k and then condition on the evidence k conjoined with the subsequent evidence e, or
- construct a probability theory, based on a measure μ_k, which models the agent's beliefs after observing k, and then condition on subsequent evidence e.

All subsequent probabilities will be identical no matter which construction was used. Building μ_k directly is sometimes easier because the model does not have to cover the cases of when k is false. Sometimes, however, it is easier to build μ and condition on k.

What is important is that there is a coherent stage where the probability model is reasonable and where every subsequent observation is conditioned on.

Bayes' rule specifies how an agent should update its belief in a proposition based on a new piece of evidence.

Suppose an agent has a current belief in proposition h based on evidence k already observed, given by $P(h|k)$, and subsequently observes e. Its new belief in h is $P(h|e \wedge k)$. Bayes' rule tells us how to update the agent's belief in hypothesis h as new evidence arrives.

Proposition 6.4. *(Bayes' rule) As long as $P(e|k) \neq 0$,*

$$P(h|e \wedge k) = \frac{P(e|h \wedge k) \times P(h|k)}{P(e|k)}.$$

This is often written with the background knowledge k implicit. In this case, if $P(e) \neq 0$, then

$$P(h|e) = \frac{P(e|h) \times P(h)}{P(e)}.$$

*$P(e|h)$ is the **likelihood** of the hypothesis h; $P(h)$ is the **prior** of the hypothesis h. Bayes' rule states that the posterior is proportional to the likelihood times the prior.*

Proof. The commutativity of conjunction means that $h \wedge e$ is equivalent to $e \wedge h$, and so they have the same probability given k. Using the rule for multiplication in two different ways,

$$
\begin{aligned}
P(h \wedge e|k) &= P(h|e \wedge k) \times P(e|k) \\
&= P(e|h \wedge k) \times P(h|k).
\end{aligned}
$$

The theorem follows from dividing the right-hand sides by $P(e|k)$. □

Often, Bayes' rule is used to compare various hypotheses (different h_i's), where it can be noticed that the denominator $P(e|k)$ is a constant that does not depend on the particular hypothesis. When comparing the relative posterior probabilities of hypotheses, we can ignore the denominator. To get the posterior probability, the denominator can be computed by reasoning by cases. If H is an exclusive and covering set of propositions representing all possible hypotheses, then

$$
\begin{aligned}
P(e|k) &= \sum_{h \in H} P(e \wedge h|k) \\
&= \sum_{h \in H} P(e|h \wedge k) \times P(h|k).
\end{aligned}
$$

Thus, the denominator of Bayes' rule is obtained by summing the numerators for all the hypotheses. When the hypothesis space is large, computing the denominator can be computationally difficult.

Generally, one of $P(e|h \wedge k)$ or $P(h|e \wedge k)$ is much easier to estimate than the other. This often occurs when you have a causal theory of a domain, and the predictions of different hypotheses – the $P(e|h_i \wedge k)$ for each hypothesis h_i – can be derived from the domain theory.

Example 6.5 Suppose the diagnostic assistant is interested in the diagnosis of the light switch s_1 of Figure 1.8 (page 34). You would expect that the modeler is able to specify how the output of a switch is a function of the input, the switch position, and the status of the switch (whether it is working, shorted, installed upside-down, etc.). Bayes' rule lets an agent infer the status of the switch given the other information.

Example 6.6 Suppose an agent has information about the reliability of fire alarms. It may know how likely it is that an alarm will work if there is a fire. If it must know the probability that there is a fire, given that there is an alarm, it can use Bayes' rule:

$$P(fire|alarm) = \frac{P(alarm|fire) \times P(fire)}{P(alarm)},$$

where $P(alarm|fire)$ is the probability that the alarm worked, assuming that there was a fire. It is a measure of the alarm's reliability. The expression $P(fire)$ is the probability of a fire given no other information. It is a measure of how fire-prone the building is. $P(alarm)$ is the probability of the alarm sounding, given no other information.

6.1.4 Expected Values

You can use the probabilities to give the expected value of any numerical random variable (i.e., one whose domain is a subset of the reals). A variable's expected value is the variable's weighted average value, where its value in each possible world is weighted by the measure of the possible world.

Suppose V is a random variable whose domain is numerical, and ω is a possible world. Define $V(\omega)$ to be the value v in the domain of V such that $\omega \models V = v$. That is, we are treating a random variable as a function on worlds.

The **expected value** of numerical variable V, written $\mathcal{E}(V)$, is

$$\mathcal{E}(V) \quad = \quad \sum_{\omega \in \Omega} V(\omega) \times \mu(\omega)$$

when finitely many worlds exist. When infinitely many worlds exist, we must integrate.

Example 6.7 If *number_of_broken_switches* is an integer-valued random variable,

$$\mathcal{E}(number\_of\_broken\_switches)$$

would give the expected number of broken switches. If the world acted according to the probability model, this would give the long-run average number of broken switches.

In a manner analogous to the semantic definition of conditional probability (page 226), the **conditional expected value** of variable X conditioned on evidence e, written $\mathcal{E}(V|e)$, is

$$\mathcal{E}(V|e) \;=\; \sum_{w \in \Omega} V(w) \times \mu_e(w).$$

Thus,

$$\mathcal{E}(V|e) \;=\; \frac{1}{P(e)} \sum_{w \models e} V(w) \times P(w)$$

$$= \sum_{w \in \Omega} V(w) \times P(w|e).$$

Example 6.8 The expected number of broken switches given that light l_1 is not lit is given by

$$\mathcal{E}(\textit{number\_of\_broken\_switches}|\neg \textit{lit}(l_1)).$$

This is obtained by averaging the number of broken switches over all of the worlds in which light l_1 is not lit.

6.1.5 Information Theory

Probability forms the basis of information theory. In this section, we give a brief overview of information theory.

A **bit** is a binary digit. Because a bit has two possible values, it can be used to distinguish two items. Often the two values are written as 0 and 1, but they can be any two different values.

Two bits can distinguish four items, each associated with either 00, 01, 10, or 11. Similarly, three bits can distinguish eight items. In general, n bits can distinguish 2^n items. Thus, we can distinguish n items with $\log_2 n$ bits. It may be surprising, but we can do better than this by taking probabilities into account.

Example 6.9 Suppose you want to design a code to distinguish the elements of the set $\{a, b, c, d\}$, with $P(a) = \frac{1}{2}$, $P(b) = \frac{1}{4}$, $P(c) = \frac{1}{8}$, and $P(d) = \frac{1}{8}$. Consider the following code:

a	0	c	110
b	10	d	111

This code sometimes uses 1 bit and sometimes uses 3 bits. On average, it uses

$$P(a) \times 1 + P(b) \times 2 + P(c) \times 3 + P(d) \times 3$$

$$= \frac{1}{2} + \frac{2}{4} + \frac{3}{8} + \frac{3}{8} = 1\frac{3}{4} \text{ bits.}$$

For example, the string *aacabbda* with 8 characters has code 00110010101110, which uses 14 bits.

With this code, $-\log_2 P(a) = 1$ bit is required to distinguish a from the other symbols. To distinguish b, you must have $-\log_2 P(b) = 2$ bits. To distinguish c, you must have $-\log_2 P(c) = 3$ bits.

It is possible to build a code that, to identify x, requires $-\log_2 P(x)$ bits (or the integer greater than this, if x is the only thing being transmitted). Suppose there is a sequence of symbols we want to transmit or store and we know the probability distribution over the symbols. A symbol x with probability $P(x)$ uses $-\log_2 P(x)$ bits. To transmit a sequence, each symbol requires, on average,

$$\sum_x -P(x) \times \log_2 P(x)$$

bits to send it. This value just depends on the probability distribution of the symbols. This is called the **information content** or **entropy** of the distribution.

Analogously to conditioning in probability, the expected number of bits it takes to describe a distribution given evidence e is

$$I(e) = \sum_x -P(x|e) \times \log_2 P(x|e).$$

If a test exists that can distinguish the cases where α is true from the cases where α is false, the **information gain** from this test is

$$I(true) - (P(\alpha) \times I(\alpha) + P(\neg\alpha) \times I(\neg\alpha)),$$

where $I(true)$ is the expected number of bits needed before the test and $P(\alpha) \times I(\alpha) + P(\neg\alpha) \times I(\neg\alpha)$ is the expected number of bits after the test.

In later sections, we use the notion of information for a number of tasks:

- In diagnosis, an agent can choose a test that provides the most information.
- In decision-tree learning (page 298), information theory provides a useful criterion for choosing which property to split on: split on the property that provides the greatest information gain. The elements it must distinguish are the different values in the target concept, and the probabilities are obtained from the proportion of each value in the training set remaining at each node.
- In Bayesian learning (page 334), information theory provides a basis for deciding which is the best model given some data.

6.2   Independence

The axioms of probability are very weak and provide few constraints on allowable conditional probabilities. For example, if there are n binary variables, there are $2^n - 1$ numbers to be assigned to give a complete probability distribution from which arbitrary conditional probabilities can be derived. To determine any probability, you may have to start with an enormous database of conditional probabilities or of probabilities of possible worlds.

Two main approaches are used to overcome the need for so many numbers:

Independence Assume that the knowledge of the truth of one proposition, Y, does not affect the agent's belief in another proposition, X, in the context of other propositions Z. We say that X is independent of Y given Z. This is defined below.

Maximum entropy or random worlds Given no other knowledge, assume that everything is as random as possible. That is, the probabilities are distributed as uniformly as possible consistent with the available information.

We consider here in detail the first of these (but see the box on page 234).

As long as the value of $P(h|e)$ is not 0 or 1, the value of $P(h|e)$ does not constrain the value of $P(h|f \wedge e)$. This latter probability could have any value in the range $[0, 1]$: It is 1 when f implies h, and it is 0 if f implies $\neg h$.

As far as probability theory is concerned, there is no reason why the name of the Queen of Canada should not be as significant as a light switch's position in determining whether the light is on. Knowledge of the domain, however, may tell us that it is irrelevant.

In this section we present a representation that allows us to model the structure of the world where relevant propositions are local and where not-directly-relevant variables can be ignored when probabilities are specified. This structure can be exploited for efficient reasoning.

A common kind of qualitative knowledge is of the form $P(h|e) = P(h|f \wedge e)$. This equality says that f is irrelevant to the probability of h given e. For example, the fact that Elizabeth is the Queen of Canada is irrelevant to the probability that w_2 is live given that switch s_1 is down. This idea can apply to random variables, as in the following definition:

Random variable X is **conditionally independent** of random variable Y **given** random variable Z if for all $x \in dom(X)$, for all $y \in dom(Y)$, for all $y' \in dom(Y)$, and for all $z \in dom(Z)$, such that $P(Y=y \wedge Z=z) > 0$ and $P(Y=y' \wedge Z=z) > 0$,

$$P(X=x|Y=y \wedge Z=z) = P(X=x|Y=y' \wedge Z=z).$$

That is, given a value of Z, knowing Y's value does not affect your belief in the value of X.

Proposition 6.5. *The following four statements are equivalent, as long as the conditional probabilities are well defined:*

1. *X is conditionally independent of Y given Z.*

2. *Y is conditionally independent of X given Z.*

3. *$P(X|Y, Z) = P(X|Z)$. That is, in the context that you are given a value for Z, if you were given a value for Y, you would have the same belief in X as if you were not given a value for Y.*

4. *$P(X, Y|Z) = P(X|Z)P(Y|Z)$.*

Reducing the Numbers

The distinction between allowing representations of independence and using maximum entropy or random worlds highlights an important difference between views of a knowledge representation:

- The first view is that a knowledge representation provides a high-level modeling language that lets us model a domain in a reasonably natural way. According to this view, it is expected that knowledge representation designers prescribe how to use the knowledge representation language. It is expected that they provide a user manual on how to describe domains of interest.

- The second view is that a knowledge representation should allow someone to add whatever knowledge they may have about a domain. The knowledge representation should fill in the rest in a commonsense manner. According to this view, it is unreasonable for a knowledge representation designer to specify how particular knowledge should be encoded.

Judging a knowledge representation by the wrong criteria does not result in a fair assessment.

A belief network is a representation for a particular independence among variables. Belief networks should be viewed as a modeling language. Many domains can be concisely and naturally represented by exploiting the independencies that belief networks compactly represent. This does not mean that we can just throw in lots of facts (or probabilities) and expect a reasonable answer. One must think about a domain and consider exactly what variables are involved and what the dependencies are among the variables. When judged by this criterion, belief networks form a useful representation scheme.

Once the network structure and the domains of the variables for a belief network are defined, exactly which numbers are required (the conditional probabilities) are prescribed. The user cannot simply add arbitrary conditional probabilities but must follow the network's structure. If the numbers that are required of a belief network are provided and are locally consistent, the whole network will be consistent.

In contrast, the maximum entropy or random worlds approaches infer the most random worlds that are consistent with a probabilistic knowledge base. They form a probabilistic knowledge representation of the second type. For the random worlds approach, any numbers that happen to be available can be added and used. However, if you allow someone to add arbitrary probabilities, it is easy for the knowledge to be inconsistent with the axioms of probability. Moreover, it is difficult to justify an answer as correct if the assumptions are not made explicit.

The proof is left as an exercise. [See Exercise 1 (page 275).]

Variables X and Y are **unconditionally independent** if $P(X, Y) = P(X)P(Y)$, that is, if they are conditionally independent given no observations. Note that X and Y being unconditionally independent does not imply they are conditionally independent given some other information Z.

Conditional independence is a useful assumption about a domain that is often natural to assess and can be exploited to give a useful representation.

6.3 Belief Networks

The notion of conditional independence can be used to give a concise representation of many domains. The idea is that, given a random variable X, a small set of variables may exist that directly affect the variable's value in the sense that X is conditionally independent of other variables given values for the directly affecting variables. The set of locally affecting variables is called the **Markov blanket**. This locality is what is exploited in a belief network. A **belief network** is a directed model of conditional dependence among a set of random variables. The precise statement of conditional independence in a belief network takes into account the directionality.

To define a belief network, start with a set of random variables that represent all of the features of the model. Suppose these variables are $\{X_1, \ldots, X_n\}$. Next, select a total ordering of the variables, $X_1, \ldots, X_n$.

The chain rule (Proposition 6.3 (page 227)) shows how to decompose a conjunction into conditional probabilities:

$$P(X_1 = v_1 \wedge X_2 = v_2 \wedge \cdots \wedge X_n = v_n)$$
$$= \prod_{i=1}^{n} P(X_i = v_i | X_1 = v_1 \wedge \cdots \wedge X_{i-1} = v_{i-1}).$$

Or, in terms of random variables and probability distributions,

$$P(X_1, X_2, \cdots, X_n) = \prod_{i=1}^{n} P(X_i | X_1, \cdots, X_{i-1}).$$

Define the **parents** of random variable X_i, written $parents(X_i)$, to be a minimal set of predecessors of X_i in the total ordering such that the other predecessors of X_i are conditionally independent of X_i given $parents(X_i)$. That is, $parents(X_i) \subseteq \{X_1, \ldots, X_{i-1}\}$ such that

$$P(X_i | X_{i-1} \ldots X_1) = P(X_i | parents(X_i)).$$

If more than one minimal set exists, any minimal set can be chosen to be the parents. There can be more than one minimal set only when some of the predecessors are deterministic functions of others.

We can put the chain rule and the definition of parents together, giving

$$P(X_1, X_2, \cdots, X_n) = \prod_{i=1}^{n} P(X_i | parents(X_i)).$$

The probability over all of the variables, $P(X_1, X_2, \cdots, X_n)$, is called the **joint probability distribution**. A belief network defines a **factorization** of the joint probability distribution, where the conditional probabilities form factors that are multiplied together.

A **belief network**, also called a **Bayesian network**, is an acyclic directed graph (DAG), where the nodes are random variables. There is an arc from each element of *parents*(X_i) into X_i. Associated with the belief network is a set of conditional probability distributions – the conditional probability of each variable given its parents (which includes the prior probabilities of those variables with no parents).

Thus, a belief network consists of

- a DAG, where each node is labeled by a random variable;

- a domain for each random variable; and

- a set of conditional probability distributions giving $P(X|parents(X))$ for each variable X.

A belief network is acyclic by construction. The way the chain rule decomposes the conjunction gives the ordering. A variable can have only predecessors as parents. Different decompositions can result in different belief networks.

Example 6.10 Suppose we want to use the diagnostic assistant to diagnose whether there is a fire in a building based on noisy sensor information and possibly conflicting explanations of what could be going on. The agent receives a report about whether everyone is leaving the building. Suppose the report sensor is noisy: It sometimes reports leaving when there is no exodus (a false positive), and it sometimes does not report when everyone is leaving (a false negative). Suppose the fire alarm going off can cause the leaving, but this is not a deterministic relationship. Either tampering or fire could affect the alarm. Fire also causes smoke to rise from the building.

Suppose we use the following variables, all of which are Boolean, in the following order:

- *Tampering* is true when there is tampering with the alarm.

- *Fire* is true when there is a fire.

- *Alarm* is true when the alarm sounds.

- *Smoke* is true when there is smoke.

- *Leaving* is true if there are many people leaving the building at once.

- *Report* is true if there is a report given by someone of people leaving. *Report* is false if there is no report of leaving.

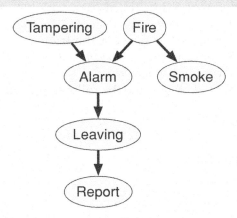

Figure 6.1: Belief network for report of leaving of Example 6.10

The variable *Report* denotes the sensor report that people are leaving. This information is unreliable because the person issuing such a report could be playing a practical joke, or no one who could have given such a report may have been paying attention. This variable is introduced to allow conditioning on unreliable sensor data. The agent knows what the sensor reports, but it only has unreliable evidence about people leaving the building.

As part of the domain, assume the following conditional independencies:

- *Fire* is conditionally independent of *Tampering* (given no other information).

- *Alarm* depends on both *Fire* and *Tampering*. That is, we are making no independence assumptions about how *Alarm* depends on its predecessors given this variable ordering.

- *Smoke* depends only on *Fire* and is conditionally independent of *Tampering* and *Alarm* given whether there is a *Fire*.

- *Leaving* only depends on *Alarm* and not directly on *Fire* or *Tampering* or *Smoke*. That is, *Leaving* is conditionally independent of the other variables given *Alarm*.

- *Report* only directly depends on *Leaving*.

The belief network of Figure 6.1 expresses these dependencies. This network represents the factorization

$$P(Tampering, Fire, Alarm, Smoke, Leaving, Report)$$
$$= \ P(Tampering) \times P(Fire) \times P(Alarm|Tampering, Fire)$$
$$\times \ P(Smoke|Fire) \times P(Leaving|Alarm) \times P(Report|Leaving).$$

We also must define the domain of each variable. Assume that the variables are Boolean; that is, they have domain {*true, false*}. We use the lower-case variant of the variable to represent the true value and use negation for the false value. Thus, for example, *Tampering* = *true* is written as *tampering*, and *Tampering* = *false* is written as ¬*tampering*.

The examples that follow assume the following conditional probabilities:

$P(tampering) = 0.02$

$P(fire) = 0.01$

$P(alarm|fire \land tampering) = 0.5$

$P(alarm|fire \land \neg tampering) = 0.99$

$P(alarm|\neg fire \land tampering) = 0.85$

$P(alarm|\neg fire \land \neg tampering) = 0.0001$

$P(smoke|fire) = 0.9$

$P(smoke|\neg fire) = 0.01$

$P(leaving|alarm) = 0.88$

$P(leaving|\neg alarm) = 0.001$

$P(report|leaving) = 0.75$

$P(report|\neg leaving) = 0.01$

Example 6.11 Consider the wiring example of Figure 1.8 (page 34). Suppose we decide to have variables for whether lights are lit, for the switch positions, for whether lights and switches are faulty or not, and for whether there is power in the wires. The variables are defined in Figure 6.2.

Let's select an ordering where the causes of a variable are before the variable in the ordering. For example, the variable for whether a light is lit comes after variables for whether the light is working and whether there is power coming into the light.

Whether light l_1 is lit depends only on whether there is power in wire w_0 and whether light l_1 is working properly. Other variables, such as the position of switch s_1, whether light l_2 is lit, or who is the Queen of Canada, are irrelevant. Thus, the parents of L_1_lit are W_0 and L_1_st.

Consider variable W_0, which represents whether there is power in wire w_0. If we knew whether there was power in wires w_1 and w_2, and we knew the position of switch s_2 and whether the switch was working properly, the value of the other variables (other than L_1_lit) would not affect our belief in whether there is power in wire w_0. Thus, the parents of W_0 should be S_2_Pos, S_2_st, W_1, and W_2.

Figure 6.2 shows the resulting belief network after the independence of each variable has been considered. The belief network also contains the domains of the variables, as given in the figure, and conditional probabilities of each variable given its parents.

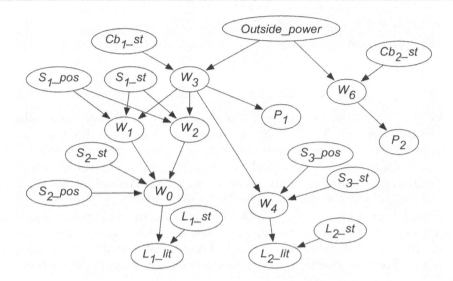

- For each wire w_i, there is a random variable, W_i, with domain $\{live, dead\}$, which denotes whether there is power in wire w_i. $W_i=live$ means wire w_i has power. $W_i=dead$ means there is no power in wire w_i.

- *Outside_power* with domain $\{live, dead\}$ denotes whether there is power coming into the building.

- For each switch s_i, variable S_i_pos denotes the position of s_i. It has domain $\{up, down\}$.

- For each switch s_i, variable S_i_st denotes the state of switch s_i. It has domain $\{ok, upside\_down, short, intermittent, broken\}$. $S_i\_st=ok$ means switch s_i is working normally. $S_i\_st=upside\_down$ means switch s_i is installed upside-down. $S_i\_st=short$ means switch s_i is shorted and acting as a wire. $S_i\_st=broken$ means switch s_i is broken and does not allow electricity to flow.

- For each circuit breaker cb_i, variable Cb_i_st has domain $\{on, off\}$. $Cb_i\_st=on$ means power can flow through cb_i and $Cb_i\_st=off$ means that power cannot flow through cb_i.

- For each light l_i, variable L_i_st with domain $\{ok, intermittent, broken\}$ denotes the state of the light. $L_i\_st=ok$ means light l_i will light if powered, $L_i\_st=intermittent$ means light l_i intermittently lights if powered, and $L_i\_st=broken$ means light l_i does not work.

Figure 6.2: Belief network for the electrical domain of Figure 1.8

For the variable W_1, the following conditional probabilities must be specified:

$P(W_1 = live|S_1\_pos = up \land S_1\_st = ok \land W_3 = live)$
$P(W_1 = live|S_1\_pos = up \land S_1\_st = ok \land W_3 = dead)$
$P(W_1 = live|S_1\_pos = up \land S_1\_st = upside\_down \land W_3 = live)$
$\vdots$
$P(W_1 = live|S_1\_pos = down \land S_1\_st = broken \land W_3 = dead).$

There are two values for S_1_pos, five values for S_1_ok, and two values for W_3, so there are $2 \times 5 \times 2 = 20$ different cases where a value for $W_1 = live$ must be specified. As far as probability theory is concerned, the probability for $W_1 = live$ for these 20 cases could be assigned arbitrarily. Of course, knowledge of the domain constrains what values make sense. The values for $W_1 = dead$ can be computed from the values for $W_1 = live$ for each of these cases.

Because the variable S_1_st has no parents, it requires a prior distribution, which can be specified as the probabilities for all but one of the values; the remaining value can be derived from the constraint that all of the probabilities sum to 1. Thus, to specify the distribution of S_1_st, four of the following five probabilities must be specified:

$P(S_1\_st = ok)$
$P(S_1\_st = upside\_down)$
$P(S_1\_st = short)$
$P(S_1\_st = intermittent)$
$P(S_1\_st = broken)$

The other variables are represented analogously.

A belief network is a graphical representation of conditional independence. The independence allows us to depict direct effects within the graph and prescribes which probabilities must be specified. Arbitrary posterior probabilities can be derived from the network.

The independence assumption embedded in a belief network is as follows: *Each random variable is conditionally independent of its non-descendants given its parents.* That is, if X is a random variable with parents $Y_1, \ldots, Y_n$, all random variables that are not descendants of X are conditionally independent of X given $Y_1, \ldots, Y_n$:

$$P(X|Y_1, \ldots, Y_n, R) = P(X|Y_1, \ldots, Y_n),$$

if R does not involve a descendant of X. For this definition, we include X as a descendant of itself. The right-hand side of this equation is the form of the probabilities that are specified as part of the belief network. R may involve ancestors of X and other nodes as long as they are not descendants of X. The independence assumption states that all of the influence of non-descendant variables is captured by knowing the value of X's parents.

Often, we refer to just the labeled DAG as a belief network. When this is done, it is important to remember that a domain for each variable and a set of conditional probability distributions are also part of the network.

The number of probabilities that must be specified for each variable is exponential in the number of parents of the variable. The independence assumption

---

Belief Networks and Causality

Belief networks have often been called **causal networks** and have been claimed to be a good representation of causality. Recall (page 204) that a causal model predicts the result of interventions. Suppose you have in mind a causal model of a domain, where the domain is specified in terms of a set of random variables. For each pair of random variables X_1 and X_2, if a direct causal connection exists from X_1 to X_2 (i.e., intervening to change X_1 in some context of other variables affects X_2 and this cannot be modeled by having some intervening variable), add an arc from X_1 to X_2. You would expect that the causal model would obey the independence assumption of the belief network. Thus, all of the conclusions of the belief network would be valid.

You would also expect such a graph to be acyclic; you do not want something eventually causing itself. This assumption is reasonable if you consider that the random variables represent particular events rather than event types. For example, consider a causal chain that "being stressed" causes you to "work inefficiently," which, in turn, causes you to "be stressed." To break the apparent cycle, we can represent "being stressed" at different stages as different random variables that refer to different times. Being stressed in the past causes you to not work well at the moment which causes you to be stressed in the future. The variables should satisfy the **clarity principle** (page 114) and have a well-defined meaning. The variables should not be seen as event types.

The belief network itself has nothing to say about causation, and it can represent non-causal independence, but it seems particularly appropriate when there is causality in a domain. Adding arcs that represent local causality tends to produce a small belief network. The belief network of Figure 6.2 (page 239) shows how this can be done for a simple domain.

A causal network models **interventions**. If someone were to artificially force a variable to have a particular value, the variable's descendants – but no other nodes – would be affected.

Finally, you can see how the causality in belief networks relates to the causal and evidential reasoning discussed in Section 5.7 (page 204). A causal belief network can be seen as a way of axiomatizing in a causal direction. Reasoning in belief networks corresponds to abducing to causes and then predicting from these. A direct mapping exists between the logic-based abductive view discussed in Section 5.7 (page 204) and belief networks: Belief networks can be modeled as logic programs with probabilities over possible hypotheses. This is described in Section 14.3 (page 611).

is useful insofar as the number of variables that directly affect another variable is small. You should order the variables so that nodes have as few parents as possible.

Note the restriction "each random variable is conditionally independent of its non-descendants given its parents" in the definition of the independence encoded in a belief network (page 240). If R contains a descendant of variable X, the independence assumption is not directly applicable.

Example 6.12 In Figure 6.2 (page 239), variables S_3_pos, S_3_st, and W_3 are the parents of variable W_4. If you know the values of S_3_pos, S_3_st, and W_3, knowing whether or not l_1 is lit or knowing the value of Cb_1_st will not affect your belief in whether there is power in wire w_4. However, even if you knew the values of S_3_pos, S_3_st, and W_3, learning whether l_2 is lit potentially changes your belief in whether there is power in wire w_1. The independence assumption is not directly applicable.

The variable S_1_pos has no parents. Thus, the independence embedded in the belief network specifies that $P(S_1\_pos = up|A) = P(S_1\_pos = up)$ for any A that does not involve a descendant of S_1_pos. If A includes a descendant of $S_1\_pos = up$ – for example, if A is $S_2\_pos = up \land L_1\_lit = true$ – the independence assumption cannot be directly applied.

A belief network specifies a joint probability distribution from which arbitrary conditional probabilities can be derived. A network can be queried by asking for the conditional probability of any variables conditioned on the values of any other variables. This is typically done by providing observations on some variables and querying another variable.

Example 6.13 Consider Example 6.10 (page 236). The prior probabilities (with no evidence) of each variable can be computed using the methods of the next section. The following conditional probabilities follow from the model of Example 6.10, to about three decimal places:

$P(tampering) = 0.02$

$P(fire) = 0.01$

$P(report) = 0.028$

$P(smoke) = 0.0189$

Observing the report gives the following:

$P(tampering|report) = 0.399$

$P(fire|report) = 0.2305$

$P(smoke|report) = 0.215$

As expected, the probability of both *tampering* and *fire* are increased by the report. Because *fire* is increased, so is the probability of *smoke*.

Suppose instead that *smoke* were observed:

$P(tampering|smoke) = 0.02$

$P(fire|smoke) = 0.476$

$P(report|smoke) = 0.320$

Note that the probability of *tampering* is not affected by observing *smoke*; however, the probabilities of *report* and *fire* are increased.

Suppose that both *report* and *smoke* were observed:

$P(tampering|report \wedge smoke) = 0.0284$

$P(fire|report \wedge smoke) = 0.964$

Observing both makes *fire* even more likely. However, in the context of the *report*, the presence of *smoke* makes *tampering* less likely. This is because the *report* is **explained away** by *fire*, which is now more likely.

Suppose instead that *report*, but not *smoke*, was observed:

$P(tampering|report \wedge \neg smoke) = 0.501$

$P(fire|report \wedge \neg smoke) = 0.0294$

In the context of the *report*, *fire* becomes much less likely and so the probability of *tampering* increases to explain the *report*.

This example illustrates how the belief net independence assumption gives commonsense conclusions and also demonstrates how explaining away is a consequence of the independence assumption of a belief network.

This network can be used in a number of ways:

- By conditioning on the knowledge that the switches and circuit breakers are ok, and on the values of the outside power and the position of the switches, this network can simulate how the lighting should work.
- Given values of the outside power and the position of the switches, the network can infer the likelihood of any outcome – for example, how likely it is that l_1 is lit.
- Given values for the switches and whether the lights are lit, the posterior probability that each switch or circuit breaker is in any particular state can be inferred.
- Given some observations, the network can be used to reason backward to determine the most likely position of switches.
- Given some switch positions, some outputs, and some intermediate values, the network can be used to determine the probability of any other variable in the network.

6.3.1 Constructing Belief Networks

To represent a domain in a belief network, the designer of a network must consider the following questions:

- What are the relevant variables? In particular, the designer must consider
  - what the agent may observe in the domain. Each feature that can be observed should be a variable, because the agent must be able to condition on all of its observations.
  - what information the agent is interested in knowing the probability of, given the observations. Each of these features should be made into a variable that can be queried.

– other **hidden variables** or **latent variables** that will not be observed or queried but that make the model simpler. These variables either account for dependencies or reduce the size of the specification of the conditional probabilities.

- What values should these variables take? This involves considering the level of detail at which the agent should reason to answer the sorts of queries that will be encountered.

    For each variable, the designer should specify what it means to take each value in its domain. What must be true in the world for a variable to have a particular value should satisfy the clarity principle (page 114). It is a good idea to explicitly document the meaning of all variables and their possible values. The only time the designer may not want to do this is when a hidden variable exists whose values the agent will want to learn from data [see Section 11.2.2 (page 460)].

- What is the relationship between the variables? This should be expressed in terms of local influence and be modeled using the parent relation.

- How does the distribution of a variable depend on the variables that locally influence it (its parents)? This is expressed in terms of the conditional probability distributions.

Example 6.14 Suppose you want the diagnostic assistant to be able to reason about the possible causes of a patient's wheezing and coughing, as in Example 5.30 (page 201).

- The agent can observe coughing, wheezing, and fever and can ask whether the patient smokes. There are thus variables for these.

- The agent may want to know about other symptoms of the patient and the prognosis of various possible treatments; if so, these should also be variables. (Although they are not used in this example).

- There are variables that are useful to predict the outcomes of patients. The medical community has named many of these and characterized their symptoms. Here we will use the variables *Bronchitis* and *Influenza*.

- Now consider what the variables directly depend on. Whether patients wheeze depends on whether they have bronchitis. Whether they cough depends on on whether they have bronchitis. Whether patients have bronchitis depends on whether they have influenza and whether they smoke. Whether they have fever depends on whether they have influenza. Figure 6.3 depicts these dependencies.

- Choosing the values for the variables involves considering the level of detail at which to reason. You could encode the severity of each of the diseases and symptoms as values for the variables. You could, for example, use the values *severe, moderate, mild,* or *absent* for the *Wheezing* variable. You could even model the disease at a lower level of abstraction, for example, by representing all subtypes of the diseases. For ease of exposition, we will model the domain at a very abstract level, only considering the presence or absence of symptoms and diseases. Each of the variables will be

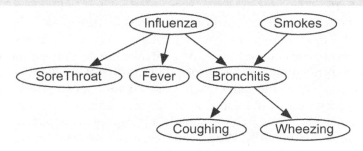

Figure 6.3: Belief network for Example 6.14

Boolean, with domain {*true, false*}, representing the presence or absence of the associated disease or symptom.

- You assess how each variable depends on its parents, which is done by specifying the conditional probabilities of each variable given its parents:

$P(influenza) = 0.05$

$P(smokes) = 0.2$

$P(soreThroat|influenza) = 0.3$

$P(soreThroat|\neg influenza) = 0.001$

$P(fever|influenza) = 0.9$

$P(fever|\neg influenza) = 0.05$

$P(bronchitis|influenza \wedge smokes) = 0.99$

$P(bronchitis|influenza \wedge \neg smokes) = 0.9$

$P(bronchitis|\neg influenza \wedge smokes) = 0.7$

$P(bronchitis|\neg influenza \wedge \neg smokes) = 0.0001$

$P(coughing|bronchitis) = 0.8$

$P(coughing|\neg bronchitis) = 0.07$

$P(wheezing|bronchitis) = 0.6$

$P(wheezing|\neg bronchitis) = 0.001$

The process of **diagnosis** is carried out by conditioning on the observed symptoms and deriving posterior probabilities of the faults or diseases.

This example also illustrates another example of explaining away and the preference for simpler diagnoses over complex ones.

Before any observations, we can compute (see the next section), to a few significant digits, $P(smokes) = 0.2$, $P(influenza) = 0.05$, and $P(bronchitis) = 0.18$. Once *wheezing* is observed, all three become more likely: $P(smokes|wheezing) = 0.79$, $P(influenza|wheezing) = 0.25$, and $P(bronchitis|wheezing) = 0.992$.

Suppose *wheezing* $\wedge$ *fever* is observed: $P(smokes|wheezing \wedge fever) = 0.32$, $P(influenza|wheezing \wedge fever) = 0.86$, and $P(bronchitis|wheezing \wedge fever) = 0.998$. Notice how, as in Example 5.30 (page 201), when *fever* is observed, influenza is indicated, and so *smokes* is **explained away**.

Example 6.15 Consider the belief network depicted in Figure 6.2 (page 239). Note the independence assumption embedded in this model: The DAG specifies that the lights, switches, and circuit breakers break independently. To model dependencies among how the switches break, you can add more arcs and perhaps more nodes. For example, if lights do not break independently because they come from the same batch, you can add an extra node that conveys the dependency. You would add a node that represents whether the lights come from a good or bad batch, which is made a parent of L_1_st and L_2_st. The lights can now break dependently. When you have evidence that one light is broken, the probability that the batch is bad may increase and thus make it more likely that the other light is bad. If you are not sure whether the lights are indeed from the same batch, you can add a node representing this, too. The important point is that the belief network provides a specification of independence that lets us model dependencies in a natural and direct manner.

The model implies that no possibility exists of there being shorts in the wires or that the house is wired differently from the diagram. In particular, it implies that w_0 cannot be shorted to w_4 so that wire w_0 can get power from wire w_4. You could add extra dependencies that let each possible short be modeled. An alternative is to add an extra node that indicates that the model is appropriate. Arcs from this node would lead to each variable representing power in a wire and to each light. When the model is appropriate, you can use the probabilities of Example 6.11 (page 238). When the model is inappropriate, you can, for example, specify that each wire and light works at random. When there are weird observations that do not fit in with the original model – they are impossible or extremely unlikely given the model – the probability that the model is inappropriate will increase.

Example 6.16 Suppose we want to develop a **help system** to determine what help page a user is interested in based on the keywords they give in a query to a help system.

The system will observe the words that the user gives. Suppose that we do not want to model the sentence structure, but assume that the set of words will be sufficient to determine the help page. The user can give multiple words. One way to represent this is to have a Boolean variable for each word. Thus, there will be nodes labeled "able", "absent", "add", ..., "zoom" that have the value *true* when the user uses that word in a query and *false* when the user does not use that word.

We are interested in which help page the user wants. Suppose that the user is interested in one and only one help page. Thus, it seems reasonable to have a node H with domain the set of all help pages, $\{h_1, \ldots, h_k\}$.

One way this can be represented is as a **naive Bayesian classifier**. A naive Bayesian classifier is a belief network that has a single node – the class – that directly influences the other variables, and the other variables are independent given the class. Figure 6.4 shows a naive Bayesian classifier for the help system where H, the help page the user is interested in, is the class, and the other nodes represent the words used in the query. In this network, the words used in a

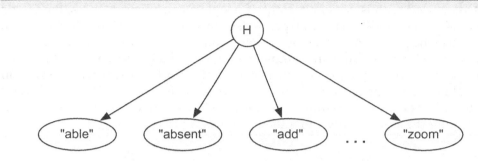

Figure 6.4: Naive belief network for Example 6.16

query depend on the help page the user is interested in, and the words are conditionally independent of each other given the help page.

This network requires $P(h_i)$ for each help page h_i, which specifies how likely it is that a user would want this help page given no information. This information could be obtained from how likely it is that users have particular problems they need help with. This network assumes the user is interested in exactly one help page, and so $\sum_i P(h_i) = 1$.

The network also requires, for each word w_j and for each help page h_i, the probability $P(w_j|h_i)$. These may seem more difficult to acquire but there are a few heuristics we can use. The average of these values should be the average number of words in a query divided by the total number of words. We would expect words that appear in the help page to be more likely to be used when asking for that help page than words not in the help page. There may also be keywords associated with the page that may be more likely to be used. There may also be some words that are just used more, independently of the help page the user is interested in. Example 7.13 (page 312) shows how the probabilities of this network can be learned from experience.

To condition on the set of words in a query, the words that appear in the query are observed to be true and the words that are not in the query are observed to be false. For example, if the help text was "the zoom is absent", the words "the", "zoom", "is", and "absent" would be observed to be true, and the other words would observed to be false. The posterior for H can then be computed and the most likely few help topics can be shown to the user.

Some words, such as "the" and "is", may not be useful in that they have the same conditional probability for each help topic and so, perhaps, would be omitted from the model. Some words that may not be expected in a query could also be omitted from the model.

Note that the conditioning was also on the words that were not in the query. For example, if page h_{73} was about printing problems, we may expect that everyone who wanted page h_{73} would use the word "print". The non-existence of the word "print" in a query is strong evidence that the user did not want page h_{73}.

The independence of the words given the help page is a very strong assumption. It probably does not apply to words like "not", where what "not" is associated with is very important. If people are asking sentences, the words would not be conditionally independent of each other given the help they need, because the probability of a word depends on its context in the sentence. There may even be words that are complementary, in which case you would expect users to use one and not the other (e.g., "type" and "write") and words you would expect to be used together (e.g., "go" and "to"); both of these cases violate the independence assumption. It is an empirical question as to how much violating the assumptions hurts the usefulness of the system.

6.4   Probabilistic Inference

The most common probabilistic inference task is to compute the posterior distribution of a query variable given some evidence. Unfortunately, even the problem of estimating the posterior probability in a belief network within an absolute error (of less than 0.5), or within a constant multiplicative factor, is NP-hard, so general efficient implementations will not be available.

The main approaches for probabilistic inference in belief networks are

- exploiting the structure of the network. This approach is typified by the variable elimination algorithm detailed later.

- search-based approaches. By enumerating some of the possible worlds, posterior probabilities can be estimated from the worlds generated. By computing the probability mass of the worlds not considered, a bound on the error in the posterior probability can be estimated. This approach works well when the distributions are extreme (all probabilities are close to zero or close to one), as occurs in engineered systems.

- **variational inference**, where the idea is to find an approximation to the problem that is easy to compute. First choose a class of representations that are easy to compute. This class could be as simple as the set of disconnected belief networks (with no arcs). Next try to find a member of the class that is closest to the original problem. That is, find an easy-to-compute distribution that is as close as possible to the posterior distribution that must be computed. Thus, the problem reduces to an optimization problem of minimizing the error.

- stochastic simulation. In these approaches, random cases are generated according to the probability distributions. By treating these random cases as a set of samples, the marginal distribution on any combination of variables can be estimated. Stochastic simulation methods are discussed in Section 6.4.2 (page 256).

This book presents only the first and fourth methods.

6.4.1   Variable Elimination for Belief Networks

This section gives an algorithm for finding the posterior distribution for a variable in an arbitrarily structured belief network. Many of the efficient exact

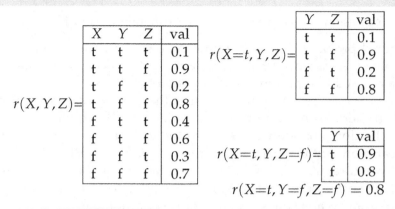

Figure 6.5: An example factor and assignments

methods can be seen as optimizations of this algorithm. This algorithm can be seen as a variant of variable elimination (VE) for constraint satisfaction problems (CSPs) (page 127) or VE for soft constraints (page 147).

The algorithm is based on the notion that a belief network specifies a factorization of the joint probability distribution (page 236).

Before we give the algorithm, we define factors and the operations that will be performed on them. Recall that $P(X|Y)$ is a function from variables (or sets of variables) X and Y into the real numbers that, given a value for X and a value for Y, gives the conditional probability of the value for X, given the value for Y. This idea of a function of variables is generalized as the notion of a factor. The VE algorithm for belief networks manipulates factors to compute posterior probabilities.

A **factor** is a representation of a function from a tuple of random variables into a number. We will write factor f on variables $X_1, \ldots, X_j$ as $f(X_1, \ldots, X_j)$. The variables $X_1, \ldots, X_j$ are the variables **of** the factor f, and f is a factor **on** $X_1, \ldots, X_j$.

Suppose $f(X_1, \ldots, X_j)$ is a factor and each v_i is an element of the domain of X_i. $f(X_1 = v_1, X_2 = v_2, \ldots, X_j = v_j)$ is a number that is the value of f when each X_i has value v_i. Some of the variables of a factor can be assigned to values to make a new factor on the other variables. For example, $f(X_1 = v_1, X_2, \ldots, X_j)$, sometimes written as $f(X_1, X_2, \ldots, X_j)_{X_1 = v_1}$, where v_1 is an element of the domain of variable X_1, is a factor on $X_2, \ldots, X_j$.

Example 6.17 Figure 6.5 shows a factor $r(X, Y, Z)$ on variables X, Y and Z as a table. This assumes that each variable is binary with domain $\{t, f\}$. The figure gives a table for the factor $r(X = t, Y, Z)$, which is a factor on Y, Z. Similarly, $r(X = t, Y, Z = f)$ is a factor on Y, and $r(X = t, Y = f, Z = f)$ is a number.

Factors can be multiplied together. Suppose f_1 and f_2 are factors, where f_1 is a factor that contains variables $X_1, \ldots, X_i$ and $Y_1, \ldots, Y_j$, and f_2 is a factor with variables $Y_1, \ldots, Y_j$ and $Z_1, \ldots, Z_k$, where $Y_1, \ldots, Y_j$ are the variables in

Representations of Conditional Probabilities and Factors

A conditional probability distribution can be seen as a function of the variables involved. A factor is a representation of a function on variables; thus, a factor can be used to represent conditional probabilities.

When the variables have finite domains, these factors can be implemented as arrays. If there is an ordering of the variables (e.g., alphabetical) and the values in the domains are mapped into the non-negative integers, there is a canonical representation of each factor as a one-dimensional array that is indexed by natural numbers. Operations on factors can be implemented efficiently using such a representation. However, this form is not a good one to present to users because the structure of the conditional is lost.

Factors do not have to be implemented as arrays. The tabular representation is often too large when there are many parents. Often, more structure exists in conditional probabilities that can be exploited.

One such structure exploits **context-specific independence**, where one variable is conditionally independent of another, given a particular value of the third variable. For example, suppose the robot can go outside or get coffee. Whether it gets wet depends on whether there is rain in the context that it went out or on whether the cup was full if it got coffee. There are a number of ways to represent the conditional probability $P(Wet|Out, Rain, Full)$ – for example as a decision tree, as rules with probabilities, or as tables with contexts:

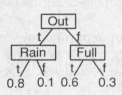

out :

Rain	Wet	Prob
t	t	0.8
t	f	0.2
f	t	0.1
f	f	0.9

$wet \leftarrow out \wedge rain : 0.8$
$wet \leftarrow out \wedge \sim rain : 0.1$
$wet \leftarrow \sim out \wedge full : 0.6$ $\sim out :$
$wet \leftarrow \sim out \wedge \sim full : 0.3$

Full	Wet	Prob
t	t	0.6
t	f	0.4
f	t	0.3
f	f	0.7

Another common representation is a **noisy or**. For example, suppose the robot can get wet from rain, coffee, sprinkler, or kids. There can be a probability that it gets wet from rain if it rains, and a probability that it gets wet from coffee if it has coffee, and so on (these probabilities give the noise). The robot gets wet if it gets wet from one of them, giving the "or".

The next chapter explores other representations that can be used for conditional probabilities.

$f_1=$

A	B	val
t	t	0.1
t	f	0.9
f	t	0.2
f	f	0.8

$f_2=$

B	C	val
t	t	0.3
t	f	0.7
f	t	0.6
f	f	0.4

$f_1 \times f_2=$

A	B	C	val
t	t	t	0.03
t	t	f	0.07
t	f	t	0.54
t	f	f	0.36
f	t	t	0.06
f	t	f	0.14
f	f	t	0.48
f	f	f	0.32

Figure 6.6: Multiplying factors example

common to f_1 and f_2. The **product** of f_1 and f_2, written $f_1 \times f_2$, is a factor on the union of the variables, namely $X_1, \ldots, X_i, Y_1, \ldots, Y_j, Z_1, \ldots, Z_k$, defined by:

$$
(f_1 \times f_2)(X_1, \ldots, X_i, Y_1, \ldots, Y_j, Z_1, \ldots, Z_k)
$$
$$
= f_1(X_1, \ldots, X_i, Y_1, \ldots, Y_j) \times f_2(Y_1, \ldots, Y_j, Z_1, \ldots, Z_k).
$$

Example 6.18 Figure 6.6 shows the product of $f_1(A, B)$ and $f_2(B, C)$, which is a factor on A, B, C. Note that $(f_1 \times f_2)(A = t, B = f, C = f) = f_1(A = t, B = f) \times f_2(B = f, C = f) = 0.9 \times 0.4 = 0.36$.

The remaining operation is to sum out a variable in a factor. Given factor $f(X_1, \ldots, X_j)$, summing out a variable, say X_1, results in a factor on the other variables, $X_2, \ldots, X_j$, defined by

$$
(\sum_{X_1} f)(X_2, \ldots, X_j) = f(X_1 = v_1, X_2, \ldots, X_j) + \cdots + f(X_1 = v_k, X_2 \ldots, X_j),
$$

where $\{v_1, \ldots, v_k\}$ is the set of possible values of variable X_1.

Example 6.19 Figure 6.7 (on the next page) gives an example of summing out variable B from a factor $f_3(A, B, C)$, which is a factor on A, C. Notice how

$$
(\sum_B f_3)(A = t, C = f) = f_3(A = t, B = t, C = f) + f_3(A = t, B = f, C = f)
$$
$$
= 0.07 + 0.36
$$
$$
= 0.43
$$

A conditional probability distribution $P(X|Y_1, \ldots, Y_j)$ can be seen as a factor f on $X, Y_1, \ldots, Y_j$, where

$$
f(X = u, Y_1 = v_1, \ldots, Y_j = v_j) = P(X = u | Y_1 = v_1 \wedge \cdots \wedge Y_j = v_j).
$$

Usually, humans prefer the $P(\cdot|\cdot)$ notation, but internally the computer just treats conditional probabilities as factors.

	A	B	C	val
	t	t	t	0.03
	t	t	f	0.07
	t	f	t	0.54
$f_3=$	t	f	f	0.36
	f	t	t	0.06
	f	t	f	0.14
	f	f	t	0.48
	f	f	f	0.32

	A	C	val
	t	t	0.57
$\sum_B f_3=$	t	f	0.43
	f	t	0.54
	f	f	0.46

Figure 6.7: Summing out a variable from a factor

The **belief network inference problem** is the problem of computing the posterior distribution of a variable, given some evidence.

The problem of computing posterior probabilities can be reduced to the problem of computing the probability of conjunctions. Given evidence $Y_1 = v_1, \ldots, Y_j = v_j$, and query variable Z:

$$P(Z|Y_1 = v_1, \ldots, Y_j = v_j)$$
$$= \frac{P(Z, Y_1 = v_1, \ldots, Y_j = v_j)}{P(Y_1 = v_1, \ldots, Y_j = v_j)}$$
$$= \frac{P(Z, Y_1 = v_1, \ldots, Y_j = v_j)}{\sum_Z P(Z, Y_1 = v_1, \ldots, Y_j = v_j)}.$$

So the agent computes the factor $P(Z, Y_1 = v_1, \ldots, Y_j = v_j)$ and normalizes. Note that this is a factor only of Z; given a value for Z, it returns a number that is the probability of the conjunction of the evidence and the value for Z.

Suppose the variables of the belief network are $X_1, \ldots, X_n$. To compute the factor $P(Z, Y_1 = v_1, \ldots, Y_j = v_j)$, sum out the other variables from the joint distribution. Suppose $Z_1, \ldots, Z_k$ is an enumeration of the other variables in the belief network – that is,

$$\{Z_1, \ldots, Z_k\} = \{X_1, \ldots, X_n\} - \{Z\} - \{Y_1, \ldots, Y_j\}.$$

The probability of Z conjoined with the evidence is

$$p(Z, Y_1 = v_1, \ldots, Y_j = v_j) = \sum_{Z_k} \cdots \sum_{Z_1} P(X_1, \ldots, X_n)_{Y_1 = v_1, \ldots, Y_j = v_j}.$$

The order that the variables Z_i are summed out is an **elimination ordering**.

Note how this is related to the possible worlds semantics of probability (page 221). There is a possible world for each assignment of a value to each variable. The **joint probability distribution**, $P(X_1, \ldots, X_n)$, gives the probability (or measure) for each possible world. The VE algorithm thus selects the worlds with the observed values for the Y_i's and sums over the possible worlds with the same value for Z. This corresponds to the definition of conditional probability (page 225). However, VE does this more efficiently than by summing over all of the worlds.

By the rule for conjunction of probabilities and the definition of a belief network,

$$P(X_1, \ldots, X_n) = P(X_1 | parents(X_1)) \times \cdots \times P(X_n | parents(X_n)),$$

where $parents(X_i)$ is the set of parents of variable X_i.

We have now reduced the belief network inference problem to a problem of summing out a set of variables from a product of factors. To solve this problem efficiently, we use the distribution law learned in high school: to compute a sum of products such as $xy + xz$ efficiently, distribute out the common factors (here x), which results in $x(y + z)$. This is the essence of the VE algorithm. We call the elements multiplied together "factors" because of the use of the term in algebra. Initially, the factors represent the conditional probability distributions, but the intermediate factors are just functions on variables that are created by adding and multiplying factors.

To compute the posterior distribution of a query variable given observations:

1. Construct a factor for each conditional probability distribution.

2. Eliminate each of the non-query variables:

   - if the variable is observed, its value is set to the observed value in each of the factors in which the variable appears,

   - otherwise the variable is summed out.

3. Multiply the remaining factors and normalize.

To sum out a variable Z from a product $f_1, \ldots, f_k$ of factors, first partition the factors into those that do not contain Z, say $f_1, \ldots, f_i$, and those that contain Z, $f_{i+1}, \ldots, f_k$; then distribute the common factors out of the sum:

$$\sum_Z f_1 \times \cdots \times f_k = f_1 \times \cdots \times f_i \times \left(\sum_Z f_{i+1} \times \cdots \times f_k \right).$$

VE explicitly constructs a representation (in terms of a multidimensional array, a tree, or a set of rules) of the rightmost factor.

Figure 6.8 (on the next page) gives pseudocode for the VE algorithm. The elimination ordering can be given a priori or can be computed on the fly. It is worthwhile to select observed variables first in the elimination ordering, because eliminating these simplifies the problem.

This assumes that the query variable is not observed. If it is observed to have a particular value, its posterior probability is just 1 for the observed value and 0 for the other values.

1: **procedure** $VE\_BN(Vs, Ps, O, Q)$
2:     **Inputs**
3:         Vs: set of variables
4:         Ps: set of factors representing the conditional probabilities
5:         O: set of observations of values on some of the variables
6:         Q: a query variable
7:     **Output**
8:         posterior distribution on Q
9:     **Local**
10:        Fs: a set of factors
11:    $Fs \leftarrow Ps$
12:    **for each** $X \in Vs - \{Q\}$ using some elimination ordering **do**
13:        **if** X is observed **then**
14:            **for each** $F \in Fs$ that involves X **do**
15:                **set** X in F to its observed value in O
16:                project F onto remaining variables
17:        **else**
18:            $Rs := \{F \in Fs : F \text{ involves } X\}$
19:            let T be the product of the factors in Rs
20:            $N := \sum_X T$
21:            $Fs := Fs \setminus Rs \cup \{N\}$
22:    let T be the product of the factors in Rs
23:    $N := \sum_Q T$
24:    **return** T/N

Figure 6.8: Variable elimination for belief networks

Example 6.20 Consider Example 6.10 (page 236) with the query

$$P(\text{Tampering}|\text{Smoke} = \text{true} \wedge \text{Report} = \text{true}).$$

After eliminating the observed variables, *Smoke* and *Report*, the following factors remain:

ConditionalProbability	Factor
$P(\text{Tampering})$	$f_0(\text{Tampering})$
$P(\text{Fire})$	$f_1(\text{Fire})$
$P(\text{Alarm}|\text{Tampering}, \text{Fire})$	$f_2(\text{Tampering}, \text{Fire}, \text{Alarm})$
$P(\text{Smoke} = \text{yes}|\text{Fire})$	$f_3(\text{Fire})$
$P(\text{Leaving}|\text{Alarm})$	$f_4(\text{Alarm}, \text{Leaving})$
$P(\text{Report} = \text{yes}|\text{Leaving})$	$f_5(\text{Leaving})$

The algorithm ignores the conditional probability reading and just works with the factors. The intermediate factors do not always represent a conditional probability.

Suppose *Fire* is selected next in the elimination ordering. To eliminate *Fire*, collect all of the factors containing *Fire* – $f_1(Fire)$, $f_2(Tampering, Fire, Alarm)$, and $f_3(Fire)$ – multiply them together, and sum out *Fire* from the resulting factor. Call this factor $F_6(Tampering, Alarm)$. At this stage, the following factors remain:

> $f_0(Tampering)$,
> $f_4(Alarm, Leaving)$,
> $f_5(Leaving)$,
> $f_6(Tampering, Alarm)$.

Suppose *Alarm* is eliminated next. VE multiplies the factors containing *Alarm* and sums out *Alarm* from the product, giving a factor, call it f_7:

$$f_7(Tampering, Leaving) = \sum_{Alarm} f_4(Alarm, Leaving) \times f_6(Tampering, Alarm)$$

It then has the following factors:

> $f_0(Tampering)$,
> $f_5(Leaving)$,
> $f_7(Tampering, Leaving)$.

Eliminating *Leaving* results in the factor

$$f_8(Tampering) = \sum_{Leaving} f_5(Leaving) \times f_7(Tampering, Leaving).$$

To determine the distribution over *Tampering*, multiply the remaining factors, giving

$$f_9(Tampering) = f_0(Tampering) \times f_8(Tampering).$$

The posterior distribution over tampering is given by

$$\frac{f_9(Tampering)}{\sum_{Tampering} f_9(Tampering)}.$$

Note that the denominator is the prior probability of the evidence.

Example 6.21 Consider the same network as in the previous example but with the following query:

> $P(Alarm|Fire{=}true)$.

When *Fire* is eliminated, the factor $P(Fire)$ becomes a factor of no variables; it is just a number, $P(Fire = true)$.

Suppose *Report* is eliminated next. It is in one factor, which represents $P(Report|Leaving)$. Summing over all of the values of *Report* gives a factor on *Leaving*, all of whose values are 1. This is because $P(Report{=}true|Leaving = v) + P(Report = false|Leaving = v) = 1$ for any value v of *Leaving*.

Similarly, if you eliminate *Leaving* next, you multiply a factor that is all 1 by a factor representing $P(Leaving|Alarm)$ and sum out *Leaving*. This, again, results in a factor all of whose values are 1.

Similarly, eliminating *Smoke* results in a factor of no variables, whose value is 1. Note that even if smoke had been observed, eliminating smoke would result in a factor of no variables, which would not affect the posterior distribution on *Alarm*.

Eventually, there is only the factor on *Alarm* that represents its prior probability and a constant factor that will cancel in the normalization.

The complexity of the algorithm depends on a measure of complexity of the network. The size of a tabular representation of a factor is exponential in the number of variables in the factor. The **treewidth** of a network, given an elimination ordering, is the maximum number of variables in a factor created by summing out a variable, given the elimination ordering. The **treewidth** of a belief network is the minimum treewidth over all elimination orderings. The treewidth depends only on the graph structure and is a measure of the sparseness of the graph. The complexity of VE is exponential in the treewidth and linear in the number of variables. Finding the elimination ordering with minimum treewidth is NP-hard, but there is some good elimination ordering heuristics, as discussed for CSP VE (page 130).

There are two main ways to speed up this algorithm. Irrelevant variables can be pruned, given the observations and the query. Alternatively, it is possible to compile the graph into a secondary structure that allows for caching of values.

6.4.2 Approximate Inference Through Stochastic Simulation

Many problems are too big for exact inference, and one must resort to approximate inference. One of the most effective methods is based on generating random samples from the (posterior) distribution that the network specifies.

Stochastic simulation is based on the idea that a set of samples can be used to compute probabilities. For example, you could interpret the probability $P(a) = 0.14$ as meaning that, out of 1,000 samples, about 140 will have a true. You can go from (enough) samples into probabilities and from probabilities into samples.

We consider three problems:

- how to generate samples,
- how to incorporate observations, and
- how to infer probabilities from samples.

We examine three methods that use sampling to compute the posterior distribution of a variable: (1) rejection sampling, (2) importance sampling, and (3) particle filtering.

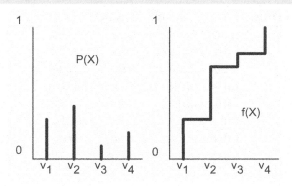

Figure 6.9: A cumulative probability distribution

Sampling from a Single Variable

To generate samples from a single discrete or real-valued variable, X, first totally order the values in the domain of X. For discrete variables, if there is no natural order, you can just create an arbitrary ordering. Given this ordering, the **cumulative probability distribution** is a function of x, defined by $f(x) = P(X \leq x)$.

To generate a random sample for X, select a random number y in the range $[0, 1]$. We select y from a uniform distribution to ensure that each number between 0 and 1 has the same chance of being chosen. Let v be the value of X that maps to y in the cumulative probability distribution. That is, v is the element of $dom(X)$ such that $f(v) = y$ or, equivalently, $v = f^{-1}(y)$. Then, $X = v$ is a random sample of X, chosen according to the distribution of X.

Example 6.22 Consider a random variable X with domain $\{v_1, v_2, v_3, v_4\}$. Suppose $P(X{=}v_1) = 0.3$, $P(X{=}v_2) = 0.4$, $P(X{=}v_3) = 0.1$, and $P(X{=}v_4) = 0.2$. First, totally order the values, say $v_1 < v_2 < v_3 < v_4$. Figure 6.9 shows $P(X)$, the distribution for X, and $f(X)$, the cumulative distribution for X. Consider value v_1; 0.3 of the range of f maps back to v_1. Thus, if a sample is uniformly selected from the Y-axis, v_1 has a 0.3 chance of being selected, v_2 has a 0.4 chance of being selected, and so forth.

Forward Sampling in Belief Networks

Forward sampling is a way to generate a sample of every variable of a belief network so that each sample is generated in proportion to it probability. Suppose $X_1, \ldots, X_n$ is a total ordering of the variables so that the parents of a variable come before the variable in the total order. Forward sampling draws a sample of all of the variables by drawing a sample of each variable $X_1, \ldots, X_n$ in order. First, it samples X_1 using the aforementioned method. For each of the other variables, due to the total ordering of variables, when it comes time to

Sample	Tampering	Fire	Alarm	Smoke	Leaving	Report
s_1	false	true	true	true	false	false
s_2	false	false	false	false	false	false
s_3	false	true	true	true	true	true
s_4	false	false	false	false	false	true
s_5	false	false	false	false	false	false
s_6	false	false	false	false	false	false
s_7	true	false	false	true	true	true
s_8	true	false	false	false	false	true
...						
s_{1000}	true	false	true	true	false	false

Figure 6.10: Sampling for a belief network

sample X_i, it already has values for all of X_i's parents. It now samples a value for X_i from the distribution of X_i given the values already assigned to the parents of X_i. Repeating this for every variable generates a sample containing values for all of the variables. The probability of selecting a particular assignment to all of the variables will be the probability of the assignment.

Example 6.23 Let us create a set of samples for the belief network of Figure 6.1 (page 237). Suppose the variables are ordered as follows: *Tampering, Fire, Alarm, Smoke, Leaving, Report*. First the algorithm samples *Tampering*, using the inverse of the cumulative distribution. Suppose it selects *Tampering = false*. Then it samples *Fire* using the same method. Suppose it selects *Fire = true*. Then it must select a value for *Alarm*, using the distribution $P(Alarm|Tampering = false, Fire = true)$. Suppose it selects *Alarm = true*. Next, it selects a value for *Smoke* using $P(Smoke|Fire = true)$. Then it selects a value for *Leaving* using the distribution for $P(Leaving|Alarm = true)$. Suppose it selects *Leaving = false*. Then it selects a value for *Report*, using the distribution $P(Report|Leaving = false)$. It has thus selected a value for each variable and created the first sample of Figure 6.10. Notice that it has selected a very unlikely combination of values. This does not happen very often; it happens in proportion to how likely the sample is. It can then repeat this until it has enough samples. In Figure 6.10, it generated 1,000 samples.

From Samples to Probabilities

Probabilities can be estimated from a set of examples using the sample average. The **sample average** of a proposition α is the number of samples where α is true divided by the total number of samples. The sample average approaches the true probability as the number of samples approaches infinity by the law of large numbers.

Hoeffding's inequality provides an estimate of the error of an unconditional probability given n samples:

Proposition 6.6 (Hoeffding). *Suppose p is the true probability, and s is the sample average from n independent samples; then*

$$P(|s - p| > \epsilon) \leq 2e^{-2n\epsilon^2}.$$

This theorem can be used to determine how many samples are required to guarantee a **probably approximately correct** estimate of the probability. To guarantee that the error is less than some $\epsilon < 0.5$, infinitely many samples are required. However, if you are willing to have an error greater than ϵ in δ of the cases, you can solve $2e^{-2n\epsilon^2} < \delta$ for n, which gives

$$n > \frac{-\ln \frac{\delta}{2}}{2\epsilon^2}.$$

For example, suppose you want an error less than 0.1, nineteen times out of twenty; that is, you are only willing to tolerate an error bigger than 0.1, in 5% of the cases. You can use Hoeffding's bound by setting ϵ to 0.1 and $\delta = 0.05$, which gives $n > 184$. Thus, you can guarantee such bounds on the error with 185 samples. If you want an error of less than 0.01 in at least 95% of the cases, 18,445 samples can be used. If you want an error of less than 0.1 in 99% of the cases, 265 samples can be used.

Rejection Sampling

Given some evidence e, rejection sampling estimates $P(h|e)$ using the formula

$$P(h|e) = \frac{P(h \wedge e)}{P(e)}.$$

This can be computed by considering only the samples where e is true and by determining the proportion of these in which h is true. The idea of **rejection sampling** is that samples are generated as before, but any sample where e is false is rejected. The proportion of the remaining, non-rejected, samples where h is true is an estimate of $P(h|e)$. If the evidence is a conjunction of assignments of values to variables, a sample can be rejected when any of the variables assigned in the sample are different from the observed value.

The error in the probability of h depends on the number of samples that are not rejected. The number of samples that are not rejected is proportional to $P(e)$. Thus, in Hoeffding's inequality, n is the number of non-rejected samples. Therefore, the error depends on $P(e)$.

Rejection sampling does not work well when the evidence is unlikely. This may not seem like that much of a problem because, by definition, unlikely

Sample	Tampering	Fire	Alarm	Smoke	Leaving	Report	
s_1	false	true	true	true	✘		
s_2	false	false	false	false	false	false	✘
s_3	false	true	true	true	✘		
s_4	false	false	false	false	false	true	✔
s_5	false	false	false	false	false	false	✘
s_6	false	false	false	false	false	false	✘
s_7	true	false	false	true	✘		
s_8	true	false	false	false	false	true	✔
...							
s_{1000}	true	false	true	true	✘		

Figure 6.11: Rejection sampling for $P(tampering|\neg smoke \wedge report)$

evidence is unlikely to occur. But, although this may be true for simple models, for complicated models with complex observations, every possible observation may be unlikely. Also, for many applications, such as in diagnosis, the user is interested in determining the probabilities because unusual observations are involved.

Example 6.24 Figure 6.11 shows how rejection sampling can be used to estimate $P(tampering|\neg smoke \wedge report)$. Any sample with $Smoke = true$ is rejected. The sample can be rejected without considering any more variables. Any sample with $Report = false$ is rejected. The sample average from the remaining samples (those marked with ✔) is used to estimate the posterior probability of $tampering$.

Because $P(\neg smoke \wedge report) = 0.0213$, we would expect about 21 samples out of the 1,000 to not be rejected. Thus, 21 can be used as n in Hoeffding's inequality, which, for example, guarantees an error for any probability computed from these samples of less than 0.2 in about 63% of the cases.

Importance Sampling

Instead of creating a sample and then rejecting it, it is possible to mix sampling with inference to reason about the probability that a sample would be rejected. In importance sampling, each sample has a weight, and the sample average is computed using the weighted average of samples. The weights of samples come from two sources:

- The samples do not have to be selected in proportion to their probability, but they can be selected according to some other distribution, called the **proposal distribution**.

- Evidence is used to update the weights and is used to compute the probability that a sample would be rejected.

Example 6.25 Consider variable A with no parents; variable E has A as its only parent, but A has other children. Suppose $P(e|a) = 0.003$, $P(e|\neg a) = 0.63$, and e is observed. Consider the samples with $A = true$. Out of 1,000 such samples, only about 3 will not be rejected. Instead of rejecting 99.7% of the samples with $A = true$, each sample with $A = true$ can be weighted by 0.003. Thus, just one sample is able to convey the information of many rejections.

Suppose $P(a) = 0.98$. If the algorithm samples according to the probability, $A = false$ would only be true in about 20 samples out of 1,000. Instead of sampling according to the probability, suppose $A = true$ is sampled 50% of the time, but each sample is weighted as follows. Each sample with $A = true$ can be weighted by $0.98/0.5 = 1.96$ and each sample with $A = false$ can be weighted by $0.02/0.5 = 0.04$. It is easy to show that the weighted sample average is the same as the probability.

In rejection sampling, given the preceding probabilities and the observation of e, A will be true in 98% of the samples and 99.7% of these will be rejected due to the evidence of e. $A = false$ would be selected in 2% of the samples and 37% of these will be rejected. Rejection sampling would thus accept only $0.98 \times 0.003 + 0.02 \times 0.63 = 0.01554$ of the samples and would reject more than 98% of the samples.

If you combine the ideas in the first two paragraphs of this example, half of the examples will have $A = true$, and these will be weighted by $1.96 \times 0.003 = 0.00588$, and the other half of the samples will have $A = false$ with a weighting of $0.04 \times 0.63 = 0.0252$. Even two such samples convey the information of many rejected samples.

Importance sampling differs from rejection sampling in two ways:

- Importance sampling does not sample all variables, only some of them. The variables that are not sampled and are not observed are summed out (i.e, some exact inference is carried out).

  In particular, you probably do not want it to sample the observed variables (although the algorithm does not preclude this). If all of the non-observed variables are sampled, it is easy to determine the probability of a sample given the evidence [see Exercise 6.10 (page 278)].

- Importance sampling does not have to sample the variables according to their prior probability; it can sample them using any distribution. The distribution that it uses to sample the variables is called the **proposal distribution**. Any distribution can be used as a proposal distribution as long as the proposal distribution does not have a zero probability for choosing some sample that is possible in the model (otherwise this part of the space will never be explored). Choosing a good proposal distribution is non-trivial.

In general, to sum over variables S from a product $f(S)q(S)$, you can choose a set of samples $\{s_1, \ldots, s_N\}$ from the distribution $q(s)$. Then

$$\sum_S f(S)q(S) = \lim_{N \to \infty} \left(\frac{1}{N} \sum_{s_i} f(s_i) \right), \tag{6.1}$$

which essentially computes the expected value (page 230) of $f(S)$, where the expectation is over the distribution $q(S)$.

In forward sampling, $q(s)$ is the uniform sample, but Equation (6.1) works for any distribution.

In importance sampling, let S be the set of variables that will be sampled. As in VE, we introduce some variables and sum them out; in this case, we sum over the sampled variables:

$$P(h|e) = \sum_S P(h|S,e)P(S|e).$$

Multiplying the top and the bottom by proposal distribution $q(S)$ gives

$$P(h|e) = \sum_S \frac{P(h|S,e)P(S|e)q(S)}{q(S)}.$$

Note that this does not give a divide-by-zero error; if $q(s) = 0$, s would never be chosen as a sample.

Using Equation (6.1), suppose $\{s_1, \ldots, s_N\}$ is the set of all samples:

$$P(h|e) = \lim_{N \to \infty} \sum_{s_i} \frac{P(h|s_i, e)P(s_i|e)}{q(s_i)}.$$

Using Bayes' rule on $P(s_i|e)$, and noting that $P(e)$ is a constant, gives

$$P(h|e) = \lim_{n \to \infty} \frac{1}{k} \sum_{s_i} \frac{P(h|s_i, e)P(e|s_i)P(s_i)}{q(s_i)},$$

where k is a normalizing constant that ensures that the posterior probabilities of the values for a mutually exclusive and covering set of hypotheses sum to 1.

Thus, for each sample, the weighting $P(s_i)/q(s_i)$ acts like a prior that is multiplied by the probability of the evidence, given the sample, to get the weight of the sample. Given many samples, the preceding formula shows how to predict the posterior on any h by getting the weighted average prediction of each sample.

Note how importance sampling generalizes rejection sampling. Rejection sampling is the case with $q(s_i) = P(s_i)$ and S includes all of the variables, including the observed variables.

Figure 6.12 shows the details of the importance sampling algorithm for computing $P(Q|e)$ for query variable Q and evidence e. The first *for* loop (line 18) creates the sample s on S. The variable p (on line 21) is the weight of sample s. The algorithm updates the weight of each value of the query variable and adds the probability of the sample s to the variable *mass*, which represents the **probability mass** – the sum of probabilities for all of the values for the query variable. Finally, it returns the probability by dividing the weight of each value of the query variable by the probability mass.

```
1: procedure IS_BN(Vs, P, e, Q, S, q, n)
2:     Inputs
3:         Vs: set of variables
4:         P: a procedure to compute conditional probabilities
5:         e: the evidence; an assignment of a value to some of the variables
6:         Q: a query variable
7:         S = {S_1, ..., S_k}: a set of variables to sample
8:         q: a distribution on S (the proposal distribution)
9:         n: number of samples to generate
10:    Output
11:        posterior distribution on Q
12:    Local
13:        array v[k], where v[i] ∈ dom(S_i)
14:        real array ans[m] where m is the size of dom(Q)
15:        s assignment of a value to each element of S
16:    mass := 0
17:    repeat n times
18:        for i = 1 : k do
19:            select v_i ∈ dom(S_i) using distribution q(S_i=v_i|S_0=v_0, ...,
       S_{i-1}=v_{i-1})
20:            s := assignment S_0=v_0, ..., S_k=v_k
21:            p := P(e|s) × P(s)/q(s)
22:            for each v_i ∈ dom(Q) do
23:                ans[i] := ans[i] + P(Q = v_i|s ∧ e) × p
24:            mass := mass + p
25:    return ans[]/mass
```

Figure 6.12: Importance sampling for belief network inference

Example 6.26 Suppose we want to use importance sampling to compute $P(alarm|smoke \land report)$. We must choose which variables to sample and the proposal distribution. Suppose we sample *Tampering*, *Fire*, and *Leaving*, and we use the following proposal distribution:

$$q(tampering) = 0.02$$
$$q(fire) = 0.5$$
$$q(Alarm|Tampering, Alarm) = P(Alarm|Tampering, Alarm)$$
$$q(Leaving|Alarm) = P(Leaving|Alarm)$$

Thus, the proposal distribution is the same as the original distribution, except for *Fire*.

The following table gives a few samples. In this table, s is the sample; e is *smoke* $\land$ *report*; $P(e|s)$ is equal to $P(smoke|Fire) \times P(report|Leaving)$, where the value for *Fire* and *Leaving* are from the sample; $P(s)/q(s)$ is 0.02 when

Fire = *true* in the sample and is 1.98 when *Fire* = *false*; $p = P(e|s) \times P(s)/q(s)$ is
the weight of the sample.

Tampering	Fire	Alarm	Leaving	$P(e|s)$	$P(s)/q(s)$	p
false	true	false	true	0.675	0.02	0.0135
true	true	true	false	0.009	0.02	0.00018
false	false	false	true	0.0075	1.98	0.01485
false	true	false	false	0.009	0.02	0.00018

$P(alarm|smoke \wedge report)$ is the weighted proportion of the samples that have
Alarm true.

The efficiency of this algorithm, in terms of how accuracy depends on the run
time, depends on

- the proposal distribution. To get the best result, the proposal distribution
  should be as close as possible to the posterior distribution. However, an
  agent typically cannot sample directly from the posterior distribution; if it
  could, it could produce posterior probabilities much more simply.

- which variables to sample. Sampling fewer variables means that there is
  more information from each sample, but each sample requires more time
  to compute the probability of the sample.

Determining the proposal distribution and which variables to sample is an art.

Particle Filtering

Importance sampling enumerates the samples one at a time and, for each sample, assigns a value to each variable. It is also possible to start with all of the
samples and, for each variable, generate a value for that variable for each of
the samples. For example, for the data of Figure 6.10 (page 258), the same data
could be generated by generating all of the values for *Tampering* before generating the values for *Fire*. The **particle filtering** algorithm generates all the
samples for one variable before moving to the next variable. It does one sweep
through the variables, and for each variable it does a sweep through all of the
samples. This algorithm has an advantage when variables are generated dynamically and there can be unboundedly many variables. It also allows for a
new operation of resampling.

Given a set of samples on some of the variables, **resampling** consists of
taking *n* samples, each with their own weighting, and generating a new set
of *n* samples, each with the same weight. Resampling can be implemented in
the same way that random samples for a single random variable are generated
(page 257), but samples, rather than values, are selected. Some of the samples
are selected multiple times and some are not selected.

A **particle** consists of an assignment of a value to a set of variables and
an associated weight. The probability of a proposition, given some evidence,
is proportional to the weighted proportion of the weights of the particles in
which the proposition is true. A set of particles is a **population**.

Particle filtering is a sampling method that starts with a population of particles, each of which assigns a value to no variables, and has a weight of 1. At each step it can

- select a variable that has not been sampled or summed out and is not observed. For each particle, it samples the variable according to some proposal distribution. The weight of the particle is updated as in importance sampling.

- select a piece of evidence to absorb. This evidence should not have been absorbed before. The weight of the particle is multiplied by the probability of the evidence given the values of the particle (and summing out any variables that are relevant and have not been sampled).

- resample the population. Resampling constructs a new population of particles, each with the same weight, by selecting particles from the population, where each particle is chosen with probability proportional to the weight of the particle. Some particles may be forgotten and some may be duplicated.

Importance sampling can be seen as being equivalent to particle filtering without resampling, but the principal difference is the order in which the particles are generated. In particle filtering, each variable is sampled for all particles, whereas, in importance sampling, each particle (sample) is sampled for all variables before the next particle is considered.

Particle filtering has two main advantages over importance sampling. First, it can be used for an unbounded number of variables (which we will see later). Second, the particles better cover the hypothesis space. Whereas importance sampling will involve some particles that have very low probability, with only a few of the particles covering most of the probability mass, resampling lets many particles more uniformly cover the probability mass.

Example 6.27 Consider using particle filtering to compute $P(Report|smoke)$ for the belief network of Figure 6.1 (page 237). First generate the particles $s_1, \ldots, s_{1000}$. For this example, we use the conditional probability of the variable being sampled given particle as the proposal distribution. Suppose it first samples *Fire*. Out of the 1,000 particles, about 10 will have *Fire* = *true* and about 990 will have *Fire* = *false* (as $P(fire) = 0.01$). It can then absorb the evidence *Smoke* = *true*. Those particles with *Fire* = *true* will be weighted by 0.9 [as $P(smoke|fire) = 0.9$] and those particles with *Fire* = *false* will be weighted by 0.01 [as $P(smoke|\neg fire) = 0.01$]. It can then resample; each particle can be chosen in proportion to its weight. The particles with *Fire* = *true* will be chosen in the ratio $990 \times 0.01 : 10 \times 0.9$. Thus, about 524 particles will be chosen with *Fire* = *true*, and the remainder with *Fire* = *false*. The other variables can be sampled, in turn, until *Report* is sampled.

Note that in particle filtering the particles are not independent, so Hoeffding's inequality (page 259), is not directly applicable.

Figure 6.13: A Markov chain as a belief network

6.5 Probability and Time

We can model a dynamic system as a belief network by treating a feature at a particular time as a random variable. We first give a model in terms of states and then show how it can be extended to features.

6.5.1 Markov Chains

A **Markov chain** is a special sort of belief network used to represent sequences of values, such as the sequence of states in a dynamic system or the sequence of words in a sentence.

Figure 6.13 shows a generic Markov chain as a belief network. The network does not have to stop at stage s_4, but it can be extended indefinitely. The belief network conveys the independence assumption

$$P(S_{t+1}|S_0,\ldots,S_t) = P(S_{t+1}|S_t),$$

which is called the **Markov assumption**.

Often, S_t represents the **state** at time t. Intuitively, S_t conveys all of the information about the history that can affect the future states. At S_t, you can see that "the future is conditionally independent of the past given the present."

A Markov chain is **stationary** if the transition probabilities are the same for each time point [i.e., for all $t > 0$, $t' > 0$, $P(S_{t+1}|S_t) = P(S_{t'+1}|S_{t'})$]. To specify a stationary Markov chain, two conditional probabilities must be specified:

- $P(S_0)$ specifies initial conditions.
- $P(S_{t+1}|S_t)$ specifies the dynamics, which is the same for each $t \geq 0$.

Stationary Markov chains are of interest because

- They provide a simple model that is easy to specify.
- The assumption of stationarity is often the natural model, because the dynamics of the world typically does not change in time. If the dynamics does change in time, it is usually because some other feature exists that could also be modeled.
- The network can extend indefinitely. Specifying a small number of parameters can give an infinite network. You can ask queries or make observations about any arbitrary points in the future or the past.

To determine the probability distribution of state S_i, VE can be used to sum out the preceding variables. Note that the variables after S_i are irrelevant to the probability of S_i and need not be considered. This computation is normally specified as matrix multiplication, but note that matrix multiplication

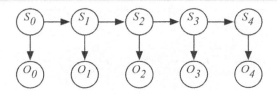

Figure 6.14: A hidden Markov model as a belief network

is a simple form of VE. Similarly, to compute $P(S_i|S_k)$, where $k > i$, only the variables before S_k need to be considered.

6.5.2 Hidden Markov Models

A **hidden Markov model (HMM)** is an augmentation of the Markov chain to include observations. Just like the state transition of the Markov chain, an HMM also includes observations of the state. These observations can be **partial** in that different states can map to the same observation and **noisy** in that the same state can stochastically map to different observations at different times.

The assumptions behind an HMM are that the state at time $t + 1$ only depends on the state at time t, as in the Markov chain. The observation at time t only depends on the state at time t. The observations are modeled using the variable O_t for each time t whose domain is the set of possible observations. The belief network representation of an HMM is depicted in Figure 6.14. Although the belief network is shown for four stages, it can proceed indefinitely.

A stationary HMM includes the following probability distributions:

- $P(S_0)$ specifies initial conditions.
- $P(S_{t+1}|S_t)$ specifies the dynamics.
- $P(O_t|S_t)$ specifies the sensor model.

There are a number of tasks that are common for HMMs.

The problem of **filtering** or belief-state **monitoring** is to determine the current state based on the current and previous observations, namely to determine

$$P(S_i|O_0, \ldots, O_i).$$

Note that all state and observation variables after S_i are irrelevant because they are not observed and can be ignored when this conditional distribution is computed.

The problem of **smoothing** is to determine a state based on past and future observations. Suppose an agent has observed up to time k and wants to determine the state at time i for $i < k$; the smoothing problem is to determine

$$P(S_i|O_0, \ldots, O_k).$$

All of the variables S_i and V_i for $i > k$ can be ignored.

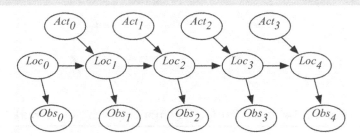

Figure 6.15: A belief network for localization

Localization

Suppose a robot wants to determine its location based on its history of actions and it sensor readings. This is the problem of **localization**. Figure 6.15 shows a belief-network representation of the localization problem. There is a variable Loc_i for each time i, which represents the robot's location at time i. There is a variable Obs_i for each time i, which represents the robot's observation made at time i. For each time i, there is a variable Act_i that represents the robot's action at time i. In this section, assume that the robot's actions are observed (we consider the case in which the robot chooses its actions in Chapter 9).

This model assumes the following dynamics: At time i, the robot is at location Loc_i, it observes Obs_i, then it acts, it observes its action Act_i, and time progresses to time $i + 1$, where it is at location Loc_{i+1}. Its observation at time t only depends on the state at time t. The robot's location at time $t + 1$ depends on its location at time t and its action at time t. Its location at time $t + 1$ is conditionally independent of previous locations, previous observations, and previous actions, given its location at time t and its action at time t.

The localization problem is to determine the robot's location as a function of its observation history:

$$P(Loc_t|Obs_0, Act_0, Obs_1, Act_1, \ldots, Act_{t-1}, Obs_t).$$

Example 6.28 Consider the domain depicted in Figure 6.16. There is a circular corridor, with 16 locations numbered 0 to 15. The robot is at one of these locations at each time. This is modeled with, for every time i, a variable Loc_i with domain $\{0, 1, \ldots, 15\}$.

- There are doors at positions 2, 4, 7, and 11 and no doors at other locations.
- The robot has a sensor that can noisily sense whether or not it is in front of a door. This is modeled with a variable Obs_i for each time i, with domain $\{door, nodoor\}$. Assume the following conditional probabilities:

$$P(Obs{=}door \mid atDoor) = 0.8$$
$$P(Obs{=}door \mid notAtDoor) = 0.1$$

where $atDoor$ is true at states 2, 4, 7, and 11 and $notAtDoor$ is true at the other states.

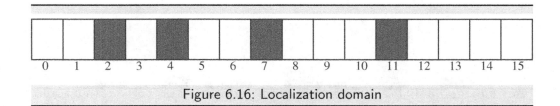

Figure 6.16: Localization domain

Thus, the observation is partial in that many states give the same observation and it is noisy in the following way: In 20% of the cases in which the robot is at a door, the sensor falsely gives a negative reading. In 10% of the cases where the robot is not at a door, the sensor records that there is a door.

- The robot can, at each time, move left, move right, or stay still. Assume that the *stay still* action is deterministic, but the dynamics of the moving actions are stochastic. Just because it carries out the *goRight* action does not mean that it actually goes one step to the right – it is possible that it stays still, goes two steps right, or even ends up at some arbitrary location (e.g., if someone picks up the robot and moves it). Assume the following dynamics, for each location L:

$$P(Loc_{t+1}=L|Act_t=goRight \wedge Loc_t=L) = 0.1$$
$$P(Loc_{t+1}=L+1|Act_t=goRight \wedge Loc_t=L) = 0.8$$
$$P(Loc_{t+1}=L+2|Act_t=goRight \wedge Loc_t=L) = 0.074$$
$$P(Loc_{t+1}=L'|Act_t=goRight \wedge Loc_t=L) = 0.002 \text{ for any other location } L'.$$

All location arithmetic is modulo 16. The action *goLeft* works the same but to the left.

The robot starts at an unknown location and must determine its location.

It may seem as though the domain is too ambiguous, the sensors are too noisy, and the dynamics is too stochastic to do anything. However, it is possible to compute the probability of the robot's current location given its history of actions and observations.

Figure 6.17 (on the next page) gives the robot's probability distribution over its locations, assuming it starts with no knowledge of where it is and experiences the following observations: observe door, go right, observe no door, go right, and then observe door. Location 4 is the most likely current location, with posterior probability of 0.42. That is, in terms of the network of Figure 6.15:

$$P(Loc_2 = 4 \quad | \quad Obs_0 = door, Act_0 = goRight, Obs_1 = nodoor,$$
$$Act_1 = goRight, Obs_2 = door) = 0.42$$

Location 7 is the second most likely current location, with posterior probability of 0.141. Locations 0, 1, 3, 8, 12, and 15 are the least likely current locations, with posterior probability of 0.011.

You can see how well this works for other sequences of observations by using the applet at the book web site.

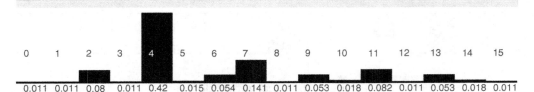

| 0 | 1 | 2 | 3 | 4 | 5 | 6 | 7 | 8 | 9 | 10 | 11 | 12 | 13 | 14 | 15 |

0.011 0.011 0.08 0.011 0.42 0.015 0.054 0.141 0.011 0.053 0.018 0.082 0.011 0.053 0.018 0.011

Figure 6.17: A distribution over locations. The locations are numbered from 0 to 15. The number at the bottom gives the posterior probability that the robot is at the location after the particular sequence of actions and observations given in Example 6.28 (page 268). The height of the bar is proportional to the posterior probability.

Example 6.29 Let us augment Example 6.28 (page 268) with another sensor. Suppose that, in addition to a door sensor, there is also a light sensor. The light sensor and the door sensor are conditionally independent given the state. Suppose the light sensor is not very informative; it can only give yes-or-no information about whether it can detect any light, and that this is very noisy, and depends on the location.

This is modeled in Figure 6.18 using the following variables:

- Loc_t is the robot's location at time t.

- Act_t is the robot's action at time t.

- D_t is the door sensor value at time t.

- L_t is the light sensor value at time t.

Conditioning on both L_i and D_i lets it combine information from the light sensor and the door sensor. This is an instance of **sensor fusion**. It is not necessary to define any new mechanisms for sensor fusion given the belief-network model; standard probabilistic inference combines the information from both sensors.

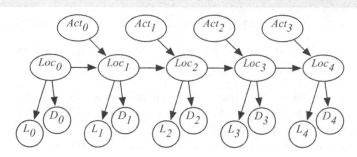

Figure 6.18: Localization with multiple sensors

6.5.3   Algorithms for Monitoring and Smoothing

You can use any standard belief-network algorithms, such as VE or particle filtering, to carry out monitoring or smoothing. However, you can take advantage of the fact that time moves forward and that you are getting observations in time and are interested in the state at the current time.

In **belief monitoring** or **filtering**, an agent computes the probability of the current state given the history of observations. In terms of the HMM of Figure 6.14 (page 267), for each i, the agent wants to compute $P(S_i|o_0, \ldots, o_i)$, which is the distribution over the state at time i given the particular observation of $o_0, \ldots, o_i$. This can easily be done using VE:

$$
\begin{aligned}
P(S_i|o_0, \ldots, o_i) \ &\propto\ P(S_i, o_0, \ldots, o_i) \\
&=\ P(o_i|S_i)P(S_i, o_0, \ldots, o_{i-1}) \\
&=\ P(o_i|S_i) \sum_{S_{i-1}} P(S_i, S_{i-1}, o_0, \ldots, o_{i-1}) \\
&=\ P(o_i|S_i) \sum_{S_{i-1}} P(S_i|S_{i-1})P(S_{i-1}, o_0, \ldots, o_{i-1}) \\
&\propto\ P(o_i|S_i) \sum_{S_{i-1}} P(S_i|S_{i-1})P(S_{i-1}|o_0, \ldots, o_{i-1}). \qquad (6.2)
\end{aligned}
$$

Suppose the agent has computed the previous belief based on the observations received up until time $i - 1$. That is, it has a factor representing $P(S_{i-1}|o_0, \ldots, o_{i-1})$. Note that this is just a factor on S_{i-1}. To compute the next belief, it multiplies this by $P(S_i|S_{i-1})$, sums out S_{i-1}, multiplies this by the factor $P(o_i|S_i)$, and normalizes.

Multiplying a factor on S_{i-1} by the factor $P(S_i|S_{i-1})$ and summing out S_{i-1} is **matrix multiplication**. Multiplying the result by $P(o_i|S_i)$ is called the **dot product**. Matrix multiplication and dot product are simple instances of VE.

Example 6.30   Consider the domain of Example 6.28 (page 268). An observation of a door involves multiplying the probability of each location L by $P(door|Loc = L)$ and renormalizing. A move right involves, for each state, doing a forward simulation of the move-right action in that state weighted by the probability of being in that state.

For many problems the state space is too big for exact inference. For these domains, particle filtering (page 264) is often very effective. With temporal models, resampling typically occurs at every time step. Once the evidence has been observed, and the posterior probabilities of the samples have been computed, they can be resampled.

Smoothing is the problem of computing the probability distribution of a state variable in an HMM given past and future observations. The use of future observations can make for more accurate predictions. Given a new observation it is possible to update all previous state estimates with one sweep through the states using VE; see Exercise 6.11 (page 279).

6.5.4   Dynamic Belief Networks

You do not have to represent the state at a particular time as a single variable. It is often more natural to represent the state in terms of features (page 112).

A **dynamic belief network** (**DBN**) is a belief network with regular repeated structure. It is like a (hidden) Markov model, but the states and the observations are represented in terms of features. Assume that time is discrete (page 46). If F is a feature, we write F_t as the random variable that represented the value of variable F at time t. A dynamic belief network makes the following assumptions:

- The set of features is the same at each time.
- For any time $t > 0$, the parents of variable F_t are variables at time t or time $t - 1$, such that the graph for any time is acyclic. The structure does not depend on the value of t (except $t = 0$ is a special case).
- The conditional probability distribution of how each variable depends on its parents is the same for every time $t > 0$.

Thus, a dynamic belief network specifies a belief network for time $t = 0$, and for each variable F_t specifies $P(F_t|parents(F_t))$, where the parents of F_t are in the same or previous time step. This is specified for t as a free parameter; the conditional probabilities can be used for any time $t > 0$. As in a belief network, directed cycles are not allowed.

The model for a dynamic belief network can be represented as a **two-step belief network** that represents the variables at the first two times (times 0 and 1). That is, for each feature F there are two variables, F_0 and F_1; $parents(F_0)$ only include variables for time 0, and $parents(F_1)$ can be variables at time 0 or 1, as long as the resulting graph is acyclic. Associated with the network are the probabilities $P(F_0|parents(F_0))$ and $P(F_1|parents(F_1))$. Because of the repeated structure, $P(F_i|parents(F_i))$, for $i > 1$, has exactly the same structure and the same conditional probability values as $P(F_1|parents(F_1))$.

Example 6.31   Suppose the trading agent (page 37) wants to model the dynamics of the price of a commodity such as printer paper. To represent this domain, the designer models what variables affect the price and the other variables. Suppose the cost of pulp and the transportation costs directly affect the price of paper. The transportation costs are affected by the weather. The pulp cost is affected by the prevalence of tree pests, which in turn depend on the weather. Suppose that each variable depends on the values of the previous time step. A two-stage dynamic belief network representing these dependencies is shown in Figure 6.19.

Note that, in this figure, the variables are initially independent.

This two-stage dynamic belief network can be expanded into a regular dynamic belief network by replicating the nodes for each time step, and the parents for future steps are a copy of the parents for the time 1 variables. An expanded belief network is shown in Figure 6.20. The subscripts represent the time that the variable is referring to.

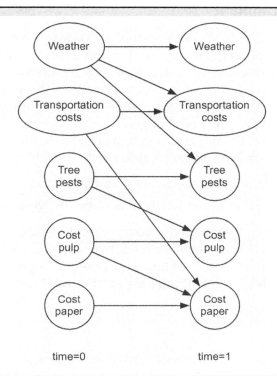

time=0   time=1

Figure 6.19: Two-stage dynamic belief network for paper pricing

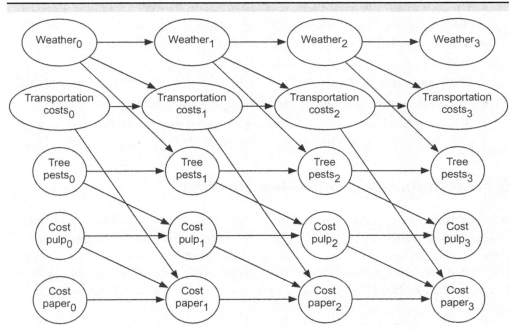

Figure 6.20: Expanded dynamic belief network for paper pricing

6.5.5   Time Granularity

One of the problems with the definition of an HMM or a dynamic belief network is that the model depends on the time granularity. The time granularity can either be fixed, for example each day or each thirtieth of a second, or it can be event-based, where a time step exists when something interesting occurs. If the time granularity were to change, for example from daily to hourly, the conditional probabilities must be changed.

One way to model the dynamics independently of the time granularity is to model, for each variable and each value for the variable,

- how long the variable is expected to keep that value and
- what value it will transition to when its value changes.

Given a discretization of time, and a time model for state transitions, such as an exponential decay, the dynamic belief network can be constructed from this information. If the discretization of time is fine enough, ignoring multiple value transitions in each time step will only result in a small error. See Exercise 6.12 (page 279).

6.6   Review

The following are the main points you should have learned from this chapter:

- Probability can be used to make decisions under uncertainty.
- The posterior probability is used to update an agent's beliefs based on evidence.
- A Bayesian belief network can be used to represent independence in a domain.
- Exact inference can be carried out for sparse graphs (with low treewidth).
- Stochastic simulation can be used for approximate inference.
- A hidden Markov model or a dynamic belief network can be used for probabilistic reasoning in time, such as for localization.

6.7   References and Further Reading

Introductions to probability theory from an AI perspective, and belief (Bayesian) networks, are by Darwiche [2009], [Koller and Friedman, 2009], Pearl [1988], Jensen [1996], and Castillo, Gutiérrez, and Hadi [1996]. Halpern [1997] reviews the relationship between logic and probability. Bacchus, Grove, Halpern, and Koller [1996] present a random worlds approach to probabilistic reasoning.

Variable elimination for evaluating belief networks is presented in Zhang and Poole [1994] and Dechter [1996]. Treewidth is discussed by Bodlaender [1993].

For comprehensive reviews of information theory, see Cover and Thomas [1991] and Grünwald [2007].

For discussions of causality, see Pearl [2000] and Spirtes et al. [2000].

For introductions to stochastic simulation, see Rubinstein [1981] and Andrieu, de Freitas, Doucet, and Jordan [2003]. The forward sampling in belief networks is based on Henrion [1988], who called it logic sampling. The use of importance sampling in belief networks described here is based on Cheng and Druzdzel [2000], who also consider how to learn the proposal distribution. There is a collection of articles on particle filtering in Doucet, de Freitas, and Gordon [2001].

HMMs are described by Rabiner [1989]. Dynamic Bayesian networks were introduced by Dean and Kanazawa [1989]. Markov localization and other issues on the relationship of probability and robotics are described by Thrun, Burgard, and Fox [2005]. The use of particle filtering for localization is due to Dellaert, Fox, Burgard, and Thrun [1999].

The annual Conference on Uncertainty in Artificial Intelligence, and the general AI conferences, provide up-to-date research results.

6.8 Exercises

Exercise 6.1 Using only the axioms of probability and the definition of conditional independence, prove Proposition 6.5 (page 233).

Exercise 6.2 Consider the belief network of Figure 6.21 (on the next page), which extends the electrical domain to include an overhead projector. Answer the following questions about how knowledge of the values of some variables would affect the probability of another variable:

(a) Can knowledge of the value of *Projector_plugged_in* affect your belief in the value of *Sam_reading_book*? Explain.

(b) Can knowledge of *Screen_lit_up* affect your belief in *Sam_reading_book*? Explain.

(c) Can knowledge of *Projector_plugged_in* affect your belief in *Sam_reading_book* given that you have observed a value for *Screen_lit_up*? Explain.

(d) Which variables could have their probabilities changed if just *Lamp_works* was observed?

(e) Which variables could have their probabilities changed if just *Power_in_projector* was observed?

Exercise 6.3 Represent the same scenario as in Exercise 5.8 (page 211) using a belief network. Show the network structure and shade the observed nodes. Give all of the initial factors, making reasonable assumptions about the conditional probabilities (they should follow the story given in that exercise, but allow some noise).

Exercise 6.4 Suppose we want to diagnose the errors school students make when adding multidigit binary numbers. Suppose we are only considering adding two two-digit numbers to form a three-digit number.

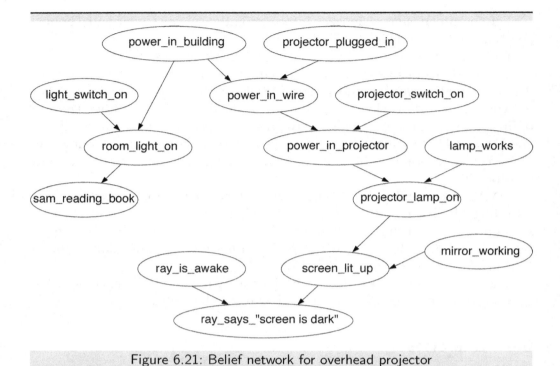

Figure 6.21: Belief network for overhead projector

That is, the problem is of the form:

$$\begin{array}{ccc} & A_1 & A_0 \\ + & B_1 & B_0 \\ \hline C_2 & C_1 & C_0 \end{array},$$

where A_i, B_i, and C_i are all binary digits.

(a) Suppose we want to model whether students know binary addition and whether they know how to carry. If they know how, they usually get the correct answer, but sometimes they make mistakes. If they don't know how to do the appropriate task, they simply guess.

What variables are necessary to model binary addition and the errors students could make? You must specify, in words, what each of the variables represents. Give a DAG that specifies the dependence of these variables.

(b) What are reasonable conditional probabilities for this domain?

(c) Implement this, perhaps by using the Alspace.org belief-network tool. Test your representation on a number of different cases.

You must give the graph, explain what each variable means, give the probability tables, and show how it works on a number of examples.

Exercise 6.5 In this question, you will build a belief network representation of the Deep Space 1 (DS1) spacecraft considered in Exercise 5.10 (page 212). Figure 5.14 (page 213) depicts a part of the actual DS1 engine design.

Suppose the following scenario:

- Valves can be *open* or *closed*.

- A value can be *ok*, in which case the gas will flow if the valve is open and not if it is closed; *broken*, in which case gas never flows; *stuck*, in which case gas flows independently of whether the valve is open or closed; or *leaking*, in which case gas flowing into the valve leaks out instead of flowing through.

- There are three gas sensors that can detect gas leaking (but not which gas); the first gas sensor detects gas from the rightmost valves ($v1 \ldots v4$), the second gas sensor detects gas from the center valves ($v5 \ldots v12$), and the third gas sensor detects gas from the leftmost valves ($v13 \ldots v16$).

(a) Build a belief-network representation of the domain. You only must consider the topmost valves (those that feed into engine $e1$). Make sure there are appropriate probabilities.

(b) Test your model on some non-trivial examples.

Exercise 6.6 Consider the following belief network:

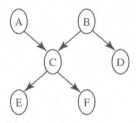

with Boolean variables (we write $A = true$ as a and $A = false$ as $\neg a$) and the following conditional probabilities:

$P(a)$	$=$	0.9	$P(d\|b)$	$=$	0.1
$P(b)$	$=$	0.2	$P(d\|\neg b)$	$=$	0.8
$P(c\|a,b)$	$=$	0.1	$P(e\|c)$	$=$	0.7
$P(c\|a, \neg b)$	$=$	0.8	$P(e\|\neg c)$	$=$	0.2
$P(c\|\neg a, b)$	$=$	0.7	$P(f\|c)$	$=$	0.2
$P(c\|\neg a, \neg b)$	$=$	0.4	$P(f\|\neg c)$	$=$	0.9

(a) Compute $P(e)$ using VE. You should first prune irrelevant variables. Show the factors that are created for a given elimination ordering.

(b) Suppose you want to compute $P(e|\neg f)$ using VE. How much of the previous computation can be reused? Show the factors that are different from those in part (a).

Exercise 6.7 Explain how to extend VE to allow for more general observations and queries. In particular, answer the following:

(a) How can the VE algorithm be extended to allow observations that are disjunctions of values for a variable (e.g., of the form $X = a \vee X = b$)?

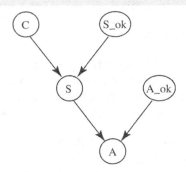

Figure 6.22: Belief network for a nuclear submarine

(b) How can the VE algorithm be extended to allow observations that are disjunctions of values for different variables (e.g., of the form $X = a \vee Y = b$)?

(c) How can the VE algorithm be extended to allow for the marginal probability on a set of variables (e.g., asking for the marginal $P(XY|e)$)?

Exercise 6.8 In a nuclear research submarine, a sensor measures the temperature of the reactor core. An alarm is triggered ($A = true$) if the sensor reading is abnormally high ($S = true$), indicating an overheating of the core ($C = true$). The alarm and/or the sensor can be defective ($S\_ok = false$, $A\_ok = false$), which can cause them to malfunction. The alarm system can be modeled by the belief network of Figure 6.22.

(a) What are the initial factors for this network? For each factor, state what it represents and what variables it is a function of.

(b) Show how VE can be used to compute the probability that the core is overheating, given that the alarm does not go off; that is, $P(c|\neg a)$.

   For each variable eliminated, show which variable is eliminated, which factor(s) are removed, and which factor(s) are created, including what variables each factor is a function of. Explain how the answer can be derived from the final factor.

(c) Suppose we add a second, identical sensor to the system and trigger the alarm when either of the sensors reads a high temperature. The two sensors break and fail independently. Give the corresponding extended belief network.

Exercise 6.9 Let's continue Exercise 5.14 (page 215).

(a) Explain what knowledge (about physics and about students) a beliefnetwork model requires.

(b) What is the main advantage of using belief networks (over using abductive diagnosis or consistency-based diagnosis) in this domain?

(c) What is the main advantage of using abductive diagnosis or consistencybased diagnosis compared to using belief networks in this domain?

Exercise 6.10 In importance sampling, every non-observed variable is sampled; a full implementation of VE is not needed. Explain how to compute the probability of a sample given the evidence in this situation. [Hint: remember that it is possible to sample children as well as parents of observed variables.]

Exercise 6.11 Consider the problem of filtering in HMMs (page 271).

(a) Give a formula for the probability of some variable X_j given future and past observations. This should involve obtaining a factor from the previous state and a factor from the next state and combining them to determine the posterior probability of X_k. How can the factor needed by X_{j-1} be computed without recomputing the message from X_{j+1}? [Hint: consider how VE, eliminating from the leftmost variable and eliminating from the rightmost variable, can be used to compute the posterior distribution for X_j.]

(b) Suppose you have computed the probability distribution for each state S_1, ..., S_k, and then you get an observation for time $k + 1$. How can the posterior probability of each variable be updated in time linear in k? [Hint: you may need to store more than just the distribution over each S_i.]

Exercise 6.12 Consider the problem of generating a dynamic belief network given a particular discretization of time and given a representation in terms of transition time, and the state transition, as in Section 6.5.5 (page 274). Suppose that there is an exponential distribution of how long each variable remains in a state and that the half-life of each variable value is specified. Give the dynamic belief network representation, assuming only a single transition in each time step.

Exercise 6.13 Suppose you get a job where the boss is interested in localization of a robot that is carrying a camera around a factory. The boss has heard of variable elimination, rejection sampling, and particle filtering and wants to know which would be most suitable for this task. You must write a report for your boss (using proper English sentences), explaining which one of these technologies would be most suitable. For the two technologies that are not the most suitable, explain why you rejected them. For the one that is most suitable, explain what information is required by that technology to use it for localization:

(a) VE (i.e., exact inference as used in HMMs),

(b) rejection sampling, or

(c) particle filtering.

Part III

Learning and Planning

Chapter 7

Learning: Overview and Supervised Learning

Whoso neglects learning in his youth, loses the past and is dead for the future.

– Euripides (484 BC – 406 BC), Phrixus, Frag. 927

Learning is the ability of an agent to improve its behavior based on experience. This could mean the following:

- The range of behaviors is expanded; the agent can do more.
- The accuracy on tasks is improved; the agent can do things better.
- The speed is improved; the agent can do things faster.

The ability to learn is essential to any intelligent agent. As Euripides pointed, learning involves an agent remembering its past in a way that is useful for its future.

This chapter considers supervised learning: given a set of training examples made up of input–output pairs, predict the output of a new input. We show how such learning may be based on one of four possible approaches: choosing a single hypothesis that fits the training examples well, predicting directly from the training examples, selecting the subset of a hypothesis space consistent with the training examples, or finding the posterior probability distribution of hypotheses conditioned on the training examples.

Chapter 11 goes beyond supervised learning and considers clustering (often called unsupervised learning), learning probabilistic models, and reinforcement learning. Section 14.2 (page 606) considers learning relational representations.

7.1 Learning Issues

The following components are part of any learning problem:

task The behavior or task that is being improved

data The experiences that are used to improve performance in the task

measure of improvement How the improvement is measured – for example, new skills that were not present initially, increasing accuracy in prediction, or improved speed

Consider the agent internals of Figure 2.9 (page 60). The problem of **learning** is to take in prior knowledge and data (e.g., about the experiences of the agent) and to create an internal representation (the knowledge base) that is used by the agent as it acts.

This internal representation could be the raw experiences themselves, but it is typically a compact representation that summarizes the data. The problem of inferring an internal representation based on examples is often called **induction** and can be contrasted with deduction (page 167), which is deriving consequences of a knowledge base, and abduction (page 199), which is hypothesizing what may be true about a particular case.

There are two principles that are at odds in choosing a representation scheme:

- *The richer the representation scheme, the more useful it is for subsequent problems solving.* For an agent to learn a way to solve a problem, the representation must be rich enough to express a way to solve the problem.

- *The richer the representation, the more difficult it is to learn.* A very rich representation is difficult to learn because it requires a great deal of data, and often many different hypotheses are consistent with the data.

The representations required for intelligence are a compromise between many desiderata [see Section 1.4 (page 11)]. The ability to learn the representation is one of them, but it is not the only one.

Learning techniques face the following issues:

Task Virtually any task for which an agent can get data or experiences can be learned. The most commonly studied learning task is **supervised learning**: given some input features, some target features, and a set of **training examples** where the input features and the target features are specified, predict the target features of a new example for which the input features are given. This is called **classification** when the target variables are discrete and **regression** when the target features are continuous.

Other learning tasks include learning classifications when the examples are not already classified (unsupervised learning), learning what to do based on rewards and punishments (reinforcement learning), learning to reason faster (analytic learning), and learning richer representations such as logic programs (inductive logic programming) or Bayesian networks.

Feedback Learning tasks can be characterized by the feedback given to the learner. In **supervised learning**, what has to be learned is specified for each example. Supervised classification occurs when a trainer provides the classification for each example. Supervised learning of actions occurs when the agent is given immediate feedback about the value of each action. **Unsupervised learning** occurs when no classifications are given and the learner must discover categories and regularities in the data. Feedback often falls between these extremes, such as in **reinforcement learning**, where the feedback in terms of rewards and punishments occurs after a sequence of actions. This leads to the **credit-assignment problem** of determining which actions were responsible for the rewards or punishments. For example, a user could give rewards to the delivery robot without telling it exactly what it is being rewarded for. The robot then must either learn what it is being rewarded for or learn which actions are preferred in which situations. It is possible that it can learn what actions to perform without actually determining which consequences of the actions are responsible for rewards.

Representation For an agent to use its experiences, the experiences must affect the agent's internal representation. Much of machine learning is studied in the context of particular representations (e.g., decision trees, neural networks, or case bases). This chapter presents some standard representations to show the common features behind learning.

Online and offline In **offline learning**, all of the training examples are available to an agent before it needs to act. In **online learning**, training examples arrive as the agent is acting. An agent that learns online requires some representation of its previously seen examples before it has seen all of its examples. As new examples are observed, the agent must update its representation. Typically, an agent never sees all of its examples. **Active learning** is a form of online learning in which the agent acts to acquire useful examples from which to learn. In active learning, the agent reasons about which examples would be useful to learn from and acts to collect these examples.

Measuring success Learning is defined in terms of improving performance based on some measure. To know whether an agent has learned, we must define a measure of success. The measure is usually not how well the agent performs on the training experiences, but how well the agent performs for new experiences.

In classification, being able to correctly classify all training examples is not the problem. For example, consider the problem of predicting a Boolean feature based on a set of examples. Suppose that there were two agents P and N. Agent P claims that all of the negative examples seen were the only negative examples and that every other instance is positive. Agent N claims that the positive examples in the training set were the only positive examples and that every other instance is negative. Both of these agents correctly classify every example in the training set but disagree on every other example. Success in learning should not be judged on correctly classifying the training set but on being able to correctly classify unseen examples. Thus, the learner must **generalize**: go beyond the specific given examples to classify unseen examples.

A standard way to measure success is to divide the examples into a training set and a test set. A representation is built using the training set, and then the predictive accuracy is measured on the test set. Of course, this is only an approximation of what is wanted; the real measure is its performance on some future task.

Bias   The tendency to prefer one hypothesis over another is called a **bias**. Consider the agents N and P defined earlier. Saying that a hypothesis is better than N's or P's hypothesis is not something that is obtained from the data – both N and P accurately predict all of the data given – but is something external to the data. Without a bias, an agent will not be able to make any predictions on unseen examples. The hypotheses adopted by P and N disagree on all further examples, and, if a learning agent cannot choose some hypotheses as better, the agent will not be able to resolve this disagreement. To have any inductive process make predictions on unseen data, an agent requires a bias. What constitutes a good bias is an empirical question about which biases work best in practice; we do not imagine that either P's or N's biases work well in practice.

Learning as search   Given a representation and a bias, the problem of learning can be reduced to one of search. Learning is a search through the space of possible representations, trying to find the representation or representations that best fits the data given the bias. Unfortunately, the search spaces are typically prohibitively large for systematic search, except for the simplest of examples. Nearly all of the search techniques used in machine learning can be seen as forms of local search (page 130) through a space of representations. The definition of the learning algorithm then becomes one of defining the search space, the evaluation function, and the search method.

Noise   In most real-world situations, the data are not perfect. Noise exists in the data (some of the features have been assigned the wrong value), there are inadequate features (the features given do not predict the classification), and often there are examples with missing features. One of the important properties of a learning algorithm is its ability to handle noisy data in all of its forms.

Interpolation and extrapolation   For cases in which there is a natural interpretation of "between," such as where the prediction is about time or space, interpolation involves making a prediction between cases for which there are data. Extrapolation involves making a prediction that goes beyond the seen examples. Extrapolation is usually much more inaccurate than interpolation. For example, in ancient astronomy, the Ptolemaic system and heliocentric system of Copernicus made detailed models of the movement of solar system in terms of epicycles (cycles within cycles). The parameters for the models could be made to fit the data very well and they were very good at interpolation; however, the models were very poor at extrapolation. As another example, it is often easy to predict a stock price on a certain day given data about the prices on the days before and the days after that day. It is very difficult to predict the price that a stock will be tomorrow, and it would be very profitable to be able to do so. An agent must be careful if its test cases mostly involve interpolating between data points, but the learned model is used for extrapolation.

Why Should We Believe an Inductive Conclusion?

When learning from data, an agent makes predictions beyond what the data give it. From observing the sun rising each morning, people predict that the sun will rise tomorrow. From observing unsupported objects repeatedly falling, a child may conclude that unsupported objects always fall (until she comes across helium-filled balloons). From observing many swans, all of which were black, someone may conclude that all swans are black. From the data of Figure 7.1 (page 289), the algorithms that follow learn a representation that predicts the user action for a case where the author is unknown, the thread is new, the length is long, and it was read at work. The data do not tell us what the user does in this case. The question arises of why an agent should ever believe any conclusion that is not a logical consequence of its knowledge.

When an agent adopts a bias, or chooses a hypothesis, it is going beyond the data – even making the same prediction about a new case that is identical to an old case in all measured respects goes beyond the data. So why should an agent believe one hypothesis over another? By what criteria can it possibly go about choosing a hypothesis?

The most common technique is to choose the simplest hypothesis that fits the data by appealing to **Ockham's razor**. William of Ockham was an English philosopher who was born in about 1285 and died, apparently of the plague, in 1349. (Note that "Occam" is the French spelling of the English town "Ockham"and is often used.) He argued for economy of explanation: "What can be done with fewer [assumptions] is done in vain with more" [Edwards, 1967, Vol. 8, p. 307].

Why should one believe the simplest hypothesis, especially because which hypothesis is simplest depends on the language used to express the hypothesis?

First, it is reasonable to assume that there is structure in the world and that an agent should discover this structure to act appropriately. A reasonable way to discover the structure of the world is to search for it. An efficient search strategy is to search from simpler hypotheses to more complicated ones. If there is no structure to be discovered, nothing will work! The fact that much structure has been found in the world (e.g., all of the structure discovered by physicists) would lead us to believe that this is not a futile search.

The fact that simplicity is language dependent should not necessarily make us suspicious. Language has evolved because it is useful; it allows people to express the structure of the world. Thus, we would expect that simplicity in everyday language would be a good measure of complexity.

The most important reason for believing inductive hypotheses is that it is useful to believe them. They help agents interact with the world and to avoid being killed; an agent that does not learn that it should not fling itself from heights will not survive long. The "simplest hypothesis" heuristic is useful because it works.

7.2   Supervised Learning

An abstract definition of **supervised learning** is as follows. Assume the learner is given the following data:

- a set of **input features**, $X_1, \ldots, X_n$;
- a set of **target features**, $Y_1, \ldots, Y_k$;
- a set of **training examples**, where the values for the input features and the target features are given for each example; and
- a set of **test examples**, where only the values for the input features are given.

The aim is to predict the values of the target features for the test examples and as-yet-unseen examples. Typically, learning is the creation of a representation that can make predictions based on descriptions of the input features of new examples.

If e is an example, and F is a feature, let $val(e, F)$ be the value of feature F in example e.

Example 7.1   Figure 7.1 shows training and test examples typical of a classification task. The aim is to predict whether a person reads an article posted to a bulletin board given properties of the article. The input features are *Author*, *Thread*, *Length*, and *WhereRead*. There is one target feature, *UserAction*. There are eighteen training examples, each of which has a value for all of the features.

In this data set, $val(e_{11}, Author) = unknown$, $val(e_{11}, Thread) = followUp$, and $val(e_{11}, UserAction) = skips$.

The aim is to predict the user action for a new example given its values for the input features.

The most common way to learn is to have a **hypothesis space** of all possible representations. Each possible representation is a **hypothesis**. The hypothesis space is typically a large finite, or countably infinite, space. A prediction is made using one of the following:

- the best hypothesis that can be found in the hypothesis space according to some measure of better,
- all of the hypotheses that are consistent with the training examples, or
- the posterior probability of the hypotheses given the evidence provided by the training examples.

One exception to this paradigm is in case-based reasoning, which uses the examples directly.

7.2.1   Evaluating Predictions

If e is an example, a **point estimate** for target feature Y is a prediction of a particular value for Y on e. Let $pval(e, Y)$ be the predicted value for target feature Y on example e. The **error** for this example on this feature is a measure of

Example	Author	Thread	Length	WhereRead	UserAction
e_1	known	new	long	home	skips
e_2	unknown	new	short	work	reads
e_3	unknown	follow Up	long	work	skips
e_4	known	follow Up	long	home	skips
e_5	known	new	short	home	reads
e_6	known	follow Up	long	work	skips
e_7	unknown	follow Up	short	work	skips
e_8	unknown	new	short	work	reads
e_9	known	follow Up	long	home	skips
e_{10}	known	new	long	work	skips
e_{11}	unknown	follow Up	short	home	skips
e_{12}	known	new	long	work	skips
e_{13}	known	follow Up	short	home	reads
e_{14}	known	new	short	work	reads
e_{15}	known	new	short	home	reads
e_{16}	known	follow Up	short	work	reads
e_{17}	known	new	short	home	reads
e_{18}	unknown	new	short	work	reads
e_{19}	unknown	new	long	work	?
e_{20}	unknown	follow Up	long	home	?

Figure 7.1: Examples of a user's preferences. These are some training and test examples obtained from observing a user deciding whether to read articles posted to a threaded discussion board depending on whether the author is known or not, whether the article started a new thread or was a follow-up, the length of the article, and whether it is read at home or at work. $e_1, \ldots, e_{18}$ are the training examples. The aim is to make a prediction for the user action on e_{19}, e_{20}, and other, currently unseen, examples.

how close $pval(e, Y)$ is to $val(e, Y)$, where $val(e, Y)$ is the actual value for feature Y in e.

For regression, when the target feature Y is real valued, both $pval(e, Y)$ and $val(e, Y)$ are real numbers that can be compared arithmetically.

For classification, when the target feature Y is a discrete variable, a number of alternatives exist:

- When Y is binary, one value can be associated with 0, the other value with 1, and a prediction can be some real number. The predicted and actual values can be compared numerically.

- When the domain of Y has more than two values, sometimes the values are totally ordered and can be scaled so a real number can be associated with each value of the domain of Y. In this case, the predicted and actual values can be compared on this scale. Often, this is not appropriate even when the values are totally ordered; for example, suppose the values are *short, medium,* and *long*. The prediction that the value is *short* ∨ *long* is very different from the prediction that the value is *medium*.

- When the domain of Y is $\{v_1, \ldots, v_k\}$, where $k > 2$, a separate prediction can be made for each v_i. This can be modeled by having a binary **indicator variable** (page 141) associated with each v_i which, for each example, has value 1 when the example has value v_i and the indicator variable has value 0 otherwise. For each training example, exactly one of the indicator variables associated with Y will be 1 and the others will be 0. A prediction gives k real numbers – one real number for each v_i.

Example 7.2 Suppose the trading agent wants to learn a person's preference for the length of holidays. Suppose the holiday can be for 1, 2, 3, 4, 5, or 6 days.

One representation is to have a real-valued variable Y that is the number of days in the holiday.

Another representation is to have six real-valued variables, $Y_1, \ldots, Y_6$, where Y_i represents the proposition that the person would like to stay for i days. For each example, $Y_i=1$ when there are i days in the holiday, and $Y_i=0$ otherwise.

The following is a sample of five data points using the two representations:

Example	Y		Example	Y_1	Y_2	Y_3	Y_4	Y_5	Y_6
e_1	1		e_1	1	0	0	0	0	0
e_2	6		e_2	0	0	0	0	0	1
e_3	6		e_3	0	0	0	0	0	1
e_4	2		e_4	0	1	0	0	0	0
e_5	1		e_5	1	0	0	0	0	0

A prediction for a new example in the first representation can be any real number, such as $Y=3.2$.

In the second representation, the learner would predict a value for each Y_i for each example. One such prediction may be $Y_1=0.5$, $Y_2=0.3$, $Y_3=0.1$, $Y_4=0.1$, $Y_5=0.1$, and $Y_6=0.5$. This is a prediction that the person may like 1 day or 6 days, but will not like a stay of 3, 4, or 5 days.

In the following definitions, E is the set of all examples and **T** is the set of target features.

There are a number of prediction measures that can be defined:

- The **absolute error** on E is the sum of the absolute errors of the predictions on each example. That is,

$$\sum_{e \in E} \sum_{Y \in \mathbf{T}} |val(e, Y) - pval(e, Y)| \, .$$

This is always non-negative, and is only zero when the predictions exactly fit the observed values.

- The **sum-of-squares error** on E is

$$\sum_{e \in E} \sum_{Y \in \mathbf{T}} (val(e, Y) - pval(e, Y))^2 \, .$$

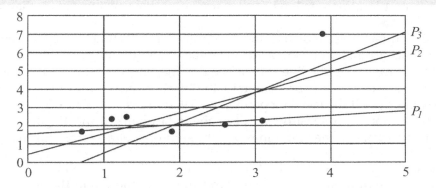

Figure 7.2: Linear predictions for a simple prediction example. Filled circles are the training examples. P_1 is the prediction that minimizes the absolute error of the training examples. P_2 is the prediction that minimizes the sum-of-squares error of the training examples. P_3 is the prediction that minimizes the worst-case error of the training examples. See Example 7.3.

This measure treats large errors as worse than small errors. An error twice as big is four times as bad, and an error 10 times as big is 100 times worse.

- The **worst-case error** on E is the maximum absolute error:

$$\max_{e \in E} \max_{Y \in \mathbf{T}} |val(e, Y) - pval(e, Y)|.$$

In this case, the learner is evaluated by how bad it can be.

Example 7.3 Suppose there is a real-valued target feature, Y, that is based on a single real-valued input feature, X. Suppose the data contains the following (X, Y) points:

$$(0.7, 1.7), (1.1, 2.4), (1.3, 2.5), (1.9, 1.7), (2.6, 2.1), (3.1, 2.3), (3.9, 7).$$

Figure 7.2 shows a plot of the training data (filled circles) and three lines, $P_1, P_2,$ and P_3, that predict the Y-value for all X points. P_1 is the line that minimizes the absolute error, P_2 is the line that minimizes the sum-of-squares error, and P_3 minimizes the worst-case error of the training examples.

  Lines P_1 and P_2 give similar predictions for $X=1.1$; namely, P_1 predicts 1.805 and P_2 predicts 1.709, whereas the data contain a data point $(1.1, 2.4)$. P_3 predicts 0.7. They give predictions within 1.5 of each other when interpolating in the range $[1, 3]$. Their predictions diverge when extrapolating from the data. P_1 and P_3 give very different predictions for $X=10$.

  The difference between the lines that minimize the various error measures is most pronounced in how they handle the outlier examples, in this case the point $(3.9, 7)$. The other points are approximately in a line.

  The prediction with the least worse-case error for this example, P_3, only depends on three data points, $(1.1, 2.4), (3.1, 2.3),$ and $(3.9, 7)$, each of which has the same worst-case error for prediction P_3. The other data points could be at different locations, as long as they are not farther away from P_3 than these three points.

In contrast, the prediction that minimizes the absolute error, P_1, does not change as a function of the actual Y-value of the training examples, as long as the points above the line stay above the line, and those below the line stay below. For example, the prediction that minimizes the absolute error would be the same, even if the last data point was $(3.9, 107)$ instead of $(3.9, 7)$.

Prediction P_2 is sensitive to all of the data points; if the Y-value for any point changes, the line that minimizes the sum-of-squares error will change.

There are a number of prediction measures that can be used for the special case where the domain of Y is $\{0, 1\}$, and the prediction is in the range $[0, 1]$. These measures can be used for Boolean domains where *true* is treated as 1, and *false* is treated as 0.

- The **likelihood of the data** is the probability of the data when the predicted value is interpreted as a probability:

$$\prod_{e \in E} \prod_{Y \in \mathbf{T}} pval(e, Y)^{val(e, Y)} (1 - pval(e, Y))^{(1 - val(e, Y))}.$$

One of $val(e, Y)$ and $(1 - val(e, Y))$ is 1, and the other is 0. Thus, this product uses $pval(e, Y)$ when $val(e, Y)=1$ and $(1 - pval(e, Y))$ when $val(e, Y)=0$. A better prediction is one with a higher likelihood. The model with the greatest likelihood is the **maximum likelihood model**.

- The **entropy** of the data is the number of bits it will take to encode the data given a code that is based on $pval(e, Y)$ treated as a probability. The entropy is

$$- \sum_{e \in E} \sum_{Y \in \mathbf{T}} [val(e, Y) \log pval(e, Y) + (1 - val(e, Y)) \log(1 - pval(e, Y))].$$

A better prediction is one with a lower entropy.

A prediction that minimizes the entropy is a prediction that maximizes the likelihood. This is because the entropy is the negative of the logarithm of the likelihood.

- Suppose the predictions are also restricted to be $\{0, 1\}$. A **false-positive error** is a positive prediction that is wrong (i.e., the predicted value is 1, and the actual value is 0). A **false-negative error** is a negative prediction that is wrong (i.e., the predicted value is 0, and the actual value is 1). Often different costs are associated with the different sorts of errors. For example, if there are data about whether a product is safe, there may be different costs for claiming it is safe when it is not safe, and for claiming it is not safe when it is safe.

We can separate the question of whether the agent has a good learning algorithm from whether it makes good predictions based on preferences that are outside of the learner. The predicting agent can at one extreme choose to only claim a positive prediction when it is sure the prediction is positive. At the other extreme, it can claim a positive prediction unless it is sure the prediction should be negative. It can often make predictions between these extremes.

One way to test the prediction independently of the decision is to consider the four cases between the predicted value and the actual value:

	actual positive	actual negative
predict positive	true positive (tp)	false positive (fp)
predict negative	false negative (fn)	true negative (tn)

Suppose tp is the number of true positives, fp is the number of false negatives, fn is the number of false negatives, and tn is the number of true negatives. The **precision** is $\frac{tp}{tp+fp}$, which is the proportion of positive predictions that are actual positives. The **recall** or **true-positive rate** is $\frac{tp}{tp+fn}$, which is the proportion of actual positives that are predicted to be positive. The **false-positive error** rate is $\frac{fp}{fp+tn}$, which is the proportion of actual negatives predicted to be positive.

An agent should try to maximize precision and recall and to minimize the false-positive rate; however, these goals are incompatible. An agent can maximize precision and minimize the false-positive rate by only making positive predictions it is sure about. However, this choice worsens recall. To maximize recall, an agent can be risky in making predictions, which makes precision smaller and the false-positive rate larger. The predicting agent often has parameters that can vary a threshold of when to make positive predictions. A **precision-recall curve** plots the precision against the recall as these parameters change. An **ROC curve**, or receiver operating characteristic curve, plots the false-positive rate against the false-negative rate as this parameter changes. Each of these approaches may be used to compare learning algorithms independently of the actual claim of the agent.

- The prediction can be seen as an action of the predicting agent. The agent should choose the action that maximizes a preference function that involves a trade-off among the costs associated with its actions. The actions may be more than true or false, but may be more complex, such as "proceed with caution" or "definitely true." What an agent should do when faced with uncertainty is discussed in Chapter 9.

Example 7.4 Consider the data of Example 7.2 (page 290). Suppose there are no input features, so all of the examples get the same prediction.

In the first representation, the prediction that minimizes the sum of absolute errors on the training data presented in Example 7.2 (page 290) is 2, with an error of 10. The prediction that minimizes the sum-of-squares error on the training data is 3.2. The prediction the minimizes the worst-case error is 3.5.

For the second representation, the prediction that minimizes the sum of absolute errors for the training examples is to predict 0 for each Y_i. The prediction that minimizes the sum-of-squares error for the training examples is $Y_1=0.4$, $Y_2=0.1$, $Y_3=0$, $Y_4=0$, $Y_5=0$, and $Y_6=0.4$. This is also the prediction that minimizes the entropy and maximizes the likelihood of the training data. The prediction that minimizes the worst-case error for the training examples is to predict 0.5 for Y_1, Y_2, and Y_6 and to predict 0 for the other features.

Thus, whichever prediction is preferred depends on how the prediction will be evaluated.

7.2.2 Point Estimates with No Input Features

The simplest case for learning is when there are no input features and where there is a single target feature. This is the base case for many of the learning algorithms and corresponds to the case where all inputs are ignored. In this case, a learning algorithm predicts a single value for the target feature for all of the examples. The prediction that minimizes the error depends on the error that is being minimized.

Suppose E is a set of examples and Y is a numeric feature. The best an agent can do is to make a single point estimate for all examples. Note that it is possible for the agent to make stochastic predictions, but these are not better; see Exercise 7.2 (page 342).

The sum-of-squares error on E of prediction v is

$$\sum_{e \in E} (val(e, Y) - v)^2.$$

The absolute error on E of prediction v is

$$\sum_{e \in E} |val(e, Y) - v|.$$

The worst-case error on E of prediction v is

$$\max_{e \in E} |val(e, Y) - v|.$$

Proposition 7.1. *Suppose V is the multiset of values of $val(e, Y)$ for $e \in E$.*

(a) *The prediction that minimizes the sum-of-squares error on E is the mean of V (the average value).*

(b) *The value that minimizes the absolute error is the median of V. In particular, any number v such that there is the same number of values of V less than v as there are values greater than v minimizes the error.*

(c) *The value that minimizes the worst-case error is $(max + min)/2$, where max is the maximum value and min is the minimum value.*

Proof. The details of the proof are left as an exercise. The basic idea follows:

(a) Differentiate the formula for the sum-of-squares error with respect to v and set to zero. This is elementary calculus. To make sure the point(s) with a derivative of zero is(are) a minimum, the end points also must be checked.

Prediction measure	Measure of prediction p for the training data	Optimal prediction for training data
absolute error	$n_0 p + n_1(1-p)$	$median(n_0, n_1)$
sum squares	$n_0 p^2 + n_1(1-p)^2$	$\frac{n_1}{n_0+n_1}$
worst case	$\begin{cases} p \text{ if } n_1 = 0 \\ 1 - p \text{ if } n_0 = 0 \\ max(p, 1-p) \text{ otherwise} \end{cases}$	$\begin{cases} 0 \text{ if } n_1 = 0 \\ 1 \text{ if } n_0 = 0 \\ 0.5 \text{ otherwise} \end{cases}$
likelihood	$p^{n_1}(1-p)^{n_0}$	$\frac{n_1}{n_0+n_1}$
entropy	$-n_1 \log p - n_0 \log(1-p)$	$\frac{n_1}{n_0+n_1}$

Figure 7.3: Optimal prediction for binary classification where the training data consist of n_0 examples of 0 and n_1 examples of 1, with no input features. $median(n_0, n_1)$ is 0 if $n_0 > n_1$, 1 if $n_0 < n_1$, and any value in $[0, 1]$ if $n_0 = n_1$.

(b) The absolute error is a piecewise linear function of v. The slope for a value that is not in V depends on the number of elements greater minus the number of elements less than that value: v is a minimum if there are the same number of elements greater than v as there are less than v.

(c) This prediction has an error of $(max - min)/2$; increasing or decreasing the prediction will increase the error. □

When the target feature has domain $\{0, 1\}$, the training examples can be summarized in two numbers: n_0, the number of examples with the value 0, and n_1, the number of examples with value 1. The prediction for each new case is the same number, p.

The optimal prediction p depends on the optimality criteria. The value of the optimality criteria for the training examples can be computed analytically and can be optimized analytically. The results are summarized in Figure 7.3.

Notice that optimizing the absolute error means predicting the median, which in this case is also the mode; this should not be surprising because the error is linear in p.

The optimal prediction for the training data for the other criteria is to predict the **empirical frequency**: the proportion of 1's in the training data, namely $\frac{n_1}{n_0+n_1}$. This can be seen as a prediction of the **probability**. The empirical frequency is often called the **maximum-likelihood estimate**.

This analysis does not specify the optimal prediction for the test data. We would *not* expect the empirical frequency of the training data to be the optimal prediction for the test data for maximizing the likelihood or minimizing the entropy. If $n_0 = 0$ or if $n_1 = 0$, all of the training data are classified the same. However, if just one of the test examples is not classified in this way, the likelihood would be 0 (its lowest possible value) and the entropy would be infinite. See Exercise 1 (page 342).

7.2.3   Learning Probabilities

For many of the prediction measures, the optimal prediction on the training data is the empirical frequency. Thus, making a point estimate can be interpreted as learning a probability. However, the empirical frequency is typically not a good estimate of the probability of new cases; just because an agent has not observed some value of a variable does not mean that the value should be assigned a probability of zero. A probability of zero means that the value is impossible.

Typically, we do not have data without any prior knowledge. There is typically a great deal of knowledge about a domain, either in the meaning of the symbols or in experience with similar examples that can be used to improve predictions.

A standard way both to solve the zero-probability problem and to take prior knowledge into account is to use a **pseudocount** or **prior count** for each value to which the training data is added.

Suppose there is a binary feature Y, and an agent has observed n_0 cases where $Y=0$ and n_1 cases where $Y=1$. The agent can use a pseudocount $c_0 \geq 0$ for $Y=0$ and a pseudocount $c_1 \geq 0$ for $Y=1$ and estimate the probability as

$$P(Y=1) = (n_1 + c_1)/(n_0 + c_0 + n_1 + c_1).$$

This takes into account both the data and the prior knowledge. This formula can be justified in terms of a prior on the parameters [see Section 7.8 (page 334)]. Choosing pseudocounts is part of designing the learner.

More generally, suppose Y has domain $\{y_1, \ldots, y_k\}$. The agent starts with a pseudocount c_i for each y_i. These counts are chosen before the agent has seen any of the data. Suppose the agent observes some training examples, where n_i is the number of data points with $Y=y_i$. It can then use

$$P(Y=y_i) = \frac{c_i + n_i}{\sum_{i'} c_{i'} + n_{i'}}.$$

To determine the pseudocounts, consider the question, "How much more should an agent believe y_i if it had seen one example with y_i true than if it had seen no examples with y_i true?" If, with no examples of y_i true, the agent believes that y_i is impossible, c_i should be zero. If not, the ratio chosen in answer to that question should be equal to the ratio $(1 + c_i) : c_i$. If the pseudocount is 1, a value that has been seen once would be twice as likely as one that has been seen no times. If the pseudocount is 10, a value observed once would be 10% more likely than a value observed no times. If the pseudocount is 0.1, a value observed once would be 11 times more likely than a value observed no times. If there is no reason to choose one value in the domain of Y over another, all of the values of c_i should be equal.

If there is no prior knowledge, Laplace [1812] suggested that it is reasonable to set $c_i=1$. See Section 7.8 (page 334) for a justification of why this may be reasonable. We will see examples where it is not appropriate, however.

The same idea can be used to learn a **conditional probability distribution** (page 227). To estimate a conditional distribution, $P(Y|X)$, of variable Y conditioned on variable(s) X, the agent can maintain a count for each pair of a value for Y and a value for X. Suppose c_{ij} is a non-negative number that will be used as a pseudocount for $Y=y_i \land X=x_j$. Suppose n_{ij} is the number of observed cases of $Y=y_i \land X=x_j$. The agent can use

$$P(Y=y_i|X=x_j) = \frac{c_{ij} + n_{ij}}{\sum_{i'} c_{i'j} + n_{i'j}},$$

but this does not work well when the denominator is small, which occurs when some values of X are rare. When X has structure – for example, when it is composed of other variables – it is often the case that some assignments to X are very rare or even do not appear in the training data. In these cases, the learner must use other methods that are discussed in this chapter.

Probabilities from Experts

The use of pseudocounts also gives us a way to combine **expert opinion** and data. Often a single agent does not have good data but may have access to multiple experts who have varying levels of expertise and who give different probabilities.

There are a number of problems with obtaining probabilities from experts:

- experts' reluctance to give an exact probability value that cannot be refined,

- representing the uncertainty of a probability estimate,

- combining the numbers from multiple experts, and

- combining expert opinion with actual data.

Rather than expecting experts to give probabilities, the experts can provide counts. Instead of giving a real number such as 0.667 for the probability of A, an expert can give a pair of numbers as $\langle n, m \rangle$ that can be interpreted as though the expert had observed n A's out of m trials. Essentially, the experts provide not only a probability but also an estimate of the size of the data set on which their opinion is based.

The counts from different experts can be combined together by adding the components to give the pseudocounts for the system. Whereas the ratio reflects the probability, different levels of confidence can be reflected in the absolute values: $\langle 2, 3 \rangle$ reflects extremely low confidence that would quickly be dominated by data or other experts' estimates. The pair $\langle 20, 30 \rangle$ reflects more confidence – a few examples would not change it much, but tens of examples would. Even hundreds of examples would have little effect on the prior counts of the pair $\langle 2000, 3000 \rangle$. However, with millions of data points, even these prior counts would have little impact on the resulting probability.

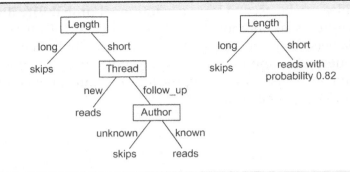

Figure 7.4: Two decision trees

7.3 Basic Models for Supervised Learning

A learned model is a representation of a function from the input features to the target features. Most supervised learning methods take the input features, the target features, and the training data and return a model that can be used for future prediction. Many of the learning methods differ in what representations are considered for representing the function. We first consider some basic models from which other composite models are built. Section 7.4 (page 313) considers more sophisticated models that are built from these basic models.

7.3.1 Learning Decision Trees

A decision tree is a simple representation for classifying examples. Decision tree learning is one of the most successful techniques for supervised classification learning. For this section, assume that all of the features have finite discrete domains, and there is a single target feature called the **classification**. Each element of the domain of the classification is called a **class**.

A **decision tree** or a **classification tree** is a tree in which each internal (non-leaf) node is labeled with an input feature. The arcs coming from a node labeled with a feature are labeled with each of the possible values of the feature. Each leaf of the tree is labeled with a class or a probability distribution over the classes.

To classify an example, filter it down the tree, as follows. For each feature encountered in the tree, the arc corresponding to the value of the example for that feature is followed. When a leaf is reached, the classification corresponding to that leaf is returned.

Example 7.5 Figure 7.4 shows two possible decision trees for the example of Figure 7.1 (page 289). Each decision tree can be used to classify examples according to the user's action. To classify a new example using the tree on the left, first determine the length. If it is long, predict skips. Otherwise, check the thread. If the thread is new, predict reads. Otherwise, check the author and predict read only if the author is known. This decision tree can correctly classify all examples in Figure 7.1 (page 289).

The tree on the right makes probabilistic predictions when the length is short. In this case, it predicts reads with probability 0.82 and so skips with probability 0.18.

A deterministic decision tree, in which all of the leaves are classes, can be mapped into a set of rules, with each leaf of the tree corresponding to a rule. The example has the classification at the leaf if all of the conditions on the path from the root to the leaf are true.

Example 7.6 The leftmost decision tree of Figure 7.4 can be represented as the following rules:

> *skips* ← *long*.
> *reads* ← *short* ∧ *new*.
> *reads* ← *short* ∧ *followUp* ∧ *known*.
> *skips* ← *short* ∧ *followUp* ∧ *unknown*.

With negation as failure (page 194), the rules for either *skips* or *reads* can be omitted, and the other can be inferred from the negation.

To use decision trees as a target representation, there are a number of questions that arise:

- Given some training examples, what decision tree should be generated? Because a decision tree can represent any function of the input features, the bias that is necessary to learn is incorporated into the preference of one decision tree over another. One proposal is to prefer the smallest tree that is consistent with the data, which could mean the tree with the least depth or the tree with the fewest nodes. Which decision trees are the best predictors of unseen data is an empirical question.

- How should an agent go about building a decision tree? One way is to search the space of decision trees for the smallest decision tree that fits the data. Unfortunately the space of decision trees is enormous (see Exercise 7.7 (page 344)). A practical solution is to carry out a local search on the space of decision trees, with the goal of minimizing the error. This is the idea behind the algorithm described below.

Searching for a Good Decision Tree

A decision tree can be incrementally built from the top down by recursively selecting a feature to split on and partitioning the training examples with respect to that feature. In Figure 7.5 (on the next page), the procedure *DecisionTreeLearner* learns a decision tree for binary attributes. The decisions regarding when to stop and which feature to split on are left undefined. The procedure *DecisionTreeClassify* takes in a decision tree produced by the learner and makes predictions for a new example.

1: **procedure** *DecisionTreeLearner*(X, Y, E)
2:    **Inputs**
3:        X: set of input features, $X = \{X_1, \ldots, X_n\}$
4:        Y: target feature
5:        E: set of training examples
6:    **Output**
7:        decision tree
8:    **if** stopping criterion is true **then**
9:        **return** *pointEstimate*(Y, E)
10:   **else**
11:       Select feature $X_i \in X$, with domain $\{v_1, v_2\}$
12:       let $E_1 = \{e \in E : val(e, X_i) = v_1\}$
13:       let $T_1 = DecisionTreeLearner(X \setminus \{X_i\}, Y, E_1)$
14:       let $E_2 = \{e \in E : val(e, X_i) = v_2\}$
15:       let $T_2 = DecisionTreeLearner(X \setminus \{X_i\}, Y, E_2)$
16:       **return** $\langle X_i = v_1, T_1, T_2 \rangle$
17:
18: **procedure** *DecisionTreeClassify*(e, X, Y, DT)
19:   **Inputs**
20:       X: set of input features, $X = \{X_1, \ldots, X_n\}$
21:       Y: target feature
22:       e: example to classify
23:       DT: decision tree
24:   **Output**
25:       prediction on Y for example e
26:   **Local**
27:       S subtree of DT
28:   $S := DT$
29:   **while** S is an internal node of the form $\langle X_i = v, T_1, T_2 \rangle$ **do**
30:       **if** $val(e, X_i) = v$ **then**
31:           $S := T_1$
32:       **else**
33:           $S := T_2$
34:   **return** S

Figure 7.5: Decision tree learning and classification for binary features

The algorithm *DecisionTreeLearner* builds a decision tree from the top down as follows: The input to the algorithm is a set of input features, a target feature, and a set of examples. The learner first tests if some stopping criterion is true. If the stopping criterion is true, it returns a point estimate (page 288) for Y, which is either a value for Y or a probability distribution over the values for Y. If the stopping criterion is not true, the learner selects a feature X_i to split on, and for each value v of this feature, it recursively builds a subtree for those examples with $X_i = v$. The returned tree is represented here in terms of triples representing an if-then-else structure.

Example 7.7 Consider applying *DecisionTreeLearner* to the classification data of Figure 7.1 (page 289). The initial call is

$decisionTreeLearner([Author, Thread, Length, WhereRead], UserAction,$
$[e_1, e_2, \ldots, e_{18}])$.

Suppose the stopping criterion is not true and the algorithm selects the feature *Length* to split on. It then calls

$decisionTreeLearner([WhereRead, Thread, Author], UserAction,$
$[e_1, e_3, e_4, e_6, e_9, e_{10}, e_{12}])$.

All of these examples agree on the user action; therefore, the algorithm returns the prediction *skips*. The second step of the recursive call is

$decisionTreeLearner([WhereRead, Thread, Author], UserAction,$
$[e_2, e_5, e_7, e_8, e_{11}, e_{13}, e_{14}, e_{15}, e_{16}, e_{17}, e_{18}])$.

Not all of the examples agree on the user action, so the algorithm selects a feature to split on. Suppose it selects *Thread*. Eventually, this recursive call returns the subtree for the case when *Length* is *short*, such as

$\langle Thread=new, reads, \langle Author=unknown, skips, reads \rangle \rangle$.

The final result is

$\langle Length=long, skips,$
$\quad \langle Thread=new, reads, \langle Author=unknown, skips, reads \rangle \rangle \rangle$,

which is a representation of the tree of Figure 7.4 (page 298).

The learning algorithm of Figure 7.5 leaves three choices unspecified:

- The stopping criterion is not defined. The learner should stop when there are no input features, when all of the examples have the same classification, or when no splitting would improve the classification ability of the resulting tree. The last is the most difficult criterion to test for; see below.

- What should be returned at the leaves is not defined. This is a point estimate (page 288) because, at this step, all of the other input features are ignored. This prediction is typically the most likely classification, the median or mean value, or a probability distribution over the classifications. [See Exercise 7.9 (page 345).]

- Which feature to select to split on is not defined. The aim is to choose the feature that will result in the smallest tree. The standard way to do this is to choose the **myopically optimal** split: if the learner were only allowed one split, which single split would result in the best classification? With the sum-of-squares error, for each feature, determine the error of the resulting tree based on a single split on that feature. For the likelihood or the entropy, the myopically optimal split is the one that gives the maximum **information gain** (page 232). Sometimes information gain is used even when the optimality criterion is the sum-of-squares error. An alternative, the **Gini index**, is investigated in Exercise 7.10 (page 345).

Example 7.8 Consider learning the user action from the data of Figure 7.1 (page 289), where we split on the feature with the maximum information gain or we myopically choose the split that minimizes the entropy or maximizes the likelihood of the data. See Section 6.1.5 (page 231) for the definition of information used here.

The information content of all examples with respect to feature *UserAction* is 1.0, because there are 9 examples with *UserAction=reads* and 9 examples with *UserAction=skips*.

Splitting on *Author* partitions the examples into $[e_1, e_4, e_5, e_6, e_9, e_{10}, e_{12}, e_{13}, e_{14}, e_{15}, e_{16}, e_{17}]$ with *Author=known* and $[e_2, e_3, e_7, e_8, e_{11}, e_{18}]$ with *Author=unknown*, each of which is evenly split between the different user actions. The information gain for the test *Author* is zero. In this case, finding out whether the author is known, by itself, provides no information about what the user action will be.

Splitting on *Thread* partitions the examples into $[e_1, e_2, e_5, e_8, e_{10}, e_{12}, e_{14}, e_{15}, e_{17}, e_{18}]$ and $[e_3, e_4, e_6, e_7, e_9, e_{11}, e_{13}, e_{16}]$. The first set of examples, those with *Thread=new*, contains 3 examples with *UserAction=skips* and 7 examples with *UserAction=reads*; thus, the information content of this set with respect to the user action is

$$-0.3 \times \log_2 0.3 - 0.7 \times \log_2 0.7 = 0.881$$

and so the information gain is 0.119.

Similarly, the examples with *Thread=old* divide up 6 : 2 according to the user action and thus have information content 0.811. The expected information gain is thus $1.0 - [(10/18) \times 0.881 + (8/18) \times 0.811] = 0.150$.

The test *Length* divides the examples into $[e_1, e_3, e_4, e_6, e_9, e_{10}, e_{12}]$ and $[e_2, e_5, e_7, e_8, e_{11}, e_{13}, e_{14}, e_{15}, e_{16}, e_{17}, e_{18}]$. The former all agree on the value of *UserAction* and so have information content zero. The user action divides the second set 9 : 2, and so the information is 0.684. Thus, the expected information gain by the test *length* is $1.0 - 11/18 \times 0.684 = 0.582$. This is the highest information gain of any test and so *Length* is chosen to split on.

In choosing which feature to split on, the information content before the test is the same for all tests, and so the learning agent can choose the test that results in the minimum expected information after the test.

The algorithm of Figure 7.5 (page 300) assumes each input feature has only two values. This restriction can be lifted in two ways:

- Allow a multiway split. To split on a multivalued variable, there would be a child for each value in the domain of the variable. This means that the representation of the decision tree becomes more complicated than the simple if-then-else form used for binary features. There are two main problems with this approach. The first is what to do with values for which there are no training examples. The second is that, for most myopic splitting heuristics, including information gain, it is generally better to split on a variable with a larger domain because it produces more children and so can fit the data better than splitting on a feature with a smaller domain. [See Exercise 7.8 (page 344).] However, splitting on a feature with a smaller domain keeps the representation more compact.

- Partition the domain into two disjoint subsets. When the domain is totally ordered, such as if the domain is a subset of the real numbers, the domain can be split into values less than some threshold and those greater than the threshold. For example, the children could correspond to $X < v$ and $X \geq v$ for some value v in the domain of X. A myopically optimal value for v can be chosen in one sweep through the data by sorting the data on the value of X and considering each split that partitions the values. When the domain does not have a natural ordering, a split can be performed on arbitrary subsets of the domain. In this case, the myopically optimal split can be found by sorting values that appear in the data on the probability of classification.

If there is noise in the data, a major problem of the preceding algorithm is **overfitting** the data. Overfitting occurs when the algorithm tries to fit distinctions that appear in the training data but do not appear in the unseen examples. This occurs when random correlations exist in the training data that are not reflected in the data set as a whole. Section 7.5 (page 320) discusses ways to detect overfitting. There are two ways to overcome the problem of overfitting in decision trees:

- Restrict the splitting to split only when the split is useful.
- Allow unrestricted splitting and then prune the resulting tree where it makes unwarranted distinctions.

The second method seems to work better in practice. One reason is that it is possible that two features together predict well but one of them, by itself, is not very useful, as shown in the following example.

Example 7.9 Suppose the aim is to predict whether a game of matching pennies is won or not. The input features are A, whether the first coin is heads or tails; B, whether the second coin is heads or tails; and C, whether there is cheering. The target feature, W, is true when there is a win, which occurs when both coins are heads or both coins are tails. Suppose cheering is correlated with winning. This example is tricky because A by itself provides no information about W, and B by itself provides no information about W. However, together they perfectly predict W. A myopic split may first split on C, because this provides the most myopic information. If all the agent is told is C, this is much more useful than A or B. However, if the tree eventually splits on A and B, the split on C is not needed. Pruning can remove C as being useful, whereas stopping early will keep the split on C.

A discussion of how to trade off model complexity and fit to the data is presented in Section 7.5 (page 320).

7.3.2   Linear Regression and Classification

Linear functions provide the basis for many learning algorithms. In this section, we first cover regression – the problem of predicting a real-valued function from training examples. Then we consider the discrete case of classification.

Linear regression is the problem of fitting a linear function to a set of input–output pairs given a set of training examples, in which the input and output features are numeric.

Suppose the input features are $X_1, \ldots, X_n$. A **linear function** of these features is a function of the form

$$f^{\overline{w}}(X_1, \ldots, X_n) = w_0 + w_1 \times X_1 + \cdots + w_n \times X_n ,$$

where $\overline{w} = \langle w_0, w_1, \ldots, w_n \rangle$ is a tuple of weights. To make w_0 not be a special case, we invent a new feature, X_0, whose value is always 1.

We will learn a function for each target feature independently, so we consider only one target, Y. Suppose a set E of examples exists, where each example $e \in E$ has values $val(e, X_i)$ for feature X_i and has an observed value $val(e, Y)$. The predicted value is thus

$$pval^{\overline{w}}(e, Y) = w_0 + w_1 \times val(e, X_1) + \cdots + w_n \times val(e, X_n)$$

$$= \sum_{i=0}^{n} w_i \times val(e, X_i) ,$$

where we have made it explicit that the prediction depends on the weights, and where $val(e, X_0)$ is defined to be 1.

The sum-of-squares error on examples E for target Y is

$$Error_E(\overline{w}) = \sum_{e \in E} (val(e, Y) - pval^{\overline{w}}(e, Y))^2$$

$$= \sum_{e \in E} \left(val(e, Y) - \sum_{i=0}^{n} w_i \times val(e, X_i) \right)^2 . \tag{7.1}$$

In this linear case, the weights that minimize the error can be computed analytically [see Exercise 7.5 (page 344)]. A more general approach, which can be used for wider classes of functions, is to compute the weights iteratively.

Gradient descent (page 149) is an iterative method to find the minimum of a function. Gradient descent starts with an initial set of weights; in each step, it decreases each weight in proportion to its partial derivative:

$$w_i := w_i - \eta \times \frac{\partial Error_E(\overline{w})}{\partial w_i}$$

where η, the gradient descent step size, is called the **learning rate**. The learning rate, as well as the features and the data, is given as input to the learning algorithm. The partial derivative specifies how much a small change in the weight would change the error.

1: **procedure** *LinearLearner*(X, Y, E, η)
2:     **Inputs**
3:         X: set of input features, $X = \{X_1, \ldots, X_n\}$
4:         Y: target feature
5:         E: set of examples from which to learn
6:         η: learning rate
7:     **Output**
8:         parameters $w_0, \ldots, w_n$
9:     **Local**
10:         $w_0, \ldots, w_n$: real numbers
11:         $pval^{\overline{w}}(e, Y) = w_0 + w_1 \times val(e, X_1) + \cdots + w_n \times val(e, X_n)$
12:     initialize $w_0, \ldots, w_n$ randomly
13:     **repeat**
14:         **for each** example e in E **do**
15:             $\delta := val(e, Y) - pval^{\overline{w}}(e, Y)$
16:             **for each** $i \in [0, n]$ **do**
17:                 $w_i := w_i + \eta \times \delta \times val(e, X_i)$
18:     **until** termination
19:     **return** $w_0, \ldots, w_n$

Figure 7.6: Gradient descent for learning a linear function

Consider minimizing the sum-of-squares error. The error is a sum over the examples. The partial derivative of a sum is the sum of the partial derivatives. Thus, we can consider each example separately and consider how much it changes the weights. The error with respect to example e has a partial derivative with respect to weight of w_i of $-2 \times [val(e, Y) - pval^{\overline{w}}(e, Y)] \times val(e, X_i)$. For each example e, let $\delta = val(e, Y) - pval^{\overline{w}}(e, Y)$. Thus, each example e updates each weight w_i:

$$w_i \quad := \quad w_i + \eta \times \delta \times val(e, X_i), \tag{7.2}$$

where we have ignored the constant 2, because we assume it is absorbed into the constant η.

Figure 7.6 gives an algorithm, *LinearLearner*(X, Y, E, η), for learning a linear function for minimizing the sum-of-squares error. Note that, in line 17, $val(e, X_0)$ is 1 for all e. Termination is usually after some number of steps, when the error is small or when the changes get small.

The algorithm presented in Figure 7.6 is sometimes called **incremental gradient descent** because of the weight change while it iterates through the examples. An alternative is to save the weights at each iteration of the while loop, use the saved weights for computing the function, and then update these saved weights after all of the examples. This process computes the true derivative of the error function, but it is more complicated and often does not work as well.

The same algorithm can be used for other error functions. For the absolute error, which is not actually differentiable at zero, the derivative can be defined to be zero at that point because the error is already at a minimum and the parameters do not have to change. See Exercise 7.12 (page 346).

Squashed Linear Functions

The use of a linear function does not work well for classification tasks. When there are only two values, say 0 and 1, a learner should never make a prediction of greater than 1 or less than 0. However, a linear function could make a prediction of, say, 3 for one example just to fit other examples better.

Initially let's consider binary classification, where the domain of the target variable is $\{0, 1\}$. If multiple binary target variables exist, they can be learned separately.

For classification, we often use a **squashed linear function** of the form

$$f^{\overline{w}}(X_1, \ldots, X_n) = f(w_0 + w_1 \times X_1 + \cdots + w_n \times X_n),$$

where f is an **activation function**, which is a function from real numbers into $[0, 1]$. Using a squashed linear function to predict a value for the target feature means that the prediction for example e for target feature Y is

$$pval^{\overline{w}}(e, Y) = f(w_0 + w_1 \times val(e, X_1) + \cdots + w_n \times val(e, X_n)).$$

A simple activation function is the **step function**, $f(x)$, defined by

$$f(x) = \begin{cases} 1 & \text{if } x \geq 0 \\ 0 & \text{if } x < 0. \end{cases}$$

A step function was the basis for the **perceptron** [Rosenblatt, 1958], which was one of the first methods developed for learning. It is difficult to adapt gradient descent to step functions because gradient descent takes derivatives and step functions are not differentiable.

If the activation is differentiable, we can use gradient descent to update the weights. The sum-of-squares error is

$$Error_E(\overline{w}) = \sum_{e \in E} \left(val(e, Y) - f\left(\sum_i w_i \times val(e, X_i)\right) \right)^2.$$

The partial derivative with respect to weight w_i for example e is

$$\frac{\partial Error_E(\overline{w})}{\partial w_i} = -2 \times \delta \times f'\left(\sum_i w_i \times val(e, X_i)\right) \times val(e, X_i).$$

where $\delta = val(e, Y) - pval^{\overline{w}}(e, Y)$, as before. Thus, each example e updates each weight w_i as follows:

$$w_i \quad := \quad w_i + \eta \times \delta \times f'\left(\sum_i w_i \times val(e, X_i)\right) \times val(e, X_i).$$

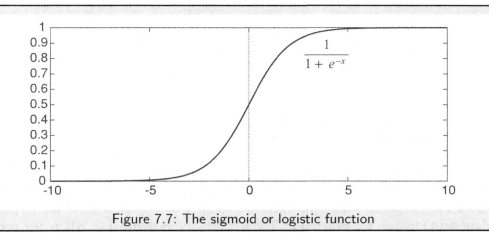

Figure 7.7: The sigmoid or logistic function

A typical differentiable activation function is the **sigmoid** or **logistic function**:

$$f(x) = \frac{1}{1 + e^{-x}} \; .$$

This function, depicted in Figure 7.7, squashes the real line into the interval $(0, 1)$, which is appropriate for classification because we would never want to make a prediction of greater than 1 or less than 0. It is also differentiable, with a simple derivative – namely, $f'(x) = f(x) \times (1 - f(x))$ – which can be computed using just the values of the outputs.

The *LinearLearner* algorithm of Figure 7.6 (page 305) can be changed to use the sigmoid function by changing line 17 to

$$w_i := w_i + \eta \times \delta \times pval^{\overline{w}}(e, Y) \times [1 - pval^{\overline{w}}(e, Y)] \times val(e, X_i) \; .$$

where $pval^{\overline{w}}(e, Y) = f(\sum_i w_i \times val(e, X_i))$ is the predicted value of feature Y for example e.

Example 7.10 Consider learning a squashed linear function for classifying the data of Figure 7.1 (page 289). One function that correctly classifies the examples is

$$Reads = f(-8 + 7 \times Short + 3 \times New + 3 \times Known) \, ,$$

where f is the sigmoid function. A function similar to this can be found with about 3,000 iterations of gradient descent with a learning rate $\eta = 0.05$. According to this function, *Reads* is true (the predicted value is closer to 1 than 0) if and only if *Short* is true and either *New* or *Known* is true. Thus, the linear classifier learns the same function as the decision tree learner. To see how this works, see the "mail reading" example of the Neural AIspace.org applet.

This algorithm with the sigmoid function as the activation function can learn any linearly separable classification in the sense that the error can be

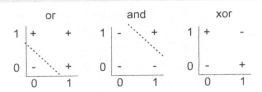

Figure 7.8: Linear separators for Boolean functions

made arbitrarily small on arbitrary sets of examples if, and only if, the target classification is linearly separable. A classification is **linearly separable** if there exists a hyperplane where the classification is true on one side of the hyperplane and false on the other side. The hyperplane is defined as where the predicted value, $f^{\overline{w}}(X_1, \ldots, X_n) = f(w_0 + w_1 \times val(e, X_1) + \cdots + w_n \times val(e, X_n))$, is 0.5. For the sigmoid activation function, this occurs when $w_0 + w_1 \times val(e, X_1) + \cdots + w_n \times val(e, X_n) = 0$ for the learned weights $\overline{w}$. On one side of this hyperplane, the prediction is greater than 0.5; on the other side, it is less than 0.5.

Figure 7.8 shows linear separators for "or" and "and". The dashed line separates the positive (true) cases from the negative (false) cases. One simple function that is not linearly separable is the **exclusive-or** (xor) function, shown on the right. There is no straight line that separates the positive examples from the negative examples. As a result, a linear classifier cannot represent, and therefore cannot learn, the exclusive-or function.

Often it is difficult to determine a priori whether a data set is linearly separable.

Example 7.11   Consider the data set of Figure 7.9, which is used to predict whether a person likes a holiday as a function of whether there is culture, whether the person has to fly, whether the destination is hot, whether there is music, and whether there is nature. In this data set, the value 1 means true and 0 means false. The linear classifier requires the numerical representation.

After 10,000 iterations of gradient descent with a learning rate of 0.05, the optimal prediction is (to one decimal point)

$$Likes = f(2.3 \times Culture + 0.01 \times Fly - 9.1 \times Hot$$
$$- 4.5 \times Music + 6.8 \times Nature + 0.01) ,$$

which approximately predicts the target value for all of the tuples in the training set except for the last and the third-to-last tuple, for which it predicts a value of about 0.5. This function seems to be quite stable with different initializations. Increasing the number of iterations makes it predict the other tuples better.

When the domain of the target variable is greater than 2 – there are more than two classes – indicator variables (page 290) can be used to convert the classification to binary variables. These binary variables could be learned separately. However, the outputs of the individual classifiers must be combined to give a prediction for the target variable. Because exactly one of the values must be

Culture	Fly	Hot	Music	Nature	Likes
0	0	1	0	0	0
0	1	1	0	0	0
1	1	1	1	1	0
0	1	1	1	1	0
0	1	1	0	1	0
1	0	0	1	1	1
0	0	0	0	0	0
0	0	0	1	1	1
1	1	1	0	0	0
1	1	0	1	1	1
1	1	0	0	0	1
1	0	1	0	1	1
0	0	0	1	0	0
1	0	1	1	0	0
1	1	1	1	0	0
1	0	0	1	0	0
1	1	1	0	1	0
0	0	0	0	1	1
0	1	0	0	0	1

Figure 7.9: Training data for which holiday a person likes

true for each example, the learner should not predict that more than one will be true or that none will be true. A classifier that predicts a probability distribution can normalize the predictions of the individual predictions. A learner that must make a definitive prediction can use the mode.

7.3.3 Bayesian Classifiers

A **Bayesian classifier** is based on the idea that the role of a (natural) class is to predict the values of features for members of that class. Examples are grouped in classes because they have common values for the features. Such classes are often called **natural kinds**. In this section, the target feature corresponds to a discrete **class**, which is not necessarily binary.

The idea behind a Bayesian classifier is that, if an agent knows the class, it can predict the values of the other features. If it does not know the class, Bayes' rule (page 227) can be used to predict the class given (some of) the feature values. In a Bayesian classifier, the learning agent builds a probabilistic model of the features and uses that model to predict the classification of a new example.

A **latent variable** is a probabilistic variable that is not observed. A Bayesian classifier is a probabilistic model where the classification is a latent variable that is probabilistically related to the observed variables. Classification then become inference in the probabilistic model.

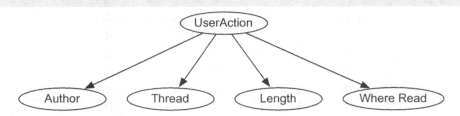

Figure 7.10: Belief network corresponding to a naive Bayesian classifier

The simplest case is the **naive Bayesian classifier**, which makes the independence assumption that the input features are conditionally independent of each other given the classification. (See page 233 for a definition of conditional independence.)

The independence of the naive Bayesian classifier is embodied in a particular belief network (page 235) where the features are the nodes, the target variable (the classification) has no parents, and the classification is the only parent of each input feature. This belief network requires the probability distributions $P(Y)$ for the target feature Y and $P(X_i|Y)$ for each input feature X_i. For each example, the prediction can be computed by conditioning on observed values for the input features and by querying the classification.

Given an example with inputs $X_1=v_1,\ldots,X_k=v_k$, Bayes' rule (page 227) is used to compute the posterior probability distribution of the example's classification, Y:

$$P(Y|X_1=v_1,\ldots,X_k=v_k)$$
$$= \frac{P(X_1=v_1,\ldots,X_k=v_k|Y) \times P(Y)}{P(X_1=v_1,\ldots,X_k=v_k)}$$
$$= \frac{P(X_1=v_1|Y) \times \cdots \times P(X_k=v_k|Y) \times P(Y)}{\sum_Y P(X_1=v_1|Y) \times \cdots \times P(X_k=v_k|Y) \times P(Y)}$$

where the denominator is a normalizing constant to ensure the probabilities sum to 1. The denominator does not depend on the class and, therefore, it is not needed to determine the most likely class.

To learn a classifier, the distributions of $P(Y)$ and $P(X_i|Y)$ for each input feature can be learned from the data, as described in Section 7.2.3 (page 296). The simplest case is to use the empirical frequency in the training data as the probability (i.e., use the proportion in the training data as the probability). However, as shown below, this approach is often not a good idea when this results in zero probabilities.

Example 7.12 Suppose an agent wants to predict the user action given the data of Figure 7.1 (page 289). For this example, the user action is the classification. The naive Bayesian classifier for this example corresponds to the belief network of Figure 7.10. The training examples are used to determine the probabilities required for the belief network.

Suppose the agent uses the empirical frequencies as the probabilities for this example. The probabilities that can be derived from these data are

$$P(UserAction=reads) = \frac{9}{18} = 0.5$$

$$P(Author=known|UserAction=reads) = \frac{2}{3}$$

$$P(Author=known|UserAction=skips) = \frac{2}{3}$$

$$P(Thread=new|UserAction=reads) = \frac{7}{9}$$

$$P(Thread=new|UserAction=skips) = \frac{1}{3}$$

$$P(Length=long|UserAction=reads) = 0$$

$$P(Length=long|UserAction=skips) = \frac{7}{9}$$

$$P(WhereRead=home|UserAction=reads) = \frac{4}{9}$$

$$P(WhereRead=home|UserAction=skips) = \frac{4}{9} .$$

Based on these probabilities, the features *Author* and *WhereRead* have no predictive power because knowing either does not change the probability that the user will read the article. The rest of this example ignores these features.

To classify a new case where the author is unknown, the thread is a follow-up, the length is short, and it is read at home,

$$P(UserAction=reads|Thread=followUp \wedge Length=short)$$
$$= P(followUp|reads) \times P(short|reads) \times P(reads) \times c$$
$$= \frac{2}{9} \times 1 \times \frac{1}{2} \times c$$
$$= \frac{1}{9} \times c$$

$$P(UserAction=skips|Thread=followUp \wedge Length=short)$$
$$= P(followUp|skips) \times P(short|skips) \times P(skips) \times c$$
$$= \frac{2}{3} \times \frac{2}{9} \times \frac{1}{2} \times c$$
$$= \frac{2}{27} \times c$$

where c is a normalizing constant that ensures these add up to 1. Thus, c must be $\frac{27}{5}$, so

$$P(UserAction=reads|Thread=followUp \wedge Length=short) = 0.6 .$$

This prediction does not work well on example e_{11}, which the agent skips, even though it is a *followUp* and is *short*. The naive Bayesian classifier summarizes the data into a few parameters. It predicts the article will be read because being short is a stronger indicator that the article will be read than being a follow-up is an indicator that the article will be skipped.

A new case where the length is long has $P(length{=}long|UserAction{=}$ $reads) = 0$. Thus, the posterior probability that the *UserAction=reads* is zero, no matter what the values of the other features are.

The use of zero probabilities can imply some unexpected behavior. First, some features become predictive: knowing just one feature value can rule out a category. If we allow zero probabilities, it is possible that some combinations of observations are impossible. See Exercise 7.13 (page 346). This is a problem not necessarily with using a Bayesian classifier but rather in using empirical frequencies as probabilities. The alternative to using the empirical frequencies is to incorporate pseudocounts (page 296). A designer of the learner should carefully choose pseudocounts, as shown in the following example.

Example 7.13 Consider how to learn the probabilities for the **help system** of Example 6.16 (page 246), where a helping agent infers what help page a user is interested in based on the keywords given by the user. The helping agent must learn the prior probability that each help page is wanted and the probability of each keyword given the help page wanted. These probabilities must be learned, because the system designer does not know a priori what words users will use. The agent can learn from the words users actually use when looking for help.

The learner must learn $P(H)$. To do this, it starts with a pseudocount (page 296) for each h_i. Pages that are a priori more likely can have a higher pseudocount. If the designer did not have any prior belief about which pages were more likely, the agent could use the same pseudocount for each page. To think about what count to use, the designer should consider how much more the agent would believe a page is the correct page after it has seen the page once; see Section 7.2.3 (page 296). It is possible to learn this pseudocount, if the designer has built another help system, by optimizing the pseudocount over the training data for that help system [or by using what is called a hierarchical Bayesian model (page 338)]. Given the pseudocounts and some data, $P(h_i)$ can be computed by dividing the count (the empirical count plus the pseudocount) associated with h_i by the sum of the counts for all of the pages.

For each word w_j and for each help page h_i, the helping agent requires two counts – the number of times w_j was used when h_i was the appropriate page (call this c_{ij}^+) and the the number of times w_j was not used when h_i was the appropriate page (call this c_{ij}^-). Neither of these counts should be zero. We expect c_{ij}^- to be bigger on average than c_{ij}^+, because we expect the average query to use a small portion of the total number of words. We may want to use different counts for those words that appear in the help page h_i than for those words that do not appear in h_i, so that the system starts with sensible behavior.

Every time a user claims they have found the help page they are interested in, the counts for that page and the conditional counts for all of the words can be updated. That is, if the user says that h_i is the correct page, the count associated with h_i can be incremented, c_{ij}^+ is incremented for each word w_j used in the query, and c_{ij}^- is incremented for each w_j not in the query.

This model does not use information about the wrong page. If the user claims that a page is not the correct page, this information is not used until the correct page is found.

The biggest challenge in building such a help system is not in the learning but in acquiring useful data. In particular, users may not know whether they have found the page they were looking for. Thus, users may not know when to stop and provide the feedback from which the system learns. Some users may never be satisfied with a page. Indeed, there may not exist a page they are satisfied with, but that information never gets fed back the learner. Alternatively, some users may indicate they have found the page they were looking for, even though there may be another page that was more appropriate. In the latter case, the correct page may have its count reduced so that it is never discovered.

Although there are some cases where the naive Bayesian classifier does not produce good results, it is extremely simple, it is easy to implement, and often it works very well. It is a good method to try for a new problem.

In general, the naive Bayesian classifier works well when the independence assumption is appropriate, that is, when the class is a good predictor of the other features and the other features are independent given the class. This may be appropriate for **natural kinds**, where the classes have evolved because they are useful in distinguishing the objects that humans want to distinguish. Natural kinds are often associated with nouns, such as the class of dogs or the class of chairs.

7.4 Composite Models

Decision trees, (squashed) linear functions, and Bayesian classifiers provide the basis for many other supervised learning techniques. Linear classifiers are very restricted in what they can represent. Although decision trees can represent any discrete function, many simple functions have very complicated decision trees. Bayesian classifiers make a priori modeling assumptions that may not be valid.

One way to make the linear function more powerful is to have the inputs to the linear function be some non-linear function of the original inputs. Adding these new features can increase the dimensionality, making some functions that were not linear (or linearly separable) in the lower-dimensional space linear in the higher-dimensional space.

Example 7.14 The exclusive-or function, x_1 xor x_2, is linearly separable in the space where the dimensions are X_1, X_2, and x_1x_2, where x_1x_2 is a feature that is true when both x_1 and x_2 are true. To visualize this, consider Figure 7.8 (page 308); with the product as the third dimension, the top-right point will be lifted out of the page, allowing for a linear separator (in this case a plane) to go underneath it.

A **support vector machine (SVM)** is used for classification. It uses functions of the original inputs as the inputs of the linear function. These functions are called **kernel functions**. Many possible kernel functions exist. An example kernel function is the product of original features; adding the products of features is enough to enable the representation of the exclusive-or function. Increasing the dimensionality can, however, cause overfitting. An SVM constructs a decision surface, which is a hyperplane that divides the positive and negative examples in this higher-dimensional space. Define the **margin** to be the minimum distance from the decision surface to any of the examples. An SVM finds the decision surface with maximum margin. The examples that are closest to the decision surface are those that support (or hold up) the decision surface. In particular, these examples, if removed, would change the decision surface. Overfitting is avoided because these support vectors define a surface that can be defined in fewer parameters than there are examples. For detailed description of SVMs see the references at the end of this chapter.

Neural networks allow the inputs to the (squashed) linear function to be a squashed linear function with parameters to be tuned. Having multiple layers of squashed linear functions as inputs to (squashed) linear functions that predict the target variables allows more complex functions to be represented. Neural networks are described in more detail later.

Another nonlinear representation is a **regression tree**, which is a decision tree with a (squashed) linear function at the leaves of the decision tree. This can represent a piecewise linear approximation. It is even possible to have neural networks or SVMs at the leaves of the decision tree. To classify a new example, the example is filtered down the tree, and the classifier at the leaves is then used to classify the example.

The naive Bayesian classifier can be expanded to allow some input features to be parents of the classification and to allow some to be children. The probability of the classification given its parents can be represented as a decision tree or a squashed linear function or a neural network. The children of the classification do not have to be independent. One representation of the children is as a **tree augmented naive Bayesian (TAN) network**, where the children are allowed to have exactly one other parent other than the classification (as long as the resulting graph is acyclic). This allows for a simple model that accounts for interdependencies among the children. An alternative is to put structure in the class variable. A **latent tree model** decomposes the class variable into a number of latent variables that are connected together in a tree structure. Each observed variable is a child of one of the latent variables. The latent variables allow a model of the dependence between the observed variables.

Another possibility is to use a number of classifiers that have each been trained on the data and to combine these using some mechanism such as voting or a linear function. These techniques are known as ensemble learning (page 319).

7.4.1 Neural Networks

Neural networks are a popular target representation for learning. These networks are inspired by the neurons in the brain but do not actually simulate neurons. Artificial neural networks typically contain many fewer than the approximately 10^{11} neurons that are in the human brain, and the artificial neurons, called **units**, are much simpler than their biological counterparts.

Artificial neural networks are interesting to study for a number of reasons:

- As part of neuroscience, to understand real neural systems, researchers are simulating the neural systems of simple animals such as worms, which promises to lead to an understanding about which aspects of neural systems are necessary to explain the behavior of these animals.

- Some researchers seek to automate not only the functionality of intelligence (which is what the field of artificial intelligence is about) but also the mechanism of the brain, suitably abstracted. One hypothesis is that the only way to build the functionality of the brain is by using the mechanism of the brain. This hypothesis can be tested by attempting to build intelligence using the mechanism of the brain, as well as without using the mechanism of the brain. Experience with building other machines – such as flying machines (page 9), which use the same principles, but not the same mechanism, that birds use to fly – would indicate that this hypothesis may not be true. However, it is interesting to test the hypothesis.

- The brain inspires a new way to think about computation that contrasts with currently available computers. Unlike current computers, which have a few processors and a large but essentially inert memory, the brain consists of a huge number of asynchronous distributed processes, all running concurrently with no master controller. One should not think that the current computers are the only architecture available for computation.

- As far as learning is concerned, neural networks provide a different measure of simplicity as a learning bias than, for example, decision trees. Multilayer neural networks, like decision trees, can represent any function of a set of discrete features. However, the functions that correspond to simple neural networks do not necessarily correspond to simple decision trees. Neural network learning imposes a different bias than decision tree learning. Which is better, in practice, is an empirical question that can be tested on different domains.

There are many different types of neural networks. This book considers one kind of neural network, the **feed-forward neural network**. Feed-forward networks can be seen as cascaded squashed linear functions. The inputs feed into a layer of hidden units, which can feed into layers of more hidden units, which eventually feed into the output layer. Each of the hidden units is a squashed linear function of its inputs.

Neural networks of this type can have as inputs any real numbers, and they have a real number as output. For regression, it is typical for the output units to be a linear function of their inputs. For classification it is typical for the output to be a sigmoid function of its inputs (because there is no point in predicting a value outside of [0,1]). For the hidden layers, there is no point in having their output be a linear function of their inputs because a linear function of a linear function is a linear function; adding the extra layers gives no added functionality. The output of each hidden unit is thus a squashed linear function of its inputs.

Associated with a network are the parameters for all of the linear functions. These parameters can be tuned simultaneously to minimize the prediction error on the training examples.

Example 7.15 Figure 7.11 shows a neural network with one hidden layer for the classification data of Figure 7.9 (page 309). As explained in Example 7.11 (page 308), this data set is not linearly separable. In this example, five Boolean inputs correspond to whether there is culture, whether the person has to fly, whether the destination is hot, whether there is music, and whether there is nature, and a single output corresponds to whether the person likes the holiday. In this network, there is one hidden layer, which contains two hidden units that have no a priori meaning. The network represents the following equations:

$$
\begin{aligned}
pval(e, Likes) &= f(w_0 + w_1 \times val(e, H1) + w_2 \times val(e, H2)) \\
val(e, H1) &= f(w_3 + w_4 \times val(e, Culture) + w_5 \times val(e, Fly) \\
&\quad + w_6 \times val(e, Hot) + w_7 \times val(e, Music) + w_8 \times val(e, Nature) \\
val(e, H2) &= f(w_9 + w_{10} \times val(e, Culture) + w_{11} \times val(e, Fly) \\
&\quad + w_{12} \times val(e, Hot) + w_{13} \times val(e, Music) \\
&\quad + w_{14} \times val(e, Nature)) ,
\end{aligned}
$$

where $f(x)$ is an activation function.

For this example, there are 15 real numbers to be learned $(w_0, \ldots, w_{14})$. The hypothesis space is thus a 15-dimensional real space. Each point in this 15-dimensional space corresponds to a function that predicts a value for *Likes* for every example with *Culture, Fly, Hot, Music,* and *Nature* given.

Given particular values for the parameters, and given values for the inputs, a neural network predicts a value for each target feature. The aim of neural network learning is, given a set of examples, to find parameter settings that minimize the error. If there are m parameters, finding the parameter settings

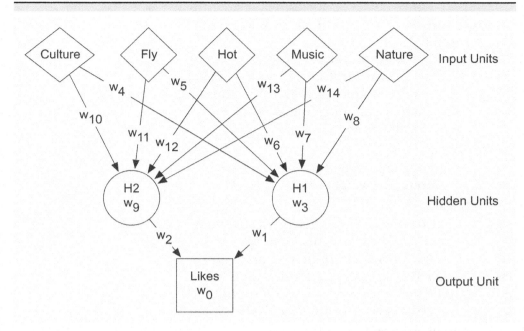

Figure 7.11: A neural network with one hidden layer. The w_i are weights. The weight inside the nodes is the weight that does not depend on an input; it is the one multiplied by 1. The meaning of this network is given in Example 7.15.

with minimum error involves searching through an m-dimensional Euclidean space.

Back-propagation learning is gradient descent search (page 149) through the parameter space to minimize the sum-of-squares error.

Figure 7.12 (on the next page) gives the incremental gradient descent version of back-propagation for networks with one layer of hidden units. This approach assumes n input features, k output features, and n_h hidden units. Both hw and ow are two-dimensional arrays of weights. Note that $0 : n_k$ means the index ranges from 0 to n_k (inclusive) and $1 : n_k$ means the index ranges from 1 to n_k (inclusive). This algorithm assumes that $val(e, X_0) = 1$ for all e.

The back-propagation algorithm is similar to the linear learner of Figure 7.6 (page 305), but it takes into account multiple layers and the activation function. Intuitively, for each example it involves simulating the network on that example, determining first the value of the hidden units (line 23) then the value of the output units (line 25). It then passes the error back through the network, computing the error on the output nodes (line 26) and the error on the hidden nodes (line 28). It then updates all of the weights based on the derivative of the error.

Gradient descent search (page 149) involves repeated evaluation of the function to be minimized – in this case the error – and its derivative. An

1: **procedure** $BackPropagationLearner(X, Y, E, n_h, \eta)$
2:     **Inputs**
3:         X: set of input features, $X = \{X_1, \ldots, X_n\}$
4:         Y: set of target features, $Y = \{Y_1, \ldots, Y_k\}$
5:         E: set of examples from which to learn
6:         n_h: number of hidden units
7:         η: learning rate
8:     **Output**
9:         hidden unit weights $hw[0:n, 1:n_h]$
10:        output unit weights $ow[0:n_h, 1:k]$
11:    **Local**
12:        $hw[0:n, 1:n_h]$ weights for hidden units
13:        $ow[0:n_h, 1:k]$ weights for output units
14:        $hid[0:n_h]$ values for hidden units
15:        $hErr[1:n_h]$ errors for hidden units
16:        $out[1:k]$ predicted values for output units
17:        $oErr[1:k]$ errors for output units
18:    initialize hw and ow randomly
19:    $hid[0] := 1$
20:    **repeat**
21:        **for each** example e in E **do**
22:            **for each** $h \in \{1, \ldots, n_h\}$ **do**
23:                $hid[h] := \sum_{i=0}^{n} hw[i, h] \times val(e, X_i)$
24:            **for each** $o \in \{1, \ldots, k\}$ **do**
25:                $out[o] := \sum_{h=0}^{n} hw[i, h] \times hid[h]$
26:                $oErr[o] := out[o] \times (1 - out[o]) \times (val(e, Y_o) - out[o])$
27:            **for each** $h \in \{0, \ldots, n_h\}$ **do**
28:                $hErr[h] := hid[h] \times (1 - hid[h]) \times \sum_{o=0}^{k} ow[h, o] \times oErr[o]$
29:                **for each** $i \in \{0, \ldots, n\}$ **do**
30:                    $hw[i, h] := hw[i, h] + \eta \times hErr[h] \times val(e, X_i)$
31:            **for each** $o \in \{1, \ldots, k\}$ **do**
32:                $ow[h, o] := ow[h, o] + \eta \times oErr[o] \times hid[h]$
33:    **until** termination
34:    **return** $w_0, \ldots, w_n$

Figure 7.12: Back-propagation for learning a neural network with a single hidden layer

evaluation of the error involves iterating through all of the examples. Back-propagation learning thus involves repeatedly evaluating the network on all examples. Fortunately, with the logistic function the derivative is easy to determine given the value of the output for each unit.

Example 7.16 The network of Figure 7.11 (page 317), with one hidden layer containing two units, trained on the data of Figure 7.9 (page 309), can perfectly fit this data.

One run of back-propagation with the learning rate $\eta = 0.05$, and taking 10,000 steps, gave weights that accurately predicted the training data:

$$H1 = f(-2.0 \times Culture - 4.43 \times Fly + 2.5 \times Hot$$
$$+ 2.4 \times Music - 6.1 \times Nature + 1.63)$$
$$H2 = f(-0.7 \times Culture + 3.0 \times Fly + 5.8 \times Hot$$
$$+ 2.0 \times Music - 1.7 \times Nature - 5.0)$$
$$Likes = f(-8.5 \times H1 - 8.8 \times H2 + 4.36) .$$

The use of neural networks may seem to challenge the **physical symbol system hypothesis** (page 15), which relies on symbols having meaning. Part of the appeal of neural networks is that, although meaning is attached to the input and output units, the designer does not associate a meaning with the hidden units. What the hidden units actually represent is something that is learned. After a neural network has been trained, it is often possible to look inside the network to determine what a particular hidden unit actually represents. Sometimes it is easy to express concisely in language what it represents, but often it is not. However, arguably, the computer has an internal meaning; it can explain its internal meaning by showing how examples map into the values of the hidden unit.

7.4.2 Ensemble Learning

In **ensemble learning**, an agent takes a number of learning algorithms and combines their output to make a prediction. The algorithms being combined are called **base-level algorithms**.

The simplest case of ensemble learning is to train the base-level algorithms on random subsets of the data and either let these vote for the most popular classification (for definitive predictions) or average the predictions of the base-level algorithm. For example, one could train a number of decision trees, each on random samples of, say, 50% of the training data, and then either vote for the most popular classification or average the numerical predictions. The outputs of the decision trees could even be inputs to a linear classifier, and the weights of this classifier could be learned.

This approach works well when the base-level algorithms are **unstable**: they tend to produce different representations depending on which subset of the data is chosen. Decision trees and neural networks are unstable, but linear classifiers tend to be stable and so would not work well with ensembles.

In **bagging**, if there are m training examples, the base-level algorithms are trained on sets of m randomly drawn, with replacement, sets of the training examples. In each of these sets, some examples are not chosen, and some are duplicated. On average, each set contains about 63% of the original examples.

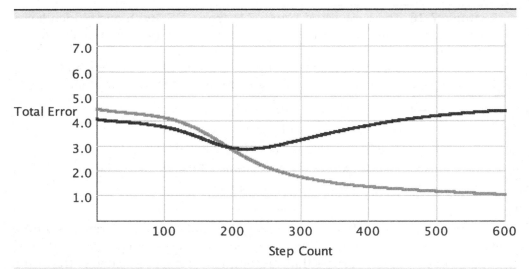

Figure 7.13: Error as a function of training time. On the x-axis is the step count of a run of back-propagation with three hidden units on the data of Figure 7.9 (page 309), using unseen examples as the test set. On the y-axis is the sum-of-squares error for the training set (gray line) and the test set (black line).

In **boosting** there is a sequence of classifiers in which each classifier uses a weighted set of examples. Those examples that the previous classifiers misclassified are weighted more. Weighting examples can either be incorporated into the base-level algorithms or can affect which examples are chosen as training examples for the future classifiers.

Another way to create base-level classifiers is to manipulate the input features. Different base-level classifiers can be trained on different features. Often the sets of features are hand-tuned.

Another way to get diverse base-level classifiers is to randomize the algorithm. For example, neural network algorithms that start at different parameter settings may find different local minima, which make different predictions. These different networks can be combined.

7.5 Avoiding Overfitting

Overfitting can occur when some regularities appear in the training data that do not appear in the test data, and when the learner uses those regularities for prediction.

Example 7.17 Figure 7.13 shows a typical plot of how the sum-of-squares error changes with the number of iterations of linear regression. The sum-of-squares error on the training set decreases as the number of iterations increases. For the test set, the error reaches a minimum and then increases as the number of iterations increases. The same behavior occurs in decision-tree learning as a function of the number of splits.

We discuss two ways to avoid overfitting. The first is to have an explicit trade-off between model complexity and fitting the data. The second approach is to use some of the training data to detect overfitting.

7.5.1 Maximum A Posteriori Probability and Minimum Description Length

One way to trade off model complexity and fit to the data is to choose the model that is most likely, given the data. That is, choose the model that maximizes the probability of the model given the data, $P(model|data)$. The model that maximizes $P(model|data)$ is called the **maximum a posteriori probability** model, or the **MAP model**.

The probability of a model (or a hypothesis) given some data is obtained by using Bayes' rule (page 227):

$$P(model|data) \;=\; \frac{P(data|model) \times P(model)}{P(data)} \,. \tag{7.3}$$

The likelihood, $P(data|model)$, is the probability that this model would have produced this data set. It is high when the model is a good fit to the data, and it is low when the model would have predicted different data. The prior $P(model)$ encodes the **learning bias** and specifies which models are a priori more likely. The prior probability of the model, $P(model)$, is required to bias the learning toward simpler models. Typically simpler models have a higher prior probability. The denominator $P(data)$ is a normalizing constant to make sure that the probabilities sum to 1.

Because the denominator of Equation (7.3) is independent of the model, it can be ignored when choosing the most likely model. Thus, the MAP model is the model that maximizes

$$P(data|model) \times P(model) \,. \tag{7.4}$$

One alternative is to choose the **maximum likelihood model** – the model that maximizes $P(data|model)$. The problem with choosing the most likely model is that, if the space of models is rich enough, a model exists that specifies that this particular data set will be produced, which has $P(data|model) = 1$. Such a model may be a priori very unlikely. However, we do not want to exclude it, because it may be the true model. Choosing the maximum-likelihood model is equivalent to choosing the maximum a posteriori model with a uniform prior over hypotheses.

MAP Learning of Decision Trees

To understand MAP learning, consider how it can be used to learn decision trees (page 298). If there are no examples with the same values for the input features and different values for the target features, there are always decision trees that fit the data perfectly. If the training examples do not cover all of the assignments to the input variables, multiple trees will fit the data perfectly.

However, with noise, none of these may be the best model. Not only do we want to compare the models that fit the data perfectly; we also want to compare those models with the models that do not necessarily fit the data perfectly. MAP learning provides a way to compare these models.

Suppose there are multiple decision trees that accurately fit the data. If *model* denotes one of those decision trees, $P(data|model) = 1$. The preference for one decision tree over another depends on the prior probabilities of the decision trees; the prior probability encodes the learning bias (page 284). The preference for simpler decision trees over more complicated decision trees occurs because simpler decision trees have a higher prior probability.

Bayes' rule gives a way to trade off simplicity and ability to handle noise. Decision trees can handle noisy data by having probabilities at the leaves. When there is noise, larger decision trees fit the training data better, because the tree can account for random regularities (noise) in the training data. In decision-tree learning, the likelihood favors bigger decision trees; the more complicated the tree, the better it can fit the data. The prior distribution can favor smaller decision trees. When there is a prior distribution over decision trees, Bayes' rule specifies how to trade off model complexity and accuracy: The posterior probability of the model given the data is proportional to the product of the likelihood and the prior.

Example 7.18 Consider the data of Figure 7.1 (page 289), where the learner is to predict the user's actions.

One possible decision tree is the one given on the left of Figure 7.4 (page 298). Call this decision tree d_2. The likelihood of the data is $P(data|d_2) = 1$. That is, d_2 accurately fits the data.

Another possible decision tree is one with no internal nodes, and a leaf that says to predict *reads* with probability $\frac{1}{2}$. This is the most likely tree with no internal nodes, given the data. Call this decision tree d_0. The likelihood of the data given this model is

$$P(data|d_0) = \left(\frac{1}{2}\right)^9 \times \left(\frac{1}{2}\right)^9 \approx 0.00000149.$$

Another possible decision tree is one on the right of Figure 7.4 (page 298), which just splits on *Length*, and with probabilities on the leaves given by $P(reads|Length=long) = 0$ and $P(reads|Length=short) = \frac{9}{11}$. Note that $\frac{9}{11}$ is the empirical frequency of *reads* among the training set with *Length=short*. Call this decision tree d_{1a}. The likelihood of the data given this model is

$$P(data|d_{1a}) = 1^7 \times \left(\frac{9}{11}\right)^9 \times \left(\frac{2}{11}\right)^2 \approx 0.0543.$$

Another possible decision tree is one that just splits on *Thread*, and with probabilities on the leaves given by $P(reads|Thread=new) = \frac{7}{10}$ (as 7 out of the 10 examples with *Thread=new* have *UserAction=reads*), and

$P(reads|Thread=followUp) = \frac{2}{8}$. Call this decision tree d_{1t}. The likelihood of the data given d_{1t} is

$$P(data|d_{1t}) = \left(\frac{7}{10}\right)^7 \times \left(\frac{3}{10}\right)^3 \times \left(\frac{6}{8}\right)^6 \times \left(\frac{2}{8}\right)^2 \approx 0.000025.$$

These are just four of the possible decision trees. Which is best depends on the prior on trees. The likelihood of the data is multiplied by the prior probability of the decision trees to determine the posterior probability of the decision tree.

Description Length

The negative of the logarithm (base 2) of Formula (7.4) is

$$(-\log_2 P(data|model)) + (-\log_2 P(model)).$$

This can be interpreted in terms of **information theory** (page 231). The left-hand side of this expression is the number of bits it takes to describe the data given the model. The right-hand side is the number of bits it takes to describe the model. A model that minimizes this sum is a **minimum description length (MDL)** model. The **MDL principle** is to choose the model that minimizes the number of bits it takes to describe both the model and the data given the model.

One way to think about the MDL principle is that the aim is to communicate the data as succinctly as possible. The use of the model is to make communication shorter. To communicate the data, first communicate the model, then communicate the data in terms of the model. The number of bits it takes to communicate the data using a model is the number of bits it takes to communicate the model plus the number of bits it takes to communicate the data in terms of the model. The MDL principle is used to choose the model that lets us communicate the data in as few bits as possible.

As the logarithm function is monotonically increasing, the MAP model is the same the MDL model. The idea of choosing a model with the highest posterior probability is the same as choosing a model with a minimum description length.

Example 7.19 In Example 7.18, the definition of the priors on decision trees was left unspecified. The notion of a description length provides a basis for assigning priors to decision trees; consider how many bits it takes to describe a decision tree [see Exercise 7.11 (page 346)]. One must be careful defining the codes, because each code should describe a decision tree, and each decision tree should be described by a code.

7.5.2 Cross Validation

The problem with the previous methods is that they require a notion of simplicity to be known before the agent has seen any data. It would seem as though an agent should be able to determine, from the data, how complicated a model needs to be. Such a method could be used when the learning agent has no prior information about the world.

The idea of **cross validation** is to split the training set into two: a set of examples to train with, and a **validation set**. The agent trains using the new training set. Prediction on the validation set is used to determine which model to use.

Consider a graph such as the one in Figure 7.13 (page 320). The error of the training set gets smaller as the size of the tree grows. The idea of cross validation is to choose the representation in which the error of the validation set is a minimum. In these cases, learning can continue until the error of the validation set starts to increase.

The validation set that is used as part of training is not the same as the test set. The test set is used to evaluate how well the learning algorithm works as a whole. It is cheating to use the test set as part of learning. Remember that the aim is to predict examples that the agent has not seen. The test set acts as a surrogate for these unseen examples, and so it cannot be used for training or validation.

Typically, we want to train on as many examples as possible, because then we get better models. However, having a small validation set means that the validation set may fit well, or not fit well, just by luck. There are various methods that have been used to reuse examples for both training and validation.

One method, k-fold cross validation, is used to determine the best model complexity, such as the depth of a decision tree or the number of hidden units in a neural network. The method of k-**fold cross validation** partitions the training set into k sets. For each model complexity, the learner trains k times, each time using one of the sets as the validation set and the remaining sets as the training set. It then selects the model complexity that has the smallest average error on the validation set (averaging over the k runs). It can return the model with that complexity, trained on all of the data.

7.6 Case-Based Reasoning

The previous methods tried to find a compact representation of the data that can be used for future prediction. In **case-based reasoning**, the training examples – the cases – are stored and accessed to solve a new problem. To get a prediction for a new example, those cases that are similar, or close to, the new example are used to predict the value of the target features of the new example. This is at one extreme of the learning problem where, unlike decision trees and neural networks, relatively little work must be done offline, and virtually all of the work is performed at query time.

Case-based reasoning can be used for classification and regression. It is also applicable when the cases are complicated, such as in legal cases, where the cases are complex legal rulings, and in planning, where the cases are previous solutions to complex problems.

If the cases are simple, one algorithm that works well is to use the *k*-**nearest neighbors** for some given number *k*. Given a new example, the *k* training examples that have the input features closest to that example are used to predict the target value for the new example. The prediction can be the mode, average, or some interpolation between the prediction of these *k* training examples, perhaps weighting closer examples more than distant examples.

For this method to work, a distance metric is required that measures the closeness of two examples. First define a metric for the domain of each feature, in which the values of the features are converted to a numerical scale that can be used to compare values. Suppose $val(e, X_i)$ is a numerical representation of the value of feature X_i for the example e. Then $(val(e_1, X_i) - val(e_2, X_i))$ is the difference between example e_1 and e_2 on the dimension defined by feature X_i. The **Euclidean distance**, the square root of the sum of the squares of the dimension differences, can be used as the distance between two examples. One important issue is the relative scales of different dimensions; increasing the scale of one dimension increases the importance of that feature. Let w_i be a non-negative real-valued parameter that specifies the weight of feature X_i. The distance between examples e_1 and e_2 is then

$$d(e_1, e_2) = \sqrt{\sum_i w_i \times (val(e_1, X_i) - val(e_2, X_i))^2} \,.$$

The feature weights can be provided as input. It is also possible to learn these weights. The learning agent can try to find a parameter setting that minimizes the error in predicting the value of each element of the training set, based on every other instance in the training set. This is called the **leave-one-out cross-validation** error measure.

Example 7.20 Consider using case-based reasoning on the data of Figure 7.1 (page 289). Rather than converting the data to a secondary representation as in decision-tree or neural-network learning, case-based reasoning uses the examples directly to predict the value for the user action in a new case.

Suppose a learning agent wants to classify example e_{20}, for which the author is unknown, the thread is a follow-up, the length is short, and it is read at home. First the learner tries to find similar cases. There is an exact match in example e_{11}, so it may want to predict that the user does the same action as for example e_{11} and thus skips the article. It could also include other close examples.

Consider classifying example e_{19}, where the author is unknown, the thread is new, the length is long, and it was read at work. In this case there are no exact matches. Consider the close matches. Examples e_2, e_8, and e_{18} agree on the features *Author*, *Thread*, and *WhereRead*. Examples e_{10} and e_{12} agree on *Thread*, *Length*, and *WhereRead*. Example e_3 agrees on *Author*, *Length*, and *WhereRead*. Examples e_2, e_8, and e_{18} predict *Reads*, but the other examples predict *Skips*. So what should be predicted? The decision-tree algorithm says that *Length* is the best predictor, and so e_2, e_8, and e_{18} should be ignored. For the sigmoid linear learning algorithm, the parameter values in Example 7.10 (page 307) similarly predict that the reader skips the article. A case-based reasoning algorithm to predict whether the user will or will not read this article must determine the relative importance of the dimensions.

One of the problems in case-based reasoning is accessing the relevant cases. A *kd*-tree is a way to index the training examples so that training examples that are close to a given example can be found quickly. Like a decision tree, a *kd*-tree splits on input features, but at the leaves are subsets of the training examples. In building a *kd*-tree from a set of examples, the learner tries to find an input feature that partitions the examples into set of approximately equal size and then builds *kd*-trees for the examples in each partition. This division stops when all of the examples at a leaf are the same. A new example can be filtered down the tree, as in a decision tree. The exact matches will be at the leaf found. However, the examples at the leaves of the *kd*-tree could possibly be quite distant from the example to be classified; they agree on the values down the branch of the tree but could disagree on the values of all other features. The same tree can be used to search for those examples that have one feature different from the ones tested in the tree. See Exercise 7.16 (page 347).

Case-based reasoning is also applicable when the cases are more complicated, for example, when they are legal cases or previous solutions to planning problems. In this scenario, the cases can be carefully chosen and edited to be useful. Case-based reasoning can be seen as a cycle of the following four tasks.

Retrieve: Given a new case, retrieve similar cases from the case base.

Reuse: Adapt the retrieved cases to fit to the new case.

Revise: Evaluate the solution and revise it based on how well it works.

Retain: Decide whether to retain this new case in the case base.

The revision can involve other reasoning techniques, such as using the proposed solution as a starting point to search for a solution, or a human could do the adaptation in an interactive system. Retaining can then save the new case together with the solution found.

Example 7.21 A common example of a case-based reasoning system is a helpdesk that users call with problems to be solved. For example, case-based reasoning could be used by the diagnostic assistant to help users diagnose problems on their computer systems. When a user gives a description of their problem, the closest cases in the case base are retrieved. The diagnostic assistant can recommend some of these to the user, adapting each case to the user's particular situation. An example of adaptation is to change the recommendation based on what software the user has, what method they use to connect to the Internet, and the brand of printer. If one of the cases suggested works, that can be recorded in the case base to make that case be more important when another user asks a similar question. If none of the cases found works, some other problem solving can be done to solve the problem, perhaps by adapting other cases or having a human help diagnose the problem. When the problem is finally fixed, what worked in that case can be added to the case base.

7.7 Learning as Refining the Hypothesis Space

So far, learning is either choosing the best representation – for example, the best decision tree or the best values for parameters in a neural network – or predicting the value of the target features of a new case from a database of previous cases. This section considers a different notion of learning, namely learning as delineating those hypotheses that are consistent with the examples. Rather than choosing a hypothesis, the aim is to find all hypotheses that are consistent. This investigation will shed light on the role of a bias and provide a mechanism for a theoretical analysis of the learning problem.

We make three assumptions:

- There is a single target feature, Y, that is Boolean. This is not really a restriction for classification, because any discrete feature can be made into Boolean features using indicator variables (page 141).
- The hypotheses make definitive predictions, predicting true or false for each example, rather than probabilistic prediction.
- There is no noise in the data.

Given these assumptions, it is possible to write a hypothesis in terms of a proposition, where the primitive propositions are assignments to the input features.

Example 7.22 The decision tree of Figure 7.4 (page 298) can be seen as a representation *reads* defined by the proposition

$$pval(e, Reads) = val(e, Short) \land (val(e, New) \lor val(e, Known)) .$$

For the rest of this section, we write this more simply as

$$reads \leftrightarrow short \land (new \lor known) .$$

The goal is to try to find a proposition on the input features that correctly classifies the training examples.

Example 7.23 Consider the trading agent trying to infer which books or articles the user reads based on keywords supplied in the article. Suppose the learning agent has the following data:

article	Crime	Academic	Local	Music	Reads
a_1	true	false	false	true	true
a_2	true	false	false	false	true
a_3	false	true	false	false	false
a_4	false	false	true	false	false
a_5	true	true	false	false	true

The aim is to learn which articles the user reads.

In this example, *reads* is the target feature, and the aim is to find a definition such as

$$reads \leftrightarrow crime \wedge (\neg academic \vee \neg music) \ .$$

This definition may be used to classify the training examples as well as future examples.

Hypothesis space learning assumes the following sets:

- I, the **instance space**, is the set of all possible examples.
- $\mathcal{H}$, the **hypothesis space**, is a set of Boolean functions on the input features.
- $E \subseteq I$ is the set of **training examples**. Values for the input features and the target feature are given for the training example.

If $h \in \mathcal{H}$ and $i \in I$, we write $h(i)$ to mean the value that h predicts for i on the target variable Y.

Example 7.24 In Example 7.23, I is the set of the $2^5 = 32$ possible examples, one for each combination of values for the features.

The hypothesis space $\mathcal{H}$ could be all Boolean combinations of the input features or could be more restricted, such as conjunctions or propositions defined in terms of fewer than three features.

In Example 7.23, the training examples are $E = \{a_1, a_2, a_3, a_4, a_5\}$. The target feature is *Reads*. Because the table specifies some of the values of this feature, and the learner will make predictions on unseen cases, the learner requires a bias (page 286). In hypothesis space learning, the bias is imposed by the hypothesis space.

Hypothesis h is **consistent** with a set of training examples E if $\forall e \in E$, h accurately predicts the target feature of e. That is, $h(e) = val(e, Y)$; the predicted value is the same as the actual value for each example. The problem is to find the subset of $\mathcal{H}$ or just an element of $\mathcal{H}$ consistent with all of the training examples.

Example 7.25 Consider the data of Example 7.23, and suppose $\mathcal{H}$ is the set of conjunctions of literals. An example hypothesis in $\mathcal{H}$ that is consistent with $\{a_1\}$ is $\neg academic \wedge music$. This hypothesis means that the person reads an article if and only if $\neg academic \wedge music$ is true of the article. This concept is not the target concept because it is inconsistent with $\{a_1, a_2\}$.

7.7.1 Version-Space Learning

Rather than enumerating all of the hypotheses, the subset of $\mathcal{H}$ consistent with the examples can be found more efficiently by imposing some structure on the hypothesis space.

Hypothesis h_1 is a **more general hypothesis** than hypothesis h_2 if h_2 implies h_1. In this case, h_2 is a **more specific hypothesis** than h_1. Any hypothesis is both more general than itself and more specific than itself.

Example 7.26 The hypothesis $\neg academic \wedge music$ is more specific than $music$ and is also more specific than $\neg academic$. Thus, $music$ is more general than $\neg academic \wedge music$. The most general hypothesis is $true$. The most specific hypothesis is $false$.

The "more general than" relation forms a partial ordering over the hypothesis space. The version-space algorithm that follows exploits this partial ordering to search for hypotheses that are consistent with the training examples.

Given hypothesis space $\mathcal{H}$ and examples E, the **version space** is the subset of $\mathcal{H}$ that is consistent with the examples.

The **general boundary** of a version space, G, is the set of maximally general members of the version space (i.e., those members of the version space such that no other element of the version space is more general). The **specific boundary** of a version space, S, is the set of maximally specific members of the version space.

These concepts are useful because the general boundary and the specific boundary completely determine the version space:

Proposition 7.2. *The version space, given hypothesis space $\mathcal{H}$ and examples E, can be derived from its general boundary and specific boundary. In particular, the version space is the set of $h \in \mathcal{H}$ such that h is more general than an element of S and more specific than an element of G.*

Candidate Elimination Algorithm

The **candidate elimination algorithm** incrementally builds the version space given a hypothesis space $\mathcal{H}$ and a set E of examples. The examples are added one by one; each example possibly shrinks the version space by removing the hypotheses that are inconsistent with the example. The candidate elimination algorithm does this by updating the general and specific boundary for each new example. This is described in Figure 7.14 (on the next page).

Example 7.27 Consider how the candidate elimination algorithm handles Example 7.23 (page 327), where $\mathcal{H}$ is the set of conjunctions of literals.

Before it has seen any examples, $G_0 = \{true\}$ – the user reads everything – and $S_0 = \{false\}$ – the user reads nothing. Note that $true$ is the empty conjunction and $false$ is the conjunction of an atom and its negation.

After considering the first example, a_1, $G_1 = \{true\}$ and

$$S_1 = \{crime \wedge \neg academic \wedge \neg local \wedge music\}.$$

Thus, the most general hypothesis is that the user reads everything, and the most specific hypothesis is that the user only reads articles exactly like this one.

1: **procedure** *CandidateEliminationLearner*$(X, Y, E, \mathcal{H})$
2:     **Inputs**
3:         X: set of input features, $X = \{X_1, \ldots, X_n\}$
4:         Y: target feature
5:         E: set of examples from which to learn
6:         $\mathcal{H}$: hypothesis space
7:     **Output**
8:         general boundary $G \subseteq \mathcal{H}$
9:         specific boundary $S \subseteq \mathcal{H}$ consistent with E
10:     **Local**
11:         G: set of hypotheses in $\mathcal{H}$
12:         S: set of hypotheses in $\mathcal{H}$
13:     Let $G = \{true\}$, $S = \{false\}$;
14:     **for each** $e \in E$ **do**
15:         **if** e is a positive example **then**
16:             Elements of G that classify e as negative are removed from G;
17:             Each element s of S that classifies e as negative is removed and replaced by the minimal generalizations of s that classify e as positive and are less general than some member of G;
18:             Non-maximal hypotheses are removed from S;
19:         **else**
20:             Elements of S that classify e as positive are removed from S;
21:             Each element g of G that classifies e as positive is removed and replaced by the minimal specializations of g that classifies e as negative and are more general than some member of S.
22:             Non-minimal hypotheses are removed from G.

Figure 7.14: Candidate elimination algorithm

After considering the first two examples, $G_2 = \{true\}$ and

$$S_2 = \{crime \wedge \neg academic \wedge \neg local\}.$$

Since a_1 and a_2 disagree on music, it has concluded that music cannot be relevant.

After considering the first three examples, the general boundary becomes

$$G_3 = \{crime, \neg academic\}$$

and $S_3 = S_2$. Now there are two most general hypotheses; the first is that the user reads anything about crime, and the second is that the user reads anything non-academic.

After considering the first four examples,

$$G_4 = \{crime, \neg academic \wedge \neg local\}$$

and $S_4 = S_3$.

After considering all five examples, we have

$$G_5 = \{crime\},$$
$$S_5 = \{crime \wedge \neg local\}.$$

Thus, after five examples, only two hypotheses exist in the version space. They differ only on their prediction on an example that has $crime \wedge local$ true. If the target concept can be represented as a conjunction, only an example with $crime \wedge local$ true will change G or S. This version space can make predictions about all other examples.

The Bias Involved in Version-Space Learning

Recall (page 286) that a bias is necessary for any learning to generalize beyond the training data. There must have been a bias in Example 7.27 (page 329) because, after observing only 5 of the 16 possible assignments to the input variables, an agent was able to make predictions about examples it had not seen.

The bias involved in version-space learning is a called a **language bias** or a **restriction bias** because the bias is obtained from restricting the allowable hypotheses. For example, a new example with crime false and music true will be classified as false (the user will not read the article), even though no such example has been seen. The restriction that the hypothesis must be a conjunction of literals is enough to predict its value.

This bias should be contrasted with the bias involved in decision-tree learning (page 298). The decision tree can represent any Boolean function. Decision-tree learning involves a **preference bias**, in that some Boolean functions are preferred over others; those with smaller decision trees are preferred over those with larger decision trees. A decision-tree learning algorithm that builds a single decision tree top-down also involves a **search bias** in that the decision tree returned depends on the search strategy used.

The candidate elimination algorithm is sometimes said to be an unbiased learning algorithm because the learning algorithm does not impose any bias beyond the language bias involved in choosing $\mathcal{H}$. It is easy for the version space to collapse to the empty set – for example, if the user reads an article with crime false and music true. This means that the target concept is not in $\mathcal{H}$. Version-space learning is not tolerant to noise; just one misclassified example can throw off the whole system.

The **bias-free** hypothesis space is where $\mathcal{H}$ is the set of all Boolean functions. In this case, G always contains one concept: the concept which says that all negative examples have been seen and every other example is positive. Similarly, S contains the single concept which says that all unseen examples are negative. The version space is incapable of concluding anything about examples it has not seen; thus, it cannot generalize. Without a language bias or a preference bias, no generalization and therefore no learning will occur.

7.7.2 Probably Approximately Correct Learning

So far, we have seen a number of different learning algorithms. This section covers some of the theoretical aspects of learning, developed in an area called **computational learning theory**.

Some relevant questions that we can ask about a theory of computational learning include the following:

- Is the learner guaranteed to converge to the correct hypothesis as the number of examples increases?
- How many examples are required to identify a concept?
- How much computation is required to identify a concept?

In general, the answer to the first question is "no," unless it can be guaranteed that the examples always eventually rule out all but the correct hypothesis. Someone out to trick the learner could choose examples that do not help discriminate correct hypotheses from incorrect hypotheses. So if such a person cannot be ruled out, a learner cannot guarantee to find a consistent hypothesis. However, given randomly chosen examples, a learner that always chooses a consistent hypothesis can get arbitrarily close to the correct concept. This requires a notion of closeness and a specification of what is a randomly chosen example.

Consider a learning algorithm that chooses a hypothesis consistent with all of the training examples. Assume a probability distribution over possible examples and that the training examples and the test examples are chosen from the same distribution. The distribution does not have to be known. We will prove a result that holds for all distributions.

Define the **error of hypothesis** $h \in \mathcal{H}$, written $error(h)$, to be the probability of choosing an element i of I such that $h(i) \neq val(i, Y)$, where $h(i)$ is the predicted value of target variable Y on possible example i, and $val(i, Y)$ is the actual value of Y. Recall that I, the instance space, is the set of all possible examples. That is,

$$error(h) = P(h(i) \neq val(i, Y) | i \in I) .$$

An agent typically does not know P or $val(i, Y)$ for all i and, thus, does not actually know the error of a particular hypothesis.

Given $\epsilon > 0$, hypothesis h is **approximately correct** if $error(h) \leq \epsilon$.

We make the following assumption.

Assumption 7.3. *The training and test examples are chosen independently from the same probability distribution as the population.*

It is still possible that the examples do not distinguish hypotheses that are far away from the concept – it is just very unlikely that they do not. A learner that chooses a hypothesis that is consistent with the training examples is **probably approximately correct** if, for an arbitrary number δ ($0 < \delta \leq 1$), the algorithm is not approximately correct in at most δ of the cases. That is, the hypothesis generated is approximately correct at least $1 - \delta$ of the time.

Under the preceding assumption, for arbitrary ϵ and δ, we can guarantee that an algorithm that returns a consistent hypothesis will find a hypothesis with error less than ϵ, in at least $1 - \delta$ of the cases. Moreover, this outcome does not depend on the probability distribution.

Suppose $\epsilon > 0$ and $\delta > 0$ are given. Partition the hypothesis space $\mathcal{H}$ into

$$\mathcal{H}_0 = \{h \in \mathcal{H} : error(h) \leq \epsilon\}$$
$$\mathcal{H}_1 = \{h \in \mathcal{H} : error(h) > \epsilon\} .$$

We want to guarantee that the learner does not choose an element of $\mathcal{H}_1$ in more than δ of the cases.

Suppose $h \in \mathcal{H}_1$, then

$$P(h \text{ is wrong for a single example}) \geq \epsilon$$
$$P(h \text{ is correct for a single example}) \leq 1 - \epsilon$$
$$P(h \text{ is correct for } m \text{ examples}) \leq (1 - \epsilon)^m$$

Thus,

$$P(\mathcal{H}_1 \text{ contains a hypothesis that is correct for } m \text{ examples})$$
$$\leq |\mathcal{H}_1| (1 - \epsilon)^m$$
$$\leq |\mathcal{H}| (1 - \epsilon)^m$$
$$\leq |\mathcal{H}| e^{-\epsilon m}$$

using the inequality that $(1 - \epsilon) \leq e^{-\epsilon}$ if $0 \leq \epsilon \leq 1$.

Thus, if we ensure that $|\mathcal{H}| e^{-\epsilon m} \leq \delta$, we guarantee that $\mathcal{H}_1$ does not contain a hypothesis that is correct for m examples in more than δ of the cases. Thus, H_0 contains all of the correct hypotheses in all but δ is the cases.

Solving for m gives

$$m \geq \frac{1}{\epsilon} \left(\ln |\mathcal{H}| + \ln \frac{1}{\delta} \right) .$$

Thus, we can conclude the following proposition.

Proposition 7.4. *If a hypothesis is consistent with at least*

$$\frac{1}{\epsilon} \left(\ln |\mathcal{H}| + \ln \frac{1}{\delta} \right)$$

training examples, it has error at most ϵ, at least $1 - \delta$ of the time.

The number of examples required to guarantee this error bound is called the **sample complexity**. The number of examples required according to this proposition is a function of ϵ, δ, and the size of the hypothesis space.

Example 7.28 Suppose the hypothesis space $\mathcal{H}$ is the set of conjunctions of literals on n Boolean variables. In this case $|\mathcal{H}| = 3^n + 1$ because, for each conjunction, each variable in is one of three states: (1) it is unnegated in the conjunction, (2) it is negated, or (3) it does not appear; the "+1" is needed to represent false, which is the conjunction of any atom and its negation. Thus, the sample complexity is $\frac{1}{\epsilon}\left(n\ln 3 + \ln\frac{1}{\delta}\right)$ examples, which is polynomial in n, $\frac{1}{\epsilon}$, and $\ln\frac{1}{\delta}$.

If we want to guarantee at most a 5% error 99% of the time and have 30 Boolean variables, then $\epsilon = 1/20$, $\delta = 1/100$, and $n = 30$. The bound says that we can guarantee this performance if we find a hypothesis that is consistent with $20 \times (30\ln 3 + \ln 100) \approx 752$ examples. This is much less than the number of possible instances, which is $2^{30} = 1,073,741,824$, and the number of hypotheses, which is $3^{30} + 1 = 205,891,132,094,650$.

Example 7.29 If the hypothesis space $\mathcal{H}$ is the set of all Boolean functions on n variables, then $|\mathcal{H}| = 2^{2^n}$; thus, we require $\frac{1}{\epsilon}\left(2^n\ln 2 + \ln\frac{1}{\delta}\right)$ examples. The sample complexity is exponential in n.

If we want to guarantee at most a 5% error 99% of the time and have 30 Boolean variables, then $\epsilon = 1/20$, $\delta = 1/100$, and $n = 30$. The bound says that we can guarantee this performance if we find a hypothesis that is consistent with $20 \times (2^{30}\ln 2 + \ln 100) \approx 14,885,222,452$ examples.

Consider the third question raised at the start of this section, namely, how quickly a learner can find the probably approximately correct hypothesis. First, if the sample complexity is exponential in the size of some parameter (e.g., n above), the computational complexity must be exponential because an algorithm must at least consider each example. To show an algorithm with polynomial complexity, we must find a hypothesis space with polynomial sample complexity and show that the algorithm uses polynomial time for each example.

7.8 Bayesian Learning

Rather than choosing the most likely model or delineating the set of all models that are consistent with the training data, another approach is to compute the posterior probability of each model given the training examples.

The idea of **Bayesian learning** is to compute the posterior probability distribution of the target features of a new example conditioned on its input features and all of the training examples.

Suppose a new case has inputs $X{=}x$ and has target features, Y; the aim is to compute $P(Y|X{=}x \wedge \mathbf{e})$, where $\mathbf{e}$ is the set of training examples. This is the probability distribution of the target variables given the particular inputs and the examples. The role of a model is to be the assumed generator of the examples. If we let M be a set of disjoint and covering models, then reasoning by cases (page 224) and the chain rule give

$$
\begin{aligned}
P(Y|x \wedge \mathbf{e}) &= \sum_{m \in M} P(Y \wedge m | x \wedge \mathbf{e}) \\
&= \sum_{m \in M} P(Y | m \wedge x \wedge \mathbf{e}) \times P(m | x \wedge \mathbf{e}) \\
&= \sum_{m \in M} P(Y | m \wedge x) \times P(m | \mathbf{e}).
\end{aligned}
$$

The first two equalities are theorems from the definition of probability (page 223). The last equality makes two assumptions: the model includes all of the information about the examples that is necessary for a particular prediction [i.e., $P(Y|m \wedge x \wedge \mathbf{e}) = P(Y|m \wedge x)$], and the model does not change depending on the inputs of the new example [i.e., $P(m|x \wedge \mathbf{e}) = P(m|\mathbf{e})$]. This formula says that we average over the prediction of all of the models, where each model is weighted by its posterior probability given the examples.

$P(m|\mathbf{e})$ can be computed using Bayes' rule:

$$P(m|\mathbf{e}) = \frac{P(\mathbf{e}|m) \times P(m)}{P(\mathbf{e})} .$$

Thus, the weight of each model depends on how well it predicts the data (the likelihood) and its prior probability. The denominator, $P(\mathbf{e})$, is a normalizing constant to make sure the posterior probabilities of the models sum to 1. Computing $P(\mathbf{e})$ can be very difficult when there are many models.

A set $\{e_1, \ldots, e_k\}$ of examples are **i.i.d. (independent and identically distributed)**, where the distribution is given by model m if, for all i and j, examples e_i and e_j are independent given m, which means $P(e_i \wedge e_j|m) = P(e_i|m) \times P(e_j|m)$. We usually assume that the examples are i.i.d.

Suppose the set of training examples $\mathbf{e}$ is $\{e_1, \ldots, e_k\}$. That is, $\mathbf{e}$ is the conjunction of the e_i, because all of the examples have been observed to be true. The assumption that the examples are i.i.d. implies

$$P(\mathbf{e}|m) = \prod_{i=1}^{k} P(e_i|m) .$$

The set of models may include structurally different models in addition to models that differ in the values of the parameters. One of the techniques of Bayesian learning is to make the parameters of the model explicit and to determine the distribution over the parameters.

Example 7.30 Consider the simplest learning task under uncertainty. Suppose there is a single Boolean random variable, Y. One of two outcomes, a and $\neg a$, occurs for each example. We want to learn the probability distribution of Y given some examples.

There is a single parameter, ϕ, that determines the set of all models. Suppose that ϕ represents the probability of $Y=true$. We treat this parameter as a real-valued random variable on the interval $[0, 1]$. Thus, by definition of ϕ, $P(a|\phi) = \phi$ and $P(\neg a|\phi) = 1 - \phi$.

Suppose an agent has no prior information about the probability of Boolean variable Y and no knowledge beyond the training examples. This ignorance can be modeled by having the prior probability distribution of the variable ϕ as a uniform distribution over the interval $[0, 1]$. This is the the probability density function labeled $n_0=0, n_1=0$ in Figure 7.15.

We can update the probability distribution of ϕ given some examples. Assume that the examples, obtained by running a number of independent experiments, are a particular sequence of outcomes that consists of n_0 cases where Y is false and n_1 cases where Y is true.

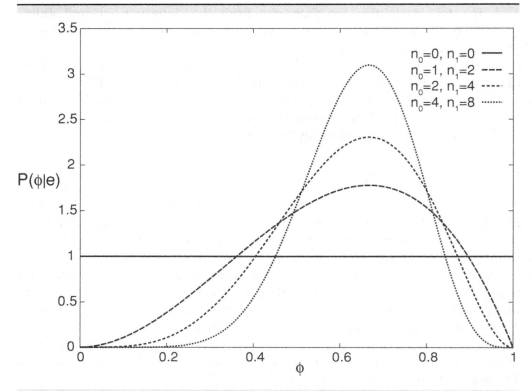

Figure 7.15: Beta distribution based on different samples

The posterior distribution for ϕ given the training examples can be derived by Bayes' rule. Let the examples $\mathbf{e}$ be the particular sequence of observation that resulted in n_1 occurrences of $Y=true$ and n_0 occurrences of $Y=false$. Bayes' rule gives us

$$P(\phi|\mathbf{e}) = \frac{P(\mathbf{e}|\phi) \times P(\phi)}{P(\mathbf{e})} .$$

The denominator is a normalizing constant to make sure the area under the curve is 1.

Given that the examples are i.i.d.,

$$P(\mathbf{e}|\phi) = \phi^{n_1} \times (1 - \phi)^{n_0}$$

because there are n_0 cases where $Y=false$, each with a probability of $1 - \phi$, and n_1 cases where $Y=true$, each with a probability of ϕ.

One possible prior probability, $P(\phi)$, is a uniform distribution on the interval $[0, 1]$. This would be reasonable when the agent has no prior information about the probability.

Figure 7.15 gives some posterior distributions of the variable ϕ based on different sample sizes, and given a uniform prior. The cases are $(n_0 = 1, n_1 = 2)$, $(n_0 = 2, n_1 = 4)$, and $(n_0 = 4, n_1 = 8)$. Each of these peak at the same place, namely at $\frac{2}{3}$. More training examples make the curve sharper.

The distribution of this example is known as the **beta distribution**; it is parametrized by two counts, α_0 and α_1, and a probability p. Traditionally, the α_i parameters for the beta distribution are one more than the counts; thus, $\alpha_i = n_i + 1$. The beta distribution is

$$Beta^{\alpha_0, \alpha_1}(p) = \frac{1}{K} p^{\alpha_1 - 1} \times (1 - p)^{\alpha_0 - 1}$$

where K is a normalizing constant that ensures the integral over all values is 1. Thus, the uniform distribution on $[0, 1]$ is the beta distribution $Beta^{1,1}$.

The generalization of the beta distribution to more than two parameters is known as the Dirichlet distribution. The **Dirichlet distribution** with two sorts of parameters, the "counts" $\alpha_1, \ldots, \alpha_k$, and the probability parameters $p_1, \ldots, p_k$, is

$$Dirichlet^{\alpha_1, \ldots, \alpha_k}(p_1, \ldots, p_k) = \frac{1}{K} \prod_{j=1}^{k} p_j^{\alpha_j - 1}$$

where K is a normalizing constant that ensures the integral over all values is 1; p_i is the probability of the ith outcome (and so $0 \leq p_i \leq 1$) and α_i is one more than the count of the ith outcome. That is, $\alpha_i = n_i + 1$. The Dirichlet distribution looks like Figure 7.15 along each dimension (i.e., as each p_j varies between 0 and 1).

For many cases, summing over all models weighted by their posterior distribution is difficult, because the models may be complicated (e.g., if they are decision trees or even belief networks). However, for the Dirichlet distribution, the expected value for outcome i (averaging over all p_j's) is

$$\frac{\alpha_i}{\sum_j \alpha_j}.$$

The reason that the α_i parameters are one more than the counts is to make this formula simple. This fraction is well defined only when the α_j are all non-negative and not all are zero.

Example 7.31 Consider Example 7.30 (page 335), which determines the value of ϕ based on a sequence of observations made up of n_0 cases where Y is false and n_1 cases where Y is true. Consider the posterior distribution as shown in Figure 7.15. What is interesting about this is that, whereas the most likely posterior value of ϕ is $\frac{n_1}{n_0 + n_1}$, the expected value (page 230) of this distribution is $\frac{n_1 + 1}{n_0 + n_1 + 2}$.

Thus, the expected value of the $n_0 = 1, n_1 = 2$ curve is $\frac{3}{5}$, for the $n_0 = 2, n_1 = 4$ case the expected value is $\frac{5}{8}$, and for the $n_0 = 4, n_1 = 8$ case it is $\frac{9}{14}$. As the learner gets more training examples, this value approaches $\frac{n}{m}$.

This estimate is better than $\frac{n}{m}$ for a number of reasons. First, it tells us what to do if the learning agent has no examples: Use the uniform prior of $\frac{1}{2}$. This is the expected value of the $n = 0, m = 0$ case. Second, consider the case where

$n=0$ and $m=3$. The agent should not use $P(y)=0$, because this says that Y is impossible, and it certainly does not have evidence for this! The expected value of this curve with a uniform prior is $\frac{1}{5}$.

An agent does not have to start with a uniform prior; it can start with any prior distribution. If the agent starts with a prior that is a Dirichlet distribution, its posterior will be a Dirichlet distribution. The posterior distribution can be obtained by adding the observed counts to the α_i parameters of the prior distribution.

The i.i.d. assumption can be represented as a belief network, where each of the e_i are independent given model m. This independence assumption can be represented by the belief network shown on the left side of Figure 7.16. If m is made into a discrete variable, any of the inference methods of the previous chapter can be used for inference in this network. A standard reasoning technique in such a network is to condition on all of the observed e_i and to query the model variable or an unobserved e_i variable.

The problem with specifying a belief network for a learning problem is that the model grows with the number of observations. Such a network can be specified before any observations have been received by using a **plate model**. A plate model specifies what variables will be used in the model and what will be repeated in the observations. The right side of Figure 7.16 shows a plate model that represents the same information as the left side. The plate is drawn as a rectangle that contains some nodes, and an index (drawn on the bottom right of the plate). The nodes in the plate are indexed by the index. In the plate model, there are multiple copies of the variables in the plate, one for each value of the index. The intuition is that there is a pile of plates, one for each value of the index. The number of plates can be varied depending on the number of observations and what is queried. In this figure, all of the nodes in the plate share a common parent. The probability of each copy of a variable in a plate given the parents is the same for each index.

A plate model lets us specify more complex relationships between the variables. In a **hierarchical Bayesian model**, the parameters of the model can

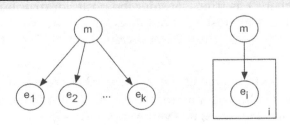

Figure 7.16: Belief network and plate models of Bayesian learning

depend on other parameters. Such a model is hierarchical in the sense that some parameters can depend on other parameters.

Example 7.32 Suppose a diagnostic assistant agent wants to model the probability that a particular patient in a hospital is sick with the flu before symptoms have been observed for this patient. This prior information about the patient can be combined with the observed symptoms of the patient. The agent wants to learn this probability, based on the statistics about other patients in the same hospital and about patients at different hospitals. This problem can range from the cases where a lot of data exists about the current hospital (in which case, presumably, that data should be used) to the case where there is no data about the particular hospital that the patient is in. A hierarchical Bayesian model can be used to combine the statistics about the particular hospital the patient is in with the statistics about the other hospitals.

Suppose that for patient X in hospital H there is a random variable S_{HX} that is true when the patient is sick with the flu. (Assume that the patient identification number and the hospital uniquely determine the patient.) There is a value ϕ_H for each hospital H that will be used for the prior probability of being sick with the flu for each patient in H. In a Bayesian model, ϕ_H is treated as a real-valued random variable with domain $[0, 1]$. S_{HX} depends on ϕ_H, with $P(S_{HX}|\phi_H) = \phi_H$. Assume that ϕ_H is distributed according to a beta distribution (page 337). We don't assume that ϕ_{h_1} and ϕ_{h_2} are independent of each other, but depend on **hyperparameters**. The hyperparameters can be the prior counts α_0 and α_1. The parameters depend on the hyperparameters in terms of the conditional probability $P(\phi_{h_i}|\alpha_0, \alpha_1) = Beta^{\alpha_0, \alpha_1}(\phi_{h_i})$; α_0 and α_1 are real-valued random variables, which require some prior distribution.

The plate model and the corresponding belief network are shown in Figure 7.17 . Part (a) shows the plate model, where there is a copy of the outside plate

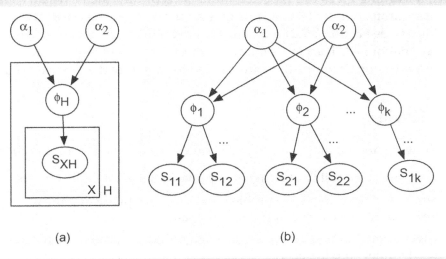

(a)   (b)

Figure 7.17: Hierarchical Bayesian model

for each hospital and a copy of the inside plate for each patient in the hospital. Part of the resulting belief network is shown in part (b). Observing some of the S_{HX} will affect the ϕ_H and so α_0 and α_1, which will in turn affect the other ϕ_H variables and the unobserved S_{HX} variables.

Sophisticated methods exist to evaluate such networks. However, if the variables are made discrete, any of the methods of the previous chapter can be used.

In addition to using the posterior distribution of ϕ to derive the expected value, we can use it to answer other questions such as: What is the probability that the posterior probability of ϕ is in the range $[a, b]$? In other words, derive $P((\phi \geq a \wedge \phi \leq b)|e)$. This is the problem that the Reverend Thomas Bayes solved more than 200 years ago [Bayes, 1763]. The solution he gave – although in much more cumbersome notation – was

$$\frac{\int_a^b p^n \times (1-p)^{m-n}}{\int_0^1 p^n \times (1-p)^{m-n}}.$$

This kind of knowledge is used in surveys when it may be reported that a survey is correct with an error of at most 5%, 19 times out of 20. It is also the same type of information that is used by probably approximately correct (PAC) learning (page 332), which guarantees an error at most ϵ at least $1 - \delta$ of the time. If an agent chooses the midpoint of the range $[a, b]$, namely $\frac{a+b}{2}$, as its hypothesis, it will have error less than or equal to $\frac{b-a}{2}$, just when the hypothesis is in $[a, b]$. The value $1 - \delta$ corresponds to $P(\phi \geq a \wedge \phi \leq b|e)$. If $\epsilon = \frac{b-a}{2}$ and $\delta = 1 - P(\phi \geq a \wedge \phi \leq b|e)$, choosing the midpoint will result in an error at most ϵ in $1 - \delta$ of the time. PAC learning gives worst-case results, whereas Bayesian learning gives the expected number. Typically, the Bayesian estimate is more accurate, but the PAC results give a guarantee of the error. The sample complexity (see Section 7.7.2) required for Bayesian learning is typically much less than that of PAC learning – many fewer examples are required to *expect to achieve* the desired accuracy than are needed to *guarantee* the desired accuracy.

7.9 Review

The following are the main points you should have learned from this chapter:

- Learning is the ability of an agent improve its behavior based on experience.
- Supervised learning is the problem that involves predicting the output of a new input, given a set of input–output pairs.
- Given some training examples, an agent builds a representation that can be used for new predictions.
- Linear classifiers, decision trees, and Bayesian classifiers are all simple representations that are the basis for more sophisticated models.

- An agent can choose the best hypothesis given the training examples, delineate all of the hypotheses that are consistent with the data, or compute the posterior probability of the hypotheses given the training examples.

7.10 References and Further Reading

For good overviews of machine learning see Mitchell [1997], Duda, Hart, and Stork [2001], Bishop [2008], and Hastie, Tibshirani, and Friedman [2009].

The collection of papers by Shavlik and Dietterich [1990] contains many classic learning papers. Michie, Spiegelhalter, and Taylor [1994] give empirical evaluation of many learning algorithms on many different problems. Briscoe and Caelli [1996] discuss many different machine learning algorithms. Weiss and Kulikowski [1991] overview techniques for classification learning. Davis and Goadrich [2006] discusses precision, recall, and ROC curves.

The approach to combining expert knowledge and data was proposed by Spiegelhalter, Franklin, and Bull [1990].

Decision-tree learning is discussed by Quinlan [1986]. For an overview of a mature decision-tree learning tool see Quinlan [1993]. The Gini index [Exercise 7.10 (page 345)] is the splitting criteria used in CART [Breiman, Friedman, Olshen, and Stone, 1984].

TAN networks are described by Friedman, Greiger, and Goldszmidt [1997]. Latent tree models are described by Zhang [2004].

For overviews of neural networks see Bishop [1995], Hertz, Krogh, and Palmer [1991], and Jordan and Bishop [1996]. Back-propagation is introduced in Rumelhart, Hinton, and Williams [1986]. Minsky and Papert [1988] analyze the limitations of neural networks.

For reviews of ensemble learning see Dietterich [2002]. Boosting is described in Schapire [2002] and Meir and Rätsch [2003].

For reviews on case-based reasoning see Aamodt and Plaza [1994], Kolodner and Leake [1996], and Lopez De Mantaras, Mcsherry, Bridge, Leake, Smyth, Craw, Faltings, Maher, Cox, Forbus, Keane, Aamodt, and Watson [2005]. For a review of nearest-neighbor algorithms, see Duda et al. [2001] and Dasarathy [1991]. The dimension-weighting learning nearest-neighbor algorithm is from Lowe [1995]. For a classical review of case-based reasoning, see Riesbeck and Schank [1989], and for recent reviews see Aha, Marling, and Watson [2005].

Version spaces were defined by Mitchell [1977]. PAC learning was introduced by Valiant [1984]. The analysis here is due to Haussler [1988]. Kearns and Vazirani [1994] give a good introduction to computational learning theory and PAC learning. For more details on version spaces and PAC learning, see Mitchell [1997].

For overviews of Bayesian learning, see Jaynes [2003], Loredo [1990], Howson and Urbach [2006], and Cheeseman [1990]. See also books on Bayesian statistics such as Gelman, Carlin, Stern, and Rubin [2004] and Bernardo and Smith [1994]. Bayesian learning of decision trees is described in Buntine [1992]. Grünwald [2007] discusses the MDL principle.

For research results on machine learning, see the journals *Journal of Machine Learning Research (JMLR)*, *Machine Learning*, the annual *International Conference on Machine Learning (ICML)*, the *Proceedings of the Neural Information Processing Society (NIPS)*, or general AI journals such as *Artificial Intelligence* and the *Journal of Artificial Intelligence Research*, and many specialized conferences and journals.

7.11   Exercises

Exercise 7.1   The aim of this exercise is to fill in the table of Figure 7.3 (page 295).

(a) Prove the optimal prediction for training data. To do this, find the minimum value of the absolute error, the sum-of-squares error, the entropy, and the value that gives the maximum likelihood. The maximum or minimum value is either an end point or where the derivative is zero.

(b) To determine the best prediction for the test data, assume that the data cases are generated stochastically according to some true parameter p_0. Try the following for a number of different values for $p_0 \in [0, 1]$. Generate k training examples (try various values for k, some small, say 5, and some large, say 1,000) by sampling with probability p_0; from these generate n_0 and n_1. Generate a test set that contains many test cases using the same parameter p_0. For each of the optimality criteria – sum of absolute values, sum of squares, and likelihood (or entropy) – which of the following gives a lower error on the test set:

   i) the mode

   ii) $n_1 / (n_0 + n_1)$

   iii) if $n_1 = 0$, use 0.001, if $n_0 = 0$, use 0.999, else use $n_1 / (n_0 + n_1)$. (Try this for different numbers when the counts are zero.)

   iv) $(n_1 + 1) / (n_0 + n_1 + 2)$

   v) $(n_1 + \alpha) / (n_0 + n_1 + 2\alpha)$ for different values of $\alpha > 0$

   vi) another predictor that is a function of n_0 and n_1.

   You may have to generate many different training sets for each parameter. (For the mathematically sophisticated, can you prove what the optimal predictor is for each criterion?)

Exercise 7.2   In the context of a point estimate of a feature with domain $\{0, 1\}$ with no inputs, it is possible for an agent to make a stochastic prediction with a parameter $p \in [0, 1]$ such that the agent predicts 1 with probability p and predicts 0 otherwise. For each of the following error measures, give the expected error on a training set with n_0 occurrences of 0 and n_1 occurrences of 1 (as a function of p). What is the value of p that minimizes the error? Is this worse or better than the prediction of Figure 7.3 (page 295)?

(a) sum of absolute errors

(b) sum-of-squares error

(c) worst-case error

Example	Comedy	Doctors	Lawyers	Guns	Likes
e_1	false	true	false	false	false
e_2	true	false	true	false	true
e_3	false	false	true	true	true
e_4	false	false	true	false	false
e_5	false	false	false	true	false
e_6	true	false	false	true	false
e_7	true	false	false	false	true
e_8	false	true	true	true	true
e_9	false	true	true	false	false
e_{10}	true	true	true	false	true
e_{11}	true	true	false	true	false
e_{12}	false	false	false	false	false

Figure 7.18: Training examples for Exercise 7.3

Exercise 7.3 Suppose we have a system that observes a person's TV watching habits in order to recommend other TV shows the person may like. Suppose that we have characterized each show by whether it is a comedy, whether it features doctors, whether it features lawyers, and whether it has guns. Suppose we are given the examples of Figure 7.18 about whether the person likes various TV shows. We want to use this data set to learn the value of *Likes* (i.e., to predict which TV shows the person would like based on the attributes of the TV show).

You may find the Alspace.org applets useful for this assignment. (Before you start, see if you can see the pattern in what shows the person likes.)

(a) Suppose the error is the sum of absolute errors. Give the optimal decision tree with only one node (i.e., with no splits). What is the error of this tree?

(b) Do the same as in part (a), but with the sum-of-squares error.

(c) Suppose the error is the sum of absolute errors. Give the optimal decision tree of depth 2 (i.e., the root node is the only node with children). For each leaf in the tree, give the examples that are filtered to that node. What is the error of this tree?

(d) Do the same as in part (c) but with the sum-of-squares error.

(e) What is the smallest tree that correctly classifies all training examples? Does a top-down decision tree that optimizes the information gain at each step represent the same function?

(f) Give two instances that do not appear in the examples of Figure 7.18 and show how they are classified using the smallest decision tree. Use this to explain the bias inherent in the tree. (How does the bias give you these particular predictions?)

(g) Is this data set linearly separable? Explain why or why not.

Exercise 7.4 Consider the decision-tree learning algorithm of Figure 7.5 (page 300) and the data of Figure 7.1 (page 289). Suppose, for this question, the stopping criterion is that all of the examples have the same classification. The tree of Figure 7.4 (page 298) was built by selecting a feature that gives the maximum information gain. This question considers what happens when a different feature is selected.

(a) Suppose you change the algorithm to always select the first element of the list of features. What tree is found when the features are in the order [*Author, Thread, Length, WhereRead*]? Does this tree represent a different function than that found with the maximum information gain split? Explain.

(b) What tree is found when the features are in the order [*WhereRead, Thread, Length, Author*]? Does this tree represent a different function than that found with the maximum information gain split or the one given for the preceding part? Explain.

(c) Is there a tree that correctly classifies the training examples but represents a different function than those found by the preceding algorithms? If so, give it. If not, explain why.

Exercise 7.5 Consider Equation (7.1) (page 304), which gives the error of a linear prediction.

(a) Give a formula for the weights that minimize the error for the case where $n = 1$ (i.e., when there is only one input feature). [Hint: For each weight, differentiate with respect to that weight and set to zero.]

(b) Give a set of equations for the weights that minimize the error for arbitrary n.

(c) Why is it hard to minimize the error analytically when using a sigmoid linear function (i.e., a squashed linear function when the activation function is a sigmoid or logistic function)?

Exercise 7.6 Suppose that, in the output of a neural network, we assign any value greater than 0.5 to be true and any less than 0.5 to be false (i.e., any positive value before the activation function is true, and a negative value is false).

Run the AIspace.org neural network learning applet on the data of Figure 7.9 (page 309) for a neural network with two hidden nodes. Given the final parameter settings found, give a logical formula (or a decision tree or a set of rules) that represents the Boolean function that is the value for the hidden units and the output units. This formula or set of rules should not refer to any real numbers.

[Hint: One brute-force method is to go through the 16 combinations of values for the inputs to each hidden unit and determine the truth value of the output. A better method is to try to understand the functions themselves.]

Does the neural network learn the same function as the decision tree?

Exercise 7.7 The aim of this exercise is to determine the size of the space of decision trees. Suppose there are n binary features in a learning problem. How many different decision trees are there? How many different functions are represented by these decision trees? Is it possible that two different decision trees give rise to the same function?

Exercise 7.8 Extend the decision-tree learning algorithm of Figure 7.5 (page 300) so that multivalued features can be represented. Make it so that the rule form of the decision tree is returned.

One problem that must be overcome is when no examples correspond to one particular value of a chosen feature. You must make a reasonable prediction for this case.

Exercise 7.9 The decision-tree learning algorithm of Figure 7.5 (page 300) has to stop if it runs out of features and not all examples agree.

Suppose that you are building a decision tree and you have come to the stage where there are no remaining features to split on and there are examples in the training set, n_1 of which are positive and n_0 of which are negative. Three strategies have been suggested:

i) Return whichever value has the most examples – return *true* if $n_1 > n_0$, *false* if $n_1 < n_0$, and either if $n_1 = n_0$.

ii) Return the empirical frequency, $n_1/(n_0 + n_1)$.

iii) Return $(n_1 + 1)/(n_0 + n_1 + 2)$.

Which of the following strategies has the least error on the training set?

(a) The error is defined as the sum of the absolute differences between the value of the example ($1 = true$ and $0 = false$) and the predicted values in the tree (either $1 = true$ and $0 = false$ or the probability).

(b) The error is defined as the sum of the squares of the differences in values.

(c) The error is the entropy of the data.

Explain how you derived this answer.

Exercise 7.10 In choosing which feature to split on in decision-tree search, an alternative heuristic to the max information split of Section 7.3.1 is to use the Gini index.

The Gini index of a set of examples (with respect to target feature Y) is a measure of the impurity of the examples:

$$gini_Y(Examples) = 1 - \sum_{Val} \left(\frac{|\{e \in Examples : val(e, Y) = Val\}|}{|Examples|} \right)^2$$

where $|\{e \in Examples : val(e, Y) = Val\}|$ is the number of examples with value Val of feature Y, and $|Examples|$ is the total number of examples. The Gini index is always non-negative and has value zero only if all of the examples have the same value on the feature. The Gini index reaches its maximum value when the examples are evenly distributed among the values of the features.

One heuristic for choosing which property to split on is to choose the split that minimizes the total impurity of the training examples on the target feature, summed over all of the leaves.

(a) Implement a decision-tree search algorithm that uses the Gini index.

(b) Try both the Gini index algorithm and the maximum information split algorithm on some databases and see which results in better performance.

(c) Find an example database where the Gini index finds a different tree than the maximum information gain heuristic. Which heuristic seems to be better for this example? Consider which heuristic seems more sensible for the data at hand.

(d) Try to find an example database where the maximum information split seems more sensible than the Gini index, and try to find another example for which the Gini index seems better. [Hint: Try extreme distributions.]

Exercise 7.11 As outlined in Example 7.18 (page 322), define a code for describing decision trees. Make sure that each code corresponds to a decision tree (for every sufficiently long sequence of bits, the initial segment of the sequence will describe a unique decision tree), and each decision tree has a code. How does this code translate into a prior distribution on trees? In particular, how much does the likelihood of introducing a new split have to increase to offset the reduction in prior probability of the split (assuming that smaller trees are easier to describe than large trees in your code)?

Exercise 7.12 Show how gradient descent can be used for learning a linear function that minimizes the absolute error. [Hint: Do a case analysis of the error. The error is differentiable at every point except when the error is zero, in which case it does not need to be updated.]

Exercise 7.13 Give an example where a naive Bayesian classifier can give inconsistent results when using empirical frequencies as probabilities. [Hint: You require two features, say A and B, and a binary classification, say C, that has domain $\{0, 1\}$. Construct a data set where the empirical probabilities give $P(a|C = 0) = 0$ and $P(b|C = 1) = 0$.] What observation is inconsistent with the model?

Exercise 7.14 Run the Alspace.org neural network learner on the data of Figure 7.1 (page 289).

(a) Suppose that you decide to use any predicted value from the neural network greater than 0.5 as true, and any value less than 0.5 as false. How many examples are misclassified initially? How many examples are misclassified after 40 iterations? How many examples are misclassified after 80 iterations?

(b) Try the same example and the same initial values, with different step sizes for the gradient descent. Try at least $\eta = 0.1$, $\eta = 1.0$, and $\eta = 5.0$. Comment on the relationship between step size and convergence.

(c) Given the final parameter values you found, give a logical formula for what each of the units is computing. You can do this by considering, for each of the units, the truth tables for the input values and by determining the output for each combination, then reducing this formula. Is it always possible to find such a formula?

(d) All of the parameters were set to different initial values. What happens if the parameter values were all set to the same (random) value? Test it out for this example, and hypothesize what occurs in general.

(e) For the neural network algorithm, comment on the following stopping criteria:

    i) Learn for a limited number of iterations, where the limit is set initially.

    ii) Stop when the sum-of-squares error is less than 0.25. Explain why 0.25 may be an appropriate number.

    iii) Stop when the derivatives all become within some ϵ of zero.

iv) Split the data into training data and test data, and stop when the error on the test data increases.

Which would you expect to better handle overfitting? Which criteria guarantee the gradient descent will stop? Which criteria would guarantee that, if it stops, the network can be used to predict the test data accurately?

Exercise 7.15 In the neural net learning algorithm, the parameters are updated for each example. To compute the derivative accurately, the parameters should be updated only after all examples have been seen. Implement such a learning algorithm and compare it to the incremental algorithm, with respect to both rate of convergence and to speed of the algorithm.

Exercise 7.16

(a) Draw a *kd*-tree for the data of Figure 7.1 (page 289). The topmost feature to split on should be the one that most divides the examples into two equal classes. Assume that you know that the *UserAction* feature does not appear in subsequent queries, and so it should not be split on. Show which training examples are at which leaf nodes.

(b) Show the locations in this tree that contain the closest training examples to a new case where the author is unknown, the thread is new, the length is long, and it was read at work.

(c) Based on this example, discuss which examples should be returned from a lookup on a *kd*-tree. Why is this different from a lookup on a decision tree?

Exercise 7.17 Implement a nearest-neighbor learning system that stores the training examples in a *kd*-tree and uses the neighbors that differ in the fewest number of features, weighted evenly. How well does this work in practice?

Chapter 8

Planning with Certainty

He who every morning plans the transaction of the day and follows out that plan, carries a thread that will guide him through the maze of the most busy life. But where no plan is laid, where the disposal of time is surrendered merely to the chance of incidence, chaos will soon reign.

– Victor Hugo (1802–1885)

Planning is about how an agent achieves its goals. To achieve anything but the simplest goals, an agent must reason about its future. Because an agent does not usually achieve its goals in one step, what it should do at any time depends on what it will do in the future. What it will do in the future depends on the state it is in, which, in turn, depends on what it has done in the past. This chapter considers how an agent can represent its actions and their effects and use these models to find a plan to achieve its goals.

In particular, this chapter considers the case where

- the agent's actions are deterministic; that is, the agent can predict the consequences of its actions.

- there are no exogenous events beyond the control of the agent that change the state of the world.

- the world is fully observable; thus, the agent can observe the current state of the world.

- time progresses discretely from one state to the next.

- goals are predicates of states that must be achieved or maintained.

Some of these assumptions are relaxed in the following chapters.

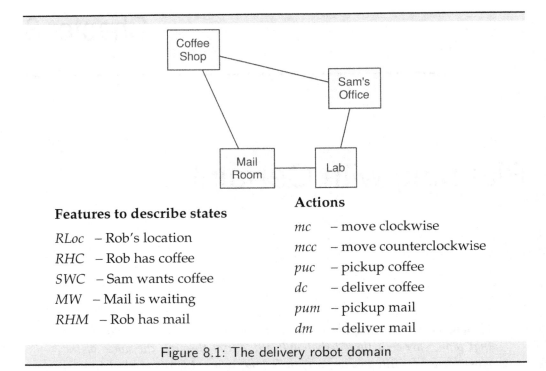

Features to describe states

RLoc – Rob's location
RHC   – Rob has coffee
SWC – Sam wants coffee
MW – Mail is waiting
RHM – Rob has mail

Actions

mc   – move clockwise
mcc   – move counterclockwise
puc   – pickup coffee
dc   – deliver coffee
pum – pickup mail
dm   – deliver mail

Figure 8.1: The delivery robot domain

8.1   Representing States, Actions, and Goals

To reason about what to do, an agent must have goals, some model of the world, and a model of the consequences of its actions.

A deterministic **action** is a partial function from states to states. It is partial because not every action can be carried out in every state. For example, a robot cannot carry out the action to pick up a particular object if it is nowhere near the object. The **precondition** of an action specifies when the action can be carried out. The **effect** of an action specifies the resulting state.

Example 8.1   Consider a delivery robot world (page 30) with mail and coffee to deliver. Assume a simplified domain with four locations as shown in Figure 8.1. The robot, called Rob, can buy coffee at the coffee shop, pick up mail in the mail room, move, and deliver coffee and/or mail. Delivering the coffee to Sam's office will stop Sam from wanting coffee. There can be mail waiting at the mail room to be delivered to Sam's office. This domain is quite simple, yet it is rich enough to demonstrate many of the problems in representing actions and in planning.

The state can be described in terms of the following features:
- the robot's location (*RLoc*), which is one of the coffee shop (*cs*), Sam's office (*off*), the mail room (*mr*), or the laboratory (*lab*).
- whether the robot has coffee (*RHC*). Let *rhc* mean Rob has coffee and $\overline{rhc}$ mean Rob does not have coffee.

- whether Sam wants coffee (*SWC*). Let *swc* mean Sam wants coffee and $\overline{swc}$ mean Sam does not want coffee.
- whether mail is waiting at the mail room (*MW*). Let *mw* mean there is mail waiting and $\overline{mw}$ mean there is no mail waiting.
- whether the robot is carrying the mail (*RHM*). Let *rhm* mean Rob has mail, and $\overline{rhm}$ mean Rob does not have mail.

Suppose Rob has six actions:

- Rob can move clockwise (*mc*).
- Rob can move counterclockwise (*mcc*).
- Rob can pick up coffee if Rob is at the coffee shop. Let *puc* mean that Rob picks up coffee. The precondition of *puc* is $\overline{rhc} \wedge RLoc = cs$; that is, Rob can pick up coffee in any state where its location is *cs*, and it is not already holding coffee. The effect of this action is to make *RHC* true. It does not affect the other features.
- Rob can deliver coffee if Rob is carrying coffee and is at Sam's office. Let *dc* mean that Rob delivers coffee. The precondition of *dc* is $rhc \wedge RLoc = off$. The effect of this action is to make *RHC* true and make *SWC* false.
- Rob can pick up mail if Rob is at the mail room and there is mail waiting there. Let *pum* mean Rob picks up the mail.
- Rob can deliver mail if Rob is carrying mail and at Sam's office. Let *dm* mean Rob delivers mail.

Assume that it is only possible for Rob to do one action at a time. We assume that a lower-level controller can implement these actions.

8.1.1 Explicit State-Space Representation

One possible representation of the effect and precondition of actions is to explicitly enumerate the states and, for each state, specify the actions that are possible in that state and, for each state–action pair, specify the state that results from carrying out the action in that state. This would require a table such as the following:

State	Action	Resulting State
s_7	act_{47}	s_{94}
s_7	act_{14}	s_{83}
s_{94}	act_5	s_{33}
...	...	...

The first tuple in this relation specifies that it is possible to carry out action act_{47} in state s_7 and, if it were to be carried out in state s_7, the resulting state would be s_{94}.

Thus, this is the explicit representation of the actions in terms of a graph. This is called a **state-space graph**. This is the sort of graph that was used in Chapter 3.

Example 8.2 In Example 8.1 (page 350), the states are the quintuples specifying the robot's location, whether the robot has coffee, whether Sam wants coffee, whether mail is waiting, and whether the robot is carrying the mail. For example, the tuple

$$\langle lab, \overline{rhc}, swc, \overline{mw}, rhm \rangle$$

represents the state where Rob is at the Lab, does not have coffee, Sam wants coffee, there is no mail waiting, and Rob has mail.

$$\langle lab, rhc, swc, mw, \overline{rhm} \rangle$$

represents the state where Rob is at the Lab, carrying coffee, Sam wants coffee, there is mail waiting, and Rob is not holding any mail.

In this example, there are $4 \times 2 \times 2 \times 2 \times 2 = 64$ states. Intuitively, all of them are possible, even if you would not expect that some of them would be reached by an intelligent robot.

There are six actions, not all of which are applicable in each state.

The actions can be defined in terms of the state transitions:

State	Action	Resulting State
$\langle lab, \overline{rhc}, swc, \overline{mw}, rhm \rangle$	mc	$\langle mr, \overline{rhc}, swc, \overline{mw}, rhm \rangle$
$\langle lab, \overline{rhc}, swc, \overline{mw}, rhm \rangle$	mcc	$\langle off, \overline{rhc}, swc, \overline{mw}, rhm \rangle$
$\langle off, \overline{rhc}, swc, \overline{mw}, rhm \rangle$	dm	$\langle off, \overline{rhc}, swc, \overline{mw}, \overline{rhm} \rangle$
$\langle off, \overline{rhc}, swc, \overline{mw}, rhm \rangle$	mcc	$\langle cs, \overline{rhc}, swc, \overline{mw}, rhm \rangle$
$\langle off, \overline{rhc}, swc, \overline{mw}, rhm \rangle$	mc	$\langle lab, \overline{rhc}, swc, \overline{mw}, rhm \rangle$
...	...	...

This table shows the transitions for two of the states. The complete problem representation includes the transitions for the other 62 states.

This is not a good representation for three main reasons:

- There are usually too many states to represent, to acquire, and to reason with.

- Small changes to the model mean a large change to the representation. Modeling another feature means changing the whole representation. For example, to model the level of power in the robot, so that it can recharge itself in the Lab, every state has to change.

- There is also usually much more structure and regularity in the effects of actions. This structure can make the specification of the preconditions and the effects of actions, and reasoning about them, more compact and efficient.

An alternative is to model the effects of actions in terms of how the actions affect the features.

8.1.2 Feature-Based Representation of Actions

A feature-based representation of actions models

- which actions are possible in a state, in terms of the values of the features of the state, and
- how the feature values in the next state are affected by the feature values of the current state and the action.

The **precondition** of an action is a proposition that must be true before the action can be carried out. In terms of constraints, the robot is constrained to only be able to choose an action for which the precondition is true.

Example 8.3 In Example 8.1 (page 350), the action of Rob to pick up coffee (*puc*) has precondition $cs \land \overline{rhc}$. That is, Rob must be at the coffee shop (*cs*), not carrying coffee ($\overline{rhc}$). As a constraint, this means that *puc* is not available for any other location or when *rhc* is true.

The action move clockwise is always possible. Its precondition is *true*.

The **feature-based representation of actions** uses rules to specify the value of each variable in the state resulting from an action. The bodies of these rules can include the action carried out and the values of features in the previous state.

The rules have two forms:

- A **causal rule** specifies when a feature gets a new value.
- A **frame rule** specifies when a feature keeps its value.

It is useful to think of these as two separate cases: what makes the feature change its value, and what makes it keep its value.

Example 8.4 In Example 8.1 (page 350), Rob's location depends on its previous location and where it moved. Let $RLoc'$ be the variable that specifies the location in the resulting state. The following rules specify the conditions under which Rob is at the coffee shop:

$$RLoc' = cs \leftarrow RLoc = off \land Act = mcc.$$
$$RLoc' = cs \leftarrow RLoc = mr \land Act = mc.$$
$$RLoc' = cs \leftarrow RLoc = cs \land Act \neq mcc \land Act \neq mc.$$

The first two rules are causal rules and the last rule is a frame rule.

Whether the robot has coffee in the resulting state depends on whether it has coffee in the previous state and its action:

$$rhc' \leftarrow rhc \land Act \neq dc.$$
$$rhc' \leftarrow Act = puc.$$

The first of these is a frame rule that specifies that the robot having coffee persists unless the robot delivers the coffee. The rule implicitly implies that the robot cannot drop the coffee or lose it, or it cannot be stolen. The second is the causal rule specifying that picking up the coffee causes the robot to have coffee in the next time step.

Causal rules and frame rules do not specify when an action is possible. What is possible is defined by the precondition of the actions.

8.1.3 The STRIPS Representation

The previous representation was feature-centric in that, for each feature, there were rules that specified its value in the state resulting from an action. An alternative is an action-centric representation which, for each action, specifies the effect of the action. One such representation is the **STRIPS representation**. STRIPS, which stands for "STanford Research Institute Problem Solver," was the planner used in Shakey, one of the first robots built using AI technology.

First, divide the features that describe the world into **primitive** and **derived** features. Definite clauses are used to determine the value of derived features from the values of the primitive features in any given state. The STRIPS representation is used to determine the values of primitive features in a state based on the previous state and the action taken by the agent.

The STRIPS representation is based on the idea that most things are not affected by a single action. For each action, STRIPS models when the action is possible and what primitive features are affected by the action. The effect of the action relies on the **STRIPS assumption**: All of the primitive features not mentioned in the description of the action stay unchanged.

The **STRIPS representation** for an action consists of

- the **precondition**, which is a set of assignments of values to features that must be true for the action to occur, and

- the **effect**, which is a set of resulting assignments of values to those primitive features that change as the result of the action.

Primitive feature V has value v after the action act if $V = v$ was on the effect list of act or if V was not mentioned in the effect list of act, and V had value v immediately before act. Non-primitive features can be derived from the values of the primitive features for each time.

When the variables are Boolean, it is sometimes useful to divide the effects into a **delete list**, which includes those variables made false, and an **add list**, which includes those variables made true.

Example 8.5 In Example 8.1 (page 350), the action of Rob to pick up coffee (*puc*) has the following STRIPS representation:

precondition $[cs, \overline{rhc}]$

effect $[rhc]$

That is, the robot must be at the coffee shop and not have coffee. After the action, *rhc* holds (i.e., $RHC = true$), and all other feature values are unaffected by this action.

Example 8.6 The action of delivering coffee (dc) can be defined by

precondition $[\mathit{off}, \mathit{rhc}]$

effect $[\overline{\mathit{rhc}}, \overline{\mathit{swc}}]$

The robot can deliver coffee when it is in the office and has coffee. It can deliver coffee whether Sam wants coffee or not. If Sam wanted coffee before the action, Sam no longer wants it after. Thus, the effects are to make $RHC = \mathit{false}$ and $SWC = \mathit{false}$.

The feature-based representation is more powerful than the STRIPS representation because it can represent anything representable in STRIPS. It can be more verbose because it requires explicit frame axioms, which are implicit in the STRIPS representation.

A STRIPS representation of a set of actions can be translated into the feature-based representation as follows. If the effects list of an action *act* is $[e_1, \ldots, e_k]$, the STRIPS representation is equivalent to the causal rules

$$e'_i \leftarrow act.$$

for each e_i that is made true by the action and the frame rules

$$c' \leftarrow c \wedge act.$$

for each condition c that does not involve a variable on the effects list. The precondition of each action in the representations is the same.

A **conditional effect** is an effect of an action that depends on the value of other features. The feature-based representation can specify conditional effects, whereas STRIPS cannot represent these directly.

Example 8.7 Consider representing the action *mc*. The effect of *mc* depends on the robot's location before *mc* was carried out.

The feature-based representation is as in Example 8.4 (page 353).

To represent this in the STRIPS representation, we construct multiple actions that differ in what is true initially. For example, *mc_cs* (move clockwise from coffee shop) has a precondition $[RLoc = cs]$ and effect $[RLoc = \mathit{off}]$.

8.1.4 Initial States and Goals

In a typical planning problem, where the world is fully observable and deterministic, the initial state is defined by specifying the value for each feature for the initial time.

There are two sorts of goals:

- An **achievement goal** is a proposition that must be true in the final state.
- A **maintenance goal** is a proposition that must be true in every state through which the agent passes. These are often **safety goals** – the goal of staying away from bad states.

There may be other kinds of goals such as transient goals (that must be achieved somewhere in the plan but do not have to hold at the end) or resource goals, such as wanting to minimize energy used or time traveled.

8.2   Forward Planning

A deterministic **plan** is a sequence of actions to achieve a **goal** from a given starting state. A deterministic **planner** is a problem solver that can produce a plan. The input to a planner is an initial world description, a specification of the actions available to the agent, and a goal description. The specification of the actions includes their preconditions and their effects.

One of the simplest planning strategies is to treat the planning problem as a path planning problem in the **state-space graph**. In a state-space graph, nodes are states, and arcs correspond to actions from one state to another. The arcs coming out of a state s correspond to all of the legal actions that can be carried out in that state. That is, for each state s, there is an arc for each action a whose precondition holds in state s, and where the resulting state does not violate a maintenance goal. A plan is a path from the initial state to a state that satisfies the achievement goal.

A **forward planner** searches the state-space graph from the initial state looking for a state that satisfies a goal description. It can use any of the search strategies described in Chapter 3.

Example 8.8   Figure 8.2 shows part of the search space starting from the state where Rob is at the coffee shop, Rob does not have coffee, Sam wants coffee, there is mail waiting, and Rob does not have mail. The search space is the same irrespective of the goal state.

Using a forward planner is not the same as making an explicit state-based representation of the actions (page 351), because the relevant part of the graph can be created dynamically from the representations of the actions.

A complete search strategy, such as A^* with multiple-path pruning or iterative deepening, is guaranteed to find a solution. The complexity of the search space is defined by the forward branching factor (page 75) of the graph. The branching factor is the set of all possible actions at any state, which may be quite large. For the simple robot delivery domain, the branching factor is 3 for the initial situation and is up to 4 for other situations. When the domain becomes bigger, the branching factor increases and so the search space explodes. This complexity may be reduced by finding good heuristics [see Exercise 8.6 (page 369)], but the heuristics have to be very good to overcome the combinatorial explosion.

A state can be represented as either

(a) *a complete world description*, in terms of an assignment of a value to each primitive proposition or as a proposition that defines the state, or

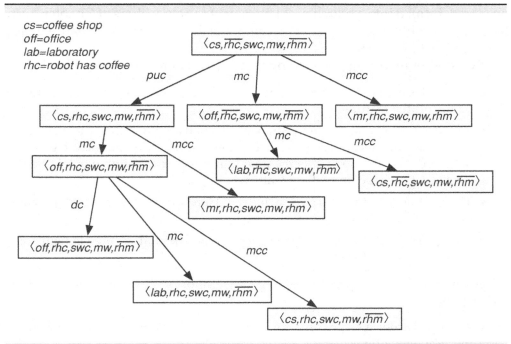

Figure 8.2: Part of the search space for a state-space planner

(b) *a path from an initial state*; that is, by the sequence of actions that were used to reach that state from the initial state. In this case, what holds in a state can be deduced from the axioms that specify the effects of actions.

The difference between representations (a) and (b) amounts to the difference between computing a whole new world description for each world created, or by calculating what holds in a world as necessary. Alternative (b) may save on space (particularly if there is a complex world description) and will allow faster creation of a new node, but it will be slower to determine what actually holds in any given world. Another difficulty with option (b) is that determining whether two states are the same (e.g., for loop detection or multiple-path pruning) is expensive.

We have presented state-space searching as a forward search method, but it is also possible to search backward from the set of states that satisfy the goal. Whereas the initial state is usually fully specified and so the frontier starts off containing a single state, the goal does not usually fully specify a state and so there would be many goal states that satisfy the goal. This would mean that the frontier is initially very large. Thus, backward search in the state space is often not practical.

8.3 Regression Planning

It is often more efficient to search in a different search space – one where the nodes are not states but rather are goals to be achieved. Once the problem has been transformed into a search problem, any of the algorithms of Chapter 3 can be used. We will only consider achievement goals and not maintenance goals; see Exercise 8.9 (page 369).

Regression planning is searching in the graph defined by the following:

- The nodes are goals that must be achieved. A goal is a set of assignments to (some of) the features.

- The arcs correspond to actions. In particular, an arc from node g to g', labeled with action act, means act is the last action that is carried out before goal g is achieved, and the node g' is the goal that must be true immediately before act so that g is true immediately after act.

- The start node is the goal to be achieved. Here we assume it is a conjunction of assignments of values to features.

- The goal condition for the search, $goal(g)$, is true if all of the elements of g are true of the initial state.

Given a node that represents goal g, a neighbor of g exists for every action act such that

- act is **possible**: it is possible for act to be carried out and for g to be true immediately after act; and

- act is **useful**: act achieves part of g.

The neighbor of g along the arc labeled with action act is the node g' defined by the weakest precondition. The **weakest precondition** for goal g to hold after action act is a goal g' such that

- g' is true before act implies that g is true immediately after act.

- g' is "weakest" in the sense that any proposition that satisfies the first condition must imply g'. This precludes, for example, having unnecessary conditions conjoined onto a precondition.

A set of assignments of values to variables is **consistent** if it assigns at most one value to any variable. That is, it is inconsistent if it assigns two different values to any variable.

Suppose goal $g = \{X_1 = v_1, \ldots, X_n = v_n\}$ is the node being considered.

Consider computing the neighbors of a node given the feature-based representation of actions. An action act is useful if there is a causal rule that achieves $X_i = v_i$ for some i, using action act. The neighbor of this node along the arc labeled with action act is the proposition

$$precondition(act) \wedge body(X_1 = v_1, act) \wedge \cdots \wedge body(X_n = v_n, act)$$

where $body(X_i = v_i, act)$ is the set of assignments of variables in the body of a rule that specifies when $X_i = v_i$ is true immediately after act. There is no such neighbor if there is no corresponding rule for some i, or if the proposition is inconsistent (i.e., assigns different values to a variable). Note that,

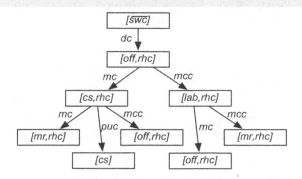

Figure 8.3: Part of the search space for a regression planner

if multiple rules are applicable for the same action, there will be multiple neighbors.

In terms of the STRIPS representation, *act* is useful for solving *g* if $X_i = v_i$ is an effect of action *act*, for some *i*. Action *act* is possible unless there is an effect $X_j = v_j$ of *act* and *g* contains $X_j = v'_j$ where $v'_j \neq v_j$. Immediately before *act*, the preconditions of *act*, as well as any $X_k = v_k$ not achieved by *act*, must hold.

Thus, the neighbor of the goal *g* on an arc labeled with *act* is

$$precondition(act) \cup (g \setminus effects(act))\}$$

as long as it is consistent.

Example 8.9 Suppose the goal is to achieve $\overline{swc}$. The start node is $[\overline{swc}]$. If this is true in the initial state, the planner stops. If not, it chooses an action that achieves $\overline{swc}$. In this case, there is only one: *dc*. The preconditions of *dc* are *off* ∧ *rhc*. Thus, there is one arc:

$$\langle [\overline{swc}], [\mathit{off}, rhc] \rangle \text{ labeled with } dc.$$

Consider the node [*off*, *rhc*]. There are two actions that can achieve *off*, namely *mc* from *cs* and *mcc* from *lab*. There is one action that can achieve *rhc*, namely *puc*. However, *puc* has as a precondition *cs* ∧ $\overline{rhc}$, but *cs* and *off* are inconsistent (because they involve different assignments to the variable *RLoc*). Thus, *puc* is not a possible last action; it is not possible that, immediately after *puc*, the condition [*off*, *rhc*] holds.

Figure 8.3 shows the first two levels of the search space (without multipath pruning or loop detection). Note that the search space is the same no matter what the initial state is. The starting state has two roles, first as a stopping criterion and second as a source of heuristics.

The following example shows how a regression planner can recognize what the last action of a plan must be.

Example 8.10 Suppose the goal was for Sam to not want coffee and for the robot to have coffee: $[\overline{swc}, rhc]$. The last action cannot be dc to achieve $\overline{swc}$, because this achieves $\overline{rhc}$. The only last action must be puc to achieve rhc. Thus, the resulting goal is $[\overline{swc}, cs]$. Again, the last action before this goal cannot be to achieve $\overline{swc}$ because this has as a precondition *off*, which is inconsistent with cs. Therefore, the second-to-last action must be a move action to achieve cs.

A problem with the regression planner is that a goal may not be achievable. Deciding whether a set of goals is achievable is often difficult to infer from the definitions of the actions. For example, you may be required to know that an object cannot be at two different places at the same time; sometimes this is not explicitly represented and is only implicit in the effects of an action, and the fact that the object is only in one position initially. To perform consistency pruning, the regression planner can use domain knowledge to prune the search space.

Loop detection and multiple-path pruning may be incorporated into a regression planner. The regression planner does not have to visit exactly the same node to prune the search. If the goal represented by a node n implies a goal on the path to n, node n can be pruned. Similarly, for multiple-path pruning, see Exercise 8.11 (page 369).

A regression planner commits to a particular total ordering of actions, even if no particular reason exists for one ordering over another. This commitment to a total ordering tends to increase the complexity of the search space if the actions do not interact much. For example, it tests each permutation of a sequence of actions when it may be possible to show that no ordering succeeds.

8.4   Planning as a CSP

In forward planning, the search is constrained by the initial state and only uses the goal as a stopping criterion and as a source for heuristics. In regression planning, the search is constrained by the goal and only uses the start state as a stopping criterion and as a source for heuristics. It is possible to go forward and backward in the same planner by using the initial state to prune what is not reachable and the goal to prune what is not useful. This can be done by converting a planning problem to a constraint satisfaction problem (CSP) and using one of the CSP methods from Chapter 4.

For the CSP representation, it is also useful to describe the actions in terms of features – to have a factored representation of actions as well as a factored representation of states. The features representing actions are called **action features** and the features representing states are called **state features**.

Example 8.11 Another way to model the actions of Example 8.1 (page 350) is that, at each step, Rob gets to choose

- whether it will pick up coffee. Let *PUC* be a Boolean variable that is true when Rob picks up coffee.

- whether it will deliver coffee. Let *DelC* be a Boolean variable that is true when Rob delivers coffee.

- whether it will pick up mail. Let *PUM* be a Boolean variable that is true when Rob picks up mail.

- whether it will deliver mail. Let *DelM* be a Boolean variable that is true when Rob delivers mail.

- whether it moves. Let *Move* be a variable with domain $\{mc, mcc, nm\}$ that specifies whether Rob moves clockwise, moves counterclockwise, or does not move (*nm* means "not move").

To construct a CSP from a planning problem, first choose a fixed **horizon**, which is the number of time steps over which to plan. Suppose this number is k. The CSP has the following variables:

- a variable for each state feature and each time from 0 to k. If there are n such features, there are $n(k + 1)$ such variables.

- a variable for each action feature for each time in the range 0 to $k - 1$. These are called action variables. The action at time t represents the action that takes the agent from the state at time t to the state at time $t + 1$.

There are a number of types of constraints:

- **State constraints** are constraints among variables at the same time step. These can include physical constraints on the state or can ensure that states that violate maintenance goals (page 355) are forbidden.

- **Precondition constraints** between state variables at time t and action variables at time t specify constraints on what actions are available from a state.

- **Effect constraints** among state variables at time t, action variables at time t, and state variables at time $t + 1$ constrain the values of the state variables at time $t + 1$ in terms of the actions and the previous state.

- **Action constraints** specify which actions cannot co-occur. These are sometimes called mutual exclusion or **mutex constraints**.

- **Initial-state constraints** are constraints on the initial state (at time 0). These constrain the initial state to be the current state of the agent. If there is a unique initial state, it can be represented as a set of domain constraints on the state variables at time 0.

- **Goal constraints** constrain the final state to be a state that satisfies the achievement goal. These are domain constraints if the goal is for certain variables to have particular values at the final step, but they can also be more general constraints – for example, if two variables must have the same value.

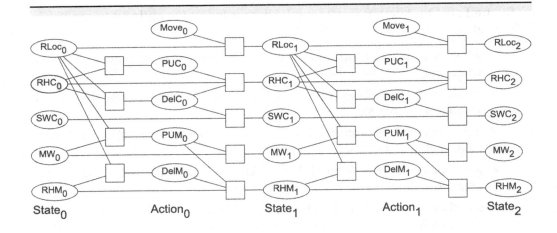

$RLoc_i$ – Rob's location $Move_i$ – Rob's move action

RHC_i – Rob has coffee PUC_i – Rob picks up coffee

SWC_i – Sam wants coffee $DelC$ – Rob delivers coffee

MW_i – Mail is waiting PUM_i – Rob picks up mail

RHM_i – Rob has mail $DelM_i$ – Rob delivers mail

Figure 8.4: The delivery robot CSP planner for a planning horizon of 2

Example 8.12 Figure 8.4 shows a CSP representation of the delivery robot example, with a planning horizon of 2. There are three copies of the state variables: one at time 0, the initial state; one at time 1; and one at time 2, the final state. There are action variables for times 0 and 1.

There are no domain constraints in this example. You could make a constraint that says Rob cannot carry both the mail and coffee, or that Rob cannot carry mail when there is mail waiting, if these were true in the domain. They are not included here.

The constraints to the left of the actions are the precondition constraints, which specify what values the action variables can take (i.e., what actions are available for each of the action variables). The $Move_i$ variables have no preconditions: all moves are available in all states. The PUM_i variable, which specifies whether Rob can pick up mail, depends on Rob's location at time i (i.e., the value of $RLoc_i$) and whether there is mail waiting at time i (MW_i). The negation of an action (e.g., $PUM_i = false$, written as $\overline{pum_i}$) is always available, assuming that the agent can choose not to perform an action. The action $PUM_i = true$, written as pum_i, is only available when the location is mr and $MW_i = true$. When the precondition of an action is a conjunction, it can be written as a set of constraints, because the constraints in a CSP are implicitly conjoined. If the precondition is a more complex proposition, it can be represented as a constraint involving more than two variables.

The constraints to the left of the state variables at times 1 and later indicate the values of the state variables as a function of the previous state and the action. For example, the following constraint is among RHC_i, DC_i, PUC_i, and whether the robot has coffee in the subsequent state, RHC_{i+1}:

RHC_i	DC_i	PUC_i	RHC_{i+1}
true	true	true	true
true	true	false	false
true	false	true	true
true	false	false	true
false	true	true	true
false	true	false	false
false	false	true	true
false	false	false	false

This table represents the same constraint as the rules of Example 8.4 (page 353).

Example 8.13 Consider finding a plan to get Sam coffee, with a planning horizon of 2.

Initially, Sam wants coffee but the robot does not have coffee. This can be represented as two domain constraints: one on SWC_0 and one on RHC_0. The goal is that Sam no longer wants coffee. This can be represented as the domain constraint $SWC_2 = false$.

Just running arc consistency on this network results in $RLoc_0 = cs$ (the robot has to start in the coffee shop), $PUC_0 = true$ (the robot has to pick up coffee initially), $Move_0 = mc$ (the robot has to move to the office), and $DC_1 = true$ (the robot has to deliver coffee at time 1).

The CSP representation assumes a fixed planning horizon (i.e., a fixed number of steps). To find a plan over any number of steps, the algorithm can be run for a horizon of $k = 0, 1, 2$, until a solution is found. For the stochastic local searching algorithm, it is possible to search multiple horizons at once, searching for all horizons, k from 0 to n, and allowing n to increase slowly. When solving the CSP using arc consistency and search, it may be possible to determine that trying a longer plan will not help. That is, by analyzing why no solution exists for a horizon of n steps, it may be possible to show that there can be no plan for any length greater than n. This will enable the planner to halt when there is no plan. See Exercise 8.12 (page 369).

8.5 Partial-Order Planning

The forward and regression planners enforce a total ordering on actions at all stages of the planning process. The CSP planner commits to the particular time that the action will be carried out. This means that those planners have to commit to an ordering of actions that cannot occur concurrently when adding them to a partial plan, even if there is no particular reason to put one action before another.

The idea of a **partial-order planner** is to have a partial ordering between actions and only commit to an ordering between actions when forced. This is sometimes also called a **non-linear planner**, which is a misnomer because such planners often produce a linear plan.

A partial ordering is a less-than relation that is transitive and asymmetric. A **partial-order plan** is a set of actions together with a partial ordering, representing a "before" relation on actions, such that any total ordering of the actions, consistent with the partial ordering, will solve the goal from the initial state. Write $act_0 < act_1$ if action act_0 is before action act_1 in the partial order. This means that action act_0 must occur before action act_1.

For uniformity, treat *start* as an action that achieves the relations that are true in the initial state, and treat *finish* as an action whose precondition is the goal to be solved. The pseudoaction *start* is before every other action, and *finish* is after every other action. The use of these as actions means that the algorithm does not require special cases for the initial situation and for the goals. When the preconditions of *finish* hold, the goal is solved.

An action, other than *start* or *finish*, will be in a partial-order plan to achieve a precondition of an action in the plan. Each precondition of an action in the plan is either true in the initial state, and so achieved by *start*, or there will be an action in the plan that achieves it.

We must ensure that the actions achieve the conditions they were assigned to achieve. Each precondition P of an action act_1 in a plan will have an action act_0 associated with it such that act_0 achieves precondition P for act_1. The triple $\langle act_0, P, act_1 \rangle$ is a **causal link**. The partial order specifies that action act_0 occurs before action act_1, which is written as $act_0 < act_1$. Any other action A that makes P false must either be before act_0 or after act_1.

Informally, a partial-order planner works as follows: Begin with the actions *start* and *finish* and the partial order *start* < *finish*. The planner maintains an agenda that is a set of $\langle P, A \rangle$ pairs, where A is an action in the plan and P is an atom that is a precondition of A that must be achieved. Initially the agenda contains pairs $\langle G, finish \rangle$, where G is an atom that must be true in the goal state.

At each stage in the planning process, a pair $\langle G, act_1 \rangle$ is selected from the agenda, where P is a precondition for action act_1. Then an action, act_0, is chosen to achieve P. That action is either already in the plan – it could be the *start* action, for example – or it is a new action that is added to the plan. Action act_0 must happen before act_1 in the partial order. It adds a causal link that records that act_0 achieves P for action act_1. Any action in the plan that deletes P must happen either before act_0 or after act_1. If act_0 is a new action, its preconditions are added to the agenda, and the process continues until the agenda is empty.

This is a non-deterministic procedure. The "choose" and the "either …or …" form choices that must be searched over. There are two choices that require search:

- which action is selected to achieve G and

- whether an action that deletes G happens before act_0 or after act_1.

The algorithm *PartialOrderPlanner* is given in Figure 8.5.

1: **non-deterministic procedure** *PartialOrderPlanner*(Gs)
2:     **Inputs**
3:         *Gs*: set of atomic propositions to achieve
4:     **Output**
5:         linear plan to achieve *Gs*
6:     **Local**
7:         *Agenda*: set of $\langle P, A \rangle$ pairs where P is atom and A an action
8:         *Actions*: set of actions in the current plan
9:         *Constraints*: set of temporal constraints on actions
10:         *CausalLinks*: set of $\langle act_0, P, act_1 \rangle$ triples
11:     $Agenda := \{ \langle G, \mathit{finish} \rangle : G \in Gs \}$
12:     $Actions := \{ start, \mathit{finish} \}$
13:     $Constraints := \{ start < \mathit{finish} \}$
14:     $CausalLinks := \{ \}$
15:     **repeat**
16:         select and remove $\langle G, act_1 \rangle$ from *Agenda*
17:         **either**
18:             choose $act_0 \in Actions$ such that act_0 achieves G
19:         **Or**
20:             choose $act_0 \notin Actions$ such that act_0 achieves G
21:             $Actions := Actions \cup \{ act_0 \}$
22:             $Constraints := add\_const(start < act_0, Constraints)$
23:             **for each** $CL \in CausalLinks$ **do**
24:                 $Constraints := protect(CL, act_0, Constraints)$
25:             $Agenda := Agenda \cup \{ \langle P, act_0 \rangle : P \text{ is a precondition of } act_0 \}$
26:         $Constraints := add\_const(act_0 < act_1, Constraints)$
27:         $CausalLinks := CausalLinks \cup \{ \langle act_o, G, act_1 \rangle \}$
28:         **for each** $A \in Actions$ **do**
29:             $Constraints := protect(\langle act_o, G, act_1 \rangle, A, Constraints)$
30:     **until** $Agenda = \{ \}$
31:     **return** total ordering of *Actions* consistent with *Constraints*

Figure 8.5: Partial-order planner

The function $add\_const(act_0 < act_1, Constraints)$ returns the constraints formed by adding the constraint $act_0 < act_1$ to *Constraints*, and it fails if $act_0 < act_1$ is incompatible with *Constraints*. There are many ways this function can be implemented. See Exercise 8.13.

The function $protect(\langle act_o, G, act_1 \rangle, A)$ checks whether $A \neq act_0$ and $A \neq act_1$ and A deletes G. If so, either $A < act_0$ is added to the set of constraints or $act_1 < A$ is added to the set of constraints. This is a non-deterministic choice that is searched over.

> **Example 8.14** Consider the goal $\overline{swc} \wedge \overline{mw}$, where the initial state contains $RLoc = lab, swc, \overline{rhc}, mw, \overline{rhm}$.
>
> Initially the agenda is
>
> $$\langle \overline{swc}, finish \rangle , \langle \overline{mw}, finish \rangle .$$
>
> Suppose $\langle \overline{swc}, finish \rangle$ is selected and removed from the agenda. One action exists that can achieve $\overline{swc}$, namely deliver coffee, dc, with preconditions *off* and *rhc*. At the end of the **repeat** loop, *Agenda* contains
>
> $$\langle off, dc \rangle , \langle rhc, dc \rangle , \langle \overline{mw}, finish \rangle .$$
>
> *Constraints* is $\{start < finish, start < dc, dc < finish\}$. There is one causal link, $\langle dc, \overline{swc}, finish \rangle$. This causal link means that no action that undoes $\overline{swc}$ is allowed to happen after dc and before *finish*.
>
> Suppose $\langle \overline{mw}, finish \rangle$ is selected from the agenda. One action exists that can achieve this, pum, with preconditions mw and $RLoc = mr$. The causal link $\langle pum, \overline{mw}, finish \rangle$ is added to the set of causal links; $\langle mw, pum \rangle$ and $\langle mr, pum \rangle$ are added to the agenda.
>
> Suppose $\langle mw, pum \rangle$ is selected from the agenda. The action *start* achieves mw, because mw is true initially. The causal link $\langle start, mw, pum \rangle$ is added to the set of causal links. Nothing is added to the agenda.
>
> At this stage, there is no ordering imposed between dc and pum.
>
> Suppose $\langle off, dc \rangle$ is removed from the agenda. There are two actions that can achieve *off*: mc_cs with preconditions cs, and mcc_lab with preconditions *lab*. The algorithm searches over these choices. Suppose it chooses mc_cs. Then the causal link $\langle mc\_cs, off, dc \rangle$ is added.
>
> The first violation of a causal link occurs when a move action is used to achieve $\langle mr, pum \rangle$. This action violates the causal link $\langle mc\_cs, off, dc \rangle$, and so must happen after dc (the robot goes to the mail room after delivering coffee) or before mc_cs.

The preceding algorithm has glossed over one important detail. It is sometimes necessary to perform some action more than once in a plan. The preceding algorithm will not work in this case, because it will try to find a partial ordering with both instances of the action occurring at the same time. To fix this problem, the ordering should be between action instances, and not actions themselves. To implement this, assign an index to each instance of an action in the plan, and the ordering is on the action instance indexes and not the actions themselves. This is left as an exercise.

8.6   Review

The following are the main points you should have learned from this chapter:

- Planning is the process of choosing a sequence of actions to achieve a goal.
- An action is a function from a state to a state. A number of representations exploit structure in representation of states. In particular, the feature-based

representation of actions represents what must be true in the previous state for a feature to have a value in the next state. The STRIPS representation is an action-based representation that specifies the effects of actions.

- Different planning algorithms can be used to convert a planning problem into a search problem.

8.7 References and Further Reading

The STRIPS representation was developed by Fikes and Nilsson [1971].

There is much ongoing research into how to plan sequences of actions. Yang [1997] presents a textbook overview of planning. For a collection of classic papers, see Allen, Hendler, and Tate [1990].

Forward planning has been used successfully for planning in the blocks world, where some good heuristics have been identified by Bacchus and Kabanza [1996]. (See Exercise 8.6 (page 369).)

Regression planning was pioneered by Waldinger [1977]. The use of weakest preconditions is based on the work of Dijkstra [1976], where it was used to define the semantics of imperative programming languages. This should not be too surprising because the commands of an imperative language are actions that change the state of the computer.

Planning as CSP is based on Graphplan [Blum and Furst, 1997] and Satplan [Kautz and Selman, 1996]. The treatment of planning as a CSP is also investigated by Lopez and Bacchus [2003] and van Beek and Chen [1999]. Bryce and Kambhampati [2007] give a recent survey.

Partial-order planning was introduced in Sacerdoti's [1975] NOAH and followed up in Tate's [1977] NONLIN system, Chapman's [1987] TWEAK algorithm, and McAllester and Rosenblitt's [1991] systematic non-linear planning (SNLP) algorithm. See Weld [1994] for an overview of partial-order planning and see Kambhampati, Knoblock, and Yang [1995] for a comparison of the algorithms. The version presented here is basically SNLP (but see Exercise 8.15).

See Wilkins [1988] for a discussion on practical issues in planning. See Weld [1999], McDermott and Hendler [1995], and Nau [2007] and associated papers for a recent overview.

8.8 Exercises

Exercise 8.1 Consider the planning domain in Figure 8.1 (page 350).

(a) Give the feature-based representation of the *MW* and *RHM* features.

(b) Give the STRIPS representations for the pick up mail and deliver mail actions.

Exercise 8.2 Suppose the robot cannot carry both coffee and mail at the same time. Give two different ways that the CSP that represents the planning problem can be changed to reflect this constraint. Test it by giving a problem where the answer is different when the robot has this limitation than when it does not.

Exercise 8.3 Write a complete description of the limited robot delivery world, and then draw a state-space representation that includes at least two instances of each of the blocks-world actions discussed in this chapter. Notice that the number of different arcs depends on the number of instances of actions.

Exercise 8.4 Change the representation of the delivery robot world [Example 8.1 (page 350)] so that

(a) the agent cannot carry both *mail* and *coffee* at the same time;

(b) the agent can carry a box in which it can place objects (so it can carry the box and the box can hold the mail and coffee).

Test it on an example that gives a different solution than the original representation.

Exercise 8.5 Suppose we must solve planning problems for cleaning a house. Various rooms can be dusted (making the room dust-free) or swept (making the room have a clean floor), but the robot can only sweep or dust a room if it is in that room. Sweeping causes a room to become dusty (i.e., not dust-free). The robot can only dust a room if the dustcloth is clean; but dusting rooms that are extra-dusty, like the garage, cause the dustcloth to become dirty. The robot can move directly from any room to any other room.

Assume there only two rooms, the garage – which, if it is dusty, it is extra-dusty – and the living room – which is not extra-dusty. Assume the following features:

- *Lr_dusty* is true when the living room is dusty.
- *Gar_dusty* is true when the garage is dusty.
- *Lr_dirty_floor* is true when the living room floor is dirty.
- *Gar_dirty_floor* is true when the garage floor is dirty.
- *Dustcloth_clean* is true when the dust cloth is clean.
- *Rob_loc* is the location of the robot.

Suppose the robot can do one of the following actions at any time:

- *move*: move to the other room,
- *dust_lr*: dust the living room (if the robot is in the living room and the living room is dusty),
- *dust_gar*: dust the garage (if the robot is in the garage and the garage is dusty),
- *sweep_lr*: sweep the living room floor (if the robot is in the living room), or
- *sweep_gar*: sweep the garage floor (if the robot is in the garage).

(a) Give the STRIPS representation for *dust_gar*.

(b) Give the feature-based representation for *lr_dusty*

(c) Suppose that, instead of the two actions *sweep_lr* and *sweep_gar*, there was just the action *sweep*, which means to sweep whatever room the robot is in. Explain how the previous answers can be modified to handle the new representation or why they cannot use the new representation.

Exercise 8.6 Suggest a good heuristic for a forward planner to use in the robot delivery domain. Implement it. How well does it work?

Exercise 8.7 Suppose you have a STRIPS representation for actions a_1 and a_2, and you want to define the STRIPS representation for the composite action $a_1; a_2$, which means that you do a_1 then do a_2.

(a) What is the effects list for this composite action?

(b) What are the preconditions for this composite action? You can assume that the preconditions are specified as a list of *Variable* = *value* pairs (rather than as arbitrary logical formulas).

(c) Using the delivery robot domain of Example 8.1 (page 350), give the STRIPS representation for the composite action *puc; mc*.

(d) Give the STRIPS representation for the composite action *puc; mc; dc* made up of three primitive actions.

(e) Give the STRIPS representation for the composite action *mcc; puc; mc; dc* made up of four primitive actions.

Exercise 8.8 In a forward planner, you can represent a state in terms of the sequence of actions that lead to that state.

(a) Explain how to check if the precondition of an action is satisfied, given such a representation.

(b) Explain how to do cycle detection in such a representation. You can assume that all of the states are legal. (Some other program has ensured that the preconditions hold.)

[Hint: Consider the composite action (Exercise 8.7) consisting of the first k or the last k actions at any stage.]

Exercise 8.9 Explain how the regression planner can be extended to include maintenance goals, for either the feature-based representation of actions or the STRIPS representation. [Hint: Consider what happens when a maintenance goal mentions a feature that does not appear in a node.]

Exercise 8.10 For the delivery robot domain, give a heuristic function for the regression planner that is non-zero and an underestimate of the actual path cost. Is it admissible?

Exercise 8.11 Explain how multiple-path pruning can be incorporated into a regression planner. When can a node be pruned?

Exercise 8.12 Give a condition for the CSP planner that, when arc consistency with search fails at some horizon, implies there can be no solutions for any longer horizon. [Hint: Think about a very long horizon where the forward search and the backward search do not influence each other.] Implement it.

Exercise 8.13 To implement the function $add\_constraint(A_0 < A_1, Constraints)$ used in the partial-order planner, you have to choose a representation for a partial ordering. Implement the following as different representations for a partial ordering:

(a) Represent a partial ordering as a set of less-than relations that entail the ordering – for example, as the list $[1 < 2, 2 < 4, 1 < 3, 3 < 4, 4 < 5]$.

(b) Represent a partial ordering as the set of all the less-than relations entailed by the ordering – for example, as the list $[1 < 2, 2 < 4, 1 < 4, 1 < 3, 3 < 4, 1 < 5, 2 < 5, 3 < 5, 4 < 5]$.

(c) Represent a partial ordering as a set of pairs $\langle E, L \rangle$, where E is an element in the partial ordering and L is the list of all elements that are after E in the partial ordering. For every E, there exists a unique term of the form $\langle E, L \rangle$. An example of such a representation is $[\langle 1, [2, 3, 4, 5] \rangle, \langle 2, [4, 5] \rangle, \langle 3, [4, 5] \rangle, \langle 4, [5] \rangle, \langle 5, [] \rangle]$.

For each of these representations, how big can the partial ordering be? How easy is it to check for consistency of a new ordering? How easy is it to add a new less-than ordering constraint? Which do you think would be the most efficient representation? Can you think of a better representation?

Exercise 8.14 The selection algorithm used in the partial-order planner is not very sophisticated. It may be sensible to order the selected subgoals. For example, in the robot world, the robot should try to achieve a *carrying* subgoal before an *at* subgoal because it may be sensible for the robot to try to carry an object as soon as it knows that it should carry it. However, the robot does not necessarily want to move to a particular place unless it is carrying everything it is required to carry. Implement a selection algorithm that incorporates such a heuristic. Does this selection heuristic actually work better than selecting, say, the last added subgoal? Can you think of a general selection algorithm that does not require each pair of subgoals to be ordered by the knowledge engineer?

Exercise 8.15 The SNLP algorithm is the same as the partial-order planner presented here but, in the *protect* procedure, the condition is

$A \neq A_0$ and $A \neq A_1$ and (A deletes G or A achieves G).

This enforces *systematicity*, which means that for every linear plan there is a unique partial-ordered plan. Explain why systematicity may or may not be a good thing (e.g., discuss how it changes the branching factor or reduces the search space). Test the different algorithms on different examples.

Chapter 9

Planning Under Uncertainty

> *A plan is like the scaffolding around a building. When you're putting up the exterior shell, the scaffolding is vital. But once the shell is in place and you start to work on the interior, the scaffolding disappears. That's how I think of planning. It has to be sufficiently thoughtful and solid to get the work up and standing straight, but it cannot take over as you toil away on the interior guts of a piece. Transforming your ideas rarely goes according to plan.*

> – Twyla Tharp [2003]

In the quote above, Tharp is referring to dance, but the same idea holds for any agent when there is uncertainty. An agent cannot just plan a sequence of steps; the result of planning needs to be more sophisticated. Planning must take into account the fact that the agent does not know what will actually happen when it acts. The agent should plan to react to its environment. What it does is determined by the plan and the actual environment encountered.

Consider what an agent should do when it does not know the exact effects of its actions. Determining what to do is difficult because what an agent should do at any time depends on what it will do in the future. However, what it will do in the future depends on what it does now and what it will observe in the future.

With uncertainty, an agent typically cannot guarantee to satisfy its goals, and even trying to maximize the probability of achieving a goal may not be sensible. For example, an agent whose goal is not to be injured in a car accident would not get in a car or travel down a sidewalk or even go to the ground floor of a building, which most people would agree is not very intelligent. An agent that does not guarantee to satisfy a goal can fail in many ways, some of which may be much worse than others.

This chapter is about how to take these issues into account simultaneously. An agent's decision on what to do depends on three things:

- *the agent's ability*. The agent has to select from the options available to it.

- *what the agent believes.* You may be tempted to say "what is true in the world," but when an agent does not know what is true in the world, it can act based only on its beliefs. Sensing the world updates an agent's beliefs by conditioning on what is sensed.

- *the agent's preferences.* When an agent must reason under uncertainty, it has to consider not only what will most likely happen but also what may happen. Some possible outcomes may have much worse consequences than others. The notion of a "goal" here is richer than the goals considered in Chapter 8 because the designer of an agent must specify trade-offs between different outcomes. For example, if some action results in a good outcome most of the time, but sometimes results in a disastrous outcome, it must be compared with performing an alternative action that results in the good outcome less

---

Whose Values?

Any computer program or person who acts or gives advice is using some value system of what is important and what is not.

> *Alice ... went on "Would you please tell me, please, which way I ought to go from here?"*
> *"That depends a good deal on where you want to get to," said the Cat.*
> *"I don't much care where –" said Alice.*
> *"Then it doesn't matter which way you go," said the Cat.*

> Lewis Carroll (1832–1898)
> *Alice's Adventures in Wonderland*, 1865

We all, of course, want computers to work on *our* value system, but they cannot act according to everyone's value system! When you build programs to work in a laboratory, this is not usually a problem. The program acts according to the goals and values of the program's designer, who is also the program's user. When there are multiple users of a system, you must be aware of whose value system is incorporated into a program. If a company sells a medical diagnostic program to a doctor, does the advice the program gives reflect the values of society, the company, the doctor, or the patient (all of whom may have very different value systems)? Does it determine the doctor's or the patient's values?

If you want to build a system that gives advice to someone, you should find out what is true as well as what their values are. For example, in a medical diagnostic system, the appropriate procedure depends not only on patients' symptoms but also on their priorities. Are they prepared to put up with some pain in order to be more aware of their surroundings? Are they willing to put up with a lot of discomfort to live a bit longer? What risks are they prepared to take? Always be suspicious of a program or person that tells you what to do if it does not ask you what you want to do! As builders of programs that do things or give advice, you should be aware of whose value systems are incorporated into the actions or advice.

often and the disastrous outcome less often and some mediocre outcome most of the time. Decision theory specifies how to trade off the desirability of outcomes with the probabilities of these outcomes.

9.1 Preferences and Utility

What an agent decides to do should depend on its preferences. In this section, we specify some intuitive properties of preferences that we want and give a consequence of these properties. The properties that we give are **axioms of rationality** from which we prove a theorem about how to measure these preferences. You should consider whether each axiom is reasonable for a **rational agent** to follow; if you accept them all as reasonable, you should accept their consequence. If you do not accept the consequence, you should question which of the axioms you are willing to give up.

An agent chooses actions based on their **outcomes**. Outcomes are whatever the agent has preferences over. If the agent does not have preferences over anything, it does not matter what the agent does. Initially, we consider outcomes without considering the associated actions. Assume there are only a finite number of outcomes.

We define a preference relation over outcomes. Suppose o_1 and o_2 are outcomes. We say that o_1 is **weakly preferred** to outcome o_2, written $o_1 \succeq o_2$, if outcome o_1 is at least as desirable as outcome o_2. The axioms that follow are arguably reasonable properties of such a preference relation.

Define $o_1 \sim o_2$ to mean $o_1 \succeq o_2$ and $o_2 \succeq o_1$. That is, $o_1 \sim o_2$ means outcomes o_1 and o_2 are equally preferred. In this case, we say that the agent is **indifferent** between o_1 and o_2.

Define $o_1 \succ o_2$ to mean $o_1 \succeq o_2$ and $o_2 \not\succeq o_1$. That is, the agent prefers outcome o_1 to outcome o_2 and is not indifferent between them. In this case, we say that o_1 is **strictly preferred** to outcome o_2.

Typically, an agent does not know the outcome of its actions. A **lottery** is defined to be a finite distribution over outcomes, written as

$$[p_1 : o_1, p_2 : o_2, \ldots, p_k : o_k],$$

where o_i are outcomes and p_i are non-negative real numbers such that

$$\sum_i p_i = 1.$$

The lottery specifies that outcome o_i occurs with probability p_i. In all that follows, assume that outcomes include lotteries. This includes the case of having lotteries over lotteries.

Axiom 9.1. *[Completeness] An agent has preferences between all pairs of outcomes:*

$$\forall o_1 \forall o_2 \; o_1 \succeq o_2 \text{ or } o_2 \succeq o_1.$$

The rationale for this axiom is that an agent must act; if the actions available to it have outcomes o_1 and o_2 then, by acting, it is explicitly or implicitly preferring one outcome over the other.

Axiom 9.2. *[Transitivity] Preferences must be transitive:*

if $o_1 \succeq o_2$ and $o_2 \succeq o_3$ then $o_1 \succeq o_3$.

To see why this is reasonable, suppose it is false, in which case $o_1 \succeq o_2$ and $o_2 \succeq o_3$ and $o_3 \succ o_1$. Because o_3 is strictly preferred to o_1, the agent should be prepared to pay some amount to get from o_1 to o_3. Suppose the agent has outcome o_3; then o_2 is at least as good so the agent would just as soon have o_2. o_1 is at least as good as o_2 so the agent would just as soon have o_1 as o_2. Once the agent has o_1 it is again prepared to pay to get to o_3. It has gone through a cycle of preferences and paid money to end up where it is. This cycle that involves paying money to go through it is known as a **money pump** because, by going through the loop enough times, the amount of money that agent must pay can exceed any finite amount. It seems reasonable to claim that being prepared to pay money to cycle through a set of outcomes is irrational; hence, a rational agent should have transitive preferences.

Also assume that monotonicity holds for mixes of $\succ$ and $\succeq$, so that if one or both of the preferences in the premise of the transitivity axiom is strict, then the conclusion is strict. That is, if $o_1 \succ o_2$ and $o_2 \succeq o_3$ then $o_1 \succ o_3$. Also, if $o_1 \succeq o_2$ and $o_2 \succ o_3$ then $o_1 \succ o_3$.

Axiom 9.3. *[Monotonicity] An agent prefers a larger chance of getting a better outcome than a smaller chance of getting the better outcome. That is, if $o_1 \succ o_2$ and $p > q$ then*

$$[p : o_1, (1 - p) : o_2] \succ [q : o_1, (1 - q) : o_2].$$

Note that, in this axiom, $\succ$ between outcomes represents the agent's preference, whereas $>$ between p and q represents the familiar comparison between numbers.

Axiom 9.4. *[Decomposability] ("no fun in gambling"). An agent is indifferent between lotteries that have the same probabilities over the same outcomes, even if one or both is a lottery over lotteries. For example:*

$$[p : o_1, (1 - p) : [q : o_2, (1 - q) : o_3]]$$
$$\sim [p : o_1, (1 - p)q : o_2, (1 - p)(1 - q) : o_3].$$

Also $o_1 \sim [1 : o_1, 0 : o_2]$ for any outcomes o_1 and o_2.

This axiom specifies that it is only the outcomes and their probabilities that define a lottery. If an agent had a preference for gambling, that would be part of the outcome space.

These axioms can be used to characterize much of an agent's preferences between outcomes and lotteries. Suppose that $o_1 \succ o_2$ and $o_2 \succ o_3$. Consider whether the agent would prefer

- o_2 or
- the lottery $[p : o_1, (1 - p) : o_3]$

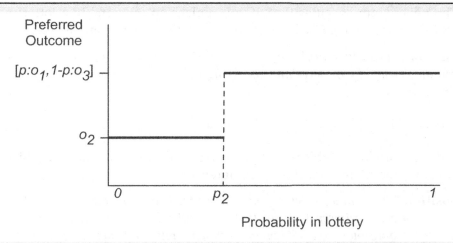

Figure 9.1: The preference between o_2 and the lottery, as a function of p.

for different values of $p \in [0,1]$. When $p = 1$, the agent prefers the lottery (because the lottery is equivalent to o_1 and $o_1 \succ o_2$). When $p = 0$, the agent prefers o_2 (because the lottery is equivalent to o_3 and $o_2 \succ o_3$). At some stage, as p is varied, the agent's preferences flip between preferring o_2 and preferring the lottery. Figure 9.1 shows how the preferences must flip as p is varied. On the X-axis is p and the Y-axis shows which of o_2 or the lottery is preferred.

Proposition 9.1. *If an agent's preferences are complete, transitive, and follow the monotonicity and decomposability axioms, and if $o_1 \succ o_2$ and $o_2 \succ o_3$, there exists a number p_2 such that $0 \leq p_2 \leq 1$ and*

- *for all $p < p_2$, the agent prefers o_2 to the lottery (i.e., $o_2 \succ [p : o_1, (1-p) : o_3]$) and*
- *for all $p > p_2$, the agent prefers the lottery (i.e., $[p : o_1, (1-p) : o_3] \succ o_2$).*

Proof. By monotonicity and transitivity, if $o_2 \succeq [p : o_1, (1-p) : o_3]$ for any p then, for all $p' < p$, $o_2 \succ [p' : o_1, (1-p') : o_3]$. Similarly, if $[p : o_1, (1-p) : o_3] \succeq o_2$ for any p then, for all $p' > p$, $[p' : o_1, (1-p') : o_3] \succ o_2$. By completeness, for each value of p, either $o_2 \succ [p : o_1, (1-p) : o_3]$, $o_2 \sim [p : o_1, (1-p) : o_3]$ or $[p : o_1, (1-p) : o_3] \succ o_2$. If there is some p such that $o_2 \sim [p : o_1, (1-p) : o_3]$, then the theorem holds. Otherwise a preference for either o_2 or the lottery with parameter p implies preferences for either all values greater than p or for all values less than p. By repeatedly subdividing the region that we do not know the preferences for, we will approach, in the limit, a value that fills the criteria for p_2. $\square$

The preceding proposition does not specify what the preference of the agent is at the point p_2. The following axiom specifies that the agent is indifferent at this point.

Axiom 9.5. *[Continuity] Suppose $o_1 \succ o_2$ and $o_2 \succ o_3$, then there exists a $p_2 \in [0,1]$ such that*

$$o_2 \sim [p_2 : o_1, (1-p_2) : o_3].$$

The next axiom specifies that, if you replace an outcome in a lottery with another outcome that is not worse, the lottery does not become worse.

Axiom 9.6. *[Substitutability] If $o_1 \succeq o_2$ then the agent weakly prefers lotteries that contain o_1 instead of o_2, everything else being equal. That is, for any number p and outcome o_3:*

$$[p : o_1, (1-p) : o_3] \succeq [p : o_2, (1-p) : o_3].$$

A direct corollary of this is that you can substitutes outcomes for which the agent is indifferent and not change preferences:

Proposition 9.2. *If an agent obeys the substitutability axiom and $o_1 \sim o_2$ then the agent is indifferent between lotteries that only differ by o_1 and o_2. That is, for any number p and outcome o_3 the following indifference relation holds:*

$$[p : o_1, (1-p) : o_3] \sim [p : o_2, (1-p) : o_3].$$

This follows because $o_1 \sim o_2$ is equivalent to $o_1 \succeq o_2$ and $o_2 \succeq o_1$.

An agent is defined to be **rational** if it obeys the completeness, transitivity, monotonicity, decomposability, continuity, and substitutability axioms.

It is up to you to determine if this technical definition of rational matches your intuitive notion of rational. In the rest of this section, we show consequences of this definition.

Although preferences may seem to be very complicated, the following theorem shows that a rational agent's value for an outcome can be measured by a real number and that these numbers can be combined with probabilities so that preferences under uncertainty can be compared using expectation. This is surprising because

- it may seem that preferences are too multifaceted to be modeled by a single number. For example, although one may try to measure preferences in terms of dollars, not everything is for sale or easily converted into dollars and cents.

- you would not expect that values could be combined with probabilities. An agent that is indifferent between $\$(px + (1-p)y)$ and the lottery $[p : \$x, (1-p)\$y]$ for all monetary values x and y and for all $p \in [0, 1]$ is known as an **expected monetary value** (EMV) agent. Most people are not EMV agents, because they have, for example, a strict preference between \$1,000,000 and the lottery $[0.5 : \$0, 0.5 : \$2,000,000]$. (Think about whether you would prefer a million dollars or a coin toss where you would get nothing if the coin lands heads or two million if the coin lands tails.) Money cannot be simply combined with probabilities, so it may be surprising that there is a value that can be.

Proposition 9.3. *If an agent is rational, then for every outcome o_i there is a real number $u(o_i)$, called the **utility** of o_i, such that*

- *$o_i \succ o_j$ if and only if $u(o_i) > u(o_j)$ and*

- *utilities are linear with probabilities:*

$$u([p_1 : o_1, p_2 : o_2, \ldots, p_k : o_k]) = p_1 u(o_1) + p_2 u(o_2) + \cdots + p_k u(o_k).$$

Proof. If the agent has no strict preferences (i.e., the agent is indifferent between all outcomes) then define $u(o) = 0$ for all outcomes o.

Otherwise, choose the best outcome, o_{best}, and the worst outcome, o_{worst}, and define, for any outcome o, the utility of o to be the value p such that

$$o \sim [p : o_{best}, (1-p) : o_{worst}].$$

The first part of the proposition follows from substitutability and monotonicity.

The second part can be proved by replacing each o_i by its equivalent lottery between o_{best} and o_{worst}. This composite lottery can be reduced to a single lottery between o_{best} and o_{worst}, with the utility given in the theorem. The details are left as an exercise. $\square$

In this proof the utilities are all in the range $[0, 1]$, but any linear scaling gives the same result. Sometimes $[0, 100]$ is a good scale to distinguish it from probabilities, and sometimes negative numbers are useful to use when the outcomes have costs. In general, a program should accept any scale that is intuitive to the user.

A linear relationship does not usually exist between money and utility, even when the outcomes have a monetary value. People often are **risk averse** when it comes to money. They would rather have $\$n$ in their hand than some randomized setup where they expect to receive $\$n$ but could possibly receive more or less.

Example 9.1 Figure 9.2 (on the next page) shows a possible money-utility trade-off for a risk-averse agent. Risk aversion corresponds to a concave utility function.

This agent would rather have $300,000 than a 50% chance of getting either nothing or $1,000,000, but would prefer the gamble on the million dollars to $275,000. They would also require more than a 73% chance of winning a million dollars to prefer this gamble to half a million dollars.

Note that, for this utility function, $u(\$999000) \approx 0.9997$. Thus, given this utility function, the person would be willing to pay $1,000 to eliminate a 0.03% chance of losing all of their money. This is why **insurance** companies exist. By paying the insurance company, say $600, the agent can change the lottery that is worth $999,000 to them into one worth $1,000,000 and the insurance companies expect to pay out, on average, about $300, and so expect to make $300. The insurance company can get its expected value by insuring enough houses. It is good for both parties.

As presented here, rationality does not impose any conditions on what the utility function looks like.

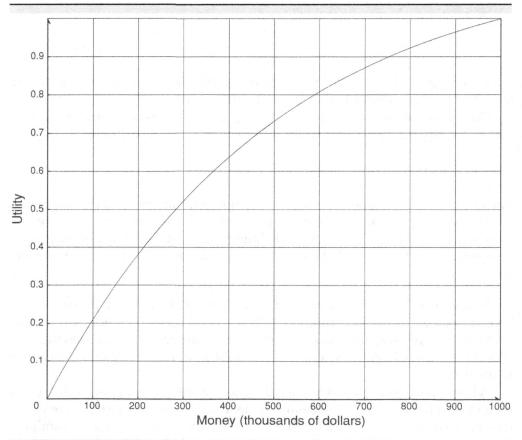

Figure 9.2: Possible money-utility trade-off for a risk-averse agent

Example 9.2 Figure 9.3 shows a possible money-utility trade-off for someone who really wants a toy worth $30, but who would also like one worth $20. Apart from these, money does not matter much to this agent. This agent is prepared to take risks to get what it wants. For example, if it had $29, it would be very happy to bet $19 of its own against a single dollar of another agent on a fair bet, such as a coin toss. It does not want more than $60, because this will leave it open to extortion.

9.1.1 Factored Utility

Utility, as defined, is a function of outcomes or states. Often too many states exist to represent this function directly in terms of states, and it is easier to specify it in terms of features.

Suppose each outcome can be described in terms of features $X_1, \ldots, X_n$. An **additive utility** is one that can be decomposed into set of factors:

$$u(X_1, \ldots, X_n) = f_1(X_1) + \cdots + f_n(X_n).$$

Such a decomposition is making the assumption of **additive independence**.

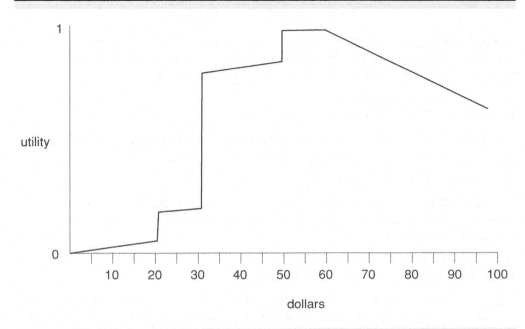

Figure 9.3: Possible money-utility trade-off from Example 9.2

When this can be done, it greatly simplifies **preference elicitation** – the problem of acquiring preferences from the user. Note that this decomposition is not unique, because adding a constant to one of the factors and subtracting it from another factor gives the same utility. To put this decomposition into canonical form, we can have a local utility function $u_i(X_i)$ that has a value of 0 for the value of X_i in the worst outcome, and 1 for the value of X_i in the best outcome, and a series of weights, w_i, that are non-negative numbers that sum to 1 such that

$$u(X_1, \ldots, X_n) = w_1 \times u_1(X_1) + \cdots + w_n \times u_n(X_n).$$

To elicit such a utility function requires eliciting each local utility function and assessing the weights. Each feature, if it is relevant, must have a best value for this feature and a worst value for this feature. Assessing the local functions and weights can be done as follows. We consider just X_1; the other features then can be treated analogously. For feature X_1, values x_1 and x'_1 for X_1, and values $x_2, \ldots, x_n$ for $X_2, \ldots, X_n$:

$$u(x_1, x_2 \ldots, x_n) - u(x'_1, x_2 \ldots, x_n) = w_1 \times (u_1(x_1) - u_1(x'_1)). \tag{9.1}$$

The weight w_1 can be derived when x_1 is the best outcome and x'_1 is the worst outcome (because then $u_1(x_1) - u_1(x'_1) = 1$). The values of u_1 for the other values in the domain of X_1 can be computed using Equation (9.1) , making x'_1 the worst outcome (as then $u_1(x'_1) = 0$).

| Challenges to Expected Utility |

There have been a number of challenges to the theory of expected utility. The **Allais Paradox**, presented in 1953 [Allais and Hagen, 1979], is as follows. Which would you prefer out of the following two alternatives?

A: $1m – one million dollars
B: lottery $[0.10 : \$2.5m, 0.89 : \$1m, 0.01 : \$0]$

Similarly, what would you choose between the following two alternatives?

C: lottery $[0.11 : \$1m, 0.89 : \$0]$
D: lottery $[0.10 : \$2.5m, 0.9 : \$0]$

It turns out that many people prefer A to B, and prefer D to C. This choice is inconsistent with the axioms of rationality. To see why, both choices can be put in the same form:

A,C: lottery $[0.11 : \$1m, 0.89 : X]$
B,D: lottery $[0.10 : \$2.5m, 0.01 : \$0, 0.89 : X]$

In A and B, X is a million dollars. In C and D, X is zero dollars. Concentrating just on the parts of the alternatives that are different seems like an appropriate strategy, but people seem to have a preference for certainty.

Tversky and Kahneman [1974], in a series of human experiments, showed how people systematically deviate from utility theory. One such deviation is the **framing effect** of a problem's presentation. Consider the following:

- A disease is expected to kill 600 people. Two alternative programs have been proposed:

  Program A: 200 people will be saved
  Program B: with probability 1/3, 600 people will be saved, and with probability 2/3, no one will be saved

  Which program would you favor?

- A disease is expected to kill 600 people. Two alternative programs have been proposed:

  Program C: 400 people will die
  Program D: with probability 1/3 no one will die, and with probability 2/3 600 will die

  Which program would you favor?

Tversky and Kahneman showed that 72% of people in their experiments chose A over B, and 22% chose C over D. However, these are exactly the same choice, just described in a different way.

An alternative to expected utility is **prospect theory**, developed by Kahneman and Tversky, that takes into account an agent's current wealth at each time. That is, a decision is based on the agent's gains and losses, rather than the outcome. However, just because this better matches a human's choices does not mean it is the best for an artificial agent, but an artificial agent that must interact with humans should take into account how humans reason.

Assuming additive independence entails making a strong independence assumption. In particular, in Equation (9.1) (page 379), the difference in utilities must be the same for all values $x_2, \ldots, x_n$ for $X_2, \ldots, X_n$.

Additive independence is often not a good assumption. Two values of two binary features are **complements** if having both is better than the sum of the two. Suppose the features are X and Y, with domains $\{x_0, x_1\}$ and $\{y_0, y_1\}$. Values x_1 and y_1 are complements if getting one when the agent has the other is more valuable than when the agent does not have the other:

$$u(x_1, y_0) - u(x_0, y_0) < u(x_1, y_1) - u(x_0, y_1).$$

Note that this implies y_1 and x_1 are also complements.

Two values for binary features are **substitutes** if having both is not worth as much as the sum of having each one. If values x_1 and y_1 are substitutes, it means that getting one when the agent has the other is less valuable than getting one when the agent does not have the other:

$$u(x_1, y_0) - u(x_0, y_0) > u(x_1, y_1) - u(x_0, y_1).$$

This implies y_1 and x_1 are also substitutes.

Example 9.3 For a purchasing agent in the travel domain, having a plane booking for a particular day and a hotel booking for the same day are complements: one without the other does not give a good outcome.

Two different outings on the same day would be substitutes, assuming the person taking the holiday would enjoy one outing, but not two, on the same day. However, if the two outings are in close proximity to each other and require a long traveling time, they may be complements (the traveling time may be worth it if the person gets two outings).

Additive utility assumes there are no substitutes or complements. When there is interaction, we require a more sophisticated model, such as a **generalized additive independence** model, which represents utility as a sum of factors. This is similar to the optimization models of Section 4.10 (page 144); however, we want to use these models to compute expected utility. Elicitation of the generalized additive independence model is much more involved than eliciting an additive model, because a feature can appear in many factors.

9.2 One-Off Decisions

Basic decision theory applied to intelligent agents relies on the following assumptions:

- Agents know what actions they can carry out.
- The effect of each action can be described as a probability distribution over outcomes.
- An agent's preferences are expressed by utilities of outcomes.

It is a consequence of Proposition 9.3 (page 376) that, if agents only act for one step, a rational agent should choose an action with the highest expected utility.

Example 9.4 Consider the problem of the delivery robot in which there is uncertainty in the outcome of its actions. In particular, consider the problem of going from position $o109$ in Figure 3.1 (page 73) to the *mail* position, where there is a chance that the robot will slip off course and fall down the stairs. Suppose the robot can get pads that will not change the probability of an accident but will make an accident less severe. Unfortunately, the pads add extra weight. The robot could also go the long way around, which would reduce the probability of an accident but make the trip much slower.

   Thus, the robot has to decide whether to wear the pads and which way to go (the long way or the short way). What is not under its direct control is whether there is an accident, although this probability can be reduced by going the long way around. For each combination of the agent's choices and whether there is an accident, there is an outcome ranging from severe damage to arriving quickly without the extra weight of the pads.

To model one-off decision making, a **decision variable** can be used to model an agent's choice. A decision variable is like a random variable, with a domain, but it does not have an associated probability distribution. Instead, an agent gets to choose a value for a decision variable. A **possible world** specifies values for both random and decision variables, and for each combination of values to decision variables, there is a probability distribution over the random variables. That is, for each assignment of a value to each decision variable, the measures of the worlds that satisfy that assignment sum to 1. Conditional probabilities are only defined when a value for every decision variable is part of what is conditioned on.

   Figure 9.4 shows a **decision tree** that depicts the different choices available to the agent and their outcomes. [These are different from the decision trees used for classification (page 298)]. To read the decision tree, start at the root (on the left in this figure). From each node one of the branches can be followed. For the decision nodes, shown as squares, the agent gets to choose which branch to take. For each random node, shown as a circle, the agent does not get to choose which branch will be taken; rather there is a probability distribution over the branches from that node. Each path to a leaf corresponds to a world, shown as w_i, which is the **outcome** that will be true if that path is followed.

Example 9.5 In Example 9.4 there are two decision variables, one corresponding to the decision of whether the robot wears pads and one to the decision of which way to go. There is one random variable, whether there is an accident or not. Eight possible worlds exist, corresponding to the eight paths in the decision tree of Figure 9.4.

   What the agent should do depends on how important it is to arrive quickly, how much the pads' weight matters, how much it is worth to reduce the damage from severe to moderate, and the likelihood of an accident.

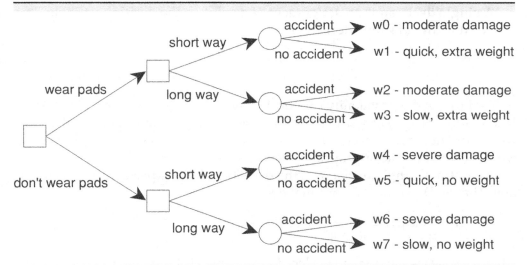

Figure 9.4: A decision tree for the delivery robot. Square boxes represent decisions that the robot can make. Circles represent random variables that the robot cannot observe before making its decision.

The proof of Proposition 9.3 (page 376) specifies how to measure the desirability of the outcomes. Suppose we decide to have utilities in the range [0,100]. First, choose the best outcome, which would be w_5, and give it a utility of 100. The worst outcome is w_6, so assign it a utility of 0. For each of the other worlds, consider the lottery between w_6 and w_5. For example, w_0 may have a utility of 35, meaning the agent is indifferent between w_0 and $[0.35 : w_5, 0.65 : w_6]$, which is slightly better than w_2, which may have a utility of 30. w_1 may have a utility of 95, because it is only slightly worse than w_5.

Example 9.6 In **diagnosis**, decision variables correspond to various treatments and tests. The utility may depend on the costs of tests and treatment and whether the patient gets better, stays sick, or dies, and whether they have short-term or chronic pain. The outcomes for the patient depend on the treatment the patient receives, the patient's physiology, and the details of the disease, which may not be known with certainty. Although we have used the vocabulary of medical diagnosis, the same approach holds for diagnosis of artifacts such as airplanes.

In a one-off decision, the agent chooses a value for each decision variable. This can be modeled by treating all the decision variables as a single composite decision variable. The domain of this decision variable is the cross product of the domains of the individual decision variables. Call the resulting composite decision variable D.

Each world ω specifies an assignment of a value to the decision variable D and an assignment of a value to each random variable.

A **single decision** is an assignment of a value to the decision variable. The **expected utility** of single decision $D = d_i$ is

$$\mathcal{E}(U|D = d_i) = \sum_{\omega \models (D=d_i)} U(\omega) \times P(\omega),$$

where $P(\omega)$ is the probability of world ω, and $U(\omega)$ is the value of the utility U in world ω; $\omega \models (D = d_i)$ means that the decision variable D has value d_i in world ω. Thus, the expected-utility computation involves summing over the worlds that select the appropriate decision.

An **optimal single decision** is the decision whose expected utility is maximal. That is, $D = d_{max}$ is an optimal decision if

$$\mathcal{E}(U|D = d_{max}) = \max_{d_i \in dom(D)} \mathcal{E}(U|D = d_i),$$

where $dom(D)$ is the domain of decision variable D. Thus,

$$d_{max} = \arg \max_{d_i \in dom(D)} \mathcal{E}(U|D = d_i).$$

Example 9.7 The delivery robot problem of Example 9.4 (page 382) is a single decision problem where the robot has to decide on the values for the variables *Wear_Pads* and *Which_Way*. The single decision is the complex decision variable $\langle$*Wear_Pads*, *Which_Way*$\rangle$. Each assignment of a value to each decision variable has an expected value. For example, the expected utility of *Wear_Pads* $= true \wedge$ *Which_Way* $= short$ is given by

$$\mathcal{E}(U|wear\_pads \wedge Which\_Way = short)$$
$$= P(accident|wear\_pads \wedge Which\_way = short) \times utility(w_0)$$
$$+ (1 - P(accident|wear\_pads \wedge Which\_way = short)) \times utility(w_1),$$

where the worlds w_0 and w_1 are as in Figure 9.4, and *wear_ pads* means *Wear_Pads* $= true$.

9.2.1 Single-Stage Decision Networks

The decision tree is a state-based representation because the worlds correspond to the resulting state. It is, however, often more natural and more efficient to represent and reason in terms of features, represented as variables.

A **single-stage decision network** is an extension of a belief network that has three kinds of nodes:

- **Decision nodes**, drawn as rectangles, represent decision variables. The agent gets to choose a value for each decision variable. Where there are multiple decision variables, we assume there is a total ordering of the decision nodes, and the decision nodes before a decision node D in the total ordering are the parents of D.

- **Chance nodes**, drawn as ovals, represent random variables. These are the same as the nodes in a belief network. Each chance node has an associated domain and a conditional probability of the variable, given its parents. As in

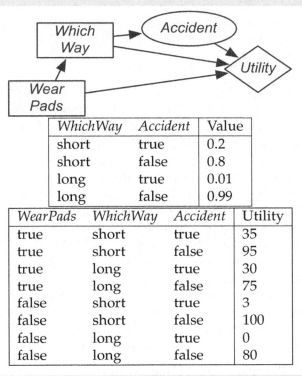

WhichWay	Accident	Value
short	true	0.2
short	false	0.8
long	true	0.01
long	false	0.99

WearPads	WhichWay	Accident	Utility
true	short	true	35
true	short	false	95
true	long	true	30
true	long	false	75
false	short	true	3
false	short	false	100
false	long	true	0
false	long	false	80

Figure 9.5: Single-stage decision network for the delivery robot

a belief network, the parents of a chance node represent conditional dependence: a variable is independent of its non-descendants, given its parents. In a decision network, both chance nodes and decision nodes can be parents of a chance node.

- A **utility node**, drawn as a diamond, represents the utility. The parents of the utility node are the variables on which the utility depends. Both chance nodes and decision nodes can be parents of the utility node.

Each chance variable and each decision variable has an associated domain. There is no domain associated with the utility node. Whereas the chance nodes represent random variables and the decision nodes represent decision variables, there are no associated utility variables. The utility provides a function of its parents.

Associated with a decision network is a conditional probability for each chance node given its parents (as in a belief network) and a representation of the utility as a function of the utility node's parents. In the specification of the network, there are no tables associated with the decision nodes.

Example 9.8 Figure 9.5 gives a decision network representation of Example 9.4 (page 382). There are two decisions to be made: which way to go and whether to wear padding. Whether the agent has an accident only depends on which way they go. The utility depends on all three variables.

This network requires two factors: a factor representing the conditional probability, $P(Accident|WhichWay)$, and a factor representing the utility as a function of *WhichWay*, *Accident*, and *WearPads*. Tables for these factors are shown in Figure 9.5.

A **policy** for a single-stage decision network is an assignment of a value to each decision variable. Each policy has an **expected utility**, which is the conditional expected value (page 231) of the utility conditioned on the policy. An **optimal policy** is a policy whose expected utility is maximal. That is, it is a policy such that no other policy has a higher expected utility.

Figure 9.6 shows how **variable elimination** can be used to find an optimal policy in a single-stage decision network. After pruning irrelevant nodes and summing out all random variables, there will be a single factor that represents the expected utility for each combination of decision variables. This factor does not have to be a factor on *all* of the decision variables; however, those decision variables that are not included are not relevant to the decision.

Example 9.9   Consider running *OptimizeSSDN* on the decision network of Figure 9.5. No nodes can be pruned, so it sums out the only random variable, *Accident*. To do this, it multiplies both factors because they both contain *Accident*, and sums out *Accident*, giving the following factor:

WearPads	WhichWay	Value
true	short	0.2* 35+ 0.8*95=83
true	long	0.01*30+0.99*75=74.55
false	short	0.2*3+0.8*100=80.6
false	long	0.01*0+0.99*80=79.2

Thus, the policy with the maximum value – the optimal policy – is to take the short way and wear pads, with an expected utility of 83.

9.3   Sequential Decisions

Generally, agents do not make decisions in the dark without observing something about the world, nor do they make just a single decision. A more typical scenario is that the agent makes an observation, decides on an action, carries out that action, makes observations in the resulting world, then makes another decision conditioned on the observations, and so on. Subsequent actions can depend on what is observed, and what is observed can depend on previous actions. In this scenario, it is often the case that the sole reason for carrying out an action is to provide information for future actions.

A **sequential decision problem** is a sequence of decisions, where for each decision you should consider

- what actions are available to the agent;
- what information is, or will be, available to the agent when it has to act;

```
1: procedure OptimizeSSDN(DN)
2:     Inputs
3:         DN a single stage decision network
4:     Output
5:         An optimal policy and the expected utility of that policy.
6:     Prune all nodes that are not ancestors of the utility node.
7:     Sum out all chance nodes.
8:     – at this stage there is a single factor F that was derived from utility
9:     Let v be the maximum value in F
10:    Let d be an assignment that gives the maximum value
11:    return d, v
```

Figure 9.6: Variable elimination for a single-stage decision network

- the effects of the actions; and
- the desirability of these effects.

Example 9.10 Consider a simple case of diagnosis where a doctor first gets to choose some tests and then gets to treat the patient, taking into account the outcome of the tests. The reason the doctor may decide to do a test is so that some information (the test results) will be available at the next stage when treatment may be performed. The test results will be information that is available when the treatment is decided, but not when the test is decided. It is often a good idea to test, even if testing itself can harm the patient.

The actions available are the possible tests and the possible treatments. When the test decision is made, the information available will be the symptoms exhibited by the patient. When the treatment decision is made, the information available will be the patient's symptoms, what tests were performed, and the test results. The effect of the test is the test result, which depends on what test was performed and what is wrong with the patient. The effect of the treatment is some function of the treatment and what is wrong with the patient. The utility includes, for example, costs of tests and treatments, the pain and inconvenience to the patient in the short term, and the long-term prognosis.

9.3.1 Decision Networks

A **decision network** (also called an **influence diagram**) is a graphical representation of a finite sequential decision problem. Decision networks extend belief networks to include decision variables and utility. A decision network extends the single-stage decision network (page 384) to allow for sequential decisions.

In particular, a **decision network** is a directed acyclic graph (DAG) with chance nodes, decision nodes, and a utility node. This extends single-stage decision networks by allowing both chance nodes and decision nodes to be

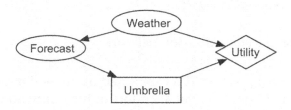

Figure 9.7: Decision network for decision of whether to take an umbrella

parents of decision nodes. Arcs coming into decision nodes represent the information that will be available when the decision is made. Arcs coming into chance nodes represents probabilistic dependence. Arcs coming into the utility node represent what the utility depends on.

A **no-forgetting agent** is an agent whose decisions are totally ordered, and the agent remembers its previous decisions and any information that was available to a previous decision. A **no-forgetting decision network** is a decision network in which the decision nodes are totally ordered and, if decision node D_i is before D_j in the total ordering, then D_i is a parent of D_j, and any parent of D_i is also a parent of D_j. Thus, any information available to D_i is available to D_j, and the action chosen for decision D_i is part of the information available at decision D_j. The no-forgetting condition is sufficient to make sure that the following definitions make sense and that the following algorithms work.

Example 9.11 Figure 9.7 shows a simple decision network for a decision of whether the agent should take an umbrella when it goes out. The agent's utility depends on the weather and whether it takes an umbrella. However, it does not get to observe the weather. It only gets to observe the forecast. The forecast probabilistically depends on the weather.

As part of this network, the designer must specify the domain for each random variable and the domain for each decision variable. Suppose the random variable *Weather* has domain {*norain, rain*}, the random variable *Forecast* has domain {*sunny, rainy, cloudy*}, and the decision variable *Umbrella* has domain {*takeIt, leaveIt*}. There is no domain associated with the utility node. The designer also must specify the probability of the random variables given their parents. Suppose $P(Weather)$ is defined by

$$P(Weather{=}rain) = 0.3.$$

$P(Forecast|Weather)$ is given by

Weather	Forecast	Probability
norain	sunny	0.7
norain	cloudy	0.2
norain	rainy	0.1
rain	sunny	0.15
rain	cloudy	0.25
rain	rainy	0.6

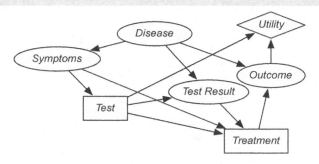

Figure 9.8: Decision network for diagnosis

Suppose the utility function, *Utility*(*Weather*, *Umbrella*), is

Weather	Umbrella	Utility
norain	takeIt	20
norain	leaveIt	100
rain	takeIt	70
rain	leaveIt	0

There is no table specified for the *Umbrella* decision variable. It is the task of the planner to determine which value of *Umbrella* to select, depending on the forecast.

Example 9.12 Figure 9.8 shows a decision network that represents the scenario of Example 9.10 (page 387). The symptoms depend on the disease. What test to perform is decided based on the symptoms. The test result depends on the disease and the test performed. The treatment decision is based on the symptoms, the test performed, and the test result. The outcome depends on the disease and the treatment. The utility depends on the costs and the side effects of the test and on the outcome.

Note that the diagnostic assistant that is deciding on the tests and the treatments never actually finds out what disease the patient has, unless the test result is definitive, which it typically is not.

Example 9.13 Figure 9.9 (on the next page) gives a decision network that is an extension of the belief network of Figure 6.1 (page 237). The agent can receive a report of people leaving a building and has to decide whether or not to call the fire department. Before calling, the agent can check for smoke, but this has some cost associated with it. The utility depends on whether it calls, whether there is a fire, and the cost associated with checking for smoke.

In this sequential decision problem, there are two decisions to be made. First, the agent must decide whether to check for smoke. The information that will be available when it makes this decision is whether there is a report of people leaving the building. Second, the agent must decide whether or not to call the fire department. When making this decision, the agent will know whether there was a report, whether it checked for smoke, and whether it can see smoke. Assume that all of the variables are binary.

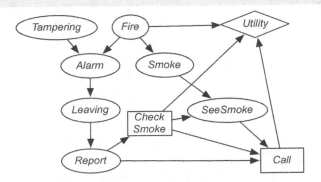

Figure 9.9: Decision network for the alarm problem

The information necessary for the decision network includes the conditional probabilities of the belief network and

- $P(SeeSmoke|Smoke, CheckSmoke)$; how seeing smoke depends on whether the agent looks for smoke and whether there is smoke. Assume that the agent has a perfect sensor for smoke. It will see smoke if and only if it looks for smoke and there is smoke. [See Exercise 9.6 (page 415).]
- $Utility(CheckSmoke, Fire, Call)$; how the utility depends on whether the agent checks for smoke, whether there is a fire, and whether the fire department is called. Figure 9.10 provides this utility information. This utility function expresses the cost structure that calling has a cost of 200, checking has a cost of 20, but not calling when there is a fire has a cost of 5,000. The utility is the negative of the cost.

9.3.2 Policies

A **policy** specifies what the agent should do under all contingencies. An agent wants to find an optimal policy – one that maximizes its expected utility.

CheckSmoke	Fire	Call	Utility
yes	yes	call	−220
yes	yes	do not call	−5020
yes	no	call	−220
yes	no	do not call	−20
no	yes	call	−200
no	yes	do not call	−5000
no	no	call	−200
no	no	do not call	0

Figure 9.10: Utility for alarm decision network

A policy consists of a decision function for each decision variable. A **decision function** for a decision variable is a function that specifies a value for the decision variable for each assignment of values of its parents. Thus, a policy specifies what the agent will do for each possible value that it could sense.

Example 9.14 In Example 9.11 (page 388), some of the policies are

- Always bring the umbrella.
- Bring the umbrella only if the forecast is "rainy."
- Bring the umbrella only if the forecast is "sunny."

There are eight different policies, because there are three possible forecasts and there are two choices for each of the forecasts.

Example 9.15 In Example 9.13 (page 389), a policy specifies a decision function for *CheckSmoke* and a decision function for *Call*. Some of the policies are

- Never check for smoke, and call only if there is a report.
- Always check for smoke, and call only if it sees smoke.
- Check for smoke if there is a report, and call only if there is a report and it sees smoke.
- Check for smoke if there is no report, and call when it does not see smoke.
- Always check for smoke and never call.

In this example, there are 1,024 different policies (given that each variable is binary). There are 4 decision functions for *CheckSmoke*. There are 2^8 decision functions for *Call*; for each of the 8 assignments of values to the parents of *Call*, the agent can choose to call or not.

Expected Utility of a Policy

A policy can be evaluated by determining its expected utility for an agent following the policy. A rational agent should adopt the policy that maximizes its expected utility.

A **possible world** specifies a value for each random variable and each decision variable. A possible world does not have a probability unless values for all of the decision variables are specified. A possible world **satisfies** a policy if the value of each decision variable in the possible world is the value selected in the decision function for that decision variable in the policy. If ω is a possible world, and π is a policy, $\omega \models \pi$ is defined to mean that possible world ω satisfies policy π.

It is important to realize that a possible world corresponds to a complete history and specifies the values of all random and decision variables, including all observed variables, for a complete sequence of actions. Possible world ω satisfies policy π if ω is one possible unfolding of history given that the agent follows policy π. The satisfiability constraint enforces the intuition that the agent will actually do the action prescribed by π for each of the possible observations.

The **expected utility of policy** π is

$$\mathcal{E}(\pi) = \sum_{\omega \models \pi} U(\omega) \times P(\omega),$$

where $P(\omega)$, the probability of world ω, is the product of the probabilities of the values of the chance nodes given their parents' values in ω, and $U(\omega)$ is the value of the utility U in world ω.

Example 9.16 In Example 9.11 (page 388), let π_1 be the policy to take the umbrella if the forecast is cloudy and to leave it at home otherwise. The expected utility of this policy is obtained by averaging the utility over the worlds that satisfy this policy:

$$\begin{aligned}
\mathcal{E}(\pi_1) = {} & P(norain)P(sunny|norain)Utility(norain, leaveIt) \\
& + P(norain)P(cloudy|norain)Utility(norain, takeIt) \\
& + P(norain)P(rainy|norain)Utility(norain, leaveIt) \\
& + P(rain)P(sunny|rain)Utility(rain, leaveIt) \\
& + P(rain)P(cloudy|rain)Utility(rain, takeIt) \\
& + P(rain)P(rainy|rain)Utility(rain, leaveIt),
\end{aligned}$$

where *norain* means *Weather = norain*, *sunny* means *Forecast = sunny*, and similarly for the other values. Notice how the value for the decision variable is the one chosen by the policy. It only depends on the forecast.

An **optimal policy** is a policy π^* such that $\mathcal{E}(\pi^*) \geq \mathcal{E}(\pi)$ for all policies $\mathcal{E}(\pi)$. That is, an optimal policy is a policy whose expected utility is maximal over all policies.

Suppose a binary decision node has n binary parents. There are 2^n different assignments of values to the parents and, consequently, there are 2^{2^n} different possible decision functions for this decision node. The number of policies is the product of the number of decision functions for each of the decision variables. Even small examples can have a huge number of policies. Thus, an algorithm that enumerates the set of policies looking for the best one will be very inefficient.

9.3.3 Variable Elimination for Decision Networks

Fortunately, we do not have to enumerate all of the policies; we can use variable elimination (VE) to find an optimal policy. The idea is to first consider the *last* decision, find an optimal decision for each value of its parents, and produce a factor of these maximum values. It then has a new decision network, with one less decision, that can be solved recursively.

1: **procedure** *VE_DN(DN)*:
2:     **Inputs**
3:         *DN* a single stage decision network
4:     **Output**
5:         An optimal policy and its expected utility
6:     **Local**
7:         *DFs*: a set of decision functions, initially empty
8:         *Fs*: a set of factors
9:     Remove all variables that are not ancestors of the utility node
10:     Create a factor in *Fs* for each conditional probability
11:     Create a factor in *Fs* for the utility
12:     **while** there are decision nodes remaining **do**
13:         Sum out each random variable that is not an ancestor of a decision node
14:         ▷ *at this stage there is one decision node D that is in a factor F with a subset of its parents*
15:         Add $\max_D F$ to *Fs*.
16:         Add $\arg\max_D F$ to *DFs*.
17:     Sum out all remaining random variables
18:     Return *DFs* and the product of remaining factors

Figure 9.11: Variable elimination for decision networks

Figure 9.11 shows how to use VE for decision networks. Essentially it computes the expected utility of an optimal decision. It eliminates the random variables that are not parents of a decision node by summing them out according to some elimination ordering. The elimination ordering does not affect correctness and so it can be chosen for efficiency.

After eliminating all of the random variables that are not parents of a decision node, there must be one decision variable that is in a factor that only contains it and some subset of its parents because of the no-forgetting condition. This is the last action in the ordering of actions.

To eliminate that decision node, *VE_DN* chooses the values for the decision that result in the maximum utility. This maximization creates a new factor on the remaining variables and a decision function for the decision variable being eliminated. This decision function created by maximizing is a component of an optimal policy.

Example 9.17 In Example 9.11 (page 388), there are three initial factors representing *P(Weather)*, *P(Forecast|Weather)*, and *Utility(Weather, Umbrella)*. First, it eliminates *Weather*: by multiplying all three factors and summing out *Weather*, giving a factor on *Forecast* and *Umbrella*,

Forecast	Umbrella	Value
sunny	takeIt	12.95
sunny	leaveIt	49.0
cloudy	takeIt	8.05
cloudy	leaveIt	14.0
rainy	takeIt	14.0
rainy	leaveIt	7.0

To maximize over *Umbrella*, for each value of *Forecast*, *VE_DN* selects the value of *Umbrella* that maximizes the value of the factor. For example, when the forecast is *sunny*, the agent should leave the umbrella at home for a value of 49.0.

VE_DN constructs an optimal decision function for *Umbrella* by selecting a value of *Umbrella* that results in the maximum value for each value of *Forecast*:

Forecast	Umbrella
sunny	leaveIt
cloudy	leaveIt
rainy	takeIt

It also creates a new factor that contains the maximal value for each value of *Forecast*:

Forecast	Value
sunny	49.0
cloudy	14.0
rainy	14.0

It now sums out *Forecast* from this factor, which gives the value 77.0. This is the expected value of the optimal policy.

Example 9.18 Consider Example 9.13 (page 389). Before summing out any variables it has the following factors:

Meaning	Factor
$P(Tampering)$	$f_0(Tampering)$
$P(Fire)$	$f_1(Fire)$
$P(Alarm\|Tampering, Fire)$	$f_2(Tampering, Fire, Alarm)$
$P(Smoke\|Fire)$	$f_3(Fire, Smoke)$
$P(Leaving\|Alarm)$	$f_4(Alarm, Leaving)$
$P(Report\|Leaving)$	$f_5(Leaving, Report)$
$P(SeeSmoke\|CheckSmoke, Smoke)$	$f_6(Smoke, SeeSmoke, CheckSmoke)$
$utility(Fire, CheckSmoke, Call)$	$f_7(Fire, CheckSmoke, Call)$

The expected utility is the product of the probability and the utility, as long as the appropriate actions are chosen.

VE_DN sums out the random variables that are not ancestors of a decision node. Thus, it sums out *Tampering, Fire, Alarm, Smoke,* and *Leaving*. After these have been eliminated, there is a single factor, part of which (to two decimal places) is:

Report	SeeSmoke	CheckSmoke	Call	Value
t	t	t	t	−1.33
t	t	t	f	−29.30
t	t	f	t	0
t	t	f	f	0
t	f	t	t	−4.86
t	f	t	f	−3.68
...	...	...	...	...

From this factor, an optimal decision function can be created for *Call* by selecting a value for *Call* that maximizes *Value* for each assignment to *Report*, *SeeSmoke*, and *CheckSmoke*. The maximum of −1.33 and −29.3 is −1.33, so when *Report* = t, *SeeSmoke* = t, and *CheckSmoke* = t, the optimal action is *Call* = t with value −1.33. The method is the same for the other values of *Report*, *SeeSmoke* and *CheckSmoke*.

An optimal decision function for *Call* is

Report	SeeSmoke	CheckSmoke	Call
t	t	t	t
t	t	f	t
t	f	t	f
...	...	...	...

Note that the value for *Call* when *SeeSmoke* = t and *CheckSmoke* = f is arbitrary. It does not matter what the agent plans to do in this situation, because the situation never arises.

The factor resulting from maximizing *Call* contains the maximum values for each combination of *Report*, *SeeSmoke*, and *CheckSmoke*:

Report	SeeSmoke	CheckSmoke	Value
t	t	t	−1.33
t	t	f	0
t	f	t	−3.68
...	...	...	...

It can then sum out *SeeSmoke*, which gives the factor

Report	CheckSmoke	Value
t	t	−5.01
t	f	−5.65
f	t	−23.77
f	f	−17.58

Maximizing *CheckSmoke* for each value of *Report* gives the decision function

Report	CheckSmoke
t	t
f	f

and the factor

Report	Value
t	−5.01
f	−17.58

Summing out *Report* gives the expected utility of −22.60 (taking into account rounding errors).

Thus, the policy returned can be seen as

> *checkSmoke* ← *report*.
>
> *call_fire_department* ← *see_smoke*.
>
> *call_fire_department* ← *report* ∧ ¬*check_smoke* ∧ ¬*see_smoke*.

The last of these rules is never used because the agent following the optimal policy does check for smoke if there is a report. However, when executing *VE_DN*, the agent does not know an optimal policy for *CheckSmoke* when it is optimizing *Call*. Only by considering what to do with the information on smoke does the agent determine whether to check for smoke.

Note also that, in this case, even though checking for smoke has a cost associated with it, checking for smoke is worthwhile because the information obtained is valuable.

The following example shows how the factor containing a decision variable can contain a subset of its parents when the VE algorithm optimizes the decision.

Example 9.19   Consider Example 9.11 (page 388), but with an extra arc from *Weather* to *Umbrella*. That is, the agent gets to observe both the weather and the forecast. In this case, there are no random variables to sum out, and the factor that contains the decision node and a subset of its parents is the original utility factor. It can then maximize *Umbrella*, giving the decision function and the factor:

Weather	Umbrella		Weather	Value
norain	leaveIt		norain	100
rain	takeIt		rain	70

Note that the forecast is irrelevant to the decision. Knowing the forecast does not give the agent any useful information.

Summing out *Forecast* gives a factor that contains ones. Summing out *Weather*, where $P(Weather=norain) = 0.7$, gives the expected utility $0.7 \times 100 + 0.3 \times 70 = 91$.

9.4   The Value of Information and Control

Example 9.20   In Example 9.18 (page 394), the action *CheckSmoke* provides information about fire. Checking for smoke costs 20 units and does not provide any direct reward; however, in an optimal policy, it is worthwhile to check for smoke when there is a report because the agent can condition its further actions on the information obtained. Thus, the information about smoke is valuable to the agent. Even though smoke provides imperfect information about whether there is fire, that information is still very useful for making decisions.

One of the important lessons from this example is that an information-seeking action, such as *check_for_smoke*, can be treated in the same way as any other action, such as *call_fire_department*. An optimal policy often includes actions whose only purpose is to find information as long as subsequent actions can condition on some effect of the action. Most actions do not just provide information; they also have a more direct effect on the world.

Information is valuable to agents because it helps them make better decisions.

The **value of information** i for decision D is the expected value of an optimal policy that can condition decision D, and subsequent decisions, on knowledge of i minus the expected value of an optimal policy that cannot observe i. Thus, in a decision network, it is the value of an optimal policy with i as a parent of D and subsequent decisions minus the value of an optimal policy without i as a parent of D.

> **Example 9.21** In Example 9.11 (page 388), consider how much it could be worth to get a better forecast. The value of getting perfect information about the weather for the decision about whether to take an umbrella is the difference between the value of the network with an arc from *Weather* to *Umbrella* which, as calculated in Example 9.19, is 91 and the original network, which, as computed in Example 9.11 (page 388), is 77. Thus, perfect information would be worth $91 - 77 = 14$. This is an upper bound on how much another sensor of the weather could be worth.

The value of information is a bound on the amount the agent would be willing to pay (in terms of loss of utility) for information i at stage d. It is an upper bound on the amount that imperfect information about the value of i at decision d would be worth. Imperfect information is, for example, information available from a noisy sensor of i. It is not worth paying more for a sensor of i than the value of information i.

The value of information has some interesting properties:

- The value of information is never negative. The worst that can happen is that the agent can ignore the information.

- If an optimal decision is to do the same thing no matter which value of i is observed, the value of information i is zero. If the value of information i is zero, there is an optimal policy that does not depend on the value of i (i.e., the same action is chosen no matter which value of i is observed).

Within a decision network, the value of information i at decision d can be evaluated by considering both

- the decision network with arcs from i to d and from i to subsequent decisions and

- the decision network without such arcs.

The differences in the values of the optimal policies of these two decision networks is the value of information i at d. Something more sophisticated must be done when adding the arc from i to d causes a cycle.

Example 9.22 In the alarm problem [Example 9.18 (page 394)], the agent may be interested in knowing whether it is worthwhile to install a relay for the alarm so that the alarm can be heard directly instead of relying on the noisy sensor of people leaving. To determine how much a relay could be worth, consider how much perfect information about the alarm would be worth. If the information is worth less than the cost of the relay, it is not worthwhile to install the relay.

The value of information about the alarm for checking for smoke and for calling can be obtained by solving the decision network of Figure 9.9 (page 390) together with the same network, but with an arc from *Alarm* to *Check_for_smoke* and an arc from *Alarm* to *Call_fire_department*. The original network has a value of −22.6. This new decision network has an optimal policy whose value is −6.3. The difference in the values of the optimal policies for the two decision networks, namely 16.3, is the value of *Alarm* for the decision *Check_for_smoke*. If the relay costs 20 units, the installation will not be worthwhile.

The value of the network with an arc from *Alarm* to *Call_fire_department* is −6.3, the same as if there was also an arc from *Alarm* to *Check_for_smoke*. In the optimal policy, the information about *Alarm* is ignored in the optimal decision function for *Check_for_smoke*; the agent never checks for smoke in the optimal policy when *Alarm* is a parent of *Call_fire_department*.

The **value of control** specifies how much it is worth to control a variable. In its simplest form, it is the change in value of a decision network where a random variable is replaced by a decision variable, and arcs are added to make it a no-forgetting network. If this is done, the change in utility is non-negative; the resulting network always has an equal or higher expected utility.

Example 9.23 In the alarm decision network of Figure 9.9 (page 390), you may be interested in the value of controlling tampering. This could, for example, be used to estimate how much it is worth to add security guards to prevent tampering. To compute this, compare the value of the decision network of Figure 9.9 (page 390) to the decision network where *Tampering* is a decision node and a parent of the other two decision nodes.

The value of the initial decision network is −22.6. First, consider the value of information. If *Tampering* is made a parent of *Call*, the value is −21.30. If *Tampering* is made a parent of *Call* and *CheckSmoke*, the value is −20.87.

To determine the value of control, turn the *Tampering* node into a decision node and make it a parent of the other two decisions. The value of the resulting network is −20.71. Notice here that control is more valuable than information.

The value of controlling tampering in the original network is −20.71 − (−22.6) = 1.89. The value of controlling tampering in the context of observing tampering is 20.71 − (−20.87) = 0.16.

The previous description applies when the parents of the random variable that is being controlled become parents of the decision variable. In this scenario, the value of control is never negative. However, if the parents of the decision node do not include all of the parents of the random variable, it is possible that control is less valuable than information. In general one must be explicit about what information will be available when considering controlling a variable.

Example 9.24   Consider controlling the variable *Smoke* in Figure 9.9 (page 390). If *Fire* is a parent of the decision variable *Smoke*, it has to be a parent of *Call* to make it a no-forgetting network. The expected utility of the resulting network with *Smoke* coming before *checkSmoke* is −2.0. The value of controlling *Smoke* in this situation is due to observing *Fire*. The resulting optimal decision is to call if there is a fire and not call otherwise.

Suppose the agent were to control *Smoke* without conditioning on *Fire*. That is, the agent has to either make smoke or not, and *Fire* is not a parent of the other decisions. This situation can be modeled by making *Smoke* a decision variable with no parents. In this case, the expected utility is −23.20, which is worse than the initial decision network, because blindly controlling *Smoke* loses its ability to act as a sensor from *Fire*.

9.5   Decision Processes

The decision networks of the previous section were for finite-stage, partially observable domains. In this section, we consider indefinite horizon and infinite horizon problems.

Often an agent must reason about an ongoing process or it does not know how many actions it will be required to do. These are called **infinite horizon** problems when the process may go on forever or **indefinite horizon** problems when the agent will eventually stop, but where it does not know when it will stop. To model these situations, we augment the Markov chain (page 266) with actions. At each stage, the agent decides which action to perform; the resulting state depends on both the previous state and the action performed.

For ongoing processes, you do not want to consider only the utility at the end, because the agent may never get to the end. Instead, an agent can receive a sequence of **rewards**. These rewards incorporate the action costs in addition to any prizes or penalties that may be awarded. Negative rewards are called **punishments**. Indefinite horizon problems can be modeled using a stopping state. A **stopping state** or **absorbing state** is a state in which all actions have no effect; that is, when the agent is in that state, all actions immediately return to that state with a zero reward. Goal achievement can be modeled by having a reward for entering such a stopping state.

We only consider **stationary** (page 266) models where the state transitions and the rewards do not depend on the time.

A **Markov decision process** or an **MDP** consists of

- *S*, a set of states of the world.
- *A*, a set of actions.

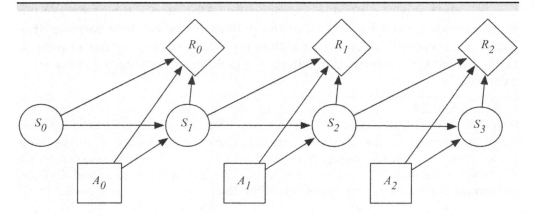

Figure 9.12: Decision network representing a finite part of an MDP

- $P : S \times S \times A \rightarrow [0,1]$, which specifies the dynamics. This is written $P(s'|s,a)$, where

$$\forall s \in S \ \forall a \in A \ \sum_{s' \in S} P(s'|s,a) = 1.$$

  In particular, $P(s'|s,a)$ specifies the probability of transitioning to state s' given that the agent is in state s and does action a.

- $R : S \times A \times S \rightarrow \Re$, where $R(s,a,s')$ gives the expected immediate reward from doing action a and transitioning to state s' from state s.

Both the dynamics and the rewards can be stochastic; there can be some randomness in the resulting state and reward, which is modeled by having a distribution over the resulting state and by R giving the *expected* reward. The outcomes are stochastic when they depend on random variables that are not modeled in the MDP.

A finite part of a Markov decision process can be depicted using a decision network as in Figure 9.12.

Example 9.25 A grid world is an idealization of a robot in an environment. At each time, the robot is at some location and can move to neighboring locations, collecting rewards and punishments. Suppose that the actions are stochastic, so that there is a probability distribution over the resulting states given the action and the state.

Figure 9.13 shows a 10×10 grid world, where the robot can choose one of four actions: up, down, left, or right. If the agent carries out one of these actions, it has a 0.7 chance of going one step in the desired direction and a 0.1 chance of going one step in any of the other three directions. If it bumps into the outside wall (i.e., the square computed as above is outside the grid), there is a penalty of 1 (i.e., a reward of -1) and the agent does not actually move. There are four rewarding states (apart from the walls), one worth $+10$ (at position $(9,8)$; 9 across and 8 down), one worth $+3$ (at position $(8,3)$), one

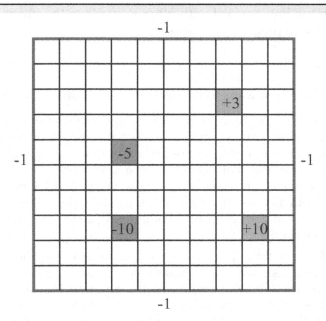

Figure 9.13: The grid world of Example 9.25

worth -5 (at position $(4, 5)$), and one worth -10 (at position $(4, 8)$). In each of these states, the agent gets the reward after it carries out an action in that state, not when it enters the state. When the agent reaches the state $(9, 8)$, no matter what it does at the next step, it is flung, at random, to one of the four corners of the grid world.

Note that, in this example, the reward is be a function of both the initial state and the final state. The way to tell if the agent bumped into the wall is if the agent did not actually move. Knowing just the initial state and the action, or just the final state and the action, does not provide enough information to infer the reward.

As with decision networks (page 387), the designer also has to consider what information is available to the agent when it decides what to do. There are two common variations:

- In a **fully observable Markov decision process**, the agent gets to observe the current state when deciding what to do.

- A **partially observable Markov decision process** (POMDP) is a combination of an MDP and a hidden Markov model (page 267). At each time point, the agent gets to make some observations that depend on the state. The agent only has access to the history of observations and previous actions when making a decision. It cannot directly observe the current state.

To decide what to do, the agent compares different sequences of rewards. The most common way to do this is to convert a sequence of rewards into a number called the **value** or the **cumulative reward**. To do this, the agent combines an immediate reward with other rewards in the future. Suppose the agent receives the sequence of rewards:

$r_1, r_2, r_3, r_4, \ldots$.

There are three common ways to combine rewards into a value V:

total reward: $V = \sum_{i=1}^{\infty} r_i$. In this case, the value is the sum of all of the rewards. This works when you can guarantee that the sum is finite; but if the sum is infinite, it does not give any opportunity to compare which sequence of rewards is preferable. For example, a sequence of \$1 rewards has the same total as a sequence of \$100 rewards (both are infinite). One case where the reward is finite is when there is a stopping state (page 399); when the agent always has a non-zero probability of entering a stopping state, the total reward will be finite.

average reward: $V = \lim_{n \to \infty} (r_1 + \cdots + r_n)/n$. In this case, the agent's value is the average of its rewards, averaged over for each time period. As long as the rewards are finite, this value will also be finite. However, whenever the total reward is finite, the average reward is zero, and so the average reward will fail to allow the agent to choose among different actions that each have a zero average reward. Under this criterion, the only thing that matters is where the agent ends up. Any finite sequence of bad actions does not affect the limit. For example, receiving \$1,000,000 followed by rewards of \$1 has the same average reward as receiving \$0 followed by rewards of \$1 (they both have an average reward of \$1).

discounted reward: $V = r_1 + \gamma r_2 + \gamma^2 r_3 + \cdots + \gamma^{i-1} r_i + \cdots$, where γ, the **discount factor**, is a number in the range $0 \leq \gamma < 1$. Under this criterion, future rewards are worth less than the current reward. If γ was 1, this would be the same as the total reward. When $\gamma = 0$, the agent ignores all future rewards. Having $0 \leq \gamma < 1$ guarantees that, whenever the rewards are finite, the total value will also be finite.

We can rewrite the discounted reward as

$$V = \sum_{i=1}^{\infty} \gamma^{i-1} r_i$$
$$= r_1 + \gamma r_2 + \gamma^2 r_3 + \cdots + \gamma^{i-1} r_i + \cdots$$
$$= r_1 + \gamma(r_2 + \gamma(r_3 + \ldots)).$$

Suppose V_k is the reward accumulated from time k:

$$V_k = r_k + \gamma(r_{k+1} + \gamma(r_{k+2} + \ldots))$$
$$= r_k + \gamma V_{k+1}.$$

To understand the properties of V_k, suppose $S = 1 + \gamma + \gamma^2 + \gamma^3 + \ldots$, then $S = 1 + \gamma S$. Solving for S gives $S = 1/(1 - \gamma)$. Thus, under the discounted reward, the value of all of the future is at most $1/(1 - \gamma)$ times as much as the maximum reward and at least $1/(1 - \gamma)$ times as much as the minimum reward. Therefore, the eternity of time from now only has a finite value compared with the immediate reward, unlike the average reward, in which the immediate reward is dominated by the cumulative reward for the eternity of time.

In economics, γ is related to the interest rate: getting \$1 now is equivalent to getting \$$(1 + i)$ in one year, where i is the interest rate. You could also see the discount rate as the probability that the agent survives; γ can be seen as the probability that the agent keeps going. The rest of this book considers a discounted reward.

A **stationary policy** is a function $\pi : S \rightarrow A$. That is, it assigns an action to each state. Given a reward criterion, a policy has an expected value for every state. Let $V^\pi(s)$ be the expected value of following π in state s. This specifies how much value the agent expects to receive from following the policy in that state. Policy π is an **optimal policy** if there is no policy π' and no state s such that $V^{\pi'}(s) > V^\pi(s)$. That is, it is a policy that has a greater or equal expected value at every state than any other policy.

For infinite horizon problems, a stationary MDP always has an optimal stationary policy. However, this is not true for finite-stage problems, where a nonstationary policy might be better than all stationary policies. For example, if the agent had to stop at time n, for the last decision in some state, the agent would act to get the largest immediate reward without considering the future actions, but for earlier decisions at the same state it may decide to get a lower reward immediately to obtain a larger reward later.

9.5.1 Value of a Policy

The expected value of a policy π for the discounted reward, with discount γ, is defined in terms of two interrelated functions, V^π and Q^π.

Let $Q^\pi(s, a)$, where s is a state and a is an action, be the expected value of doing a in state s and then following policy π. Recall that $V^\pi(s)$, where s is a state, is the expected value of following policy π in state s.

Q^π and V^π can be defined recursively in terms of each other. If the agent is in state s, performs action a, and arrives in state s', it gets the immediate reward of $R(s, a, s')$ plus the discounted future reward, $\gamma V^\pi(s')$. When the agent is planning it does not know the actual resulting state, so it uses the expected value, averaged over the possible resulting states:

$$Q^\pi(s, a) = \sum_{s'} P(s'|s, a)(R(s, a, s') + \gamma V^\pi(s')). \tag{9.2}$$

$V^\pi(s)$ is obtained by doing the action specified by π and then acting following π:

$$V^\pi(s) = Q^\pi(s, \pi(s)).$$

9.5.2 Value of an Optimal Policy

Let $Q^*(s,a)$, where s is a state and a is an action, be the expected value of doing a in state s and then following the optimal policy. Let $V^*(s)$, where s is a state, be the expected value of following an optimal policy from state s.

Q^* can be defined analogously to Q^π:

$$Q^*(s,a) = \sum_{s'} P(s'|s,a)(R(s,a,s') + \gamma V^*(s')). \tag{9.3}$$

$V^*(s)$ is obtained by performing the action that gives the best value in each state:

$$V^*(s) = \max_a Q^*(s,a).$$

An optimal policy π^* is one of the policies that gives the best value for each state:

$$\pi^*(s) = \arg\max_a Q^*(s,a).$$

Note that $\arg\max_a Q^*(s,a)$ is a function of state s, and its value is one of the a's that results in the maximum value of $Q^*(s,a)$.

9.5.3 Value Iteration

Value iteration is a method of computing an optimal MDP policy and its value.

Value iteration starts at the "end" and then works backward, refining an estimate of either Q^* or V^*. There is really no end, so it uses an arbitrary end point. Let V_k be the value function assuming there are k stages to go, and let Q_k be the Q-function assuming there are k stages to go. These can be defined recursively. Value iteration starts with an arbitrary function V_0 and uses the following equations to get the functions for $k+1$ stages to go from the functions for k stages to go:

$$Q_{k+1}(s,a) = \sum_{s'} P(s'|s,a)(R(s,a,s') + \gamma V_k(s')) \text{ for } k \geq 0$$

$$V_k(s) = \max_a Q_k(s,a) \text{ for } k > 0.$$

It can either save the $V[S]$ array or the $Q[S,A]$ array. Saving the V array results in less storage, but it is more difficult to determine an optimal action, and one more iteration is needed to determine which action results in the greatest value.

Figure 9.14 shows the value iteration algorithm when the V array is stored. This procedure converges no matter what is the initial value function V_0. An initial value function that approximates V^* converges quicker than one that does not. The basis for many abstraction techniques for MDPs is to use some heuristic method to approximate V^* and to use this as an initial seed for value iteration.

1: **procedure** *Value_Iteration*(S, A, P, R, θ)
2:     **Inputs**
3:         S is the set of all states
4:         A is the set of all actions
5:         P is state transition function specifying $P(s'|s, a)$
6:         R is a reward function $R(s, a, s')$
7:         θ a threshold, $\theta > 0$
8:     **Output**
9:         $\pi[S]$ approximately optimal policy
10:         $V[S]$ value function
11:     **Local**
12:         real array $V_k[S]$ is a sequence of value functions
13:         action array $\pi[S]$
14:     assign $V_0[S]$ arbitrarily
15:     $k := 0$
16:     **repeat**
17:         $k := k + 1$
18:         **for each** state s **do**
19:             $V_k[s] = \max_a \sum_{s'} P(s'|s, a)(R(s, a, s') + \gamma V_{k-1}[s'])$
20:     **until** $\forall s \, |V_k[s] - V_{k-1}[s]| < \theta$
21:     **for each** state s **do**
22:         $\pi[s] = \arg\max_a \sum_{s'} P(s'|s, a)(R(s, a, s') + \gamma V_k[s'])$
23:     **return** π, V_k

Figure 9.14: Value iteration for MDPs, storing V

Example 9.26 Consider the 9 squares around the $+10$ reward of Example 9.25 (page 400). The discount is $\gamma = 0.9$. Suppose the algorithm starts with $V_0[s] = 0$ for all states s.

The values of V_1, V_2, and V_3 (to one decimal point) for these nine cells is

0	0	−0.1
0	10	−0.1
0	0	−0.1

0	6.3	−0.1
6.3	9.8	6.2
0	6.3	−0.1

4.5	6.2	4.4
6.2	9.7	6.6
4.5	6.1	4.4

After the first step of value iteration, the nodes get their immediate expected reward. The center node in this figure is the $+10$ reward state. The right nodes have a value of $−0.1$, with the optimal actions being up, left, and down; each of these has a 0.1 chance of crashing into the wall for a reward of $−1$.

The middle grid shows V_2, the values after the second step of value iteration. Consider the node that is immediately to the left of the $+10$ rewarding state. Its optimal value is to go to the right; it has a 0.7 chance of getting a reward of 10 in the following state, so that is worth 9 (10 times the discount of 0.9) to it now. The expected reward for the other possible resulting states is 0. Thus, the value of this state is $0.7 \times 9 = 6.3$.

Consider the node immediately to the right of the +10 rewarding state after the second step of value iteration. The agent's optimal action in this state is to go left. The value of this state is

Prob	Reward		Future Value	
0.7 × (	0	+	0.9 × 10)	*Agent goes left*
+ 0.1 × (	0	+	0.9 × −0.1)	*Agent goes up*
+ 0.1 × (	−1	+	0.9 × −0.1)	*Agent goes right*
+ 0.1 × (	0	+	0.9 × −0.1)	*Agent goes down*

which evaluates to 6.173.

Notice also how the +10 reward state now has a value less than 10. This is because the agent gets flung to one of the corners and these corners look bad at this stage.

After the next step of value iteration, shown on the right-hand side of the figure, the effect of the +10 reward has progressed one more step. In particular, the corners shown get values that indicate a reward in 3 steps.

An applet is available on the book web site showing the details of value iteration for this example.

The value iteration algorithm of Figure 9.14 has an array for each stage, but it really only must store the current and the previous arrays. It can update one array based on values from the other.

A common refinement of this algorithm is **asynchronous value iteration**. Rather than sweeping through the states to create a new value function, asynchronous value iteration updates the states one at a time, in any order, and store the values in a single array. Asynchronous value iteration can store either the $Q[s,a]$ array or the $V[s]$ array. Figure 9.15 shows asynchronous value iteration when the Q array is stored. It converges faster and uses less space than value iteration and is the basis of some of the algorithms for reinforcement learning (page 463). Termination can be difficult to determine if the agent must guarantee a particular error, unless it is careful about how the actions and states are selected. Often, this procedure is run indefinitely and is always prepared to give its best estimate of the optimal action in a state when asked.

Asynchronous value iteration could also be implemented by storing just the $V[s]$ array. In that case, the algorithm selects a state s and carries out the update:

$$V[s] = \max_a \sum_{s'} P(s'|s,a)(R(s,a,s') + \gamma V[s']).$$

Although this variant stores less information, it is more difficult to extract the policy. It requires one extra backup to determine which action a results in the maximum value. This can be done using

$$\pi[s] = \arg\max_a \sum_{s'} P(s'|s,a)(R(s,a,s') + \gamma V[s']).$$

1: **procedure** *Asynchronous_Value_Iteration(S, A, P, R)*
2:     **Inputs**
3:         S is the set of all states
4:         A is the set of all actions
5:         P is state transition function specifying $P(s'|s, a)$
6:         R is a reward function $R(s, a, s')$
7:     **Output**
8:         $\pi[s]$ approximately optimal policy
9:         $Q[S, A]$ value function
10:     **Local**
11:         real array $Q[S, A]$
12:         action array $\pi[S]$
13:     assign $Q[S, A]$ arbitrarily
14:     **repeat**
15:         select a state s
16:         select an action a
17:         $Q[s, a] = \sum_{s'} P(s'|s, a)(R(s, a, s') + \gamma \max_{a'} Q[s', a'])$
18:     **until** termination
19:     **for each** state s **do**
20:         $\pi[s] = \arg\max_a Q[s, a]$
21:     **return** π, Q

Figure 9.15: Asynchronous value iteration for MDPs

Example 9.27 In Example 9.26 (page 405), the state one step up and one step to the left of the +10 reward state only had its value updated after three value iterations, in which each iteration involved a sweep through all of the states.

In asynchronous value iteration, the +10 reward state can be chosen first. Then the node to its left can be chosen, and its value will be $0.7 \times 0.9 \times 10 = 6.3$. Then the node above that node could be chosen, and its value would become $0.7 \times 0.9 \times 6.3 = 3.969$. Note that it has a value that reflects that it is close to a +10 reward after considering 3 states, not 300 states, as does value iteration.

9.5.4 Policy Iteration

Policy iteration starts with a policy and iteratively improves it. It starts with an arbitrary policy π_0 (an approximation to the optimal policy works best) and carries out the following steps starting from $i = 0$.

- Policy evaluation: determine $V^{\pi_i}(S)$. The definition of V^π is a set of $|S|$ linear equations in $|S|$ unknowns. The unknowns are the values of $V^{\pi_i}(S)$. There is an equation for each state. These equations can be solved by a linear

```
 1: procedure Policy_Iteration(S, A, P, R)
 2:     Inputs
 3:         S is the set of all states
 4:         A is the set of all actions
 5:         P is state transition function specifying P(s'|s, a)
 6:         R is a reward function R(s, a, s')
 7:     Output
 8:         optimal policy π
 9:     Local
10:         action array π[S]
11:         Boolean variable noChange
12:         real array V[S]
13:     set π arbitrarily
14:     repeat
15:         noChange ← true
16:         Solve V[s] = ∑_{s'∈S} P(s'|s, π[s])(R(s, a, s') + γV[s'])
17:         for each s ∈ S do
18:             Let QBest = V[s]
19:             for each a ∈ A do
20:                 Let Qsa = ∑_{s'∈S} P(s'|s, a)(R(s, a, s') + γV[s'])
21:                 if Qsa > QBest then
22:                     π[s] ← a
23:                     QBest ← Qsa
24:                     noChange ← false
25:     until noChange
26:     return π
```

Figure 9.16: Policy iteration for MDPs

equation solution method (such as Gaussian elimination) or they can be solved iteratively.

- Policy improvement: choose $\pi_{i+1}(s) = \arg\max_a Q^{\pi_i}(s, a)$, where the Q-value can be obtained from V using Equation (9.2) (page 403). To detect when the algorithm has converged, it should only change the policy if the new action for some state improves the expected value; that is, it should set $\pi_{i+1}(s)$ to be $\pi_i(s)$ if $\pi_i(s)$ is one of the actions that maximizes $Q^{\pi_i}(s, a)$.

- Stop if there is no change in the policy – that is, if $\pi_{i+1} = \pi_i$ – otherwise increment i and repeat.

The algorithm is shown in Figure 9.16. Note that it only keeps the latest policy and notices if it has changed. This algorithm always halts, usually in a small number of iterations. Unfortunately, solving the set of linear equations is often time consuming.

A variant of policy iteration, called **modified policy iteration**, is obtained by noticing that the agent is not required to evaluate the policy to improve it; it can just carry out a number of backup steps [using Equation (9.2) (page 403)] and then do an improvement.

The idea behind policy iteration is also useful for systems that are too big to be represented directly as MDPs. Suppose a controller has some parameters that can be varied. An estimate of the derivative of the cumulative discounted reward of a parameter a in some context s, which corresponds to the derivative of $Q(a, s)$, can be used to improve the parameter. Such an iteratively improving controller can get into a local maximum that is not a global maximum. Policy iteration for MDPs does not result in non-optimal local maxima, because it is possible to improve an action for a state without affecting other states, whereas updating parameters can affect many states at once.

9.5.5 Dynamic Decision Networks

The MDP is a state-based representation. In this section, we consider a feature-based extension of MDPs, which forms the basis for what is known as **decision-theoretic planning**.

The representation of a **dynamic decision network** (DDN) can be seen in a number of different ways:

- a factored representation of MDPs, where the states are described in terms of features;

- an extension of decision networks to allow repeated structure for ongoing actions and state changes;

- an extension of dynamic belief networks (page 272) to include actions and rewards; and

- an extension of the feature-based representation of actions (page 353) to allow for uncertainty in the effect of actions.

A fully observable dynamic decision network consists of

- a set of state features, each with a domain;

- a set of possible actions forming a decision node A, with domain the set of actions;

- a two-stage belief network with an action node A, nodes F_0 and F_1 for each feature F (for the features at time 0 and time 1, respectively), and a conditional probability $P(F_1|parents(F_1))$ such that the parents of F_1 can include A and features at times 0 and 1 as long as the resulting network is acyclic; and

- a reward function that can be a function of the action and any of the features at times 0 or 1.

As in a dynamic belief network, the features at time 1 can be replicated for each subsequent time.

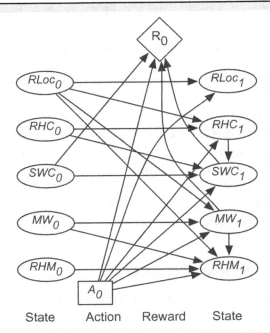

Figure 9.17: Dynamic decision network showing the two-stage belief network and the reward structure

Example 9.28 Consider representing a stochastic version of Example 8.1 (page 350) as a dynamic decision network. We use the same features as in that example.

The parents of $RLoc_1$ are $Rloc_0$ and A. The parents of RHC_1 are RHC_0, A, and $RLoc_0$; whether the robot has coffee depends on whether it had coffee before, what action it performed, and its location.

The parents of SWC_1 include SWC_0, RHC_0, A, and $RLoc_0$. You would not expect RHC_1 and SWC_1 to be independent because they both depend on whether or not the coffee was successfully delivered. This could be modeled by having one be a parent of the other. The two-stage belief network of how the state variables at time 1 depends on the action and the other state variables is shown in Figure 9.17. This figure also shows the reward as a function of the action, whether Sam stopped wanting coffee, and whether there is mail waiting.

An alternative way to model the dependence between RHC_1 and SWC_1 is to introduce a new variable, CSD_1, which represents whether coffee was successfully delivered at time 1. This variable is a parent of both RHC_1 and SWC_1. Whether Sam wants coffee is a function of whether Sam wanted coffee before and whether coffee was successfully delivered. Whether the robot has coffee depends on the action and the location, to model the robot picking up coffee. Similarly, the dependence between MW_1 and RHM_1 can be modeled by introducing a variable MPU_1, which represents whether the mail was successfully picked up. The resulting DDN replicated to a horizon of 2, but omitting the reward, is shown in Figure 9.18.

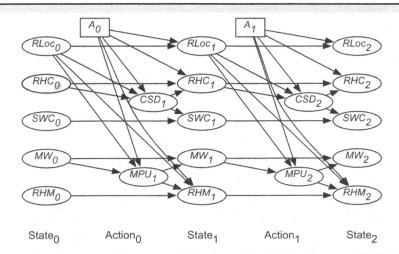

Figure 9.18: Dynamic decision network with intermediate variables for a horizon of 2, omitting the reward nodes

As part of such a decision network, we should also model the information available to the actions and the rewards. In a **fully observable dynamic decision network**, the parents of the action are all the previous state variables. Because this can be inferred, the arcs are typically not explicitly drawn. If the reward comes only at the end, variable elimination for decision networks, shown in Figure 9.11 (page 393), can be applied directly. Note that we do not require the no-forgetting condition for this to work; the fully observable condition suffices. If rewards are accrued at each time step, the algorithm must be augmented to allow for the addition of rewards. See Exercise 9.12 (page 418).

9.5.6 Partially Observable Decision Processes

A **partially observable Markov decision process (POMDP)** is a combination of an MDP (page 399) and a hidden Markov model (page 267). Instead of assuming that the state is observable, we assume that there are some partial and/or noisy observations of the state that the agent gets to observe before it has to act.

A POMDP consists of the following:

- S, a set of states of the world;
- A, a set of actions;
- O, a set of possible observations;
- $P(S_0)$, which gives the probability distribution of the starting state;
- $P(S'|S,A)$, which specifies the dynamics – the probability of getting to state S' by doing action A from state S;
- $R(S,A,S')$, which gives the expected reward of starting in state S, doing action A, and transitioning to state S'; and
- $P(O|S)$, which gives the probability of observing O given the state is S.

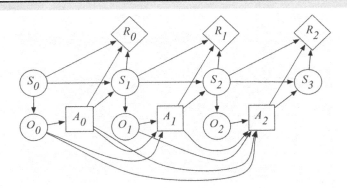

Figure 9.19: A POMDP as a dynamic decision network

A finite part of a POMDP can be depicted using the decision diagram as in Figure 9.19.

There are three main ways to approach the problem of computing the optimal policy for a POMDP:

- Solve the associated dynamic decision network using variable elimination for decision networks [Figure 9.11 (page 393), extended to include discounted rewards]. The policy created is a function of the history of the agent (page 48). The problem with this approach is that the history is unbounded, and the number of possible histories is exponential in the planning horizon.

- Make the policy a function of the belief state – a probability distribution over the states. Maintaining the belief state is the problem of filtering (page 267). The problem with this approach is that, with n states, the set of belief states is an $(n-1)$-dimensional real space. However, because the value of a sequence of actions only depends on the states, the expected value is a linear function of the values of the states. Because plans can be conditional on observations, and we only consider optimal actions for any belief state, the optimal policy for any finite look-ahead, is piecewise linear and convex.

- Search over the space of controllers for the best controller (page 48). Thus, the agent searches over what to remember and what to do based on its belief state and observations. Note that the first two proposals are instances of this approach: the agent remembers all of its history or the agent has a belief state that is a probability distribution over possible states. In general, the agent may want to remember some parts of its history but have probabilities over some other features. Because it is unconstrained over what to remember, the search space is enormous.

9.6   Review

- Utility is a measure of preference that combines with probability.
- A decision network can represent a finite stage partially observable sequential decision problem in terms or features.

- An MDP can represent an infinite stage or indefinite stage sequential decision problem in terms of states.
- A fully observable MDP can be solved with value iteration or policy iteration.
- A dynamic decision network allows for the representation of an MDP in terms of features.

9.7 References and Further Reading

Utility theory, as presented here, was invented by Neumann and Morgenstern [1953] and was further developed by Savage [1972]. Keeney and Raiffa [1976] discuss utility theory, concentrating on multiattribute (feature-based) utility functions. For work on graphical models of utility, see Bacchus and Grove [1995] and Boutilier, Brafman, Domshlak, Hoos, and Poole [2004]. For a recent survey, see Walsh [2007].

Decision networks or influence diagrams were invented by Howard and Matheson [1984]. A method using dynamic programming for solving influence diagrams can be found in Shachter and Peot [1992]. The value of information and control is discussed by Matheson [1990].

MDPs were invented by Bellman [1957] and are discussed by Puterman [1994] and Bertsekas [1995]. See Boutilier, Dean, and Hanks [1999] for a review of lifting MDPs to features known as decision-theoretic planning.

9.8 Exercises

Exercise 9.1 Students have to make decisions about how much to study for each course. The aim of this question is to investigate how to use decision networks to help them make such decisions.

Suppose students first have to decide how much to study for the midterm. They can study a lot, study a little, or not study at all. Whether they pass the midterm depends on how much they study and on the difficulty of the course. As a first-order approximation, they pass if they study hard or if the course is easy and they study a bit. After receiving their midterm grade, they have to decide how much to study for the final exam. Again, the final exam result depends on how much they study and on the difficulty of the course. Their final grade depends on which exams they pass; generally they get an A if they pass both exams, a B if they only pass the final, a C if they only pass the midterm, or an F if they fail both. Of course, there is a great deal of noise in these general estimates.

Suppose that their final utility depends on their total effort and their final grade. Suppose the total effort is obtained by adding the effort in studying for the midterm and the final.

(a) Draw a decision network for a student decision based on the preceding story.
(b) What is the domain of each variable?
(c) Give appropriate conditional probability tables.

(d) What is the best outcome (give this a utility of 100) and what is the worst outcome (give this a utility of 0)?

(e) Give an appropriate utility function for a student who just wants to pass (not get an F). What is an optimal policy for this student?

(f) Give an appropriate utility function for a student who wants to do really well. What is an optimal policy for this student?

Exercise 9.2 Consider the following decision network:

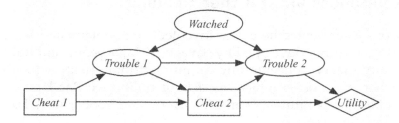

This diagram models a decision about whether to cheat at two different time instances.

Suppose $P(watched) = 0.4$, $P(trouble1|cheat1, watched) = 0.8$, and *Trouble1* is true with probability 0 for the other cases. Suppose the conditional probability $P(Trouble2|Cheat2, Trouble1, Watched)$ is given by the following table:

Cheat2	Trouble1	Watched	$P(Trouble2 = t)$
t	t	t	1.0
t	t	f	0.3
t	f	t	0.8
t	f	f	0.0
f	t	t	0.3
f	t	f	0.3
f	f	t	0.0
f	f	f	0.0

Suppose the utility is given by

Trouble2	Cheat2	Utility
t	t	30
t	f	0
f	t	100
f	f	70

(a) What is an optimal decision function for the variable *Cheat2*? Show what factors are created. Please try to do it by hand, and then check it with the AIspace.org applet.

(b) What is an optimal policy? What is the value of an optimal policy? Show the tables created.

(c) What is an optimal policy if the probability of being watched goes up?

(d) What is an optimal policy when the rewards for cheating are reduced?

(e) What is an optimal policy when the instructor is less forgiving (or less forgetful) of previous cheating?

Exercise 9.3 Suppose that, in a decision network, the decision variable *Run* has parents *Look* and *See*. Suppose you are using VE to find an optimal policy and, after eliminating all of the other variables, you are left with the factor

Look	See	Run	Value
true	true	yes	23
true	true	no	8
true	false	yes	37
true	false	no	56
false	true	yes	28
false	true	no	12
false	false	yes	18
false	false	no	22

(a) What is the resulting factor after eliminating *Run*? [Hint: You do not sum out *Run* because it is a decision variable.]

(b) What is the optimal decision function for *Run*?

Exercise 9.4 Suppose that, in a decision network, there were arcs from random variables "contaminated specimen" and "positive test" to the decision variable "discard sample." Sally solved the decision network and discovered that there was a unique optimal policy:

contaminated specimen	positive test	discard sample
true	true	yes
true	false	no
false	true	yes
false	false	no

What can you say about the value of information in this case?

Exercise 9.5 How sensitive are the answers from the decision network of Example 9.13 (page 389) to the probabilities? Test the program with different conditional probabilities and see what effect this has on the answers produced. Discuss the sensitivity both to the optimal policy and to the expected value of the optimal policy.

Exercise 9.6 In Example 9.13 (page 389), suppose that the fire sensor was noisy in that it had a 20% false-positive rate,

$$P(see\_smoke|report \land \neg smoke) = 0.2,$$

and a 15% false negative-rate:

$$P(see\_smoke|report \land smoke) = 0.85.$$

Is it still worthwhile to check for smoke?

Exercise 9.7 Consider the belief network of Exercise 6.8 (page 278). When an alarm is observed, a decision is made whether to shut down the reactor. Shutting down the reactor has a cost c_s associated with it (independent of whether the core was overheating), whereas not shutting down an overheated core incurs a cost c_m that is much higher than c_s.

(a) Draw the decision network to model this decision problem for the original system (i.e., with only one sensor).

(b) Specify the tables for all new factors that must be defined (you should use the parameters c_s and c_m where appropriate in the tables). Assume that the *utility* is the negative of *cost*.

Exercise 9.8 Explain why we often use discounting of future rewards in MDPs. How would an agent act differently if the discount factor was 0.6 as opposed to 0.9?

Exercise 9.9

Consider a game world:

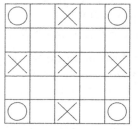

The robot can be at one of the 25 locations on the grid. There can be a treasure on one of the circles at the corners. When the robot reaches the corner where the treasure is, it collects a reward of 10, and the treasure disappears. When there is no treasure, at each time step, there is a probability $P_1 = 0.2$ that a treasure appears, and it appears with equal probability at each corner. The robot knows its position and the location of the treasure.

There are monsters at the squares marked with an X. Each monster randomly and independently, at each time step, checks if the robot is on its square. If the robot is on the square when the monster checks, it has a reward of -10 (i.e., it loses 10 points). At the center point, the monster checks at each time step with probability $p_2 = 0.4$; at the other 4 squares marked with an X, the monsters check at each time step with probability $p_3 = 0.2$.

Assume that the rewards are immediate upon entering a state: that is, if the robot enters a state with a monster, it gets the (negative) reward on entering the state, and if the robot enters the state with a treasure, it gets the reward upon entering the state, even if the treasure arrives at the same time.

The robot has 8 actions corresponding to the 8 neighboring squares. The diagonal moves are noisy; there is a $p_4 = 0.6$ probability of going in the direction chosen and an equal chance of going to each of the four neighboring squares closest to the desired direction. The vertical and horizontal moves are also noisy; there is a $p_5 = 0.8$ chance of going in the requested direction and an equal chance of going to one of the adjacent diagonal squares. For example, the actions up-left and up have the following result:

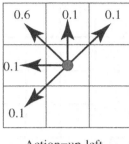 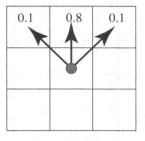

Action=up-left   Action=up

If the action would result in crashing into a wall, the robot has a reward of -2 (i.e., loses 2) and does not move.

There is a discount factor of $p_6 = 0.9$.

(a) How many states are there? (Or how few states can you get away with?) What do they represent?

(b) What is an optimal policy?

(c) Suppose the game designer wants to design different instances of the game that have non-obvious optimal policies for a game player. Give three assignments to the parameters p_1 to p_6 with different optimal policies. If there are not that many different optimal policies, give as many as there are and explain why there are no more than that.

Exercise 9.10 Consider a 5×5 grid game similar to the game of the previous question. The agent can be at one of the 25 locations, and there can be a treasure at one of the corners or no treasure.

In this game the "up" action has dynamics given by the following diagram:

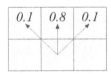

That is, the agent goes up with probability 0.8 and goes up-left with probability 0.1 and up-right with probability 0.1.

If there is no treasure, a treasure can appear with probability 0.2. When it appears, it appears randomly at one of the corners, and each corner has an equal probability of treasure appearing. The treasure stays where it is until the agent lands on the square where the treasure is. When this occurs the agent gets an immediate reward of $+10$ and the treasure disappears in the next state transition. The agent and the treasure move simultaneously so that if the agent arrives at a square at the same time the treasure appears, it gets the reward.

Suppose we are doing asynchronous value iteration and have the value for each state as in the following grid. The numbers in the square represent the value of that state and empty squares have a value of zero. It is irrelevant to this question how these values got there.

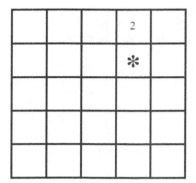 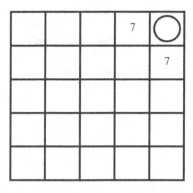

The left grid shows the values for the states where there is no treasure and the right grid shows the values of the states when there is a treasure at the top-right corner. There are also states for the treasures at the other three corners, but you assume that the current values for these states are all zero.

Consider the next step of asynchronous value iteration. For state s_{13}, which is marked by $*$ in the figure, and the action a_2, which is "up," what value is assigned to $Q[s_{13}, a_2]$ on the next value iteration? You must show all work but do not have to do any arithmetic (i.e., leave it as an expression). Explain each term in your expression.

Exercise 9.11 In a decision network, suppose that there are multiple utility nodes, where the values must be added. This lets us represent a generalized additive utility function. How can the VE for decision networks algorithm, shown in Figure 9.11 (page 393), be altered to include such utilities?

Exercise 9.12 How can variable elimination for decision networks, shown in Figure 9.11 (page 393), be modified to include additive discounted rewards? That is, there can be multiple utility (reward) nodes, having to be added and discounted. Assume that the variables to be eliminated are eliminated from the latest time step forward.

Exercise 9.13 This is a continuation of Exercise 6.8 (page 278).

(a) When an alarm is observed, a decision is made whether to shut down the reactor. Shutting down the reactor has a cost c_s associated with it (independent of whether the core was overheating), whereas not shutting down an overheated core incurs a cost c_m, which is much higher than c_s. Draw the decision network modeling this decision problem for the original system (i.e., only one sensor). Specify any new tables that must be defined (you should use the parameters c_s and c_m where appropriate in the tables). You can assume that the *utility* is the negative of *cost*.

(b) For the decision network in the previous part, determine the expected utility of shutting down the reactor versus not shutting it down when an alarm goes off. For each variable eliminated, show which variable is eliminated, how it is eliminated (through summing or maximization), which factors are removed, what factor is created, and what variables this factor is over. You are not required to give the tables.

Exercise 9.14 One of the decisions we must make in real life is whether to accept an invitation even though we are not sure we can or want to go to an event. The following figure represents a decision network for such a problem:

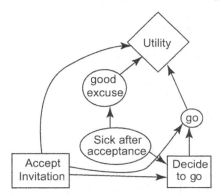

Suppose that all of the decision and random variables are Boolean (i.e., have domain {*true, false*}). You can accept the invitation, but when the time comes, you still must decide whether or not to go. You might get sick in between accepting the invitation and having to decide to go. Even if you decide to go, if you haven't accepted the invitation you may not be able to go. If you get sick, you have a good excuse not to go. Your utility depends on whether you accept, whether you have a good excuse, and whether you actually go.

(a) Give a table representing a possible utility function. Assume the unique best outcome is that you accept the invitation, you don't have a good excuse, but you do go. The unique worst outcome is that you accept the invitation, you don't have a good excuse, and you don't go. Make your other utility values reasonable.

(b) Suppose that that you get to observe whether you are sick before accepting the invitation. Note that this is a different variable than if you are sick after accepting the invitation. Add to the network so that this situation can be modeled. You must not change the utility function, but the new observation must have a positive value of information. The resulting network must be one for which the decision network solving algorithm works.

(c) Suppose that, after you have decided whether to accept the original invitation and before you decide to go, you can find out if you get a better invitation (to an event that clashes with the original event, so you cannot go to both). Suppose you would rather go to the better invitation than go to the original event you were invited to. (The difficult decision is whether to accept the first invitation or wait until you get a better invitation, which you may not get.) Unfortunately, having another invitation does not provide a good excuse. On the network, add the node "better invitation" and all relevant arcs to model this situation. [You do not have to include the node and arcs from part (b).]

(d) If you have an arc between "better invitation" and "accept invitation" in part (c), explain why (i.e., what must the world be like to make this arc appropriate). If you did not have such an arc, which way could it go to still fit the preceding story; explain what must happen in the world to make this arc appropriate.

(e) If there was no arc between "better invitation" and "accept invitation" (whether or not you drew such an arc), what must be true in the world to make this lack of arc appropriate.

Exercise 9.15 Consider the following decision network:

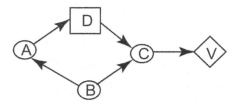

(a) What are the initial factors. (You do not have to give the tables; just give what variables they depend on.)

(b) Show what factors are created when optimizing the decision function and computing the expected value, for one of the legal elimination orderings. At each step explain which variable is being eliminated, whether it is being summed out or maximized, what factors are being combined, and what factors are created (give the variables they depend on, not the tables).

(c) If the value of information of A at decision D is zero, what does an optimal policy look like? (Please give the most specific statement you can make about any optimal policy.)

Exercise 9.16 What is the main difference between asynchronous value iteration and standard value iteration? Why does asynchronous value iteration often work better than standard value iteration?

Exercise 9.17 Consider a grid world where the action "up" has the following dynamics:

0.1	0.8	0.1

That is, it goes up with probability 0.8, up-left with probability 0.1, and up-right with probability 0.1. Suppose we have the following states:

s_{12}	s_{13}	s_{14}
s_{17}	s_{18}	s_{19}

There is a reward of $+10$ upon entering state s_{14}, and a reward of -5 upon entering state s_{19}. All other rewards are 0.

The discount is 0.9.

Suppose we are doing asynchronous value iteration, storing $Q[S, A]$, and we have the following values for these states:

$$V(s_{12}) = 5 \quad V(s_{13}) = 7 \quad V(s_{14}) = -3$$
$$V(s_{17}) = 2 \quad V(s_{18}) = 4 \quad V(s_{19}) = -6$$

Suppose, in the next step of asynchronous value iteration, we select state s_{18} and action up. What is the resulting updated value for $Q[s_{18}, up]$? Give the numerical formula, but do not evaluate or simplify it.

Chapter 10

Multiagent Systems

Imagine a personal software agent engaging in electronic commerce on your behalf. Say the task of this agent is to track goods available for sale in various online venues over time, and to purchase some of them on your behalf for an attractive price. In order to be successful, your agent will need to embody your preferences for products, your budget, and in general your knowledge about the environment in which it will operate. Moreover, the agent will need to embody your knowledge of other similar agents with which it will interact (e.g., agents who might compete with it in an auction, or agents representing store owners) – including their own preferences and knowledge. A collection of such agents forms a multiagent system.

– Yoav Shoham and Kevin Leyton-Brown [2008, page xvii]

What should an agent do when there are other agents, with their own values, who are also reasoning about what to do? An intelligent agent should not ignore other agents or treat them as noise in the environment. We consider the problems of determining what an agent should do given a mechanism that specifies how the world works, and of designing a mechanism that has useful properties.

10.1 Multiagent Framework

In this chapter, we consider the case in which there are multiple agents, where

- the agents can act autonomously, each with its own information about the world and the other agents.

- the outcome depends on the actions of all of the agents. A **mechanism** specifies how the actions of the agents lead to outcomes.
- each agent can have its own utility that depends on the outcome.

Each agent decides what to do based on its own utilities, but it also has to interact with other agents. An agent acts **strategically** when it decides what to do based on its goals or utilities.

Sometimes we treat **nature** as an agent. Nature is defined as being a special agent that does not have values and does not act strategically. It just acts, perhaps stochastically. Nature may be seen as including of all of the agents that are not acting strategically. In terms of the agent architecture shown in Figure 1.3 (page 11), nature and the other agents form the environment for an agent. A strategic agent cannot treat other strategic agents as part of nature because it should reason about their utility and actions, and because the other agents are perhaps available to cooperate and negotiate with.

There are two extremes in the study of multiagent systems:

- fully **cooperative**, where the agents share the same utility function, and
- fully **competitive**, when one agent can only win when another loses. These are often called **zero-sum games** when the utility can be expressed in a form such that the sum of the utilities for the agents is zero for every outcome.

Most interactions are between these two extremes, where the agents' utilities are synergistic in some aspects, competing in some, and other aspects are independent. For example, two commercial agents with stores next door to each other may both share the goal of having the street area clean and inviting; they may compete for customers, but may have no preferences about the details of the other agent's store. Sometimes their actions do not interfere with each other, and sometimes they do. Often agents can be better off if they coordinate their actions through cooperation and negotiation.

Multiagent interactions have mostly been studied using the terminology of games following the seminal work of Neumann and Morgenstern [1953]. Many issues of interaction between agents can be studied in terms of games. Even quite small games can highlight deep issues. However, the study of games is meant to be about general multiagent interactions, not just artificial games.

Multiagent systems are ubiquitous in artificial intelligence. From parlor games such as checkers, chess, backgammon, and Go, to robot soccer, to interactive computer games, to having agents that act in complex economic systems, games are integral to AI. Games were one of the first applications of AI. One of the first reinforcement learning systems was for the game of checkers by Samuel [1959], with the first operating checkers program dating back to 1952. There was great fanfare when Deep Blue beat the world chess champion in 1997. Computers have also been successful at checkers and backgammon, but less so in the game Go because of the size of the search space and the availability of good heuristics. Although large, these games are conceptually simple because the agents can observe the state of the world (they are fully observable). In most real-world interactions, the state of the world is not observable.

There is now much interest in partially observable games like poker, where the environment is predictable (even if stochastic), and robot soccer, where the environment is not very predictable. But all of these games are much simpler than the multiagent interactions people perform in their daily lives, let alone the strategizing needed for bartering in marketplaces or on the Internet, where the rules are less well defined and the utilities are much more multifaceted.

10.2 Representations of Games

To be able to reason about a multiagent interaction, we represent the options available to the agents and the payoffs for their actions. There are many representation schemes for games, and multiagent interactions in general, that have been proposed in economics and AI. In AI, these representation schemes typically try to represent some aspect of games that can be exploited for computational gain.

We present three representations; two of these are classic representations from economics. The first abstracts away all structure of the policies of the agents. The second models the sequential structure of games and is the foundation for much work on representing board games. The third representation moves away from the state-based representation to allow the representation of games in terms of features.

10.2.1 Normal Form of a Game

The most basic representation of games is the **strategic form of a game** or a **normal-form game**. The strategic form of a game consists of

- a finite set I of agents, typically identified with the integers $I = \{1, \ldots, n\}$.
- a set of actions A for each agent $i \in I$. An assignment of an action in A_i to each agent $i \in I$ is an **action profile**. We can view an action profile as a tuple $\langle a_1, \ldots, a_n \rangle$, which specifies that agent i carries out action a_i.
- a utility function u_i for each agent $i \in I$ that, given an action profile, returns the expected utility for agent i given the action profile.

The joint action of all the agents (an action profile) produces an **outcome**. Each agent has a utility over each outcome. The utility for an agent is meant to encompass everything that the agent is interested in, including fairness and societal well-being. Thus, we assume that each agent is trying to maximize its own utility, without reference to the utility of other agents.

Example 10.1   The game rock-paper-scissors is a common game played by children, and there is even a world championship of rock-paper-scissors. Suppose there are two agents (players), Alice and Bob. There are three actions for each agent, so that

$$A_{Alice} = A_{Bob} = \{rock, paper, scissors\}.$$

		Bob		
		rock	*paper*	*scissors*
Alice	*rock*	0,0	−1,1	1,−1
	paper	1,−1	0,0	−1,1
	scissors	−1,1	1,−1	0,0

Figure 10.1: Strategic form for the rock-paper-scissors game

For each combination of an action for Alice and an action for Bob there is a utility for Alice and a utility for Bob. This is often drawn in a table as in Figure 10.1. This is called a **payoff matrix**. Alice chooses a row and Bob chooses a column, simultaneously. This gives a pair of numbers: the first number is the payoff to the row player (Alice) and the second gives the payoff to the column player (Bob). Note that the utility for each of them depends on what both players do. An example of an action profile is $\langle scissors_{Alice}, rock_{Bob}\rangle$, where Alice chooses scissors and Bob chooses rock. In this action profile, Alice receives the utility of −1 and Bob receives the utility of 1. This game is a zero-sum game because one person wins only when the other loses.

This representation of a game may seem very restricted, because it only gives a one-off payoff for each agent based on single actions, chosen simultaneously, for each agent. However, the interpretation of an action in the definition is very general.

Typically, an "action" is not just a simple choice, but a **strategy**: a specification of what the agent will do under the various contingencies. The normal form, essentially, is a specification of the utilities given the possible strategies of the agents. This is why it is called the strategic form of a game.

In general, the "action" in the definition of a normal-form game can be a **controller** (page 48) for the agent. Thus, each agent chooses a controller and the utility gives the expected outcome of the controllers run for each agent in an environment. Although the examples that follow are for simple actions, the general case has an enormous number of possible actions (possible controllers) for each agent.

10.2.2   Extensive Form of a Game

Whereas the normal form of a game represents controllers as single units, it if often more natural to specify the unfolding of a game through time. The extensive form of a game is an extension of a single-agent **decision tree** (page 382). We first give a definition that assumes the game is fully observable (called *perfect information* in game theory).

A **perfect information game** in **extensive form** or a **game tree** is a finite tree where the nodes are states and the arcs correspond to actions by the agents. In particular:

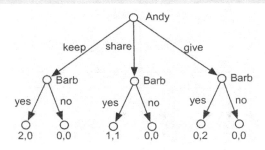

Figure 10.2: Extensive form of the sharing game

- Each internal node is labeled with an agent (or with *nature*). The agent is said to control the node.
- Each arc out of a node labeled with agent i corresponds to an action for agent i.
- Each internal node labeled with *nature* has a probability distribution over its children.
- The leaves represent final outcomes and are labeled with a utility for each agent.

The extensive form of a game specifies a particular unfolding of the game. Each path to a leaf, called a **run**, specifies one particular way that the game could proceed depending on the choices of the agents and nature.

A pure **strategy** for agent i is a function from nodes controlled by agent i into actions. That is, a pure strategy selects a child for each node that agent i controls. A **strategy profile** consists of a strategy for each agent.

Example 10.2 Consider a sharing game where there are two agents, Andy and Barb, and there are two identical items to be divided between them. Andy first selects how they will be divided: Andy keeps both items, they share and each person gets one item, or he gives both items to Barb. Then Barb gets to either reject the allocation and they both get nothing, or accept the allocation and they both get the allocated amount.

The extensive form of the sharing game is shown in Figure 10.2. Andy has 3 strategies. Barb has 8 pure strategies; one for each combination of assignments to the nodes she controls. As a result, there are 24 strategy profiles.

Given a strategy profile, each node has a utility for each agent. The utility for an agent at a node is defined recursively from the bottom up:

- The utility for each agent at a leaf is given as part of the leaf.
- The utility for agent j of a node controlled by agent i is the utility for agent j of the child node that is selected by agent i's strategy.
- The utility for agent i for a node controlled by nature is the expected value of the utility for agent i of the children. That is, $u_i(n) = \sum_c P(c)u_i(c)$, where the sum is over the children c of node n, and $P(c)$ is the probability that nature will choose child c.

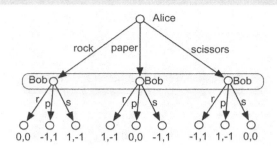

Figure 10.3: Extensive form of the rock-paper-scissors game

Example 10.3   In the sharing game, suppose we have the following strategy profile: Andy chooses *keep* and Barb chooses *no, yes, yes* for each of the nodes she gets to choose for. Under this strategy profile, the utility for Andy at the leftmost internal node is 0, the utility for Andy at the center internal node is 1, and the utility for Andy at the rightmost internal node is 0. The utility for Andy at the root is 0.

The preceding definition of the extensive form of a game assumes that the agents can observe the state of the world (i.e., they know what node they are at each step). This means that the state of the game must be fully observable. In a **partially observable game** or an **imperfect information game**, the agents do not necessarily know the state of the game. To model these games in an extensive form, we introduce the notion of information sets. An **information set** is a set of nodes, all controlled by the same agent and all with the same set of available actions. The idea is that the agent cannot distinguish the elements of the information set. The agent only knows the game state is at one of the nodes of the information set, not which node. In a strategy, the agent chooses one action for each information set; the same action is carried out at each node in the information set. Thus, in the extensive form, a strategy specifies a function from information sets to actions.

Example 10.4   Figure 10.3 gives the extensive form for the rock-paper-scissors game of Example 10.1 (page 425). The elements of the information set are in a rounded rectangle. Bob must choose the same action for each node in the information set.

10.2.3   Multiagent Decision Networks

The extensive form of a game can be seen as a state-based representation of a game. As we have seen before, it is often more concise to describe states in terms of features. A **multiagent decision network** is a factored representation of a multiagent decision problem. It islike a **decision network** (page 387),

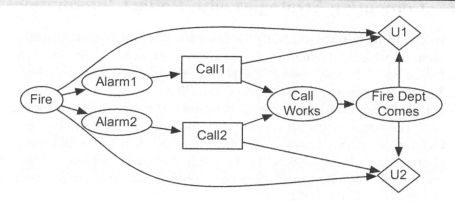

Figure 10.4: Multiagent decision network for the fire example

except that each decision node is labeled with an agent that gets to choose a value for the node. There is a utility node for each agent specifying the utility for that agent. The parents of a decision node specify the information that will be available to the agent when it has to act.

Example 10.5 Figure 10.4 gives a multiagent decision network for a fire department example. In this scenario, there are two agents, Agent 1 and Agent 2. Each has its own noisy sensor of whether there is a fire. However, if they both call, it is possible that their calls will interfere with each other and neither call will work. Agent 1 gets to choose a value for decision variable *Call*1 and can only observe the value for the variable *Alarm*1. Agent 2 gets to choose a value for decision variable *Call*2 and can only observe the value for the variable *Alarm*2. Whether the call works depends on the values of *Call*1 and *Call*2. Whether the fire department comes depends on whether the call works. Agent 1's utility depends on whether there was a fire, whether the fire department comes, and whether they called – similarly for Agent 2.

A multiagent decision network can be converted into a normal-form game; however, the number of strategies can be enormous. If a decision variable has d states and n binary parents, there are 2^n assignments of values to parents and so d^{2^n} strategies. That is just for a single decision node; more complicated networks are even bigger when converted to normal form. Therefore, the algorithms that we present that are exponential in the number of strategies are impractical for anything but the smallest multiagent decision networks.

Other representations exploit other structures in multiagent settings. For example, the utility of an agent may depend on the number of other agents who do some action, but not on their identities. An agent's utility may depend on what a few other agents do, not directly on the actions of all other agents. An agent's utility may only depend on what the agents at neighboring locations do, and not on the identity of these agents or on what other agents do.

10.3   Computing Strategies with Perfect Information

The equivalent to full observability with multiple agents is called **perfect information**. In perfect information games, agents act sequentially and, when an agent has to act, it gets to observe the state of the world before deciding what to do. Each agent acts to maximize its own utility.

A perfect information game can be represented as an extensive form game where the information sets all contain a single node. They can also be represented as a multiagent decision network where the decision nodes are totally ordered and, for each decision node, the parents of that decision node include the preceding decision node and all of their parents [i.e., they are no-forgetting decision networks (page 388)].

Perfect information games are solvable in a manner similar to fully observable single-agent systems. We can either do it backward using dynamic programming or forward using search. The difference from the single-agent case is that the multiagent algorithm maintains a utility for each agent and, for each move, it selects an action that maximizes the utility of the agent making the move. The dynamic programming variant, called **backward induction**, essentially follows the definition of the utility of a node for each agent, but, at each node, the agent who controls the node gets to choose the action that maximizes its utility.

> **Example 10.6** Consider the sharing game of Figure 10.2 (page 427). For each of the nodes labeled with Barb, she gets to choose the value that maximizes her utility. Thus, she will choose "yes" for the right two nodes she controls, and would choose either for the leftmost node she controls. Suppose she chooses "no" for this node; then Andy gets to choose one of his actions: *keep* has utility 0 for him, *share* has utility 1, and *give* has utility 0, so he chooses to share.

In the case where two agents are competing so that a positive reward for one is a negative reward for the other agent, we have a two-agent **zero-sum game**. The value of such a game can be characterized by a single number that one agent is trying to maximize and the other agent is trying to minimize. Having a single value for a two-agent zero-sum game leads to a **minimax** strategy. Each node is either a MAX node, if it is controlled by the agent trying to maximize, or is a MIN node if it is controlled by the agent trying to minimize.

Backward induction can be used to find the optimal minimax strategy. From the bottom up, backward induction maximizes at MAX nodes and minimizes at MIN nodes. However, backward induction requires a traversal of the whole game tree. It is possible to prune part of the search tree by showing that some part of the tree will never be part of an optimal play.

> **Example 10.7** Consider searching in the game tree of Figure 10.5. In this figure, the square MAX nodes are controlled by the maximizing agent, and the round MIN nodes are controlled by the minimizing agent.
>
> Suppose the values of the leaf nodes are given or can be computed given the definition of the game. The numbers at the bottom show some of these values.

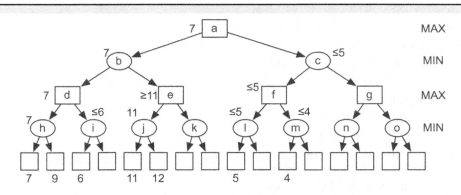

Figure 10.5: A zero-sum game tree showing which nodes can be pruned

The other values are irrelevant, as we show here. Suppose we are doing a left-first depth-first traversal of this tree. The value of node h is 7, because it is the minimum of 7 and 9. Just by considering the leftmost child of i with a value of 6, we know that the value of i is less than or equal to 6. Therefore, at node d, the maximizing agent will go left. We do not have to evaluate the other child of i. Similarly, the value of j is 11, so the value of e is at least 11, and so the minimizing agent at node b will choose to go left.

The value of l is less than or equal to 5, and the value of m is less than or equal to 4; thus, the value of f is less than or equal to 5, so the value of c will be less than or equal to 5. So, at a, the maximizing agent will choose to go left. Notice that this argument did not depend on the values of the unnumbered leaves. Moreover, it did not depend on the size of the subtree that was not explored.

The previous example analyzed what can be pruned. Minimax with **alpha-beta (α-β) pruning** is a depth-first search algorithm that prunes by passing pruning information down in terms of parameters α and β. In this depth-first search, a node has a "current" value, which has been obtained from some of its descendants. This current value can be updated as it gets more information about the value of its other descendants.

The parameter α can be used to prune MIN nodes. Initially, it is the highest current value for all MAX ancestors of the current node. Any MIN node whose current value is less than or equal to its α value does not have to be explored further. This cutoff was used to prune the other descendants of nodes l, m, and c in the previous example.

The dual is the β parameter, which can be used to prune MAX nodes.

The minimax algorithm with α-β pruning is given in Figure 10.6 (on the next page). It is called, initially, with

$$MinimaxAlphaBeta(R, -\infty, \infty),$$

where R is the root node. Note that it uses α as the current value for the MAX nodes and β as the current value for the MIN nodes.

1: **procedure** *MinimaxAlphaBeta*(N, α, β)
2:     **Inputs**
3:         N a node in a game tree
4:         α, β real numbers
5:     **Output**
6:         The value for node N
7:     **if** N is a leaf node **then**
8:         **return** value of N
9:     **else if** N is a MAX node **then**
10:        **for each** child C of N **do**
11:            Set α ← max(α, *MinimaxAlphaBeta*(C, α, β))
12:            **if** α ≥ β **then**
13:                **return** β
14:        **return** α
15:    **else**
16:        **for each** child C of N **do**
17:            Set β ← min(β, *MinimaxAlphaBeta*(C, α, β))
18:            **if** α ≥ β **then**
19:                **return** α
20:        **return** β

Figure 10.6: Minimax with α-β pruning

Example 10.8 Consider running *MinimaxAlphaBeta* on the tree of Figure 10.5. We will show the recursive calls. Initially, it calls

$$MinimaxAlphaBeta(a, -\infty, \infty),$$

which then calls, in turn,

$$MinimaxAlphaBeta(b, -\infty, \infty)$$

$$MinimaxAlphaBeta(d, -\infty, \infty)$$

$$MinimaxAlphaBeta(h, -\infty, \infty).$$

This last call finds the minimum of both of its children and returns 7. Next the procedure calls

$$MinimaxAlphaBeta(i, 7, \infty),$$

which then gets the value for the first of i's children, which has value 6. Because $\alpha \geq \beta$, it returns 6. The call to d then returns 7, and it calls

$$MinimaxAlphaBeta(e, -\infty, 7).$$

Node e's first child returns 11 and, because $\alpha \geq \beta$, it returns 11. Then b returns 7, and the call to a calls

$$MinimaxAlphaBeta(c, 7, \infty),$$

which in turn calls

$$MinimaxAlphaBeta(f, 7, \infty),$$

which eventually returns 5, and so the call to c returns 5, and the whole procedure returns 7.

By keeping track of the values, the maximizing agent knows to go left at a, then the minimizing agent will go left at b, and so on.

The amount of pruning provided by this algorithm depends on the ordering of the children of each node. It works best if a highest-valued child of a MAX node is selected first and if a lowest-valued child of a MIN node is returned first. In implementations of real games, much of the effort is made to try to ensure this outcome.

Most real games are too big to carry out minimax search, even with α-β pruning. For these games, instead of only stopping at leaf nodes, it is possible to stop at any node. The value returned at the node where the algorithm stops is an estimate of the value for this node. The function used to estimate the value is an **evaluation function**. Much work goes into finding good evaluation functions. There is a trade-off between the amount of computation required to compute the evaluation function and the size of the search space that can be explored in any given time. It is an empirical question as to the best compromise between a complex evaluation function and a large search space.

10.4 Partially Observable Multiagent Reasoning

Partial observability means that an agent does not know the state of the world or that the agents act simultaneously.

Partial observability for the multiagent case is more complicated than the fully observable multiagent case or the partially observable single-agent case. The following simple examples show some important issues that arise even in the case of two agents, each with a few choices.

Example 10.9 Consider the case of a penalty kick in soccer as depicted in Figure 10.7. If the kicker kicks to his right and the goalkeeper jumps to his right, the probability of a goal is 0.9, and similarly for the other combinations of actions, as given in the figure.

What should the kicker do, given that he wants to maximize the probability of a goal and that the goalkeeper wants to minimize the probability of a goal? The kicker could think that it is better kicking to his right, because the pair of

		goalkeeper	
		left	right
kicker	left	0.6	0.2
	right	0.3	0.9

Probability of a goal

Figure 10.7: Soccer penalty kick. The kicker can kick to his left or right. The goalkeeper can jump to his left or right.

numbers for his right kick is higher than the pair for the left. The goalkeeper could then think that if the kicker will kick right, then he should jump left. However, if the kicker thinks that the goalkeeper will jump left, he should then kick left. But then, the goalkeeper should jump right. Then the kicker should kick right.

Each agents is potentially faced with an infinite regression of reasoning about what the other agent will do. At each stage in their reasoning, the agents reverse their decision. One could imagine cutting this off at some depth; however, the actions then are purely a function of the arbitrary depth. Even worse, if the kicker knew the depth limit of reasoning for the goalkeeper, he could exploit this knowledge to determine what the kicker will do and choose his action appropriately.

An alternative is for the agents to choose actions stochastically. You could imagine that the kicker and the goalkeeper each secretly toss a coin to decide what to do. You then should think about whether the coins should be biased. Suppose that the kicker decides to kick to his right with probability p_k and that the goalkeeper decides to jump to his right with probability p_j. The probability of a goal is then

$$0.9 p_k p_j + 0.3 p_k (1 - p_j) + 0.2 (1 - p_k) p_j + 0.6 (1 - p_k)(1 - p_j).$$

Figure 10.8 shows the probability of a goal as a function of p_k. The different lines correspond to different values of p_j.

There is something special about the value $p_k = 0.4$. At this value, the probability of a goal is 0.48, independent of the value of p_j. That is, no matter what the goalkeeper does, the kicker expects to get a goal with probability 0.48. If the kicker deviates from $p_k = 0.4$, he could do better or he could do worse, depending on what the goalkeeper does.

The plot for p_j is similar, with all of the lines meeting at $p_j = 0.3$. Again, when $p_j = 0.3$, the probability of a goal is 0.48.

The strategy with $p_k = 0.4$ and $p_j = 0.3$ is special in the sense that neither agent can do better by unilaterally deviating from the strategy. However, this does not mean that they cannot do better; if one of the agents deviates from this equilibrium, the other agent can do better by deviating from the equilibrium.

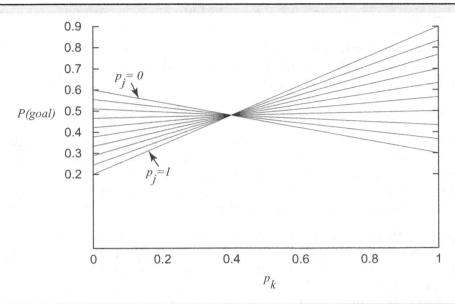

Figure 10.8: Probability of a goal as a function of action probabilities

However, this equilibrium is safe for an agent in the sense that, even if the other agent knew the agent's strategy, the other agent cannot force a worse outcome for the agent. Playing this strategy means that an agent does not have to worry about double-guessing the other agent. He will get the best payoff he can guarantee to obtain.

Let us now extend the definition of a strategy to include randomized strategies.

Consider the normal form of a game where each agent gets to choose an action simultaneously. Each agent chooses an action without knowing what the other agents choose.

A **strategy** for an agent is a probability distribution over the actions for this agent. If the agent is acting deterministically, one of the probabilities will be 1 and the rest will be 0; this is called a **pure strategy**. If the agent is not following a pure strategy, none of the probabilities will be 1, and more than one action will have a non-zero probability; this is called a **stochastic strategy**. The set of actions with a non-zero probability in a strategy is called the **support set** of the strategy.

A **strategy profile** is an assignment of a strategy to each agent. If σ is a strategy profile, let σ_i be the strategy of agent i in σ, and let σ_{-i} be the strategies of the other agents. Then σ is $\sigma_i \sigma_{-i}$. If the strategy profile is made up of pure strategies, it is often called an **action profile**, because each agent is playing a particular action.

A strategy profile σ has a utility for each agent. Let $utility(\sigma, i)$ be the utility of strategy profile σ for agent i. The utility of a stochastic strategy profile can be computed by computing the expected utility given the utilities of the basic actions that make up the profile and the probabilities of the actions.

A **best response** for an agent i to the strategies σ_{-i} of the other agents is a strategy that has maximal utility for that agent. That is, σ_i is a best response to σ_{-i} if, for all other strategies σ_i' for agent i,

$$utility(\sigma_i\sigma_{-i}, i) \geq utility(\sigma_i'\sigma_{-i}, i).$$

A strategy profile σ is a **Nash equilibrium** if, for each agent i, strategy σ_i is a best response to σ_{-i}. That is, a Nash equilibrium is a strategy profile such that no agent can be better by unilaterally deviating from that profile.

One of the great results of game theory, proved by Nash [1950], is that every finite game has at least one Nash equilibrium.

Example 10.10 In Example 10.9 (page 433), there is a unique Nash equilibrium where $p_k = 0.4$ and $p_j = 0.3$. This has the property that, if the kicker is playing $p_k = 0.4$, it does not matter what the goalkeeper does; the goalkeeper will have the same payoff, and so $p_j = 0.3$ is a best response (as is any other strategy). Similarly, if the goalkeeper is playing $p_j = 0.3$, it does not matter what the kicker does; and so every strategy, including $p_k = 0.4$, is a best response. The only reason an agent would consider randomizing between two actions is if the actions have the same expected utility. All probabilistic mixtures of the two actions have the same utility. The reason to choose a particular value for the probability of the mixture is to prevent the other agent from exploiting a deviation.

There are examples with multiple Nash equilibria. Consider the following two-agent, two-action game.

Example 10.11 Suppose there is a resource that two agents may want to fight over. Each agent can choose to act as a hawk or as a dove. Suppose the resource is worth R units, where $R > 0$. If both agents act as doves, they share the resource. If one agent acts as a hawk and the other as a dove, the hawk agent gets the resource and the dove agent gets nothing. If they both act like hawks, there is destruction of the resource and the reward to both is $-D$, where $D > 0$. This can be depicted by the following payoff matrix:

		Agent 2	
		dove	hawk
Agent 1	dove	R/2,R/2	0,R
	hawk	R,0	-D,-D

In this matrix, Agent 1 gets to choose the row, Agent 2 gets to choose the column, and the payoff in the cell is a pair consisting of the reward to Agent 1 and the reward to Agent 2. Each agent is trying to maximize its own reward.

In this game there are three Nash equilibria:

- In one equilibrium, Agent 1 acts as a hawk and Agent 2 as a dove. Agent 1 does not want to deviate because then they have to share the resource. Agent 2 does not want to deviate because then there is destruction.

- In the second equilibrium, Agent 1 acts as a dove and Agent 2 as a hawk.
- In the third equilibrium, both agents act stochastically. In this equilibrium, there is some chance of destruction. The probability of acting like a hawk goes up with the value R of the resource and goes down as the value D of destruction increases. See Exercise 1 (page 450).

In this example, you could imagine each agent doing some posturing to try to indicate what it will do to try to force an equilibrium that is advantageous to it.

Having multiple Nash equilibria does not come from being adversaries, as the following example shows.

Example 10.12 Suppose there are two people who want to be together. Agent 1 prefers they both go to the football game and Agent 2 prefers they both go shopping. They both would be unhappy if they are not together. Suppose they both have to choose simultaneously what activity to do. This can be depicted by the following payoff matrix:

		Agent 2	
		football	shopping
Agent 1	football	2,1	0,0
	shopping	0,0	1,2

In this matrix, Agent 1 chooses the row, and Agent 2 chooses the column.

In this game, there are three Nash equilibria. One equilibrium is where they both go shopping, one is where they both go to the football game, and one is a randomized strategy.

This is a **coordination** problem. Knowing the set of equilibria does not actually tell either agent what to do, because what an agent should do depends on what the other agent will do. In this example, you could imagine conversations to determine which equilibrium they would choose.

Even when there is a unique Nash equilibrium, that Nash equilibrium does not guarantee the maximum payoff to each agent. The following example is a variant of what is known as the **prisoner's dilemma**.

Example 10.13 Imagine you are on a game show with a stranger that you will never see again. You each have the choice of

- taking $100 for yourself or
- giving $1,000 to the other person.

This can be depicted as the following payoff matrix:

		Player 2	
		take	give
Player 1	take	100,100	1100,0
	give	0,1100	1000,1000

No matter what the other agent does, each agent is better off if it takes rather than gives. However, both agents are better off if they both give rather than if they both take.

Thus, there is a unique Nash equilibrium, where both agents take. This strategy profile results in each player receiving $100. The strategy profile where both players give results in each player receiving $1,000. However, in this strategy profile, each agent is rewarded for deviating.

There is a large body of research on the prisoner's dilemma, because it does not seem to be so rational to be greedy, where each agent tries to do the best for itself, resulting in everyone being worse off. One case where giving becomes preferred is when the game is played a number of times. This is known as the **sequential prisoner's dilemma**. One strategy for the sequential prisoner's dilemma is **tit-for-tat**: each player *gives* initially, then does the other agent's previous action at each step. This strategy is a Nash equilibrium as long as there is no last action that both players know about. [See Exercise 10.3 (page 450).]

Having multiple Nash equilibria not only arises from partial observability. It is even possible to have multiple equilibria with a perfect information game, and it is even possible to have infinitely many Nash equilibria, as the following example shows.

Example 10.14   Consider the sharing game of Example 10.2 (page 427). In this game there are infinitely many Nash equilibria. There is a set of equilibria where Andy shares, and Barb says "yes" to sharing for the center choice and can randomize between the other choices, as long as the probability of saying "yes" in the left-hand choice is less than or equal to 0.5. In these Nash equilibria, they both get 1. There is another set of Nash equilibria where Andy keeps, and Barb randomizes among her choices so that the probability of saying yes in the left branch is greater than or equal to 0.5. In these equilibria, Barb gets 0, and Andy gets some value in range $[1, 2]$ depending on Barb's probability. There is a third set of Nash equilibria where Barb has a 0.5 probability of selecting *yes* at the leftmost node, selects *yes* at the center node, and Andy randomizes between *keep* and *share* with any probability.

Suppose the sharing game were modified slightly so that Andy offered a small bribe for Barb to say "yes." This can be done by changing the 2, 0 payoff to be 1.9, 0.1. Andy may think, "Given the choice between 0.1 and 0, Barb will choose 0.1, so then I should keep." But Barb could think, "I should say *no* to 0.1, so that Andy shares and I get 1." In this example (even ignoring the rightmost branch), there are multiple pure Nash equilibria, one where Andy keeps, and Barb says *yes* at the leftmost branch. In this equilibrium, Andy gets 1.9 and Barb gets 0.1. There is another Nash equilibrium where Barb says *no* at the leftmost choice node and *yes* at the center branch and Andy chooses *share*. In this equilibrium, they both get 1. It would seem that this is the one preferred by Barb. However, Andy could think that Barb is making an empty **threat**. If he actually decided to *keep*, Barb, acting to maximize her utility, would not actually say *no*.

The backward induction algorithm only finds one of the equilibria in the modified sharing game. It computes a **subgame-perfect equilibrium**, where it is assumed that the agents choose the action with greatest utility for them at every node where they get to choose. It assumes that agents do not carry out threats that it is not in their interest to carry out at the time. In the modified sharing game of the previous example, it assumes that Barb will say "yes" to the small bribe. However, when dealing with real opponents, we must be careful of whether they will follow through with threats that we may not think rational.

10.4.1 Computing Nash Equilibria

To compute a Nash equilibrium for a game in strategic form, there are three steps:

1. Eliminate dominated strategies.
2. Determine which actions will have non-zero probabilities; this is called the **support set**.
3. Determine the probability for the actions in the support set.

It turns out that the second of these is the most difficult.

Eliminating Dominated Strategies

A strategy s_1 for a agent A **dominates** strategy s_2 for A if, for every action of the other agents, the utility of s_1 for agent A is higher than the utility of s_2 for agent A. Any pure strategy dominated by another strategy can be eliminated from consideration. The dominating strategy can be a randomized strategy. This can be done repeatedly.

Example 10.15 Consider the following payoff matrix, where the first agent chooses the row and the second agent chooses the column. In each cell is a pair of payoffs: the payoff for Agent 1 and the payoff for Agent 2. Agent 1 has actions $\{a_1, b_1, c_1\}$. Agent 2 has possible actions $\{d_2, e_2, f_2\}$.

Agent 2

		d_2	e_2	f_2
	a_1	3,5	5,1	1,2
Agent 1	b_1	1,1	2,9	6,4
	c_1	2,6	4,7	0,8

(Before looking at the solution try to work out what each agent should do.)

Action c_1 can be removed because it is dominated by action a_1: Agent 1 will never do c_1 if action a_1 is available to it. You can see that the payoff for Agent 1 is greater doing a_1 than doing c_1, no matter what the other agent does.

Once action c_1 is eliminated, action f_2 can be eliminated because it is dominated by the randomized strategy $0.5 \times d_2 + 0.5 \times e_2$.

Once c_1 and f_2 have been eliminated, b_1 is dominated by a_1, and so Agent 1 will do action a_1. Given that Agent 1 will do a_1, Agent 2 will do d_2. Thus, the payoff in this game will be 3 for Agent 1 and 5 for Agent 2.

Strategy s_1 **strictly dominates** strategy s_2 for Agent i if, for all action profiles σ_{-i} of the other agents,

$$utility(s_1\sigma_{-i}, i) > utility(s_2\sigma_{-i}, i).$$

It is clear that, if s_2 is a pure strategy that is strictly dominated by some strategy s_1, then s_2 can never be in the support set of any Nash equilibrium. This holds even if s_1 is a stochastic strategy. Repeated elimination of strictly dominated strategies gives the same result, irrespective of the order in which the strictly dominated strategies are removed.

There are also weaker notions of domination, where the greater-than symbol in the preceding formula is replaced by greater than or equal. If the weaker notion of domination is used, there is always a Nash equilibrium with support of the non-dominated strategies. However, some Nash equilibria can be lost. Moreover, which equilibria are lost can depend on the order in which the dominated strategies are removed.

Computing Randomized Strategies

We can use the fact that an agent will only randomize between actions if the actions all have the same utility to the agent (given the strategies of the other agent). This forms a set of constraints that can be solved to give a Nash equilibrium. If these constraints can be solved with numbers in the range $(0, 1)$, and the mixed strategies computed for each agent are not dominated by another strategy for the agent, then this strategy profile is a Nash equilibrium.

Recall that a support set (page 435) is a set of pure strategies that each have non-zero probability in a Nash equilibrium.

Once dominated strategies have been eliminated, we can search over support sets to determine whether the support sets form a Nash equilibrium. Note that, if there are n actions available to an agent, there are $2^n - 1$ non-empty subsets, and we have to search over combinations of support sets for the various agents. So this is not very feasible unless there are few non-dominated actions or there are Nash equilibria with small support sets. To find simple (in terms of the number of actions in the support set) equilibria, we can search from smaller support sets to larger sets.

Suppose agent i is randomizing between actions $a_i^1, \ldots, a_i^{k_i}$ in a Nash equilibrium. Let p_i^j be the probability that agent i does action a_i^j. Let $\sigma_{-i}(p_{-i})$ be the strategies for the other agents as a function of their probabilities. The fact that this is a Nash equilibrium gives the following constraints: $p_i^j > 0$, $\sum_{j=1}^{k_i} p_i^j = 1$, and, for all j, j'

$$utility(a_i^j \sigma_{-i}(p_{-i}), i) = utility(a_i^{j'} \sigma_{-i}(p_{-i}), i).$$

We also require that the utility of doing a_i^j is not less than the utility of doing an action outside of the support set. Thus, for all $a' \notin \{a_i^1, \ldots, a_i^{k_i}\}$,

$$utility(a_i^j \sigma_{-i}(p_{-i}), i) \geq utility(a' \sigma_{-i}(p_{-i}), i).$$

Example 10.16 In Example 10.9 (page 433), suppose the goalkeeper jumps right with probability p_j and the kicker kicks right with probability p_k.

If the goalkeeper jumps right, the probability of a goal is

$$0.9p_k + 0.2(1 - p_k).$$

If the goalkeeper jumps left, the probability of a goal is

$$0.3p_k + 0.6(1 - p_k).$$

The only time the goalkeeper would randomize is if these are equal; that is, if

$$0.9p_k + 0.2(1 - p_k) = 0.3p_k + 0.6(1 - p_k).$$

Solving for p_k gives $p_k = 0.4$.

Similarly, for the kicker to randomize, the probability of a goal must be the same whether the kicker kicks left or right:

$$0.2p_j + 0.6(1 - p_j) = 0.9p_j + 0.3(1 - p_j).$$

Solving for p_j gives $p_j = 0.3$.

Thus, the only Nash equilibrium is where $p_k = 0.4$ and $p_j = 0.3$.

10.4.2 Learning to Coordinate

Due to the existence of multiple equilibria, in many cases it is not clear what an agent should actually do, even if it knows all of the outcomes for the game and the utilities of the agents. However, most real strategic encounters are much more difficult, because the agents do not know the outcomes or the utilities of the other agents.

An alternative to the deep strategic reasoning implied by computing the Nash equilibria is to try to learn what actions to perform. This is quite different from the standard setup for learning covered in Chapter 7, where an agent was learning about some unknown but fixed concept; here, an agent is learning to interact with other agents who are also learning.

This section presents a simple algorithm that can be used to iteratively improve an agent's policy. We assume that the agents are repeatedly playing the same game and are learning what to do based on how well they do. We assume that each agent is always playing a mixed strategy; the agent updates the probabilities of the actions based on the payoffs received. For simplicity, we assume a single state; the only thing that changes between times is the randomized policies of the other agents.

1: **procedure** *PolicyImprovement*(A, α, δ)
2:      **Inputs**
3:          A a set of actions
4:          α step size for action estimate
5:          δ step size for probability change
6:      **Local**
7:          n the number of elements of A
8:          $P[A]$ a probability distribution over A
9:          $Q[A]$ an estimate of the value of doing A
10:         *a_best* the current best action
11:     $n \leftarrow |A|$
12:     $P[A]$ assigned randomly such that $P[a] > 0$ and $\sum_{a \in A} P[a] = 1$
13:     $Q[a] \leftarrow 0$ for each $a \in A$
14:     **repeat**
15:         **select** action a based on distribution P
16:         **do** a
17:         **observe** *payoff*
18:         $Q[a] \leftarrow Q[a] + \alpha(payoff - Q[a])$
19:         $a\_best \leftarrow \arg\max(Q)$
20:         $P[a\_best] \leftarrow P[a\_best] + n \times \delta$
21:         **for each** $a' \in A$ **do**
22:             $P[a'] \leftarrow P[a'] - \delta$
23:             **if** $P[a'] < 0$ **then**
24:                 $P[a\_best] \leftarrow P[a\_best] + P[a']$
25:                 $P[a'] \leftarrow 0$
26:     **until** termination

Figure 10.9: Learning to coordinate

The algorithm *PolicyImprovement* of Figure 10.9 gives a controller for a learning agent. It maintains its current stochastic policy in the P array and an estimate of the payoff for each action in the Q array. The agent carries out an action based on its current policy and observes the action's payoff. It then updates its estimate of the value of that action and modifies its current strategy by increasing the probability of its best action.

In this algorithm, n is the number of actions (the number of elements of A). First, it initializes P randomly so that it is a probability distribution; Q is initialized arbitrarily to zero.

At each stage, the agent chooses an action a based on the current distribution P. It carries out the action a and observes the payoff it receives. It then updates its estimate of the payoff from doing a. It is doing gradient descent (page 149) with learning rate α to minimize the error in its estimate of the payoff of action a. If the payoff is more than its previous estimate, it increases its

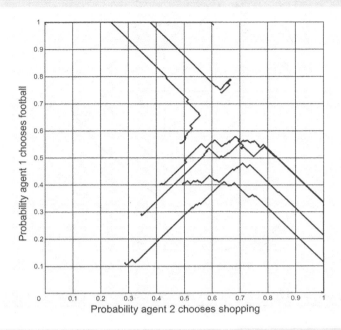

Figure 10.10: Learning for the football–shopping coordination example

estimate in proportion to the error. If the payoff is less than its estimate, it decreases its estimate.

It then computes *a_best*, which is the current best action according to its estimated Q-values. (Assume that, if there is more than one best action, one is chosen at random to be *a_best*.) It increases the probability of the best action by $(n - 1)\delta$ and reduces the probability of the other actions by δ. The *if* condition on line 23 is there to ensure that the probabilities are all non-negative and sum to 1.

Even when P has some action with probability 0, it is useful to try that action occasionally to update its current value. In the following examples, we assume that the agent chooses a random action with probability 0.05 at each step and otherwise chooses each action according to the probability of that action in P.

An open-source Java applet that implements this learning controller is available from the book's web site.

Example 10.17 Figure 10.10 shows a plot of the learning algorithm for Example 10.12 (page 437). This figure plots the relative probabilities for agent 1 choosing football and agent 2 choosing shopping for 7 runs of the learning algorithm. Each line is one run. Each of the runs ends at the top-left corner or the bottom-right corner. In these runs, the policies are initialized randomly, $\alpha = 0.1$, and $\delta = 0.01$.

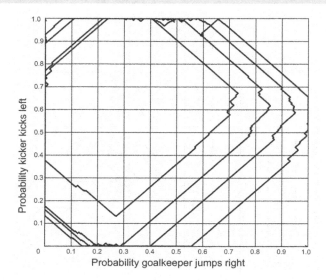

Figure 10.11: Learning for the soccer penalty kick example

If the other agents are playing a fixed strategy (even if it is a stochastic strategy), this algorithm converges to a best response to that strategy (as long as α and δ are small enough, and as long as the agent randomly tries all of the actions occasionally).

The following discussion assumes that all agents are using this learning controller.

If there is a unique Nash equilibrium in pure strategies, and all of the agents use this algorithm, they will converge to this equilibrium. Dominated strategies will have their probability set to zero. In Example 10.15 (page 439), it will find the Nash equilibrium. Similarly for the prisoner's dilemma in Example 10.13 (page 437), it will converge to the unique equilibrium where both agents take. Thus, this algorithm does *not* learn to **cooperate**, where cooperating agents will both *give* in the prisoner's dilemma to maximize their payoffs.

If there are multiple pure equilibria, this algorithm will converge to one of them. The agents thus learn to **coordinate**. In the football–shopping game of Example 10.12 (page 437), it will converge to one of the equilibria of both shopping or both going to the football game. Which one it converges to depends on the initial strategies.

If there is only a randomized equilibrium, as in the penalty kick game of Example 10.9 (page 433), this algorithm tends to cycle around the equilibrium.

Example 10.18 Figure 10.11 shows a plot of two players using the learning algorithm for Example 10.9 (page 433). This figure plots the relative probabilities for the goalkeeper jumping right and the kicker kicking left for one run of the learning algorithm. In this run, $\alpha = 0.1$ and $\delta = 0.001$. The learning algorithm cycles around the equilibrium, never actually reaching the equilibrium.

Consider the two-agent competitive game where there is only a randomized Nash equilibrium. If an agent A is playing another agent, B, that is playing a Nash equilibrium, it does not matter which action in its support set is performed by agent A; they all have the same value to A. Thus, agent A will tend to wander off the equilibrium. Note that, when A deviates from the equilibrium strategy, the best response for agent B is to play deterministically. This algorithm, when used by agent B eventually, notices that A has deviated from the equilibrium and agent B changes its policy. Agent B will also deviate from the equilibrium. Then agent A can try to exploit this deviation. When they are both using this controller, each agents's deviation can be exploited, and they tend to cycle.

There is nothing in this algorithm to keep the agents on a randomized equilibrium. One way to try to make agents not wander too far from an equilibrium is to adopt a **win or learn fast (WoLF)** strategy: when the agent is winning it takes small steps (δ is small), and when the agent is losing it takes larger steps (δ is increased). While it is winning, it tends to stay with the same policy, and while it is losing, it tries to move quickly to a better policy. To define winning, a simple strategy is for an agent to see whether it is doing better than the average payoff it has received so far.

Note that there is no perfect learning strategy. If an opposing agent knew the exact strategy (whether learning or not) agent A was using, and could predict what agent A would do, it could exploit that knowledge.

10.5 Group Decision Making

Often groups of people have to make decisions about what the group will do. Societies are the classic example, where voting is used to ascertain what the group wants. It may seem that voting is a good way to determine what a group wants, and when there is a clear most-preferred choice, it is. However, there are major problems with voting when there is not a clear preferred choice, as shown in the following example.

Example 10.19 Consider a purchasing agent that has to decide on a holiday destination for a group of people, based on their preference. Suppose there are three people, Alice, Bob and Cory, and three destinations, X, Y, and Z. Suppose the agents have the following preferences, where $\succ$ means strictly prefers (page 373):

- Alice: $X \succ Y \succ Z$.
- Bob: $Y \succ Z \succ X$.
- Cory: $Z \succ X \succ Y$.

Given these preferences, in a pairwise vote, $X \succ Y$ because two out of the three prefer X to Y. Similarly, in the voting, $Y \succ Z$ and $Z \succ X$. Thus, the preferences obtained by voting are not transitive. This example is known as the **Condorcet paradox**. Indeed, it is not clear what a group outcome should be in this case, because it is symmetric between the outcomes.

A **social preference function** gives a preference relation for a group. We would like a social preference function to depend on the preferences of the individuals in the group. It may seem that the Condorcet paradox is a problem with pairwise voting; however, the following result shows that such paradoxes occur with any social preference function.

Proposition 10.1. *(Arrow's impossibility theorem) If there are three or more outcomes, the following properties cannot simultaneously hold for any social preference function:*

- *The social preference function is complete and transitive (page 373).*
- *Every individual preference that is complete and transitive is allowed.*
- *If every individual prefers outcome o_1 to o_2, the group prefers o_1 to o_2.*
- *The group preference between outcomes o_1 and o_2 depends only on the individual preferences on o_1 and o_2 and not on the individuals' preferences on other outcomes.*
- *No individual gets to unilaterally decide the outcome (nondictatorship).*

When building an agent that takes the individual preferences and gives a social preference, we have to be aware that we cannot have all of these intuitive and desirable properties. Rather than giving a group preference that has undesirable properties, it may be better to point out to the individuals how their preferences cannot be reconciled.

10.6   Mechanism Design

The earlier discussion on agents choosing their actions assumed that each agent gets to play in a predefined game. The problem of **mechanism design** is to design a game with desirable properties for various agents to play.

A **mechanism** specifies the actions available to each agent and the distribution of outcomes of each action profile. We assume that agents have utilities over outcomes.

There are two common properties that are desirable for a mechanism:

- A mechanism should be easy for agents to use. Given an agent's utility, it should be easy for the agent to determine what to do. A **dominant strategy** is a strategy for an agent that is best for the agent, no matter what the other agents do. If an agent has a dominant strategy, it can do its best action without the complicated strategic reasoning described in the previous section. A mechanism is dominant-strategy **truthful** if it has a dominant strategy for each agent and, in the dominant strategy, an agent's best strategy is to declare its true preferences. In a mechanism that is dominant-strategy truthful, an agent simply declares its true preferences; the agent cannot do better by trying to manipulate the mechanism for its own gain.

- A mechanism should give the best outcome aggregated over all of the agents. For example, a mechanism is **economically efficient** if the outcome chosen is one that maximizes the sum of the utilities of the agents.

Example 10.20 Suppose you want to design a meeting scheduler, where users input the times they are available and the scheduler chooses a time for the meeting. One mechanism is for the users to specify when they are available or not, and for the scheduler to select the time that has the most people available. A second mechanism is for the users to specify their utility for the various times, and the scheduler chooses the time that maximizes the sum of the utilities. Neither of these mechanisms is dominant-strategy truthful.

For the first mechanism, users may declare that they are unavailable at some time to force a time they prefer. It is not clear that being available at a certain time is well defined; at some stage, users must decide whether it is easier to reschedule what they would have otherwise done at some particular time. Different people may have different thresholds as to what other activities can be moved.

For the second mechanism, suppose there are three people, Alice, Bob, and Cory, and they have to decide whether to meet on Monday, Tuesday, or Wednesday. Suppose they have the following utilities for the meeting days:

	Monday	Tuesday	Wednesday
Alice	0	8	10
Bob	3	4	0
Cory	11	7	6

The economically efficient outcome is to meet on Tuesday. However, if Alice were to change her evaluation of Tuesday to be 2, the mechanism would choose Wednesday. Thus, Alice has an incentive to misrepresent her values. It is not in Alice's interest to be honest.

Note that, if there is a mechanism that has dominant strategies, there is a mechanism that is dominant-strategy truthful. This is known as the **revelation principle**. To implement a dominant-strategy truthful mechanism, we can, in principle, write a program that accepts from an agent its actual preferences and provides to the original mechanism the optimal input for that agent. Essentially, this program can optimally lie for the agent.

It turns out that it is essentially impossible to design a reasonable mechanism that is dominant-strategy truthful. As long as there are three or more outcomes that are possible to be chosen, the only mechanisms with dominant strategies have a **dictator**: there is one agent whose preferences determine the outcome. This is the Gibbard–Satterthwaite theorem.

One way to obtain dominant-strategy truthful mechanisms is to introduce money. Assume that money can be added to utility so that, for any two outcomes o_1 and o_2, for each agent there is some (possibly negative) amount d such that the agent is indifferent between the outcomes o_1 and $o_2 + d$. By allowing an agent to be paid to accept an outcome they would not otherwise prefer, or to pay for an outcome they want, we can ensure the agent does not gain by lying.

In a **VCG mechanism**, or a Vickrey–Clarke–Groves mechanism, the agents get to declare their values for each of the outcomes. The outcome that maximizes the sum of the declared values is chosen. Agents pay according to how much their participation affects the outcome. Agent i pays the sum of the value for the other agents for the chosen outcome minus the sum of the values for the other agents if i had not participated. The VCG mechanism is both economically efficient and dominant-strategy truthful, assuming that agents only care about their utility and not about other agents' utilities or other agents' payments.

Example 10.21   Consider the values of Example 10.20. Suppose the values given can be interpreted as equivalent to dollars; for example, Alice is indifferent between meeting on Monday or meeting on Tuesday and paying $8.00 (she is prepared to pay $7.99 to move the meeting from Monday to Tuesday, but not $8.01). Given these declared values, Tuesday is chosen as the meeting day. If Alice had not participated, Monday would have been chosen, and so the other agents have a net loss of 3, so Alice has to pay $3.00. The net value to her is then 5; the utility of 8 for the Tuesday minus the payment of 3. The declarations, payments, and net values are given in the following table:

	Monday	Tuesday	Wednesday	Payment	Net Value
Alice	0	8	10	3	5
Bob	3	4	0	1	3
Cory	11	7	6	0	7
Total	14	19	16		

Consider what would happen if Alice had changed her evaluation of Tuesday to 2. In this case, Wednesday would be the chosen day, but Alice would have had to pay $8.00, with a new value of 2, and so would be worse off. Alice cannot gain an advantage by lying to the mechanism.

One common mechanism for selling an item, or a set of items, is an **auction**. A common auction type for selling a single item is an ascending auction, where there is a current offering price for the item that increases by a predetermined increment when the previous offering price has been met. Offering to buy the item at the current price is called a bid. Only one person may put in a bid for a particular price. The item goes to the person who put in the highest bid, and the person pays the amount of that bid.

Consider a VCG mechanism for selling a single item. Suppose there are a number of agents who each put in a bid for how much they value an item. The outcome that maximizes the payoffs is to give the item to the person who had the highest bid. If they had not participated, the item would have gone to the second-highest bidder. Therefore, according to the VCG mechanism, the top bidder should get the item and pay the value of the second-highest bid. This is known as a **second-price auction**. The second price auction is equivalent (up to bidding increments) to having an ascending auction, where people use a proxy bid, and there is an agent to convert the proxy bid into real bids. Bidding in a second-price auction is straightforward because the agents do not have to do complex strategic reasoning. It is also easy to determine a winner and the appropriate payment.

10.7   Review

This chapter has touched on some of the issues that arise with multiple agents. The following are the main points to remember:

- A multiagent system consists of multiple agents who can act autonomously and have their own utility over outcomes. The outcomes depend on the actions of all agents. Agents can compete, cooperate, coordinate, communicate, and negotiate.

- The strategic form of a game specifies the expected outcome given controllers for each agent.

- The extensive form of a game models agents' actions and information through time in terms of game trees.

- A multiagent decision network models probabilistic dependency and information availability.

- Perfect information games can be solved by backing up values in game trees or searching the game tree using minimax with α-β pruning.

- In partially observable domains, sometimes it is optimal to act stochastically.

- A Nash equilibrium is a strategy profile for each agent such that no agent can increase its utility by unilaterally deviating from the strategy profile.

- Agents can learn to coordinate by playing the same game repeatedly, but it is difficult to learn a randomized strategy.

- By introducing payments, it is possible to design a mechanism that is dominant-strategy truthful and economically efficient.

10.8   References and Further Reading

For overviews of multiagent systems see Shoham and Leyton-Brown [2008], Stone and Veloso [2000], Wooldridge [2002], and Weiss [1999]. Nisan, Roughgarden, Tardos, and Vazirani [2007] overview current research frontiers in algorithmic game theory.

Multiagent decision networks are based on the MAIDs of Koller and Milch [2003].

Minimax with α-β pruning was first published by Hart and Edwards [1961]. Knuth and Moore [1975] and Pearl [1984] analyze α-β pruning and other methods for searching game trees. Ballard [1983] discusses how minimax can be combined with chance nodes.

The Deep Blue chess computer is described by Campbell, Hoane Jr., and Hse [2002].

The learning of games and the WoLF strategy is based on Bowling and Veloso [2002].

Mechanism design is described by Shoham and Leyton-Brown [2008], Nisan [2007] and in microeconomics textbooks such as Mas-Colell, Whinston, and Green [1995]. Ordeshook [1986] has a good description of group decision making and game theory.

10.9 Exercises

Exercise 10.1 For the hawk–dove game of Example 10.11 (page 436), where $D > 0$ and $R > 0$, each agent is trying to maximize its utility. Is there a Nash equilibrium with a randomized strategy? What are the probabilities? What is the expected payoff to each agent? (These should be expressed as functions of R and D). Show your calculation.

Exercise 10.2 In Example 10.12 (page 437), what is the Nash equilibrium with randomized strategies? What is the expected value for each agent in this equilibrium?

Exercise 10.3 In the sequential prisoner's dilemma (page 438), suppose there is a discount factor of γ, which means there is a probability γ of stopping at each stage. Is tit-for-tat a Nash equilibrium for all values of γ? If so, prove it. If not, for which values of γ is it a Nash equilibrium?

Chapter 11

Beyond Supervised Learning

Learning without thought is labor lost; thought without learning is perilous.

Confucius (551 BC – 479 BC), The Confucian Analects

This chapter goes beyond the supervised learning of Chapter 7. It covers learning richer representation and learning what to do; this enables learning to be combined with reasoning. First we consider unsupervised learning in which the classifications are not given in the training set. This is a special case of learning belief network, which is considered next. Finally, we consider reinforcement learning, in which an agent learns how to act while interacting with an environment.

11.1 Clustering

Chapter 7 considered supervised learning, where the target features that must be predicted from input features are observed in the training data. In **clustering** or **unsupervised learning**, the target features are not given in the training examples. The aim is to construct a natural classification that can be used to cluster the data.

The general idea behind clustering is to partition the examples into **clusters** or **classes**. Each class predicts feature values for the examples in the class. Each clustering has a prediction error on the predictions. The best clustering is the one that minimizes the error.

Example 11.1 A diagnostic assistant may want to group the different treatments into groups that predict the desirable and undesirable effects of the treatment. The assistant may not want to give a patient a drug because similar drugs may have had disastrous effects on similar patients.

> An intelligent tutoring system may want to cluster students' learning be-
> havior so that strategies that work for one member of a class may work for
> other members.

In **hard clustering**, each example is placed definitively in a class. The class
is then used to predict the feature values of the example. The alternative to
hard clustering is **soft clustering**, in which each example has a probability distribution over its class. The prediction of the values for the features of an example is the weighted average of the predictions of the classes the example is
in, weighted by the probability of the example being in the class.

11.1.1   Expectation Maximization

The **expectation maximization (EM)** algorithms can be used for clustering.
Given the data, EM learns a theory that specifies how each example should
be classified and how to predict feature values for each class. The general idea
is to start with a random theory or randomly classified data and to repeat two
steps until they converge on a coherent theory:

E: Classify the data using the current theory.

M: Generate the best theory using the current classification of the data.

Step E generates the expected classification for each example. Step M generates
the most likely theory given the classified data. The M step is the problem of
supervised learning. As an iterative algorithm, it can get stuck in local optima;
different initializations can affect the theory found.

The next two sections consider two instances of the EM algorithm.

11.1.2 k-Means

The **k-means algorithm** is used for hard clustering. The training examples and
the number of classes, k, are given as input. The output is a set of k classes,
a prediction of a value for each feature for each class, and an assignment of
examples to classes.

The algorithm assumes that each feature is given on a numerical scale, and
it tries to find classes that minimize the sum-of-squares error when the predicted values for each example are derived from the class to which it belongs.

Suppose E is the set of all examples, and the input features are $X_1, \ldots, X_n$.
Let $val(e, X_j)$ be the value of input feature X_j for example e. We assume that
these are observed. We will associate a class with each integer $i \in \{1, \ldots, k\}$.

The k-means algorithm outputs

- a function $class : E \rightarrow \{1, \ldots, k\}$, which means that $class(e)$ is the classification of example e. If $class(e) = i$, we say that e is in class i.
- a *pval* function such that for each class $i \in \{1, \ldots, k\}$, and for each feature
  X_j, $pval(i, X_j)$ is the prediction for each example in class i for feature X_j.

Given a particular *class* function and *pval* function the **sum-of-squares error** is

$$\sum_{e \in E} \sum_{j=1}^{n} \left(pval(class(e), X_j) - val(e, X_j)\right)^2.$$

The aim is to find a *class* function and a *pval* function that minimize the sum-of-squares error.

As shown in Proposition 7.1 (page 294), to minimize the sum-of-squares error, the prediction of a class should be the mean of the prediction of the examples in the class. Unfortunately, there are too many partitions of the examples into k classes to search through to find the optimal partitioning.

The k-means algorithm iteratively improves the sum-of-squares error. Initially, it randomly assigns the examples to the classes. Then it carries out the following two steps:

M: For each class i and feature X_j, assign to $pval(i, X_j)$ the mean value of $val(e, X_j)$ for each example e in class i:

$$pval(i, X_j) \leftarrow \frac{\sum_{e:class(e)=i} val(e, X_j)}{|\{e : class(e) = i\}|},$$

where the denominator is the number of examples in class i.

E: Reassign each example to a class: assign each e to the class i that minimizes

$$\sum_{j=1}^{n} \left(pval(i, X_j) - val(e, X_j)\right)^2.$$

These two steps are repeated until the second step does not change the assignment of any example.

An assignment of examples to classes is **stable** if running both the M step and the E step does not change the assignment. Note that any permutation of the labels of a stable assignment is also a stable assignment.

This algorithm will eventually converge to a stable local minimum. This is easy to see because the sum-of-squares error keeps reducing and there are only a finite number of reassignments. This algorithm often converges in a few iterations. It is not guaranteed to converge to a global minimum. To try to improve the value, it can be run a number of times with different initial assignments.

Example 11.2 An agent has observed the following $\langle X, Y \rangle$ pairs:

$(0.7, 5.1)$, $(1.5, 6)$, $(2.1, 4.5)$, $(2.4, 5.5)$, $(3, 4.4)$, $(3.5, 5)$, $(4.5, 1.5)$, $(5.2, 0.7)$, $(5.3, 1.8)$, $(6.2, 1.7)$, $(6.7, 2.5)$, $(8.5, 9.2)$, $(9.1, 9.7)$, $(9.5, 8.5)$.

These data points are plotted in part (a) of Figure 11.1 (on the next page). Suppose the agent wants to cluster the data points into two classes.

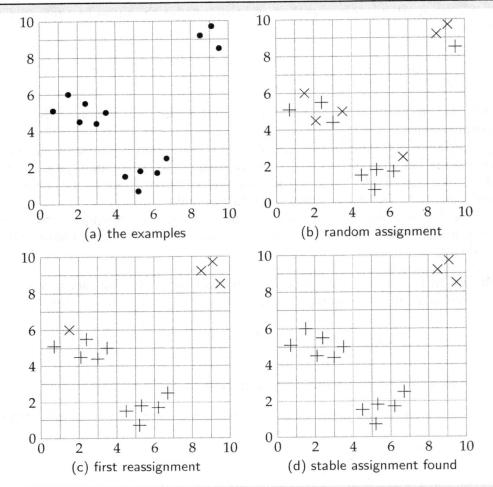

Figure 11.1: A trace of the k-means algorithm for $k = 2$ for Example 11.2

In part (b), the points are randomly assigned into the classes; one class is depicted as + and the other as ×. The mean of the points marked with + is $\langle 4.6, 3.65 \rangle$. The mean of the points marked with × is $\langle 5.2, 6.15 \rangle$.

In part (c), the points are reassigned according to the closer of the two means. After this reassignment, the mean of the points marked with + is then $\langle 3.96, 3.27 \rangle$. The mean of the points marked with × is $\langle 7.15, 8.34 \rangle$.

In part (d), the points are reassigned to the closest mean. This assignment is stable in that no further reassignment will change the assignment of the examples.

A different initial assignment to the points can give different clustering. One clustering that arises in this data set is for the lower points (those with a Y-value less than 3) to be in one class, and for the other points to be in another class.

Running the algorithm with three classes would separate the data into the top-right cluster, the left-center cluster, and the lower cluster.

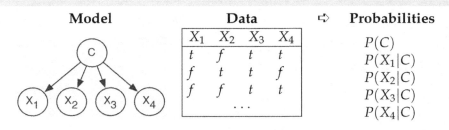

Figure 11.2: EM algorithm: Bayesian classifier with hidden class

One problem with the k-means algorithm is the relative scale of the dimensions. For example, if one feature is *height*, another feature is *age*, and another is a binary feature, you must scale the different domains so that they can be compared. How they are scaled relative to each other affects the classification.

To find an appropriate number of classes, an agent can search over the number of classes. Note that $k + 1$ classes can always result in a lower error than k classes as long as more than k different values are involved. A *natural* number of classes would be a value k when there is a large reduction in error going from $k - 1$ classes to k classes, but in which there is only gradual reduction in error for larger values. Note that the optimal division into three classes, for example, may be quite different from the optimal division into two classes.

11.1.3   EM for Soft Clustering

The **EM** algorithm can be used for soft clustering. Intuitively, for clustering, EM is like the k-means algorithm, but examples are probabilistically in classes, and probabilities define the distance metric. We assume here that the features are discrete.

As in the k-means algorithm, the training examples and the number of classes, k, are given as input.

When clustering, the role of the categorization is to be able to predict the values of the features. To use EM for soft clustering, we can use a **naive Bayesian classifier** (page 310), where the input features probabilistically depend on the class and are independent of each other given the class. The class variable has k values, which can be just $\{1, \ldots, k\}$.

Given the naive Bayesian model and the data, the EM algorithm produces the probabilities needed for the classifier, as shown in Figure 11.2. The class variable is C in this figure. The probability distribution of the class and the probabilities of the features given the class are enough to classify any new example.

To initialize the EM algorithm, augment the data with a class feature, C, and a count column. Each original tuple gets mapped into k tuples, one for each class. The counts for these tuples are assigned randomly so that they

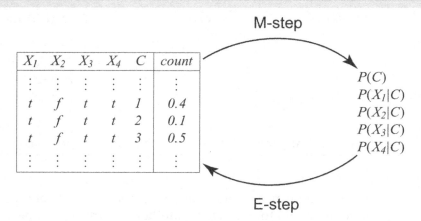

M-step

X_1	X_2	X_3	X_4	C	count
⋮	⋮	⋮	⋮	⋮	⋮
t	f	t	t	1	0.4
t	f	t	t	2	0.1
t	f	t	t	3	0.5
⋮	⋮	⋮	⋮	⋮	⋮

$P(C)$
$P(X_1|C)$
$P(X_2|C)$
$P(X_3|C)$
$P(X_4|C)$

E-step

Figure 11.3: EM algorithm for unsupervised learning

sum to 1. For example, for four features and three classes, we could have the following:

X_1	X_2	X_3	X_4
⋮	⋮	⋮	⋮
t	f	t	t
⋮	⋮	⋮	⋮

$\longrightarrow$

X_1	X_2	X_3	X_4	C	Count
⋮	⋮	⋮	⋮	⋮	⋮
t	f	t	t	1	0.4
t	f	t	t	2	0.1
t	f	t	t	3	0.5
⋮	⋮	⋮	⋮	⋮	⋮

If the set of training examples contains multiple tuples with the same values on the input features, these can be grouped together in the augmented data. If there are m tuples in the set of training examples with the same assignment of values to the input features, the sum of the counts in the augmented data with those feature values is equal to m.

The EM algorithm, illustrated in Figure 11.3, maintains both the probability tables and the augmented data. In the E step, it updates the counts, and in the M step it updates the probabilities.

The algorithm is presented in Figure 11.4. In this figure, $A[X_1, \ldots, X_n, C]$ contains the augmented data; $M_i[X_i, C]$ is the marginal probability, $P(X_i, C)$, derived from A; and $P_i[X_i, C]$ is the conditional probability $P(X_i|C)$. It repeats two steps:

- **E step**: Update the augmented data based on the probability distribution. Suppose there are m copies of the tuple $\langle X_1 = v_1, \ldots, X_n = v_n \rangle$ in the original data. In the augmented data, the count associated with class c, stored in $A[v_1, \ldots, v_n, c]$, is updated to

$$m \times P(C = c | X_1 = v_1, \ldots, X_n = v_n).$$

1: **procedure** $EM(X, D, k)$
2:     **Inputs**
3:         X set of features $X = \{X_1, \ldots, X_n\}$
4:         D data set on features $\{X_1, \ldots, X_n\}$
5:         k number of classes
6:     **Output**
7:         $P(C), P(X_i|C)$ for each $i \in \{1 : n\}$, where $C = \{1, \ldots, k\}$.
8:     **Local**
9:         real array $A[X_1, \ldots, X_n, C]$
10:        real array $P[C]$
11:        real arrays $M_i[X_i, C]$ for each $i \in \{1 : n\}$
12:        real arrays $P_i[X_i, C]$ for each $i \in \{1 : n\}$
13:    $s :=$ number of tuples in D
14:    Assign $P[C], P_i[X_i, C]$ arbitrarily
15:    **repeat**
16:   ▷ E Step
17:        **for each** assignment $\langle X_1 = v_1, \ldots, X_n = v_n\rangle \in D$ **do**
18:           let $m \leftarrow |\langle X_1 = v_1, \ldots, X_n = v_n\rangle \in D|$
19:           **for each** $c \in \{1 : k\}$ **do**
20:              $A[v_1, \ldots, v_n, c] \leftarrow m \times P(C = c | X_1 = v_1, \ldots, X_n = v_n)$
21:   ▷ M Step
22:        **for each** $i \in \{1 : n\}$ **do**
23:           $M_i[X_i, C] = \sum_{X_1, \ldots, X_{i-1}, X_{i+1}, \ldots, X_n} A[X_1, \ldots, X_n, C]$
24:           $P_i[X_i, C] = \dfrac{M_i[X_i, C]}{\sum_C M_i[X_i, C]}$
25:        $P[C] = \sum_{X_1, \ldots, X_n} A[X_1, \ldots, X_n, C]/s$
26:    **until** termination

Figure 11.4: EM for unsupervised learning

Note that this step involves probabilistic inference, as shown below.

- **M step**: Infer the maximum-likelihood probabilities for the model from the augmented data. This is the same problem as learning probabilities from data (page 296).

The EM algorithm presented starts with made-up probabilities. It could have started with made-up counts. EM will converge to a local maximum of the likelihood of the data. The algorithm can terminate when the changes are small enough.

This algorithm returns a probabilistic model, which can be used to classify an existing or new example. The way to classify a new example, and the way to evaluate line 20, is to use the following:

$$P(C = c | X_1 = v_1, \ldots, X_n = v_n)$$
$$= \frac{P(C = c) \times \prod_{i=1}^{n} P(X_i = v_i | C = c)}{\sum_{c'} P(C = c') \times \prod_{i=1}^{n} P(X_i = v_i | C = c')} .$$

The probabilities in this equation are specified as part of the model learned.

Notice the similarity with the k-means algorithm. The E step (probabilistically) assigns examples to classes, and the M step determines what the classes predict.

Example 11.3 Consider Figure 11.3 (page 456). Let E' be the augmented examples (i.e., with C and the *count* columns). Suppose there are m examples. Thus, at all times the sum of the counts in E' is m.

In the M step, $P(C = i)$ is set to the proportion of the counts with $C = i$, which is

$$\frac{\sum_{X_1, \ldots, X_n} A[X_1, \ldots, X_n, C = i]}{m} ,$$

which can be computed with one pass through the data.

$M_1[X_1, C]$, for example, becomes

$$\sum_{X_2, X_3, X_4} A[X_1, \ldots, X_4, C].$$

It is possible to update all of the $M_i[X_i, C]$ arrays with one pass though the data. See Exercise 11.3 (page 486). The conditional probabilities represented by the P_i arrays can be computed from the M_i arrays by normalizing.

The E step updates the counts in the augmented data. It will replace the 0.4 in Figure 11.3 (page 456) with

$$P(C = 1 | x_1 \wedge \neg x_2 \wedge x_3 \wedge x_4)$$
$$= \frac{P(x_1 | C = 1) P(\neg x_2 | C = 1) P(x_3 | C = 1) P(x_4 | C = 1) P(C = 1)}{\sum_{i=1}^{3} P(x_1 | C = i) P(\neg x_2 | C = i) P(x_3 | C = i) P(x_4 | C = i) P(C = i)} .$$

Each of these probabilities is provided as part of the learned model.

Note that, as long as $k > 1$, EM virtually always has multiple local maxima. In particular, any permutation of the class labels of a local maximum will also be a local maximum.

11.2 Learning Belief Networks

A **belief network** (page 235) gives a probability distribution over a set of random variables. We cannot always expect an expert to be able to provide an accurate model; often we want to learn a network from data.

Learning a belief network from data can mean many different things depending on how much prior information is known and how complete the data

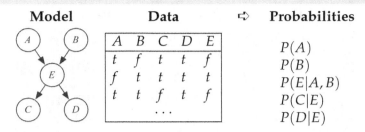

Figure 11.5: From the model and the data, learning the probabilities

set is. In the simplest case, the structure is given, all of the variables are observed in each example, and only the probabilities must be learned. At the other extreme, you may not even know what variables should be hypothesized to account for the data, and there may be missing data, which cannot be assumed to be missing at random.

11.2.1 Learning the Probabilities

The simplest case is when we are given the structure of the model and all of the variables have been observed. In this case, we must learn only the probabilities. This is very similar to the case of learning probabilities in Section 7.3.3 (page 309).

Each conditional probability distribution can be learned separately using the empirical data and pseudocounts (page 296) or in terms of the Dirichlet distribution (page 337).

Example 11.4 Figure 11.5 shows a typical example. We are given the model and the data, and we must infer the probabilities.

For example, one of the elements of $P(E|AB)$ is

$$P(E = t|A = t \land B = f)$$
$$= \frac{(\#\text{examples: } E = t \land A = t \land B = f) + c_1}{(\#\text{examples: } A = t \land B = f) + c},$$

where c_1 is a pseudocount of the number of cases where $E = t \land A = t \land B = f$, and c is a pseudocount of the number of cases where $A = t \land B = f$. Note that $c_1 \leq c$.

If a variable has many parents, using the counts and pseudo counts can suffer from overfitting (page 303). Overfitting is most severe when there are few examples for some of the combinations of the parent variables. In that case, the techniques of Chapter 7 can be used: for example, learning decision trees with probabilities at the leaves, sigmoid linear functions, or neural networks. To use supervised learning methods for learning conditional probabilities of a variable X given its parents, the parents become the input nodes and X becomes the

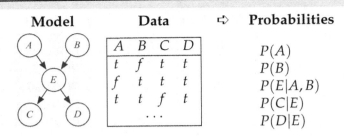

Figure 11.6: Deriving probabilities with missing data

target feature. Decision trees can be used for arbitrary discrete variables. Sigmoid linear functions and neural networks can represent a conditional probability of a binary variable given its parents. For non-binary variables, indicator variables (page 290) can be used.

11.2.2 Unobserved Variables

The next simplest case is one in which the model is given, but not all variables are observed. A **hidden variable** or a **latent variable** is a variable in the belief network models whose value is not observed. That is, there is no column in the data corresponding to that variable.

Example 11.5 Figure 11.6 shows a typical case. Assume that all of the variables are binary. The model contains a variable E that is not in the database. The data set does not contain the variable E, but the model does. We want to learn the parameters of the model that includes the hidden variable E. There are 10 parameters to learn.

Note that, if E were missing from the model, the algorithm would have to learn $P(A)$, $P(B)$, $P(C|AB)$, $P(D|ABC)$, which has 14 parameters. The reason to introduce hidden variables is to make the model simpler and, therefore, less prone to overfitting.

The **EM** algorithm for learning belief networks with hidden variables is essentially the same as the EM algorithm for clustering (page 455). The E step can involve more complex probabilistic inference as, for each example, it infers the probability of the hidden variable(s) given the observed variables for that example. The M step of inferring the probabilities of the model from the augmented data is the same as the fully observable case discussed in the previous section, but, in the augmented data, the counts are not necessarily integers.

11.2.3 Missing Data

Data can be incomplete in ways other than having an unobserved variable. A data set can simply be missing the values of some variables for some of the tuples. When some of the values of the variables are missing, one must be very

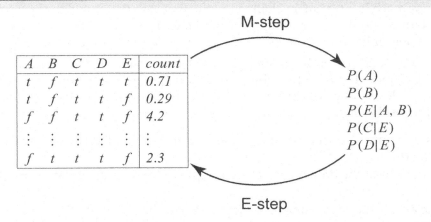

Figure 11.7: EM algorithm for belief networks with hidden variables

careful in using the data set because the missing data may be correlated with the phenomenon of interest.

Example 11.6 Suppose you have a (claimed) treatment for a disease that does not actually affect the disease or its symptoms. All it does is make sick people sicker. If you were to randomly assign patients to the treatment, the sickest people would drop out of the study, because they become too sick to participate. The sick people who took the treatment would drop out at a faster rate than the sick people who did not take the treatment. Thus, if the patients for whom the data is missing are ignored, it looks like the treatment works; there are fewer sick people in the set of those who took the treatment and remained in the study!

If the data is **missing at random**, the missing data can be ignored. However, "missing at random" is a strong assumption. In general, an agent should construct a model of why the data is missing or, preferably, it should go out into the world and find out why the data is missing.

11.2.4 Structure Learning

Suppose we have complete data and no hidden variables, but we do not know the structure of the belief network. This is the setting for **structure learning** of belief networks.

There are two main approaches to structure learning:

- The first is to use the definition of a belief network in terms of conditional independence (page 235). Given a total ordering of variables, make the parents of a variable X be a subset of the variables that are predecessors of X in the total ordering that render the other variables independent of X. This approach has two main challenges: the first is to determine the best total ordering; the second is to find a way to measure independence. It is difficult to determine conditional independence when there is limited data.

- The second method is to have a score for networks, for example, using the MAP model (page 321), which takes into account fit to the data and model complexity. Given such a measure, you can search for the structure that minimizes this error.

In this section we concentrate on the second method, often called a **search and score** method.

Assume that the data is a set E of examples, where each example has a value for each variable.

The aim of the search and score method is to choose a model that maximizes

$$P(model|data) \propto P(data|model)P(model).$$

The likelihood, $P(data|model)$, is the product of the probability of each example. Using the product decomposition, the product of each example given the model is the product of the probability of each variable given its parents in the model. Thus,

$$
\begin{aligned}
&P(data|model)P(model) \\
&= (\prod_{e \in E} P(e|model))P(model) \\
&= (\prod_{e \in E} \prod_{X_i} P^e_{model}(X_i|par(X_i, model)))P(model),
\end{aligned}
$$

where $par(X_i, model)$ denotes the parents of X_i in the model, and $P^e_{model}(\cdot)$ denotes the probability of example e as specified in the model.

This is maximized when its logarithm is maximized. When taking logarithms, products become sums:

$$
\begin{aligned}
&\log P(data|model) + \log P(model) \\
&= \sum_{e \in E} \sum_{X_i} \log P^e_{model}(X_i|par(X_i, model))) + \log P(model).
\end{aligned}
$$

To make this approach feasible, assume that the prior probability of the model decomposes into components for each variable. That is, we assume probability of the model decomposes into a product of probabilities of local models for each variable. Let $model(X_i)$ be the local model for variable X_i.

Thus, we want to maximize the following:

$$
\begin{aligned}
&\sum_{e \in E} \sum_{X_i} \log P^e_{model}(X_i|par(X_i, model))) + \sum_{X_i} \log P(model(X_i)) \\
&= \sum_{X_i} (\sum_{e \in E} \log P^e_{model}(X_i|par(X_i, model))) + \sum_{X_i} \log P(model(X_i)) \\
&= \sum_{X_i} (\sum_{e \in E} \log P^e_{model}(X_i|par(X_i, model)) + \log P(model(X_i)).
\end{aligned}
$$

We could optimize this by optimizing each variable separately, except for the fact that the parent relation is constrained by the acyclic condition of the belief network. However, given a total ordering of the variables, we have a classification problem in which we want to predict the probability of each variable given the predecessors in the total ordering. To represent $P(X_i|par(X_i, model))$ we could use, for example, a decision tree with probabilities of the leaves [as described in Section 7.5.1 (page 321)] or learn a squashed linear function. Given the preceding score, we can search over total orderings of the variables to maximize this score.

11.2.5 General Case of Belief Network Learning

The general case is with unknown structure, hidden variables, and missing data; we do not even know what variables exist. Two main problems exist. The first is the problem of missing data discussed earlier. The second problem is computational; although there is a well-defined search space, it is prohibitively large to try all combinations of variable ordering and hidden variables. If one only considers hidden variables that simplify the model (as seems reasonable), the search space is finite, but enormous.

One can either select the best model (e.g, the model with the highest a posteriori probability) or average over all models. Averaging over all models gives better predictions, but it is difficult to explain to a person who may have to understand or justify the model.

The problem with combining this approach with missing data seems to be much more difficult and requires more knowledge of the domain.

11.3 Reinforcement Learning

Imagine a robot that can act in a world, receiving rewards and punishments and determining from these what it should do. This is the problem of **reinforcement learning**. This chapter only considers fully observable, single-agent reinforcement learning [although Section 10.4.2 (page 441) considered a simple form of multiagent reinforcement learning].

We can formalize reinforcement learning in terms of Markov decision processes (page 399), but in which the agent, initially, only knows the set of possible states and the set of possible actions. Thus, the dynamics, $P(s'|a, s)$, and the reward function, $R(s, a, s')$, are initially unknown. An agent can act in a world and, after each step, it can observe the state of the world and observe what reward it obtained. Assume the agent acts to achieve the optimal discounted reward (page 402) with a discount factor γ.

Example 11.7 Consider the tiny reinforcement learning problem shown in Figure 11.8 (on the next page). There are six states the agent could be in, labeled as $s_0, \ldots, s_5$. The agent has four actions: *UpC, Up, Left, Right*. That is all the agent

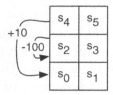

Figure 11.8: The environment of a tiny reinforcement learning problem

knows before it starts. It does not know how the states are configured, what the actions do, or how rewards are earned.

Figure 11.8 shows the configuration of the six states. Suppose the actions work as follows:

upC (for "up carefully") The agent goes up, except in states s_4 and s_5, where the agent stays still, and has a reward of -1.

right The agent moves to the right in states s_0, s_2, s_4 with a reward of 0 and stays still in the other states, with a reward of -1.

left The agent moves one state to the left in states s_1, s_3, s_5. In state s_0, it stays in state s_0 and has a reward of -1. In state s_2, it has a reward of -100 and stays in state s_2. In state s_4, it gets a reward of 10 and moves to state s_0.

up With a probability of 0.8 it acts like *upC*, except the reward is 0. With probability 0.1 it acts as a *left*, and with probability 0.1 it acts as *right*.

Suppose there is a discounted reward (page 402) with a discount of 0.9. This can be translated as having a 0.1 chance of the agent leaving the game at any step, or as a way to encode that the agent prefers immediate rewards over future rewards.

Example 11.8 Figure 11.9 shows the domain of a more complex game. There are 25 grid locations the agent could be in. A prize could be on one of the corners, or there could be no prize. When the agent lands on a prize, it receives

P_0	R			P_1
		M		
				M
M	M		M	
P_2				P_3

Figure 11.9: The environment of a grid game

a reward of 10 and the prize disappears. When there is no prize, for each time step there is a probability that a prize appears on one of the corners. Monsters can appear at any time on one of the locations marked M. The agent gets damaged if a monster appears on the square the agent is on. If the agent is already damaged, it receives a reward of -10. The agent can get repaired (i.e., so it is no longer damaged) by visiting the repair station marked R.

In this example, the state consists of four components: $\langle X, Y, P, D \rangle$, where X is the X-coordinate of the agent, Y is the Y-coordinate of the agent, P is the position of the prize ($P = 0$ if there is a prize on P_0, $P = 1$ if there is a prize on P_1, similarly for 2 and 3, and $P = 4$ if there is no prize), and D is Boolean and is true when the agent is damaged. Because the monsters are transient, it is not necessary to include them as part of the state. There are thus $5 \times 5 \times 5 \times 2 = 250$ states. The environment is fully observable, so the agent knows what state it is in. But the agent does not know the meaning of the states; it has no idea initially about being damaged or what a prize is.

The agent has four actions: *up*, *down*, *left*, and *right*. These move the agent one step – usually one step in the direction indicated by the name, but sometimes in one of the other directions. If the agent crashes into an outside wall or one of the interior walls (the thick lines near the location R), it remains where is was and receives a reward of -1.

The agent does not know any of the story given here. It just knows there are 250 states and 4 actions, which state it is in at every time, and what reward was received each time.

This game is simple, but it is surprisingly difficult to write a good controller for it. There is a Java applet available on the book web site that you can play with and modify. Try to write a controller by hand for it; it is possible to write a controller that averages about 500 rewards for each 1,000 steps. This game is also difficult to learn, because visiting R is seemingly innocuous until the agent has determined that being damaged is bad, and that visiting R makes it not damaged. It must stumble on this while trying to collect the prizes. The states where there is no prize available do not last very long. Moreover, it has to learn this without being given the concept of *damaged*; all it knows, initially, is that there are 250 states and 4 actions.

Reinforcement learning is difficult for a number of reasons:

- The **blame attribution problem** is the problem of determining which action was responsible for a reward or punishment. The responsible action may have occurred a long time before the reward was received. Moreover, not a single action but rather a combination of actions carried out in the appropriate circumstances may be responsible for the reward. For example, you could teach an agent to play a game by rewarding it when it wins or loses; it must determine the brilliant moves that were needed to win. You may try to train a dog by saying "bad dog" when you come home and find a mess. The dog has to determine, out of all of the actions it did, which of them were the actions that were responsible for the reprimand.

- Even if the dynamics of the world does not change, the effect of an action of the agent depends on what the agent will do in the future. What may initially seem like a bad thing for the agent to do may end up being an optimal action because of what the agent does in the future. This is common among planning problems, but it is complicated in the reinforcement learning context because the agent does not know, a priori, the effects of its actions.

- The explore–exploit dilemma: if the agent has worked out a good course of actions, should it continue to follow these actions (exploiting what it has determined) or should it explore to find better actions? An agent that never explores may act forever in a way that could have been much better if it had explored earlier. An agent that always explores will never use what it has learned. This dilemma is discussed further in Section 11.3.4 (page 472).

11.3.1 Evolutionary Algorithms

One way to solve reinforcement algorithms is to treat this as an optimization problem (page 144), with the aim of selecting a policy that maximizes the expected reward collected. One way to do this via **policy search**. The aim is to search through the space of all policies to find the best policy. A policy is a controller (page 48) that can be evaluated by running it in the agent acting in the environment.

Policy search is often solved as a stochastic local search algorithm (page 134) by searching in the space of policies. A policy can be evaluated by running it in the environment a number of times.

One of the difficulties is in choosing a representation of the policy. Starting from an initial policy, the policy can be repeatedly evaluated in the environment and iteratively improved. This process is called an **evolutionary algorithm** because the agent, as a whole, is evaluated on how well it survives. This is often combined with genetic algorithms (page 142), which take us one step closer to the biological analogy of competing agents mutating genes. The idea is that crossover provides a way to combine the best features of policies.

Evolutionary algorithms have a number of issues. The first is the size of the state space. If there are n states and m actions, there are m^n policies. For example, for the game described in Example 11.7 (page 463), there are $4^6 = 4,096$ different policies. For the game of Example 11.8 (page 464), there are 250 states, and so $4^{250} \approx 10^{150}$ policies. This is a very small game, but it has more policies than there are particles in the universe.

Second, evolutionary algorithms use experiences very wastefully. If an agent was in state s_2 of Example 11.7 (page 463) and it moved left, you would like it to learn that it is bad to go left from state s_2. But evolutionary algorithms wait until the agent has finished and judge the policy as a whole. Stochastic local search will randomly try doing something else in state s_2 and so may eventually determine that that action was not good, but it is very indirect. Genetic algorithms are slightly better in that the policies that have the agent going left in state s_2 will die off, but again this is very indirect.

Third, the performance of evolutionary algorithms can be very sensitive to the representation of the policy. The representation for a genetic algorithm should be such that crossover preserves the good parts of the policy. The representations are often tuned for the particular domain.

An alternative pursued in the rest of this chapter is to learn after every action. The components of the policy are learned, rather than the policy as a whole. By learning what do in each state, we can make the problem linear in the number of states rather than exponential in the number of states.

11.3.2 Temporal Differences

To understand how reinforcement learning works, first consider how to average experiences that arrive to an agent sequentially.

Suppose there is a sequence of numerical values, $v_1, v_2, v_3, \ldots$, and the goal is to predict the next value, given all of the previous values. One way to do this is to have a running approximation of the expected value of the v's. For example, given a sequence of students' grades and the aim of predicting the next grade, a reasonable prediction is to predict the average grade.

Let A_k be an estimate of the expected value based on the first k data points $v_1, \ldots, v_k$. A reasonable estimate is the sample average:

$$A_k = \frac{v_1 + \cdots + v_k}{k}.$$

Thus,

$$
\begin{aligned}
kA_k &= v_1 + \cdots + v_{k-1} + v_k \\
&= (k-1)A_{k-1} + v_k.
\end{aligned}
$$

Dividing by k gives

$$A_k = \left(1 - \frac{1}{k}\right) A_{k-1} + \frac{v_k}{k}.$$

Let $\alpha_k = \frac{1}{k}$; then

$$
\begin{aligned}
A_k &= (1 - \alpha_k)A_{k-1} + \alpha_k v_k \\
&= A_{k-1} + \alpha_k(v_k - A_{k-1}).
\end{aligned}
\tag{11.1}
$$

The difference, $v_k - A_{k-1}$, is called the **temporal difference error** or **TD error**; it specifies how different the new value, v_k, is from the old prediction, A_{k-1}. The old estimate, A_{k-1}, is updated by α_k times the TD error to get the new estimate, A_k. The qualitative interpretation of the temporal difference formula is that if the new value is higher than the old prediction, increase the predicted value; if the new value is less than the old prediction, decrease the predicted value. The change is proportional to the difference between the new value and the old prediction. Note that this equation is still valid for the first value, $k = 1$.

This analysis assumes that all of the values have an equal weight. However, suppose you are keeping an estimate of the expected value of students' grades. If schools start giving higher grades, the newer values are more useful for the estimate of the current situation than older grades, and so they should be weighted more in predicting new grades.

In reinforcement learning, the latter values of v_i (i.e., the more recent values) are more accurate than the earlier values and should be weighted more. One way to weight later examples more is to use Equation (11.1), but with α as a constant ($0 < \alpha \leq 1$) that does not depend on k. Unfortunately, this does not converge to the average value when variability exists in the values in the sequence, but it can track changes when the underlying process generating the values changes.

You could reduce α more slowly and potentially have the benefits of both approaches: weighting recent observations more and still converging to the average. You can guarantee convergence if

$$\sum_{k=1}^{\infty} \alpha_k = \infty \text{ and } \sum_{k=1}^{\infty} \alpha_k^2 < \infty.$$

The first condition is to ensure that random fluctuations and initial conditions get averaged out, and the second condition guarantees convergence.

Note that guaranteeing convergence to the average is not compatible with being able to adapt to make better predictions when the underlying process generating the values keeps changing.

For the rest of this chapter, α without a subscript is assumed to be a constant. With a subscript it is a function of the number of cases that have been combined for the particular estimate.

11.3.3   Q-learning

In Q-learning and related algorithms, an agent tries to learn the optimal policy from its history of interaction with the environment. A **history** of an agent is a sequence of state-action-rewards:

$$\langle s_0, a_0, r_1, s_1, a_1, r_2, s_2, a_2, r_3, s_3, a_3, r_4, s_4 \ldots \rangle ,$$

which means that the agent was in state s_0 and did action a_0, which resulted in it receiving reward r_1 and being in state s_1; then it did action a_1, received reward r_2, and ended up in state s_2; then it did action a_2, received reward r_3, and ended up in state s_3; and so on.

We treat this history of interaction as a sequence of experiences, where an **experience** is a tuple

$$\langle s, a, r, s' \rangle ,$$

which means that the agent was in state s, it did action a, it received reward r, and it went into state s'. These experiences will be the data from which the agent can learn what to do. As in decision-theoretic planning, the aim is for the agent to maximize its value, which is usually the discounted reward (page 402).

1: **controller** *Q-learning*(S, A, γ, α)
2:     **Inputs**
3:         S is a set of states
4:         A is a set of actions
5:         γ the discount
6:         α is the step size
7:     **Local**
8:         real array $Q[S, A]$
9:         previous state s
10:        previous action a
11:     initialize $Q[S, A]$ arbitrarily
12:     observe current state s
13:     **repeat**
14:         select and carry out an action a
15:         observe reward r and state s'
16:         $Q[s, a] \leftarrow Q[s, a] + \alpha \left(r + \gamma \max_{a'} Q[s', a'] - Q[s, a]\right)$
17:         $s \leftarrow s'$
18:     **until** termination

Figure 11.10: Q-learning controller

Recall (page 404) that $Q^*(s, a)$, where a is an action and s is a state, is the expected value (cumulative discounted reward) of doing a in state s and then following the optimal policy.

Q-learning uses temporal differences to estimate the value of $Q^*(s, a)$. In Q-learning, the agent maintains a table of $Q[S, A]$, where S is the set of states and A is the set of actions. $Q[s, a]$ represents its current estimate of $Q^*(s, a)$.

An experience $\langle s, a, r, s' \rangle$ provides one data point for the value of $Q(s, a)$. The data point is that the agent received the future value of $r + \gamma V(s')$, where $V(s') = \max_{a'} Q(s', a')$; this is the actual current reward plus the discounted estimated future value. This new data point is called a **return**. The agent can use the temporal difference equation (11.1) to update its estimate for $Q(s, a)$:

$$Q[s, a] \leftarrow Q[s, a] + \alpha \left(r + \gamma \max_{a'} Q[s', a'] - Q[s, a]\right)$$

or, equivalently,

$$Q[s, a] \leftarrow (1 - \alpha) Q[s, a] + \alpha \left(r + \gamma \max_{a'} Q[s', a']\right).$$

Figure 11.10 shows the Q-learning controller. This assumes that α is fixed; if α is varying, there will be a different count for each state–action pair and the algorithm would also have to keep track of this count.

Q-learning learns an optimal policy no matter which policy the agent is actually following (i.e., which action a it selects for any state s) as long as there is no bound on the number of times it tries an action in any state (i.e., it does not always do the same subset of actions in a state). Because it learns an optimal policy no matter which policy it is carrying out, it is called an **off-policy** method.

Example 11.9 Consider the domain Example 11.7 (page 463), shown in Figure 11.8 (page 464). Here is a sequence of $\langle s, a, r, s' \rangle$ experiences, and the update, where $\gamma = 0.9$ and $\alpha = 0.2$, and all of the Q-values are initialized to 0 (to two decimal points):

s	a	r	s'	Update
s_0	upC	-1	s_2	$Q[s_0, upC] = -0.2$
s_2	up	0	s_4	$Q[s_2, up] = 0$
s_4	$left$	10	s_0	$Q[s_4, left] = 2.0$
s_0	upC	-1	s_2	$Q[s_0, upC] = -0.36$
s_2	up	0	s_4	$Q[s_2, up] = 0.36$
s_4	$left$	10	s_0	$Q[s_4, left] = 3.6$
s_0	up	0	s_2	$Q[s_0, upC] = 0.06$
s_2	up	-100	s_2	$Q[s_2, up] = -19.65$
s_2	up	0	s_4	$Q[s_2, up] = -15.07$
s_4	$left$	10	s_0	$Q[s_4, left] = 4.89$

Notice how the reward of -100 is averaged in with the other rewards. After the experience of receiving the -100 reward, $Q[s_2, up]$ gets the value

$$0.8 \times 0.36 + 0.2 \times (-100 + 0.9 \times 0.36) = -19.65$$

At the next step, the same action is carried out with a different outcome, and $Q[s_2, up]$ gets the value

$$0.8 \times -19.65 + 0.2 \times (0 + 0.9 \times 3.6) = -15.07$$

After more experiences going up from s_2 and not receiving the reward of -100, the large negative reward will eventually be averaged in with the positive rewards and eventually have less influence on the value of $Q[s_2, up]$, until going up in state s_2 once again receives a reward of -100.

It is instructive to consider how using α_k to average the rewards works when the earlier estimates are much worse than more recent estimates. The following example shows the effect of a sequence of deterministic actions. Note that when an action is deterministic we can use $\alpha = 1$.

Example 11.10 Consider the domain Example 11.7 (page 463), shown in Figure 11.8 (page 464). Suppose that the agent has the experience

$$\langle s_0, right, 0, s_1, upC, -1, s_3, upC, -1, s_5, left, 0, s_4, left, 10, s_0 \rangle$$

and repeats this sequence of actions a number of times. (Note that a real Q-learning agent would not keep repeating the same actions, particularly when

This is a trace of Q-learning described in Example 11.10.

(a) Q-learning for a deterministic sequence of actions with a separate α_k-value for each state–action pair, $\alpha_k = 1/k$.

Iteration	$Q[s_0, right]$	$Q[s_1, upC]$	$Q[s_3, upC]$	$Q[s_5, left]$	$Q[s_4, left]$
1	0	−1	−1	0	10
2	0	−1	−1	4.5	10
3	0	−1	0.35	6.0	10
4	0	−0.92	1.36	6.75	10
10	0.03	0.51	4	8.1	10
100	2.54	4.12	6.82	9.5	11.34
1000	4.63	5.93	8.46	11.3	13.4
10,000	6.08	7.39	9.97	12.83	14.9
100,000	7.27	8.58	11.16	14.02	16.08
1,000,000	8.21	9.52	12.1	14.96	17.02
10,000,000	8.96	10.27	12.85	15.71	17.77
∞	11.85	13.16	15.74	18.6	20.66

(b) Q-learning for a deterministic sequence of actions with $\alpha = 1$:

Iteration	$Q[s_0, right]$	$Q[s_1, upC]$	$Q[s_3, upC]$	$Q[s_5, left]$	$Q[s_4, left]$
1	0	−1	−1	0	10
2	0	−1	−1	9	10
3	0	−1	7.1	9	10
4	0	5.39	7.1	9	10
5	4.85	5.39	7.1	9	14.37
6	4.85	5.39	7.1	12.93	14.37
10	7.72	8.57	10.64	15.25	16.94
20	10.41	12.22	14.69	17.43	19.37
30	11.55	12.83	15.37	18.35	20.39
40	11.74	13.09	15.66	18.51	20.57
∞	11.85	13.16	15.74	18.6	20.66

(c) Q-values after full exploration and convergence:

Iteration	$Q[s_0, right]$	$Q[s_1, upC]$	$Q[s_3, upC]$	$Q[s_5, left]$	$Q[s_4, left]$
∞	19.5	21.14	24.08	27.87	30.97

Figure 11.11: Updates for a particular run of Q-learning

some of them look bad, but we will assume this to let us understand how Q-learning works.)

Figure 11.11 shows how the Q-values are updated though a repeated execution of this action sequence. In both of these tables, the Q-values are initialized to 0.

(a) In the top run there is a separate α_k-value for each state–action pair. Notice how, in iteration 1, only the immediate rewards are updated. In iteration

2, there is a one-step backup from the positive rewards. Note that the -1 is not backed up because another action is available that has a Q-value of 0. In the third iteration, there is a two-step backup. $Q[s_3, upC]$ is updated because of the reward of 10, two steps ahead; its value is the average of its experiences: $(-1 + -1 + (-1 + 0.9 \times 6))/3$.

(b) The second run is where $\alpha = 1$; thus, it only takes into account the current estimate. Again, the reward is backed up one step in each iteration. In the third iteration, $Q[s_3, upC]$ is updated because of the reward of 10 two steps ahead, but with $\alpha = 1$, the algorithm ignores its previous estimates and uses its new experience, $-1 + 0.9 \times 0.9$. Having $\alpha = 1$ converges much faster than when $\alpha_k = 1/k$, but $\alpha = 1$ only converges when the actions are deterministic because $\alpha = 1$ implicitly assumes that the last reward and resulting state are representative of future ones.

(c) If the algorithm is run allowing the agent to explore, as is normal, some of the Q-values after convergence are shown in part (c). Note that, because there are stochastic actions, α cannot be 1 for the algorithm to converge. Note that the Q-values are larger than for the deterministic sequence of actions because these actions do not form an optimal policy.

The final policy after convergence is to do *up* in state s_0, *upC* in state s_2, *up* in states s_1 and s_3, and *left* in states s_4 and s_5.

You can run the applet for this example that is available on the book web site. Try different initializations, and try varying α.

11.3.4   Exploration and Exploitation

The Q-learning algorithm does not specify what the agent should actually do. The agent learns a Q-function that can be used to determine an optimal action. There are two things that are useful for the agent to do:

- **exploit** the knowledge that it has found for the current state s by doing one of the actions a that maximizes $Q[s, a]$.

- **explore** in order to build a better estimate of the optimal Q-function. That is, it should select a different action from the one that it currently thinks is best.

There have been a number of suggested ways to trade off exploration and exploitation:

- The ϵ-greedy strategy is to select the greedy action (one that maximizes $Q[s, a]$) all but ϵ of the time and to select a random action ϵ of the time, where $0 \leq \epsilon \leq 1$. It is possible to change ϵ through time. Intuitively, early in the life of the agent it should select a more random strategy to encourage initial exploration and, as time progresses, it should act more greedily.

- One problem with an ϵ-greedy strategy is that it treats all of the actions, apart from the best action, equivalently. If there are two seemingly good actions and more actions that look less promising, it may be more sensible to select among the good actions: putting more effort toward determining which of these promising actions is best, rather than putting in effort to explore the actions that look bad. One way to do that is to select action a with a probability depending on the value of $Q[s, a]$. This is known as a **soft-max** action selection. A common method is to use a **Gibbs** or **Boltzmann distribution**, where the probability of selecting action a in state s is proportional to $e^{Q[s,a]/\tau}$. That is, in state s, the agent selects action a with probability

$$\frac{e^{Q[s,a]/\tau}}{\sum_a e^{Q[s,a]/\tau}}$$

where $\tau > 0$ is the **temperature** specifying how randomly values should be chosen. When τ is high, the actions are chosen in almost equal amounts. As the temperature is reduced, the highest-valued actions are more likely to be chosen and, in the limit as $\tau \rightarrow 0$, the best action is always chosen.

- An alternative is "optimism in the face of uncertainty": initialize the Q-function to values that encourage exploration. If the Q-values are initialized to high values, the unexplored areas will look good, so that a greedy search will tend to explore. This does encourage exploration; however, the agent can hallucinate that some state–action pairs are good for a long time, even though there is no real evidence for it. A state only gets to look bad when all its actions look bad; but when all of these actions lead to states that look good, it takes a long time to get a realistic view of the actual values. This is a case where old estimates of the Q-values can be quite bad estimates of the actual Q-value, and these can remain bad estimates for a long time. To get fast convergence, the initial values should be as close as possible to the final values; trying to make them an overestimate will make convergence slower. Relying only on optimism in the face if uncertainty is not useful if the dynamics can change, because it is treating the initial time period as the time to explore and, after this initial exploration, there is no more exploration.

It is interesting to compare the interaction of the exploration strategies with different choices for how α is updated. See Exercise 11.8 (page 487).

11.3.5 Evaluating Reinforcement Learning Algorithms

We can judge a reinforcement learning algorithm by how good a policy it finds and how much reward it receives while acting in the world. Which is more important depends on how the agent will be deployed. If there is sufficient time for the agent to learn safely before it is deployed, the final policy may be the most important. If the agent has to learn while being deployed, it may never get to the stage where it has learned the optimal policy, and the reward it receives while learning may be what the agent wants to maximize.

One way to show the performance of a reinforcement learning algorithm is to plot the cumulative reward (the sum of all rewards received so far) as a function of the number of steps. One algorithm dominates another if its plot is consistently above the other.

Example 11.11 Figure 11.12 (on the next page) compares four runs of Q-learning on the game of Example 11.8 (page 464). These plots were generated

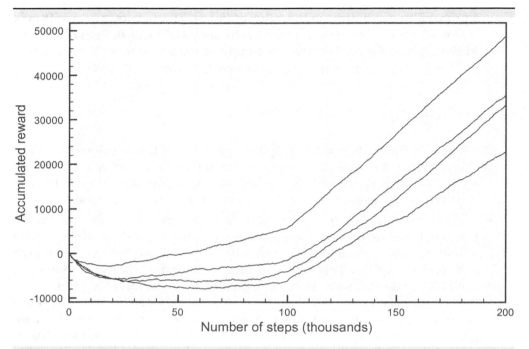

Figure 11.12: Cumulative reward as a function of the number of steps

using the "trace on console" of the applet available on the course web site and then plotting the resulting data.

The plots are for different runs that varied according to whether α was fixed, according to the initial values of the Q-function, and according to the randomness in the action selection. They all used greedy exploit of 80% (i.e., $\epsilon = 0.2$) for the first 100,000 steps, and 100% (i.e., $\epsilon = 0.0$) for the next 100,000 steps. The top plot dominated the others.

There is a great deal variability of each algorithm on different runs, so to actually compare these algorithms one must run the same algorithm multiple times. For this domain, the cumulative rewards depend on whether the agent learns to visit the repair station, which it does not always learn. The cumulative reward therefore tends to be bimodal for this example. See Exercise 11.8 (page 487).

There are three statistics of this plot that are important:

- The asymptotic slope shows how good the policy is after the algorithm has stabilized.
- The minimum of the curve shows how much reward must be sacrificed before it starts to improve.
- The zero crossing shows how long it takes until the algorithm has recouped its cost of learning.

The last two statistics are applicable when both positive and negative rewards are available and having these balanced is reasonable behavior. For other cases, the cumulative reward should be compared with reasonable behavior that is appropriate for the domain; see Exercise 11.7 (page 487).

One thing that should be noted about the cumulative reward plot is that it measures total reward, yet the algorithms optimize discounted reward at each step. In general, you should optimize for, and evaluate your algorithm using, the optimality criterion that is most appropriate for the domain.

11.3.6 On-Policy Learning

Q-learning learns an optimal policy no matter what the agent does, as long as it explores enough. There may be cases where ignoring what the agent actually does is dangerous (there will be large negative rewards). An alternative is to learn the value of the policy the agent is actually carrying out so that it can be iteratively improved. As a result, the learner can take into account the costs associated with exploration.

An **off-policy learner** learns the value of the optimal policy independently of the agent's actions. Q-learning is an off-policy learner. An **on-policy learner** learns the value of the policy being carried out by the agent, including the exploration steps.

SARSA (so called because it uses state-action-reward-state-action experiences to update the Q-values) is an *on-policy* reinforcement learning algorithm that estimates the value of the policy being followed. An experience in SARSA is of the form $\langle s, a, r, s', a' \rangle$, which means that the agent was in state s, did action a, received reward r, and ended up in state s', from which it decided to do action a'. This provides a new experience to update $Q(s, a)$. The new value that this experience provides is $r + \gamma Q(s', a')$.

Figure 11.13 gives the SARSA algorithm.

SARSA takes into account the current exploration policy which, for example, may be greedy with random steps. It can find a different policy than Q-learning in situations when exploring may incur large penalties. For example, when a robot goes near the top of stairs, even if this is an optimal policy, it may be dangerous for exploration steps. SARSA will discover this and adopt a policy that keeps the robot away from the stairs. It will find a policy that is optimal, taking into account the exploration inherent in the policy.

Example 11.12 In Example 11.10 (page 470), the optimal policy is to go up from state s_0 in Figure 11.8 (page 464). However, if the agent is exploring, this may not be a good thing to do because exploring from state s_2 is very dangerous.

If the agent is carrying out the policy that includes exploration, "when in state s, 80% of the time select the action a that maximizes $Q[s, a]$, and 20% of the time select an action at random," going up from s_0 is not optimal. An on-policy learner will try to optimize the policy the agent is following, not the optimal policy that does not include exploration.

If you were to repeat the experiment of Figure 11.11 (page 471), SARSA would back up the -1 values, whereas Q-learning did not because actions with an estimated value of 0 were available. The Q-values in parts (a) and (b) of that figure would converge to the same values, because they both converge to the value of that policy.

The Q-values of the optimal policy are less in SARSA than in Q-learning. The values for SARSA corresponding to part (c) of Figure 11.11 (page 471), are as follows:

Iteration	$Q[s_0, right]$	$Q[s_1, upC]$	$Q[s_3, upC]$	$Q[s_5, left]$	$Q[s_4, left]$
∞	9.2	10.1	12.7	15.7	18.0

The optimal policy using SARSA is to go right at state s_0. This is the optimal policy for an agent that does 20% exploration, because exploration is dangerous. If the rate of exploration were reduced, the optimal policy found would change. However, with less exploration, it would take longer to find an optimal policy.

SARSA is useful when you want to optimize the value of an agent that is exploring. If you want to do offline learning, and then use that policy in an agent that does not explore, Q-learning may be more appropriate.

---

controller SARSA(S, A, γ, α)
inputs:
    S is a set of states
    A is a set of actions
    γ the discount
    α is the step size
internal state:
    real array $Q[S, A]$
    previous state s
    previous action a
begin
    initialize $Q[S, A]$ arbitrarily
    observe current state s
    select action a using a policy based on Q
    repeat forever:
        carry out an action a
        observe reward r and state s'
        select action a' using a policy based on Q
        $Q[s, a] \leftarrow Q[s, a] + \alpha\,(r + \gamma Q[s', a'] - Q[s, a])$
        $s \leftarrow s'$
        $a \leftarrow a'$
    end-repeat
end

Figure 11.13: SARSA: on-policy reinforcement learning

11.3.7 Assigning Credit and Blame to Paths

In Q-learning and SARSA, only the previous state–action pair has its value revised when a reward is received. Intuitively, when an agent takes a number of steps that lead to a reward, all of the steps along the way could be held responsible and so receive some of the credit or the blame for a reward. This section gives an algorithm that assigns the credit and blame for all of the steps that lead to a reward.

Example 11.13 Suppose there is an action *right* that visits the states s_1, s_2, s_3, and s_4 in this order and a reward is only given when the agent enters s_4 from s_3, and any action from s_4 returns to state s_1. There is also an action *left* that moves to the left except in state s_4. In Q-learning and SARSA, after traversing right through the states s_1, s_2, s_3, and s_4 and receiving the reward, only the value of $Q[s_3, right]$ is updated. If the same sequence of states is visited again, the value of $Q[s_2, right]$ will be updated when it transitions into s_3. The value of $Q[s_1, right]$ is only updated after the next transition from state s_1 to s_2. In this sense, we say that Q-learning does a one-step backup.

Consider updating the value of $Q[s_3, right]$ based on the reward for entering state s_4. From the perspective of state s_4, the algorithm is doing a one-step backup. From the perspective of state s_3, it is doing a one-step look-ahead. To make the algorithm allow the blame to be associated with more than the previous step, the reward from entering step s_4 could do a two-step backup to update s_2 or, equivalently, a two-step look-ahead from s_2 and update s_2's value when the reward from entering s_4 is received. We will describe the algorithm in terms of a look-ahead but implement it using a backup.

With a two-step look-ahead, suppose the agent is in state s_t, does action a_t, ends up in state s_{t+1}, and receives reward r_{t+1}, then does action a_{t+1}, resulting in state s_{t+2} and receiving reward r_{t+2}. A two-step look-ahead at time t gives the return $R_t^{(2)} = r_{t+1} + \gamma r_{t+2} + \gamma^2 V(s_{t+2})$, thus giving the TD error

$$\delta_t = r_{t+1} + \gamma r_{t+2} + \gamma^2 V(s_{t+2}) - Q[s_t, a_t],$$

where $V(s_{t+2})$ is an estimate of the value of s_{t+2}. The two-step update is

$$Q[s_t, a_t] \leftarrow Q[s_t, a_t] + \alpha \delta_t.$$

Unfortunately, this is not a good estimate of the optimal Q-value, Q^*, because action a_{t+1} may not be an optimal action. For example, if action a_{t+1} was the action that takes the agent into a position with a reward of -10, and better actions were available, the agent should not update $Q[s_0, a_0]$. However, this multiple-step backup provides an improved estimate of the policy that the agent is actually following. If the agent is following policy π, this backup gives an improved estimate of Q^π. Thus multiple-step backup can be used in an on-policy method such as SARSA.

Suppose the agent is in state s_t, and it performs action a_t resulting in reward r_{t+1} and state s_{t+1}. It then does action a_{t+1}, resulting in reward r_{t+2} and state

s_{t+2}, and so forth. An n-step return at time t, where $n \geq 1$, written $R_t^{(n)}$, is a data point for the estimated future value of the action at time t, given by looking n steps ahead, is

$$R_t^{(n)} = r_{t+1} + \gamma r_{t+2} + \gamma^2 r_{t+3} + \cdots + \gamma^{n-1} r_{t+n} + \gamma^n V(s_{t+n}).$$

This could be used to update $Q[s_t, a_t]$ using the TD error $R_t^{(n)} - Q[s_t, a_t]$. However, it is difficult to know which n to use. Instead of selecting one particular n and looking forward n steps, it is possible to have an average of a number of n-step returns. One way to do this is to have a weighted average of all n-step returns, in which the returns in the future are exponentially decayed, with a decay of λ. This is the intuition behind the method called SARSA(λ); when a reward is received, the values of all of the visited states are updated. Those states farther in the past receive less of the credit or blame for the reward.

Let

$$R_t^\lambda = (1 - \lambda) \sum_{n=1}^\infty \lambda^{n-1} R_t^{(n)},$$

where $(1 - \lambda)$ is a normalizing constant to ensure we are getting an average. The following table gives the details of the sum:

look-ahead	Weight	Return
1 step	$1 - \lambda$	$r_{t+1} + \gamma V(s_{t+1})$
2 step	$(1 - \lambda)\lambda$	$r_{t+1} + \gamma r_{t+2} + \gamma^2 V(s_{t+2})$
3 step	$(1 - \lambda)\lambda^2$	$r_{t+1} + \gamma r_{t+2} + \gamma^2 r_{t+3} + \gamma^3 V(s_{t+3})$
4 step	$(1 - \lambda)\lambda^3$	$r_{t+1} + \gamma r_{t+2} + \gamma^2 r_{t+3} + \gamma^3 r_{t+4} + \gamma^4 V(s_{t+3})$
$\cdots$	$\cdots$	$\cdots$
n step	$(1 - \lambda)\lambda^{n-1}$	$r_{t+1} + \gamma r_{t+2} + \gamma^2 r_{t+3} + \cdots + \gamma^n V(s_{t+n})$
$\cdots$	$\cdots$	$\cdots$
total	1	

Collecting together the common r_{t+i} terms gives

$$\begin{aligned} R_t^\lambda = \ & r_{t+1} + \gamma V(s_{t+1}) - \lambda \gamma V(s_{t+1}) \\ & + \lambda \gamma r_{t+2} + \lambda \gamma^2 V(s_{t+2}) - \lambda^2 \gamma^2 V(s_{t+2}) \\ & + \lambda^2 \gamma^2 r_{t+3} + \lambda^2 \gamma^3 V(s_{t+3}) - \lambda^3 \gamma^3 V(s_{t+3}) \\ & + \lambda^3 \gamma^3 r_{t+4} + \lambda^3 \gamma^4 V(s_{t+4}) - \lambda^4 \gamma^4 V(s_{t+4}) \\ & + \cdots . \end{aligned}$$

This will be used in a version of SARSA in which the future estimate of $V(s_{t+i})$ is the value of $Q[s_{t+i}, a_{t+i}]$. The TD error – the return minus the state estimate –

is

$$
\begin{aligned}
R_t^\lambda - Q[s_t, a_t] \;=\; & r_{t+1} + \gamma Q[s_{t+1}, a_{t+1}] - Q[s_t, a_t] \\
& + \lambda\gamma(r_{t+2} + \gamma Q[s_{t+2}, a_{t+2}] - Q[s_{t+1}, a_{t+1}]) \\
& + \lambda^2\gamma^2(r_{t+3} + \gamma Q[s_{t+3}, a_{t+3}] - Q[s_{t+2}, a_{t+2}]) \\
& + \lambda^3\gamma^3(r_{t+4} + \gamma Q[s_{t+4}, a_{t+4}] - Q[s_{t+3}, a_{t+3}]) \\
& + \dots .
\end{aligned}
$$

Instead of waiting until the end, which may never occur, SARSA(λ) updates the value of $Q[s_t, a_t]$ at every time in the future. When the agent receives reward r_{t+i}, it can use the appropriate sum in the preceding equation to update $Q[s_t, a_t]$. The preceding description refers to all times; therefore, the update $r_{t+3} + \gamma Q[s_{t+3}, a_{t+3}] - Q[s_{t+2}, a_{t+2}]$ can be used to update all previous states. An agent can do this by keeping an **eligibility trace** that specifies how much a state–action pair should be updated at each time step. When a state–action pair is first visited, its eligibility is set to 1. At each subsequent time step its eligibility is reduced by a factor of $\lambda\gamma$. When the state–action pair is subsequently visited, 1 is added to its eligibility.

The eligibility trace is implemented by an array $e[S, A]$, where S is the set of all states and A is the set of all actions. After every action is carried out, the Q-value for every state–action pair is updated.

The algorithm, known as **SARSA(λ)**, is given in Figure 11.14 (on the next page).

Although this algorithm specifies that $Q[s, a]$ is updated for every state s and action a whenever a new reward is received, it may be much more efficient and only slightly less accurate to only update those values with an eligibility over some threshold.

11.3.8   Model-Based Methods

In many applications of reinforcement learning, plenty of time is available for computation between each action. For example, a physical robot may have many seconds between each action. Q-learning, which only does one backup per action, will not make full use of the available computation time.

An alternative to just learning the Q-values is to use the data to learn the model. That is, an agent uses its experience to explicitly learn $P(s'|s, a)$ and $R(s, a, s')$. For each action that the agent carries out in the environment, the agent can then do a number of steps of asynchronous value iteration (page 406) to give a better estimate of the Q-function.

Figure 11.15 (page 481) shows a generic model-based reinforcement learner. As with other reinforcement learning programs, it keeps track of $Q[S, A]$, but it also maintains a model of the dynamics, represented here as T, where $T[s, a, s']$ is the count of the number of times that the agent has done a in state s and ended up in state s'. The counts are added to prior counts, as in a Dirichlet distribution (page 337), to compute probabilities. The algorithm assumes

controller SARSA$(\lambda, S, A, \gamma, \alpha)$
inputs:
    S is a set of states
    A is a set of actions
    γ the discount
    α is the step size
    λ is the decay rate
internal state:
    real array $Q[S, A]$
    real array $e[S, A]$
    previous state s
    previous action a
begin
    initialize $Q[S, A]$ arbitrarily
    initialize $e[s, a] = 0$ for all s, a
    observe current state s
    select action a using a policy based on Q
    repeat forever:
        carry out an action a
        observe reward r and state s'
        select action a' using a policy based on Q
        $\delta \leftarrow r + \gamma Q[s', a'] - Q[s, a]$
        $e[s, a] \leftarrow e[s, a] + 1$
        for all s'', a'' :
            $Q[s'', a''] \leftarrow Q[s'', a''] + \alpha \delta e[s'', a'']$
            $e[s'', a''] \leftarrow \gamma \lambda e[s'', a'']$
        $s \leftarrow s'$
        $a \leftarrow a'$
    end-repeat
end

Figure 11.14: SARSA(λ)

a common prior count. The $R[s, a, s']$ array maintains the average reward for transitioning from state s, doing action a, and ending up in state s'.

After each action, the agent observes the reward r and the resulting state s'. It then updates the transition-count matrix T and the average reward R. It then does a number of steps of asynchronous value iteration, using the updated probability model derived from T and the updated reward model. There are three main undefined parts to this algorithm:

- Which Q-values should be updated? It seems reasonable that the algorithm should at least update $Q[s, a]$, because more data have been received on the transition probability and reward. From there it can

controller ModelBasedReinforementLearner(S, A, γ, c)
inputs:
 S is a set of states
 A is a set of actions
 γ the discount
 c is prior count
internal state:
 real array $Q[S, A]$
 real array $R[S, A, S]$
 integer array $T[S, A, S]$
 state s, s'
 action a
initialize $Q[S, A]$ arbitrarily
initialize $R[S, A, S]$ arbitrarily
initialize $T[S, A, S]$ to zero
observe current state s
select and carry out action a
repeat forever:
 observe reward r and state s'
 select and carry out action a
 $T[s, a, s'] \leftarrow T[s, a, s'] + 1$
 $R[s, a, s'] \leftarrow R[s, a, s'] + \dfrac{r - R[s, a, s']}{T[s, a, s']}$
 $s \leftarrow s'$
 repeat
  select state s_1, action a_1
  let $P = \sum\limits_{s_2}(T[s_1, a_1, s_2] + c)$
  $Q[s_1, a_1] \leftarrow \sum\limits_{s_2} \dfrac{T[s_1, a_1, s_2] + c}{P}\left(R[s_1, a_1, s_2] + \gamma \max\limits_{a_2} Q[s_2, a_2]\right)$
 until an observation arrives

Figure 11.15: Model-based reinforcement learner

either do random updates or determine which Q-values would change the most. The elements that potentially have their values changed the most are the $Q[s_1, a_1]$ with the highest probability of ending up at a Q-value that has changed the most (i.e., where $Q[s_1, a_2]$ has changed the most). This can be implemented by keeping a priority queue of Q-values to consider.

- How many steps of asynchronous value iteration should be done between actions? An agent should continue doing steps of value iteration until it has to act or until it gets new information. Figure 11.15 assumes that the agent acts and then waits for an observation to arrive. When an observation arrives, the agent acts as soon as possible. There are may variants, including a more relaxed agent that runs the repeat loop in parallel with observing and acting. Such an agent acts when it must, and it updates the transition and reward model when it observes.

- What should be the initial values for $R[S, A, S]$ and $Q[S, A]$? Once the agent has observed a reward for a particular $\langle s, a, s' \rangle$ transition, it will use the average of all of the rewards received for that transition. However, it requires some value for the transitions it has never experienced when updating Q. If it is using the exploration strategy of optimism in the face of uncertainty, it can use *Rmax*, the maximum reward possible, as the initial value for R, to encourage exploration. As in value iteration (page 404), it is best to initialize Q to be as close as possible to the final Q-value.

The algorithm in Figure 11.15 assumes that the prior count is the same for all $\langle s, a, s' \rangle$ transitions. If some prior knowledge exists that some transitions are impossible or some are more likely, the prior count should not be uniform.

This algorithm assumes that the rewards depend on the initial state, the action, and the final state. Moreover, it assumes that the reward for a $\langle s, a, s' \rangle$ transition is unknown until that exact transition has been observed. If the reward only depends on the initial state and the action, it is more efficient to have an $R[S, A]$. If there are separate action costs and rewards for entering a state, and the agent can separately observe the costs and rewards, the reward function can be decomposed into $C[A]$ and $R[S]$, leading to more efficient learning.

It is difficult to directly compare the model-based and model-free reinforcement learners. Typically, model-based learners are much more efficient in terms of experience; many fewer experiences are needed to learn well. However, the model-free methods often use less computation time. If experience was cheap, a different comparison would be needed than if experience was expensive.

11.3.9   Reinforcement Learning with Features

Usually, there are too many states to reason about explicitly. The alternative to reasoning explicitly in terms of states is to reason in terms of features. In this section, we consider reinforcement learning that uses an approximation of the Q-function using a linear combination of features of the state and the action. This is the simplest case and often works well. However, this approach requires careful selection of features; the designer should find features adequate to represent the Q-function. This is often a difficult engineering problem.

SARSA with Linear Function Approximation

You can use a linear function of features to approximate the Q-function in SARSA. This algorithm uses the on-policy method SARSA, because the agent's experiences sample the reward from the policy the agent is actually following, rather than sampling an optimum policy.

A number of ways are available to get a feature-based representation of the Q-function. In this section, we use features of both the state and the action to provide features for the linear function.

Suppose $F_1, \ldots, F_n$ are numerical features of the state and the action. Thus, $F_i(s, a)$ provides the value for the ith feature for state s and action a. These features are typically binary, with domain $\{0, 1\}$, but they can also be other numerical features. These features will be used to represent the Q-function.

$$Q_{\overline{w}}(s, a) = w_0 + w_1 F_1(s, a) + \cdots + w_n F_n(s, a)$$

for some tuple of weights, $\overline{w} = \langle w_0, w_1, \ldots, w_n \rangle$. Assume that there is an extra feature F_0 whose value is always 1, so that w_0 does not have to be a special case.

Example 11.14 In the grid game of Example 11.8 (page 464), some possible features are the following:

- $F_1(s, a)$ has value 1 if action a would most likely take the agent from state s into a location where a monster could appear and has value 0 otherwise.

- $F_2(s, a)$ has value 1 if action a would most likely take the agent into a wall and has value 0 otherwise.

- $F_3(s, a)$ has value 1 if step a would most likely take the agent toward a prize.

- $F_4(s, a)$ has value 1 if the agent is damaged in state s and action a takes it toward the repair station.

- $F_5(s, a)$ has value 1 if the agent is damaged and action a would most likely take the agent into a location where a monster could appear and has value 0 otherwise. That is, it is the same as $F_1(s, a)$ but is only applicable when the agent is damaged.

- $F_6(s, a)$ has value 1 if the agent is damaged in state s and has value 0 otherwise.

- $F_7(s, a)$ has value 1 if the agent is not damaged in state s and has value 0 otherwise.

- $F_8(s, a)$ has value 1 if the agent is damaged and there is a prize ahead in direction a.

- $F_9(s, a)$ has value 1 if the agent is not damaged and there is a prize ahead in direction a.

- $F_{10}(s, a)$ has the value of the x-value in state s if there is a prize at location P_0 in state s. That is, it is the distance from the left wall if there is a prize at location P_0.

- $F_{11}(s, a)$ has the value $4 - x$, where x is the horizontal position in state s if there is a prize at location P_0 in state s. That is, it is the distance from the right wall if there is a prize at location P_0.

- $F_{12}(s,a)$ to $F_{29}(s,a)$ are like F_{10} and F_{11} for different combinations of the prize location and the distance from each of the four walls. For the case where the prize is at location P_0, the y-distance could take into account the wall.

An example linear function is

$$Q(s,a)$$
$$= 2.0 - 1.0 * F_1(s,a) - 0.4 * F_2(s,a) - 1.3 * F_3(s,a)$$
$$- 0.5 * F_4(s,a) - 1.2 * F_5(s,a) - 1.6 * F_6(s,a) + 3.5 * F_7(s,a)$$
$$+ 0.6 * F_8(s,a) + 0.6 * F_9(s,a) - 0.0 * F_{10}(s,a) + 1.0 * F_{11}(s,a) + \ldots .$$

These are the learned values (to one decimal place) for one run of the algorithm that follows.

An experience in SARSA of the form $\langle s,a,r,s',a' \rangle$ (the agent was in state s, did action a, and received reward r and ended up in state s', in which it decided to do action a') provides the new estimate of $r + \gamma Q(s',a')$ to update $Q(s,a)$. This experience can be used as a data point for **linear regression** (page 304). Let $\delta = r + \gamma Q(s',a') - Q(s,a)$. Using Equation (7.2) (page 305), weight w_i is updated by

$$w_i \leftarrow w_i + \eta \delta F_i(s,a).$$

This update can then be incorporated into SARSA, giving the algorithm shown in Figure 11.16.

Selecting an action a could be done using an ϵ-greedy function: with probability ϵ, an agent selects a random action and otherwise it selects an action that maximizes $Q_{\overline{w}}(s,a)$.

Although this program is simple to implement, **feature engineering** – choosing what features to include – is non-trivial. The linear function must not only convey the best action to carry out, it must also convey the information about what future states are useful.

Many variations of this algorithm exist. Different function approximations, such as a neural network or a decision tree with a linear function at the leaves, could be used. A common variant is to have a separate function for each action. This is equivalent to having the Q-function approximated by a decision tree that splits on actions and then has a linear function. It is also possible to split on other features.

A linear function approximation can also be combined with other methods such as SARSA(λ), Q-learning, or model-based methods. Note that some of these methods have different convergence guarantees and different levels of performance.

Example 11.15 On the AIspace web site, there is an open-source implementation of this algorithm for the game of Example 11.8 (page 464) with the features of Example 11.14. Try stepping through the algorithm for individual steps, trying to understand how each step updates each parameter. Now run it for a number of steps. Consider the performance using the evaluation measures of Section 11.3.5 (page 473). Try to make sense of the values of the parameters learned.

11.4 Review

The following are the main points you should have learned from this chapter:

- EM is an iterative method to learn the parameters of models with hidden variables (including the case in which the classification is hidden).
- The probabilities and the structure of belief networks can be learned from complete data. The probabilities can be derived from counts. The structure can be learned by searching for the best model given the data.
- Missing values in examples are often not missing at random. Why they are missing is often important to determine.
- A Markov decision process is an appropriate formalism for reinforcement learning. A common method is to learn an estimate of the value of doing each action in a state, as represented by the $Q(S, A)$ function.
- In reinforcement learning, an agent should trade off exploiting its knowledge and exploring to improve its knowledge.

1: **controller** $SARSA\text{-}FA(\overline{F}, \gamma, \eta)$
2:     **Inputs**
3:         $\overline{F} = \langle F_1, \ldots, F_n \rangle$: a set of features
4:         $\gamma \in [0, 1]$: discount factor
5:         $\eta > 0$: step size for gradient descent
6:     **Local**
7:         weights $\overline{w} = \langle w_0, \ldots, w_n \rangle$, initialized arbitrarily
8:     observe current state s
9:     select action a
10:     **repeat**
11:         carry out action a
12:         observe reward r and state s'
13:         select action a' (using a policy based on $Q_{\overline{w}}$)
14:         let $\delta = r + \gamma Q_{\overline{w}}(s', a') - Q_{\overline{w}}(s, a)$
15:         **for** $i = 0$ **to** n **do**
16:             $w_i \leftarrow w_i + \eta \delta F_i(s, a)$
17:         $s \leftarrow s'$
18:         $a \leftarrow a'$
19:     **until** termination

Figure 11.16: SARSA with linear function approximation

- Off-policy learning, such as Q-learning, learns the value of the optimal policy. On-policy learning, such as SARSA, learns the value of the policy the agent is actually carrying out (which includes the exploration).
- Model-based reinforcement learning separates learning the dynamics and reward models from the decision-theoretic planning of what to do given the models.

11.5 References and Further Reading

Unsupervised learning is discussed by Fisher [1987] and Cheeseman, Kelly, Self, Stutz, Taylor, and Freeman [1988]. Bayesian classifiers are discussed by Duda et al. [2001] and Langley, Iba, and Thompson [1992]. Friedman and Goldszmidt [1996a] discuss how the naive Bayesian classifier can be generalized to allow for more appropriate independence assumptions.

For an overview of learning belief networks, see Heckerman [1999], Darwiche [2009], and [Koller and Friedman, 2009]. Structure learning using decision trees is based on Friedman and Goldszmidt [1996b].

For an introduction to reinforcement learning, see Sutton and Barto [1998] or Kaelbling, Littman, and Moore [1996]. Bertsekas and Tsitsiklis [1996] investigate function approximation and its interaction with reinforcement learning.

11.6 Exercises

Exercise 11.1 Consider the unsupervised data of Figure 11.1 (page 454).

(a) How many different stable assignments of examples to classes does the k-means algorithm find when $k = 2$? [Hint: Try running the algorithm on the data with a number of different starting points, but also think about what assignments of examples to classes are stable.] Do not count permutations of the labels as different assignments.

(b) How many different stable assignments are there when $k = 3$?

(c) How many different stable assignments are there when $k = 4$?

(d) Why might someone suggest that three is the natural number of classes in this example? Give a definition for "natural" number of classes, and use this data to justify the definition.

Exercise 11.2 Suppose the k-means algorithm is run for an increasing sequence of values for k, and that it is run for a number of times for each k to find the assignment with a global minimum error. Is it possible that a number of values of k exist for which the error plateaus and then has a large improvement (e.g., when the error for $k = 3$, $k = 4$, and $k = 5$ are about the same, but the error for $k = 6$ is much lower)? If so, give an example. If not, explain why.

Exercise 11.3 Give an algorithm for EM for unsupervised learning [Figure 11.4 (page 457)] that does not store an A array, but rather recomputes the appropriate value for the M step. Each iteration should only involve one sweep through the data set. [Hint: For each tuple in the data set, update all of the relevant M_i-values.]

Exercise 11.4 Suppose a Q-learning agent, with fixed α and discount γ, was in state 34, did action 7, received reward 3, and ended up in state 65. What value(s) get updated? Give an expression for the new value. (Be as specific as possible.)

Exercise 11.5 Explain what happens in reinforcement learning if the agent always chooses the action that maximizes the Q-value. Suggest two ways to force the agent to explore.

Exercise 11.6 Explain how Q-learning fits in with the agent architecture of Section 2.2.1 (page 46). Suppose that the Q-learning agent has discount factor γ, a step size of α, and is carrying out an ϵ-greedy exploration strategy.

(a) What are the components of the belief state of the Q-learning agent?

(b) What are the percepts?

(c) What is the command function of the Q-learning agent?

(d) What is the belief-state transition function of the Q-learning agent?

Exercise 11.7 For the plot of the total reward as a function of time as in Figure 11.12 (page 474), the minimum and zero crossing are only meaningful statistics when balancing positive and negative rewards is reasonable behavior. Suggest what should replace these statistics when zero is not an appropriate definition of reasonable behavior. [Hint: Think about the cases that have only positive reward or only negative reward.]

Exercise 11.8 Compare the different parameter settings for the game of Example 11.8 (page 464). In particular compare the following situations:

(a) α varies, and the Q-values are initialized to 0.0.

(b) α varies, and the Q-values are initialized to 5.0.

(c) α is fixed to 0.1, and the Q-values are initialized to 0.0.

(d) α is fixed to 0.1, and the Q-values are initialized to 5.0.

(e) Some other parameter settings.

For each of these, carry out multiple runs and compare the distributions of minimum values, zero crossing, the asymptotic slope for the policy that includes exploration, and the asymptotic slope for the policy that does not include exploration. To do the last task, after the algorithm has converged, set the exploitation parameter to 100% and run a large number of additional steps.

Exercise 11.9 Consider four different ways to derive the value of α_k from k in Q-learning (note that for Q-learning with varying α_k, there must be a different count k for each state–action pair).

i) Let $\alpha_k = 1/k$.

ii) Let $\alpha_k = 10/(9 + k)$.

iii) Let $\alpha_k = 0.1$.

iv) Let $\alpha_k = 0.1$ for the first 10,000 steps, $\alpha_k = 0.01$ for the next 10,000 steps, $\alpha_k = 0.001$ for the next 10,000 steps, $\alpha_k = 0.0001$ for the next 10,000 steps, and so on.

(a) Which of these will converge to the true Q-value in theory?

(b) Which converges to the true Q-value in practice (i.e., in a reasonable number of steps)? Try it for more than one domain.

(c) Which can adapt when the environment adapts slowly?

Exercise 11.10 Suppose your friend presented you with the following example where SARSA(λ) seems to give unintuitive results. There are two states, A and B. There is a reward of 10 coming into state A and no other rewards or penalties. There are two actions: *left* and *right*. These actions only make a difference in state B. Going left in state B goes directly to state A, but going right has a low probability of going into state A. In particular:

- $P(A|B, left) = 1$; reward is 10.

- $P(A|B, right) = 0.01$; reward is 10. $P(B|B, right) = 0.99$; reward is 0.

- $P(A|A, left) = P(A|A, right) = 0.999$ and $P(B|A, left) = P(B|A, right) = 0.001$. This is small enough that the eligibility traces will be close enough to zero when state B is entered.

- γ and λ are 0.9 and α is 0.4.

Suppose that your friend claimed that that $Q(\lambda)$ does not work in this example, because the eligibility trace for the action *right* in state B ends up being bigger than the eligibility trace for action *left* in state B and the rewards and all of the parameters are the same. In particular, the eligibility trace for action *right* will be about 5 when it ends up entering state A, but it be 1 for action *left*. Therefore, the best action will be to go right in state B, which is not correct.

What is wrong with your friend's argument? What does this example show?

Exercise 11.11 In SARSA with linear function approximators, if you use linear regression to minimize $r + \gamma Q_{\overline{w}}(s', a') - Q_{\overline{w}}(s, a)$, you get a different result than we have here. Explain what you get and why what is described in the text may be preferable (or not).

Exercise 11.12 In Example 11.14 (page 483), some of the features are perfectly correlated (e.g., F_6 and F_7). Does having such correlated features affect what functions can be represented? Does it help or hurt the speed at which learning occurs?

Part IV

Reasoning About Individuals and Relations

Chapter 12

Individuals and Relations

There is a real world with real structure. The program of mind has been trained on vast interaction with this world and so contains code that reflects the structure of the world and knows how to exploit it. This code contains representations of real objects in the world and represents the interactions of real objects. The code is mostly modular..., with modules for dealing with different kinds of objects and modules generalizing across many kinds of objects.... The modules interact in ways that mirror the real world and make accurate predictions of how the world evolves....

You exploit the structure of the world to make decisions and take actions. Where you draw the line on categories, what constitutes a single object or a single class of objects for you, is determined by the program of your mind, which does the classification. This classification is not random but reflects a compact description of the world, and in particular a description useful for exploiting the structure of the world.

– Eric B. Baum [2004, pages 169–170]

This chapter is about how to represent individuals (things, objects) and relationships among them. As Baum suggests in the quote above, the real world contains objects and we want compact representations of those objects. Such representations can be much more compact than representations in terms of features alone. This chapter considers logical representations and gives a detailed example of how such representations can be used for natural language interfaces to databases, without uncertainty. Later chapters address ontologies and the meaning of symbols, relational learning, and probabilistic relational models.

491

12.1   Exploiting Structure Beyond Features

One of the main lessons of AI is that successful agents exploit the structure of the world. The previous chapters considered states represented in terms of features. Using features is much more compact than representing the states explicitly, and algorithms can exploit this compactness. There is, however, usually much more structure in features that can be exploited for representation and inference. In particular, this chapter considers reasoning in terms of

- **individuals** – things in the domain, whether they are concrete individuals such as people and buildings, imaginary individuals such as unicorns and fairies, or abstract concepts such as courses and times.

- **relations** – what is true about these individuals. This is meant to be as general as possible and includes unary relations that are true or false of single individuals, in addition to relationships among multiple individuals.

> **Example 12.1**   In Example 5.5 (page 164), the propositions up_s_2, up_s_3, and ok_s_2 have no internal structure. There is no notion that the proposition up_s_2 and up_s_3 are about the same relation, but with different individuals, or that up_s_2 and ok_s_2 are about the same switch. There is no notion of individuals and relations.
>
> An alternative is to explicitly represent the individual switches s_1, s_2, s_3, and the properties or relations, up and ok. Using this representation, "switch s_2 is up" is represented as $up(s_2)$. By knowing what up and s_1 represent, we do not require a separate definition of $up(s_1)$. A binary relation, like $connected\_to$, can be used to relate two individuals, such as $connected\_to(w_1, s_1)$.

A number of reasons exist for using individuals and relations instead of just features:

- It is often the natural representation. Often features are properties of individuals, and this internal structure is lost in converting to features.

- An agent may have to model a domain without knowing what the individuals are, or how many there will be, and, thus, without knowing what the features are. At run time, the agent can construct the features when it finds out which individuals are in the particular environment.

- An agent can do some reasoning without caring about the particular individuals. For example, it may be able to derive that something holds for all individuals without knowing what the individuals are. Or, an agent may be able to derive that some individual exists that has some properties, without caring about other individuals. There may be some queries an agent can answer for which it does not have to distinguish the individuals.

- The existence of individuals could depend on actions or could be uncertain. For example, in planning in a manufacturing context, whether there is a working component may depend on many other subcomponents working and being put together correctly; some of these may depend on the agent's actions, and some may not be under the agent's control. Thus, an agent may have to act without knowing what features there are or what features there will be.

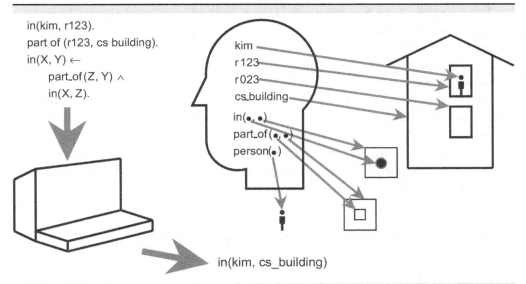

in(kim, r123).
part of (r123, cs building).
in(X, Y) ←
    part_of(Z, Y) ∧
    in(X, Z).

kim
r123
r023
cs_building
in(•, •)
part_of(•, •)
person(•)

in(kim, cs_building)

Figure 12.1: The role of semantics. The meaning of the symbols are in the user's head. The computer takes in symbols and outputs symbols. The output can be interpreted by the user according to the meaning the user places on the symbols.

- Often there are infinitely many individuals an agent is reasoning about, and so infinitely many features. For example, if the individuals are sentences, the agent may only have to reason about a very limited set of sentences (e.g., those that could be meant by a person speaking, or those that may be sensible to generate), even though there may be infinitely many possible sentences, and so infinitely many features.

12.2 Symbols and Semantics

Chapter 5 was about reasoning with symbols that represent propositions. In this section, we expand the semantics to reason about individuals and relations. A symbol will denote an individual or a relation. We still have propositions; atomic propositions now have internal structure in terms of relations and individuals.

Figure 12.1 illustrates the general idea of semantics with individuals and relations. The person who is designing the knowledge base has a meaning for the symbols. The person knows what the symbols *kim*, *r123*, and *in* refer to in the domain and supplies a knowledge base of sentences in the representation language to the computer. These sentences have meaning to that person. She can ask questions using these symbols and with the particular meaning she has for them. The computer takes these sentences and questions, and it computes answers. The computer does not know what the symbols mean. However, the person who supplied the information can use the meaning associated with the symbols to interpret the answer with respect to the world.

The mapping between the symbols in the mind and the individuals and relations denoted by these symbols is called a **conceptualization**. In this chapter, we assume that the conceptualization is in the user's head, or written informally, in comments. Making conceptualizations explicit is the role of a formal ontology (page 563).

Under this view, what is the correct answer is defined independently of how it is computed. The correctness of a knowledge base is defined by the semantics, not by a particular algorithm for proving queries. As long as the inference is faithful to the semantics, the proof procedure can be optimized for efficiency. This separation of meaning from computation lets an agent optimize performance while maintaining correctness.

12.3   Datalog: A Relational Rule Language

This section expands the syntax for the propositional definite clause language (page 163). The syntax is based on normal mathematical notation for predicate symbols but follows Prolog's convention for variables.

The **syntax** of **Datalog** is given by the following, where a **word** is a sequence of letters, digits, or an underscore ("_"):

- A logical **variable** is a word starting with an upper-case letter or the underscore.

  For example X, *Room*, *B4*, *Raths*, and *The_big_guy* are all variables.

  Logical variables are not the same as algebraic variables (page 113) or random variables (page 221).

- A **constant** is a word that starts with a lower-case letter, or is a number constant or a string.

- A **predicate symbol** is a word that starts with a lower-case letter. Constants and predicate symbols are distinguishable by their context in a knowledge base.

  For example, *kim*, *r123*, f, *grandfather*, and *borogroves* can be constants or predicate symbols, depending on the context; *725* is a constant.

- A **term** is either a variable or a constant.

  For example X, *kim*, *cs422*, *mome*, or *Raths* can be terms.

- We expand the definition of **atomic symbol**, or simply an **atom**, to be of the form p or $p(t_1, \ldots, t_n)$, where p is a predicate symbol and each t_i is a term. Each t_i is called an **argument** to the predicate.

  For example, *teaches(sue, cs422)*, *in(kim, r123)*, *sunny*, *father(bill, Y)*, *happy(C)*, and *outgrabe(mome, Raths)* can all be atoms. From context in the atom *outgrabe(mome, Raths)*, we know that *outgrabe* is a predicate symbol and *mome* is a constant.

The notions of **definite clause**, **rule**, **query**, and **knowledge base** are the same as for propositional definite clauses (page 163) but with the expanded definition of atom. The definitions are repeated here.

Relationships to Traditional Programming Languages

The notion of logical semantics presented in this chapter should be contrasted with the procedural semantics of traditional programming languages like Fortran, C++, Lisp, or Java. The semantics for these languages specify the meaning of the language constructs in terms of what the computer will compute based on the program. This corresponds more closely to the proof theory presented here. Logical semantics gives a way to specify the relationships of the symbols to the world, and a way to specify the result of a program independently of how it is computed.

The definitions of semantics and reasoning theory correspond to the notions of a Tarskian semantics and proof in mathematical **logic**. Logic allows us to define knowledge independently of how it is used. Knowledge base designers or users can verify the correctness of knowledge if they know its meaning. People can debate the truth of sentences in the language and observe the world to verify the statements. The same semantics can be used to establish the correctness of an implementation.

The notion of an individual is similar to the definition of an object in **object-oriented languages** such as Smalltalk, C++, or Java. The main difference is that the objects in object-oriented languages are computational objects rather than real physical objects. In an object-oriented language, a "person" object is a representation of a person; it is not the actual person. However, in the representation and reasoning systems considered in AI, an individual "person" can denote the actual person. In object-oriented languages, objects send each other messages. In the logical view, not only do we want to interact with objects, but we also want to reason about them. We may want to be able to predict what an object will do without getting the object to do it. We may want to predict the internal state from the observed behavior, for example, in a diagnostic task. We even want to reason about, and predict the behavior of, individuals who may be deliberately concealing information and may not want us to know what they are doing. For example, consider a "person" object: although there can be some interaction with the person, there is often much information that we do not know. Because we cannot keep asking them for the information (which they may not know or may not want to tell us), we require some external representation of the information about that individual. It is even harder to interact with a chair or a disease, but we still may want to reason about them.

Many programming languages have facilities for dealing with designed objects, perhaps even with a single purpose in mind. For example, in Java, objects have to fit into a single class hierarchy, whereas real-world individuals may have many roles and be in many classes; it is the complex interaction of these classes that specifies the behavior. A knowledge base designer may not know, a priori, how these classes will interact.

- A **body** is an atom or a conjunction of atoms.
- A **definite clause** is either an atom, called a **atomic clause**, or of the form $a \leftarrow b$, called a **rule**, where a, the **head**, is an atom and b is a body. We will end clauses with a period.
- A **knowledge base** is a set of definite clauses.
- A **query** is of the form ask b, where b is a body.
- An **expression** is either a term, an atom, a definite clause, or a query.

In our examples, we will follow the Prolog convention that comments, which are ignored by the system, extend from a "%" to the end of the line.

Example 12.2 The following is a knowledge base:

$$in(kim, R) \leftarrow teaches(kim, cs422) \wedge in(cs422, R).$$
$$grandfather(sam, X) \leftarrow father(sam, Y) \wedge parent(Y, X).$$
$$slithy(toves) \leftarrow mimsy \wedge borogroves \wedge outgrabe(mome, Raths).$$

From context, *kim*, *cs422*, *sam*, *toves*, and *mome* are constants; *in*, *teaches*, *grandfather*, *father*, *parent*, *slithy*, *mimsy*, *borogroves*, and *outgrabe* are predicate symbols; and X, Y, and *Raths* are variables.

The first two clauses about Kim and Sam may make some intuitive sense, even though we have not explicitly provided any formal specification for the meaning of sentences of the definite clause language. However, regardless of the mnemonic names' suggestiveness, as far as the computer is concerned, the first two clauses have no more meaning than the third. Meaning is provided only by virtue of a semantics.

An expression is **ground** if it does not contain any variables. For example, *teaches(fred, cs322)* is ground, but *teaches(Prof, Course)* is not ground.

The next section defines the semantics. We first consider ground expressions and then extend the semantics to include variables.

12.3.1 Semantics of Ground Datalog

The first step in giving the semantics of Datalog is to give the semantics for the ground (variable-free) case.

An **interpretation** is a triple $I = \langle D, \phi, \pi \rangle$, where

- D is a non-empty set called the **domain**. Elements of D are **individuals**.
- ϕ is a mapping that assigns to each constant an element of D.
- π is a mapping that assigns to each n-ary predicate symbol a function from D^n into $\{true, false\}$.

ϕ is a function from names into individuals in the world. The constant c is said to **denote** the individual $\phi(c)$. Here c is a symbol but $\phi(c)$ can be anything: a real physical object such as a person or a virus, an abstract concept such as a course, love, or the number 2, or even a symbol.

$\pi(p)$ specifies whether the relation denoted by the n-ary predicate symbol p is true or false for each n-tuple of individuals. If predicate symbol p has no arguments, then $\pi(p)$ is either *true* or *false*. Thus, for predicate symbols with no arguments, this semantics reduces to the semantics of propositional definite clauses (page 159).

Example 12.3 Consider the world consisting of three objects on a table:

These are drawn in this way because they are things in the world, not symbols. ✂ is a pair of scissors, ☎ is a telephone, and ✎ is a pencil.

Suppose the constants in our language are *phone*, *pencil*, and *telephone*. We have the predicate symbols *noisy* and *left_of*. Assume *noisy* is a unary predicate (it takes a single argument) and that *left_of* is a binary predicate (it takes two arguments).

An example interpretation that represents the objects on the table is

- $D = \{✂, ☎, ✎\}$.
- $\phi(phone) = ☎$, $\phi(pencil) = ✎$, $\phi(telephone) = ☎$.
- $\pi(noisy)$:

$\langle ✂ \rangle$	*false*	$\langle ☎ \rangle$	*true*	$\langle ✎ \rangle$	*false*

$\pi(left\_of)$:

$\langle ✂,✂ \rangle$	*false*	$\langle ✂,☎ \rangle$	*true*	$\langle ✂,✎ \rangle$	*true*
$\langle ☎,✂ \rangle$	*false*	$\langle ☎,☎ \rangle$	*false*	$\langle ☎,✎ \rangle$	*true*
$\langle ✎,✂ \rangle$	*false*	$\langle ✎,☎ \rangle$	*false*	$\langle ✎,✎ \rangle$	*false*

Because *noisy* is unary, it takes a singleton individual and has a truth value for each individual.

Because *left_of* is a binary predicate, it takes a pair of individuals and is true when the first element of the pair is left of the second element. Thus, for example, $\pi(left\_of)(\langle ✂, ☎ \rangle) = true$, because the scissors are to the left of the telephone; $\pi(left\_of)(\langle ✎, ✎ \rangle) = false$, because the pencil is not to the left of itself.

Note how the D is a set of things in the world. The relations are among the objects in the world, not among the names. As ϕ specifies that *phone* and *telephone* refer to the same object, exactly the same statements are true about them in this interpretation.

Example 12.4 Consider the interpretation of Figure 12.1 (page 493).

D is the set with four elements: the person Kim, room 123, room 023, and the CS building. This is not a set of four symbols, but it is the set containing the actual person, the actual rooms, and the actual building. It is difficult to write down this set and, fortunately, you never really have to. To remember the meaning and to convey the meaning to another person, knowledge base designers typically describe D, ϕ, and π by pointing to the physical individuals or a depiction of them (as is done in Figure 12.1) and describe the meaning in natural language.

The constants are *kim*, *r123*, *r023*, and *cs_building*. The mapping ϕ is defined by the gray arcs from each of these constants to an object in the world in Figure 12.1.

The predicate symbols are *person, in,* and *part_of.* The meaning of these are meant to be conveyed in the figure by the arcs from the predicate symbols.

Thus, the person called Kim is in the room *r*123 and is also in the CS building, and these are the only instances of the *in* relation that are true. Similarly, room *r*123 and room *r*023 are part of the CS building, and there are no other *part_of* relationships that are true in this interpretation.

It is important to emphasize that the elements of *D* are the real physical individuals, and not their names. The name *kim* is not in the name *r*123 but, rather, the person denoted by *kim* is in the room denoted by *r*123.

Each ground term denotes an individual in an interpretation. A constant *c* denotes in *I* the individual $\phi(c)$.

A ground atom is either true or false in an interpretation. Atom $p(t_1, \ldots, t_n)$ is **true** in *I* if $\pi(p)(\langle t_1', \ldots, t_n' \rangle) = true$, where t_i' is the individual denoted by term t_i, and is **false** in *I* otherwise.

Example 12.5 The atom *in*(*kim, r*123) is true in the interpretation of Example 12.4, because the person denoted by *kim* is indeed in the room denoted by *r*123. Similarly, *person*(*kim*) is true, as is *part_of*(*r*123, *cs_building*). The atoms *in*(*cs_building, r*123) and *person*(*r*123) are false in this interpretation.

12.3.2 Interpreting Variables

When a variable appears in a clause, the clause is true in an interpretation only if the clause is true for all possible values of that variable. The variable is said to be **universally quantified** within the scope of the clause. If a variable *X* appears in a clause *C*, then claiming that *C* is true in an interpretation means that *C* is true no matter which individual from the domain is denoted by *X*.

To formally define semantics of variables, a **variable assignment**, ρ, is a function from the set of variables into the domain *D*. Thus, a variable assignment assigns an element of the domain to each variable. Given ϕ and a variable assignment ρ, each term denotes an individual in the domain. If the term is a constant, the individual denoted is given by ϕ. If the term is a variable, the individual denoted is given by ρ. Given an interpretation and a variable assignment, each atom is either true or false, using the same definition as earlier. Similarly, given an interpretation and a variable assignment, each clause is either true or false.

A clause is true in an interpretation if it is true for all variable assignments. This is called a **universal quantification**. The variables are said to be **universally quantified** in the scope of the clause. Thus, a clause is false in an interpretation means there is a variable assignment under which the clause is false. The scope of the variable is the whole clause, which means that the same variable assignment is used for all instances of a variable in a clause.

Example 12.6 The clause

$$part\_of(X, Y) \leftarrow in(X, Y).$$

is false in the interpretation of Example 12.4 (page 497), because under the variable assignment with X denoting Kim and Y denoting Room 123, the clause's body is true and the clause's head is false.

The clause

$$in(X, Y) \leftarrow part\_of(Z, Y) \wedge in(X, Z).$$

is true, because in all variable assignments where the body is true, the head is also true.

Logical consequence is defined as in Section 5.1.2 (page 160): ground body g is a **logical consequence** of KB, written $KB \models g$, if g is true in every model of KB.

Example 12.7 Suppose the knowledge base KB is

$in(kim, r123).$
$part\_of(r123, cs\_building).$
$in(X, Y) \leftarrow$
     $part\_of(Z, Y) \wedge$
     $in(X, Z).$

The interpretation defined in Example 12.4 (page 497) is a model of KB, because each clause is true in that interpretation.

$KB \models in(kim, r123)$, because this is stated explicitly in the knowledge base. If every clause of KB is true in an interpretation, then $in(kim, r123)$ must be true in that interpretation.

$KB \not\models in(kim, r023)$. The interpretation defined in Example 12.4 is a model of KB, in which $in(kim, r023)$ is false.

$KB \not\models part\_of(r023, cs\_building)$. Although $part\_of(r023, cs\_building)$ is true in the interpretation of Example 12.4 (page 497), there is another model of KB in which $part\_of(r023, cs\_building)$ is false. In particular, the interpretation which is like the interpretation of Example 12.4 (page 497), but where
$\pi(part\_of)(\langle\langle\phi(r023), \phi(cs\_building)\rangle\rangle) = false,$
is a model of KB in which $part\_of(r023, cs\_building)$ is false.

$KB \models in(kim, cs\_building)$. If the clauses in KB are true in interpretation I, it must be the case that $in(kim, cs\_building)$ is true in I, otherwise there is an instance of the third clause of KB that is false in I – a contradiction to I being a model of KB.

Notice how the semantics treats variables appearing in a clause's body but not in its head [see Example 12.8 (on the next page)].

Example 12.8 In Example 12.7, the variable Y in the clause defining *in* is universally quantified at the level of the clause; thus, the clause is true for all variable assignments. Consider particular values c_1 for X and c_2 for Y. The clause

$$in(c_1, c_2) \leftarrow$$
$$part\_of(Z, c_2) \land$$
$$in(c_1, Z).$$

is true for all variable assignments to Z. If there exists a variable assignment c_3 for Z such that $part\_of(Z, c_2) \land in(c_1, Z)$ is true in an interpretation, then $in(c_1, c_2)$ must be true in that interpretation. Therefore, you can read the last clause of Example 12.7 as "for all X and for all Y, $in(X, Y)$ is true if there exists a Z such that $part\_of(Z, Y) \land in(X, Z)$ is true."

When we want to make the quantification explicit, we write $\forall X\, p(X)$, which reads, "**for all** X, $p(X)$," to mean $p(X)$ is true for every variable assignment for X. We write $\exists X\, p(X)$ and read "**there exists** X such that $p(X)$" to mean $p(X)$ is true for some variable assignment for X. X is said to be an **existentially quantified variable**.

The rule $P(X) \leftarrow Q(X, Y)$ means

$$\forall X\, \forall Y\, (P(X) \leftarrow Q(X, Y)),$$

which is equivalent to

$$\forall X\, (P(X) \leftarrow \exists Y\, Q(X, Y)).$$

Thus, free variables that only appear in the body are existentially quantified in the scope of the body.

It may seem as though there is something peculiar about talking about the clause being true for cases where it does not make sense.

Example 12.9 Consider the clause

$$in(cs422, love) \leftarrow$$
$$part\_of(cs422, sky) \land$$
$$in(sky, love).$$

where $cs422$ denotes a course, *love* denotes an abstract concept, and *sky* denotes the sky. Here, the clause is vacuously true in the intended interpretation according to the truth table for $\leftarrow$, because the clause's right-hand side is false in the intended interpretation.

As long as whenever the head is non-sensical, the body is also, the rule can never be used to prove anything non-sensical. When checking for the truth of a clause, you must only be concerned with those cases in which the clause's body is true. Using the convention that a clause is true whenever the body is false, even if it does not make sense, makes the semantics simpler and does not cause any problems.

Humans' View of Semantics

The formal description of semantics does not tell us why semantics is interesting or how it can be used as a basis to build intelligent systems. The basic idea behind the use of logic is that, when knowledge base designers have a particular world they want to characterize, they can select that world as an **intended interpretation**, select denotations for the symbols with respect to that interpretation, and write, as clauses, what is true in that world. When the system computes a logical consequence of a knowledge base, the knowledge base designer or a user can interpret this answer with respect to the intended interpretation. Because the intended interpretation is a model, and a logical consequence is true in all models, a logical consequence must be true in the intended interpretation.

Informally, the methodology for designing a representation of the world and how it fits in with the formal semantics is as follows:

Step 1 Select the task domain or world to represent. This could be some aspect of the real world (for example, the structure of courses and students at a university, or a laboratory environment at a particular point in time), some imaginary world (for example, the world of Alice in Wonderland, or the state of the electrical environment if a switch breaks), or an abstract world (for example, the world of numbers and sets). Within this world, let the domain D be the set of all individuals or things that you want to be able to refer to and reason about. Also, select which relations to represent.

Step 2 Associate constants in the language with individuals in the world that you want to name. For each element of D you want to refer to by name, assign a constant in the language. For example, you may select the name "*kim*" to denote a particular professor, the name "*cs322*" for a particular introductory AI course, the name "*two*" for the number that is the successor of the number one, and the name "*red*" for the color of stoplights. Each of these names denotes the corresponding individual in the world.

Step 3 For each relation that you may want to represent, associate a predicate symbol in the language. Each n-ary predicate symbol denotes a function from D^n into $\{true, false\}$, which specifies the subset of D^n for which the relation is true. For example, the predicate symbol "*teaches*" of two arguments (a teacher and a course) may correspond to the binary relation that is true when the individual denoted by the first argument teaches the course denoted by the second argument. These relations need not be binary. They could have any number of (zero or more) arguments. For example, "*is_red*" may be a predicate that has one argument.

These associations of symbols with their meanings forms an intended interpretation.

Step 4 You now write clauses that are true in the intended interpretation. This is often called **axiomatizing** the domain, where the given clauses are the **axioms** of the domain. If the person who is denoted by the symbol *kim* actually teaches the course denoted by the symbol *cs502*, you can assert the clause *teaches*(*kim*, *cs502*) as being true in the intended interpretation.

Step 5 Now you are able to ask questions about the intended interpretation and to interpret the answers using the meaning assigned to the symbols.

Following this methodology, the knowledge base designer does not actually tell the computer anything until step 4. The first three steps are carried out in the head of the designer. Of course, the designer should document the denotations to make their knowledge bases understandable to other people, so that they remember each symbol's denotation, and so that they can check the truth of the clauses. This is not necessarily something to which the computer has access.

The world, itself, does not prescribe what the individuals are.

Example 12.10 In one conceptualization of a domain, *pink* may be a predicate symbol of one argument that is true when the individual denoted by that argument is pink. In another conceptualization, *pink* may be an individual that is the color pink, and it may be used as the second argument to a binary predicate *color*, which says that the individual denoted by the first argument has the color denoted by the second argument. Alternatively, someone may want to describe the world at a level of detail where various shades of red are not distinguished, and so the color pink would not be included. Someone else may describe the world in more detail, in which pink is too general a term, for example by using the terms coral and salmon.

It is important to realize that the denotations are in the head of the knowledge base designer. The denotations are sometimes not even written down and are often written in natural language to convey the meaning to other people. When the individuals in the domain are real physical objects, it is usually difficult to give the denotation without physically pointing at the individual. When the individual is an abstract individual – for example, a university course or the concept of love – it is virtually impossible to write the denotation. However, this does not prevent the system from representing and reasoning about such concepts.

Example 12.11 Example 5.5 (page 164) represented the electrical environment of Figure 1.8 (page 34) using just propositions. Using individuals and relations can make the representation more intuitive, because the general knowledge about how switches work can be clearly separated from the knowledge about a specific house.

To represent this domain, we first decide what the individuals are in the domain. In what follows, we assume that each switch, each light, and each power outlet is an individual. We also represent each wire between two switches and between a switch and a light as an individual. Someone may claim that, in fact, there are pairs of wires joined by connectors and that the electricity flow must obey Kirchhoff's laws. Someone else may decide that even that level of abstraction is inappropriate because we should model the flow of electrons. However, an appropriate level of abstraction is one that is appropriate for the task at hand. A resident of the house may not know the whereabouts of the connections between the individual strands of wire or even the voltage. Therefore, we assume a flow model of electricity, where power flows from the outside of the house through wires to lights. This model is appropriate for the task of determining whether a light should be lit or not, but it may not be appropriate for all tasks.

Next, give names to each individual to which we want to refer. This is done in Figure 1.8 (page 34). For example, the individual w_0 is the wire between light l_1 and switch s_2.

Next, choose which relationships to represent. Assume the following predicates with their associated intended interpretations:

- *light*(L) is true if the individual denoted by L is a light.
- *lit*(L) is true if the light L is lit and emitting light.
- *live*(W) is true if there is power coming into W; that is, W is live.
- *up*(S) is true if switch S is up.
- *down*(S) is true if switch S is down.
- *ok*(E) is true if E is not faulty; E can be either a circuit breaker or a light.
- *connected_to*(X, Y) is true if component X is connected to Y such that current would flow from Y to X.

At this stage, the computer has not been told anything. It does not know what the predicates are, let alone what they mean. It does not know what individuals exist or their names.

Before anything about the particular house is known, the system can be told general rules such as

$$lit(L) \leftarrow light(L) \wedge live(L) \wedge ok(L).$$

Recursive rules let you state what is live from what is connected to what:

$$live(X) \leftarrow connected\_to(X, Y) \wedge live(Y).$$
$$live(outside).$$

For the particular house, given a particular configuration of components and their connections, the following facts about the world can be told to the computer:

$$light(l_1).$$
$$light(l_2).$$
$$down(s_1).$$
$$up(s_2).$$
$$connected\_to(w_0, w_1) \leftarrow up(s_2).$$
$$connected\_to(w_0, w_2) \leftarrow down(s_2).$$
$$connected\_to(w_1, w_3) \leftarrow up(s_1).$$

These rules and atomic clauses are all that the computer is told. It does not know the meaning of these symbols. However, it can now answer questions about this particular house.

12.3.3 Queries with Variables

Queries are used to ask whether something is a logical consequence of a knowledge base. With propositional queries (page 166), a user can ask yes-or-no questions. Queries with variables allow the system to return the values of the variables that make the query a logical consequence of the knowledge base.

An **instance** of a query is obtained by substituting terms for the variables in the query. Different occurrences of a variable must be replaced by the same term. Given a query with free variables, an **answer** is either an instance of the query that is a logical consequence of the knowledge base, or *"no"*, meaning that no instances of the query logically follow from the knowledge base. Instances of the query are specified by providing values for the variables in the query. Determining which instances of a query follow from a knowledge base is known as **answer extraction**.

Example 12.12 Consider the clauses of Figure 12.2. The person who wrote these clauses presumably has some meaning associated with the symbols, and has written the clauses because they are true in some, perhaps imaginary, world. The computer knows nothing about rooms or directions. All it knows are the clauses it is given; and it can compute their logical consequences.

The user can ask the following query:

> ask *imm_west*($r105, r107$).

and the answer is *yes*. The user can ask the query

> ask *imm_east*($r107, r105$).

and the answer is, again, *yes*. The user can ask the query

> ask *imm_west*($r205, r207$).

and the answer is *no*. This means it is not a logical consequence, not that it is false. There is not enough information in the database to determine whether or not $r205$ is immediately west of $r207$.

The query

> ask *next_door*($R, r105$).

has two answers. One answer, with $R = r107$, means *next_door*($r107, r105$) is a logical consequence of the clauses. The other answer is for $R = r103$. The query

> ask *west*($R, r105$).

has two answers: one for $R = r103$ and one for $R = r101$. The query

> ask *west*($r105, R$).

has three answers: one for $R = r107$, one for $R = r109$, and one for $R = r111$. The query

> ask *next_door*(X, Y).

% *imm_west*(W, E) is true if room W is immediately west of room E.

> *imm_west*($r101, r103$).
> *imm_west*($r103, r105$).
> *imm_west*($r105, r107$).
> *imm_west*($r107, r109$).
> *imm_west*($r109, r111$).
> *imm_west*($r131, r129$).
> *imm_west*($r129, r127$).
> *imm_west*($r127, r125$).

% *imm_east*(E, W) is true if room E is immediately east of room W.

> *imm_east*(E, W) ←
>   *imm_west*(W, E).

% *next_door*($R1, R2$) is true if room $R1$ is next door to room $R2$.

> *next_door*(E, W) ←
>   *imm_east*(E, W).
> *next_door*(W, E) ←
>   *imm_west*(W, E).

% *two_doors_east*(E, W) is true if room E is two doors east of room W.

> *two_doors_east*(E, W) ←
>   *imm_east*(E, M) ∧
>   *imm_east*(M, W).

% *west*(W, E) is true if room W is west of room E.

> *west*(W, E) ←
>   *imm_west*(W, E).
> *west*(W, E) ←
>   *imm_west*(W, M) ∧
>   *west*(M, E).

Figure 12.2: A knowledge base about rooms

---

has 16 answers, including

> $X = r103, Y = r101$
> $X = r105, Y = r103$
> $X = r101, Y = r103$
> $\cdots$.

12.4 Proofs and Substitutions

Both the bottom-up and top-down propositional proof procedures of Section 5.2.2 (page 167) can be extended to Datalog.

An **instance** of a clause is obtained by uniformly substituting terms for variables in the clause. All occurrences of a particular variable are replaced by the same term. The proof procedure extended for variables must account for the fact that a free variable in a clause means that any instance of the clause is true. A proof may have to use different instances of the same clause in a single proof. The specification of what value is assigned to each variable is called a substitution.

A **substitution** is a finite set of the form $\{V_1/t_1, \ldots, V_n/t_n\}$, where each V_i is a distinct variable and each t_i is a term. The element V_i/t_i is a **binding** for variable V_i. A substitution is in **normal form** if no V_i appears in any t_j.

Example 12.13 For example, $\{X/Y, Z/a\}$ is a substitution in normal form that binds X to Y and binds Z to a. The substitution $\{X/Y, Z/X\}$ is not in normal form, because the variable X occurs both on the left and on the right of a binding.

The **application** of a substitution $\sigma = \{V_1/t_1, \ldots, V_n/t_n\}$ to expression e, written $e\sigma$, is an expression that is like the original expression e but with every occurrence of V_i in e replaced by the corresponding t_i. The expression $e\sigma$ is called an **instance** of e. If $e\sigma$ does not contain any variables, it is called a **ground instance** of e.

Example 12.14 Some applications of substitutions are

$$p(a, X)\{X/c\} = p(a, c).$$
$$p(Y, c)\{Y/a\} = p(a, c).$$
$$p(a, X)\{Y/a, Z/X\} = p(a, X).$$
$$p(X, X, Y, Y, Z))\{X/Z, Y/t\} = p(Z, Z, t, t, Z).$$

Substitutions can apply to clauses, atoms, and terms. For example, the result of applying the substitution $\{X/Y, Z/a\}$ to the clause

$$p(X, Y) \leftarrow q(a, Z, X, Y, Z)$$

is the clause

$$p(Y, Y) \leftarrow q(a, a, Y, Y, a).$$

A substitution σ is a **unifier** of expressions e_1 and e_2 if $e_1\sigma$ is identical to $e_2\sigma$. That is, a unifier of two expressions is a substitution that when applied to each expression results in the same expression.

Example 12.15 $\{X/a, Y/b\}$ is a unifier of $t(a, Y, c)$ and $t(X, b, c)$ as

$$t(a, Y, c)\{X/a, Y/b\} = t(X, b, c)\{X/a, Y/b\} = t(a, b, c).$$

Expressions can have many unifiers.

Example 12.16 Atoms $p(X, Y)$ and $p(Z, Z)$ have many unifiers, including $\{X/b, Y/b, Z/b\}$, $\{X/c, Y/c, Y/c\}$, and $\{X/Z, Y/Z\}$. The third unifier is more general than the first two, because the first two both have X the same as Z and Y the same as Z but make more commitments in what these values are.

Substitution σ is a **most general unifier (MGU)** of expressions e_1 and e_2 if

- σ is a unifier of the two expressions, and
- if another substitution σ' exists that is also a unifier of e_1 and e_2, then $e\sigma'$ must be an instance of $e\sigma$ for all expressions e.

Expression e_1 is a **renaming** of e_2 if they differ only in the names of variables. In this case, they are both instances of each other.

If two expressions have a unifier, they have at least one MGU. The expressions resulting from applying the MGUs to the expressions are all renamings of each other. That is, if σ and σ' are both MGUs of expressions e_1 and e_2, then $e_1\sigma$ is a renaming of $e_1\sigma'$.

Example 12.17 $\{X/Z, Y/Z\}$ and $\{Z/X, Y/X\}$ are both MGUs of $p(X, Y)$ and $p(Z, Z)$. The resulting applications

$$p(X, Y)\{X/Z, Y/Z\} = p(Z, Z)$$
$$p(X, Y)\{Z/X, Y/X\} = p(X, X)$$

are renamings of each other.

12.4.1   Bottom-up Procedure with Variables

The propositional bottom-up proof procedure (page 167) can be extended to Datalog by using ground instances of the clauses. A **ground instance** of a clause is obtained by uniformly substituting constants for the variables in the clause. The constants required are those appearing in the knowledge base or in the query. If there are no constants in the knowledge base or the query, one must be invented.

Example 12.18 Suppose the knowledge base is

> $q(a)$.
> $q(b)$.
> $r(a)$.
> $s(W) \leftarrow r(W)$.
> $p(X, Y) \leftarrow q(X) \wedge s(Y)$.

The set of all ground instances is

> $q(a)$.
> $q(b)$.
> $r(a)$.
> $s(a) \leftarrow r(a)$.
> $s(b) \leftarrow r(b)$.
> $p(a, a) \leftarrow q(a) \wedge s(a)$.
> $p(a, b) \leftarrow q(a) \wedge s(b)$.
> $p(b, a) \leftarrow q(b) \wedge s(a)$.
> $p(b, b) \leftarrow q(b) \wedge s(b)$.

The propositional bottom-up proof procedure of Section 5.2.2 (page 167) can be applied to the grounding to derive $q(a), q(b), r(a), s(a), p(a, a)$, and $p(b, a)$ as the ground instances that are logical consequences.

Example 12.19 Suppose the knowledge base is

> $p(X, Y)$.
> $g \leftarrow p(W, W)$.

The bottom-up proof procedure must invent a new constant symbol, say c. The set of all ground instances is then

> $p(c, c)$.
> $g \leftarrow p(c, c)$.

The propositional bottom-up proof procedure will derive $p(c, c)$ and g.

If the query was ask $p(a, d)$, the set of ground instances would change to reflect these constants.

The bottom-up proof procedure applied to the grounding of the knowledge base is sound, because each instance of each rule is true in every model. This procedure is essentially the same as the variable-free case, but it uses the set of ground instances of the clauses, all of which are true by definition.

This procedure is also complete for ground atoms. That is, if a ground atom is a consequence of the knowledge base, it will eventually be derived. To prove this, as in the propositional case (page 169), we construct a particular generic model. A model must specify what the constants denote. A **Herbrand interpretation** is an interpretation where the the domain is symbolic and consists of all constants of the language. An individual is invented if there are no constants. In a Herbrand interpretation, each constant denotes itself.

Consider the Herbrand interpretation where the ground instances of the relations that are eventually derived by the bottom-up procedure with a fair selection rule are true. It is easy to see that this Herbrand interpretation is a model of the rules given. As in the variable-free case (page 167), it is a **minimal model** in that it has the fewest true atoms of any model. If $KB \models g$ for ground atom g, then g is true in the minimal model and, thus, is eventually derived.

Example 12.20 Consider the clauses of Figure 12.2 (page 505). The bottom-up proof procedure can immediately derive each instance of *imm_west* given as a fact. Then you can add the *imm_east* clauses:

> *imm_east*($r103, r101$)
> *imm_east*($r105, r103$)
> *imm_east*($r107, r105$)
> *imm_east*($r109, r107$)
> *imm_east*($r111, r109$)
> *imm_east*($r129, r131$)
> *imm_east*($r127, r129$)
> *imm_east*($r125, r127$)

Next, the *next_door* relations that follow can be added to the set of consequences, including

> *next_door*($r101, r103$)
> *next_door*($r103, r101$)

The *two_door_east* relations can be added to the set of consequences, including

> *two_door_east*($r105, r101$)
> *two_door_east*($r107, r103$)

Finally, the *west* relations that follow can be added to the set of consequences.

12.4.2 Definite Resolution with Variables

The propositional top-down proof procedure (page 169) can be extended to the case with variables by allowing instances of rules to be used in the derivation.

A **generalized answer clause** is of the form

$$yes(t_1, \ldots, t_k) \leftarrow a_1 \wedge a_2 \wedge \ldots \wedge a_m,$$

where $t_1, \ldots, t_k$ are terms and $a_1, \ldots, a_m$ are atoms. The use of *yes* enables **answer extraction**: determining which instances of the query variables are a logical consequence of the knowledge base.

Initially, the generalized answer clause for query q is

$$yes(V_1, \ldots, V_k) \leftarrow q,$$

where $V_1, \ldots, V_k$ are the variables that appear in q. Intuitively this means that an instance of $yes(V_1, \ldots, V_k)$ is true if the corresponding instance of the query is true.

The proof procedure maintains a current generalized answer clause.

At each stage, the algorithm selects an atom a_i in the body of the generalized answer clause. It then chooses a clause in the knowledge base whose head unifies with a_i. The **SLD resolution** of the generalized answer clause $yes(t_1, \ldots, t_k) \leftarrow a_1 \wedge a_2 \wedge \ldots \wedge a_m$ on a_i with the chosen clause

$$a \leftarrow b_1 \wedge \ldots \wedge b_p,$$

where a_i and a have most general unifier σ, is the answer clause

$$(yes(t_1, \ldots, t_k) \leftarrow a_1 \wedge \ldots \wedge a_{i-1} \wedge b_1 \wedge \ldots \wedge b_p \wedge a_{i+1} \wedge \ldots \wedge a_m)\sigma,$$

where the body of the chosen clause has replaced a_i in the answer clause, and the MGU is applied to the whole answer clause.

An **SLD derivation** is a sequence of generalized answer clauses $\gamma_0, \gamma_1, \ldots, \gamma_n$ such that

- γ_0 is the answer clause corresponding to the original query. If the query is q, with free variables $V_1, \ldots, V_k$, the initial generalized answer clause γ_0 is

    $$yes(V_1, \ldots, V_k) \leftarrow q.$$

- γ_i is obtained by selecting an atom a_i in the body of γ_{i-1}; choosing a *copy* of a clause $a \leftarrow b_1 \wedge \ldots \wedge b_p$ in the knowledge base whose head, a, unifies with a_i; replacing a_i with the body, $b_1 \wedge \ldots \wedge b_p$; and applying the unifier to the whole resulting answer clause.

    The main difference between this and the propositional top-down proof procedure (page 169) is that, for clauses with variables, the proof procedure must take *copies* of clauses from the knowledge base. The copying renames the variables in the clause with new names. This is both to remove name clashes between variables and because a single proof may use different instances of a clause.

- γ_n is an answer. That is, it is of the form

    $$yes(t_1, \ldots, t_k) \leftarrow \, .$$

When this occurs, the algorithm returns the answer

$$V_1 = t_1, \ldots, V_k = t_k.$$

Notice how the answer is extracted; the arguments to *yes* keep track of the instances of the variables in the initial query that lead to a successful proof.

A non-deterministic procedure that answers queries by finding SLD derivations is given in Figure 12.3. This is non-deterministic (page 170) in the sense that all derivations can be found by making appropriate choices that do not fail. If all choices fail, the algorithm fails, and there are no derivations. The choose is implemented using search. This algorithm assumes that $unify(a_i, a)$ returns an MGU of a_i and a, if there is one, and $\perp$ if they do not unify. Unification is defined in the next section.

1: **non-deterministic procedure** *FODCDeductionTD*(KB,q)
2:     **Inputs**
3:         *KB*: a set definite clauses
4:         Query q: a set of atoms to prove, with variables $V_1, \ldots, V_k$
5:     **Output**
6:         substitution θ if $KB \models q\theta$ and fail otherwise
7:     **Local**
8:         G is a generalized answer clause
9:     Set G to generalized answer clause $yes(V_1, \ldots, V_k) \leftarrow q$
10:     **while** G is not an answer **do**
11:         Suppose G is $yes(t_1, \ldots, t_k) \leftarrow a_1 \wedge a_2 \wedge \ldots \wedge a_m$
12:         **select** atom a_i in the body of G
13:         **choose** clause $a \leftarrow b_1 \wedge \ldots \wedge b_p$ in KB
14:         Rename all variables in $a \leftarrow b_1 \wedge \ldots \wedge b_p$ to have new names
15:         Let σ be *unify*(a_i, a). Fail if *unify* returns $\bot$.
16:         assign G the answer clause: $(yes(t_1, \ldots, t_k) \leftarrow a_1 \wedge \ldots \wedge a_{i-1} \wedge b_1 \wedge \ldots \wedge b_p \wedge a_{i+1} \wedge \ldots \wedge a_m)\sigma$
17:     **return** $V_1 = t_1, \ldots, V_k = t_k$ where G is $yes(t_1, \ldots, t_k) \leftarrow$

Figure 12.3: Top-down definite clause proof procedure

Example 12.21 Consider the database of Figure 12.2 (page 505) and the query

ask *two_doors_east*$(R, r107)$.

Figure 12.4 (on the next page) shows a successful derivation with answer $R = r111$.

Note that this derivation used two instances of the rule

$$imm\_east(E, W) \leftarrow imm\_west(W, E).$$

One instance eventually substituted $r111$ for E, and one instance substituted $r109$ for E.

Some choices of which clauses to resolve against may have resulted in a partial derivation that could not be completed.

Unification

The preceding algorithms assumed that we could find the **most general unifier** of two atoms. The problem of **unification** is the following: given two atoms, determine if they unify, and, if they do, return an MGU of them.

The unification algorithm is given in Figure 12.5 (page 513). E is a set of equality statements implying the unification, and S is a set of equalities of the correct form of a substitution. In this algorithm, if x/y is in the substitution S,

$yes(R) \leftarrow two\_doors\_east(R, r107)$
    resolve with $two\_doors\_east(E_1, W_1) \leftarrow$
                  $imm\_east(E_1, M_1) \wedge imm\_east(M_1, W_1)$.
    substitution: $\{E_1/R, W_1/r107\}$
$yes(R) \leftarrow imm\_east(R, M_1) \wedge imm\_east(M_1, r107)$
    select leftmost conjunct
    resolve with $imm\_east(E_2, W_2) \leftarrow imm\_west(W_2, E_2)$
    substitution: $\{E_2/R, W_2/M_1\}$
$yes(R) \leftarrow imm\_west(M_1, R) \wedge imm\_east(M_1, r107)$
    select leftmost conjunct
    resolve with $imm\_west(r109, r111)$
    substitution: $\{M_1/r109, R/r111\}$
$yes(r111) \leftarrow imm\_east(r109, r107)$
    resolve with $imm\_east(E_3, W_3) \leftarrow imm\_west(W_3, E_3)$
    substitution: $\{E_3/r109, W_3/r107\}$
$yes(r111) \leftarrow imm\_west(r107, r109)$
    resolve with $imm\_west(r107, r109)$
    substitution: $\{\}$
$yes(r111) \leftarrow$

Figure 12.4: A derivation for query ask $two\_doors\_east(R, r107)$.

then, by construction, x is a variable that does not appear elsewhere in S or in E. In line 20, x and y must have the same predicate and the same number of arguments; otherwise the unification fails.

Example 12.22 Suppose we want to unify $p(X, Y, Y)$ with $p(a, Z, b)$. Initially E is $\{p(X, Y, Y) = p(a, Z, b)\}$. The first time through the while loop, E becomes $\{X = a, Y = Z, Y = b\}$. Suppose $X = a$ is selected next. Then S becomes $\{X/a\}$ and E becomes $\{Y = Z, Y = b\}$. Suppose $Y = Z$ is selected. Then Y is replaced by Z in S and E. S becomes $\{X/a, Y/Z\}$ and E becomes $\{Z = b\}$. Finally $Z = b$ is selected, Z is replaced by b, S becomes $\{X/a, Y/b, Z/b\}$, and E becomes empty. The substitution $\{X/a, Y/b, Z/b\}$ is returned as an MGU.

12.5 Function Symbols

Datalog requires a name, using a constant, for every individual about which the system reasons. Often it is simpler to identify an individual in terms of its components, rather than requiring a separate constant for each individual.

```
 1: procedure Unify(t₁, t₂)
 2:     Inputs
 3:         t₁, t₂: atoms
 4:     Output
 5:         most general unifier of t₁ and t₂ if it exists or ⊥ otherwise
 6:     Local
 7:         E: a set of equality statements
 8:         S: substitution
 9:     E ← {t₁ = t₂}
10:     S = {}
11:     while E ≠ {} do
12:         select and remove x = y from E
13:         if y is not identical to x then
14:             if x is a variable then
15:                 replace x with y everywhere in E and S
16:                 S ← {x/y} ∪ S
17:             else if y is a variable then
18:                 replace y with x everywhere in E and S
19:                 S ← {y/x} ∪ S
20:             else if x is f(x₁, ..., xₙ) and y is f(y₁, ..., yₙ) then
21:                 E ← E ∪ {x₁ = y₁, ..., xₙ = yₙ}
22:             else
23:                 return ⊥
24:     return S
```

Figure 12.5: Unification algorithm for Datalog

Example 12.23 In many domains, you want to be able to refer to a time as an individual. You may want to say that some course is held at 11:30 a.m. You do not want a separate constant for each possible time. It is better to define times in terms of, say, the number of hours past midnight and the number of minutes past the hour. Similarly, you may want to reason with facts that mention particular dates. You do not want to give a constant for each date. It is easier to define a date in terms of the year, the month, and the day.

Using a constant to name each individual means that the knowledge base can only represent a finite number of individuals, and the number of individuals is fixed when the knowledge base is designed. However, many cases exist in which you want to reason about a potentially infinite set of individuals.

Example 12.24 Suppose you want to build a system that takes questions in English and that answers them by consulting an online database. In this case, each sentence is considered an individual. You do not want to have to give each sentence its own name, because there are too many English sentences to name them all. It may be better to name the words and then to specify a sentence in terms of the sequence of words in the sentence. This approach may be more practical because there are far fewer words to name than sentences, and each word has it own natural name. You may also want to specify the words in terms of the letters in the word or in terms of their constituent parts.

Example 12.25 You may want to reason about lists of students. For example, you may be required to derive the average mark of a class of students. A class list of students is an individual that has properties, such as its length and its seventh element. Although it may be possible to name each list, it is very inconvenient to do so. It is much better to have a way to describe lists in terms of their elements.

Function symbols allow you to describe individuals indirectly. Rather than using a constant to describe an individual, an individual is described in terms of other individuals.

Syntactically a **function symbol** is a word starting with a lower-case letter. We extend the definition of a term (page 494) so that a **term** is either a variable, a constant, or of the form $f(t_1, \ldots, t_n)$, where f is a function symbol and each t_i is a term. Apart from extending the definition of terms, the language stays the same.

Terms only appear within predicate symbols. You do not write clauses that imply terms. You may, however, write clauses that include atoms that use function symbols as ways to describe individuals.

The semantics must be changed to reflect the new syntax. The only thing we change is the definition of ϕ (page 496). We extend ϕ so that ϕ is a mapping that assigns to each constant an element of D and to each n-ary function symbol a function from D^n into D. Thus, ϕ specifies the mapping denoted by each function symbol. In particular, ϕ specifies which individual is denoted by each ground term.

A knowledge base consisting of clauses with function symbols can compute any computable function. Thus, a knowledge base can be interpreted as a program, called a **logic program**.

This slight expansion of the language has a major impact. With just one function symbol and one constant, infinitely many different terms and infinitely many different atoms exist. The infinite number of terms can be used to describe an infinite number of individuals.

Example 12.26 Suppose you want to define times during the day as in Example 12.23. You can use the function symbol am so that $am(H, M)$ denotes the time $H{:}M$ a.m., when H is an integer between 1 and 12 and M is an integer between 0 and 59. For example, $am(10, 38)$ denotes the time 10:38 a.m.; am denotes a function from pairs of integers into times. Similarly, you can define the symbol pm to denote the times after noon.

The only way to use the function symbol is to write clauses that define relations using the function symbol. There is no notion of *defining* the *am* function; times are not in a computer any more than people are.

To use function symbols, you can write clauses that are quantified over the arguments of the function symbol. For example, the following defines the $before(T_1, T_2)$ relation that is true if time T_1 is before time T_2 in a day:

$before(am(H1, M1), pm(H2, M2))$.
$before(am(12, M1), am(H2, M2)) \leftarrow$
    $H2 < 12$.
$before(am(H1, M1), am(H2, M2)) \leftarrow$
    $H1 < H2 \wedge$
    $H2 < 12$.
$before(am(H, M1), am(H, M2)) \leftarrow$
    $M1 < M2$.
$before(pm(12, M1), pm(H2, M2)) \leftarrow$
    $H2 < 12$.
$before(pm(H1, M1), pm(H2, M2)) \leftarrow$
    $H1 < H2 \wedge$
    $H2 < 12$.
$before(pm(H, M1), pm(H, M2)) \leftarrow$
    $M1 < M2$.

This is complicated because the morning and afternoon hours start with 12, then go to 1, so that, for example, 12:37 a.m. is before 1:12 a.m.

Function symbols are used to build data structures.

Example 12.27 A tree is a useful data structure. You could use a tree to build a syntactic representation of a sentence for a natural language processing system. We could decide that a labeled tree is either of the form $node(N, LT, RT)$ or of the form $leaf(L)$. Thus, *node* is a function from a name, a left tree, and a right tree into a tree. The function symbol *leaf* denotes a function from a node into a tree.

The relation $at\_leaf(L, T)$ is true if label L is the label of a leaf in tree T. It can be defined by

$at\_leaf(L, leaf(L))$.
$at\_leaf(L, node(N, LT, RT)) \leftarrow$
    $at\_leaf(L, LT)$.
$at\_leaf(L, node(N, LT, RT)) \leftarrow$
    $at\_leaf(L, RT)$.

This is an example of a structural recursive program. The rules cover all of the cases for each of the structures representing trees.

516 12. Individuals and Relations

The relation $in\_tree(L, T)$, which is true if label L is the label of an interior node of tree T, can be defined by

$in\_tree(L, node(L, LT, RT))$.

$in\_tree(L, node(N, LT, RT)) \leftarrow$
    $in\_tree(L, LT)$.

$in\_tree(L, node(N, LT, RT)) \leftarrow$
    $in\_tree(L, RT)$.

Example 12.28 You can reason about **lists** without any notion of a list being built in. A list is either the empty list or an element followed by a list. You can invent a constant to denote the empty list. Suppose you use the constant *nil* to denote the empty list. You can choose a function symbol, say $cons(Hd, Tl)$, with the intended interpretation that it denotes a list with first element *Hd* and rest of the list *Tl*. The list containing the elements a, b, c would then be represented as

$cons(a, cons(b, cons(c, nil)))$.

To use lists, one must write predicates that do something with them. For example, the relation $append(X, Y, Z)$ that is true when X, Y, and Z are lists, such that Z contains the elements of X followed by the elements of Z, can be defined recursively by

$append(nil, L, L)$.

$append(cons(Hd, X), Y, cons(Hd, Z)) \leftarrow$
    $append(X, Y, Z)$.

There is nothing special about *cons* or *nil*; we could have just as well used *foo* and *bar*.

12.5.1 Proof Procedures with Function Symbols

The proof procedures with variables carry over for the case with function symbols. The main difference is that the class of terms is expanded to include function symbols.

The use of function symbols involves infinitely many terms. This means that, when forward chaining on the clauses, we have to ensure that the selection criterion for selecting clauses is fair (page 170).

Example 12.29 To see why fairness is important, consider the following clauses as part of a larger program:

$num(0)$.

$num(s(N)) \leftarrow num(N)$.

An unfair strategy could initially select the first of these clauses to forward chain on and, for every subsequent selection, select the second clause. The second clause can always be used to derive a new consequence. This strategy never selects any other clauses and thus never derives the consequences of these other clauses.

First-Order and Second-Order Logic

First-order predicate calculus is a logic that extends propositional calculus (page 157) to include atoms with function symbols and logical variables. All logical variables must have explicit quantification in terms of "for all" ($\forall$) and "there exists" ($\exists$) (page 500). The semantics of first-order predicate calculus is like the semantics of logic programs presented in this chapter, but with a richer set of operators.

The language of logic programs forms a pragmatic subset of first-order predicate calculus, which has been developed because it is useful for many tasks. First-order predicate calculus can be seen as a language that adds disjunction and explicit quantification to logic programs.

First-order logic is of first order because it allows quantification over individuals in the domain. First-order logic allows neither predicates as variables nor quantification over predicates.

Second-order logic allows for quantification over first-order relations and predicates whose arguments are first-order relations. These are second-order relations. For example, the second-order logic formula

$$\forall R \; symmetric(R) \leftrightarrow (\forall X \forall Y \; R(X,Y) \rightarrow R(Y,X))$$

defines the second-order relation *symmetric*, which is true if its argument is a symmetric relation.

Second-order logic seems necessary for many applications because transitive closure is not first-order definable. For example, suppose you want *before* to be the transitive closure of *next*, where $next(X, s(X))$ is true. Think of *next* meaning the "next millisecond" and *before* denoting "before." The natural first-order definition would be the definition

$$\forall X \forall Y \; before(X,Y) \leftrightarrow (Y = s(X) \lor before(s(X),Y)) . \tag{12.1}$$

This expression does not accurately capture the definition, because, for example,

$$\forall X \forall Y \; before(X,Y) \rightarrow \exists W \; Y = s(W)$$

does not logically follow from Formula (12.1), because there are nonstandard models of Formula (12.1) with Y denoting *infinity*. To capture the transitive closure, you require a formula stating that *before* is the minimal predicate that satisfies the definition. This can be stated using second-order logic.

First-order logic is **recursively enumerable**, which means that a sound and complete proof procedure exists in which every true statement can be proved by a sound proof procedure on a Turing machine. Second-order logic is not recursively enumerable, so there does not exist a sound and complete proof procedure that can be implemented on a Turing machine.

This problem of ignoring some clauses forever is known as **starvation**. A **fair** selection criterion is one such that any clause available to be selected will eventually be selected. The bottom-up proof procedure is complete only if it is fair.

The top-down proof procedure is the same as for Datalog [see Figure 12.3 (page 511)]. Unification becomes more complicated, because it must recursively descend into the structure of terms. There is one change to the unification algorithm: a variable X does not unify with a term t in which X occurs and is not X itself. Checking for this condition is known as the **occurs check**. If the occurs check is not used and a variable is allowed to unify with a term in which it appears, the proof procedure becomes unsound, as shown in the following example.

Example 12.30 Consider the knowledge base with only one clause:

$$lt(X, s(X)).$$

Suppose the intended interpretation is the domain of integers in which lt means "less than" and $s(X)$ denotes the integer after X. The query ask $lt(Y, Y)$ should fail because it is false in our intended interpretation that there is no number less than itself. However, if X and $s(X)$ could unify, this query would succeed. In this case, the proof procedure would be unsound because something could be derived that is false in a model of the axioms.

The unification algorithm of Figure 12.5 (page 513) finds the MGU of two terms with function symbols with one change. The algorithm should return $\perp$ if it selects an equality $x = y$, where x is a variable and y is a term that is not x, but contains x. This last step is the occurs check. The occurs check is sometimes omitted (e.g., in Prolog), because removing it makes the proof procedure more efficient, even though removing it makes the proof procedure unsound.

The following example shows the details of SLD resolution with function symbols.

Example 12.31 Consider the clauses

$$append(c(A, X), Y, c(A, Z)) \leftarrow$$
$$\qquad append(X, Y, Z).$$
$$append(nil, Z, Z).$$

For now, ignore what this may mean. Like the computer, treat this as a problem of symbol manipulation. Consider the following query:

$$ask\ append(F, c(L, nil), c(l, c(i, c(s, c(t, nil))))).$$

The following is a derivation:

$yes(F, L) \leftarrow append(F, c(L, nil), c(l, c(i, c(s, c(t, nil)))))$

 resolve with $append(c(A_1, X_1), Y_1, c(A_1, Z_1)) \leftarrow append(X_1, Y_1, Z_1)$

 substitution: $\{F/c(l, X_1), Y_1/c(L, nil), A_1/l, Z_1/c(i, c(s, c(t, nil)))\}$

$yes(c(l, X_1), L) \leftarrow append(X_1, c(L, nil), c(i, c(s, c(t, nil))))$

 resolve with $append(c(A_2, X_2), Y_2, c(A_2, Z_2)) \leftarrow append(X_2, Y_2, Z_2)$

 substitution: $\{X_1/c(i, X_2), Y_2/c(L, nil), A_2/i, Z_2/c(s, c(t, nil))\}$

$yes(c(l, c(i, X_2)), L) \leftarrow append(X_2, c(L, nil), c(s, c(t, nil)))$

 resolve with $append(c(A_3, X_3), Y_3, c(A_3, Z_3)) \leftarrow append(X_3, Y_3, Z_3)$

 substitution: $\{X_2/c(s, X_3), Y_3/c(L, nil), A_3/s, Z_3/c(t, nil)\}$

$yes(c(l, c(i, c(s, X_3))), L) \leftarrow append(X_3, c(L, nil), c(t, nil))$

At this stage both clauses are applicable. Choosing the first clause gives

 resolve with $append(c(A_4, X_4), Y_4, c(A_4, Z_4)) \leftarrow append(X_4, Y_4, Z_4)$

 substitution: $\{X_3/c(t, X_4), Y_4/c(L, nil), A_4/t, Z_4/nil\}$

$yes(c(l, c(i, c(s, X_3))), L) \leftarrow append(X_4, c(L, nil), nil)$

At this point, there are no clauses whose head unifies with the atom in the generalized answer clause's body. The proof fails.

 Choosing the second clause instead of the first gives

 resolve with $append(nil, Z_5, Z_5)$.

 substitution: $\{Z_5/c(t, nil), X_3/nil, L/t\}$

$yes(c(l, c(i, c(s, nil))), t) \leftarrow$

At this point, the proof succeeds, with answer $F = c(l, c(i, c(s, nil))), L = t$.

For the rest of this chapter, we use the "syntactic sugar" notation of Prolog for representing lists. The empty list, *nil*, is written as $[\,]$. The list with first element E and the rest of the list R, which was $cons(E, R)$, is now written as $[E|R]$. There is one notational simplification: $[X|[Y]]$ is written as $[X, Y]$, where Y can be a sequence of values. For example, $[a|[\,]]$ is written as $[a]$, and $[b|[a|[\,]]]$ is written as $[b, a]$; $[a|[b|c]]$ is written as $[a, b|c]$.

Example 12.32 Using the list notation, *append* from the previous example can be written as

$append([A|X], Y, [A|Z]) \leftarrow$
 $append(X, Y, Z)$.
$append([\,], Z, Z)$.

The query

ask $append(F, [L], [l, i, s, t])$

has an answer $F = [l, i, s], L = t$. The proof is exactly as in the previous example. As far as the proof procedure is concerned, nothing has changed; there is just a renamed function symbol and constant.

12.6   Applications in Natural Language Processing

Natural language processing is an interesting and difficult domain in which to develop and evaluate representation and reasoning theories. All of the problems of AI arise in this domain; solving "the natural language problem" is as difficult as solving "the AI problem" because any domain can be expressed in natural language. The field of **computational linguistics** has a wealth of techniques and knowledge. In this book, we can only give an overview.

There are at least three reasons for studying natural language processing:

- You want a computer to communicate with users in their terms; you would rather not force users to learn a new language. This is particularly important for casual users and those users, such as managers and children, who have neither the time nor the inclination to learn new interaction skills.

- There is a vast store of information recorded in natural language that could be accessible via computers. Information is constantly generated in the form of books, news, business and government reports, and scientific papers, many of which are available online. A system requiring a great deal of information must be able to process natural language to retrieve much of the information available on computers.

- Many of the problems of AI arise in a very clear and explicit form in natural language processing and, thus, it is a good domain in which to experiment with general theories.

The development of natural language processing provides the possibility of natural language interfaces to knowledge bases and natural language translation. We show in the next section how to write a natural language query answering system that is applicable to very narrow domains for which stylized natural language is adequate and in which little, if any, ambiguity exists. At the other extreme are shallow but broad systems, such as the help system presented in Example 6.16 (page 246) and Example 7.13 (page 312). Example 7.13 (page 312). Developing useful systems that are both deep and broad is difficult.

There are three major aspects of any natural language understanding theory:

Syntax   The syntax describes the form of the language. It is usually specified by a grammar. Natural language is much more complicated than the formal languages used for the artificial languages of logics and computer programs.

Semantics   The semantics provides the meaning of the utterances or sentences of the language. Although general semantic theories exist, when we build a natural language understanding system for a particular application, we try to use the simplest representation we can. For example, in the development that follows, there is a fixed mapping between words and concepts in the knowledge base, which is inappropriate for many domains but simplifies development.

Pragmatics The pragmatic component explains how the utterances relate to the world. To understand language, an agent should consider more than the sentence; it has to take into account the context of the sentence, the state of the world, the goals of the speaker and the listener, special conventions, and the like.

To understand the difference among these aspects, consider the following sentences, which might appear at the start of an AI textbook:

- *This book is about artificial intelligence.*
- *The green frogs sleep soundly.*
- *Colorless green ideas sleep furiously.*
- *Furiously sleep ideas green colorless.*

The first sentence would be quite appropriate at the start of such a book; it is syntactically, semantically, and pragmatically well formed. The second sentence is syntactically and semantically well formed, but it would appear very strange at the start of an AI book; it is thus not pragmatically well formed for that context. The last two sentences are attributed to linguist Noam Chomsky [1957]. The third sentence is syntactically well formed, but it is semantically non-sensical. The fourth sentence is syntactically ill formed; it does not make any sense – syntactically, semantically, or pragmatically.

In this book, we are not attempting to give a comprehensive introduction to computational linguistics. See the references at the end of the chapter for such introductions.

12.6.1 Using Definite Clauses for Context-Free Grammars

This section shows how to use definite clauses to represent aspects of the syntax and semantics of natural language.

Languages are defined by their legal sentences. Sentences are sequences of symbols. The legal sentences are specified by a grammar.

Our first approximation of natural language is a context-free grammar. A **context-free grammar** is a set of **rewrite rules**, with **non-terminal** symbols transforming into a sequence of terminal and non-terminal symbols. A sentence of the language is a sequence of **terminal** symbols generated by such rewriting rules. For example, the grammar rule

$$sentence \longmapsto noun\_phrase, verb\_phrase$$

means that a non-terminal symbol *sentence* can be a *noun_phrase* followed by a *verb_phrase*. The symbol "$\longmapsto$" means "can be rewritten as." If a sentence of natural language is represented as a list of words, this rule means that a list of words is a sentence if it is a noun phrase followed by a verb phrase:

$$sentence(S) \leftarrow noun\_phrase(N), verb\_phrase(V), append(N, V, S).$$

To say that the word "computer" is a noun, you would write

$noun([computer])$.

There is an alternative, simpler representation of context-free grammar rules using definite clauses that does not require an explicit *append*, known as a **definite clause grammar (DCG)**. Each non-terminal symbol s becomes a predicate with two arguments, $s(T_1, T_2)$, which means that list T_2 is an ending of the list T_1 such that all of the words in T_1 before T_2 form a sequence of words of the category s. Lists T_1 and T_2 together form a **difference list** of words that make the class given by the non-terminal symbol, because it is the difference of these that forms the syntactic category.

Example 12.33   Under this representation, $noun\_phrase(T_1, T_2)$ is true if list T_2 is an ending of list T_1 such that all of the words in T_1 before T_2 form a noun phrase. T_2 is the rest of the sentence. You can think of T_2 as representing a position in a list that is after position T_1. The difference list represents the words between these positions.

The atomic symbol

$noun\_phrase([the, student, passed, the, course, with, a, computer],$
$\qquad [passed, the, course, with, a, computer])$

is true in the intended interpretation because "the student" forms a noun phrase.

The grammar rule

$sentence \longmapsto noun\_phrase, verb\_phrase$

means that there is a sentence between some T_0 and T_2 if there exists a noun phrase between T_0 and T_1 and a verb phrase between T_1 and T_2:

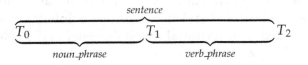

This grammar rule can be specified as the following clause:

$sentence(T_0, T_2) \leftarrow$
$\qquad noun\_phrase(T_0, T_1) \wedge$
$\qquad verb\_phrase(T_1, T_2)$.

In general, the rule

$h \longmapsto b_1, b_2, \ldots, b_n$

says that h is composed of a b_1 followed by a b_2, ..., followed by a b_n, and is written as the definite clause

$$\begin{aligned} & h(T_0, T_n) \leftarrow \\ & \quad b_1(T_0, T_1) \land \\ & \quad b_2(T_1, T_2) \land \\ & \quad \vdots \\ & \quad b_n(T_{n-1}, T_n). \end{aligned}$$

using the interpretation

$$\overbrace{\underbrace{T_0 \qquad}_{b_1}\underbrace{T_1 \qquad}_{b_2} T_2 \cdots \underbrace{T_{n-1} \qquad}_{b_n}}^{h} T_n$$

where the T_i are new variables.

To say that non-terminal h gets mapped to the terminal symbols, $t_1, \ldots, t_n$, one would write

$$h([t_1, \cdots, t_n | T], T)$$

using the interpretation

$$\overbrace{t_1, \cdots, t_n}^{h} T$$

Thus, $h(T_1, T_2)$ is true if $T_1 = [t_1, \ldots, t_n | T_2]$.

Example 12.34 The rule that specifies that the non-terminal h can be rewritten to the non-terminal a followed by the non-terminal b followed by the terminal symbols c and d, followed by the non-terminal symbol e followed by the terminal symbol f and the non-terminal symbol g, can be written as

$$h \longmapsto a, b, [c, d], e, [f], g$$

and can be represented as

$$\begin{aligned} & h(T_0, T_6) \leftarrow \\ & \quad a(T_0, T_1) \land \\ & \quad b(T_1, [c, d | T_3]) \land \\ & \quad e(T_3, [f | T_5]) \land \\ & \quad g(T_5, T_6). \end{aligned}$$

Note that the translations $T_2 = [c, d | T_3]$ and $T_4 = [f | T_5]$ were done manually.

Figure 12.6 (on the next page) axiomatizes a simple grammar of English. Figure 12.7 (page 525) gives a simple dictionary of words and their parts of speech, which can be used with this grammar.

% A sentence is a noun phrase followed by a verb phrase.

$$sentence(T_0, T_2) \leftarrow$$
$$noun\_phrase(T_0, T_1) \land$$
$$verb\_phrase(T_1, T_2).$$

% A noun phrase is a determiner followed by modifiers followed by a noun
% followed by an optional prepositional phrase.

$$noun\_phrase(T_0, T_4) \leftarrow$$
$$det(T_0, T_1) \land$$
$$modifiers(T_1, T_2) \land$$
$$noun(T_2, T_3) \land$$
$$pp(T_3, T_4).$$

% Modifiers consist of a (possibly empty) sequence of adjectives.

$$modifiers(T, T).$$
$$modifiers(T_0, T_2) \leftarrow$$
$$adjective(T_0, T_1) \land$$
$$modifiers(T_1, T_2).$$

% An optional prepositional phrase is either nothing or a preposition followed
% by a noun phrase.

$$pp(T, T).$$
$$pp(T_0, T_2) \leftarrow$$
$$preposition(T_0, T_1) \land$$
$$noun\_phrase(T_1, T_2).$$

% A verb phrase is a verb followed by a noun phrase and an optional
% prepositional phrase.

$$verb\_phrase(T_0, T_3) \leftarrow$$
$$verb(T_0, T_1) \land$$
$$noun\_phrase(T_1, T_2) \land$$
$$pp(T_2, T_3).$$

Figure 12.6: A context-free grammar for a very restricted subset of English

$det(T, T)$.
$det([a|T], T)$.
$det([the|T], T)$.
$noun([student|T], T)$.
$noun([course|T], T)$.
$noun([computer|T], T)$.
$adjective([practical|T], T)$.
$verb([passed|T], T)$.
$preposition([with|T], T)$.

Figure 12.7: A simple dictionary

Example 12.35 For the grammar of Figure 12.6 and the dictionary of Figure 12.7, the query

ask $noun\_phrase([the, student, passed, the, course, with, a, computer], R)$.

will return

$R = [passed, the, course, with, a, computer]$.

The sentence "The student passed the course with a computer." has two different parses, one using the clause instance

$verb\_phrase([passed, the, course, with, a, computer], []) \leftarrow$
  $verb([passed, the, course, with, a, computer],$
    $[the, course, with, a, computer]) \wedge$
  $noun\_phrase([the, course, with, a, computer], []) \wedge$
  $pp([], [])$

and one using the instance

$verb\_phrase([passed, the, course, with, a, computer], []) \leftarrow$
  $verb([passed, the, course, with, a, computer],$
    $[the, course, with, a, computer]) \wedge$
  $noun\_phrase([the, course, with, a, computer], [with, a, computer]) \wedge$
  $pp([with, a, computer], [])$.

In the first of these, the prepositional phrase modifies the noun phrase (i.e., the course is with a computer); and in the second, the prepositional phrase modifies the verb phrase (i.e., the course was passed with a computer).

12.6.2   Augmenting the Grammar

A context-free grammar does not adequately express the complexity of the grammar of natural languages, such as English. Two mechanisms can be added to this grammar to make it more expressive:

- extra arguments to the non-terminal symbols and
- arbitrary conditions on the rules.

The extra arguments will enable us to do several things: to construct a parse tree, to represent the semantic structure of a sentence, to incrementally build a query that represents a question to a database, and to accumulate information about phrase agreement (such as number, tense, gender, and person).

12.6.3   Building Structures for Non-terminals

You can add an extra argument to the predicates to represent a parse tree, forming a rule such as

$$sentence(T_0, T_2, s(NP, VP)) \leftarrow$$
$$noun\_phrase(T_0, T_1, NP) \land$$
$$verb\_phrase(T_1, T_2, VP).$$

which means that the parse tree for a sentence is of the form $s(NP, VP)$, where NP is the parse tree for the noun phrase and VP is the parse tree for the verb phrase.

This is important if you want some result from the syntactic analysis, not just to know whether the sentence is syntactically valid. The notion of a parse tree is a simplistic form of what is required because it does not adequately represent the meaning or "deep structure" of a sentence. For example, you would really like to recognize that "Alex taught the AI course" and "the AI course was taught by Alex" have the same meaning, only differing in the active or passive voice.

12.6.4   Canned Text Output

There is nothing in the definition of the grammar that requires English input and the parse tree as output. A query of grammar rule with the meaning of the sentence bound and a free variable representing the sentence can produce a sentence that matches the meaning.

One such use of grammar rules is to provide canned text output from logic terms; the output is a sentence in English that matches the logic term. This is useful for producing English versions of atoms, rules, and questions that a user – who may not know the intended interpretation of the symbols, or even the syntax of the formal language – can easily understand.

% $trans(Term, T0, T1)$ is true if $Term$ translates into the words contained in the
% difference list $T0 - T1$.

$trans(scheduled(S, C, L, R), T_1, T_8) \leftarrow$
    $trans(session(S), T_1, [of|T_3]) \land$
    $trans(course(C), T_3, [is, scheduled, at|T_5]) \land$
    $trans(time(L), T_5, [in|T_7]) \land$
    $trans(room(R), T_7, T_8).$
$trans(session(w11), [the, winter, 2011, session|T], T).$
$trans(course(cs422), [the, advanced, artificial, intelligence, course|T], T).$
$trans(time(clock(0, M)), [12, :, M, am|T], T).$
$trans(time(clock(H, M)), [H, :, M, am|T], T) \leftarrow$
    $H > 0 \land H < 12.$
$trans(time(clock(12, M)), [12, :, M, pm|T], T).$
$trans(time(clock(H, M)), [H1, :, M, pm|T], T) \leftarrow$
    $H > 12 \land$
    $H1$ is $H - 12.$
$trans(room(above(R)), [the, room, above|T_1], T_2) \leftarrow$
    $trans(room(R), T_1, T_2).$
$trans(room(csci333), [the, computer, science, department, office|T], T).$

Figure 12.8: Grammar for output of canned English

Example 12.36 Figure 12.8 shows a grammar for producing canned text on schedule information. For example, the query

    ask $trans(scheduled(w11, cs422, clock(15, 30), above(csci333)), T, []).$

produces the answer $T = [the, winter, 2011, session, of, the, advanced, artificial, intelligence, course, is, scheduled, at, 3, :, 30, pm, in, the, room, above, the, computer, science, department, office]$. This list could be written as a sentence to the user.

This grammar would probably not be useful for understanding natural language, because it requires a very stylized form of English; the user would have to use the exact translation of a term to get a legal parse.

12.6.5 Enforcing Constraints

Natural language imposes constraints which, for example, disallow sentences such as "a students eat." Words in a sentence must satisfy some agreement criteria. "A students eat" fails to satisfy the criterion of number agreement, which specifies whether the nouns and verbs are singular or plural.

Number agreement can be enforced in the grammar by parametrizing the non-terminals by the number and making sure that the numbers of the different parts of speech agree. You only add an extra argument to the relevant non-terminals.

Example 12.37 The grammar of Figure 12.9 does not allow "a students," "the student eat," or "the students eats," because all have number disagreement, but it allows "a green student eats," "the students," or "the student," because "the" can be either singular or plural.

To parse the sentence "the student eats," you issue the query

> ask *sentence*([*the, student, eats*], [ ], *Num, T*)

and the answer returned is

> $Num = singular$,
> $T = s(np(definite, [ ], student, nopp), vp(eat, nonp, nopp))$.

To parse the sentence "the students eat," you issue the query

> ask *sentence*([*the, students, eat*], [ ], *Num, T*)

and the answer returned is

> $Num = plural$,
> $T = s(np(definite, [ ], student, nopp), vp(eat, nonp, nopp))$.

To parse the sentence "a student eats," you issue the query

> ask *sentence*([*a, student, eats*], [ ], *Num, T*)

and the answer returned is

> $Num = singular$,
> $T = s(np(indefinite, [ ], student, nopp), vp(eat, nonp, nopp))$.

Note that the only difference between the answers is whether the subject is singular and whether the determiner is definite.

12.6.6 Building a Natural Language Interface to a Database

You can augment the preceding grammar to implement a simple natural language interface to a database. The idea is that, instead of transforming subphrases into parse trees, you transform them into a form that can be queried on a database. For example, a noun phrase becomes an individual with a set of predicates defining it.

Example 12.38 The phrase "a female student enrolled in a computer science course" could be translated into

> $answer(X) \leftarrow$
> $\quad female(X) \land student(X) \land enrolled\_in(X, Y) \land course(Y)$
> $\quad \land department(Y, comp\_science)$.

% A sentence is a noun phrase followed by a verb phrase.

$sentence(T_0, T_2, Num, s(NP, VP)) \leftarrow$
  $noun\_phrase(T_0, T_1, Num, NP) \wedge$
  $verb\_phrase(T_1, T_2, Num, VP).$

% A noun phrase is empty or a determiner followed by modifiers followed by
% a noun followed by an optional prepositional phrase.

$noun\_phrase(T, T, Num, nonp).$
$noun\_phrase(T_0, T_4, Num, np(Det, Mods, Noun, PP)) \leftarrow$
  $det(T_0, T_1, Num, Det) \wedge$
  $modifiers(T_1, T_2, Mods) \wedge$
  $noun(T_2, T_3, Num, Noun) \wedge$
  $pp(T_3, T_4, PP).$

% A verb phrase is a verb, followed by a noun phrase, followed by an optional
% prepositional phrase.

$verb\_phrase(T_0, T_3, Num, vp(V, NP, PP)) \leftarrow$
  $verb(T_0, T_1, Num, V) \wedge$
  $noun\_phrase(T_1, T_2, N2, NP) \wedge$
  $pp(T_2, T_3, PP).$

% An optional prepositional phrase is either nothing or a preposition followed
% by a noun phrase. Only the null case is given here.

$pp(T, T, nopp).$

% Modifiers is a sequence of adjectives. Only the null case is given.

$modifiers(T, T, [\,]).$

% The dictionary.

$det([a|T], T, singular, indefinite).$
$det([the|T], T, Num, definite).$
$noun([student|T], T, singular, student).$
$noun([students|T], T, plural, student).$
$verb([eats|T], T, singular, eat).$
$verb([eat|T], T, plural, eat).$

Figure 12.9: Grammar to enforce number agreement and build parse tree

% A noun phrase is a determiner followed by modifiers followed by a noun
% followed by an optional prepositional phrase.

$noun\_phrase(T_0, T_4, Obj, C_0, C_4) \leftarrow$
  $det(T_0, T_1, Obj, C_0, C_1) \wedge$
  $modifiers(T_1, T_2, Obj, C_1, C_2) \wedge$
  $noun(T_2, T_3, Obj, C_2, C_3) \wedge$
  $pp(T_3, T_4, Obj, C_3, C_4).$

% Modifiers consist of a sequence of adjectives.

$modifiers(T, T, Obj, C, C).$
$modifiers(T_0, T_2, Obj, C_0, C_2) \leftarrow$
  $adjective(T_0, T_1, Obj, C_0, C_1) \wedge$
  $modifiers(T_1, T_2, Obj, C_1, C_2).$

% An optional prepositional phrase is either nothing or a preposition followed
% by a noun phrase.

$pp(T, T, Obj, C, C).$
$pp(T_0, T_2, O_1, C_0, C_2) \leftarrow$
  $preposition(T_0, T_1, O_1, O_2, C_0, C_1) \wedge$
  $noun\_phrase(T_1, T_2, O_2, C_1, C_2).$

Figure 12.10: A grammar that constructs a query

Let us ignore the problems of quantification, such as how the words "all," "a,"
and "the" get translated into quantifiers. You can construct a query by allowing
noun phrases to return an individual and a list of constraints imposed by the
noun phrase on the individual. Appropriate grammar rules are specified in
Figure 12.10, and they are used with the dictionary of Figure 12.11.

In this grammar,

$noun\_phrase(T_0, T_1, O, C_0, C_1)$

means that list T_1 is an ending of list T_0, and the words in T_0 before T_1 form
a noun phrase. This noun phrase refers to the individual O. C_0 is an ending of
C_1, and the formulas in C_1, but not in C_0, are the constraints on individual O
imposed by the noun phrase.

Example 12.39 The query

  ask $noun\_phrase([a, computer, science, course], [\,], Obj, [\,], C).$

will return

  $C = [course(Obj), dept(Obj, comp\_science)].$

The query

> ask *noun_phrase*([*a, female, student, enrolled, in, a, computer,*
>   *science, course*], [ ], *P*, [ ], *C*).

returns

> *C* = [*course*(*X*), *dept*(*X*, *comp_science*), *enrolled*(*P*, *X*), *student*(*P*),
>   *female*(*P*)].

If the elements of list *C* are queried against a database that uses these relations and constants, precisely the female students enrolled in a computer science course could be found.

12.6.7 Limitations

Thus far, we have assumed a very simple form of natural language. Our aim was to show what could be easily accomplished with simple tools rather than with a comprehensive study of natural language. Useful front ends to databases can be built with the tools presented by, for example, constraining the domain sufficiently and asking the user, if necessary, which of multiple competing interpretations are intended.

This discussion of natural language processing assumes that natural language is compositional; the meaning of the whole can be derived from the meaning of the parts. Compositionality is, in general, a false assumption. You usually must know the context in the discourse and the situation in the world to discern what is meant by an utterance. Many types of ambiguity exist that can only be resolved by understanding the context of the words.

---

det(*T, T, O, C, C*).
det([*a*|*T*], *T, O, C, C*).
det([*the*|*T*], *T, O, C, C*).
noun([*course*|*T*], *T, O, C*, [*course*(*O*)|*C*]).
noun([*student*|*T*], *T, O, C*, [*student*(*O*)|*C*]).
noun([*john*|*T*], *T, john, C, C*).
noun([*cs312*|*T*], *T, 312, C, C*).
adjective([*computer, science*|*T*], *T, O, C*, [*dept*(*O, comp_science*)|*C*]).
adjective([*female*|*T*], *T, O, C*, [*female*(*O*)|*C*]).
preposition([*enrolled, in*|*T*], *T, O*$_1$*, O*$_2$*, C*, [*enrolled*(*O*$_1$, *O*$_2$)|*C*]).

Figure 12.11: A dictionary for constructing a query

For example, you cannot always determine the correct reference of a description without knowledge of the context and the situation. A description does not always refer to a uniquely determined individual.

Example 12.40 Consider the following paragraph:

> The student took many courses. Two computer science courses and one mathematics course were particularly difficult. *The mathematics course. . .*

The referent is defined by the context and not just the description "*The mathematics course.*" There could be more mathematics courses, but we know from context that the phrase is referring to the particularly difficult one taken by the student.

Many problems of reference arise in database applications if the use of "*the*" or "*it*" is allowed or if words that have more than one meaning are permitted. Context is used to disambiguate references in natural language. Consider:

> *Who is the head of the mathematics department?*
> *Who is her secretary?*

It is clear from the previous sentence who "her" refers to, as long as the reader understands that heads are people who have a gender, but departments do not.

12.7 Equality

Sometimes it is useful to use more than one term to name a single individual. For example, the terms 4×4, 2^4, $273 - 257$, and 16 may denote the same number. Sometimes, you want to have each name refer to a different individual. For example, you may want a separate name for different courses in a university. Sometimes you do not know whether or not two names denote the same individual – for example, whether the 8 a.m. delivery person is the same as the 1 p.m. delivery person.

This section considers the role of equality, which allows us to represent whether or not two terms denote the same individual in the world. Note that, in the definite clause language presented earlier in the chapter, all of the answers were valid whether or not terms denoted the same individuals.

Equality is a special predicate symbol with a standard domain-independent intended interpretation.

Term t_1 **equals** term t_2, written $t_1 = t_2$, is true in interpretation I if t_1 and t_2 denote the same individual in I.

Equality does *not* mean similarity. If a and b are constants and $a = b$, it is not the case that there are two things that are similar or even identical. Rather, it means there is one thing with two names.

chair 1   chair 2

Figure 12.12: Two chairs

Example 12.41 Consider the world of two chairs given in Figure 12.12. In this world it is not true that *chair1* = *chair2*, even though the two chairs may be identical in all respects; without representing the exact position of the chairs, they cannot be distinguished. It may be the case that *chairOnRight* = *chair2*. It is not the case that the chair on the right is *similar* to chair2. It *is* chair2.

12.7.1 Allowing Equality Assertions

If you do not allow equality assertions, the only thing that is equal to a term is itself. This can be captured as though you had the assertion $X = X$. This means that for any ground term t, t denotes the same individual as t.

If you want to permit equality assertions (e.g., stating that *chairOnRight* = *chair2*), the representation and reasoning system must be able to derive what follows from a knowledge base that includes clauses with equality in the head. There are two major ways of doing this. The first is to axiomatize equality like any other predicate. The second is to build special-purpose inference machinery for equality. Both of these ways are considered here.

Axiomatizing Equality

Equality can be axiomatized as follows. The first three axioms state that equality is reflexive, symmetric, and transitive:

$$X = X.$$
$$X = Y \leftarrow Y = X.$$
$$X = Z \leftarrow X = Y \wedge Y = Z.$$

The other axioms depend on the set of function and relation symbols in the language; thus, they form what is called an **axiom schema**. The general idea is that you can substitute a term with a term that is equal in functions and in relations. For each n-ary function symbol f, there is a rule of the form

$$f(X_1, \ldots, X_n) = f(Y_1, \ldots, Y_n) \leftarrow X_1 = Y_1 \wedge \cdots \wedge X_n = Y_n.$$

For each n-ary predicate symbol p, there is a rule of the form

$$p(X_1, \ldots, X_n) \leftarrow p(Y_1, \ldots, Y_n) \wedge X_1 = Y_1 \wedge \cdots \wedge X_n = Y_n.$$

> **Example 12.42** The binary function $cons(X, Y)$ requires the axiom
>
> $$cons(X_1, X_2) = cons(Y_1, Y_2) \leftarrow X_1 = Y_1 \wedge X_2 = Y_2.$$
>
> The ternary relationship $prop(I, P, V)$ requires the axiom
>
> $$prop(I_1, P_1, V_1) \leftarrow prop(I_2, P_2, V_2) \wedge I_1 = I_2 \wedge P_1 = P_2 \wedge V_1 = V_2.$$

Having these axioms explicit as part of the knowledge base turns out to be very inefficient. The use of these rules is not guaranteed to halt using a top-down depth-first interpreter. For example, the symmetric axiom will cause an infinite loop unless identical subgoals are noticed.

Special-Purpose Equality Reasoning

Paramodulation is a way to augment a proof procedure to implement equality. The general idea is that, if $t_1 = t_2$, any occurrence of t_1 can be replaced by t_2. Equality can thus be treated as a **rewrite rule**, substituting equals for equals. This approach works best if you can select a **canonical representation** for each individual, which is a term that other representations for that individual can be mapped into.

One classic example is the representation of numbers. There are many terms that represent the same number (e.g., 4×4, $13 + 3$, $273 - 257$, 2^4, 4^2, 16), but typically we treat the sequence of digits (in base ten) as the canonical representation of the number.

Universities invented student numbers to provide a canonical representation for each student. Different students with the same name are distinguishable and different names for the same person can be mapped to the person's student number.

12.7.2 Unique Names Assumption

Instead of being agnostic about the equality of each term and expecting the user to axiomatize which names denote the same individual and which denote different individuals, it is often easier to have the convention that different ground terms denote different individuals.

> **Example 12.43** Consider a student database example where a student must have two courses as science electives. Suppose a student has passed *math302* and *psyc303*; then you only know whether they have passed two courses if you know *math302* $\neq$ *psyc303*. That is, the constants *math302* and *psyc303* denote different courses. Thus, you must know which course numbers denote different courses. Rather than writing $n \times (n - 1)$ inequality axioms for n individuals, it may be better to have the convention that every course number denotes a different course and thus the use of inequality axioms is avoided.

This approach to handling equality is known as the unique names assumption.

The **unique names assumption (UNA)** is the assumption that distinct ground terms denote different individuals. That is, for every pair of distinct ground terms t_1 and t_2, assume $t_1 \neq t_2$, where "$\neq$" means "not equal to."

Note that this does not follow from the semantics for the definite clause language (page 159). As far as that semantics was concerned, distinct ground terms t_1 and t_2 could denote the same individual or could denote different individuals.

In the logic presented thus far, the unique names assumption only matters if explicit inequalities exist in the bodies of clauses or equality in the head of clauses. With the unique names assumption, equality does not appear in the head of clauses, other than in the clauses defining equality presented earlier. Other clauses implying equality would be either tautologies or inconsistent with the unique name axioms.

The unique names assumption can be axiomatized with the following axiom schema for inequality, which consists of the axiom schema for equality (page 533) together with the axiom schema:

- $c \neq c'$ for any distinct constants c and c'.
- $f(X_1, \ldots, X_n) \neq g(Y_1, \ldots, Y_m)$ for any distinct function symbols f and g.
- $f(X_1, \ldots, X_n) \neq f(Y_1, \ldots, Y_n) \leftarrow X_i \neq Y_i$, for any function symbol f. There are n instances of this schema for every n-ary function symbol f (one for each i such that $1 \leq i \leq n$).
- $f(X_1, \ldots, X_n) \neq c$ for any function symbol f and constant c.
- $t \neq X$ for any term t in which X appears (where t is not the term X).

With this axiomatization, two ground terms are not equal if and only if they do not unify, because ground terms are identical if and only if they unify. This is not the case for non-ground terms. For example, $a \neq X$ has some instances that are true – for example, when X has value b – and an instance which is false, namely, when X has value a.

The unique names assumption is very useful for database applications, in which you do not, for example, want to have to state that $kim \neq sam$ and $kim \neq chris$ and $chris \neq sam$. The unique names assumption allows us to use the convention that each name denotes a different individual.

Sometimes the unique names assumption is inappropriate – for example, $2 + 2 \neq 4$ is wrong, nor may it be the case that $clark\_kent \neq superman$.

Top-Down Procedure for the Unique Names Assumption

The top-down procedure incorporating the unique names assumption should not treat inequality as just another predicate, mainly because too many different individuals exist for any given individual.

If there is a subgoal $t_1 \neq t_2$, for terms t_1 and t_2 there are three cases:

1. t_1 and t_2 do not unify. In this case, $t_1 \neq t_2$ succeeds.

   For example, the inequality $f(X, a, g(X)) \neq f(t(X), X, b)$ succeeds because the two terms do not unify.

2. t_1 and t_2 are identical, including having the same variables in the same positions. In this case, $t_1 \neq t_2$ fails.

For example, $f(X,a,g(X)) \neq f(X,a,g(X))$ fails.

Note that, for any pair of ground terms, one of these first two cases must occur.

3. Otherwise, there are instances of $t_1 \neq t_2$ that succeed and instances of $t_1 \neq t_2$ that fail.

For example, consider the subgoal $f(W,a,g(Z)) \neq f(t(X),X,Y)$. The MGU of $f(W,a,g(Z))$ and $f(t(X),X,Y)$ is $\{X/a,\ W/t(a),\ Y/g(Z)\}$. Some instances of the inequality, such as the ground instances consistent with the unifier, should fail. Any instance that is not consistent with the unifier should succeed. Unlike other goals, you do not want to enumerate every instance that succeeds because that would mean unifying X with every function and constant different than a, as well as enumerating every pair of values for Y and Z where Y is different than $g(Z)$.

The top-down proof procedure can be extended to incorporate the unique names assumption. Inequalities of the first type can succeed and those of the second type can fail. Inequalities the third type can be **delayed**, waiting for subsequent goals to unify variables so that one of the first two cases occur. To delay a goal in the proof procedure of Figure 12.3 (page 511), when selecting an atom in the body of ac, the algorithm should select one of the atoms that is not being delayed. If there are no other atoms to select, and neither of the first two cases is applicable, the query should succeed. There is always an instance of the inequality that succeeds, namely, the instance where every variable gets a different constant that does not appear anywhere else. When this occurs, the user has to be careful when interpreting the free variables in the answer. The answer does not mean that it is true for every instance of the free variables, but rather that it is true for some instance.

Example 12.44   Consider the rules that specify whether a student has passed at least two courses:

$$passed\_two\_courses(S) \leftarrow$$
$$\qquad C_1 \neq C_2 \land$$
$$\qquad passed(S,C_1) \land$$
$$\qquad passed(S,C_2).$$
$$passed(S,C) \leftarrow$$
$$\qquad grade(S,C,M) \land$$
$$\qquad M \geq 50.$$
$$grade(mike,engl101,87).$$
$$grade(mike,phys101,89).$$

For the query

ask $passed\_two\_courses(mike),$

the subgoal $C_1 \neq C_2$ cannot be determined and so must be delayed. The top-down proof procedure can, instead, select $passed(mike, C_1)$, which binds $engl101$ to C_1. It can then call $passed(mike, C_2)$, which in turn calls $grade(mike, C_2, M)$, which can succeed with substitution $\{C_2/engl101, M/87\}$. At this stage, the variables for the delayed inequality are bound enough to determine that the inequality should fail.

Another clause can be chosen for $grade(mike, C_2, M)$, returning substitution $\{C_2/phys101, M/89\}$. The variables in the delayed inequality are bound enough to test the inequality and, this time, the inequality succeeds. It can then go on to prove that $89 > 50$, and the goal succeeds.

One question that may arise from this example is "why not simply make the inequality the last call, because then it does not need to be delayed?" There are two reasons. First, it may be more efficient to delay. In this example, the delayed inequality can be tested before checking whether $87 > 50$. Although this particular inequality test may be fast, in many cases substantial computation can be avoided by noticing violated inequalities as soon as possible. Second, if a sub-proof were to return one of the values before it is bound, the proof procedure should still remember the inequality constraint, so that any future unification that violates the constraint can fail.

12.8 Complete Knowledge Assumption

To extend the complete knowledge assumption of Section 5.5 (page 193) to logic programs with variables and functions symbols, we require axioms for equality, and the domain closure, and a more sophisticated notion of the completion. Again, this defines a form of **negation as failure**.

Example 12.45 Suppose a *student* relation is defined by

> $student(mary)$.
> $student(john)$.
> $student(ying)$.

The complete knowledge assumption would say that these three are the only students; that is,

> $student(X) \leftrightarrow X = mary \lor X = john \lor X = ying$.

That is, if X is *mary*, *john*, or *ying*, then X is a student, and if X is a student, X must be one of these three. In particular, Kim is not a student.

Concluding $\neg student(kim)$ requires proving prove $kim \neq mary \land kim \neq john \land kim \neq ying$. To derive the inequalities, the unique names assumption (page 534) is required.

The complete knowledge assumption includes the unique names assumption. As a result, we assume the axioms for equality (page 533) and inequality (page 534) for the rest of this section.

The **Clark normal form** of the clause

$$p(t_1, \ldots, t_k) \leftarrow B.$$

is the clause

$$p(V_1, \ldots, V_k) \leftarrow \exists W_1 \ldots \exists W_m \, V_1 = t_1 \wedge \ldots \wedge V_k = t_k \wedge B.$$

where $V_1, \ldots, V_k$ are k variables that did not appear in the original clause, and $W_1, \ldots, W_m$ are the original variables in the clause. "$\exists$" means "there exists" (page 500). When the clause is an atomic clause (page 496), B is *true*.

Suppose all of the clauses for p are put into Clark normal form, with the same set of introduced variables, giving

$$p(V_1, \ldots, V_k) \leftarrow B_1.$$

$$\vdots$$

$$p(V_1, \ldots, V_k) \leftarrow B_n.$$

which is equivalent to

$$p(V_1, \ldots, V_k) \leftarrow B_1 \vee \ldots \vee B_n.$$

This implication is logically equivalent to the set of original clauses.

Clark's completion of predicate p is the equivalence

$$\forall V_1 \ldots \forall V_k \, p(V_1, \ldots, V_k) \leftrightarrow B_1 \vee \ldots \vee B_n$$

where negations as failure ($\sim$) in the bodies are replaced by standard logical negation ($\neg$). The completion means that $p(V_1, \ldots, V_k)$ is true if and only if at least one body B_i is true.

Clark's completion of a knowledge base consists of the completion of every predicate symbol along with the axioms for equality (page 533) and inequality (page 534).

Example 12.46 For the clauses

> *student*(*mary*).
> *student*(*john*).
> *student*(*ying*).

the Clark normal form is

> $student(V) \leftarrow V = mary.$
> $student(V) \leftarrow V = john.$
> $student(V) \leftarrow V = ying.$

which is equivalent to

> $student(V) \leftarrow V = mary \vee V = john \vee V = ying.$

The completion of the *student* predicate is

> $\forall V \, student(V) \leftrightarrow V = mary \vee V = john \vee V = ying.$

Example 12.47 Consider the following recursive definition:

$passed\_each([\,], St, MinPass).$
$passed\_each([C|R], St, MinPass) \leftarrow$
    $passed(St, C, MinPass) \wedge$
    $passed\_each(R, St, MinPass).$

In Clark normal form, this can be written as

$passed\_each(L, S, M) \leftarrow L = [\,].$
$passed\_each(L, S, M) \leftarrow$
    $\exists C \, \exists R \, L = [C|R] \wedge$
    $passed(S, C, M) \wedge$
    $passed\_each(R, S, M).$

Here we have removed the equalities that specify renaming of variables and have renamed the variables as appropriate. Thus, Clark's completion of *passed_each* is

$\forall L \, \forall S \, \forall M \, passed\_each(L, S, M) \leftrightarrow L = [\,] \vee$
    $\exists C \, \exists R \, (L = [C|R] \wedge$
    $passed(S, C, M) \wedge$
    $passed\_each(R, S, M)).$

Under the complete knowledge assumption, relations that cannot be defined using only definite clauses can now be defined.

Example 12.48 Suppose you are given a database of *course*(C) that is true if C is a course, and *enrolled*(S, C), which means that student S is enrolled in course C. Without the complete knowledge assumption, you cannot define *empty_course*(C) that is true if there are no students enrolled in course C. This is because there is always a model of the knowledge base where someone is enrolled in every course.

Using negation as failure, *empty_course*(C) can be defined by

$empty\_course(C) \leftarrow course(C) \wedge {\sim}has\_Enrollment(C).$
$has\_Enrollment(C) \leftarrow enrolled(S, C).$

The completion of this is

$\forall C \, empty\_course(C) \leftrightarrow course(C) \wedge \neg has\_Enrollment(C).$
$\forall C \, has\_Enrollment(C) \leftrightarrow \exists S \, enrolled(S, C).$

Here we offer a word of caution. You should be very careful when you include free variables within negation as failure. They usually do not mean what you think they might. We introduced the predicate *has_Enrollment* in the previous example to avoid having a free variable within a negation as failure. Consider what would have happened if you had not done this:

Example 12.49 One may be tempted to define *empty_course* in the following manner:

$$empty\_course(C) \leftarrow course(C) \land \sim enrolled(S,C).$$

which has the completion

$$\forall C\ empty\_course(C) \leftrightarrow \exists S\ course(C) \land \neg enrolled(S,C).$$

This is not correct. Given the clauses

$$course(cs422).$$
$$course(cs486).$$
$$enrolled(mary,cs422).$$
$$enrolled(sally,cs486).$$

the clause

$$empty\_course(cs422) \leftarrow course(cs422) \land \sim enrolled(sally,cs422)$$

is an instance of the preceding clause for which the body is true, and the head is false, because *cs422* is not an empty course. This is a contradiction to the truth of the preceding clause.

Note that the completion of the definition in Example 12.48 is equivalent to

$$\forall C\ empty\_course(C) \leftrightarrow course(C) \land \neg \exists S\ enrolled(S,C).$$

The existence is in the scope of the negation, so this is equivalent to

$$\forall C\ empty\_course(C) \leftrightarrow course(C) \land \forall S\ \neg enrolled(S,C).$$

12.8.1 Complete Knowledge Assumption Proof Procedures

The top-down proof procedure for negation as failure with the variables and functions is much like the top-down procedure for propositional negation as failure (page 199). As with the unique names assumption, a problem arises when there are free variables in negated goals.

Example 12.50 Consider the clauses

$$p(X) \leftarrow \sim q(X) \land r(X).$$
$$q(a).$$
$$q(b).$$
$$r(d).$$

According to the semantics, there is only one answer to the query ask $p(X)$, which is $X = d$. As $r(d)$ follows, so does $\sim q(d)$ and so $p(d)$ logically follows from the knowledge base.

When the top-down proof procedure encounters $\sim q(X)$, it should not try to prove $q(X)$, which succeeds (with substitution $\{X/a\}$), and so fail $\sim q(X)$. This would make the goal $p(X)$ fail, when it should succeed. Thus, the proof procedure would be incomplete. Note that, if the knowledge base contained $s(X) \leftarrow \sim q(X)$, the failure of $q(X)$ would mean $s(X)$ succeeding. Thus, with negation as failure, incompleteness leads to unsoundness.

As with the unique names assumption [Section 12.7.2 (page 534)], a sound proof procedure should delay the negated subgoal until the free variable is bound.

We require a more complicated top-down procedure when there are calls to negation as failure with free variables:

- Negation as failure goals that contain free variables must be delayed (page 590) until the variables become bound.

- If the variables never become bound, the goal **flounders**. In this case, you cannot conclude anything about the goal. The following example shows that you should do something more sophisticated for the case of floundering goals.

Example 12.51 Consider the clauses:

$$p(X) \leftarrow \sim q(X)$$
$$q(X) \leftarrow \sim r(X)$$
$$r(a)$$

and the query

ask $p(X)$.

The completion of the knowledge base is

$$p(X) \leftrightarrow \neg q(X),$$
$$q(X) \leftrightarrow \neg r(X),$$
$$r(X) \leftrightarrow X = a.$$

Substituting $X = a$ for r gives $q(X) \leftrightarrow \neg X = a$, and so $p(X) \leftrightarrow X = a$. Thus, there is one answer, namely $X = a$, but delaying the goal will not help find it. A proof procedure should analyze the cases for which the goal failed to derive this answer. However, such a procedure is beyond the scope of this book.

12.9   Review

The following are the main points you should have learned from this chapter:

- In domains characterized by individuals and relations, constants denoting individuals and predicate symbols denoting relations can be reasoned with to determine what is true in the domain.

- Datalog is a logical language with constants, universally quantified variables, relations, and rules.

- Substitutions are used to make instances of atoms and rules. Unification makes atoms identical for use in proofs.

- Function symbols are used to denote a possibly infinite set of individuals described in terms of other individuals. Function symbols can be used to build data structures.

- It is possible to use definite clauses to represent natural language grammars.

- Equality between terms means that the terms denote the same individual.

- Clark's completion can be used to define the semantics of negation as failure under the complete knowledge assumption.

12.10 References and Further Reading

Datalog and logic programs are described by Kowalski [1979], Sterling and Shapiro [1986], and Garcia-Molina, Ullman, and Widom [2009]. The history of logic programming is described by Kowalski [1988] and Colmerauer and Roussel [1996].

The work on negation as failure (page 193), as well as the unique names assumption (page 534), is based on the work of Clark [1978]. See the book by Lloyd [1987] for a formal treatment of logic programming in general and negation as failure in particular. Apt and Bol [1994] provide a survey of different techniques for handling negation as failure.

For introductions to computational linguistics see Jurafsky and Martin [2008] and Manning and Schütze [1999]. The use of definite clauses for describing natural language is described by Pereira and Shieber [2002] and Dahl [1994].

12.11 Exercises

Exercise 12.1 Consider a domain with two individuals ($\prec$ and ☎), two predicate symbols (p and q), and three constants (a, b, and c). The knowledge base KB is defined by

$$p(X) \leftarrow q(X).$$
$$q(a).$$

(a) Give one interpretation that is a model of KB.

(b) Give one interpretation that is not a model of KB.

(c) How many interpretations are there? Give a brief justification for your answer.

(d) How many of these interpretations are models of KB? Give a brief justification for your answer.

Exercise 12.2 Consider the language that contains the constant symbols a, b, and c; the predicate symbols p and q; and no function symbols. We have the following knowledge bases built from this language:

$$\mathrm{KB}_1 = \{\ p(a)\ \}.$$
$$\mathrm{KB}_2 = \{\ p(X) \leftarrow q(X)\ \}.$$
$$\mathrm{KB}_3 = \{\ p(X) \leftarrow q(X),$$
$$p(a),$$
$$q(b)\ \}.$$

Now consider possible interpretations for this language of the form $I = \langle D, \pi, \phi \rangle$, where $D = \{ \mathrel{\vcenter{\hbox{$\mathord{\prec}$}}}, \mathbf{\Phi}, \mathbf{+}, \diamond \}$.

(a) How many interpretations with the four domain elements exist for our simple language? Give a brief justification for your answer. [Hint: Consider how many possible assignments ϕ exist for the constant symbols, and consider how many extensions predicates p and q can have to determine how many assignments π exist.] Do not try to enumerate all possible interpretations.

(b) Of the interpretations outlined above, how many are models of KB_1? Give a brief justification for your answer.

(c) Of the interpretations outlined above, how many are models of KB_2? Give a brief justification for your answer.

(d) Of the interpretations outlined above, how many are models of KB_3? Give a brief justification for your answer.

Exercise 12.3 Consider the following knowledge base:

$r(a)$.
$r(e)$.
$p(c)$.
$q(b)$.
$s(a, b)$.
$s(d, b)$.
$s(e, d)$.
$p(X) \leftarrow q(X) \wedge r(X)$.
$q(X) \leftarrow s(X, Y) \wedge q(Y)$.

Show the set of ground atomic consequences derivable from this knowledge base. Assume that a bottom-up proof procedure is used and that at each iteration the first applicable clause is selected in the order shown. Furthermore, applicable constant substitutions are chosen in "alphabetic order" if more than one applies to a given clause; for example, if X/a and X/b are both applicable for a clause at some iteration, derive $q(a)$ first. In what order are consequences derived?

Exercise 12.4 In Example 12.21 (page 511), the algorithm fortuitously chose $imm\_west(r109, r111)$ as the clause to resolve against. What would have happened if another clause had been chosen? Show the sequence of resolutions that arise, and either show a different answer or give a generalized answer clause that cannot resolve with any clause in the knowledge base.

Exercise 12.5 In Example 12.21, we always selected the leftmost conjunct to resolve on. Is there a selection rule (a selection of which conjunct in the query to resolve against) that would have resulted in only one choice for this example? Give a general rule that – for this example, at least – results in fewer failing branches being made. Give an example where your rule does not work.

Exercise 12.6 In a manner similar to Example 12.21 (page 511), show derivations of the following queries:

   (a) ask $two\_doors\_east(r107, R)$.

   (b) ask $next\_door(R, r107)$.

   (c) ask $west(R, r107)$.

   (d) ask $west(r107, R)$.

Give all answers for each query.

Exercise 12.7 Consider the following knowledge base:

$$has\_access(X, library) \leftarrow student(X).$$
$$has\_access(X, library) \leftarrow faculty(X).$$
$$has\_access(X, library) \leftarrow has\_access(Y, library) \wedge parent(Y, X).$$
$$has\_access(X, office) \leftarrow has\_keys(X).$$
$$faculty(diane).$$
$$faculty(ming).$$
$$student(william).$$
$$student(mary).$$
$$parent(diane, karen).$$
$$parent(diane, robyn).$$
$$parent(susan, sarah).$$
$$parent(sarah, ariel).$$
$$parent(karen, mary).$$
$$parent(karen, todd).$$

   (a) Provide an SLD derivation of the query ask $has\_access(todd, library)$.

   (b) The query ask $has\_access(mary, library)$ has two SLD derivations. Give both of them.

   (c) Does there exist an SLD derivation for ask $has\_access(ariel, library)$? Explain why or why not.

   (d) Explain why the set of answers to the query ask $has\_access(X, office)$ is empty.

   (e) Suppose following the clause is added to the knowledge base:

$$has\_keys(X) \leftarrow faculty(X).$$

What are the answers to the query ask $has\_access(X, office)$?

Exercise 12.8 What is the result of the following application of substitutions:

(a) $f(A, X, Y, X, Y)\{A/X, Z/b, Y/c\}$.

(b) $yes(F, L) \leftarrow append(F, c(L, nil), c(l, c(i, c(s, c(t, nil)))))$
$\qquad \{F/c(l, X_1), Y_1/c(L, nil), A_1/l, Z_1/c(i, c(s, c(t, nil)))\}$.

(c) $append(c(A_1, X_1), Y_1, c(A_1, Z_1)) \leftarrow append(X_1, Y_1, Z_1)$
$\qquad \{F/c(l, X_1), Y_1/c(L, nil), A_1/l, Z_1/c(i, c(s, c(t, nil)))\}$.

Exercise 12.9 Give a most general unifier of the following pairs of expressions:

(a) $p(f(X), g(g(b)))$ and $p(Z, g(Y))$

(b) $g(f(X), r(X), t)$ and $g(W, r(Q), Q)$

(c) $bar(val(X, bb), Z)$ and $bar(P, P)$

Exercise 12.10 For each of the following pairs of atoms, either give a most general unifier or explain why one does not exist:

(a) $p(X, Y, a, b, W)$
$p(E, c, F, G, F)$

(b) $p(X, Y, Y)$
$p(E, E, F)$

(c) $p(Y, a, b, Y)$
$p(c, F, G, F)$

(d) $ap(F0, c(b, c(B0, L0)), c(a, c(b, c(b, c(a, emp)))))$
$ap(c(H1, T1), L1, c(H1, R1))$

Exercise 12.11 List all of the ground atomic logical consequences of the following knowledge base:

$q(Y) \leftarrow s(Y, Z) \wedge r(Z)$.
$p(X) \leftarrow q(f(X))$.
$s(f(a), b)$.
$s(f(b), b)$.
$s(c, b)$.
$r(b)$.

Exercise 12.12 Consider the following logic program:

$f(empty, X, X)$.
$f(cons(X, Y), W, Z) \leftarrow$
$\qquad f(Y, W, cons(X, Z))$.

Give each top-down derivation, showing substitutions (as in Example 12.31) for the query

$\text{ask } f(cons(a, cons(b, cons(c, empty))), L, empty)$.

What are all of the answers?

Exercise 12.13 Consider the following logic program:

$$rd(cons(H, cons(H, T)), T).$$
$$rd(cons(H, T), cons(H, R)) \leftarrow$$
$$\quad rd(T, R).$$

Give a top-down derivation, showing all substitutions for the query

ask $rd(cons(a, cons(cons(a, X), cons(B, cons(c, Z)))), W)$.

What is the answer corresponding to this derivation?
   Is there a second answer? If yes, show the derivation; if not, explain why.

Exercise 12.14 Consider the following logic program:

$$ap(emp, L, L).$$
$$ap(c(H, T), L, c(H, R)) \leftarrow$$
$$\quad ap(T, L, R).$$
$$adj(A, B, L) \leftarrow$$
$$\quad ap(F, c(A, c(B, E)), L).$$

(a) Give a top-down derivation (including all substitutions) for one answer to
   the query

   ask $adj(b, Y, c(a, c(b, c(b, c(a, emp)))))$.

(b) Are there any other answers? If so, explain where a different choice could be
   made in the derivation in the previous answer, and continue the derivation,
   showing another answer. If there are no other answers, explain why not.

[You are meant to do this exercise as would a computer, without knowing what
the symbols mean. If you want to give a meaning to this program, you could read
ap as *append*, *c* as *cons*, *emp* as *empty*, and *adj* as *adjacent*.]

Exercise 12.15 The aim of this question is to get practice writing simple logic
programs.

(a) Write a relation *remove*(E, L, R) that is true if R is the resulting list of removing one instance of E from list L. The relation is false if E is not a member
   of L.

(b) Give all of the answers to the following queries:

   ask *remove*$(a, [b, a, d, a], R)$.
   ask *remove*$(E, [b, a, d, a], R)$.
   ask *remove*$(E, L, [b, a, d])$.
   ask *remove*$(p(X), [a, p(a), p(p(a)), p(p(p(a)))], R)$.

(c) Write a relation *subsequence*$(L1, L2)$ that is true if list $L1$ contains a subset of
   the elements of $L2$ in the same order.

(d) How many different proofs are there for each of the following queries:

> ask *subsequence*([a, d], [b, a, d, a]).
> ask *subsequence*([b, a], [b, a, d, a]).
> ask *subsequence*([X, Y], [b, a, d, a]).
> ask *subsequence*(S, [b, a, d, a]).

Explain why there are that many.

Exercise 12.16 In this question, you are to write a definite clause knowledge base for the design of custom video presentations.

Assume that the video is annotated using the relation

> *segment*(SegId, Duration, Covers),

where *SegId* is an identifier for the segment. (In a real application this will be enough information to extract the video segment). *Duration* is the time of the segment (in seconds). *Covers* is a list of topics covered by the video segment. An example of a video annotation is the database

> *segment*(seg0, 10, [welcome]).
> *segment*(seg1, 30, [skiing, views]).
> *segment*(seg2, 50, [welcome, computational intelligence, robots]).
> *segment*(seg3, 40, [graphics, dragons]).
> *segment*(seg4, 50, [skiing, robots]).

A presentation is a sequence of segments. You will represent a presentation by a list of segment identifiers.

(a) Axiomatize a predicate

> *presentation*(MustCover, Maxtime, Segments)

that is true if *Segments* is a presentation whose total running time is less than or equal to *Maxtime* seconds, such that all of the topics in the list *MustCover* are covered by a segment in the presentation. The aim of this predicate is to design presentations that cover a certain number of topics within a time limit.

For example, the query

> ask *presentation*([welcome, skiing, robots], 90, Segs).

should return at least the following two answers (perhaps with the segments in some other order):

> *presentation*([welcome, skiing, robots], 90, [seg0, seg4]).
> *presentation*([welcome, skiing, robots], 90, [seg2, seg1]).

Give the intended interpretation of all symbols used and demonstrate that you have tested your axiomatization (including finding all answers to your query) in AILog or Prolog. Explain briefly why each answer is an answer.

(b) Assuming you have a good user interface and a way to actually view the presentations, list *three* things that the preceding program does not do that you may want in such a presentation system. (There is no correct answer for this part. You must be creative to get full marks).

Exercise 12.17 Construct a knowledge base and a dictionary [based on Figure 12.11 (page 531)] to answer geographical questions such as that given in Figure 1.2 (page 8). For each query, either show how it can be answered or explain why it is difficult to answer given the tools presented in this chapter.

Chapter 13

Ontologies and Knowledge-Based Systems

The most serious problems standing in the way of developing an adequate theory of computation are as much ontological as they are semantical. It is not that the semantic problems go away; they remain as challenging as ever. It is just that they are joined – on center stage, as it were – by even more demanding problems of ontology.

– Smith [1996, p. 14]

How do you go about representing knowledge about a world so it is easy to acquire, debug, maintain, communicate, share, and reason with? This chapter explores how to specify the meaning of symbols in intelligent agents, how to use the meaning for knowledge-based debugging and explanation, and, finally, how an agent can represent its own reasoning and how this may be used to build knowledge-based systems. As Smith points out in the quote above, the problems of ontology are central for building intelligent computational agents.

13.1 Knowledge Sharing

Having an appropriate representation is only part of the story of building a knowledge-based agent. We also should be able to ensure that the knowledge can be acquired, particularly when the knowledge comes from diverse sources and at multiple points in time and should interoperate with other knowledge. We should also ensure that the knowledge can be reasoned about effectively.

Recall (page 61) that an **ontology** is a specification of the meanings of the symbols in an information system. Here an information system is a knowledge base or some source of information, such as a thermometer. The meaning is sometimes just in the mind of the knowledge-base designer or in comments with the knowledge base. Increasingly, the specification of the meaning is in machine-interpretable form. This formal specification is important for **semantic interoperability** – the ability of different knowledge bases to work together.

Example 13.1 A purchasing agent has to know, when a web site claims it has a good price on "chips," whether these are potato chips, computer chips, wood chips, or poker chips. An ontology would specify meaning of the terminology used by the web site. Instead of using the symbol "chip", a web site that adheres to ontologies may use the symbol "WoodChipMixed" as defined by some particular organization that has published an ontology. By using this symbol and declaring which ontology it is from, it should be unambiguous as to which use of the word *chip* is meant. A formal representation of the web page would use "WoodChipMixed", which may get translated into English simply as "chip". If another information source uses the symbol "ChipOfWood", some third party may declare that the use of the term "ChipOfWood" in that information source corresponds to "WoodChipMixed" and therefore enable the information sources to be combined.

Before discussing how ontologies are specified, we first discuss how the logic of the previous chapter (with variables, terms, and relations) can be used to build flexible representations. These flexible representations allow for the modular addition of knowledge, including adding arguments to relations.

Given a specification of the meaning of the symbols, an agent can use that meaning for knowledge acquisition, explanation, and debugging at the knowledge level.

13.2 Flexible Representations

The first part of this chapter considers a way to build flexible representations using the tools of logic. These flexible representations are the basis of modern ontologies.

13.2.1 Choosing Individuals and Relations

Given a logical representation language, such as the one developed in the previous chapter, and a world to reason about, the people designing knowledge bases have to choose what, in the world, to refer to. That is, they have to choose what individuals and relations there are. It may seem that they can just refer to the individuals and relations that exist in the world. However, the world does not determine what individuals there are. How the world is divided into individuals is invented by whomever is modeling the world. The modeler divides up the world up into things so that the agent can refer to parts of the world that make sense for the task at hand.

Example 13.2 It may seem as though "*red*" is a reasonable property to ascribe to things in the world. You may do this because you want to tell the delivery robot to go and get the red parcel. In the world, there are surfaces absorbing some frequencies and reflecting other frequencies of light. Some user may have decided that, for some application, some particular set of reflectance properties should be called "red." Some other modeler of the domain might decide on another mapping of the spectrum and use the terms *pink, scarlet, ruby,* and *crimson*, and yet another modeler may divide the spectrum into regions that do not correspond to words in any language but are those regions most useful to distinguish different categories of individuals.

Just as modelers choose what individuals to represent, they also choose what relations to use. There are, however, some guiding principles that are useful for choosing relations and individuals. These will be demonstrated through a sequence of examples.

Example 13.3 Suppose you decide that "red" is an appropriate category for classifying individuals. You can treat the name *red* as a unary relation and write that parcel *a* is red:

$$red(a).$$

If you represent the color information in this way, then you can easily ask what is red:

$$?red(X).$$

The *X* returned are the red individuals.

   With this representation, it is hard to ask the question, "What color is parcel *a*?" In the syntax of definite clauses, you cannot ask

$$ask\ X(a).$$

because, in languages based on first-order logic (page 517), predicate names cannot be variables. In second-order or higher-order logic, this would return any property of *a*, not just its color.

   There are alternative representations that allow you to ask about the color of parcel *a*. There is nothing in the world that forces you to make *red* a predicate. You could just as easily say that colors are individuals too, and you could use the constant *red* to denote the color red. Given that *red* is a constant, you can use the predicate *color* where *color*(*Ind, Val*) means that physical individual *Ind* has color *Val*. "Parcel *a* is red" can now be written as

$$color(a, red).$$

What you have done is reconceive the world: the world now consists of colors as individuals that you can name. There is now a new binary relation *color* between physical individuals and colors. Under this new representation you can ask, "What color is block *a*?" with the query

$$?color(a, C).$$

To make an abstract concept into an object is to **reify** it. In the preceding example, we reified the color *red*.

Example 13.4   It seems as though there is no disadvantage to the new representation of colors in the previous example. Everything that could be done before can be done now. It is not much more difficult to write $color(X, red)$ than $red(X)$, but you can now ask about the color of things. So the question arises of whether you can do this to every relation, and what do you end up with?

You can do a similar analysis for the *color* predicate as for the *red* predicate in Example 13.3. The representation with *color* as a predicate does not allow you to ask the question, "Which property of parcel *a* has value *red*?," where the appropriate answer is "color." Carrying out a similar transformation to that of Example 13.3, you can view properties such as *color* as individuals, and you can invent a relation *prop* and write "individual *a* has the *color* of *red*" as

$$prop(a, color, red).$$

This representation allows for all of the queries of this and the previous example. You do not have to do this again, because you can write all relations in terms of the *prop* relation.

The **individual-property-value** representation is in terms of a single relation *prop* where

$$prop(Ind, Prop, Val)$$

means that individual *Ind* has value *Val* for property *Prop*. This is also called the **triple representation** because all of the relations are represented as **triples**. The first element of the triple is called the **subject**, the second is the **verb**, and the third is the **object**, using the analogy that a triple is a simple three-word sentence.

The verb of a triple is a **property**. The **domain** of property p is the set of individuals that can appear as the subject of a triple when p is the verb. The **range** of a property p is the set of values that can appear as the object of a triple that has p as the verb.

An **attribute** is a property–value pair. For example, an attribute of a parcel may be that its color is red. Two parcels may be identical if they have the same attributes – the same values for their properties.

There are some predicates that may seem to be too simple for the triple representation:

Example 13.5   To transform $parcel(a)$, which means that *a* is a parcel, there do not seem to be appropriate properties or values. There are two ways to transform this into the triple representation. The first is to reify the concept parcel and to say that *a* is a parcel:

$$prop(a, type, parcel).$$

Here *type* is a special property that relates an individual to a class. The constant *parcel* denotes the class that is the set of all, real or potential, things that are parcels. This triple specifies that the individual *a* is in the class *parcel*.

The second is to make parcel a property and write "*a* is a parcel" as

$prop(a, parcel, true)$.

In this representation, *parcel* is a Boolean property which is true of things that are parcels.

A **Boolean property** is a property whose range is {*true*, *false*}, where *true* and *false* are constant symbols in the language.

Some predicates may seem to be too complicated for the triple representation:

Example 13.6 Suppose you want to represent the relation

$scheduled(C, S, T, R)$,

which is to mean that section *S* of course *C* is scheduled to start at time *T* in room *R*. For example, "section 2 of course *cs*422 is scheduled to start at 10:30 in room *cc*208" is written as

$scheduled(cs422, 2, 1030, cc208)$.

To represent this in the triple representation, you can invent a new individual, a *booking*. Thus, the *scheduled* relationship is reified into a booking individual.

A booking has a number of properties, namely a course, a section, a start time, and a room. To represent "section 2 of course *cs*422 is scheduled at 10:30 in room *cc*208," you name the booking, say, the constant *b*123, and write

$prop(b123, course, cs422)$.
$prop(b123, section, 2)$.
$prop(b123, start\_time, 1030)$.
$prop(b123, room, cc208)$.

This new representation has a number of advantages. The most important is that it is modular; which values go with which properties can easily be seen. It is easy to add new properties such as the instructor or the duration. With the new representation, it is easy to add that "Fran is teaching section 2 of course *cs*422, scheduled at 10:30 in room *cc*208" or that the duration is 50 minutes:

$prop(b123, instructor, fran)$.
$prop(b123, duration, 50)$.

With *scheduled* as a predicate, it was very difficult to add the instructor or duration because it required adding extra arguments to every instance of the predicate.

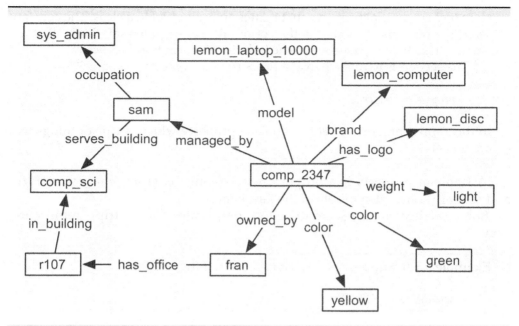

Figure 13.1: A semantic network

13.2.2   Graphical Representations

You can interpret the *prop* relation in terms of a graph, where the relation

  prop(Ind, Prop, Val)

is depicted with *Ind* and *Val* as nodes with an arc labeled with *Prop* between them. Such a graph is called a **semantic network**. Given such a graphical representation, there is a straightforward mapping into a knowledge base using the *prop* relation.

Example 13.7 Figure 13.1 shows a semantic network for the delivery robot showing the sort of knowledge that the robot may have about a particular computer. Some of the knowledge represented in the network is

  prop(comp_2347, owned_by, fran).
  prop(comp_2347, managed_by, sam).
  prop(comp_2347, model, lemon_laptop_10000).
  prop(comp_2347, brand, lemon_computer).
  prop(comp_2347, has_logo, lemon_disc).
  prop(comp_2347, color, green).
  prop(comp_2347, color, yellow).
  prop(comp_2347, weight, light).
  prop(fran, has_office, r107).
  prop(r107, in_building, comp_sci).

The network also shows how the knowledge is structured. For example, it is easy to see that computer number 2347 is owned by someone (Fran) whose office (r107) is in the *comp_sci* building. The direct indexing evident in the graph can be used by humans and machines.

This graphical notation has a number of advantages:

- It is easy for a human to see the relationships without being required to learn the syntax of a particular logic. The graphical notation helps the builders of knowledge bases to organize their knowledge.

- You can ignore the labels of nodes that just have meaningless names – for example, the name *b*123 in Example 13.6 (page 553), or *comp_2347* in Figure 13.1. You can just leave these nodes blank and make up an arbitrary name if you must map to the logical form.

Terse Language for Triples

Turtle is a simple language for representing **triples**. It is one of the languages invented for the **semantic web** (page 564). It is one of the syntaxes used for the **Resource Description Framework**, or **RDF**, growing out of a similar language called **Notation 3** or **N3**.

In Turtle and RDF everything – including individuals, classes, and properties – is a **resource**. A **Uniform Resource Identifier** (**URI**) is a unique name that can be used to identify anything. A URI is written within angle brackets, and it often has the form of a URL because URLs are unique. For example, ⟨http://aispace.org⟩ can be a URI. A "#" in a URI denotes an individual that is referred to in a web page. For example, ⟨http://cs.ubc.ca/~poole/foaf.rdf#david⟩ denotes the individual *david* referred to in http://cs.ubc.ca/~poole/foaf.rdf. The URI ⟨⟩ refers to the current document, so the URI ⟨#comp_2347⟩ denotes an individual defined in the current document.

A triple is written simply as

    Subject Verb Object.

where *Subject* and *Verb* are URIs, and *Object* is either a URI or a literal (string or number). *Verb* denotes a property. *Object* is the value of the property *Verb* for *Subject*.

Example 13.8 The triples of Example 13.7 are written in Turtle as follows:

    ⟨#comp_2347⟩ ⟨#owned_by⟩ ⟨#fran⟩ .
    ⟨#comp_2347⟩ ⟨#managed_by⟩ ⟨#sam⟩ .
    ⟨#comp_2347⟩ ⟨#model⟩ ⟨#lemon_laptop_10000⟩ .
    ⟨#comp_2347⟩ ⟨#brand⟩ ⟨#lemon_computer⟩ .

$\langle$#comp_2347$\rangle$ $\langle$#has_logo$\rangle$ $\langle$#lemon_disc$\rangle$.
$\langle$#comp_2347$\rangle$ $\langle$#color$\rangle$ $\langle$#green$\rangle$.
$\langle$#comp_2347$\rangle$ $\langle$#color$\rangle$ $\langle$#yellow$\rangle$.
$\langle$#fran$\rangle$ $\langle$#has_office$\rangle$ $\langle$#r107$\rangle$.
$\langle$#r107$\rangle$ $\langle$#serves_building$\rangle$ $\langle$#comp_sci$\rangle$.

The identifier "fran" does not tell us the name of the individual. If we wanted to say that the person's name is Fran, we would write

$\langle$#fran$\rangle$ $\langle$#name$\rangle$ "Fran".

There are some useful abbreviations used in Turtle. A comma is used to group objects with the same subject and verb. That is,

$S\ V\ O_1, O_2.$

is an abbreviation for

$S\ V\ O_1.$
$S\ V\ O_2.$

A semicolon is used to group verb–object pairs for the same subject. That is,

$S\ V_1\ O_1; V_2\ O_2.$

is an abbreviation for

$S\ V_1\ O_1.$
$S\ V_2\ O_2.$

Square brackets are to define an individual that is not given an identifier. This unnamed resource is used as the object of some triple, but otherwise cannot be referred to. Both commas and semicolons can be used to give this resource properties. Thus,

$[V_1\ O_1; V_2\ O_2]$

is an individual that has value O_1 on property V_1 and has value O_2 on property V_2. Such descriptions of unnamed individuals are sometimes called **frames**. The verbs are sometimes called **slots** and the objects are **fillers**.

Example 13.9   The Turtle sentence

$\langle$comp_3645$\rangle$ $\langle$#owned_by$\rangle$ $\langle$#fran$\rangle$;
                $\langle$#color$\rangle$ $\langle$#green$\rangle$, $\langle$#yellow$\rangle$;
                $\langle$#managed_by$\rangle$ [$\langle$#occupation$\rangle$ $\langle$#sys_admin$\rangle$;
                               $\langle$#serves_building$\rangle$ $\langle$#comp_sci$\rangle$].

says that $\langle$comp_3645$\rangle$ is owned by $\langle$#fran$\rangle$, its color is green and yellow, and it is managed by a resource whose occupation is system administration and who serves the *comp_sci* building.

This is an abbreviation for the triples

⟨comp_3645⟩ ⟨#owned_by⟩ ⟨#fran⟩ .
⟨comp_3645⟩ ⟨#color⟩ ⟨#green⟩ .
⟨comp_3645⟩ ⟨#color⟩ ⟨#yellow⟩ .
⟨comp_3645⟩ ⟨#managed_by⟩ ⟨i2134⟩ .
⟨i2134⟩ ⟨#occupation⟩ ⟨#sys_admin⟩ .
⟨i2134⟩ ⟨#serves_building⟩ ⟨#comp_sci⟩ .

but where the made-up URI, ⟨i2134⟩, cannot be referred to elsewhere.

It is difficult for a reader to know what the authors mean by a particular URI such as ⟨#name⟩ and how the use of this term relates to other people's use of the same term. There are, however, people who have agreed on certain meaning for specific terms. For example, the property ⟨http://xmlns.com/foaf/0.1/#name⟩ has a standard definition as the name of an object. Thus, if we write

⟨#fran⟩ ⟨http://xmlns.com/foaf/0.1/#name⟩ "Fran".

we mean the particular *name* property having that agreed-on definition.

It does not matter what is at the URL http://xmlns.com/foaf/0.1/, as long as those who use the URI ⟨http://xmlns.com/foaf/0.1/#name⟩ all mean the same property. That URL, at the time of writing, just redirects to a web page. However, the "friend of a friend" project (which is what "foaf" stands for) uses that name space to mean something. This works simply because people use it that way.

In Turtle, URIs can be abbreviated using a "name:" to replace a URL and the angle brackets, using an "@prefix" declaration. For example,

@prefix foaf: ⟨http://xmlns.com/foaf/0.1/#⟩

lets "foaf:name" be an abbreviation for ⟨http://xmlns.com/foaf/0.1/#name⟩. Similarly,

@prefix : ⟨#⟩

lets us write ⟨#color⟩ as :color.

Turtle also allows for parentheses for arguments to functions that are not reified. It also uses the abbreviation "a" for "rdf:type", but we do not follow that convention.

13.2.3 Primitive Versus Derived Relations

Typically, you know more about a domain than a database of facts; you know general rules from which other facts can be derived. Which facts are explicitly given and which are derived is a choice to be made when designing and building a knowledge base.

Primitive knowledge is knowledge that is defined explicitly by facts. **Derived knowledge** is knowledge that can be inferred from other knowledge. Derived knowledge is usually specified in terms of rules.

The use of rules allows for a more compact representation of knowledge. Derived relations allow for conclusions to be drawn from observations of the

---

| Classes in Knowledge Bases and Object-Oriented Programming |

The use of "individuals" and "classes" in knowledge-based systems is very similar to the use of "objects" and "classes" in **object-oriented programming (OOP) languages** such as **Smalltalk** or **Java**. This should not be too surprising because they have an interrelated history. There are important differences that tend to make the direct analogy often more confusing than helpful:

- Objects in OOP are computational objects; they are data structures and associated programs. A "person" object in Java is not a person. However, individuals in a knowledge base (KB) are (typically) things in the real world. A "person" individual in a KB can be a real person. A "chair" individual can be a real chair you can actually sit in; it can hurt you if you bump into it. You can send a message to, and get answers from, a "chair" object in Java, whereas a chair in the real world tends to ignore what you tell it. A KB is not typically used to interact with a chair, but to reason *about* a chair. A real chair stays where it is unless it is moved by a physical agent.
- In a KB, a representation of an object is only an approximation at one (or a few) levels of abstraction. Real objects tend to be much more complicated than what is represented. We typically do not represent the individual fibers in a chair. In an OOP system, there are only the represented properties of an object. The system can know everything about a Java object, but not about a real individual.
- The class structure of Java is intended to represent designed objects. A systems analyst or a programmer gets to create a design. For example, in Java, an object is only a member of one lowest-level class. There is no multiple inheritance. Real objects are not so well behaved. The same person could be a football coach, a mathematician, and a mother.
- A computer program cannot be uncertain about its data structures; it has to select particular data structures to use. However, we can be uncertain about the types of things in the world.
- The representations in a KB do not actually do anything. In an OOP system, objects do computational work. In a KB, they just represent – that is, they just refer to objects in the world.
- Whereas an object-oriented modeling language, like **UML**, may be used for representing KBs, it may not be the best choice. A good OO modeling tool has facilities to help build good designs. However, the world being modeled may not have a good design at all. Trying to force a good design paradigm on a messy world may not be productive.

domain. This is important because you do not directly observe everything about a domain. Much of what is known about a domain is inferred from the observations and more general knowledge.

A standard way to use derived knowledge is to put individuals into classes. We give general properties to classes so that individuals inherit the properties of classes. The reason we group individuals into classes is because the members of a class have attributes in common, or they have common properties that make sense for them (see the box on page 567).

A **class** is the set of those actual and potential individuals that would be members of the class. In logic, this is an **intensional** set, defined by a **characteristic function** that is true of members of the set and false of other individuals. The alternative is an **extensional** set, which is defined by listing its elements.

For example, the class *chair* is the set of all things that would be chairs. We do not want the definition to be the set of things that *are* chairs, because chairs that have not yet been built also fall into the class of chairs. We do not want two classes to be equivalent just because they have the same members. For example, the class of green unicorns and the class of chairs that are exactly 124 meters high are different classes, even though they contain the same elements; they are both empty.

The definition of class allows any set that can be described to be a class. For example, the set consisting of the number 17, the Tower of London, and Julius Caesar's left foot may be a class, but it is not very useful. A **natural kind** is a class where describing objects using the class is more succinct than describing objects without the class. For example, "mammal" is a natural kind, because describing the common attributes of mammals makes a knowledge base that uses "mammal" more succinct than one that does not use "mammal" and repeats the attributes for every individual.

We use the property *type* to mean "is a member of class." Thus, in the language of definite clauses,

$$prop(X, type, C)$$

means that individual X is a member of class C.

The people who created **RDF** and **RDF Schema** used exactly the property we want to use here for membership in a class. In the language Turtle, we can define the abbreviation

@prefix rdf: ⟨http://www.w3.org/1999/02/22-rdf-syntax-ns#⟩ .

@prefix rdfs: ⟨http://www.w3.org/2000/01/rdf-schema#⟩ .

Given these declarations, **rdf:type** means the type property that relates an individual to a class of which it is a member. By referring to the definition of **type** at that URI, this becomes a standard definition that can be used by others and can be distinguished from other meanings of the word "type."

The property **rdfs:subClassOf** between classes specifies that one class is a subset of another. In Turtle,

S rdfs:subClassOf C.

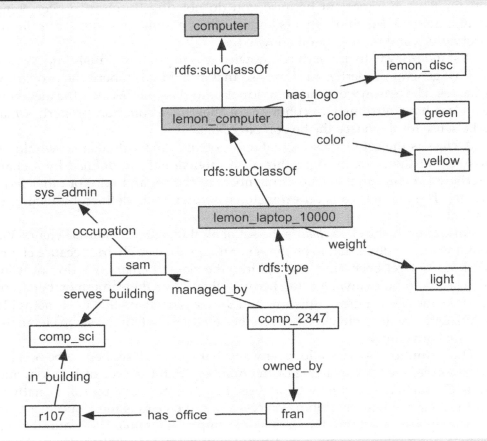

Figure 13.2: A semantic network allowing inheritance

means that class S is a subclass of class C. In terms of sets, this means that S is a subset of C. That is, every individual of type S is of type C.

Example 13.10   Example 13.7 explicitly specified that the logo for computer *comp_2347* was a lemon disc. You may, however, know that all Lemon-brand computers have this logo. An alternative representation is to associate the logo with *lemon_computer* and derive the logo of *comp_2347*. The advantage of this representation is that if you find another Lemon-brand computer, you can infer its logo.

In Turtle,

:lemon_computer rdfs:subClassOf :computer.

:lemon_laptop_10000 rdfs:subClassOf :lemon_computer.

:comp_2347 rdf:type :lemon_laptop_10000.

says that a lemon computer is a computer, a lemon laptop 10000 is a lemon computer, and that *comp_2347* is a lemon laptop 10000. An extended example is shown in Figure 13.2, where the shaded rectangles are classes, and arcs from classes are not the properties of the class but properties of the members of the class.

The relationship between types and subclasses can be written as a definite clause:

$$prop(X, type, C) \leftarrow$$
$$prop(X, type, S) \land$$
$$prop(S, subClassOf, C)$$

You can treat *type* and *subClassOf* as special properties that allow **property inheritance**. Property inheritance is when a value for a property is specified at the class level and inherited by the members of the class. If all members of class *c* have value *v* for property *p*, this can be written in Datalog as

$$prop(Ind, p, v) \leftarrow$$
$$prop(Ind, type, c).$$

which, together with the aforementioned rule that relates types and subclasses, can be used for property inheritance.

Example 13.11   All lemon computers have a lemon disc as a logo and have color yellow and color green (see the *logo* and *color* arcs in Figure 13.2). This can be represented by the following Datalog program:

$$prop(X, has\_logo, lemon\_disc) \leftarrow$$
$$prop(X, type, lemon\_computer).$$
$$prop(X, color, green) \leftarrow$$
$$prop(X, type, lemon\_computer).$$
$$prop(X, color, yellow) \leftarrow$$
$$prop(X, type, lemon\_computer).$$

The *prop* relations that can be derived from these clauses are essentially the same as that which can be derived from the flat semantic network of Figure 13.1 (page 554). With the structured representation, to incorporate a new Lemon Laptop 10000, you only declare that it is a Lemon Laptop 10000 and the color and logo properties can be derived through inheritance.

RDF and Turtle do not have definite clauses. In these languages, instead of treating the membership in a class as a predicate, classes are sets. To say that all of the elements of a set *S* have value *v* for a predicate *p*, we say that *S* is a subset of the set of all things with value *v* for predicate *p*.

Example 13.12   To state that all lemon computers have a lemon disc as a logo, we say that the set of lemon computers is a subset of the set of all things for which the property *has_logo* value *lemon_disc*.

A representation of this is shown in Figure 13.3 (on the next page). :computer and :logo are both classes. :lemon_disc is member of the class :logo. :has_logo is a property, with domain :computer and range :logo. :lemon_computer

```
@prefix rdfs:    <http://www.w3.org/2000/01/rdf-schema#>.
@prefix rdf:     <http://www.w3.org/1999/02/22-rdf-syntax-ns#>.
@prefix owl:     <http://www.w3.org/2002/07/owl#>.
@prefix :        <#>.


:computer      rdf:type    rdfs:Class.
:logo          rdf:type    rdfs:Class.
:lemon_disc    rdf:type    :logo.
:has_logo
       rdf:type        rdf:Property ;
       rdfs:domain  :computer ;
       rdfs:range   :logo.
:lemon_computer
       rdf:type            rdfs:Class ;
       rdfs:subClassOf  :computer ;
       rdfs:subClassOf
            owl:ObjectHasValue(:has_logo :lemon_disc).
```

Figure 13.3: Turtle representation of Example 13.12

is a subclass of :computer. It is also a subclass of the set of all individuals that have value :lemon_disc for the property :has_logo.

owl:ObjectHasValue is a class constructor for OWL (see below), such that owl:ObjectHasValue(:has_logo :lemon_disc) is the class of all individuals that have the value :lemon_disc for the property :has_logo.

Some general guidelines are useful for deciding what should be primitive and what should be derived:

- When associating an attribute with an individual, select the most general class C, such that the individual is in C and all members of C have that attribute, and associate the attribute with class C. Inheritance can be used to derive the attribute for the individual and all members of class C. This representation methodology tends to make knowledge bases more concise, and it means that it is easier to incorporate new individuals because they automatically inherit the attribute if they are a member of class C.

- Do not associate a contingent attribute of a class with the class. A **contingent attribute** is one whose value changes when circumstances change. For example, it may be true of the current computer environment that all of the computers come in brown boxes. However, it may not be a good idea to put that as an attribute of the *computer* class, because it would not be expected to be true as other computers are bought.

- Axiomatize in the causal direction (page 204). If a choice exists between making the cause primitive or the effect primitive, make the cause primitive. The information is then more likely to be stable when the domain changes.

13.3 Ontologies and Knowledge Sharing

Building large knowledge-based systems is complex because

- Knowledge often comes from multiple sources and must be integrated. Moreover, these sources may not have the same division of the world. Often knowledge comes from different fields that have their own distinctive terminology and divide the world according to their own needs.

- Systems evolve over time and it is difficult to anticipate all future distinctions that should be made.

- The people involved in designing a knowledge base must choose what individuals and relationships to represent. The world is not divided into individuals; that is something done by intelligent agents to understand the world. Different people involved in a knowledge-based system should agree on this division of the world.

- It is difficult to remember what your own notation means, let alone to discover what someone else's notation means. This has two aspects:

  - given a symbol used in the computer, determining what it means;
  - given a concept in someone's mind, determining what symbol they should use; that is, determining whether the concept has been used before and, if it has, discovering what notation has been used for it.

To share and communicate knowledge, it is important to be able to come up with a common vocabulary and an agreed-on meaning for that vocabulary.

A **conceptualization** is a mapping between symbols used in the computer (i.e., the vocabulary) and the individuals and relations in the world. It provides a particular abstraction of the world and notation for that abstraction. A conceptualization for small knowledge bases can be in the head of the designer or specified in natural language in the documentation. This informal specification of a conceptualization does not scale to larger systems where the conceptualization must be shared.

In philosophy, **ontology** is the study of what exists. In AI, an **ontology** is a specification of the meanings of the symbols in an information system. That is, it is a specification of a conceptualization. It is a specification of what individuals and relationships are assumed to exist and what terminology is used for them. Typically, it specifies what types of individuals will be modeled, specifies what properties will be used, and gives some axioms that restrict the use of that vocabulary.

Example 13.13 An ontology of individuals that could appear on a map could specify that the symbol "ApartmentBuilding" will represent apartment buildings. The ontology will not *define* an apartment building, but it will describe it well enough so that others can understand the definition. We want other people, who may be inclined to use different symbols, tobe able to use the

The Semantic Web

The **semantic web** is a way to allow machine-interpretable knowledge to be distributed on the World Wide Web. Instead of just serving HTML pages that are meant to be read by humans, web sites will also provide information that can be used by computers.

At the most basic level, **XML** (the Extensible Markup Language) provides a syntax designed to be machine readable, but which is possible for humans to read. It is a text-based language, where items are tagged in a hierarchical manner. The syntax for XML can be quite complicated, but at the simplest level, the scope of a tag is either in the form $\langle tag \ldots / \rangle$, or in the form $\langle tag \ldots \rangle \ldots \langle / tag \rangle$.

A **URI** (a **Uniform Resource Identifier**) is used to uniquely identify a resource. A **resource** is anything that can be uniquely identified. A URI is a string that refers to a resource, such as a web page, a person, or a corporation. Often URIs use the syntax of web addresses.

RDF (the **Resource Description Framework**) is a language built on XML, providing individual-property-value triples.

RDF-S (RDF Schema) lets you define resources (and so also properties) in terms of other resources (e.g., using *subClassOf*). RDF-S also lets you restrict the domain and range of properties and provides containers (sets, sequences, and alternatives – one of which must be true).

RDF allows sentences in its own language to be reified. This means that it can represent arbitrary logical formulas and so is not decidable in general. Undecidability is not necessarily a bad thing; it just means that you cannot put a bound on the time a computation may take. Simple logic programs with function symbols and virtually all programming languages are undecidable.

OWL (the **Web Ontology Language**) is an ontology language for the World Wide Web. It defines some classes and properties with a fixed interpretation that can be used for describing classes, properties, and individuals. It has built-in mechanisms for equality of individuals, classes, and properties, in addition to restricting domains and ranges of properties and other restrictions on properties (e.g., transitivity, cardinality).

There have been some efforts to build large universal ontologies, such as **cyc** (www.cyc.com), but the idea of the semantic web is to allow communities to converge on ontologies. Anyone can build an ontology. People who want to develop a knowledge base can use an existing ontology or develop their own ontology, usually built on existing ontologies. Because it is in their interest to have semantic interoperability, companies and individuals should tend to converge on standard ontologies for their domain or to develop mappings from their ontologies to others' ontologies.

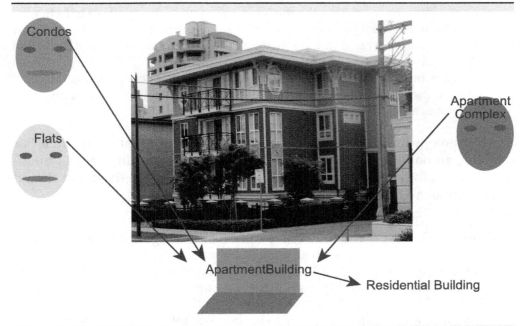

Figure 13.4: Mapping from a conceptualization to a symbol

ontology to find the appropriate symbol to use (see Figure 13.4). Multiple people are able to use the symbol consistently. An ontology should also enable a person to verify what a symbol means. That is, given a concept, they want to be able to find the symbol, and, given the symbol, they want to be able to determine what it means.

An ontology may give axioms to restrict the use of some symbol. For example, it may specify that apartment buildings are buildings, which are human-constructed artifacts. It may give some restriction on the size of buildings so that shoeboxes cannot be buildings or that cities cannot be buildings. It may state that a building cannot be at two geographically dispersed locations at the same time (so if you take off some part of the building and move it to a different location, it is no longer a single building). Because apartment buildings are buildings, these restrictions also apply to apartment buildings.

Ontologies are usually written independently of a particular application and often involve a community to agree on the meanings of symbols. An ontology consists of

- a vocabulary of the categories of the things (both classes and properties) that a knowledge base may want to represent;

- an organization of the categories, for example into an inheritance hierarchy using *subClassOf* or *subPropertyOf*, or using Aristotelian definitions (page 567); and

- a set of axioms restricting the meanings of some of the symbols to better reflect their meaning – for example, that some property is transitive, or that the domain and range are restricted, or that there are some restriction on the number of values a property can take for each individual. Sometimes relationships are defined in terms of more primitive relationships but, ultimately, the relationships are grounded out into **primitive** relationships that are not actually defined.

An ontology does not specify the individuals not known at design time. For example, an ontology of buildings would typically not include actual buildings. An ontology would specify those individuals that are fixed and should be shared, such as the days of the week, or colors.

Example 13.14 Consider a trading agent that is designed to find accommodations. Users could use such an agent to describe what accommodation they want. The trading agent could search multiple knowledge bases to find suitable accommodations or to notify users when some appropriate accommodation becomes available. An ontology is required to specify the meaning of the symbols for the user and to allow the knowledge bases to interoperate. It provides the semantic glue to tie together the users' needs with the knowledge bases.

In such a domain, houses and apartment buildings may both be residential buildings. Although it may be sensible to suggest renting a house or an apartment in an apartment building, it may not be sensible to suggest renting an apartment building to someone who does not actually specify that they want to rent the whole building. A "living unit" could be defined to be the collection of rooms that some people, who are living together, live in. A living unit may be what a rental agency offers to rent. At some stage, the designer may have to decide whether a room for rent in a house is a living unit, or even whether part of a shared room that is rented separately is a living unit. Often the boundary cases – cases that may not be initially anticipated – are not clearly delineated but become better defined as the ontology evolves.

The ontology would not contain descriptions of actual houses or apartments because the actual available accommodation would change over time and would not change the meaning of the vocabulary.

The primary purpose of an ontology is to document what the symbols mean – the mapping between symbols (in a computer) and concepts (in someone's head). Given a symbol, a person is able to use the ontology to determine what it means. When someone has a concept to be represented, the ontology is used to find the appropriate symbol or to determine that the concept does not exist in the ontology. The secondary purpose, achieved by the use of axioms, is to allow inference or to determine that some combination of values is inconsistent. The main challenge in building an ontology is the organization of the concepts to allow a human to map concepts into symbols in the computer, and for the computer to infer useful new knowledge from stated facts.

Aristotelian Definitions

Categorizing objects, the basis for modern ontologies, has a long history. Aristotle [350 B.C.] suggested the definition of a class C in terms of

- **Genus**: a superclass of C. The plural of genus is genera.
- **Differentia**: the properties that make members of the class C different from other members of the superclass of C.

He anticipated many of the issues that arise in definitions:

> *If genera are different and co-ordinate, their differentiae are themselves different in kind. Take as an instance the genus "animal" and the genus "knowledge". "With feet", "two-footed", "winged", "aquatic", are differentiae of "animal"; the species of knowledge are not distinguished by the same differentiae. One species of knowledge does not differ from another in being "two-footed".* [Aristotle, 350 B.C.]

Note that "co-ordinate" here means neither is subordinate to the other.

In the style of modern ontologies, we would say that "animal" is a class, and "knowledge" is a class. The property "two-footed" has domain "animal". If something is an instance of knowledge, it does not have a value for the property "two-footed".

To build an ontology based on **Aristotelian definitions**:

- For each class you may want to define, determine a relevant superclass, and then select those attributes that distinguish the class from other subclasses. Each attribute gives a property and a value.
- For each property, define the most general class for which it makes sense, and define the domain of the property to be this class. Make the range another class that makes sense (perhaps requiring this range class to be defined, either by enumerating its values or by defining it using an Aristotelian definition).

This can get quite complicated. For example, defining "luxury furniture", perhaps the superclass you want is "furniture" and the distinguishing characteristics are cost is high and luxury furniture is soft. The softness of furniture is different than the softness of rocks. You also probably want to distinguish the squishiness from the texture (both of which may be regarded as soft).

This methodology does not, in general, give a tree hierarchy of classes. Objects can be in many classes. Each class does not have a single most-specific superclass. However, it is still straightforward to check whether one class is a subclass of another, to check the meaning of a class, and to determine the class that corresponds to a concept in your head.

In rare cases, this results in a tree structure, most famously in the **Linnaean taxonomy** of living things. It seems that the reason this is a tree is because of evolution. Trying to force a tree structure in other domains has been much less successful.

13.3.1 Description Logic

A **Uniform Resource Identifier** has some meaning because someone published that it has that meaning and because people use it with that meaning. This works, but we want more. We would like to have meanings that allow a computer to do some inference.

Modern ontology languages such as **OWL** (page 564) are based on **description logics**. A description logic is used to describe classes, properties, and individuals. One of the main ideas behind a description logic is to separate

- a **terminological knowledge base** that describes the terminology, which should remain constant as the domain being modeled changes, and

- an **assertional knowledge base** that describes what is true in some domain at some point in time.

Usually, the terminological knowledge base is defined at the design time of the system and defines the ontology, and it only changes as the meaning of the vocabulary changes, which should be rare. The assertional knowledge base usually contains the knowledge that is situation-specific and is only known at run time.

It is typical to use triples (page 552) to define the assertional knowledge base and a language such as OWL to define the terminological knowledge base.

OWL describes domains in terms of the following:

- **Individuals** are things in the world that is being described (e.g., a particular house or a particular booking may be individuals).

- **Classes** are sets of individuals. A class is the set of all real or potential things that would be in that class. For example, the class "House" may be the set of all things that would be classified as a house, not just those houses that exist in the domain of interest.

- **Properties** are used to describe individuals. A **datatype property** has values that are primitive data types, such as integers or strings. For example, "streetName" may be a datatype property between a street and string. An **object property** has values that are other individuals. For example, "nextTo" may be a property between two houses, and "onStreet" may be a property between a house and a street.

OWL comes in three variants that differ in restrictions imposed on the classes and properties. In OWL-DL and OWL-Lite, a class cannot be an individual or a property, and a property is not an individual. In OWL-Full, the categories of individuals, properties, and classes are not necessarily disjoint. OWL-Lite has some syntactic restrictions that do not affect the meaning but can make reasoning simpler.

OWL does not make the unique names assumption (page 534); two names do not necessarily denote different individuals or different classes. It also does not make the complete knowledge assumption (page 193); it does not assume that all relevant facts have been stated.

C_k are classes, P_k are properties, I_k are individuals, and n is an integer. #S is the number of elements in set S:

Class	Class Contains
owl:Thing	all individuals
owl:Nothing	no individuals (empty set)
owl:ObjectIntersectionOf$(C_1, \ldots, C_k)$	individuals in $C_1 \cap \cdots \cap C_k$
owl:ObjectUnionOf$(C_1, \ldots, C_k)$	individuals in $C_1 \cup \cdots \cup C_k$
owl:ObjectComplementOf(C)	the individuals not in C
owl:ObjectOneOf$(I_1, \ldots, I_k)$	$I_1, \ldots, I_k$
owl:ObjectHasValue(P, I)	individuals with value I on property P, i.e., $\{x : x P I\}$
owl:ObjectAllValuesFrom(P, C)	individuals with all values in C on property P; i.e., $\{x : x P y \rightarrow y \in C\}$
owl:ObjectSomeValuesFrom(P, C)	individuals with some values in C on property P; i.e., $\{x : \exists y \in C$ such that $x P y\}$
owl:ObjectMinCardinality(n, P, C)	individuals x with at least n individuals of class C related to x by P, i.e., $\{x : \#\{y|xPy$ and $y \in C\} \geq n\}$
owl:ObjectMaxCardinality(n, P, C)	individuals x with at most n individuals of class C related to x by P, i.e., $\{x : \#\{y|xPy$ and $y \in C\} \leq n\}$

Figure 13.5: Some OWL built-in classes and class constructors

Figure 13.5 gives some primitive classes and some class constructors. This figure uses set notation to define the set of individuals in a class. Figure 13.6 (on the next page) gives primitive predicates of OWL. The owl: prefixes are from OWL. To use these properties and classes in an ontology, you include the appropriate URI abbreviations:

```
@prefix rdfs:  <http://www.w3.org/2000/01/rdf-schema#>.
@prefix rdf:   <http://www.w3.org/1999/02/22-rdf-syntax-ns#>.
@prefix owl:   <http://www.w3.org/2002/07/owl#>.
```

In these figures, xPy is a triple. Note that this is meant to define the meaning of the predicates, rather than any syntax. The predicates can be used with different syntaxes, such as XML, Turtle, or traditional relations notation.

There is one property constructor: owl:ObjectInverseOf(P), which is the inverse property of P; that is, it is the property P^{-1} such that $yP^{-1}x$ iff xPy. Note that it is only applicable to object properties; datatype properties do not have inverses, because data types cannot be the subject of a triple.

The list of classes and statements in these figures is not complete. There are corresponding datatype classes for datatype properties, where appropriate.

OWL has the following predicates with a fixed interpretation, where C_k are classes, P_k are properties, and I_k are individuals; x and y are universally quantified variables.

Statement	Meaning
rdf:type(I, C)	$I \in C$
rdfs:subClassOf(C_1, C_2)	$C_1 \subseteq C_2$
owl:EquivalentClasses(C_1, C_2)	$C_1 \equiv C_2$
owl:DisjointClasses(C_1, C_2)	$C_1 \cap C_2 = \{\}$
rdfs:domain(P, C)	if xPy then $x \in C$
rdfs:range(P, C)	if xPy then $y \in C$
rdfs:subPropertyOf(P_1, P_2)	xP_1y implies xP_2y
owl:EquivalentObjectProperties(P_1, P_2)	xP_1y if and only if xP_2y
owl:DisjointObjectProperties(P_1, P_2)	xP_1y implies not xP_2y
owl:InverseObjectProperties(P_1, P_2)	xP_1y if and only if yP_2x
owl:SameIndividual$(I_1, \ldots, I_n)$	$\forall j \forall k \; I_j = I_k$
owl:DifferentIndividuals$(I_1, \ldots, I_n)$	$\forall j \forall k \; j \neq k$ implies $I_j \neq I_k$
owl:FunctionalObjectProperty(P)	if xPy_1 and xPy_2 then $y_1 = y_2$
owl:InverseFunctionalObjectProperty(P)	if x_1Py and x_2Py then $x_1 = x_2$
owl:TransitiveObjectProperty(P)	if xPy and yPz then xPz
owl:SymmetricObjectProperty(P)	if xPy then yPx

Figure 13.6: Some RDF, RDF-S, and OWL built-in predicates

For example, owl:DataSomeValuesFrom and owl:EquivalentDataProperties have the same definitions as the corresponding object symbols, but are for datatype properties. There are also other constructs in OWL to define properties, comments, annotations, versioning, and importing other ontologies.

Example 13.15 As an example of a class constructor in Turtle notation, which uses spaces between arguments,

> owl:MinCardinality(2 :owns :building)

is the class of all individuals who own two or more buildings. That is, it is the set $\{x : \exists i_1 \exists i_2 \; x \text{ :owns } i_1 \text{ and } x \text{ :owns } i_2 \text{ and } i_1 \neq i_2\}$. This class constructor must be used in a statement, for example, to say that some individual is a member of this class or to say that this is equivalent to some other class.

Example 13.16 Consider an Aristotelian definition (page 567) of an apartment building. We can say that an apartment building is a residential building with multiple units and the units are rented. (This is in contrast to a condominium building, where the units are individually sold, or a house, where there is only one unit). Suppose we have the class *ResidentialBuilding* that is a subclass of *Building*.

We first define the functional object property *numberOfUnits*, with domain *ResidentialBuilding* and range {*one, two, moreThanTwo*}. In Turtle this is written

```
:numberOfUnits rdf:type    owl:FunctionalObjectProperty;
               rdfs:domain :ResidentialBuilding;
               rdfs:range  owl:OneOf(:one :two :moreThanTwo).
```

The functional object property *ownership* with domain *ResidentialBuilding*, and range {*rental, ownerOccupied, coop*} can be defined similarly.

We can define an apartment building as a *ResidentialBuilding* where the *numberOfUnits* property has the value *moreThanTwo* and the *ownership* property has the value rental. To specify this in OWL, we define the class of things that have value *moreThanTwo* for the property *numberOfUnits*, the class of things that have value *rental* for the property *ownership*, and say that *ApartmentBuilding* is equivalent to the intersection of these classes. In Turtle, this is

```
:ApartmentBuilding
   owl:EquivalentClasses
       owl:ObjectIntersectionOf (
           owl:ObjectHasValue(:numberOfUnits :moreThanTwo)
           owl:ObjectHasValue(:onwership :rental)
           :ResidentialBuilding).
```

This definition can be used to answer questions about apartment buildings, such as the ownership and the number of units.

Note that the previous example did not really define *ownership*. The system has no idea what this actually means. Hopefully, a user will know what it means. Someone who wants to adopt an ontology should ensure that they use a property and a class to mean the same thing as other users of the ontology.

A **domain ontology** is an ontology about a particular domain of interest. Most existing ontologies are in a narrow domain that people write for specific applications. There are some guidelines that have evolved for writing domain ontologies to enable knowledge sharing:

- If possible, use an existing ontology. This means that your knowledge base will be able to interact with others who use the same ontology.
- If an existing ontology does not exactly match your needs, import it and add to it. Do not start from scratch, because then others who want to use the best ontology will have to choose. If your ontology includes and improves the other, others who want to adopt an ontology will choose yours, because their application will be able to interact with adopters of either ontology.
- Make sure that your ontology integrates with neighboring ontologies. For example, an ontology about resorts will have to interact with ontologies about food, beaches, recreation activities, and so on. Try to make sure that it uses the same terminology for the same things.
- Try to fit in with higher-level ontologies (see below). This will make it much easier for others to integrate their knowledge with yours.
- If you must design a new ontology, consult widely with other potential users. This will make it most useful and most likely to be adopted.

- Follow naming conventions. For example, call a class by the singular name of its members. For example, call a class "Resort" not "Resorts". Resist the temptation to call it "ResortConcept" (thinking it is only the concept of a resort, not a resort; see the box on page 572). When naming classes and properties, think about how they will be used. It sounds better to say that "$r1$ is of type Resort" than "$r1$ is of type Resorts", which is better than "$r1$ is of type ResortConcept".

- As a last option, specify the matching between ontologies. Sometimes ontology matching has to be done when ontologies are developed independently. It is best if matching can be avoided; it makes knowledge using the ontologies much more complicated because there are multiple ways to say the same thing.

OWL, when written in Turtle, is much easier to read than when using XML. However, OWL is at a lower level than most people will want to specify or read. It is designed to be a machine-readable specification. There are many editors

---

Classes and Concepts

It is tempting to call the classes **concepts**, because symbols represent concepts: mappings from the internal representation into the object or relations that the symbols represent.

For example, it may be tempting to call the class of unicorns "unicornConcept" because there are no unicorns, only the concept of a unicorn. However, unicorns and the concept of unicorns are very different; one is an animal and one is a subclass of knowledge. A unicorn has four legs and a horn coming out of its head. The concept of a unicorn does not have legs or horns. You would be very surprised if a unicorn appeared in a class about ontologies, but you should not be surprised if the concept of a unicorn appeared. There are no instances of unicorns, but there are many instances of the concept of a unicorn. If you mean a unicorn, you should use the term "unicorn". If you mean the concept of a unicorn, you should use "concept of a unicorn". You should not say that a unicorn concept has four legs, because instances of knowledge do not have legs; only animals (and furniture) have legs.

As another example, consider a tectonic plate, which is part of the Earth's crust. The plates are millions of years old. The concept of a plate is less than a hundred years old. Someone can have the concept of a tectonic plate in their head, but they cannot have a tectonic plate in their head. It should be very clear that a tectonic plate and the concept of a tectonic plate are very different things, with very different properties. You should not use "concept of a tectonic plate" when you mean "tectonic plate" or vice versa.

Calling objects concepts is a common error in building ontologies. Although you are free to call things by whatever name you want, it is only useful for knowledge sharing if other people adopt your ontology. They will not adopt it if it does not make sense to them.

that let you edit OWL representation. One example is Protégé (http://protege. stanford.edu/). An ontology editor should support the following:

- It should provide a way for people to input ontologies at the level of abstraction that makes the most sense.

- Given a concept a user wants to use, an ontology editor should facilitate finding the terminology for that concept or determining that there is no corresponding term.

- It should be straightforward for someone to determine the meaning of a term.

- It should be as easy as possible to check that the ontology is correct (i.e., matches the user's intended interpretation for the terms).

- It should create an ontology that others can use. This means that it should use a standardized language as much as possible.

13.3.2 Top-Level Ontologies

Example 13.16 (page 570) defines a domain ontology designed to be used by people who want to write a knowledge base that refers to apartment buildings. Each domain ontology implicitly or explicitly assumes a higher-level ontology that it can fit into. There is interest in building a coherent top-level ontology to which other ontologies can refer and into which they can fit. Fitting the domain ontologies into a higher-level ontology should make it easier to allow them to interoperate.

One such ontology is **BFO**, the **Basic Formal Ontology**. The categories of BFO are given in Figure 13.7 (on the next page).

At the top is **entity**. OWL calls the top of the hierarchy **thing**. Essentially, everything is an entity.

Entities are either **continuants** or **occurrents**. A continuant is something existing at an instant in time, such as a person, a country, a smile, the smell of a flower, or an email. Continuants maintain their identity though time. An occurrent is something that has temporal parts such as a life, smiling, the opening of a flower, and sending an email. One way to think about the difference is to consider the entity's parts: a finger is part of a person, but is not part of a life; infancy is part of a life, but is not part of a person. Continuants participate in occurrents. Processes that last through time and events that occur at an instant in time are also both occurrents.

A continuant is an **independent continuant**, a **dependent continuant**, or a **spatial region**. An independent continuant is an entity that can exist by itself or is part of another entity. For example, a person, a face, a pen, the surface of an apple, the equator, a country, and the atmosphere are independent continuants. A dependent continuant only exists by virtue of another entity and is not a part of that entity. For example, a smile, the smell of a flower, or the ability to laugh can only exist in relation to another object. A spatial region is a region in space,

entity
    continuant
        independent continuant
            site
            object aggregate
            object
            fiat part of object
            boundary of object
        dependent continuant
            realizable entity
                function
                role
                disposition
            quality
        spatial region
            volume
            surface
            line
            point
    occurrent
        temporal region
            connected temporal region
                temporal interval
                temporal instant
            scattered temporal region
        spatio-temporal region
            connected spatio-temporal region
                spatio-temporal interval
                spatio-temporal instant
            scattered spatio-temporal region
        processual entity
            process
            process aggregate
            processual context
            fiat part of process
            boundary of process

Figure 13.7: Categories of Basic Formal Ontology (BFO). The indentation shows the subclass relationship. Each category is an immediate subclass of the lowest category above it that is less indented.

for example, the space occupied by a doughnut now, the boundary of a county, or the point in a landscape that has the best view.

An **independent continuant** can further be subdivided into the following:

- A **site** is a shape that is defined by some other continuants. For example, the hole in a donut, a city, someone's mouth, or a room are all sites. Whereas sites may be at a spatial region at every instance, they move with the object that contains them.

- An **object aggregate** is made up of other objects, such as a flock of sheep, a football team, or a heap of sand.

- An **object** is a self-connected entity that maintains its identity through time even if it gains or loses parts (e.g., a person who loses some hair, a belief, or even a leg, is still the same person). Common objects are cups, people, emails, the theory of relativity, or the knowledge of how to tie shoelaces.

- A **fiat part of an object** is part of an object that does not have clear boundaries, such as the dangerous part of a city, a tissue sample, or the secluded part of a beach.

- The **boundary of an object** is a lower-dimensional part of some continuant, for example the surface of the Earth, or a cell boundary.

A **spatial region** is three-dimensional (a volume), two-dimensional (a surface), one-dimensional (a line), or zero-dimensional (a point). These are parts of space that do not depend on other objects to give them identity. They remain static, as opposed to sites and boundaries that move with the objects that define them.

A **dependent continuant** is a quality or a realizable entity. A **quality** is something that all objects of a particular type have for all of the time they exist – for example, the mass of a bag of sugar, the shape of a hand, the fragility of a cup, the beauty of a view, the brightness of a light, and the smell of the ocean. Although these can change, the bag of sugar always has a mass and the hand always has a shape. This is contrasted with a **realizable entity**, where the value does not need to exist and the existence can change though time. A realizable entity is one of the following:

- A **function** specifies the purpose of a object. For example, the function of a cup may be to hold coffee; the function of the heart is to pump blood.

- A **role** specifies a goal that is not essential to the object's design but can be carried out. Examples of roles include the role of being a judge, the role of delivering coffee, or the role of a desk to support a computer monitor.

- A **disposition** is something that can happen to an object, for example, the disposition of a cup to break if dropped, the disposition of vegetables to rot if not refrigerated, and the disposition of matches to light if they are not wet.

The other major category of entities is the occurrent. An **occurrent** is any of the following:

- A **temporal region** is a region of time. A temporal region is either connected (if two points are in the region, so is every point in between) or scattered.

Connected temporal regions are either intervals or instants (time points). Tuesday, March 1, 2011, is a temporal interval; 3:31 p.m. on that day is a temporal point. Tuesdays from 3:00 to 4:00 is a scattered temporal region.

- A **spatio-temporal region** is a region of multidimensional space-time. Spatio-temporal regions are either scattered or connected. Some examples of spatio-temporal regions are the space occupied by a human life, the border between Canada and the United States in 1812, and the region occupied by the development of a cancer tumor.

- A **processual entity** is something that occurs or happens, has temporal parts (as well as, perhaps, spatial parts), and depends on a continuant. For example, Joe's life has parts such as infancy, childhood, adolescence, and adulthood and involves a continuant, Joe. A processual entity is any of the following:

    - A **process** is something that happens over time and has distinct ends, such as a life, a holiday, or a diagnostic session.

    - A **process aggregate** is a collection of processes such as the playing of the individuals in a band, or the flying of a set of planes in a day.

    - A **fiat part of process** is part of a process having no distinct ends, such as the most interesting part of a holiday, or the most serious part of an operation.

    - A **processual context** is the setting for some other occurrent, for example, relaxation as the setting for rejuvenation, or a surgery as a setting for an infection.

    - A **boundary of a process** is the instantaneous temporal boundary of a process, such as when a robot starts to clean up the lab, or a birth.

The claim is that this is a useful categorization on which to base other ontologies. Making it explicit how domain ontologies fit into an upper-level ontology promises to facilitate the integration of these ontologies. The integration of ontologies is necessary to allow applications to refer to multiple knowledge bases, each of which may each use different ontologies.

Designing a top-level ontology is difficult. It probably will not satisfy everyone who must use one. There always seem to be some problematic cases. In particular, boundary cases are often not well specified. However, using a standard top-level ontology should help in connecting ontologies together.

13.4 Querying Users and Other Knowledge Sources

As discussed in Section 5.3.2 (page 175), users are not experts in the domain of the knowledge base; however, they often know details about a particular case and so provide one source of knowledge. Users, typically, do not know what is relevant or what vocabulary to use and so they cannot be expected to tell the system what they know. One aspect of the problem of knowledge acquisition is how to most effectively extract knowledge from a user.

The simplest form of a question is the yes-or-no question presented in Section 5.3.2 (page 175). When variables and function symbols are involved, more sophisticated questions can be asked of the user.

Example 13.17 Consider the knowledge base of Example 12.11 (page 502), but without the rules for *up* or *down*. Suppose the user can observe the positions of the switches. To enable the user to be asked the position of switches, $up(S)$ and $down(S)$ can be askable. The following is a possible dialog for a top-down proof procedure for the query $?lit(L)$, where the user is asked the askable goals. User responses are in bold:

> Is $up(s_2)$ true? **yes.**
> Is $up(s_1)$ true? **no.**
> Is $down(s_2)$ true? **no.**
> Is $up(s_3)$ true? **yes.**
> Answer: $L = l_2$.

In this example, *up* and *down* are not explicitly related, and so the system asks both.

In this example, the ontology was simple; we assumed that the user can understand the questions. In general, asking users is not as simple; the questions have to be framed in such a way that the user can understand what the question means and what answer is expected.

13.4.1 Functional Relations

One case in which the system may know the answer to an askable goal, even though it has not been directly answered by the user, is when a relation is functional. Relation $r(X, Y)$ is functional if, for every X, there is a unique Y such that $r(X, Y)$ is true. If the system has already found one Y for a particular X for which $r(X, Y)$ is true, it should not re-ask for more instances.

Example 13.18 In the preceding example, it is redundant to ask the question "Is $down(s_2)$ true?" when the user has already told the system that $up(s_2)$ is true. It may be better to have a relation $pos(Sw, Pos)$, where the position is a function of the switch. The system must be told that pos is functional; each switch only has one position. Once the system has determined the position of a switch, it does not have to ask any more questions about the position of that switch.

It is usually very inefficient to ask yes-or-no questions of a functional relation. Rather than enumerating every possible position of the switch and asking whether or not the switch is in that position, it may be better to ask once for the position of the switch and not ask this question again. If the system wants to know the age of a person, it would be better to ask outright for the age of the person rather than to enumerate all of the ages and ask true-or-false questions.

Asking these kinds of more general questions probably would not be appropriate for non-functional relations. For example, if the switch could be in many positions at once, then it would probably be better to ask for each position that is required.

A complication arises with respect to the vocabulary of answers. The user may not know what vocabulary is expected by the knowledge engineer. There are two sensible solutions to this problem:

- The system designer provides a menu of items from which the user selects the best fit. This works when there are few items or when the items can be arranged in a narrow hierarchy.

- The system designer provides a large dictionary to anticipate all possible answers. When the user gives an answer, the answer is mapped into the internal forms expected by the system. An assumption would be made that the vocabulary used by the user would be normal language or some abbreviated form. Thus, the user may not expect the system to understand such terms as "giganormous" (meaning "very big," of course).

Which of these works better is an empirical question. Such questions about how a computer can best interact with people is studied in the field of **human–computer interaction (HCI)**.

13.4.2   More General Questions

Yes-or-no questions and functional relations do not cover all of the cases of a query. The general form of a query occurs when free variables are present in a query that is to be asked of the user.

Example 13.19   For the subgoal $p(a, X, f(Z))$ the user should be asked something like

> for which X, Z is $p(a, X, f(Z))$ true?

which, of course, should be put in terms that the user can understand.

The user would then be expected to give bindings for X and Z that make the subgoal true, or to reply *no*, meaning that there are no more instances. This follows the spirit of the query protocol for asking questions of the system.

A number of issues arise:

- Should users be expected to give all instances that are true, or should they give the instances one at a time, with the system prompting for new instances? One of the major criteria for acceptance of a knowledge-based system is in how sensible it appears. Asking questions in a natural, logical way is a big part. For this reason, it may be better to get one instance and then prompt when another instance is needed. In this way, the system can, for example, probe into one individual in depth before considering the next individual. How well this works depends on the structure of the knowledge base.

- When should you not ask/re-ask a question? For example, consider the question

> For which X is $p(X)$ true?

to which the user replies with an answer that means $X = f(Z)$, (i.e., "for all values of Z, $p(f(Z))$ is true"). In this case, the user should not be asked about whether $p(f(b))$ is true or whether $p(f(h(W)))$ is true but should be asked about whether $p(a)$ or even whether $p(X)$ is true (asking for a different instance). If the user subsequently replies *no* to the question

> For which X is $p(X)$ true?

what is meant is that there are no more answers to this question, rather than that $p(X)$ is false for all X (because the system has already been told that $X = f(b)$ is a true instance).

The general rule is that the system should not ask a question that is more specific than a positive answer that has already been given or is more specific than a question to which the user has replied *no*.

- Should the system ask the question as soon as it is encountered in the proof process, or should it delay the goal until more variables are bound? There may be some goals that will subsequently fail no matter what the user answers. For these goals, it may be better to find this out rather than asking the user at all. There may also be free variables in a query that, subsequently, will become bound. Rather than asking the user to enumerate the possibilities until they stumble on the instance that does not fail, it may be better to delay the goal (page 536).

  Consider the query $?p(X) \wedge q(X)$, where $p(X)$ is askable. If there is only one instance of q that is true, say $q(k)$, it may be better to delay asking the $p(X)$ question until X is bound to k. Then the system can ask $p(k)$ directly instead of asking the user to enumerate all of the p's until they stumble on $p(k)$ being true. However, if there is a large database of instances of $q(X)$ and few values of X for which $p(X)$ is true, it may be better to ask for instances of $p(X)$ and then to check them with the database rather than asking a yes-or-no question for each element of the database. Which is better depends on the estimated number of individuals for which $p(X)$ is true, the estimated number of individuals for which $q(X)$ is true, and the costs associated with asking the user.

These pragmatic questions are very important when designing a user-friendly interface to a KB system.

13.5 Implementing Knowledge-Based Systems

It may be useful for an agent to be able to represent its own reasoning. Such reasoning about an agent's own representations is called **reflection**. Explicitly representing its own reasoning enables the agent to reason more flexibly so that the designer can craft the most appropriate language for each application.

This section considers one use of reflection, namely, implementing lightweight tools for building new languages with features that are required for particular applications. By making it easy to implement new languages and tools, the best language for each application can be used. The language and tools can evolve as the application evolves.

A **meta-interpreter** for a language is an interpreter for the language written in the same language. Such an interpreter is useful because modifications allow for quick prototyping of new languages with useful features. Once the language has proven its utility, a compiler for the language can be developed to improve efficiency.

When implementing one language inside another, the language being implemented is called the **base language**, or sometimes the **object language**, and the language in which it is implemented is called the **metalanguage**. Expressions in the base language are said to be at the **base level**, and expressions in the metalanguage are at the **meta-level**. We first define a meta-interpreter for the definite clause language presented in Chapter 12. We then show how the base language can be modified or extended, and tools such as explanation and debugging facilities can be provided by modifying the meta-interpreter.

13.5.1 Base Languages and Metalanguages

We require a representation of the base-level expressions that can be manipulated by the interpreter to produce answers. Initially, the base language will also be the language of definite clauses. Recall (page 163) that the definite clause language is made up of terms, atoms, bodies, and clauses.

The metalanguage refers to these syntactic elements of the base language. Thus, meta-level symbols will denote base-level terms, atoms, bodies, and clauses. Base-level terms will denote objects in the domain being modeled, and base-level predicates will denote relations in the domain.

One of the advantages of a meta-interpreter over writing an interpreter for a whole new language is that the object level can use the meta-level constructs. When writing a logic programming meta-interpreter, there is a choice of how to represent variables. In the **non-ground representation**, base-level terms are represented as the same term in the metalanguage, so in particular, base-level variables are represented as meta-level variables. This is in contrast to the **ground representation**, where base language variables are represented as constants in the metalanguage. The non-ground representation means that meta-level unification is available to be used for unifying base-level terms. The ground representation allows the implementation of more sophisticated models of unification.

Example 13.20 In a non-ground representation, the base-level term $foo(X, f(b), X)$ will be represented as the meta-level term $foo(X, f(b), X)$.

In a ground representation, the base-level term $foo(X, f(b), X)$ may be represented as $foo(var(x), f(b), var(x))$, where var is a meta-level function symbol that denotes the variable with the name given as its argument.

We will develop a non-ground representation for definite clauses. The metalanguage must be able to represent all of the base-level constructs.

The base-level variables, constants, and function symbols are represented as the corresponding meta-level variables, constants, and function symbols.

Thus, all terms in the base level are represented by the same term in the meta-level. A base-level predicate symbol p is represented by the corresponding meta-level function symbol p. Thus, the base-level atom $p(t_1, \ldots, t_k)$ is represented as the meta-level term $p(t_1, \ldots, t_k)$.

Base-level bodies are also represented as meta-level terms. If e_1 and e_2 are meta-level terms that denote base-level atoms or bodies, let the meta-level term $oand(e_1, e_2)$ denote the base-level conjunction of e_1 and e_2. Thus, $oand$ is a meta-level function symbol that denotes base-level conjunction.

Base-level clauses are represented as meta-level atoms. Base-level rule "h if b" is represented as the meta-level atom $clause(h, b')$, where b' is the representation of body b. A base-level atomic clause a is represented as the meta-level atom $clause(a, true)$, where the meta-level constant $true$ represents the base-level empty body.

Example 13.21 The base-level clauses from Example 12.11 (page 502),

$connected\_to(l_1, w_0).$
$connected\_to(w_0, w_1) \leftarrow up(s_2).$
$lit(L) \leftarrow light(L) \wedge ok(L) \wedge live(L).$

can be represented as the meta-level facts

$clause(connected\_to(l_1, w_0), true).$
$clause(connected\_to(w_0, w_1), up(s_2)).$
$clause(lit(L), oand(light(L), oand(ok(L), live(L)))).$

To make the base level more readable, we use the infix function symbol "&" rather than $oand$. Instead of writing $oand(e_1, e_2)$, we write $e_1 \& e_2$. The conjunction symbol "&" is an infix function symbol of the metalanguage that denotes an operator, between atoms, of the base language. This is just a syntactic variant of the "$oand$" representation. This use of infix operators makes it easier to read base-level formulas.

Instead of writing $clause(h, b)$, we write $h \Leftarrow b$, where $\Leftarrow$ is an infix meta-level predicate symbol. Thus, the base-level clause "$h \leftarrow a_1 \wedge \cdots \wedge a_n$" is represented as the meta-level atom

$$h \Leftarrow a_1 \& \cdots \& a_n.$$

This meta-level atom is true if the corresponding base-level clause is part of the base-level knowledge base. In the meta-level, this atom can be used like any other atom.

Figure 13.8 summarizes how the base language is represented in the meta-level.

Syntactic construct		Meta-level representation of the syntactic construct	
variable	X	variable	X
constant	c	constant	c
function symbol	f	function symbol	f
predicate symbol	p	function symbol	p
"and" operator	$\wedge$	function symbol	$\&$
"if" operator	$\leftarrow$	predicate symbol	$\Leftarrow$
clause	$h \leftarrow a_1 \wedge \cdots \wedge a_n.$	atom	$h \Leftarrow a_1 \& \cdots \& a_n.$
clause	$h.$	atom	$h \Leftarrow true.$

Figure 13.8: The non-ground representation for the base language

---

Example 13.22 Using the infix notation, the base-level clauses of Example 13.21 are represented as the meta-level facts

$$connected\_to(l_1, w_0) \Leftarrow true.$$
$$connected\_to(w_0, w_1) \Leftarrow up(s_2).$$
$$lit(L) \Leftarrow light(L) \& ok(L) \& live(L).$$

This notation is easier for humans to read than the meta-level facts of Example 13.21, but as far as the computer is concerned, it is essentially the same.

The meta-level function symbol "&" and the meta-level predicate symbol "⇐" are not predefined symbols of the meta-level. You could have used any other symbols. They are written in infix notation for readability.

13.5.2   A Vanilla Meta-interpreter

This section presents a very simple **vanilla meta-interpreter** for the definite clause language written in the definite clause language. Subsequent sections augment this meta-interpreter to provide extra language constructs and knowledge engineering tools. It is important to first understand the simple case before considering the more sophisticated meta-interpreters presented later.

Figure 13.9 defines a meta-interpreter for the definite clause language. This is an axiomatization of the relation *prove*; *prove*(G) is true when base-level body G is a logical consequence of the base-level clauses.

As with axiomatizing any other relation, we write the clauses that are true in the intended interpretation, ensuring that they cover all of the cases and that there is some simplification through recursion. This meta-interpreter essentially covers each of the cases allowed in the body of a clause or in a query, and it specifies how to solve each case. A body is either empty, a conjunction, or an atom. The empty base-level body *true* is trivially proved. To prove the base-level conjunction $A \& B$, prove A and prove B. To prove atom H, find a base-level clause with H as the head, and prove the body of the clause.

% *prove*(*G*) is true if base-level body *G* is a logical consequence of the base-level
% clauses that are defined using the predicate symbol "⇐ ".

> *prove*(*true*).
> *prove*((*A* & *B*)) ←
>> *prove*(*A*) ∧
>> *prove*(*B*).
> *prove*(*H*) ←
>> (*H* ⇐ *B*) ∧
>> *prove*(*B*).

Example 13.23 Consider the meta-level representation of the base-level
knowledge base in Figure 13.10 (on the next page). This knowledge base is
adapted from Example 12.11 (page 502). This knowledge base consists of meta-
level atoms, all with the same predicate symbol, namely "⇐ ". Here, we describe how a top-down implementation works given the knowledge base that
consists of the vanilla meta-interpreter and the clauses for "⇐ ".

The base-level goal *live*(w_5) is asked with the following query:

> ?*prove*(*live*(w_5)).

The third clause of *prove* is the only clause matching this query. It then looks for
a clause of the form *live*(w_5) ⇐ *B* and finds

> *live*(*W*) ⇐ *connected_to*(*W*, W_1) & *live*(W_1).

W unifies with w_5, and *B* unifies with *connected_to*(w_5, W_1) & *live*(W_1). It then
tries to prove

> *prove*((*connected_to*(w_5, W_1) & *live*(W_1))).

The second clause for *prove* is applicable. It then tries to prove

> *prove*(*connected_to*(w_5, W_1)).

Using the third clause for *prove*, it looks for a clause with a head to unify with

> *connected_to*(w_5, W_1) ⇐ *B*,

and find *connected_to*(w_5, *outside*) ⇐ *true*, binding W_1 to *outside*. It then tries to
prove *prove*(*true*), which succeeds using the first clause for *prove*.

The second half of the conjunction, *prove*(*live*(W_1)) with W_1 = *outside*, reduces to *prove*(*true*) which is, again, immediately solved.

$lit(L) \Leftarrow$
    $light(L) \,\&$
    $ok(L) \,\&$
    $live(L).$
$live(W) \Leftarrow$
    $connected\_to(W, W_1) \,\&$
    $live(W_1).$
$live(outside) \Leftarrow true.$
$light(l_1) \Leftarrow true.$
$light(l_2) \Leftarrow true.$
$down(s_1) \Leftarrow true.$
$up(s_2) \Leftarrow true.$
$up(s_3) \Leftarrow true.$
$connected\_to(l_1, w_0) \Leftarrow true.$
$connected\_to(w_0, w_1) \Leftarrow up(s_2) \,\& ok(s_2).$
$connected\_to(w_0, w_2) \Leftarrow down(s_2) \,\& ok(s_2).$
$connected\_to(w_1, w_3) \Leftarrow up(s_1) \,\& ok(s_1).$
$connected\_to(w_2, w_3) \Leftarrow down(s_1) \,\& ok(s_1).$
$connected\_to(l_2, w_4) \Leftarrow true.$
$connected\_to(w_4, w_3) \Leftarrow up(s_3) \,\& ok(s_3).$
$connected\_to(p_1, w_3) \Leftarrow true.$
$connected\_to(w_3, w_5) \Leftarrow ok(cb_1).$
$connected\_to(p_2, w_6) \Leftarrow true.$
$connected\_to(w_6, w_5) \Leftarrow ok(cb_2).$
$connected\_to(w_5, outside) \Leftarrow true.$
$ok(X) \Leftarrow true.$

Figure 13.10: A base-level knowledge base for house wiring

13.5.3 Expanding the Base Language

The base language can be changed by modifying the meta-interpreter. Adding
clauses is used to increase what can be proved. Adding extra conditions to the
meta-interpreter rules can restrict what can be proved.

In all practical systems, not every predicate is defined by clauses. For example, it would be impractical to axiomatize arithmetic on current machines that
can do arithmetic quickly. Instead of axiomatizing such predicates, it is better
to call the underlying system directly. Assume the predicate $call(G)$ evaluates

G directly. Writing $call(p(X))$ is the same as writing $p(X)$. The predicate *call* is required because the definite clause language does not allow free variables as atoms.

Built-in procedures can be evaluated at the base level by defining the meta-level relation $built\_in(X)$ that is true if all instances of X are to be evaluated directly; X is a meta-level variable that must denote a base-level atom. Do not assume that "*built_in*" is provided as a built-in relation. It can be axiomatized like any other relation.

The base language can be expanded to allow for disjunction (inclusive or) in the body of a clause.

The **disjunction**, $A \lor B$, is true in an interpretation I when either A is true in I or B is true in I (or both are true in I).

Allowing disjunction in the body of base-level clauses does not require disjunction in the metalanguage.

Example 13.24 An example of the kind of base-level rule you can now interpret is

$$can\_see \Leftarrow eyes\_open \,\&\, (lit(l_1) \lor lit(l_2)),$$

which says that *can_see* is true if *eyes_open* is true and either $lit(l_1)$ or $lit(l_2)$ is true (or both).

Figure 13.11 shows a meta-interpreter that allows built-in procedures to be evaluated directly and allows disjunction in the bodies of rules. This requires a database of built-in assertions and assumes that $call(G)$ is a way to prove G in the meta-level.

Given such an interpreter, the meta-level and the base level are different languages. The base level allows disjunction in the body. The meta-level does not require disjunction to provide it for the base language. The meta-level requires a way to interpret $call(G)$, which the base level cannot handle. The base level, however, can be made to interpret the command $call(G)$ by adding the following meta-level clause:

$$prove(call(G)) \leftarrow$$
$$\quad prove(G).$$

13.5.4 Depth-Bounded Search

The previous section showed how adding extra meta-level clauses can be used to expand the base language. This section shows how adding extra conditions to the meta-level clauses can reduce what can be proved.

A useful meta-interpreter is one that implements depth-bounded search. This can be used to look for short proofs or as part of an iterative-deepening searcher (page 95), which carries out repeated depth-bounded, depth-first searches, increasing the bound at each stage.

% *prove*(*G*) is true if base-level body *G* is a logical consequence of the base-level
% knowledge base.

> *prove*(*true*).
> *prove*((*A* & *B*)) ←
>   *prove*(*A*) ∧
>   *prove*(*B*).
> *prove*((*A* ∨ *B*)) ←
>   *prove*(*A*).
> *prove*((*A* ∨ *B*)) ←
>   *prove*(*B*).
> *prove*(*H*) ←
>   *built_in*(*H*) ∧
>   *call*(*H*).
> *prove*(*H*) ←
>   (*H* ⇐ *B*) ∧
>   *prove*(*B*).

Figure 13.11: A meta-interpreter that uses built-in calls and disjunction

Figure 13.12 gives an axiomatization of the relation $bprove(G, D)$, which is true if G can be proved with a proof tree of depth less than or equal to nonnegative integer D. This figure uses Prolog's infix predicate symbol "is", where "V is E" is true if V is the numerical value of expression E. Within the expression, "$-$" is the infix subtraction function symbol. Thus, "D_1 is $D - 1$" is true if D_1 is one less than the number D.

One aspect of this meta-interpreter is that, if D is bound to a number in the query, this meta-interpreter will never go into an infinite loop. It will miss proofs whose depth is greater than D. As a result, this interpreter is incomplete when D is set to a fixed number. However, every proof that can be found for the *prove* meta-interpreter can be found for this meta-interpreter if the value D is set large enough. The idea behind an iterative-deepening (page 95) searcher is to exploit this fact by carrying out repeated depth-bounded searches, each time increasing the depth bound. Sometimes the depth-bounded meta-interpreter can find proofs that *prove* cannot. This occurs when the *prove* meta-interpreter goes into an infinite loop before exploring all proofs.

This is not the only way to build a bounded meta-interpreter. An alternative measure of the size of proof trees could also be used. For example, you could use the number of nodes in the tree instead of the maximum depth of the proof tree. You could also make conjunction incur a cost by changing the second rule. (See Exercise 13.7.)

% *bprove*(*G*, *D*) is true if *G* can be proved with a proof tree of depth less than or
% equal to number *D*.

>*bprove*(*true*, *D*).
>*bprove*((*A* & *B*), *D*) ←
>   *bprove*(*A*, *D*) ∧
>   *bprove*(*B*, *D*).
>*bprove*(*H*, *D*) ←
>   *D* ≥ 0 ∧
>   *D*₁ is *D* − 1 ∧
>   (*H* ⇐ *B*) ∧
>   *bprove*(*B*, *D*₁).

Figure 13.12: A meta-interpreter for depth-bounded search

13.5.5 Meta-interpreter to Build Proof Trees

To implement the how command of Section 5.3.3 (page 177), the interpreter
maintains a representation of the proof tree for a derived answer. Our meta-
interpreter can be extended to build a proof tree. Figure 13.13 gives a meta-
interpreter that implements built-in predicates and builds a representation of a
proof tree. This proof tree can be traversed to implement how questions.

% *hprove*(*G*, *T*) is true if base-level body *G* is a logical consequence of the base-
% level knowledge base, and *T* is a representation of the proof tree for the cor-
% responding proof.

>*hprove*(*true*, *true*).
>*hprove*((*A* & *B*), (*L* & *R*)) ←
>   *hprove*(*A*, *L*) ∧
>   *hprove*(*B*, *R*).
>*hprove*(*H*, *if*(*H*, *built_in*)) ←
>   *built_in*(*H*) ∧
>   *call*(*H*).
>*hprove*(*H*, *if*(*H*, *T*)) ←
>   (*H* ⇐ *B*) ∧
>   *hprove*(*B*, *T*).

Figure 13.13: A meta-interpreter that builds a proof tree

Example 13.25   Consider the base-level clauses for the wiring domain (page 502) and the base-level query $?lit(L)$. There is one answer, namely $L = l_2$. The meta-level query $?hprove(lit(L), T)$ returns the answer $L = l_2$ and the tree

$$T = if(lit(l_2),$$
$$\qquad if(light(l_2), true)\ \&$$
$$\qquad if(ok(l_2), true)\ \&$$
$$\qquad if(live(l_2),$$
$$\qquad\qquad if(connected\_to(l_2, w_4), true)\ \&$$
$$\qquad\qquad if(live(w_4),$$
$$\qquad\qquad\qquad if(connected\_to(w_4, w_3),$$
$$\qquad\qquad\qquad\qquad if(up(s_3), true))\ \&$$
$$\qquad\qquad\qquad if(live(w_3),$$
$$\qquad\qquad\qquad\qquad if(connected\_to(w_3, w_5),$$
$$\qquad\qquad\qquad\qquad\qquad if(ok(cb_1), true))\ \&$$
$$\qquad\qquad\qquad\qquad if(live(w_5),$$
$$\qquad\qquad\qquad\qquad\qquad if(connected\_to(w_5, outside), true)\ \&$$
$$\qquad\qquad\qquad\qquad\qquad if(live(outside), true)))))).$$

Although this tree can be understood if properly formatted, it requires a skilled user to understand it. The how questions of Section 5.3.3 (page 177) traverse this tree. The user only has to see clauses, not this tree. See Exercise 13.12 (page 595).

13.5.6   Ask the User Meta-interpreter

Figure 13.14 gives a pseudocode interpreter that incorporates querying the user. This interpreter assumes that there is some extralogical external database recording answers to queries. The database is updated as queries are answered. Meta-level facts of the form $answered(H, Ans)$ are being added. $ask(H, Ans)$ is true if H is asked of the user; and Ans, either *yes* or *no*, is given by the user as a reply. $unanswered(H)$ means $answered(H, Ans)$ is not in the database for any Ans. Note that the intended meaning of the fourth clause is that it succeeds only if the answer is *yes*, but the answer gets recorded whether the user answered *yes* or *no*.

Figure 13.15 gives a meta-interpreter that can be used to find the list of ancestor rules for a why question. The second argument to *wprove* is a list of clauses of the form $(H \Leftarrow B)$ for each head of a rule in the current part of the proof tree. This meta-interpreter can be combined with the meta-interpreter of Figure 13.14 that actually asks questions. When the user is asked a question and responds with "why," the list can be used to give the set of rules used to generate the current subgoal. The "why" described in Section 5.3.3 (page 178) can be implemented by stepping through the list and, thus, up the proof tree, one step at a time.

% *aprove*(*G*) is true if base-level body *G* is a logical consequence of the base-
% level knowledge base and the answers provided by asking the user yes/no
  questions.

> *aprove*(*true*).
> *aprove*((*A* & *B*)) ←
>   *aprove*(*A*) ∧
>   *aprove*(*B*).
> *aprove*(*H*) ←
>   *askable*(*H*) ∧
>   *answered*(*H*, *yes*).
> *aprove*(*H*) ←
>   *askable*(*H*) ∧
>   *unanswered*(*H*) ∧
>   *ask*(*H*, *Ans*) ∧
>   *record*(*answered*(*H*, *Ans*)) ∧
>   *Ans* = *yes*.
> *aprove*(*H*) ←
>   (*H* ⇐ *B*) ∧
>   *aprove*(*B*).

Figure 13.14: An ask-the-user interpreter in pseudocode

% *wprove*(*G*, *A*) is true if base-level body *G* is a logical consequence of the base-
% level knowledge base, and *A* is a list of ancestors for *G* in the proof tree for
% the original query.

> *wprove*(*true*, *Anc*).
> *wprove*((*A* & *B*), *Anc*) ←
>   *wprove*(*A*, *Anc*) ∧
>   *wprove*(*B*, *Anc*).
> *wprove*(*H*, *Anc*) ←
>   (*H* ⇐ *B*) ∧
>   *wprove*(*B*, [(*H* ⇐ *B*)|*Anc*]).

Figure 13.15: Meta-interpreter to collect ancestor rules for why questions

% *dprove*(*G*, D_0, D_1) is true if D_0 is an ending of D_1 and *G* logically follows from
% the conjunction of the delayable atoms in D_1.

> *dprove*(*true*, *D*, *D*).
>
> *dprove*((*A* & *B*), D_1, D_3) ←
>> *dprove*(*A*, D_1, D_2) ∧
>> *dprove*(*B*, D_2, D_3).
>
> *dprove*(*G*, *D*, [*G*|*D*]) ←
>> *delay*(*G*).
>
> *dprove*(*H*, D_1, D_2) ←
>> (*H* ⇐ *B*) ∧
>> *dprove*(*B*, D_1, D_2).

Figure 13.16: A meta-interpreter that collects delayed goals

13.5.7 Delaying Goals

One of the most useful abilities of a meta-interpreter is to **delay** goals. Some
goals, rather than being proved, can be collected in a list. At the end of the
proof, the system derives the implication that, if the delayed goals were all
true, the computed answer would be true.

A number of reasons exist for providing a facility for collecting goals that
should be delayed:

- to implement consistency-based diagnosis (page 187) and abduction
  (page 199), the assumables are delayed;

- to delay (page 536) subgoals with variables, in the hope that subsequent
  calls will ground the variables (page 537); and

- to create new rules that leave out intermediate steps – for example, if the
  delayed goals are to be asked of a user or queried from a database. This
  is called **partial evaluation** and is used for explanation-based learning to
  leave out intermediate steps in a proof.

Figure 13.16 gives a meta-interpreter that provides delaying. A base-level atom
G can be made delayable using the meta-level fact *delay*(*G*). The delayable
atoms can be collected into a list without being proved.

Suppose you can prove *dprove*(*G*, [ ], *D*). Let *D'* be the conjunction of base-
level atoms in the list of delayed goals *D*. Then you know that the implication
G ← *D'* is a logical consequence of the clauses, and *delay*(*d*) is true for all *d* ∈ *D*.

> **Example 13.26** As an example of delaying for consistency-based diagnosis,
> consider the base-level knowledge base of Figure 13.10 (page 584), but without
> the rules for *ok*. Suppose, instead, that *ok*(*G*) is delayable. This is represented

as the meta-level fact

$$delay(ok(G)).$$

The query

ask $dprove(live(p_1), [\,], D)$.

has one answer, namely, $D = [ok(cb_1)]$. If $ok(cb_1)$ were true, then $live(p_1)$ would be true.

The query

ask $dprove((lit(l_2) \ \& \ live(p_1)), [\,], D)$.

has the answer $D = [ok(cb_1), ok(cb_1), ok(s_3)]$. If cb_1 and s_3 are ok, then l_2 will be lit and p_1 will be live.

Note that $ok(cb_1)$ appears as an element of this list twice. *dprove* does not check for multiple instances of delayables in the list. A less naive version of *dprove* would not add duplicate delayables. See Exercise 13.8 (page 594).

13.6 Review

The following are the main points you should have learned from this chapter:

- Individual-property-value triples form a flexible, universal representation for relations.
- Ontologies are required for knowledge sharing.
- OWL ontologies are built from individuals, classes, and properties. A class is a set of real and potential individuals. A property links an individual to a data type or an individual.
- The ability to explain reasoning and debug knowledge in terms of semantic content can improve the usability of a knowledge-based system.
- A meta-interpreter can be used to build a light-weight implementation of a knowledge-based system that can be customized to fit the requirements of the representation language.

13.7 References and Further Reading

Brachman and Levesque [2004] give an overview of knowledge representation. Davis [1990] is an accessible introduction to a wealth of knowledge representation issues in commonsense reasoning. Brachman and Levesque [1985] present many classic knowledge representation papers. See Woods [2007] for a recent overview of semantic networks.

For an overview of the philosophical and computational aspects of ontologies, see Smith [2003]. For an overview of the semantic web see Antoniou and van Harmelen [2008]; Berners-Lee, Hendler, and Lassila [2001]; and Hendler,

Berners-Lee, and Miller [2002]. The description of OWL in this chapter is based
on OWL-2; see Hitzler, Krötzsch, Parsia, Patel-Schneider, and Rudolph [2009];
Motik, Patel-Schneider, and Parsia [2009b]; and Motik, Patel-Schneider, and
Grau [2009a]. Turtle is presented in Beckett and Berners-Lee [2008].

BFO is described in Grenon and Smith [2004]. Other top-level ontologies
include DOLCE [Gangemi, Guarino, Masolo, and Oltramari, 2003], SUMO
[Niles and Pease, 2001], and Cyc [Panton, Matuszek, Lenat, Schneider, Witbrock, Siegel, and Shepard, 2006]. Noy and Hafner [1997] compare a number
of different top-level ontologies.

Meta-interpreters for logic are discussed by Bowen [1985] and Kowalski
[1979]. See the collection by Abramson and Rogers [1989].

13.8 Exercises

Exercise 13.1 The aim of this exercise is to explore multiple representations for
the same domain.

Tic-tac-toe is a game played on a 3×3 grid. Two players, X and O, alternately
place their marks in an unoccupied position. X wins if, during its turn, it can place
an X in an unoccupied position to make three X's in a row. For example, from the
state of the game

X	O	O
	X	
X		O

X can win by moving into the left middle position.

Fred, Jane, Harold, and Jennifer have all written programs to determine if,
given a state of the game, X is able to win in the next move. Each of them has
decided on a different representation of the state of the game. The aim of this
question is to compare their representations.

Fred decides to represent a state of the game as a list of three rows, where each
row is a list containing three elements, either x, o, or b (for blank). Fred represents
the above state as the list

$$[[x,o,o],[b,x,b],[x,b,o]].$$

Jane decides that each position on the square could be described by two numbers, the position across and the position up. The top left X is in position $pos(1,3)$,
the bottom left X is in position $pos(1,1)$, and so forth. She represents the state of
the game as a pair $ttt(XPs, OPs)$ where XPs is the list of X's positions and OPs is
the list of O's positions. Thus, Jane represents the above state as

$$ttt([pos(1,3),pos(2,2),pos(1,1)],[pos(2,3),pos(3,3),pos(3,1)]).$$

Harold and Jennifer both realize that the positions on the tic-tac-toe board
could be represented in terms of a so-called magic square:

6	7	2
1	5	9
8	3	4

The game is transformed into one where the two players alternately select a digit. No digit can be selected twice, and the player who first selects three digits summing to 15 wins.

Harold decides to represent a state of game as a list of nine elements, each of which is x, o, or b, depending on whether the corresponding position in the magic square is controlled by X, controlled by O, or is blank. Thus, Harold represents the game state above as the list

$$[b, o, b, o, x, x, o, x, b].$$

Jennifer decides to represent the game as a pair consisting of the list of digits selected by X and the list of digits selected by O. She represents the state of the game above as

$$magic([6, 5, 8], [7, 2, 4]).$$

(a) For each of the four representations, write the relation to determine whether X has won based on that representation, such as $x\_won\_fred(State)$, with the intended interpretation that X has won the game in state $State$ based on Fred's representation (and similarly for the other three representations).

(b) Which representation is easier to use? Explain why.

(c) Which representation is more efficient to determine a win?

(d) Which representation would result in the simplest algorithm to make sure a player does not lose on the next move, if such a move exists?

(e) Which do you think is the best representation? Explain why. Suggest a better representation.

Exercise 13.2 Sam has proposed that any n-ary relation $P(X_1, X_2, X_3, \ldots, X_n)$ can be reexpressed as $n - 1$ binary relations, namely,

$P_1(X_1, X_2)$.
$P_2(X_2, X_3)$.
$P_3(X_3, X_4)$.

$\vdots$

$P_{n-1}(X_{n-1}, X_n)$.

Explain to Sam why this may not be such a good idea. What problems would arise if Sam tried to do this?

Exercise 13.3 Write an ontology for the objects that often appear on your desk that may be useful for a robot that is meant to tidy your desk. Think of the categories that (a) the robot can perceive and (b) should be distinguished for the task.

Exercise 13.4 Suppose a "beach resort" is a resort that is near a beach that the resort guests can use. The beach has to be near the sea or a lake, where swimming is permitted. A resort must have places to sleep and places to eat. Write a definition of beach resort on OWL.

Exercise 13.5 A luxury hotel has multiple rooms to rent, each of which is comfortable and has a view. The hotel must also have more than one restaurant. There must be menu items for vegetarians and for meat eaters to eat in the restaurants.

(a) Define a luxury hotel in OWL, based on this description. Make reasonable assumptions where the specification is ambiguous.

(b) Suggest three other properties you would expect of a luxury hotel. For each, give the natural language definition and the OWL specification.

Exercise 13.6 For the following, explain how each is categorized by BFO:

(a) your skin

(b) the period at the end of the previous sentence

(c) the excitement a child has before a vacation

(d) the trip home from a vacation

(e) a computer program

(f) summer holidays

(g) the ring of a telephone

(h) the dust on your desk

(i) the task of cleaning your office

(j) the diagnosis of flu in a person

Based on this experience, suggest and justify a modification of BFO. Think about what distinctions in BFO either don't cover the cases you need or are not exclusive.

Exercise 13.7 Modify the depth-bound meta-interpreter of Figure 13.12 (page 587) so that

(a) the bound is on the total length of the proof, where the length is the total number of instances of base-level atoms that appear in the proof.

(b) different base-level atoms can incur different costs on the bound. For example, most atoms could have zero cost, and some atoms could incur a positive cost.

Discuss why either of these may be better or worse than using the depth of the tree.

What conditions on the atom costs would guarantee that, when a positive bound is given, the proof procedure does not go into an infinite loop?

Exercise 13.8 The program of Figure 13.16 (page 590) allows duplicate delayed goals. Write a version of *dprove* that returns minimal sets of delayed goals, in their simplest forms.

Exercise 13.9 Write a meta-interpreter that can ask multiple sources for information. Suppose that each source is identified by a universal resource identifier (URI). Suppose you have the predicates

- *can_answer*(*Q, URI*) is true if the source given by *URI* can answer questions that unify with *Q*.

- *reliability*(*URI, R*) is true if *R* is some numerical measure of reliability of URI. You can assume that *R* is in the range $[-100, 100]$, in which the higher number means that it is more reliable.

- *askSite*(*URI, Q, Answer*) is true when you ask the source *URI* a question *Q*, it gives the *Answer* that is one of {*yes, no, unknown*}. Note that although *can_answer* and *reliability* can be simple databases, *askSite* is a sophisticated program that accesses the web or asks a human a question.

Write a meta-interpreter that can utilize multiple information sources and returns a reliability of the answer, where the reliability of an answer is the minimum of the reliabilities of the information sources used. You must have some convention for when no external sources were used (e.g., a reliability of 200). You can only ask an information source a question that you have recorded that it can answer.

Exercise 13.10 Write a meta-interpreter that allows for asking the users yes-or-no questions. Make sure it does not ask questions to which it already knows the answer.

Exercise 13.11 Extend the ask-the-user meta-interpreter to have questions that ask for instances. You should be able to interpret declarations that say that a predicate is functional and respond accordingly.

Exercise 13.12 Write a program that takes in a tree produced from the meta-interpreter that builds proof trees as shown in Figure 13.13 (page 587) and lets someone traverse the tree using how questions.

Exercise 13.13 Write a meta-interpreter that allows both how and why questions. In particular, it should allow the user to ask how questions about a goal that has been proved after a why question. Explain how such a program may be useful.

Exercise 13.14 Write a meta-interpreter for definite clauses that does iterative deepening search. Make sure that it only returns one answer for each proof and that the system says *no* whenever the depth-first searcher says *no*. This should be based on the depth-bounded meta-interpreter (page 587) and the iterative-deepening search algorithm (page 97).

Exercise 13.15 Build an iterative deepening abductive reasoning system to find minimal consistent sets of assumables to imply a goal. This can be based on the depth-bounded meta-interpreter of Figure 13.12 (page 587), and the delaying meta-interpreter of Figure 13.16 (page 590) to collect assumptions. The depth bound should be based on the number of assumables used in the proof. Assume that the assumables are all ground.

This should be done in two parts:

(a) Find the minimal sets of assumables that imply some *g* using iterative deepening on the number of assumables. When *g* is *false*, this program finds the minimal conflicts.

(b) Based on part (a), find the minimal explanations of *g* by interleaving finding conflicts and finding minimal sets of assumables that imply *g*.

Exercise 13.16 In this question, you will write a meta-interpreter for para-metrized logic programs. These are logic programs that can use constants in arithmetic expressions. The values for the constants are given as part of the input to the meta-interpreter.

Assume that an environment is a list of terms of the form $val(Parm, Val)$, where Val is the value associated with parameter $Parm$. Assume that each parameter only appears once in an environment. An example environment is $[val(a, 7), val(b, 5)]$.

In AILog, you can use <= as the base-level implication and & as the base-level conjunction. AILog has <= defined as an infix operator and $number$ is a built-in predicate.

(a) Write a predicate $lookup(Parm, Val, Env)$ that is true if parameter $Parm$ has value Val in environment Env.

(b) Write a predicate $eval(Exp, Val, Env)$ that is true if parametrized arithmetic expression Exp evaluates to number Val in environment Env. An expression is either

- of the form $(E_1 + E_2)$, $(E_1 * E_2)$, (E_1/E_2), $(E_1 - E_2)$, where E_1 and E_2 are parameterized arithmetic expressions;

- a number; or

- a parameter.

Assume that the operators have their usual meaning, that numbers evaluate to themselves, and that parameters evaluate to their value in the environment. You can use the AILog predicates is, use infix as N is E, which is true if (unparametrized) expression E evaluates to number N, and $number(E)$, which is true if E is a number.

(c) Write a predicate $pprove(G, Env)$ that is true if goal G is a logical consequence of the base-level KB, where parameters are interpreted in environment Env. An example interaction with AILog is

```
ailog: tell f(X,Y) <= Y is 2*a+b*X.
ailog: ask pprove(f(3,Z),[val(a,7),val(b,5)]).
Answer: pprove(f(3,29),[val(a,7),val(b,5)]).
  [ok,more,how,help]: ok.
ailog:  ask pprove(f(3,Z),[val(a,5),val(b,7)]).
Answer: pprove(f(3,31),[val(a,5),val(b,7)]).
  [ok,more,how,help]: ok.
ailog: tell dsp(X,Y) <= Z is X*X*a & Y is Z*Z*b.
ailog: ask pprove(dsp(3,Z),[val(a,7),val(b,5)]).
Answer: pprove(dsp(3,19845),[val(a,7),val(b,5)]).
  [ok,more,how,help]: ok.
ailog: ask pprove(dsp(3,Z),[val(a,5),val(b,7)]).
Answer: pprove(dsp(3,14175),[val(a,5),val(b,7)]).
  [ok,more,how,help]: ok.
```

Chapter 14

Relational Planning, Learning, and Probabilistic Reasoning

What is now required is to give the greatest possible development to mathematical logic, to allow to the full the importance of relations, and then to found upon this secure basis a new philosophical logic, which may hope to borrow some of the exactitude and certainty of its mathematical foundation. If this can be successfully accomplished, there is every reason to hope that the near future will be as great an epoch in pure philosophy as the immediate past has been in the principles of mathematics. Great triumphs inspire great hopes; and pure thought may achieve, within our generation, such results as will place our time, in this respect, on a level with the greatest age of Greece.

– Bertrand Russell [1917]

The representation scheme dimension (page 20) has, as its top level, reasoning in terms of individuals and relations. Reasoning in terms of relations allows for compact representations that can be built before the agent encounters particular individuals. When an agent is introduced to a new individual, it can infer relationships about that individual. This chapter outlines how, in three areas of AI, feature-based representations are expandable to (also) deal with individuals and relations. In each of these areas, the relational representation benefits from being able to be built before the individuals are known and, therefore, before the features are known. As Russell points out in the quote above, relational reasoning brings great advantages over propositional (and feature-based) representations.

14.1 Planning with Individuals and Relations

An agent's goals and its environment are often described in terms of individuals and relations. When the agent's knowledge base is built, and before the agent knows the objects it should reason about, it requires a representation that is independent of the individuals. Thus, it must go beyond feature-based representations. When the individuals become known, it is possible to ground out the representations in terms of features. Often, it is useful to reason in terms of the non-grounded representations.

With a relational representation, we can reify time. **Time** can be represented in terms of individuals that are points in time or temporal intervals. This section presents two relational representations that differ in how time is reified.

14.1.1 Situation Calculus

The idea behind **situation calculus** is that (reachable) states are definable in terms of the actions required to reach them. These reachable states are called situations. What is true in a situation can be defined in terms of relations with the situation as an argument. Situation calculus can be seen as a relational version of the feature-based representation of actions (page 353).

Here we only consider single agents, a fully observable environment, and deterministic actions.

Situation calculus is defined in terms of situations. A **situation** is either

- *init*, the initial situation, or
- $do(A, S)$, the situation resulting from doing action A in situation S, if it is possible to do action A in situation S.

Example 14.1 Consider the domain of Figure 3.1 (page 73). Suppose in the initial situation, *init*, the robot, Rob, is at location *o109* and there is a key *k1* at the mail room and a package at *storage*.

$$do(move(rob, o109, o103), init)$$

is the situation resulting from Rob moving from position *o109* in situation *init* to position *o103*. In this situation, Rob is at *o103*, the key *k1* is still at *mail*, and the package is at *storage*.

The situation

$$do(move(rob, o103, mail),$$
$$do(move(rob, o109, o103),$$
$$init))$$

is one in which the robot has moved from position *o109* to *o103* to *mail* and is currently at mail. Suppose Rob then picks up the key, *k1*. The resulting situation is

$$do(pickup(rob, k1),$$
$$do(move(rob, o103, mail),$$

$$do(move(rob, o109, o103),$$
$$init))).$$

> In this situation, Rob is at position *mail* carrying the key *k1*.

A situation can be associated with a state. There are two main differences between situations and states:

- Multiple situations may refer to the same state if multiple sequences of actions lead to the same state. That is, equality between situations is not the same as equality between states.

- Not all states have corresponding situations. A state is **reachable** if a sequence of actions exists that can reach that state from the initial state. States that are not reachable do not have a corresponding situation.

Some $do(A, S)$ terms do not correspond to any state. However, sometimes an agent must reason about such a (potential) situation without knowing if A is possible in state S, or if S is possible.

> **Example 14.2** The term $do(unlock(rob, door1), init)$ does not denote a state at all, because it is not possible for Rob to unlock the door when Rob is not at the door and does not have the key.

A **static** relation is a relation for which the truth value does not depend on the situation; that is, its truth value is unchanging through time. A **dynamic** relation is a relation for which the truth value depends on the situation. To represent what is true in a situation, predicate symbols denoting dynamic relations have a situation argument so that the truth can depend on the situation. A predicate symbol with a situation argument is called a **fluent**.

> **Example 14.3** The relation $at(O, L, S)$ is true when object O is at location L in situation S. Thus, at is a fluent.
> The atom
>
> $at(rob, o109, init)$
>
> is true if the robot *rob* is at position *o109* in the initial situation. The atom
>
> $at(rob, o103, do(move(rob, o109, o103), init))$
>
> is true if robot *rob* is at position *o103* in the situation resulting from *rob* moving from position *o109* to position *o103* from the initial situation. The atom
>
> $at(k1, mail, do(move(rob, o109, o103), init))$
>
> is true if *k1* is at position *mail* in the situation resulting from *rob* moving from position *o109* to position *o103* from the initial situation.

A dynamic relation is axiomatized by specifying the situations in which it is true. Typically, this is done inductively in terms of the structure of situations.

- Axioms with *init* as the situation parameter are used to specify what is true in the initial situation.
- A **primitive** relation is defined by specifying when it is true in situations of the form $do(A, S)$ in terms of what is true in situation S. That is, primitive relations are defined in terms of what is true at the previous situation.
- A **derived** relation is defined using clauses with a variable in the situation argument. The truth of a derived relation in a situation depends on what else is true in the same situation.
- Static relations are defined without reference to the situation.

Example 14.4 Suppose the delivery robot, Rob, is in the domain depicted in Figure 3.1 (page 73). Rob is at location *o109*, the parcel is in the storage room, and the key is in the mail room. The following axioms describe this initial situation:

> $at(rob, o109, init)$.
> $at(parcel, storage, init)$.
> $at(k1, mail, init)$.

The *adjacent* relation is a dynamic, derived relation defined as follows:

> $adjacent(o109, o103, S)$.
> $adjacent(o103, o109, S)$.
> $adjacent(o109, storage, S)$.
> $adjacent(storage, o109, S)$.
> $adjacent(o109, o111, S)$.
> $adjacent(o111, o109, S)$.
> $adjacent(o103, mail, S)$.
> $adjacent(mail, o103, S)$.
> $adjacent(lab2, o109, S)$.
> $adjacent(P_1, P_2, S) \leftarrow$
> $between(Door, P_1, P_2) \wedge$
> $unlocked(Door, S)$.

Notice the free S variable; these clauses are true for all situations. We cannot omit the S because which rooms are adjacent depends on whether a door is unlocked. This can change from situation to situation.

The *between* relation is static and does not require a situation variable:

> $between(door1, o103, lab2)$.

We also distinguish whether or not an agent is being carried. If an object is not being carried, we say that the object is sitting at its location. We distinguish this case because an object being carried moves with the object carrying it. An object is at a location if it is sitting at that location or is being carried by an object at that location. Thus, *at* is a derived relation:

$$at(Ob, P, S) \leftarrow$$
$$\quad sitting\_at(Ob, P, S).$$
$$at(Ob, P, S) \leftarrow$$
$$\quad carrying(Ob1, Ob, S) \wedge$$
$$\quad at(Ob1, P, S).$$

Note that this definition allows for Rob to be carrying a bag, which, in turn, is carrying a book.

The **precondition** (page 350) of an action specifies when it is possible to carry out the action. The relation $poss(A, S)$ is true when action A is possible in situation S. This is typically a derived relation.

Example 14.5 An agent can always put down an object it is carrying:

$$poss(putdown(Ag, Obj), S) \leftarrow$$
$$\quad carrying(Ag, Obj, S).$$

For the *move* action, an autonomous agent can move from its current position to an adjacent position:

$$poss(move(Ag, P_1, P_2), S) \leftarrow$$
$$\quad autonomous(Ag) \wedge$$
$$\quad adjacent(P_1, P_2, S) \wedge$$
$$\quad sitting\_at(Ag, P_1, S).$$

The precondition for the unlock action is more complicated. The agent must be at the correct side of the door and carrying the appropriate key:

$$poss(unlock(Ag, Door), S) \leftarrow$$
$$\quad autonomous(Ag) \wedge$$
$$\quad between(Door, P_1, P_2) \wedge$$
$$\quad at(Ag, P_1, S) \wedge$$
$$\quad opens(Key, Door) \wedge$$
$$\quad carrying(Ag, Key, S).$$

We do not assume that the *between* relation is symmetric. Some doors can only open one way.

We define what is true in each situation recursively in terms of the previous situation and of what action occurred between the situations. As in the feature-based representation of actions (page 353), **causal rules** specify when a relation becomes true and **frame rules** specify when a relation remains true.

Example 14.6 The primitive *unlocked* relation can be defined by specifying how different actions can affect its being true. The door is unlocked in the situation resulting from an unlock action, as long as the unlock action was possible. This is represented using the following causal rule:

$$unlocked(Door, do(unlock(Ag, Door), S)) \leftarrow$$
$$poss(unlock(Ag, Door), S).$$

Suppose the only action to make the door locked is to lock the door. Thus, *unlocked* is true in a situation following an action if it was true before, if the action was not to lock the door, and if the action was possible:

$$unlocked(Door, do(A, S)) \leftarrow$$
$$unlocked(Door, S) \wedge$$
$$A \neq lock(Door) \wedge$$
$$poss(A, S).$$

This is a frame rule.

Example 14.7 The *carrying* predicate can be defined as follows.
An agent is carrying an object after picking up the object:

$$carrying(Ag, Obj, do(pickup(Ag, Obj), S)) \leftarrow$$
$$poss(pickup(Ag, Obj), S).$$

The only action that undoes the *carrying* predicate is the *putdown* action. Thus, *carrying* is true after an action if it was true before the action, and the action was not to put down the object. This is represented in the frame rule:

$$carrying(Ag, Obj, do(A, S)) \leftarrow$$
$$carrying(Ag, Obj, S) \wedge$$
$$poss(A, S) \wedge$$
$$A \neq putdown(Ag, Obj).$$

Example 14.8 The atom *sitting_at*(Obj, Pos, S_1) is true in a situation S_1 resulting from object *Obj* moving to *Pos*, as long as the action was possible:

$$sitting\_at(Obj, Pos, do(move(Obj, Pos_0, Pos), S)) \leftarrow$$
$$poss(move(Obj, Pos_0, Pos), S).$$

The other action that makes *sitting_at* true is the *putdown* action. An object is sitting at the location where the agent who put it down was located:

$$sitting\_at(Obj, Pos, do(putdown(Ag, Obj), S)) \leftarrow$$
$$poss(putdown(Ag, Obj), S) \wedge$$
$$at(Ag, Pos, S).$$

The only other time that *sitting_at* is true in a (non-initial) situation is when it was true in the previous situation and it was not undone by an action. The only actions that undo *sitting_at* is a *move* action or a *pickup* action. This can be specified by the following frame axiom:

$sitting\_at(Obj, Pos, do(A, S)) \leftarrow$
    $poss(A, S) \wedge$
    $sitting\_at(Obj, Pos, S) \wedge$
    $\forall Pos_1 \ A \neq move(Obj, Pos, Pos_1) \wedge$
    $\forall Ag \ A \neq pickup(Ag, Obj).$

Note that the quantification in the body is not the standard quantification for rules. This can be represented using negation as failure (page 537):

$sitting\_at(Obj, Pos, do(A, S)) \leftarrow$
    $poss(A, S) \wedge$
    $sitting\_at(Obj, Pos, S) \wedge$
    $\sim move\_action(A, Obj, Pos) \wedge$
    $\sim pickup\_action(A, Obj).$
$move\_action(move(Obj, Pos, Pos_1), Obj, Pos).$
$pickup\_action(pickup(Ag, Obj), Obj).$

These clauses are designed not to have a free variable in the scope of the negation.

Example 14.9 Situation calculus can represent more complicated actions than can be represented with simple addition and deletion of propositions in the state description.

Consider the *drop_everything* action in which an agent drops everything it is carrying. In situation calculus, the following axiom can be added to the definition of *sitting_at* to say that everything the agent was carrying is now on the ground:

$sitting\_at(Obj, Pos, do(drop\_everything(Ag), S)) \leftarrow$
    $poss(drop\_everything(Ag), S) \wedge$
    $at(Ag, Pos, S) \wedge$
    $carrying(Ag, Obj, S).$

A frame axiom for *carrying* specifies that an agent is not carrying an object after a *drop_everything* action.

$carrying(Ag, Obj, do(A, S)) \leftarrow$
    $poss(A, S) \wedge$
    $carrying(Ag, Obj, S) \wedge$
    $A \neq drop\_everything(Ag) \wedge$
    $A \neq putdown(Ag, Obj).$

The *drop_everything* action thus affects an unbounded number of objects.

Situation calculus is used for **planning** by asking for a situation in which a goal is true. Answer extraction (page 504) is used to find a situation in which the goal is true. This situation can be interpreted as a sequence of actions for the agent to perform.

Example 14.10 Suppose the goal is for the robot to have the key $k1$. The following query asks for a situation where this is true:

$$?carrying(rob, k1, S).$$

This query has the following answer:

$$S = do(pickup(rob, k1),$$
$$do(move(rob, o103, mail),$$
$$do(move(rob, o109, o103),$$
$$init))).$$

The preceding answer can be interpreted as a way for Rob to get the key: it moves from $o109$ to $o103$, then to *mail*, where it picks up the key.

The goal of delivering the parcel (which is, initially, in the lounge, lng) to $o111$ can be asked with the query

$$?at(parcel, o111, S).$$

This query has the following answer:

$$S = do(move(rob, o109, o111),$$
$$do(move(rob, lng, o109),$$
$$do(pickup(rob, parcel),$$
$$do(move(rob, o109, lng), init)))).$$

Therefore, Rob should go to the lounge, pick up the parcel, go back to $o109$, and then go to $o111$.

Using the top-down proof procedure (page 509) on the situation calculus definitions is very inefficient, because a frame axiom is almost always applicable. A complete proof procedure, such as iterative deepening, searches through all permutations of actions even if they are not relevant to the goal. The use of answer extraction does not negate the necessity for efficient planners, such as the ones in Chapter 8.

14.1.2 Event Calculus

The second representation, **event calculus**, models how the truth value of relations changes because of events occurring at certain times. Time can be modeled as either continuous or discrete.

Events are modeled as occurring at particular times. Event E occurring at time T is written as $event(E, T)$.

Events make some relations true and some no longer true:

- $initiates(E, R, T)$ is true if event E makes primitive relation R true at time T.

- $terminates(E, R, T)$ is true if event E makes primitive relation R no longer true at time T.

Time T is a parameter to *initiates* and *terminates* because the effect of an event can depend on what else is true at the time. For example, the effect of attempting to unlock a door depends on the position of the robot and whether it is carrying the appropriate key.

Relations are either true or false at any time. In event calculus, relations are reified, where $holds(R, T)$ means that relation R is true at time T. This is analogous to having T as the last argument to R in situation calculus. The use of the meta-predicate *holds* allows general rules that are true for all relations.

Derived relations are defined in terms of primitive relations and other derived relations for the same time.

Primitive relation R holds at time T if an event occurred before T that made R true, and there was no intervening event that made R no longer true. This can be specified as follows:

$$holds(R, T) \leftarrow$$
$$\quad event(E, T_0) \land$$
$$\quad T_0 < T \land$$
$$\quad initiates(E, R, T_0) \land$$
$$\quad \sim clipped(R, T_0, T).$$
$$clipped(R, T_0, T) \leftarrow$$
$$\quad event(E_1, T_1) \land$$
$$\quad terminates(E_1, R, T_1) \land$$
$$\quad T_0 < T_1 \land$$
$$\quad T_1 < T.$$

The atom $clipped(R, T_0, T)$ means there is an event between times T_0 and T that makes R no longer true; $T_0 < T_1$ is true if time T_0 is before time T_1. Here $\sim$ indicates negation as failure (page 193), and so these clauses mean their completion.

Actions are represented in terms of what properties they initiate and terminate. As in situation calculus, the preconditions of actions are specified using the *poss* relation.

Example 14.11 The *pickup* action initiates a *carrying* relation, and it terminates a *sitting_at* relation as long as the preconditions for *pickup* are true:

$$initiates(pickup(Ag, Obj), carrying(Ag, Obj), T) \leftarrow$$
$$\quad poss(pickup(Ag, Obj), T).$$
$$terminates(pickup(Ag, Obj), sitting\_at(Obj, Pos), T) \leftarrow$$
$$\quad poss(pickup(Ag, Obj), T).$$
$$poss(pickup(Ag, Obj), T) \leftarrow$$
$$\quad autonomous(Ag) \land$$
$$\quad Ag \neq Obj \land$$
$$\quad holds(at(Ag, Pos), T) \land$$
$$\quad holds(sitting\_at(Obj, Pos), T).$$

This implies that if a *pickup* is attempted when the preconditions do not hold, nothing happens. It is also possible to write clauses that specify what happens under different circumstances, such as when a pickup is attempted for an object that is being held by something else.

Given particular action occurrences, and making the complete knowledge assumption that all intervening events are specified, the top-down proof procedure with negation as failure can be used to prove what is true. For planning, the agent can use abduction (page 199).

14.2 Learning with Individuals and Relations

Learning in terms of individuals and relations allows for learning where the structure of relationships is important for prediction. The learning methods presented in Chapter 7 assumed that the feature values are meaningful; something useful could be predicted about a case by using the values of features. However, when the examples are about individuals and relations, the value of a property may be a meaningless name of an individual. It is only by considering the attributes of the individual that the name denotes, and its relationship to other individuals, that an agent is able produce meaningful predictions. The learned knowledge can also be applied to individuals that did not appear in the training set.

Because much of this work has been done in the context of logic programming, it is often called **inductive logic programming**.

Example 14.12 Suppose a trading agent the following data set, in terms of the individual-property-value **triples** (page 552), about which resorts a person likes:

Individual	Property	Value
joe	*likes*	*resort_14*
joe	*dislikes*	*resort_35*
...	...	...
resort_14	*type*	*resort*
resort_14	*near*	*beach_18*
beach_18	*type*	*beach*
beach_18	*covered_in*	*ws*
ws	*type*	*sand*
ws	*color*	*white*
...	...	...

The agent wants to learn what Joe likes. What is important is not the value of the *likes* property, which is just a meaningless name, but the properties of the individual denoted by the name. Feature-based representations cannot do anything with this data set beyond learning that Joe likes *resort_14*, but not *resort_35*.

The sort of theory the agent should learn is that Joe likes resorts near sandy beaches. This theory can be expressed as a logic program:

$$prop(joe, likes, R) \leftarrow$$
$$\quad prop(R, type, resort) \wedge$$
$$\quad prop(R, near, B) \wedge$$
$$\quad prop(B, type, beach) \wedge$$
$$\quad prop(B, covered\_in, S) \wedge$$
$$\quad prop(S, type, sand).$$

Logic programs provide the ability to be able to represent deterministic theories about individuals and relations. This rule can be applied to resorts and beaches that Joe has not visited.

The input to an inductive logic programming learner includes the following:

- A is a set of atoms whose definitions the agent is learning.

- E^+ is the set of ground instances of elements of A, called the **positive examples**, that are observed to be true.

- E^- is the set of ground instances of elements of A, called the **negative examples**, that are observed to be false.

- B, the **background knowledge**, is a set of clauses that define relations that can be used in the learned logic programs.

- H is a space of possible hypotheses. H is often represented implicitly as a set of operators that can generate the possible hypotheses. We assume that each hypothesis is a logic program.

Example 14.13 In Example 14.12 (page 606), suppose the agent wants to learn what Joe likes. In this case, the inputs are

- $A = \{prop(joe, likes, R)\}$
- $E^+ = \{prop(joe, likes, resort\_14), \dots\}$. For the example that follows, we assume there are many such items that Joe likes.
- $E^- = \{prop(joe, likes, resort\_35), \dots\}$. Note that these are written in the positive form; they have been observed to be false.
- $B = \{prop(resort\_14, type, resort), prop(resort\_14, near, beach\_18), \dots\}$. This set contains all of the facts about the world that are not instances of A. The agent is not learning about these.
- H is a set of logic programs defining $prop(joe, likes, R)$. The heads of the clauses unify with $prop(joe, likes, R)$. H is too big to enumerate.

All of these, except for H, are given explicitly in the formulation of the problem.

The aim is to find a simplest hypothesis $h \in H$ such that

$$B \wedge h \models E^+ \text{ and}$$
$$B \wedge h \not\models E^-.$$

That is, the hypothesis implies the positive evidence and does not imply the negative evidence. It must be **consistent** with the negative evidence being false.

We, thus, want to find an element of the version space (page 328). This is similar to the definition of abduction (page 199), in which the knowledge base in abduction corresponds to the background knowledge. The hypothesis space of inductive logic programming is the set of logic programs. The second condition corresponds to consistency.

For the rest of this section, assume that there is a single target n-ary relation whose definition we want to learn, and for which we use the predicate symbol t. That is, $A = \{t(X_1, \dots, X_n)\}$. The hypothesis space consists of possible definitions for this relation using a logic program.

There are two main strategies used in inductive logic programming:

- The first strategy is to start with the simplest hypothesis and make it more complicated to fit the data. Because the logic program only states positive facts, the simplest hypothesis is the most general hypothesis (page 329), which is simply that $t(X_1, \dots, X_n)$ is always true. This hypothesis implies the positive examples, but it also implies the negative examples, if any exist. This strategy involves a general-to-specific search. It tries to find the simplest hypothesis that fits the data by searching the hypothesis space from the simplest hypothesis to more complex hypotheses, always implying the positive examples, until a hypothesis that does not imply the negative examples is found.
- The second strategy is to start with a hypothesis that fits the data and to make it simpler while still fitting the data. A hypothesis that fits the data is the set of positive examples. This strategy involves a specific-to-general search: start with the very specific hypothesis in which only the positive

examples are true, and then generalize the clauses, avoiding the negative cases.

We will expand on the general-to-specific search for definite clauses. The initial hypothesis contains a single clause:

$$\{t(X_1, \ldots, X_n) \leftarrow\}.$$

A **specialization operator** takes a set G of clauses and returns a set S of clauses that specializes G. To specialize means that $S \models G$.

The following are three primitive specialization operators:

- Split a clause in G on condition c. Clause $a \leftarrow b$ in G is replaced by two clauses: $a \leftarrow b \wedge c$ and $a \leftarrow b \wedge \neg c$.

- Split a clause $a \leftarrow b$ in G on a variable X that appears in a or b. Clause $a \leftarrow b$ is replaced by the clauses

  $$a \leftarrow b \wedge X = t_1.$$

  $$\ldots$$

  $$a \leftarrow b \wedge X = t_k.$$

  where the t_i are terms.

- Remove a clause that is not necessary to prove the positive examples.

The last operation changes the predictions of the clause set. Those cases no longer implied by the clauses are false.

These primitive specialization operators are used together to form the operators of H. The operators of H are combinations of primitive specialization operations designed so that progress can be evaluated using a **greedy** look-ahead. That is, the operators are defined so that one step is adequate to evaluate progress.

The first two primitive specialization operations should be carried out judiciously to ensure that the simplest hypothesis is found. An agent should carry out the splitting operations only if they make progress. Splitting is only useful when combined with clause removal. For example, adding an atom to the body of a clause is equivalent to splitting on the atom and then removing the clause containing the negation of the atom. A higher-level specialization operator may be to split on the atom $prop(X, type, T)$ for some variable X that appears in the clause, split on the values of T, and remove the resulting clauses that are not required to imply the positive examples. This operator makes progress on determining which types are useful.

Figure 14.1 (on the next page) shows a **local search** algorithm for the top-down induction of a logic program. It maintains a single hypothesis that it iteratively improves until finding a hypothesis that fits the data or until it fails to find such a hypothesis.

1: **procedure** $TDInductiveLogicProgram(t, B, E^+, E^-, R)$
2:      **Inputs**
3:         t: an atom whose definition is to be learned
4:         B: background knowledge is a logic program
5:         E^+: positive examples
6:         E^-: negative examples
7:         R: set of specialization operators
8:      **Output**
9:         logic program that classifies E^+ positively and E^- negatively or $\perp$ if no program can be found
10:      **Local**
11:         H is a set of clauses
12:      $H \leftarrow \{t(X_1, \ldots, X_n) \leftarrow\}$
13:      **while** there is $e \in E^-$ such that $B \cup H \models e$ **do**
14:         **if** there is $r \in R$ such that $B \cup r(H) \models E^+$ **then**
15:             Select $r \in R$ such that $B \cup r(H) \models E^+$
16:             $H \leftarrow r(H)$
17:         **else**
18:             **return** $\perp$
19:      **return** H

Figure 14.1: Top-down induction of a logic program

At each time step it chooses an operator to apply with the constraint that every hypothesis entails the positive examples. This algorithm glosses over two important details:

- which operators to consider and
- which operator to select.

The operators should be at a level so that they can be evaluated according to which one is making progress toward a good hypothesis. In a manner similar to decision-tree learning (page 301), the algorithm can perform a myopically optimal choice. That is, it chooses the operator that makes the most progress in minimizing the error. The error of a hypothesis can be the number of negative examples that are implied by the hypothesis.

Example 14.14   Consider Example 14.12 (page 606), in which the agent must learn about Joe's likes and dislikes.

The first hypothesis is that Joe likes everything:

$$\{prop(joe, likes, R) \leftarrow \},$$

which is inconsistent with the negative evidence.

It can split on properties that contain the individuals that Joe likes. The only way for the specialization to make progress – to prove fewer negative examples while implying all positive examples – is to contain the variable R in the body. Thus, it must consider triples in which R is the subject or the object.

- It could consider splitting on the property *type*, splitting on the value of *type*, and keeping only those that are required to prove the positive examples. This results in the following clause (assuming the positive examples only include resorts):

$$\{prop(joe, likes, R) \leftarrow prop(R, type, resort)\}.$$

There can be other clauses if the positive examples include things other than resorts that Joe likes. If the negative examples include non-resorts, this split would be useful in reducing the error.

- It could consider splitting on other properties that can be used in proofs of the positive examples, such as *near*, resulting in

$$\{prop(joe, likes, R) \leftarrow prop(R, near, B)\}$$

if all of the positive examples are near something. If some of the negative examples are not near anything, this specialization could be useful in reducing the error.

It could then choose whichever of these splits makes the most progress. In the next step it could add the other one, other properties of R, or properties of B.

14.3 Probabilistic Relational Models

The belief network probability models of Chapter 6 were defined in terms of features. Many domains are best modeled in terms of individuals and relations. Agents must often build probabilistic models before they know what individuals are in the domain and, therefore, before they know what random variables exist. When the probabilities are being learned, the probabilities often do not depend on the individuals. Although it is possible to learn about an individual, an agent must also learn general knowledge that it can apply when it finds out about a new individual.

Example 14.15 Consider the problem of an intelligent tutoring system diagnosing students' arithmetic errors. From observing a student's performance on a number of examples, the tutor should try to determine whether or not the student understands the task and, if not, work out what the student is doing wrong so that appropriate remedies can be applied.

Consider the case of diagnosing two-digit addition of the form

$$\begin{array}{ccc} & x_1 & x_0 \\ + & y_1 & y_0 \\ \hline z_2 & z_1 & z_0 \end{array}$$

The student is given the values for the x's and the y's and provides values for the z's.

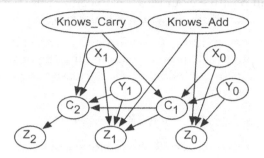

Figure 14.2: Belief network for two-digit addition

Students' answers depend on whether they know basic addition and whether they know how to carry. A belief network for this example is shown in Figure 14.2 . The carry into digit i, given by the variable C_i, depends on the x-value, the y-value, and the carry for the previous digit, and on whether the student knows how to carry. The z-value for digit i, given by the variable Z_i, depends on the x-value, the y-value, and the carry for digit i, in addition to whether the student knows basic addition.

By observing the value of the x's and the y's in the problem and the value of z's given by the student, the posterior probability that the student knows addition and knows how to carry can be inferred. One feature of the belief network model is that it allows students to make random errors; even though they know arithmetic, they can still get the wrong answer.

The problem with this representation is that it is inflexible. A flexible representation would allow for the addition of multiple digits, multiple problems, multiple students, and multiple times. Multiple digits require the replication of the network for the digits. Multiple times allow for modeling how students' knowledge and their answers change over time, even if the problems do not change over time.

If the conditional probabilities were stored as tables, the size of these tables would be enormous. For example, if the X_i, Y_i, and Z_i variables each have a domain size of 11 (the digits 0 to 9 or the blank), and the C_i and *Knows_Add* variables are binary, a tabular representation of

$$P(Z_1|X_1, Y_1, C_1, \textit{Knows\_Add})$$

would have a size greater than 4,000. There is much more structure in the conditional probability than is expressed in the tabular representation. The representation that follows allows for both relational probabilistic models and compact descriptions of conditional probabilities.

A **probabilistic relational model (PRM)** or a **relational probability model** is a model in which the probabilities are specified on the relations, independently of the actual individuals. Different individuals share the probability parameters.

A **parametrized random variable** is either a logical atom or a term (page 494). That is, it is of the form $p(t_1, \ldots, t_n)$, where each t_i is a logical variable or a constant. The parametrized random variable is said to be parametrized by the logical variables that appear in it. A ground instance of a parametrized random variable is obtained by substituting constants for the logical variables in the parametrized random variable. The ground instances of a parametrized random variable correspond to random variables. The random variables are Boolean if p is a predicate symbol. If p is a function symbol, the domain of the random variables is the range of p.

We use the convention that logical variables are in upper case. Random variables correspond to ground atoms and ground terms, so, for this section, these are written in lower case.

Example 14.16 For a PRM of the multidigit arithmetic problem of the previous example, there is a separate x-variable for each digit D and for each problem P, represented by the parametrized random variable $x(D, P)$. Thus, for example, $x(1, prob17)$ may be a random variable representing the x-value of the first digit of problem 17. Similarly there is a parametrized random variable, $y(D, P)$, which represents a random variable for each digit D and problem P.

There is a variable for each student S and time T that represents whether S knows how to add properly at time T. The parametrized random variable $knows\_add(S, T)$ represents whether student S knows addition at time T. The random variable $knows\_add(fred, mar23)$ is true if Fred knows addition on March 23. Similarly, there is a parametrized random variable $knows\_carry(S, T)$.

There is a different z-value and a different carry for each digit, problem, student, and time. These values are represented by the parametrized random variables $z(D, P, S, T)$ and $carry(D, P, S, T)$. So, $z(1, prob17, fred, mar23)$ is a random variable representing the answer Fred gave on March 23 for digit 1 of problem 17. Function z has range $\{0, \ldots, 9, blank\}$, so the random variables all have this set as their domain.

A **plate model** consists of

- a directed graph in which the nodes are parameterized random variables,
- a population of individuals for each logical variable, and
- a conditional probability of each node given its parents.

A plate model means its grounding – the belief network in which nodes are all ground instances of the parametrized random variables (each logical variable replaced by an individual in its population). The conditional probabilities of the belief network are the corresponding instances of the plate model.

Example 14.17 Figure 7.17 (page 339) gives a hierarchical Bayesian model as (a) a plate model and (b) its grounding. The plate representation, on the left of the figure, has four parametrized random variables: $s(X, H)$, $\phi(H)$, α_1, and α_2. The population for X is the set of all patients. The population for H is the set of all hospitals. The grounding of the network is shown on the right of the

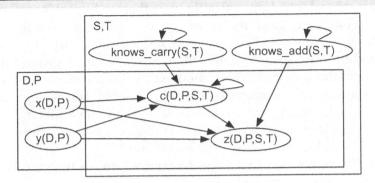

Figure 14.3: Belief network with plates for multidigit addition

figure. There is a separate random variable $\phi(h)$ for each hospital h, and a separate random variable $s(x, h)$ for each patent x and hospital h. There is a conditional probability of each $s(x, h)$ given the corresponding $\phi(h)$, a conditional probability of each $\phi(h)$ given α_1 and α_2, and prior probabilities of α_1 and α_1. The $s(x, h)$ variables in the grounding all have the same conditional probability given parent. The variables $s(x_1, h)$ and $s(x_1, h)$, for different patients x_1 and x_2, are independent of each other given $\phi(h)$. The variables $s(x_1, h_1)$ and $s(x_2, h_2)$, for different hospitals h_1 and h_2, are independent of each other given α_1 and α_2.

Example 14.18 A plate model with the parametrized random variables of Example 14.16 is shown in Figure 14.3. The rectangles correspond to plates. For the plate labeled with D, P, an instance of each variable exists for each digit D and person P. One way to view this is that the instances come out of the page, like a stack of plates. Similarly, for the plate labeled S, T, there is a copy of the variables for each student S and each time T. For the variables in the intersection of the plates, there is a random variable for each digit D, person P, student S, and time T. Note that the notation here is redundant; the plates provide the same information as the explicit parameters; the parameters for c have to be D, P, S, T because these are the plates it is in.

The plate representation denotes the same independence as a belief network (page 240); each node is independent of its non-descendants given its parents. In this case, the diagram describes its grounding. Thus, for particular values $d \in dom(D), p \in dom(P), s \in dom(S)$, and $t \in dom(T), z(d, p, s, t)$ is a random variable, with parents $x(d, p), y(d, p), c(d, p, s, t)$ and $knows\_add(s, t)$. There is a loop in the plate model on the $c(D, P, S, T)$ parametrized random variable because the carry for one digit depends on the carry for the previous digit for the same problem, student, and time. Similarly, whether students know how to carry at some time depends on whether they knew how to carry at the previous time. However, the conditional probability tables are such that the ground network is acyclic.

> There is a conditional probability of each parametrized random variable, given its parents. This conditional probability is shared among its ground instances.

Unfortunately, the plate representation is not adequate when the dependency occurs among different instances of the same relation. In the preceding example, $c(D, P, S, T)$ depends, in part, on $c(D - 1, P, S, T)$, that is, on the carry from the previous digit (and there is some other case for the first digit). A more complex example is to determine the probability that two authors are collaborators, which depends on whether they have written a paper in common. To represent such examples, it is useful to be able to specify how the logical variables interact, as is done in logic programs.

One representation that combines the ideas of belief networks, plates, and logic programs is the **independent choice logic (ICL)**. The ICL consists of a set of independent choices, a logic program that gives the consequences of the choices, and probability distributions over the choices. In more detail, the ICL is defined as follows:

An **alternative** is a set of atoms (page 494) all sharing the same logical variables. A **choice space** is a set of alternatives such that none of the atoms in the alternatives unify with each other. An ICL theory contains

- a choice space C. Let C' be the set of ground instances of the alternatives. Thus, C' is a set of sets of ground atoms.
- an acyclic logic program (that can include negation as failure), in which the head of the clauses doesn't unify with an element of an alternative in the choice space.
- a probability distribution over each alternative.

The atoms in the logic program and the choice space can contain constants, variables, and function symbols.

A **selector function** selects a single element from each alternative in C'. There exists a **possible world** for each selector function. The logic program specifies what is true in each possible world. Atom g is true in a possible world if it follows from the atoms selected by the selector function added to the logic program. The probability of proposition g is given by a measure over sets of possible worlds, where the atoms in different ground instances of the alternatives are probabilistically independent. The instances of an alternative share the same probabilities, and the probabilities of different instances are multiplied.

The acyclicity of the logic program means that only a finite number of alternatives exist with atoms involved in proofs of any ground g. So, although there may be infinitely many possible worlds, for any g, the probability measure can be defined on the sets of possible worlds that are describable in terms of a finite number of alternatives. A description of these worlds can be found by making the atoms in the alternatives assumable (page 187), with different atoms in the same alternative inconsistent, and by using abduction (page 199) to find descriptions of the sets of worlds in which g is true.

An ICL theory can be seen as a causal model (page 206) in which the causal mechanism is specified as a logic program and the background variables, corresponding to the alternatives, have independent probability distributions over them. It may seem that this logic, with only unconditionally independent atoms and a deterministic logic program, is too weak to represent the sort of knowledge required. However, even without logical variables, the independent choice logic can represent anything that can be represented in a belief network.

Example 14.19   Consider representing the belief network of Example 6.10 (page 236) in the ICL. The same technique works for any belief network.

Fire and tampering have no parents, so they can be represented directly as alternatives:

>   {*fire, nofire*},
>
>   {*tampering, notampering*}.

The probability distribution over the first alternative is $P(\textit{fire}) = 0.01$, $P(\textit{nofire}) = 0.99$. Similarly, $P(\textit{tampering}) = 0.02$, $P(\textit{notampering}) = 0.89$.

The dependence of *Smoke* on *Fire* can be represented using two alternatives:

>   {*smokeWhenFire, nosmokeWhenFire*},
>
>   {*smokeWhenNoFire, nosmokeWhenNoFire*},

with $P(\textit{smokeWhenFire}) = 0.9$ and $P(\textit{smokeWhenNoFire}) = 0.01$. Two rules can be used to specify when there is smoke:

>   *smoke* ← *fire* ∧ *smokeWhenFire*.
>
>   *smoke* ← ∼*fire* ∧ *smokeWhenNoFire*.

To represent how *Alarm* depends on *Fire* and *Tampering*, there are four alternatives:

>   {*alarmWhenTamperingFire, noalarmWhenTamperingFire*},
>
>   {*alarmWhenNoTamperingFire, noalarmWhenNoTamperingFire*},
>
>   {*alarmWhenTamperingNoFire, noalarmWhenTamperingNoFire*},
>
>   {*alarmWhenNoTamperingNoFire, noalarmWhenNoTamperingNoFire*},

where $P(\textit{alarmWhenTamperingFire}) = 0.5$, $P(\textit{alarmWhenNoTamperingFire}) = 0.99$, and similarly for the other atoms using the probabilities from Example 6.10 (page 236). There are also rules specifying when *alarm* is true, depending on tampering and fire:

>   *alarm* ← *tampering* ∧ *fire* ∧ *alarmWhenTamperingFire*.
>
>   *alarm* ← ∼*tampering* ∧ *fire* ∧ *alarmWhenNoTamperingFire*.
>
>   *alarm* ← *tampering* ∧ ∼*fire* ∧ *alarmWhenTamperingNoFire*.
>
>   *alarm* ← ∼*tampering* ∧ ∼*fire* ∧ *alarmWhenNoTamperingNoFire*.

Other random variables are represented analogously, using the same number of alternatives as there are assignments of values to the parents of a node.

An ICL representation of a conditional probability can be seen as a rule form of a decision tree (page 298) with probabilities at the leaves. There is a rule and an alternative for each branch. Non-binary alternatives are useful when non-binary variables are involved.

The independent choice logic may not seem very intuitive for representing standard belief networks, but it can make complicated relational models much simpler, as in the following example.

Example 14.20 Consider the parametrized version of the multidigit addition of Example 14.16 (page 613). The plates correspond to logical variables.

There are three cases for the value of $z(D, P, S, T)$. The first is when the student knows addition at this time, and the student did not make a mistake. In this case, they get the correct answer:

$$z(D, P, S, T, V) \leftarrow$$
$$x(D, P, Vx) \wedge$$
$$y(D, P, Vy) \wedge$$
$$carry(D, P, S, T, Vc) \wedge$$
$$knowsAddition(S, T) \wedge$$
$$\sim mistake(D, P, S, T) \wedge$$
$$V \text{ is } (Vx + Vy + Vc) \text{ div } 10.$$

Here we write the atom $z(D, P, S, T, V)$ to mean that the parametrized random variable $z(D, P, S, T)$ has value V. This is a standard logical rule and has the same meaning as a definite clause.

There is an alternative for whether or not the student happened to make a mistake in this instance:

$$\forall P \forall S \forall T \{noMistake(D, P, S, T), mistake(D, P, S, T)\},$$

where the probability of $mistake(D, P, S, T)$ is 0.05, assuming students make an error in 5% of the cases even when they know how to do arithmetic.

The second case is when the student knows addition at this time but makes a mistake. In this case, we assume that the students are equally likely to pick each of the digits:

$$z(D, P, S, T, V) \leftarrow$$
$$knowsAddition(S, T) \wedge$$
$$mistake(D, P, S, T) \wedge$$
$$selectDig(D, P, S, T, V).$$

There is an alternative that specifies which digit the student chose:

$$\forall P \forall S \forall T \{selectDig(D, P, S, T, V) \mid V \in \{0..9\}\}.$$

Suppose that, for each v, the probability of $selectDig(D, P, S, T, v)$ is 0.1.

The final case is when the student does not know addition. In this case, the student selects a digit at random:

$$z(D, P, S, T) = V \leftarrow$$
$$\sim knowsAddition(S, T) \wedge$$
$$selectDig(D, P, S, T) = V.$$

These three rules cover all of the rules for z; it is much simpler than the table of size greater than 4,000 that was required for the tabular representation and it also allows for arbitrary digits, problems, students, and times. Different digits and problems give different values for $x(D, P)$, and different students and times have different values for whether they know addition.

The rules for *carry* are similar. The main difference is that the carry in the body of the rule depends on the previous digit.

Whether a student knows addition at any time depends on whether they know addition at the previous time. Presumably, the student's knowledge also depends on what actions occur (what the student and the teacher do). Because the ICL allows standard logic programs (with "noise"), either of the representations for modeling change introduced at the start of this chapter can be used.

AILog, as used in the previous chapters, also implements ICL.

14.4   Review

The following are the main points you should have learned from this chapter:

- Relational representations are used when an agent requires models to be given or learned before it knows what individuals it will encounter.
- Many of the representations in earlier chapters can be made relational.
- Situation calculus represents time in terms of the action of an agent, using the *init* constant and the *do* function.
- Event calculus allows for continuous and discrete time and axiomatizes what follows from the occurrence of events.
- Inductive logic programming can be used to learn relational models, even when the values of features are meaningless names.
- The independent choice logic allows for the specification of probabilistic models before the individuals are known.

14.5   References and Further Reading

Situation calculus was proposed by McCarthy and Hayes [1969]. The form of the frame axioms presented here can be traced back to Kowalski [1979], Schubert [1990], and Reiter [1991]. Reiter [2001] presents a comprehensive overview of situation calculus; see also Brachman and Levesque [2004]. There have been many other suggestions about how to solve the **frame problem**, which is the problem of concisely specifying what does not change during an action. Event

Relational, Identity, and Existence Uncertainty

The models presented in Section 14.3 are concerned with **relational uncertainty**; uncertainty about whether a relation is true of some individuals. For example, we could have a probabilistic model of $likes(X, Y)$ for the case where $X \neq Y$, which models when different people like each other. This could depend on external characteristic of X and Y. We could also have a probabilistic model for $likes(X, X)$, which models whether someone likes themselves. This could depend on internal characteristics of themselves. Such models would be useful for a tutoring system to determine whether two people should work together, or whether a student's errors are due to the difficulty of the material or the student's personality.

Given individuals *sam* and *chris*, we can use the first of these models for $likes(sam, chris)$ only if we know that Sam and Chris are different people. The problem of **identity uncertainty** concerns uncertainty of whether, or not, two terms denote the same individual. This is a problem for medical systems, where it is important to determine whether the person who is interacting with the system now is the same person as one who visited yesterday. This problem is particularly difficult if the patient is non-communicative or wants to deceive the system, for example to get drugs. In the medical community, this is the problem of **record linkage**, as the problem is to determine which medical records are for the same people.

In all of the above cases, the individuals are known to exist; to give names to Chris and Sam presupposes that they exist. Given a description, the problem of determining if there exists an individual that fits the description is the problem of **existence uncertainty**. Existence uncertainty is problematic because there may be no individuals who fit the description or there may be multiple individuals. We cannot give properties to non-existent individuals, because individuals that do not exist do not have properties. If we want to give a name to an individual exists, we need to be concerned about which individual we are referring to if there are multiple individuals that exist. One particular case of existence uncertainty is **number uncertainty**, about the number of individuals that exist. For example, a purchasing agent may be uncertain about the number of people who would be interested in a package tour, and whether to offer the tour depends on the number of people who may be interested.

Reasoning about existence uncertainty can be very tricky if there are complex roles involved, and the problem is to determine if there are individuals to fill the roles. Consider a purchasing agent who must find an apartment for Sam and her son Chris. Whether Sam wants an apartment probabilistically depends, in part, on the size of her room and the color of Chris' room. However, individual apartments do not come labeled with Sam's room and Chris' room, and there may not exist a room for each of them. Given a model of an apartment Sam would want, it isn't obvious how to even condition on the observations.

calculus was proposed by Kowalski and Sergot [1986]. Shanahan [1997] provides an excellent introduction to the issues involved in representing change and to the frame problem in particular.

For overviews of inductive logic programming see Muggleton and De Raedt [1994], Muggleton [1995], and Quinlan and Cameron-Jones [1995].

Independent choice logic was proposed by Poole [1993, 1997]. De Raedt, Frasconi, Kersting, and Muggleton [2008] and Getoor and Taskar [2007] are collections of papers that provide overviews on probabilistic relational models and how they can be learned.

14.6   Exercises

Exercise 14.1   Add to the situation calculus example (also available from the course web page) the ability to paint an object. In particular, add the predicate

$color(Obj, Col, Sit)$

that is true if object *Obj* has color *Col* in situation *Sit*.

The parcel starts off blue. Thus, we have an axiom:

$color(parcel, blue, init)$.

There is an action $paint(Obj, Col)$ to paint object *Obj* with color *Col*. For this question, assume objects can only be painted red, and they can only be painted when the object and the robot are both at position *o109*. Colors accumulate on the robot (there is nothing that undoes an object being a color; if you paint the parcel red, it is both red and blue – of course this is unrealistic, but it makes the problem simpler).

Axiomatize the predicate *color* and the action *paint* using situation calculus.

You can do this without using more than three clauses (as well as the aforementioned clause defining the color in the initial situation), where none of the clauses has more than two atomic symbols in the body. You do not require equality, inequality, or negation as failure. Test it in AILog.

Your output should look something like the following:

```
ailog: bound 12.
ailog: ask color(parcel,red,S).
Answer:  color(parcel,red, do(paint(parcel,red),
                        do(move(rob,storage,o109),
                           do(pickup(rob,parcel),
                              do(move(rob,o109,storage),
                                 init)))))).
```

Exercise 14.2   In this question, you will add a more complicated paint action than in previous exercise.

Suppose the object *paint_can(Color)* denotes a can of paint of color *Color*.

Add the action $paint(Obj, Color)$ that results in the object changing its color to *Color*. (Unlike the previous question, the object only has one color). The painting can only be carried out if the object is sitting at *o109* and an autonomous agent is at position *o109* carrying the can of paint of the appropriate color.

Exercise 14.3 AILog performs depth-bounded search. You will notice that the processing time for the previous questions was slow, and we required a depth bound that was close to the actual depth bound to make it work in a reasonable amount of time.

In this question, estimate how long an iterative deepening search will take to find a solution to the following query:

```
ask sitting_at(parcel,lab2,S).
```

(Do not bother to try it – it takes too long to run.)

(a) Estimate the smallest bound necessary to find a plan. [Hint: How many steps are needed to solve this problem? How does the number of steps relate to the required depth bound?] Justify your estimate.

(b) Estimate the branching factor of the search tree. To do this you should look at the time for a complete search at level $k + 1$ versus a complete search at level k. You should justify your answer both experimentally (by running the program) and theoretically (by considering what is the branching factor). You do not have to run cases with a large run time to do this problem.

(c) Based on your answers to parts (a) and (b), and the time you found for some run of the program for a small bound, estimate the time for a complete search of the search tree at a depth one less than that required to find a solution. Justify your solution.

Exercise 14.4 In this question, you will investigate using event calculus for the robot delivery domain.

(a) Represent the *move* action in the event calculus.

(b) Represent each of the sequences of actions in Example 14.10 (page 604) in the event calculus.

(c) Show that event calculus can derive the appropriate goals from the sequence of actions given in part (b).

Exercise 14.5 Suppose that, in event calculus, there are two actions, *Open* and *Close*, and a relation *opened* that is initially, at time 0, false. Action *Open* makes *opened* true, and action *Close* makes *opened* false. Suppose that action *Open* occurs at time 5, and action *Close* occurs at time 10.

(a) Represent this in event calculus.

(b) Is *opened* true at time 3? Show the derivation.

(c) Is *opened* true at time 7? Show the derivation.

(d) Is *opened* true at time 13? Show the derivation.

(e) Is *opened* true at time 5? Explain.

(f) Is *opened* true at time 10? Explain.

(g) Suggest an alternative axiomatization for *holds* that has different behavior at times 5 and 10.

(h) Argue for one axiomatization as being more sensible than the other.

Exercise 14.6 Give some concrete specialization operators that can be used for top-down inductive logic programming. They should be defined so that making progress can be evaluated myopically. Explain under what circumstances the operators will make progress.

Exercise 14.7 For the representation of addition in Example 14.20 (page 617), it was assumed that observed z-values would all be digits. Change the representation so that the observed values can be digits, a blank, or *other*. Give appropriate probabilities.

Exercise 14.8 Represent the electrical domain of previous chapters in ICL, so that it will run in AILog. The representation should include the probabilistic dependencies of Example 6.11 (page 238) and the relations of Example 12.11 (page 502).

Part V

The Big Picture

Chapter 15

Retrospect and Prospect

Computation is the fire in our modern-day caves. By 2056, the computational revolution will be recognised as a transformation as significant as the industrial revolution. The evolution and widespread diffusion of computation and its analytical fruits will have major impacts on socioeconomics, science and culture.

– Eric Horvitz [2006]

In this chapter, we stand back and give a big-picture view of what we have covered. By placing many of the representation schemes in the design space we introduced earlier, the relationships among the representations become more apparent. This allows us to see where the frontier of AI research now lies and to get a sense of the evolution of the field. We also consider some of the many social and ethical consequences that have arisen from the development and application of intelligent computational agents. As Horvitz points out in the quote above, computation is changing the world; we must be aware of its positive and negative impacts.

15.1 Dimensions of Complexity Revisited

What has AI research achieved? Where do the current frontier issues lie? To get a systematic sense of the big picture, we use the design space for AI systems presented in Section 1.5 (page 19). There, we described nine dimensions that span part of that design space. In this section, we show how some of the representations presented in the book can be positioned in that space.

Figure 15.1 (on the next page) reviews the dimensions of complexity and extends Figure 1.6 (page 28) to include a key, in terms of numbers of stars, that is used in the subsequent figure.

Dimension	key	Value
Modularity	*	flat
	**	modular
	***	hierarchical
Representation scheme	*	states
	**	features
	***	relations
Planning horizon	*	non-planning
	**	finite stage
	***	indefinite stage
	****	infinite stage
Sensing Uncertainty	*	fully observable
	**	partially observable
Effect Uncertainty	*	deterministic
	**	stochastic
Preference	*	goals
	**	complex preferences
Learning	*	knowledge is given
	**	knowledge is learned
Number of agents	*	single agent
	**	multiple agents
Computational limits	*	perfect rationality
	**	bounded rationality

Figure 15.1: Dimensions of complexity

Figure 15.2 classifies, in terms of the values for each dimension, some of the representations covered in this book.

State-space search, as presented in Chapter 3, allows for an indefinite horizon but otherwise gives the simplest value in all the other dimensions. Regression planning (page 357), using either the feature-based representation or the STRIPS representation, extends state-space search to reason in terms of features. Constraint satisfaction problem (CSP) planning allows for better efficiency but at the cost of planning for only a finite stage.

Decision networks (page 387) allow for the representation of features, stochastic effects, partial observability, and complex preferences in terms of utilities. However, as with CSP planning, these networks only reason for a finite stage planning horizon.

Markov decision processes (MDPs) (page 399) allow for indefinite and infinite stage problems with stochastic actions and complex preferences; however, they are state-based representations that assume the state is fully observable. Partially observable MDPs (POMDPs) (page 411) allow for a partially observable state but are much more difficult to solve. Dynamic decision networks

Dimension	Modularity	Representation Scheme	Planning Horizon	Sensing Uncertainty	Effect Uncertainty	Preference	Learning	Number of Agents	Computational Limits
State-Space Search	*	*	***	*	*	*	*	*	*
Regression Planning	*	**	***	*	*	*	*	*	*
CSP Planning	*	**	**	*	*	*	*	*	*
Decision Networks	*	**	**	**	**	**	*	*	*
MDPs	*	*	****	*	**	**	*	*	*
POMDPs	*	*	****	**	**	**	*	*	*
Dynamic DNs	*	**	****	*	**	**	*	*	*
Multiagent DNs	*	**	**	**	**	**	*	**	*
Policy Improvement	*	*	*	*	*	**	**	**	*
Reinforcement Learning	*	**	****	*	**	**	**	*	*
Situation Calculus	*	***	***	*	*	*	*	*	*
Indep. Choice Logic	*	***	***	**	**	**	*	*	*

Figure 15.2: Some representations rated by dimensions of complexity

(page 409) extend MDPs to allow for a feature-based representation of states. They extend decision networks to allow for indefinite or infinite horizons, but they do not model sensing uncertainty.

Multiagent decision networks (page 428) extend decision networks to allow for multiple agents. The policy improvement algorithm (page 442) allows for learning with multiple agents, but it only allows a single state and a planning horizon of 1 (it plays a repeated single-step game); the only uncertainty is in the actions of the other agents. It can be seen as a reinforcement learning algorithm with a single state but with multiple agents.

Reinforcement learning (page 463) extends MDPs to allow for learning. Reinforcement learning with features is discussed in Section 11.3.9 (page 482).

Situation calculus (page 598) and event calculus (page 604) allow for the representation of individuals and relations and an indefinite planning horizon, but they do not represent uncertainty.

Independent choice logic (page 615) is a relational representation that allows for the representation of uncertainty in the effect of actions, sensing uncertainty, and utilities; however, in this most general framework, reasoning is not efficient.

The dimension that adds the most difficulty to building an agent is sensing uncertainty. Most of the representations that allow sensing uncertainty work by making actions a function of the history of the agent, which only works for finite stages. How to extend planning with sensing uncertainty and indefinite and infinite horizon problems is discussed in the context of POMDPs (page 411), but the suggested solutions rely on explicit states. How to handle sensing in all of its forms is one of the most active areas of current AI research.

None of representations presented in the preceding table handle hierarchical decomposition. However, large bodies of work on hierarchical planning and hierarchical reinforcement learning are not presented in this book.

Bounded rationality underlies many of the approximation methods used for applications; however, making the explicit trade-off between thinking and acting, in which the agent reasons about whether it should act immediately or think more, is still relatively rare.

As can be seen, we have presented a very small part of the design space of AI. The current frontier of research goes well beyond what is covered in this textbook. There is much active research in all areas of AI. There have been and continue to be impressive advances in planning, learning, perception, natural language understanding, robotics, and other subareas of AI. In terms of the dimensions presented here, much of this is very deep work in what is still only a small part of the design space of AI.

A divide has traditionally existed between relational reasoning, typically in terms of first-order logic or frames, and reasoning under uncertainty in terms of probability. This divide is being bridged, but it is still evident in conferences and research papers.

The decomposition of AI into subareas is not surprising. The design space is too big to explore all at once. Once a researcher has decided to handle, say, relational domains and reasoning about the existence of objects, it is difficult to add sensor uncertainty. If a researcher starts with learning with infinite horizons, it is difficult to add features or hierarchical reasoning, let alone learning with infinite horizons and relations together with hierarchies.

Some particular points in design space that have been at the frontier of research over the past few years include the following:

- hierarchical reinforcement learning, where the agent learns at multiple levels of abstraction at once;

- multiagent reinforcement learning;

- relational probabilistic learning;

- natural understanding that takes into account ambiguity, context, and pragmatics to give appropriate answers;

- robot cars that can drive through uncertain environments; and

- intelligent tutoring systems that take into account noisy sensors of students' emotions.

We still do not know how to build an agent that learns about relations for infinite-stage, partially observable domains in which there are multiple agents. Arguably humans do this, perhaps by reasoning hierarchically and approximately. So although we may not yet be able to build an intelligent artificial agent with human-level performance, we seem to have the building blocks to develop one. The main challenge is handling the complexity of the real world. However, so far there seem to be no intrinsic obstacles to building computational embodied agents capable of human-level performance.

15.2 Social and Ethical Consequences

As the science and technology of AI develops, smart artifacts are increasingly being deployed and their widespread deployment will have profound ethical, psychological, social, economic, and legal consequences for human society and our planet. Here we can only raise, and skim the surface of, some of these issues. Artificial autonomous agents are, in one sense, simply the next stage in the development of technology. In that sense, the normal concerns about the impact of technological development apply, but in another sense they represent a profound discontinuity. Autonomous agents perceive, decide, and act on their own. This is a radical, qualitative change in our technology and in our image of technology. This development raises the possibility that these agents could take unanticipated actions beyond our control. As with any disruptive technology, there must be substantial positive and negative consequences – many that will be difficult to judge and many that we simply will not, or cannot, foresee.

The familiar example of the autonomous vehicle is a convenient starting point for consideration. Experimental autonomous vehicles are seen by many as precursors to robot tanks, cargo movers, and automated warfare. Although there may be, in some sense, significant benefits to robotic warfare, there are also very real dangers. Luckily, these are, so far, only the nightmares of science fiction.

Thrun [2006] presents an optimistic view of such vehicles. The positive impact of having intelligent cars would be enormous. Consider the potential ecological savings of using highways so much more efficiently instead of paving over farmland. There is the safety aspect of reducing the annual carnage on the roads: it is estimated that 1.2 million people are killed, and more than 50 million are injured, in traffic accidents each year worldwide. Cars could communicate and negotiate at intersections. Besides the consequent reduction in accidents, there could be up to three times the traffic throughput. Elderly and disabled people would be able to get around on their own. People could dispatch their cars to the parking warehouse autonomously and then recall them later. There would indeed be automated warehouses for autonomous cars instead of using surface land for parking. Truly, the positive implications of success in this area are most encouraging. That there are two radically different, but not inconsistent, scenarios for the outcomes of the development of autonomous vehicles suggests the need for wise ethical consideration of their use. The stuff of science fiction is rapidly becoming science fact.

AI is now mature, both as a science and, in its technologies and applications, as an engineering discipline. Many opportunities exist for AI to have a positive impact on our planet's environment. AI researchers and development engineers have a unique perspective and the skills required to contribute practically to addressing concerns of global warming, poverty, food production, arms control, health, education, the aging population, and demographic issues. We could, as a simple example, improve access to tools for learning about AI so that people could be empowered to try AI techniques on their own problems, rather than relying on experts to build opaque systems for them. Games and competitions based on AI systems can be very effective learning, teaching, and research environments, as shown by the success of RoboCup for robot soccer.

We have already considered some of the environmental impact of intelligent cars and smart traffic control. Work on combinatorial auctions, already applied to spectrum allocation and logistics, could further be applied to supplying carbon offsets and to optimizing energy supply and demand. There could be more work on smart energy controllers using distributed sensors and actuators that would improve energy use in buildings. We could use qualitative modeling techniques for climate scenario modeling. The ideas behind constraint-based systems can be applied to analyze sustainable systems. A system is sustainable if it is in balance with its environment: satisfying short-term and long-term constraints on the resources it consumes and the outputs it produces.

Assistive technology for disabled and aging populations is being pioneered by many researchers. Assisted cognition is one application but also assisted perception and assisted action in the form of, for example, smart wheelchairs and companions for older people and nurses' assistants in long-term care facilities. However, Sharkey [2008] warns of some of the dangers of relying on robotic assistants as companions for the elderly and the very young. As with autonomous vehicles, researchers must ask cogent questions about the use of their creations.

Indeed, can we trust robots? There are some real reasons why we cannot yet rely on robots to do the right thing. They are not fully trustworthy and reliable, given the way they are built now. So, can they do the right thing? Will they do the right thing? What *is* the right thing? In our collective subconscious, the fear exists that eventually robots may become completely autonomous, with free will, intelligence, and consciousness; they may rebel against us as Frankenstein-like monsters.

What about ethics at the robot–human interface? Do we require ethical codes, for us and for them? It seems clear that we do. Many researchers are working on this issue. Indeed, many countries have come to realize that this is an important area of debate. There are already robot liability and insurance issues. There will have to be legislation that targets robot issues. There will have to be professional codes of ethics for robot designers and engineers just as there are for engineers in all other disciplines. We will have to factor the issues around what we should do ethically in designing, building, and deploying robots. How should robots make decisions as they develop more autonomy? What should we do ethically and what ethical issues arise for us as we interact with robots? Should we give them any rights? We have a human rights code; will there be a robot rights code?

To factor these issues, let us break them down into three fundamental questions that must be addressed. First, what should we humans do ethically in designing, building, and deploying robots? Second, how should robots ethically decide, as they develop autonomy and free will, what to do? Third, what ethical issues arise for us as we interact with robots?

In considering these questions we shall consider some interesting, if perhaps naïve, proposals put forward by the science fiction novelist Isaac Asimov [1950], one of the earliest thinkers about these issues. His Laws of Robotics are a good basis from which to start because, at first glance, they seem logical and succinct. His original three Laws are

I. A robot may not harm a human being, or, through inaction, allow a human being to come to harm.

II. A robot must obey the orders given to it by human beings except where such orders would conflict with the First Law.

III. A robot must protect its own existence, as long as such protection does not conflict with the First or Second Laws.

Asimov's answers to the three questions posed above are as follows. First, you must put those laws into every robot and, by law, manufacturers would have to do that. Second, robots should always have to follow the prioritized laws. But he did not say much about the third question. Asimov's plots arise mainly from the conflict between what the humans intend the robot to do and what it actually does; or between literal and sensible interpretations of the laws, because they are not codified in any formal language. Asimov's fiction explored many hidden implicit contradictions in the laws and their consequences.

There is much discussion of robot ethics now, but much of the discussion presupposes technical abilities that we just do not yet have. In fact, Bill Joy [2000] was so concerned about our inability to control the dangers of new technologies that he called, unsuccessfully, for a moratorium on the development of robotics (and AI), nanotechnology, and genetic engineering. In this book we have presented a coherent view of the design space and clarified the design principles for intelligent agents, including robots. We hope this will lead to a more technically informed framework for the development of social and ethical codes for intelligent agents.

However, robotics may not even be the AI technology with the greatest impact. Consider the embedded, ubiquitous, distributed intelligence in the World Wide Web and other global computational networks. This amalgam of human and artificial intelligence can be seen as evolving to become a World Wide Mind. The impact of this global net on the way we discover and communicate new knowledge is already comparable to the effects of the development of the printing press. As Marshall McLuhan argued, "We first shape the tools and thereafter our tools shape us" [McLuhan, 1964]. Although he was thinking more of books, advertising, and television, this concept applies even more to the global net and autonomous agents. The kinds of agents we build, and the kinds of agents we decide to build, will change us as much as they will change our society; we should make sure it is for the better. Margaret Somerville [2006] is an ethicist who argues that the species *Homo sapiens* is evolving into *Techno sapiens* as we project our abilities out into our technology at an accelerating rate. Many of our old social and ethical codes are broken; they do not work in this new world. As creators of the new science and technology of AI, it is our joint responsibility to pay serious attention.

15.3   References and Further Reading

Hierarchical planning is discussed by Nau [2007]. Hierarchical reinforcement learning is covered by Dietterich [2000]. Multiagent reinforcement learning is addressed by Stone [2007].

Mackworth [2009] presents some of the dangers and potential of AI.

The dangers of robotic warfare are outlined by Sharkey [2008] and Singer [2009a,b]. The estimate of traffic accidents is from Peden [2004] and the estimate of the increase in traffic throughput is from Dresner and Stone [2008].

The development of RoboCup is sketched by Visser and Burkhard [2007].

Assistive technology systems are described by Pollack [2005], Liu, Hile, Kautz, Borriello, Brown, Harniss, and Johnson [2006] and Yang, and Mackworth [2007]. Smart wheelchairs are discussed by Mihailidis, Boger, Candido, and Hoey [2007] and Viswanathan, Mackworth, Little, and Mihailidis [2007].

Shelley [1818] wrote about Dr. Frankenstein and his monster. Anderson and Leigh Anderson [2007] discusses robot ethics. World Wide Mind is cited by Hillis [2008] and Kelly [2008].

Mathematical Preliminaries and Notation

This appendix gives some definitions of fundamental mathematical concepts that are used in AI, but are traditionally taught in other courses. It also introduces some notation and data structures that are used in various parts of the book.

A.1 Discrete Mathematics

The mathematical concepts we build on include:

sets A **set** has elements (members). We write $s \in S$ if s is an element of set S. The elements in a set define the set, so that two sets are equal if they have the same elements.

tuples An n-tuple is an ordered grouping of n elements, written $\langle x_1, \ldots, x_n \rangle$. A 2-tuple is a **pair**, and a 3-tuple is a **triple**. Two n-tuples are equal if they have the same members in the corresponding positions. If S is a set, S^n is the set of n-tuples $\langle x_1, \ldots, x_n \rangle$ where x_i is a member of S. $S_1 \times S_2 \times \cdots \times S_n$ is the set of n-tuples $\langle x_1, \ldots, x_n \rangle$ where each x_i is in S_i.

relations A **relation** is a set of n-tuples. The tuples in the relation are said to be *true* of the relation.

functions A **function**, or **mapping**, f from set D, the **domain** of f, into set R, the **range** of f, written $f : D \rightarrow R$, is a subset of $D \times R$ such that for every $d \in D$ there is a unique $r \in R$ such that $\langle d, r \rangle \in f$. We write $f(d) = r$ if $\langle d, r \rangle \in f$.

While these may seem like obscure definitions for common-sense concepts, you can now use the common-sense concepts comfortable in the knowledge that if you are unsure about something, you can check the definitions.

A.2 Functions, Factors, and Arrays

Many of the algorithms in this book manipulate representations of functions. We extend the standard definition of function on sets to include functions on (sets of) variables. A **factor** is a representation of a function. An **array** is an explicit representation of a function that can have its individual components modified.

If S is a set, we write $f(S)$ to be a function, with domain S. Thus, if $c \in S$, then $f(c)$ is a value in the range of f. $f[S]$ is like $f(S)$, but individual components can be updated. This notation is based on that of C and Java (but these languages only allow for the case where S is the set of integers $\{0, \ldots, n-1\}$ for arrays of size n). Thus $f[c]$ is a value in the range of f. If $f[c]$ is assigned a new value, it will return that new value.

This notation can be extended to (algebraic) variables. If X is an algebraic variable with domain D, then $f(X)$ is a function that given a value $x \in D$, returns a value in the range of f. This value is often written as $f(X = x)$ or simply as $f(x)$. Similarly, $f[X]$ is an array indexed by X, that is, it is a function of X whose components can be modified.

This notation can also be extended to set of variables. $f(X_1, X_2, \ldots, X_n)$ is a function such that given a value v_1 for X_1, a value v_2 for X_2, $\ldots$, and a value v_n for X_n returns a value in the range of f. Note that it is the name of the variable that is important, not the position. This factor applied to the specific values is written as $f(X_1 = v_1, X_2 = v_2, \ldots, X_n = v_n)$. The set of variables, $X_1, X_2, \ldots, X_n$ is called the **scope** of f. The array $f[X_1, X_2, \ldots, X_n]$ is a function on $X_1, X_2, \ldots, X_n$ where the values can be updated.

Assigning just some of the variables gives a function on the remaining variables. Thus, for example, if f is a function with scope $X_1, X_2, \ldots, X_n$, then $f(X_1 = v_1)$ is a function of $X_2, \ldots, X_n$, such that

$$(f(X_1 = v_1))(X_2 = v_2, \ldots, X_n = v_n) = f(X_1 = v_1, X_2 = v_2, \ldots, X_n = v_n)$$

Factors can be added, multiplied or composed with any other operation level on the elements. If f_1 and f_2 is a factor, then $f_1 + f_2$ is a factor with scope the union of the scopes of f_1 and f_2, defined pointwise:

$$(f_1 + f_2)(X_1 = v_1, X_2 = v_2, \ldots, X_n = v_n)$$
$$= f_1(X_1 = v_1, X_2 = v_2, \ldots, X_n = v_n) + f_2(X_1 = v_1, X_2 = v_2, \ldots, X_n = v_n)$$

where we assume that f_1 and f_2 ignore variables not in their scope. Multiplication and other binary operators work similarly.

Example 1.1 Suppose $f_1(X, Y) = X + Y$ and $f_2(Y, Z) = Y + Z$. Then $f_1 + f_2$ is $X + 2Y + Z$, which is a function of X, Y and Z. Similarly $f_1 \times f_2 = (X + Y) \times (Y + Z)$.

$f_1(X = 2)$ is a function of Y, defined by $2 + Y$.

Suppose that variable W has domain $\{0,1\}$ and X has domain $\{1,2\}$, the factor $f_3(W,X)$ can be defined by a table such as:

W	X	value
0	1	2
0	2	1
1	1	0
1	2	3

$f_3 + f_1$ is a function on W, X, Y, such that, for example,

$$(f_3 + f_1)(W = 1, X = 2, Y = 3) = 3 + 5 = 8$$

Similarly, $(f_3 \times f_1)(W = 1, X = 2, Y = 3) = 3 \times 5 = 15$.

Other operations on factors are defined in the book.

A.3 Relations and the Relational Algebra

Relations are common in AI and database systems. The **relational algebra** defines operations on relations and is the basis of relational databases.

A **scope** S is a set of variables. A **tuple** t on scope S, has a value on each variable in its scope. We write $val(t, X)$ to be the value of tuple t on variable X. The value of $val(t, X)$ must be in $dom(X)$. This is like the mathematical notion of tuple, except the index is given by a variable, not by an integer.

A **relation** is a set of tuples, all with the same scope. A relation is often given a name. The scope of the tuples is often called the relation **scheme**. A **relational database** is a set of relations. A scheme of a relational database is the set of pairs of relation names and relation schemes.

A relation with scope $X_1, \ldots, X_n$ can be seen as a Boolean factor on $X_1, \ldots, X_n$, where the true elements are represented as tuples.

Often a relation is written as a table.

Example 1.2 The following is a tabular depiction of a relation, *enrolled*:

Course	Year	Student	Grade
cs322	2008	fran	77
cs111	2009	billie	88
cs111	2009	jess	78
cs444	2008	fran	83
cs322	2009	jordan	92

The heading gives the scheme, namely $\{Course, Year, Student, Grade\}$, and every other row is a tuple. The first tuple, call it t_1 is defined by $val(t_1, Course) = cs322$, $val(t_1, Year) = 2008$, $val(t_1, Student) = fran$, $val(t_1, Grade) = 77$.

The order of the columns and the order of the rows is not significant.

If r a relation with scheme S, and c is a condition on the variables in S, the **selection** of c in r, written $\sigma_c(r)$, is the set of tuples in r for which c holds. The selection has the same scheme as r.

If r is a relation with scheme S, and $S_0 \subseteq S$, the **projection** of r onto S_0, written $\pi_{S_0}(r)$, is the set of tuples of r where the scope is restricted to S_0.

Example 1.3 Suppose *enrolled* is the relation given in Example A.2.

The relation $\sigma_{Grade>79}(enrolled)$ selects those tuples in *enrolled* where the grade is over 79. This is the relation:

Course	Year	Student	Grade
cs111	2009	billie	88
cs444	2008	fran	83
cs322	2009	jordan	92

The relation $\pi_{\{Student,Year\}}(enrolled)$ specifies what years students were enrolled:

Student	Year
fran	2008
billie	2009
jess	2009
jordan	2009

Notice how the first and the fourth tuple of *enrolled* become the same tuple in the projection; they represent the same function on $\{Student, Year\}$.

If two relations on the same scheme, the **union, intersection** and **set difference** of these are defined as the corresponding operations on the set of tuples.

If r_1 and r_2 are two relations, the natural **join** of r_1 and r_2, written $r_1 \bowtie r_2$ is a relation where

- the scheme of the join is the union of the scheme of r_1 and the scheme of r_2,
- a tuple is in the join, if the tuple restricted to the scope of r_1 is in the relation r_1 and the tuple restricted to the scope of r_2 is in the relation r_2.

Example 1.4 Consider the relation *assisted*:

Course	Year	TA
cs322	2008	yuki
cs111	2009	sam
cs111	2009	chris
cs322	2009	yuki

The join of *enrolled* and *assisted*, written *enrolled* $\bowtie$ *assisted* is the relation:

Course	Year	Student	Grade	TA
cs322	2008	fran	77	yuki
cs111	2009	billie	88	sam
cs111	2009	jess	78	sam
cs111	2009	billie	88	chris
cs111	2009	jess	78	chris
cs322	2009	jordan	92	yuki

Note how in the join, the information about *cs444* was lost, as there was no TA in that course.

Bibliography

Aamodt, A. and Plaza, E. (1994). Case-based reasoning: foundational issues, methodological variations, and system approaches. *AI Communications*, 7(1): 39–59. 341

Abelson, H. and DiSessa, A. (1981). *Turtle Geometry: The Computer as a Medium for Exploring Mathematics*. MIT Press, Cambridge, MA. 66

Abramson, H. and Rogers, M.H. (Eds.) (1989). *Meta-Programming in Logic Programming*. MIT Press, Cambridge, MA. 592

Agre, P.E. (1995). Computational research on interaction and agency. *Artificial Intelligence*, 72: 1–52. 66

Aha, D.W., Marling, C., and Watson, I. (Eds.) (2005). *The Knowledge Engineering Review, special edition on case-based reasoning*, volume 20 (3). Cambridge University Press. 341

Albus, J.S. (1981). *Brains, Behavior and Robotics*. BYTE Publications, Peterborough, NH. 66

Allais, M. and Hagen, O. (Eds.) (1979). *Expected Utility Hypothesis and the Allais Paradox*. Reidel, Boston, MA. 380

Allen, J., Hendler, J., and Tate, A. (Eds.) (1990). *Readings in Planning*. Morgan Kaufmann, San Mateo, CA. 367

Anderson, M. and Leigh Anderson, S.L. (2007). Machine ethics: Creating an ethical intelligent agent. *AI Magazine*, 28(4): 15–26. 632

Andrieu, C., de Freitas, N., Doucet, A., and Jordan, M.I. (2003). An introduction to MCMC for machine learning. *Machine Learning*, 50(1–2): 5–43. 275

Antoniou, G. and van Harmelen, F. (2008). *A Semantic Web Primer*. MIT Pres, Cambridge, MA, 2nd edition. 591

Apt, K. and Bol, R. (1994). Logic programming and negation: A survey. *Journal of Logic Programming*, 19,20: 9–71. 207, 542

Aristotle (350 B.C.). *Categories*. Translated by E. M. Edghill, http://www.classicallibrary.org/Aristotle/categories/. 567

Asimov, I. (1950). *I, Robot*. Doubleday, Garden City, NY. 631

Bacchus, F. and Grove, A. (1995). Graphical models for preference and utility. In *Uncertainty in Artificial Intelligence (UAI-95)*, pp. 3–10. 413

Bacchus, F., Grove, A.J., Halpern, J.Y., and Koller, D. (1996). From statistical knowledge bases to degrees of belief. *Artificial Intelligence*, 87(1-2): 75–143. 274

Bacchus, F. and Kabanza, F. (1996). Using temporal logic to control search in a forward chaining planner. In M. Ghallab and A. Milani (Eds.), *New Directions in AI Planning*, pp. 141–153. ISO Press, Amsterdam. 367

Bäck, T. (1996). *Evolutionary Algorithms in Theory and Practice*. Oxford University Press, New York, NY. 152

Ballard, B.W. (1983). The *-minimax search procedure for trees containing chance nodes. *Artificial Intelligence*, 21(3): 327–350. 449

Baum, E.B. (2004). *What is Thought?* MIT Press. 491

Bayes, T. (1763). An essay towards solving a problem in the doctrine of chances. *Philosophical Transactions of the Royal Society of London*, 53: 370–418. Reprinted in *Biometrika* 45, 298–315, 1958. Reprinted in S. J. Press, *Bayesian Statistics*, 189–217, Wiley, New York, 1989. 340

Beckett, D. and Berners-Lee (2008). Turtle – terse RDF triple language. http://www.w3 .org/TeamSubmission/turtle/. 592

Bell, J.L. and Machover, M. (1977). *A Course in Mathematical Logic*. North-Holland, Amsterdam. 207

Bellman, R. (1957). *Dynamic Programming*. Princeton University Press, Princeton, NJ. 413

Bernardo, J.M. and Smith, A.F.M. (1994). *Bayesian Theory*. Wiley. 341

Berners-Lee, T., Hendler, J., and Lassila, O. (2001). The semantic web: A new form of web content that is meaningful to computers will unleash a revolution of new possibilities. *Scientific American*, pp. 28–37. 591

Bertelè, U. and Brioschi, F. (1972). *Nonserial dynamic programming*, volume 91 of *Mathematics in Science and Engineering*. Academic Press. 151

Bertsekas, D.P. (1995). *Dynamic Programming and Optimal Control*. Athena Scientific, Belmont, Massachusetts. Two volumes. 413

Bertsekas, D.P. and Tsitsiklis, J.N. (1996). *Neuro-Dynamic Programming*. Athena Scientific, Belmont, Massachusetts. 486

Besnard, P. and Hunter, A. (2008). *Elements Of Argumentation*. MIT Press, Cambridge, MA. 208

Bishop, C.M. (1995). *Neural Networks for Pattern Recognition*. Oxford University Press, Oxford, England. 341

Bishop, C.M. (2008). *Pattern Recognition and Machine Learning*. Springer-Verlag, New York. 341

Blum, A. and Furst, M. (1997). Fast planning through planning graph analysis. *Artificial Intelligence*, 90: 281–300. 367

Bobrow, D.G. (1993). Artificial intelligence in perspective: a retrospective on fifty volumes of Artificial Intelligence. *Artificial Intelligence*, 59: 5–20. 41

Bobrow, D.G. (1967). Natural language input for a computer problem solving system. In M. Minsky (Ed.), *Semantic Information Processing*, pp. 133–215. MIT Press, Cambridge MA. 8

Boddy, M. and Dean, T.L. (1994). Deliberation scheduling for problem solving in time-constrained environments. *Artificial Intelligence*, 67(2): 245–285. 41

Bodlaender, H.L. (1993). A tourist guide through treewidth. *Acta Cybernetica*, 11(1-2): 1–21. 274

Boutilier, C., Brafman, R.I., Domshlak, C., Hoos, H.H., and Poole, D. (2004). Cp-nets: A tool for representing and reasoning with conditional ceteris paribus preference statements. *Journal of Artificial Intelligence Research*, 21: 135–191. 413

Boutilier, C., Dean, T., and Hanks, S. (1999). Decision-theoretic planning: Structual assumptions and computational leverage. *Journal of Artificial Intelligence Research*, 11: 1–94. 413

Bowen, K.A. (1985). Meta-level programming and knowledge representation. *New Generation Computing*, 3(4): 359–383. 592

Bowling, M. and Veloso, M. (2002). Multiagent learning using a variable learning rate. *Artificial Intelligence*, 136(2): 215–250. 449

Brachman, R.J. and Levesque, H.J. (Eds.) (1985). *Readings in Knowledge Representation*. Morgan Kaufmann, San Mateo, CA. 41, 591, 646

Brachman, R. and Levesque, H. (2004). *Knowledge Representation and Reasoning*. Morgan Kaufmann. 591, 618

Breiman, L., Friedman, J.H., Olshen, R.A., and Stone, C.J. (1984). *Classification and Regression Trees*. Wadsworth and Brooks, Monterey, CA. 341

Briscoe, G. and Caelli, T. (1996). *A Compendium of Machine Learning, Volume 1: Symbolic Machine Learning*. Ablex, Norwood, NJ. 341

Brooks, R.A. (1986). A robust layered control system for a mobile robot. *IEEE Journal of Robotics and Automation*, 2(1): 14–23. Reprinted in Shafer and Pearl [1990]. 66

Brooks, R.A. (1991). Intelligence without representation. *Artificial Intelligence*, 47: 139–159. 66

Brooks, R. (1990). Elephants don't play chess. *Robotics and Autonomous Systems*, 6: 3–15. 41

Bryce, D. and Kambhampati, S. (2007). A tutorial on planning graph based reachability heuristics. *AI Magazine*, 28(47-83): 1. 367

Buchanan, B. and Shortliffe, E. (Eds.) (1984). *Rule-Based Expert Systems: The MYCIN Experiments of the Stanford Heuristic Programming Project*. Addison-Wesley, Reading, MA. 9

Buchanan, B.G. and Feigenbaum, E.A. (1978). Dendral and meta-dendral: Their applications dimension. *Artificial Intelligence*, 11: 5–24. 9

Buchanan, B.G. (2005). A (very) brief history of artificial intelligence. *AI Magazine*, 26(4): 53–60. 3

Buntine, W. (1992). Learning classification trees. *Statistics and Computing*, 2: 63–73. 341

Burch, R. (2008). Charles Sanders Peirce. *The Stanford Encyclopedia of Philosophy*. http://plato.stanford.edu/archives/spr2008/entries/peirce/. 207

Campbell, M., Hoane Jr., A.J., and Hse, F.h. (2002). Deep blue. *Artificial Intelligence*, 134(1-2): 57–83. 449

Castillo, E., Gutiérrez, J.M., and Hadi, A.S. (1996). *Expert Systems and Probabilistic Network Models*. Springer Verlag, New York. 274

Chapman, D. (1987). Planning for conjunctive goals. *Artificial Intelligence*, 32(3): 333–377. 367

Cheeseman, P. (1990). On finding the most probable model. In J. Shranger and P. Langley (Eds.), *Computational Models of Scientific Discovery and Theory Formation*, chapter 3, pp. 73–95. Morgan Kaufmann, San Mateo, CA. 341

Cheeseman, P., Kelly, J., Self, M., Stutz, J., Taylor, W., and Freeman, D. (1988). Autoclass: A Bayesian classification system. In *Proc. Fifth International Conference on Machine Learning*, pp. 54–64. Ann Arbor, MI. Reprinted in Shavlik and Dietterich [1990]. 486

Cheng, J. and Druzdzel, M. (2000). AIS-BN: An adaptive importance sampling algorithm for evidential reasoning in large Bayesian networks. *Journal of Artificial Intelligence Research*, 13: 155–188. 275

Chesnevar, C., Maguitman, A., and Loui, R. (2000). Logical models of argument. *ACM Comput. Surv.*, 32(4): 337–383. 208

Chomsky, N. (1957). *Syntactic Structures*. Mouton and Co., The Hague. 521

Chrisley, R. and Begeer, S. (2000). *Artificial intelligence: Critical Concepts in Cognitive Science*. Routledge, London and New York. 41, 645

Clark, K.L. (1978). Negation as failure. In H. Gallaire and J. Minker (Eds.), *Logic and Databases*, pp. 293–322. Plenum Press, New York. 207, 542

Cohen, P.R. (2005). If not Turing's test, then what? *AI Magazine*, 26(4): 61–67. 40

Colmerauer, A., Kanoui, H., Roussel, P., and Pasero, R. (1973). Un système de communication homme-machine en français. Technical report, Groupe de Researche en Intelligence Artificielle, Université d'Aix-Marseille. 207

Colmerauer, A. and Roussel, P. (1996). The birth of Prolog. In T.J. Bergin and R.G. Gibson (Eds.), *History of Programming Languages*. ACM Press/Addison-Wesley. 9, 542

Copi, I.M. (1982). *Introduction to Logic*. Macmillan, New York, sixth edition. 207

Cormen, T.H., Leiserson, C.E., Rivest, R.L., and Stein, C. (2001). *Introduction to Algorithms*. MIT Press and McGraw-Hill, second edition. 106

Cover, T.M. and Thomas, J.A. (1991). *Elements of information theory*. Wiley, New York. 275

Culberson, J. and Schaeffer, J. (1998). Pattern databases. *Computational Intelligence*, 14(3): 318–334. 106

Dahl, V. (1994). Natural language processing and logic programming. *Journal of Logic Programming*, 19,20: 681–714. 542

Darwiche, A. (2009). *Modeling and Reasoning with Bayesian Networks*. Cambridge University Press. 274, 486

Dasarathy, B.V. (1991). NN concepts and techniques. In B.V. Dasarathy (Ed.), *Nearest Neighbour (NN) Norms: NN Pattern Classification Techniques*, pp. 1–30. IEEE Computer Society Press, New York. 341

Davis, E. (1990). *Representations of Commonsense Knowledge*. Morgan Kaufmann, San Mateo, CA. 591

Davis, J. and Goadrich, M. (2006). The relationship between precision-recall and roc curves. In *Proceedings of the 23rd international conference on Machine Learning*, pp. 233–240. 341

Davis, M., Logemann, G., and Loveland, D. (1962). A machine program for theorem proving. *Communications of the ACM*, 5(7): 394–397. 151

Davis, M. and Putnam, H. (1960). A computing procedure for quantification theory. *Journal of the ACM*, 7(3): 201–215. 151

de Kleer, J. (1986). An assumption-based TMS. *Artificial Intelligence*, 28(2): 127–162. 207, 208

de Kleer, J., Mackworth, A.K., and Reiter, R. (1992). Characterizing diagnoses and systems. *Artificial Intelligence*, 56: 197–222. 207

De Raedt, L., Frasconi, P., Kersting, K., and Muggleton, S.H. (Eds.) (2008). *Probabilistic Inductive Logic Programming*. Springer. 620

Dean, T. and Kanazawa, K. (1989). A model for reasoning about persistence and causation. *Computational Intelligence*, 5(3): 142–150. 275

Dean, T.L. and Wellman, M.P. (1991). *Planning and Control*. Morgan Kaufmann, San Mateo, CA. 41, 66

Dechter, R. (1996). Bucket elimination: A unifying framework for probabilistic inference. In E. Horvitz and F. Jensen (Eds.), *Proc. Twelfth Conf. on Uncertainty in Artificial Intelligence (UAI-96)*, pp. 211–219. Portland, OR. 274

Dechter, R. (2003). *Constraint Processing*. Morgan Kaufmann. 151

Dellaert, F., Fox, D., Burgard, W., and Thrun, S. (1999). Monte Carlo localization for mobile robots. In *IEEE International Conference on Robotics and Automation (ICRA99)*. 275

Dietterich, T.G. (2000). Hierarchical reinforcement learning with the maxq value function decomposition. *Journal of Artificial Intelligence Research*, 13: 227–303. 632

Dietterich, T.G. (2002). Ensemble learning. In M. Arbib (Ed.), *The Handbook of Brain Theory and Neural Networks*, pp. 405–408. MIT Press, Cambridge, MA, second edition. 341

Dijkstra, E.W. (1976). *A discipline of programming*. Prentice-Hall, Englewood Cliffs, NJ. 367

Dijkstra, E.W. (1959). A note on two problems in connexion with graphs. *Numerische Mathematik*, 1: 269–271. 106

Doucet, A., de Freitas, N., and Gordon, N. (Eds.) (2001). *Sequential Monte Carlo in Practice*. Springer-Verlag. 275

Doyle, J. (1979). A truth maintenance system. AI Memo 521, MIT Artificial Intelligence Laboratory. 207

Dresner, K. and Stone, P. (2008). A multiagent approach to autonomous intersection management. *Journal of Artificial Intelligence Research*, 31: 591–656. 632

Duda, R.O., Hart, P.E., and Stork, D.G. (2001). *Pattern Classification*. Wiley-Interscience, 2nd edition. 341, 486

Dung, P. (1995). On the acceptability of arguments and its fundamental role in nonmonotonic reasoning, logic programming and n-person games. *Artificial Intelligence*, 77(2): 321–357. 207

Dung, P., Mancarella, P., and Toni, F. (2007). Computing ideal sceptical argumentation. *Artificial Intelligence*, 171(10-15): 642–674. 207

Edwards, P. (Ed.) (1967). *The Encyclopedia of Philosophy*. Macmillan, New York. 287

Enderton, H.B. (1972). *A Mathematical Introduction to Logic*. Academic Press, Orlando, FL. 207

Felner, A., Korf, R.E., and Hanan, S. (2004). Additive pattern database heuristics. *Journal of Artificial Intelligence Research (JAIR)*, 22: 279–318. 106

Fikes, R.E. and Nilsson, N.J. (1971). STRIPS: A new approach to the application of theorem proving to problem solving. *Artificial Intelligence*, 2(3-4): 189–208. 367

Fisher, D. (1987). Knowledge acquisition via incremental conceptual clustering. *Machine Learning*, 2: 139–172. Reprinted in Shavlik and Dietterich [1990]. 486

Forbus, K.D. (1996). Qualitative reasoning. In *CRC Hand-book of Computer Science and Engineering*. CRC Press. 66

Freuder, E.C. and Mackworth, A.K. (2006). Constraint satisfaction: An emerging paradigm. In P.V.B. F. Rossi and T. Walsh (Eds.), *Handbook of Constraint Programming*, pp. 13–28. Elsevier. 151

Friedman, N. and Goldszmidt, M. (1996a). Building classifiers using Bayesian networks. In *Proc. 13th National Conference on Artificial Intelligence*, pp. 1277–1284. Portland, OR. 486

Friedman, N. and Goldszmidt, M. (1996b). Learning Bayesian networks with local structure. In *Proc. Twelfth Conf. on Uncertainty in Artificial Intelligence (UAI-96)*, pp. 252–262. 486

Friedman, N., Greiger, D., and Goldszmidt, M. (1997). Bayesian network classifiers. *Machine Learning*, 29: 103–130. 341

Gabbay, D.M., Hogger, C.J., and Robinson, J.A. (Eds.) (1993). *Handbook of Logic in Artificial Intelligence and Logic Programming*. Clarendon Press, Oxford, England. 5 volumes. 207

Gangemi, A., Guarino, N., Masolo, C., and Oltramari, A. (2003). Sweetening wordnet with dolce. *AI Magazine*, 24(3): 13–24. 592

Garcia-Molina, H., Ullman, J.D., and Widom, J. (2009). *Database Systems: The Complete Book*. Prentice Hall, 2nd edition. 542

Gardner, H. (1985). *The Mind's New Science*. Basic Books, New York. 41

Gelman, A., Carlin, J.B., Stern, H.S., and Rubin, D.B. (2004). *Bayesian Data Analysis*. Chapman and Hall/CRC, 2nd edition. 341

Getoor, L. and Taskar, B. (Eds.) (2007). *Introduction to Statistical Relational Learning*. MIT Press, Cambridge, MA. 620

Goldberg, D.E. (1989). *Genetic Algorithms in Search, Optimization and Machine Learning*. Addison-Wesley, Reading, MA. 152

Goldberg, D.E. (2002). *The Design of Innovation: Lessons from and for Competent Genetic Algorithms*. Addison-Wesley, Reading, MA. 152

Green, C. (1969). Application of theorem proving to problem solving. In *Proc. 1st International Joint Conf. on Artificial Intelligence*, pp. 219–237. Washington, DC. Reprinted in Webber and Nilsson [1981]. 207

Grenon, P. and Smith, B. (2004). Snap and span: Towards dynamic spatial ontology. *Spatial Cognition and Computation*, 4(1): 69–103. 592

Grünwald, P.D. (2007). *The Minimum Description Length Principle*. The MIT Press, Cambridge, MA. 275, 341

Halpern, J. (1997). A logical approach to reasoning about uncertainty: A tutorial. In X. Arrazola, K. Kortha, and F. Pelletier (Eds.), *Discourse, Interaction and Communication*. Kluwer. 274

Hart, P.E., Nilsson, N.J., and Raphael, B. (1968). A formal basis for the heuristic determination of minimum cost paths. *IEEE Transactions on Systems Science and Cybernetics*, 4(2): 100–107. 106

Hart, T.P. and Edwards, D.J. (1961). The tree prune (TP) algorithm. Memo 30, MIT Artificial Intelligence Project, Cambridge MA. 449

Hastie, T., Tibshirani, R., and Friedman, J. (2009). *The Elements of Statistical Learning: Data Mining, Inference, and Prediction*. Springer, second edition. 341

Haugeland, J. (1985). *Artificial Intelligence: The Very Idea*. MIT Press, Cambridge, MA. 6, 41, 66

Haugeland, J. (Ed.) (1997). *Mind Design II: Philosohpy, Psycholgy, Artificial Intelligence*. MIT Press, Cambridge, MA, revised and enlarged edition. 40, 646, 647, 651

Haussler, D. (1988). Quantifying inductive bias: AI learning algorithms and Valiant's learning framework. *Artificial Intelligence*, 36(2): 177–221. Reprinted in Shavlik and Dietterich [1990]. 341

Hayes, P.J. (1973). Computation and deduction. In *Proc. 2nd Symposium on Mathematical Foundations of Computer Science*, pp. 105–118. Czechoslovak Academy of Sciences. 207

Heckerman, D. (1999). A tutorial on learning with Bayesian networks. In M. Jordan (Ed.), *Learning in Graphical Models*. MIT press. 486

Hendler, J., Berners-Lee, T., and Miller, E. (2002). Integrating applications on the semantic web. *Journal of the Institute of Electrical Engineers of Japan*, 122(10): 676–680. 591

Henrion, M. (1988). Propagating uncertainty in Bayesian networks by probabilistic logic sampling. In J.F. Lemmer and L.N. Kanal (Eds.), *Uncertainty in Artificial Intelligence 2*, pp. 149–163. Elsevier Science Publishers B.V. 275

Hertz, J., Krogh, A., and Palmer, R.G. (1991). *Introduction to the Theory of Neural Computation*. Lecture Notes, Volume I, Santa Fe Institute Studies in the Sciences of Complexity. Addison-Wesley, Reading, MA. 341

Hewitt, C. (1969). Planner: A language for proving theorems in robots. In *Proc. 1st International Joint Conf. on Artificial Intelligence*, pp. 295–301. Washington, DC. 207

Hillis, W.D. (2008). A forebrain for the world mind. *Edge: World Question Center*. http://www.edge.org/q2009/q09_12.html#hillis. 632

Hitzler, P., Krötzsch, M., Parsia, B., Patel-Schneider, P.F., and Rudolph, S. (2009). *OWL 2 Web Ontology Language Primer*. W3C. http://www.w3.org/TR/owl2-primer/. 592

Hobbs, J.R., Stickel, M.E., Appelt, D.E., and Martin, P. (1993). Interpretation as abduction. *Artificial Intelligence*, 63(1–2): 69–142. 207

Holland, J.H. (1975). *Adaption in Natural and Artificial Systems: an introductory analysis with applications to biology, control, and artificial intelligence*. University of Michigan Press, Ann Arbor, MI. 152

Hoos, H.H. and Stützle, T. (2004). *Stochastic Local Search: Foundations and Applications*. Morgan Kaufmann / Elsevier. 152

Horvitz, E.J. (1989). Reasoning about beliefs and actions under computational resource constraints. In L. Kanal, T. Levitt, and J. Lemmer (Eds.), *Uncertainty in Artificial Intelligence 3*, pp. 301–324. Elsevier, New York. 41

Horvitz, E. (2006). Eric Horvitz forecasts the future. *New Scientist*, 2578: 72. 625

Howard, R.A. and Matheson, J.E. (1984). Influence diagrams. In R.A. Howard and J.E. Matheson (Eds.), *The Principles and Applications of Decision Analysis*. Strategic Decisions Group, Menlo Park, CA. 413

Howson, C. and Urbach, P. (2006). *Scientific Reasoning: the Bayesian Approach*. Open Court, Chicago, Illinois, 3rd edition. 341

Jaynes, E.T. (2003). *Probability Theory: The Logic of Science*. Cambridge University Press. 341

Jensen, F.V. (1996). *An Introduction to Bayesian Networks*. Springer Verlag, New York. 274

Jordan, M. and Bishop, C. (1996). Neural networks. Memo 1562, MIT Artificial Intelligence Lab, Cambridge, MA. 341

Joy, B. (2000). Why the future doesn't need us. *Wired*. http://www.wired.com/wired/archive/8.04/joy.html. 631

Jurafsky, D. and Martin, J.H. (2008). *Speech and Language Processing: An Introduction to Natural Language Processing, Computational Linguistics, and Speech Recognition*. Prentice Hall, second edition. 542

Kaelbling, L.P., Littman, M.L., and Moore, A.W. (1996). Reinforcement learning: A survey. *Journal of Artificial Intelligence Research*, 4: 237–285. 486

Kakas, A. and Denecker, M. (2002). Abduction in logic programming. In A. Kakas and F. Sadri (Eds.), *Computational Logic: Logic Programming and Beyond*, number 2407 in LNAI, pp. 402–436. Springer Verlag. 207

Kakas, A.C., Kowalski, R.A., and Toni, F. (1993). Abductive logic programming. *Journal of Logic and Computation*, 2(6): 719–770. 207

Kambhampati, S., Knoblock, C.A., and Yang, Q. (1995). Planning as refinement search: a unified framework for evaluating design tradeoffs in partial order planning. *Artificial Intelligence*, 76: 167–238. Special issue on Planning and Scheduling. 367

Kautz, H. and Selman, B. (1996). Pushing the envelope: Planning, propositional logic and stochastic search. In *Proc. 13th National Conference on Artificial Intelligence*, pp. 1194–1201. Portland, OR. 367

Kearns, M. and Vazirani, U. (1994). *An Introduction to Computational Learning Theory*. MIT Press, Cambridge, MA. 341

Keeney, R.L. and Raiffa, H. (1976). *Decisions with Multiple Objectives*. John Wiley and Sons. 413

Kelly, K. (2008). A new kind of mind. *Edge: World Question Center*. http://www.edge.org/q2009/q09_1.html#kelly. 632

Kirkpatrick, S., Gelatt, C.D., and Vecchi, M.P. (1983). Optimization by simulated annealing. *Science*, 220: 671–680. 152

Kirsh, D. (1991a). Foundations of AI: the big issues. *Artificial Intelligence*, 47: 3–30. 41

Kirsh, D. (1991b). Today the earwig, tomorrow man? *Artificial Intelligence*, 47: 161–184. 66

Knuth, D.E. and Moore, R.W. (1975). An analysis of alpha-beta pruning. *Artificial Intelligence*, 6(4): 293–326. 449

Koller, D. and Friedman, N. (2009). *Probabilsitic Graphical Models: Principles and Techniques*. MIT Press. 274, 486

Koller, D. and Milch, B. (2003). Multi-agent influence diagrams for representing and solving games. *Games and Economic Behavior*, 45(1): 181–221. 449

Kolodner, J. and Leake, D. (1996). A tutorial introduction to case-based reasoning. In D. Leake (Ed.), *Case-Based Reasoning: Experiences, Lessons, and Future Directions*, pp. 31–65. AAAI Press/MIT Press. 341

Korf, K.E. (1985). Depth-first iterative deepening: An optimal admissible tree search. *Artificial Intelligence*, 27(1): 97–109. 106

Kowalski, R. (1979). *Logic for Problem Solving*. Artificial Intelligence Series. North-Holland, New York. 542, 592, 618

Kowalski, R. and Sergot, M. (1986). A logic-based calculus of events. *New Generation Computing*, 4(1): 67–95. 620

Kowalski, R.A. (1974). Predicate logic as a programming language. In *Information Processing 74*, pp. 569–574. North-Holland, Stockholm. 207

Kowalski, R.A. (1988). The early history of logic programming. *CACM*, 31(1): 38–43. 9, 542

Koza, J.R. (1992). *Genetic Programming: On the Programming of Computers by Means of Natural Selection*. MIT Press, Cambridge, MA. 152

Kuipers, B. (2001). Qualitative simulation. In R.A. Meyers (Ed.), *Encyclopedia of Physical Science and Technology*, pp. 287–300. Academic Press, NY, third edition. 66

Langley, P., Iba, W., and Thompson, K. (1992). An analysis of Bayesian classifiers. In *Proc. 10th National Conference on Artificial Intelligence*, pp. 223–228. San Jose, CA. 486

Laplace, P. (1812). *Théorie Analytique de Probabilités*. Courcier, Paris. 219, 223, 296

Latombe, J.C. (1991). *Robot Motion Planning*. Kluwer Academic Publishers, Boston. 66

Lawler, E.L. and Wood, D.E. (1966). Branch-and-bound methods: A survey. *Operations Research*, 14(4): 699–719. 106

Leibniz, G.W. (1677). *The Method of Mathematics: Preface to the General Science*. Selections reprinted by Chrisley and Begeer [2000]. 157

Lenat, D.B. and Feigenbaum, E.A. (1991). On the thresholds of knowledge. *Artificial Intelligence*, 47: 185–250. 41

Levesque, H.J. (1984). Foundations of a functional approach to knowledge representation. *Artificial Intelligence*, 23(2): 155–212. 207

Liu, A.L., Hile, H., Kautz, H., Borriello, G., Brown, P.A., Harniss, M., and Johnson, K. (2006). Indoor wayfinding: Developing a functional interface for individuals with cognitive impairments. In *Proceedings of the 8th International ACM SIGACCESS Conference on Computers and Accessibility*, pp. 95–102. Association for Computing Machinery, New York. 632

Lloyd, J.W. (1987). *Foundations of Logic Programming*. Symbolic Computation Series. Springer-Verlag, Berlin, second edition. 207, 542

Lopez, A. and Bacchus, F. (2003). Generalizing GraphPlan by formulating planning as a CSP. In *IJCAI-03*, pp. 954–960. 367

Lopez De Mantaras, R., Mcsherry, D., Bridge, D., Leake, D., Smyth, B., Craw, S., Faltings, B., Maher, M.L., Cox, M.T., Forbus, K., Keane, M., Aamodt, A., and Watson, I. (2005). Retrieval, reuse, revision and retention in case-based reasoning. *The Knowledge Engineering Review*, 20(3): 215–240. 341

Loredo, T. (1990). From Laplace to supernova SN 1987A: Bayesian inference in astrophysics. In P. Fougère (Ed.), *Maximum Entropy and Bayesian Methods*, pp. 81–142. Kluwer Academic Press, Dordrecht, The Netherlands. 341

Lowe, D.G. (1995). Similarity metric learning for a variable-kernel classifier. *Neural Computation*, 7: 72–85. 341

Luenberger, D.G. (1979). *Introduction to Dynamic Systems: Theory, Models and Applications*. Wiley, New York. 66

Mackworth, A.K. (1993). On seeing robots. In A. Basu and X. Li (Eds.), *Computer Vision: Systems, Theory, and Applications*, pp. 1–13. World Scientific Press, Singapore. 66

Mackworth, A.K. (2009). Agents, bodies, constraints, dynamics and evolution. *AI Magazine*. 632

Mackworth, A.K. (1977). On reading sketch maps. In *Proc. Fifth International Joint Conf. on Artificial Intelligence*, pp. 598–606. MIT, Cambridge, MA. 151

Manning, C. and Schütze, H. (1999). *Foundations of Statistical Natural Language Processing*. MIT Press, Cambridge, MA. 542

Mas-Colell, A., Whinston, M.D., and Green, J.R. (1995). *Microeconomic Theory*. Oxford University Press, New York, NY. 449

Matheson, J.E. (1990). Using influence diagrams to value information and control. In R.M. Oliver and J.Q. Smith (Eds.), *Influence Diagrams, Belief Nets and Decision Analysis*, chapter 1, pp. 25–48. Wiley. 413

McAllester, D. and Rosenblitt, D. (1991). Systematic nonlinear planning. In *Proc. 9th National Conference on Artificial Intelligence*, pp. 634–639. 367

McCarthy, J. (1986). Applications of circumscription to formalizing common-sense knowledge. *Artificial Intelligence*, 28(1): 89–116. 207

McCarthy, J. and Hayes, P.J. (1969). Some philosophical problems from the standpoint of artificial intelligence. In M. Meltzer and D. Michie (Eds.), *Machine Intelligence 4*, pp. 463–502. Edinburgh University Press. 8, 618

McCulloch, W. and Pitts, W. (1943). A logical calculus of ideas immanent in nervous activity. *Bulletin of Mathematical Biophysics*, 5: 115–133. 7

McDermott, D. and Hendler, J. (1995). Planning: What it is, what it could be, an introduction to the special issue on planning and scheduling. *Artificial Intelligence*, 76: 1–16. 367

McLuhan, M. (1964). *Understanding Media: The Extensions of Man*. New American Library, New York. 632

Meir, R. and Rätsch, G. (2003). An introduction to boosting and leveraging. In *In Advanced Lectures on Machine Learning (LNAI2600)*, pp. 119–184. Springer. 341

Mendelson, E. (1987). *Introduction to Mathematical Logic*. Wadsworth and Brooks, Monterey, CA, third edition. 207

Michie, D., Spiegelhalter, D.J., and Taylor, C.C. (Eds.) (1994). *Machine Learning, Neural and Statistical Classification*. Series in Artificial Intelligence. Ellis Horwood, Hemel Hempstead, Hertfordshire, England. 341

Mihailidis, A., Boger, J., Candido, M., and Hoey, J. (2007). The use of an intelligent prompting system for people with dementia. *ACM Interactions*, 14(4): 34–37. 632

Minsky, M. (1961). Steps towards artificial intelligence. *Proceedings of the IEEE*, 49: 8–30. 106

Minsky, M. (1986). *The Society of Mind*. Simon and Schuster, New York. 29

Minsky, M. and Papert, S. (1988). *Perceptrons: An Introduction to Computational Geometry*. MIT Press, Cambridge, MA, expanded edition. 7, 341

Minsky, M.L. (1975). A framework for representing knowledge. In P. Winston (Ed.), *The Psychology of Computer Vision*, pp. 211–277. McGraw-Hill, New York. Alternative version is in Haugeland [1997], and reprinted in Brachman and Levesque [1985]. 8

Minsky, M. (1952). A neural-analogue calculator based upon a probability model of reinforcement. Technical report, Harvard University Psychological Laboratories, Cambridge, MA. 7

Minton, S., Johnston, M.D., Philips, A.B., and Laird, P. (1992). Minimizing conflicts: a heuristic repair method for constraint satisfaction and scheduling problems. *Artificial Intelligence*, 58(1-3): 161–205. 152

Mitchell, M. (1996). *An Introduction to Genetic Algorithms*. MIT Press, Cambridge, MA. 152

Mitchell, T. (1997). *Machine Learning*. McGraw-Hill, New York. 341

Mitchell, T.M. (1977). Version spaces: A candidate elimination approach to rule learning. In *Proc. 5th International Joint Conf. on Artificial Intelligence*, pp. 305–310. Cambridge, MA. 341

Motik, B., Patel-Schneider, P.F., and Grau, B.C. (Eds.) (2009a). *OWL 2 Web Ontology Language Direct Semantics*. W3C. http://www.w3.org/TR/owl2-semantics/. 592

Motik, B., Patel-Schneider, P.F., and Parsia, B. (Eds.) (2009b). *OWL 2 Web Ontology Language Structural Specification and Functional-Style Syntax*. W3C. http://www.w3.org/TR/owl2-syntax/. 592

Muggleton, S. (1995). Inverse entailment and Progol. *New Generation Computing*, 13(3,4): 245–286. 620

Muggleton, S. and De Raedt, L. (1994). Inductive logic programming: Theory and methods. *Journal of Logic Programming*, 19,20: 629–679. 620

Muscettola, N., Nayak, P., Pell, B., and Williams, B. (1998). Remote agent: to boldly go where no AI system has gone before. *Artificial Intelligence*, 103: 5–47. 212

Nash, Jr., J.F. (1950). Equilibrium points in n-person games. *Proceedings of the National Academy of Sciences of the United States of America*, 36: 48–49. 436

Nau, D.S. (2007). Current trends in automated planning. *AI Magazine*, 28(4): 43–58. 367, 632

Neumann, J.V. and Morgenstern, O. (1953). *Theory of Games and Economic Behavior*. Princeton University Press, Princeton, NJ, third edition. 413, 424

Newell, A. and Simon, H.A. (1976). Computer science as empirical enquiry: Symbols and search. *Communications of the ACM*, 19: 113–126. Reprinted in Haugeland [1997]. 15, 41

Newell, A. and Simon, H.A. (1956). The logic theory machine: A complex information processing system. Technical Report P-868, The Rand Corporation. 7

Niles, I. and Pease, A. (2001). Towards a standard upper ontology. In C. Welty and B. Smith (Eds.), *Proceedings of the 2nd International Conference on Formal Ontology in Information Systems (FOIS-2001)*. Ogunquit, Maine. 592

Nilsson, N. (2007). The physical symbol system hypothesis: Status and prospects. In e.a. M. Lungarella (Ed.), *50 Years of AI, Festschrift*, volume 4850 of *LNAI*, pp. 9–17. Springer. 41

Nilsson, N.J. (1971). *Problem-Solving Methods in Artificial Intelligence*. McGraw-Hill, New York. 106

Nilsson, N.J. (2009). *The Quest for Artificial Intelligence: A History of Ideas and Achievements*. Cambridge University Press, Cambridge, England. 40

Nisan, N. (2007). Introduction to mechanisn design (for computer scientists). In N.N. et al. (Ed.), *Algorithmic Game Theory*, chapter 9, pp. 209–242. Cambridge University Press, Cambridge, England. 449

Nisan, N., Roughgarden, T., Tardos, E., and Vazirani, V.V. (Eds.) (2007). *Algorithmic Game Theory*. Cambridge University Press. 449

Noy, N.F. and Hafner, C.D. (1997). The state of the art in ontology design: A survey and comparative review. *AI Magazine*, 18(3): 53–74. 592

Ordeshook, P.C. (1986). *Game theory and political theory: An introduction*. Cambridge University Press, New York. 449

Panton, K., Matuszek, C., Lenat, D., Schneider, D., Witbrock, M., Siegel, N., and Shepard, B. (2006). Common sense reasoning – from Cyc to intelligent assistant. In Y. Cai and J. Abascal (Eds.), *Ambient Intelligence in Everyday Life*, LNAI 3864, pp. 1–31. Springer. 592

Pearl, J. (1984). *Heuristics*. Addison-Wesley, Reading, MA. 106, 449

Pearl, J. (1988). *Probabilistic Reasoning in Intelligent Systems: Networks of Plausible Inference*. Morgan Kaufmann, San Mateo, CA. 274

Pearl, J. (2000). *Causality: Models, Reasoning and Inference*. Cambridge University Press. 208, 275

Peden, M.e.a. (Ed.) (2004). *World Report on Road Traffic Injury Prevention*. World Health Organization, Geneva. 632

Peng, Y. and Reggia, J.A. (1990). *Abductive Inference Models for Diagnostic Problem-Solving*. Symbolic Computation – AI Series. Springer-Verlag, New York. 207

Pereira, F.C.N. and Shieber, S.M. (2002). *Prolog and Natural-Language Analysis*. Microtome Publishing. 542

Pollack, M.E. (2005). Intelligent technology for an aging population: The use of ai to assist elders with cognitive impairment. *AI Magazine*, 26(2): 9–24. 632

Poole, D. (1993). Probabilistic Horn abduction and Bayesian networks. *Artificial Intelligence*, 64(1): 81–129. 620

Poole, D. (1997). The independent choice logic for modelling multiple agents under uncertainty. *Artificial Intelligence*, 94: 7–56. Special issue on economic principles of multi-agent systems. 620

Poole, D., Goebel, R., and Aleliunas, R. (1987). Theorist: A logical reasoning system for defaults and diagnosis. In N. Cercone and G. McCalla (Eds.), *The Knowledge Frontier: Essays in the Representation of Knowledge*, pp. 331–352. Springer-Verlag, New York, NY. 207

Poole, D., Mackworth, A., and Goebel, R. (1998). *Computational Intelligence: A Logical Approach*. Oxford University Press, New York. xiv

Posner, M.I. (Ed.) (1989). *Foundations of Cognitive Science*. MIT Press, Cambridge, MA. 41

Price, C.J., Travé-Massuyàs, L., Milne, R., Ironi, L., Forbus, K., Bredeweg, B., Lee, M.H., Struss, P., Snooke, N., Lucas, P., Cavazza, M., and Coghill, G.M. (2006). Qualitative futures. *The Knowledge Engineering Review*, 21(04): 317–334. 66

Puterman, M. (1994). *Markov Decision Processes: Discrete Stochastic Dynamic Programming*. John Wiley and Sons, New York. 413

Quinlan, J.R. (1986). Induction of decision trees. *Machine Learning*, 1: 81–106. Reprinted in Shavlik and Dieterich [1990]. 341

Quinlan, J.R. (1993). *C4.5 Programs for Machine Learning*. Morgan Kaufmann, San Mateo, CA. 341

Quinlan, J.R. and Cameron-Jones, R.M. (1995). Induction of logic programs: FOIL and related systems. *New Generation Computing*, 13(3,4): 287–312. 620

Rabiner, L. (1989). A tutorial on hidden Markov models and selected applications in speech recognition. *Proceedings of the IEEE*, 77(2): 257–286. 275

Reiter, R. (1991). The frame problem in the situation calculus: A simple solution (sometimes) and a completeness result for goal regression. In V. Lifschitz (Ed.), *Artificial Intelligence and Mathematical Theory of Computation: Papers in Honor of John McCarthy*, pp. 359–380. Academic Press, San Diego, CA. 618

Reiter, R. (2001). *Knowledge in Action: Logical Foundations for Specifying and Implementing Dynamical Systems*. MIT Press. 618

Riesbeck, C. and Schank, R. (1989). *Inside Case-Based Reasoning*. Lawrence Erlbaum, Hillsdale, NJ. 341

Robinson, J.A. (1965). A machine-oriented logic based on the resolution principle. *Journal ACM*, 12(1): 23–41. 207

Rosenblatt, F. (1958). The perceptron: A probabilistic model for information storage and organization in the brain. *Psychological Review*, 65(6): 386–408. 7, 306

Rosenschein, S.J. and Kaelbling, L.P. (1995). A situated view of representation and control. *Artificial Intelligence*, 73: 149–173. 66

Rubinstein, R.Y. (1981). *Simulation and the Monte Carlo Method*. John Wiley and Sons. 275

Rumelhart, D.E., Hinton, G.E., and Williams, R.J. (1986). Learning internal representations by error propagation. In D.E. Rumelhart and J.L. McClelland (Eds.), *Parallel Distributed Processing*, chapter 8, pp. 318–362. MIT Press, Cambridge, MA. Reprinted in Shavlik and Dietterich [1990]. 341

Russell, B. (1917). *Mysticism and Logic and Other Essays*. G. Allen and Unwin, London. 597

Russell, S. and Norvig, P. (2010). *Artificial Intelligence: A Modern Approach*. Series in Artificial Intelligence. Prentice-Hall, Englewood Cliffs, NJ, third edition. 41

Russell, S. (1997). Rationality and intelligence. *Artificial Intelligence*, 94: 57–77. 41

Sacerdoti, E.D. (1975). The nonlinear nature of plans. In *Proc. 4th International Joint Conf. on Artificial Intelligence*, pp. 206–214. Tbilisi, Georgia, USSR. 367

Samuel, A.L. (1959). Some studies in machine learning using the game of checkers. *IBM Journal on Research and Development*, 3(3): 210–229. 7, 424

Sandholm, T. (2007). Expressive commerce and its application to sourcing: How we conducted $35 billion of generalized combinatorial auctions. *AI Magazine*, 28(3): 45–58. 41

Savage, L.J. (1972). *The Foundation of Statistics*. Dover, New York, 2nd edition. 413

Schank, R.C. (1990). What is AI, anyway? In D. Partridge and Y. Wilks (Eds.), *The Foundations of Artificial Intelligence*, pp. 3–13. Cambridge University Press, Cambridge, England. 41

Schapire, R.E. (2002). The boosting approach to machine learning: An overview. In *MSRI Workshop on Nonlinear Estimation and Classification*. Springer Verlag. 341

Schubert, L.K. (1990). Monotonic solutions to the frame problem in the situation calculus: An efficient method for worlds with fully specified actions. In H.E. Kyburg, R.P. Loui, and G.N. Carlson (Eds.), *Knowledge Representation and Defeasible Reasoning*, pp. 23–67. Kluwer Academic Press, Boston, MA. 618

Shachter, R. and Peot, M.A. (1992). Decision making using probabilistic inference methods. In *Proc. Eighth Conf. on Uncertainty in Artificial Intelligence (UAI-92)*, pp. 276–283. Stanford, CA. 413

Shafer, G. and Pearl, J. (Eds.) (1990). *Readings in Uncertain Reasoning*. Morgan Kaufmann, San Mateo, CA. 639

Shanahan, M. (1989). Prediction is deduction, but explanation is abduction. In *Proc. 11th International Joint Conf. on Artificial Intelligence (IJCAI-89)*, pp. 1055–1060. Detroit, MI. 207

Shanahan, M. (1997). *Solving the Frame Problem: A Mathematical Investigation of the Common Sense Law of Inertia*. MIT Press, Cambridge, MA. 620

Shapiro, S.C. (Ed.) (1992). *Encyclopedia of Artificial Intelligence*. Wiley, New York, second edition. 41

Sharkey, N. (2008). The ethical frontiers of robotics. *Science*, 322(5909): 1800–1801. 630, 632

Shavlik, J.W. and Dietterich, T.G. (Eds.) (1990). *Readings in Machine Learning*. Morgan Kaufmann, San Mateo, CA. 341, 640, 642, 643, 648, 649, 651

Shelley, M.W. (1818). *Frankenstein; or, The Modern Prometheus*. Lackington, Hughes, Harding, Mavor and Jones, London. 632

Shoham, Y. and Leyton-Brown, K. (2008). *Multiagent Systems: Algorithmic, Game Theoretic, and Logical Foundations*. Cambridge University Press. 423, 449

Simon, H.A. (1995). Artificial intelligence: an empirical science. *Artificial Intelligence*, 77(1): 95–127. 41

Simon, H. (1996). *The Sciences of the Artificial*. MIT Press, Cambridge, MA, third edition. 41, 43, 66

Singer, P.W. (2009a). Robots at war: The new battlefield. *The Wilson Quarterly*. http://www.wilsoncenter.org/index.cfm?fuseaction=wq.essay&essay_id=496613. 632

Singer, P.W. (2009b). *Wired for War: The Robotics Revolution and Conflict in the 21st Century*. Penguin, New York. 632

Smith, B. (2003). Ontology. In L. Floridi (Ed.), *Blackwell Guide to the Philosophy of Computing and Information*, pp. 155—166. Oxford: Blackwell. 591

Smith, B.C. (1991). The owl and the electric encyclopedia. *Artificial Intelligence*, 47: 251–288. 41

Smith, B.C. (1996). *On the Origin of Objects*. MIT Press, Cambridge, MA. 549

Somerville, M. (2006). *The Ethical Imagination: Journeys of the Human Spirit*. House of Anansi Press, Toronto. 632

Spall, J.C. (2003). *Introduction to Stochastic Search and Optimization: Estimation, Simulation*. Wiley. 152

Spiegelhalter, D.J., Franklin, R.C.G., and Bull, K. (1990). Assessment, criticism and improvement of imprecise subjective probabilities for a medical expert system. In M. Henrion, R.D. Shachter, L. Kanal, and J. Lemmer (Eds.), *Uncertainty in Artificial Intelligence 5*, pp. 285–294. North-Holland, Amsterdam, The Netherlands. 341

Spirtes, P., Glymour, C., and Scheines, R. (2000). *Causation, Prediction, and Search*. MIT Press, Cambridge MA, 2nd edition. 208, 275

Sterling, L. and Shapiro, E. (1986). *The Art of Prolog*. MIT Press, Cambridge, MA. 542

Stillings, N.A., Feinstein, M.H., Garfield, J.L., Rissland, E.L., Rosenbaum, D.A., Weisler, S.E., and Baker-Ward, L. (1987). *Cognitive Science: An Introduction*. MIT Press, Cambridge, MA. 41

Stone, P. (2007). Learning and multiagent reasoning for autonomous agents. In *The 20th International Joint Conference on Artificial Intelligence (IJCAI-07)*, pp. 13–30. 632

Stone, P. and Veloso, M. (2000). Multiagent systems: A survey from a machine learning perspective. *Autonomous Robots*, 8: 345–383. 449

Sutton, R.S. and Barto, A.G. (1998). *Reinforcement Learning: An Introduction*. MIT Press, Canbridge, MA. 486

Tarski, A. (1956). *Logic, Semantics, Metamathematics*. Clarendon Press, Oxford, England. Papers from 1923 to 1938 collected and translated by J. H. Woodger. 207

Tate, A. (1977). Generating project networks. In *Proc. 5th International Joint Conf. on Artificial Intelligence*, pp. 888–893. Cambridge, MA. 367

Tharp, T. (2003). *The Creative Habit: Learn It and Use It for Life*. Simon and Schuster. 371

Thrun, S. (2006). Winning the darpa grand challenge. In *Innovative Applications of Artificial Intelligence Conference, (IAAI-06)*, pp. 16–20. Boston, MA. 629

Thrun, S., Burgard, W., and Fox, D. (2005). *Probabilistic Robotics*. MIT Press, Cambridge, MA. 275

Turing, A. (1950). Computing machinery and intelligence. *Mind*, 59: 433–460. Reprinted in Haugeland [1997]. 5, 40

Tversky, A. and Kahneman, D. (1974). Judgment under uncertainty: Heuristics and biases. *Science*, 185: 1124–1131. 380

Valiant, L.G. (1984). A theory of the learnable. *Communications of the ACM*, 27: 1134–1142. Reprinted in Shavlik and Dietterich [1990]. 341

van Beek, P. and Chen, X. (1999). Cplan: A constraint programming approach to planning. In *AAAI-99*, pp. 585–590. 367

van Emden, M.H. and Kowalski, R.A. (1976). The semantics of predicate logic as a programming language. *Journal ACM*, 23(4): 733–742. 207

Visser, U. and Burkhard, H.D. (2007). Robocup: 10 years of achievements and challenges. *AI Magazine*, 28(2): 115–130. 632

Viswanathan, P., Mackworth, A.K., Little, J.J., and Mihailidis, A. (2007). Intelligent wheelchairs: Collision avoidance and navigation assistance for older adults with cognitive impairment. In *Proc. Workshop on Intelligent Systems for Assisted Cognition*. Rochester, NY. 632

Waldinger, R. (1977). Achieving several goals simultaneously. In E. Elcock and D. Michie (Eds.), *Machine Intelligence 8: Machine Representations of Knowledge*, pp. 94–136. Ellis Horwood, Chichester, England. 367

Walsh, T. (2007). Representing and reasoning with preferences. *AI Magazine*, 28(4): 59–69. 413

Warren, D.H.D. and Pereira, F.C.N. (1982). An efficient easily adaptable system for interpreting natural language queries. *Computational Linguistics*, 8(3-4): 110–122. 8

Webber, B.L. and Nilsson, N.J. (Eds.) (1981). *Readings in Artificial Intelligence*. Morgan Kaufmann, San Mateo, CA. 41, 642

Weiss, G. (Ed.) (1999). *Multiagent Systems: A Modern Approach to Distributed Artificial Intelligence*. MIT Press, Cambridge, MA. 449

Weiss, S. and Kulikowski, C. (1991). *Computer Systems that Learn: Classification and Prediction Methods from Statistics, Neural Nets, Machine Learning, and Expert Systems*. Morgan Kaufmann, San Mateo, CA. 341

Weld, D. (1999). Recent advances in AI planning. *AI Magazine*, 20(2). 367

Weld, D.S. (1992). Qualitative physics: Albatross or eagle? *Computational Intelligence*, 8(2): 175–186. Introduction to special issue on the future of qualitative physics. 66

Weld, D.S. (1994). An introduction to least commitment planning. *AI Magazine*, 15(4): 27–61. 367

Weld, D. and de Kleer, J. (Eds.) (1990). *Readings in Qualitative Reasoning about Physical Systems*. Morgan Kaufmann, San Mateo, CA. 66

Whitley, D. (2001). An overview of evolutionary algorithms. *Journal of Information and Software Technology*, 43: 817–831. 152

Wilkins, D.E. (1988). *Practical Planning: Extending the Classical AI Planning Paradigm*. Morgan Kaufmann, San Mateo, CA. 367

Winograd, T. (1990). Thinking machines: Can there be? Are we? In D. Partridge and Y. Wilks (Eds.), *The Foundations of Artificial Intelligence: A Sourcebook*, pp. 167–189. Cambridge University Press, Cambridge, England. 41

Winograd, T. (1972). *Understanding Natural Language*. Academic Press, New York. 8

Woods, W.A. (2007). Meaning and links. *AI Magazine*, 28(4): 71–92. 591

Wooldridge, M. (2002). *An Introduction to Multiagent Systems*. John Wiley and Sons, Chichester, England. 449

Yang, Q. (1997). *Intelligent Planning: A Decomposition and Abstraction-Based Approach*. Springer–Verlag, New York. 367

Yang, S., and Mackworth, A.K. (2007). Hierarchical shortest pathfinding applied to route-planning for wheelchair users. In *Proc. Canadian Conf. on Artificial Intelligence, AI-2007*. Montreal, PQ. 632

Zhang, N.L. and Poole, D. (1994). A simple approach to Bayesian network computations. In *Proc. of the Tenth Canadian Conference on Artificial Intelligence*, pp. 171–178. 274

Zhang, N.L. (2004). Hierarchical latent class models for cluster analysis. *Journal of Machine Learning Research*, 5(6): 697–723. 341

Zhang, Y. and Mackworth, A.K. (1995). Constraint nets: A semantic model for hybrid dynamic systems. *Theoretical Computer Science*, 138: 211–239. 66

Zilberstein, S. (1996). Using anytime algorithms in intelligent systems. *AI Magazine*, 17(3): 73–83. 41

Index

$=$ (equals), 532
A^* search, 89
$\wedge$ (and), 163
$\Leftarrow$ (base-level if), 581
$\leftarrow$ (if), 163, 496
$\models$ (entails), 160, 499
$\models$ (true in), 222
$\neq$ (not equal to), 535
ϕ (denotation of terms), 496, 514
π (denotation of predicate symbols), 496
π (meaning of atoms), 159
$\longmapsto$ (rewritten as), 521
$\vdash$ (derive), 167
$\vee$ (or), 585
% (comment), 496
& (base-level and), 581

abduction, 199, 200
abductive diagnosis, 201
abilities, 11
absolute error, 290
absorbing state, 399
abstractions, 15
achievement goal, 25, 355
action, 45, 350
action constraints, 361
action features, 360
action function, 74
action profile, 425, 435
activation function, 306
active learning, 285
active sensor, 64
acts, 4
actuator, 44, 45
acyclic, 184, 195
acyclic directed graph, 75
add list, 354

additive independence, 378
additive utility, 378
admissibility, 91
aerodynamics, 10
agent, 4, 10, 43, 45
    embedded, 59
    purposive, 44
agent system, 45
agent system model, 59
AI, 3
algebra, 222
algebraic variable, 113
Allais Paradox, 380
alpha-beta (α-β) pruning, 431
alternative, 615
analysis, 4
Analytical Engine, 7
ancestor, 184
annealing schedule, 138
answer, 166, 171, 187, 504
answer clause, 171
answer extraction, 504, 509
anytime algorithm, 26
application of substitution, 506
approximately correct, 332
approximately optimal, 14
approximately optimal solution, 14
arc, 75
arc consistent, 121
argument, 197, 494
Aristotelian definition, 567
array, 634
Arrow's impossibility theorem, 446
artificial intelligence, 3
ask, 161, 166
ask-the-user, 175, 576
askable, 175

653

assertional knowledge base, 568
assignment space, 118
assumable, 187, 200
assumption-based truth maintenance system,
        207
asymptotic complexity, 83
asynchronous value iteration, 406
ATMS, 207
atom, 158, 163
atomic clause, 163, 496
atomic proposition, 158, 163
atomic symbol, 494
attribute, 552
auction, 448
autonomous delivery robot, 30
average reward, 402
axiom, 160, 161, 501
axiom schema, 533
axiomatizing, 161, 501
axioms
        of probability, 224
        of rationality, 373

back-propagation learning, 317
background knowledge, 17, 607
background variables, 206
backtracking, 80, 120
backward induction, 430
bagging, 319
base language, 580
base level, 580
base-level algorithms, 319
Basic Formal Ontology, 573
Bayes' rule, 229
Bayesian classifier, 309
Bayesian learning, 334
Bayesian network, *see* belief network
Bayesian probability, 220
beam search, 141
belief, 49
belief monitoring, 271
belief network, 235, 236, 458
        causality, 241
        inference problem, 252
belief state, 48, 61
belief state transition function, 49
best response, 436
best-first search, 88
beta distribution, 337
BFO, 573
bias, 286, 321, 331
bias-free, 331
bidirectional search, 101
binary constraint, 116
binary feature, 112
biology, 6
bit, 231
blame attribution problem, 465
body, 44
        agent, 45
        rule, 163, 496
Boltzmann distribution, 142, 473
Boolean property, 553
Boolean variable, 113, 126, 158

boosting, 320
bottom-up proof procedure, 167
boundary of a process, 576
boundary of an object, 575
bounded rationality, 26
branch-and-bound, 98
branching factor, 77
breadth-first search, 84

candidate elimination algorithm, 329
canonical representation, 534
cardinal, 14
cardinal preference, 25
case analysis, 125
case-based reasoning, 324
causal, 48
causal link, 364
causal mechanism, 206
causal model, 204, 206
causal network, 241
causal rule, 353, 601
causal transduction, 48
causality, 204, 241
central limit theorem, 223
chain rule, 227
chance node, 384
characteristic function, 559
children, 142
choice space, 615
choose, 170
Church-Turing thesis, 7
clarity principle, 114, 241
Clark normal form, 538
Clark's completion, 194, 538
class, 298, 309, 451, 559, 568
classification, 284, 298
classification tree, 298
clause, 126
        definite, 163, 494, 496
        Horn, 185
closed list, 94
closed-world assumption, 193
cluster, 451
clustering, 451
cognitive science, 10
command, 45
command function, 49
command trace, 46
commonsense reasoning, 13
competitive, 424
complements, 381
complete, 131, 167
        bottom-up derivation, 169
complete knowledge assumption, 193
completeness
        of preferences, 373
complex preference, 25
complexity, 83
compositional measure of belief, 226
compound proposition, 158
computational, 4
computational learning theory, 332
computational limits dimension, 26
computational linguistics, 520

concept, 572
conceptualization, 494, 563
conditional effect, 355
conditional
        expected value, 231
conditional probability, 225
conditional probability distribution, 227, 297
conditionally independent, 233
Condorcet paradox, 445
conflict, 132, 187
conjunction, 158
consequence set, 167
consistency-based diagnosis, 187, 189
consistent, 328, 358, 608
constant, 494
constrained optimization problem, 144
constraint, 115
constraint network, 121
constraint optimization problem, 145
constraint satisfaction problem, 117
context-free grammar, 521
context-specific independence, 250
contingent attribute, 562
continuant, 573
continuous variable, 113
controller, 45, 48, 426
cooperate, 444
cooperative, 424
cooperative system, 196
coordinate, 444
coordination, 437
cost, 76
credit-assignment problem, 285
cross validation, 324, 325
crossover, 142
CSP, *see* constraint satisfaction problem
culture, 6
cumulative probability distribution, 257
cumulative reward, 401
cyc, 564
cycle, 75
cycle check, 93
cyclic, 184

DAG, 75
Datalog, 494
datatype property, 568
DBN, *see* dynamic belief network
DCG, *see* definite clause grammar
dead reckoning, 58
debugging, 179
        incorrect answers, 180
        infinite loops, 184
        missing answers, 182
decision
        sequential, 386
        single, 384
decision function, 391
decision network, 384, 387, 428
decision node, 384
decision tree, 298, 382, 426
        learning, 298, 321
decision tree learning, 232
decision variable, 382

decision-theoretic planning, 409
deduction, 167, 200
Deep Space One, 212
default, 176, 196
definite clause, 163, 494, 496
definite clause grammar (DCG), 522
definite clause resolution, 169
delay, 536, 590
delete list, 354
delivery robot, 30
DENDRAL, 9
denote, 496
dense, 46
dependent continuant, 573, 575
depth-bounded meta-interpreter, 587
depth-first search, 80
derivation, 167, 171, 510
derived, 167, 204, 354, 600
        knowledge, 558
description logic, 568
design, 4, 202
design space, 19
design time reasoning, 17
desire, 49
deterministic, 24
diagnosis, 201
        abductive, 201
        consistency-based, 187
        decision theoretic, 383
        probabilistic, 245
diagnostic assistant, 30, 33
dictator, 447
difference list, 522
differentia, 567
dimension
        computational limits, 26
        effect uncertainty, 24
        learning, 26
        modularity, 19
        number of agents, 25
        planning horizon, 22
        preference, 24
        representation scheme, 20
        sensing uncertainty, 23
directed acyclic graph, 75
directed graph, 75
Dirichlet distribution, 337
discount factor, 402
discounted reward, 402
discrete, 46
discrete variable, 113
disjunction, 158, 185, 585
disjunctive normal form, 189
disposition, 575
distribution
        normal, 223
do, 598
domain, 112, 113, 496, 552, 633
domain consistent, 121
domain expert, 63
domain ontology, 571
domain splitting, 125
dominant strategy, 446

dominates, 439
don't-care non-determinism, 170
don't-know non-determinism, 170
dot product, 271
DPLL, 127
dynamic, 599
dynamic belief network, 272
dynamic decision network, 409
dynamic programming, 103

economically efficient, 446
effect, 350, 354
effect constraints, 361
effect uncertainty dimension, 24
effectively computable, 7
effector, 44
efficient, 446
eligibility trace, 479
elimination ordering, 252
EM, 452, 455, 460
embedded agent, 59
embodied, 44
empirical frequency, 295
endogenous variables, 206
engineering goal, 4
ensemble learning, 319
entails, 160
entity, 573
entropy, 232, 292
environment, 10
epistemological, 221
epistemology, 9
equal, 532
error, 288
        absolute, 290
        sum squares, 290
        worst case, 291
error of hypothesis, 332
Euclidean distance, 95, 325
evaluation, 145
evaluation function, 132, 433
event calculus, 604
evidence, 225
evidential model, 205
evolutionary algorithm, 466
exclusive-or, 308
existence uncertainty, 619
existentially quantified variable, 500
exogenous variables, 206
expanding, 78
expectation maximization (EM), 452
expected monetary value, 376
expected utility, 386, 392
expected value, 230
        of utility of a policy, 392
experience, 468
expert opinion, 297
expert system, 9, 10, 61
explained away, 201, 243, 245
explanation, 201
exploit, 472
explore, 472
expression, 496
extensional, 559

extensionally, 116
extensive form, 426
external knowledge source, 65
extrapolation, 286

$f(p)$, 89
factor, 249, 634
factored finite state machine, 50
factored representation, 50
factorization, 236
fail, 170
failing naturally, 96
failing unnaturally, 96
failure, 197
fair, 170, 518
fairness, 19
false, 159, 498
false-negative error, 14, 182, 292
false-positive error, 14, 180, 292, 293
fault, 187
feature engineering, 484
feature-based representation of actions, 353
features, 21, 112
feed-forward neural network, 316
fiat part of an object, 575
fiat part of process, 576
filler, 556
filtering, 58, 267, 271
finite failure, 199
finite horizon, 23
finite state controller, 50
finite state machine, 50
first-order predicate calculus, 517
fixed point, 169
flat, 20
floundering goal, 541
fluent, 599
flying machines, 9
for all, 500
forward chaining, 167
forward planner, 356
frame, 556
frame problem, 618
frame rule, 353, 601
framing effect, 380
frequentist, 220
fringe, 77
frontier, 77
fully observable, 23
fully observable dynamic decision network, 411
fully observable Markov decision process, 401
function, 575, 633
        symbol, 514
fuzzy terms, 52

gambling, 220
game tree, 426
Gaussian distribution, 223
general boundary, 329
M ized additive independence, 381
generalize, 285
generalized answer clause, 509

generalized arc consistency algorithm, 122
generate and test, 118, 146
genetic algorithms, 142
genus, 567
Gibbs distribution, 142, 473
Gini index, 302, 345
global minimum, 149
goal, 11, 25, 49, 171, 356
    node, 75
goal constraints, 361
gradient descent, 149, 304
grammar, 521
    context-free, 521
    definite clause, 522
graph, 75
greedy, 23, 609
greedy ascent, 132
greedy descent, 132
ground, 496
ground instance, 506, 507
ground representation, 580

$h(n)$, 87
hard clustering, 452
hard constraint, 111, 115
head, 163, 496
help system, 246, 312
Herbrand interpretation, 508
heuristic
    function, 87
    knowledge, 72
    search, 87
heuristic depth-first search, 88
hidden Markov model (HMM), 267
hidden variable, 244, 460
hierarchical, 20
hierarchical Bayesian model, 338
hierarchical control, 50
hill climbing, 132
history, 10, 48, 468
HMM, *see* hidden Markov model
Hoeffding's inequality, 259
horizon, 361
Horn clause, 185
how, 17
how question, 177
human-computer interaction (HCI), 578
hyperparameters, 339
hypothesis, 288
hypothesis space, 288, 328

identity uncertainty, 619
imperfect information game, 428
implication, 158
incoming arc, 75
inconsistent, 186
incorrect answer, 180
incremental gradient descent, 305
indefinite horizon, 23, 399
independent, 233
independent and identically distributed (i.i.d.), 335
independent choice logic (ICL), 615

independent continuant, 573, 575
indicator variable, 141, 290
indifferent, 373
individual, 22, 141, 492, 496, 568
individual-property-value, 552
induction, 200, 284
inductive logic programming, 606
inference, 167
infinite horizon, 23, 399
influence diagram, 387
information content, 232
information gain, 232, 302
information set, 428
information theory, 231, 323
init, 598
initial-state constraints, 361
input features, 288
insects, 18
instance, 504, 506
    ground, 507
instance space, 328
insurance, 377
integrity constraint, 185
intelligent action, 4
intelligent tutoring system, 35
intended interpretation, 161, 501
intensional, 559
intensionally, 116
intention, 49
interpolation, 286
interpretation, 159, 496
intersection, 636
intervention, 204, 206, 241
involve, 115
island, 102
island-driven search, 101
iterative best improvement, 132
iterative deepening, 95
    A^*, 98

Java, 495, 558
join, 636
joint probability distribution, 236, 252

k-fold cross validation, 324
k-means algorithm, 452
kd-tree, 326
kernel functions, 314
knowledge, 12, 60
knowledge base, 12, 17, 60, 160, 163, 494, 496
knowledge engineers, 63
knowledge is given, 26
knowledge is learned, 26
knowledge level, 16, 176
knowledge-based system, 60
knowledge-level debugging, 180

landmarks, 52
language, 521
    natural, 520
language bias, 331
latent tree model, 314
latent variable, 244, 309, 460

learning, 61, 283–347, 441–445, 451–488, 606–611
    Bayesian, 334
    bias, 331
    case-based, 324
    decision trees, 232, 298
    decision tree, 321
    multiagent, 441
    neural network, 315
    PAC, 332, 340
    relational, 606
    supervised, 284
    to coordinate, 441
    unsupervised, 285, 451
    version space, 329
learning bias, 321
learning dimension, 26
learning rate, 304
leave-one-out cross-validation, 325
leaves, 75
level of abstraction, 15
life-long learning, 6
likelihood, 229
likelihood of the data, 292
linear function, 304
linear regression, 304, 484
linearly separable, 308
Linnaean taxonomy, 567
lists, 516
literal, 126, 194
liveness, 18
local minimum, 149
local optimum, 132
local search, 130, 131, 609
localization, 268
logic, 495
logic program, 514
logic programming, 207
logical consequence, 160, 499
logical variable, 494
logically follows, 160
logistic function, 307
long-term memory, 61
loop check, 93
lottery, 373
lowest-cost-first search, 86

M features, 360
M system, 51
machine learning, *see* learning
maintenance goal, 25, 355
MAP model, 321
mapping, 633
margin, 314
Markov assumption, 266
Markov blanket, 235
Markov chain, 266
Markov decision process, 399, 463
matrix multiplication, 271
maximum a posteriori probability, 321
maximum entropy, 233, 234
maximum likelihood model, 292, 321
maximum-likelihood estimate, 295
MDL principle, 323
MDP, *see* Markov decision process

measure, 221
mechanism, 424, 446
mechanism design, 446
meta-interpreter, 579, 580, 582
    ask the user, 589
    build proof tree, 587
    built-in predicates, 586
    delayed goals, 590
    depth-bounded, 587
    disjunction, 586
    vanilla, 583
meta-level, 580
metalanguage, 580
MGU, 507
min-factor elimination ordering, 130
minimal
    conflict, 187
    model, 169
minimal diagnosis, 189
minimal explanation, 201
minimal model, 509
minimax, 430
minimum deficiency elimination ordering, 130
minimum description length (MDL), 323
minimum fixed point, 169
missing at random, 461
model, 15, 57, 116, 160
modular, 20
modularity, 19
modularity dimension, 20
modus ponens, 167
money pump, 374
monitoring, 267, 271
monotone restriction, 95
monotonic, 196
more general hypothesis, 329
more specific hypothesis, 329
most general unifier, 507, 511
multiagent decision network, 428
multiple agent, 25
multiple-path pruning, 93, 94
mutex constraint, 361
MYCIN, 9
myopic, 23
myopically optimal, 301

N3, 555
naive Bayesian classifier, 246, 310, 455
Nash equilibrium, 436
natural kind, 309, 313, 559
natural language processing, 520
nature, 44, 424
nearest neighbors, 325
negation, 158, 185
negation as failure, 194, 199, 537
negative examples, 607
neighbor, 75, 131
neural network, 315
no, 166
no-forgetting agent, 388
no-forgetting decision network, 388
node, 75
noisy, 267
noisy or, 250

non-deterministic, 170
non-deterministic procedure, 170
non-ground representation, 580
non-monotonic, 196
non-parametric distribution, 223
non-planning, 23
non-serial dynamic programming, 151
non-terminal symbol, 521
nonlinear planning, 364
normal distribution, 223
normal-form game, 425
Notation 3, 555
NP, 170
NP-complete, 170
NP-hard, 170
number of agents dimension, 25
number uncertainty, 619

object, 552, 575
object aggregate, 575
object language, 580
object property, 568
object-oriented languages, 495
object-oriented programming (OOP) languages, 558
objective function, 144
observation, 11, 17, 174, 225
occurrent, 573, 575
occurs check, 518
Ockham's razor, 287
off policy, 470
off-policy learner, 475
offline, 61
offline computation, 17
offline learning, 285
omniscient agent, 114
on-policy learner, 475
one-point crossover, 142
online, 60, 64
online computation, 17
online learning, 285
ontological, 221
ontology, 61, 161, 175, 549, 563
OOP, *see* object-oriented programming
open-world assumption, 193
optimal, 74
optimal algorithm, 105
optimal policy, 386, 392, 403
optimal solution, 13, 76
optimality criterion, 144
optimization problem, 144
oracle, 170
orders of magnitude reasoning, 52
ordinal, 13
ordinal preference, 25
organizations, 6
outcome, 373, 382, 425
outgoing arc, 75
overfitting, 303
OWL, 564, 568

PAC learning, 332, 340
pair, 633
parametric distribution, 223
parametrized random variable, 613

paramodulation, 534
parents, 235
partial, 267
partial evaluation, 590
partial-order planning, 363
partially observable, 23
partially observable game, 428
partially observable Markov decision process, 401, 411
particle, 264
particle filtering, 264, 265
passive sensor, 64
past experience, 11
path, 75
    consistency, 125
payoff matrix, 426
percept, 45
percept stream, 46
percept trace, 46
perception, 58
perceptron, 306
perfect information, 430
perfect information game, 426
perfect rationality, 26
philosophy, 9
physical symbol system, 15
physical symbol system hypothesis, 15, 319
pixels, 45
plan, 356
planner, 356
planning, 356–370, 604
    as a CSP, 360
    forward, 356
    partial-order, 363
    regression, 357
planning horizon, 22
planning horizon dimension, 23
plate model, 338, 613
point estimate, 288
policy, 103, 386, 390
policy iteration, 407
policy search, 466
POMDP, *see* partially observable Markov decision process
population, 141, 264
positive examples, 607
possible, 358
possible world, 113, 115, 382, 391, 615
posterior probability, 225
pragmatics, 521
precision, 293
precision-recall curve, 293
precondition, 350, 353, 354, 601
precondition constraints, 361
predicate symbol, 494
preference, 144
preference bias, 331
preference dimension, 25
preference elicitation, 379
primitive, 204, 354, 566, 600
    knowledge, 558
prior count, 296
prior knowledge, 10

prior probability, 225
prisoner's dilemma, 437
probabilistic independence, 233
probabilistic inference, 248
probabilistic relational model (PRM), 612
probability, 219–275, 295
    axioms, 224
    conditional, 225
    posterior, 225
    prior, 225
    semantics, 222
probability density function, 223
probability distribution, 222
probability mass, 262
probability measure, 221
probable solution, 14
probably approximately correct, 259, 332
probably approximately correct learning, 332
process, 23, 576
process aggregate, 576
processual context, 576
processual entity, 576
projection, 636
Prolog, 9, 494, 496
proof, 167
    bottom-up, 167
    top-down, 169
proof procedure, 167
proof tree, 179
prop, 552
property, 552, 568
property inheritance, 561
proposal distribution, 260, 261
proposition, 21, 158
propositional calculus, 158
propositional definite clause resolution, 169
propositional definite clauses, 163
propositional satisfiability, 126
prospect theory, 380
proved, 167
pseudocount, 296
psychology, 9
punishment, 399
pure strategy, 435
pure symbol, 127
purposive agent, 44

Q^*, 404
Q-learning, 469
Q-value, 404, 469
Q^π, 403
qualitative derivatives, 52
qualitative reasoning, 52
quality, 575
quantitative reasoning, 52
query, 166, 494, 496
querying the user, 175

random initialization, 131
random restart, 131
random sampling, 132
random variable, 221
random walk, 132
random worlds, 233, 234

range, 552, 633
rational, 376
rational agent, 373
RDF, 555, 559, 564
RDF Schema, 559
RDF-S, 564
rdf:type, 559
rdfs:subClassOf, 559
reachable, 599
realizable entity, 575
reasoning, 17
recall, 293
recognition, 201
record linkage, 619
recursively enumerable, 517
reflection, 579
regression, 284, 304
regression planning, 357, 358
regression tree, 314
reify, 552
reinforcement learning, 285, 463
rejection sampling, 259
relation, 22, 492, 633, 635
relational algebra, 635
relational database, 635
relational descriptions, 22
relational probability model, 612
relational uncertainty, 619
representation, 12
representation scheme, 12
representation scheme dimension, 20, 22
resampling, 264
resolution, 169, 171
    SLD, 169, 510
resolvent, 171
resource, 555, 564
Resource Description Framework, 555, 564
restriction bias, 331
return, 469
revelation principle, 447
reward, 399
rewrite rule, 521, 534
risk averse, 377
robot, 10, 30, 44
ROC curve, 293
role, 63, 575
root, 75
rule, 163, 494, 496
rule of inference, 167
run, 427
run-time distribution, 138

safety goal, 18, 355
sample average, 258
sample complexity, 333
SARSA(λ), 479
satisfiable, 201
satisficing, 14
satisficing solution, 14
satisfies, 116
    policy, 391
satisfy, 115
scenario, 201
scheme, 115, 635

scientific goal, 4
scope, 115, 145, 634, 635
search, 71–110
    A^*, 89
    best-first, 88
    bidirectional, 101
    breadth-first, 84
    cycle-checking, 93
    depth first, 80
    dynamic programming, 103
    gradient descent, 149
    heuristic, 87
    island driven, 101
    iterative deepening, 95
    local search, 130
    lowest-cost-first, 86
search and score, 462
search bias, 331
second-order logic, 517
second-price auction, 448
select, 170
selection, 635
selector function, 615
semantic interoperability, 65, 550
semantic network, 554
semantic web, 555, 564
semantics, 159, 520
    propositional calculus, 159
    variables, 496
sensing uncertainty dimension, 23
sensor, 44, 45, 64
sensor fusion, 270
separable control problem, 58
sequential decision problem, 386
sequential prisoner's dilemma, 438
set, 633
set difference, 636
short-term memory, 61
sigmoid, 307
simulated agent, 59
simulated annealing, 136
single agent, 25
single decision, 384
single-stage decision network, 384
site, 575
situation, 598
situation calculus, 598
SLD derivation, 171, 510
SLD resolution, 169, 510
slot, 556
Smalltalk, 558
smoothing, 267, 271
SNLP, 370
social preference function, 446
society, 6
soft clustering, 452
soft constraint, 111, 145
soft-max, 473
software agent, 10
software engineer, 63
software engineering, 13
solution, 73, 75
sound, 167

spatial region, 573, 575
spatio-temporal region, 576
specialization operator, 609
specific boundary, 329
squashed linear function, 306
stable, 453
stack, 80
stage, 23
start node, 75
start states, 74
starvation, 170, 518
state, 20, 72
state constraints, 361
state space, 72
state-space graph, 351, 356
state-space problem, 74
static, 599
stationary, 266, 399
stationary policy, 403
step function, 306
step size, 150, 151
stimuli, 45
stochastic, 24
stochastic beam search, 142
stochastic local search, 134
stochastic simulation, 256
stochastic strategy, 435
stopping state, 399
strategic form of a game, 425
strategically, 424
strategy, 426, 427, 435
strategy profile, 427, 435
strictly dominated, 147
strictly dominates, 440
strictly preferred, 373
STRIPS assumption, 354
STRIPS representation, 354
structure learning, 461
subClassOf, 559
subgame-perfect equilibrium, 439
subgoal, 171
subject, 552
subjective probability, 220
substitutes, 381
substitution, 506
sum-of-squares error, 290, 453
supervised learning, 284, 288
support set, 435, 439
support vector machine (SVM), 314
SVM, *see* support vector machine
symbol, 15, 114
symbol level, 17
symbol system, 15
syntax, 520
    Datalog, 494
    propositional definite clauses, 163
synthesis, 4
systematicity, 370

tabu list, 135
target features, 288
TD error, 467
tell, 161
temperature, 473

temporal difference error, 467
temporal region, 575
term, 494, 514
terminal symbol, 521
terminological knowledge base, 568
test examples, 288
theorem, 167
there exists, 500
thing, 573
thinking, 4
threat, 438
time, 46, 598
tit-for-tat, 438
top-down proof procedure, 169
total assignment, 115
total reward, 402
trading agent, 30, 37
training examples, 284, 288, 328
transduction, 48
transitivity of preferences, 374
tree, 75
tree augmented naive Bayesian (TAN) network, 314
treewidth, 130, 256
triple, 552, 555, 606, 633
triple representation, 552
true, 159, 498, 633
true-positive rate, 293
truth maintenance system, 207
truth value, 159
truthful, 446
try, 131
tuple, 115, 633, 635
Turing test, 5
Turtle, 555
tutoring system, 30
two-step belief network, 272
type, 559
type, 553, 559

UML, 558
unary constraint, 116
unconditionally independent, 235
unification, 511
unifier, 507
Uniform Resource Identifier, 555, 564, 568
uninformed search strategies, 80
union, 636
unique names assumption, 535
unit resolution, 127
units, 315
universally quantified, 498
universally quantified variable, 498
unsatisfiable, 186
unstable, 319
unsupervised learning, 285, 451

URI, *see* Uniform Resource Identifier
useful, 358
user, 64, 114, 175
utility, 14, 376
utility node, 385

V^π, 403
V^*, 404
validation set, 324
value, 401
value of control, 398
value of information, 397
vanilla meta-interpreter, 582, 583
variable, 113
    algebraic, 113
    Boolean, 113
    continuous, 113
    decision, 382
    discrete, 113
    existentially quantified, 500
    logical, 494
    random, 221
    universally quantified, 498
variable assignment, 498
variable elimination, 386
    belief networks, 248
    CSPs, 127
    decision networks, 392
    optimizing soft constraints, 147
variational inference, 248
VCG mechanism, 447
VE, *see* variable elimination
verb, 552
version space, 329
virtual body, 50

walk, 131
weakest precondition, 358
weakly dominated, 147
weakly preferred, 373
Web Ontology Language, 564
what, 17
why question, 177
whynot question, 177
win or learn fast (WoLF), 445
word, 494
world, 10
worst-case error, 291
wrapper, 65

XML, 564

yes, 166

zero-sum game, 424, 430

CPSIA information can be obtained at www.ICGtesting.com
Printed in the USA
LVOW03*1312291114

415960LV00002B/5/P